# YALE JUDAICA SERIES

### EDITOR

## LEON NEMOY

#### ASSOCIATE EDITORS
## JUDAH GOLDIN    SAUL LIEBERMAN


## VOLUME XXII


## INTRODUCTION TO THE
## CODE OF MAIMONIDES

### (*MISHNEH TORAH*)

# Introduction to the Code of Maimonides
## (*Mishneh Torah*)

BY

ISADORE TWERSKY

NATHAN LITTAUER PROFESSOR OF HEBREW
LITERATURE AND PHILOSOPHY
HARVARD UNIVERSITY

NEW HAVEN AND LONDON, YALE UNIVERSITY PRESS

Published with assistance from the
National Endowment for the Humanities.

Copyright © 1980 by Yale University.
All rights reserved. This book may not be
reproduced in whole or in part, in any form
(beyond that copying permitted by Sections 107
and 108 of the U.S. Copyright Law and except by
reviewers for the public press), without written
permission from the publishers.

Set in Garamond type.
Printed in the United States of America

*Library of Congress Cataloging in Publication Data*

Twersky, Isadore.
   Introduction to the Code of Maimonides (Mishneh Torah)

   (Yale Judaica series; v. 22)
   Bibliography: p.
   Includes index.
   1. Moses ben Maimon, 1135–1204. Mishneh Torah.
2. Jewish law.  3. Philosophy, Jewish.  I. Title.  II. Series.
BM520.84.T83 1980    296.1'72    79–10347
ISBN 978-0-300-02846-1
10  9  8

To
ATARAH

# CONTENTS

Preface     xi
I. Introduction: The *Mishneh Torah* in the Life and Work of Maimonides     1
    Maimonides' literary oeuvre: unity and diversity     6
        Three sources of information: introduction to the *Commentary on the Mishnah;* responsum to R. Nehorai had-Dayyan; introduction to *Sefer ham-Miṣwot*     7
        Centrality of the *Mishneh Torah*     14
    His accounts of the purposes and features of the *Mishneh Torah*     20
        Seven statements: *Sefer ham-Miṣwot; Mishneh Torah;* letter to R. Phinehas ben Meshullam; letter to R. Jonathan hak-Kohen of Lunel; letter to R. Joseph ben Judah; treatise on resurrection; anonymous apologia; references in the *Moreh Nĕḇukim*     24
        Five major characteristics     48
    Sources of the *Mishneh Torah:* erudition and originality     49
    Motives and goals of the *Mishneh Torah*     61
        Historical motive: response to contemporary need     62
        Literary-systematic motive: jurisprudential need     74
        Philosophic-ideological motive: rationalistic-spiritual need     77
    The mid-twelfth-century scene: institutional-religious-literary realities; five salient features     81
    History and halakah: on the study of the *Mishneh Torah*     92

II. Form     97
    Anonymity and authority. The purpose and value of codification: brief, uniform, undocumented norms     97
    Reactions to the Code: stricture and supplement     102
    A second look: exceptions to the austere codificatory form     108
        (1) Attribution to original authorities, anecdotes and quotations     109
        (2) Original views, personal preferences, autobiographical statements     116
        (3) Multiple opinions     121
        (4) Variant customs     124
        (5) Value judgments: counsels of perfection     134
        (6) Pedagogic devices: direct address, introductory generalization, exempla     135
    The impossibility of absolute finality     139
    The Code as commentary: expository-exegetical material     143
    Maimonides' redefinition of a code: role of theoretical knowledge and explication     165
    Maimonides' *mĕleket šamayim*: rigidity and resilience     170
    Appendix: Examples of expository-exegetical material     176

### III. SCOPE — 188
- Comprehensiveness of the Code — 188
- Restricted scope of study — 192
- Halakic pragmatism and spirituality — 195
- Maimonides' intellectual breakthrough — 204
- Motives for the unification of theoretical and practical — 208
- Unity of all learning — 215
- The historical dimension — 220
- Temporary laws — 229
- Omissions — 234

### IV. CLASSIFICATION — 238
- Options for classification — 238
  - Mishnaic-Talmudic sequence — 238
  - Listing of commandments: the *Sefer ham-Miṣwot* approach — 245
  - Independent topical-conceptual arrangement — 254
- The fourteen books of the *Mishneh Torah* — 259
  - Novelty of this classification — 273
- Conceptualization and classification: splitting of halakic units — 276
  - Stresses and strains in this system — 281
- Differences between topical-conceptual and philosophic-teleological classification — 300
- Internal sequence and classification — 308
- Problem of contradictions — 311
- Appendix: Relationship between the classifications of the *Mishneh Torah* and the *Guide* — 321

### V. LANGUAGE AND STYLE — 324
- Three options — 325
  - The missing option: Arabic — 333
- In praise of brevity — 337
  - Exceptions: cases of amplification — 339
- Precision and elegance — 346
- Other features: synonymy, symmetry, neologism — 349
- Stylistic continuity and consistency — 352
- The successful fusion of content and form: literary features and codificatory needs — 354

### VI. LAW AND PHILOSOPHY — 356
- Complementarity and reciprocity of halakah and philosophy — 359
- Maimonides' continuous preoccupation with Rabbinics and metaphysics — 365
- Philosophy and law in the *Mishneh Torah* — 371
- *Ṭa'ăme ham-miṣwot* in the Maimonidean oeuvre — 374
  - Proofs that commandments have reasons — 374
    - Philosophic proof: wise=good=purposive — 378
    - Exegetical-historical proof — 380
    - Novel Maimonidean interpretation of Deut. 4:6 — 385

| | |
|---|---|
| Are the reasons for the commandments knowable? | 387 |
| Should the reasons be investigated and discovered?—dangers of antinomianism | 391 |
| Reasons for the law and mysteries of the Torah | 397 |
| Should knowledge of the reasons remain esoteric? | 400 |
| Reasons—absolute or relative? | 401 |
| *Ṭaʿăme miṣwot* and polemics | 403 |
| Reasons of the law in the *Mishneh Torah* | 407 |
| *Mĕʿilah*, viii, 8: a mandate for inquiry | 407 |
| *Tĕmurah*, iv, 13: the mandate repeated and applied | 415 |
| Widespread emphasis upon teleological role of *miṣwot* | 418 |
| Differences between *Mishneh Torah* and the *Guide* | 430 |
| Concern with ethical perfection | 440 |
| Socially-oriented explanations | 443 |
| The unity or duality of Maimonides' teaching: contradictions or divergent emphases | 447 |
| Attitude toward asceticism | 459 |
| Overt acknowledgment of elitism | 468 |
| Other features: explanation of decrees | 471 |
| Interpolation of *ḥokmah* | 473 |
| Attitude to "popular religion" | 479 |
| Personal-philosophic inclinations and halakic formulations | 485 |
| Philosophy as an integral part of Talmud | 489 |
| Nobility of philosophical knowledge | 500 |
| Conclusion | 507 |
| VII. Epilogue | 515 |
| A true classic: unprecedented and unrivaled | 515 |
| Rapid dissemination of the *Mishneh Torah:* critics and commentators | 518 |
| Design and reality: the actual impact | 526 |
| The *Mishneh Torah* and subsequent codification | 531 |
| Adherence and divergence: the example of *talmud Torah* | 535 |
| An original, dynamic force in Jewish life | 536 |
| Abbreviations | 539 |
| General | 539 |
| Personal names | 539 |
| Tractates of Mishnah, Tosefta, and Talmud | 540 |
| Works by Maimonides | 540 |
| List of treatise titles in MT | 542 |
| Glossary | 544 |
| Bibliography | 561 |
| General Index | 611 |
| Index of Maimonidean Passages | 622 |

# PREFACE

This book is a literary-historical study of the *Mishneh Torah*, Maimonides' great Code of Jewish law, organized around five characteristics repeatedly emphasized by Maimonides himself: codificatory form, scope, classification, language and style, philosophy and law. The analysis attempts to correlate his own self-perception, his own characterization and evaluation of his work, with the actual product—an objective assessment of the constructs, categories, and conclusions of his work, shaken free of stereotypes and preconceptions. When possible or appropriate, the author's statements are integrated with historical or phenomenological insights. The pivot around which it revolves is the *Mishneh Torah* itself, studied, I must confess, rather closely, for like history and science, the subject matter of halakah demands patient attention to detail. Just as the observance of halakah is predicated upon the indispensability and worth of all minutiae, so in its study no item is too trivial or inconsequential. Obviously, only a plethora of facts is capable of sustaining a soaring generalization or imaginative evaluation. Ranke observed that there are only two ways of acquiring knowledge: through the perception of the particular and through abstraction. The two, needless to say, are not mutually exclusive but complementary. Nevertheless, in order not to conceal the forest for the trees, I have tried to avoid excessive detail which might become cumbersome. Examples mentioned or discussed are representative rather than exhaustive; passages quoted from Maimonides are accompanied by the briefest commentary, while subtleties of text analysis are usually alluded to only in the notes, where additional references and cross-references chart the course of more comprehensive interpretation. In this way the book will hopefully be of interest and use to the general reader, whom the Yale Judaica Series has in mind, while also sustaining a scholarly dialogue concerning the nature, purpose, meaning, and influence of the *Mishneh Torah*. My hope, God willing, is to elaborate some of this material in a companion Hebrew volume, which provides a more natural context for expansive textual studies.

The first chapter contains a medley of biographical-bibliographical explorations and an analysis of Maimonides' declared motives in composing the Code, and concludes with a few succinct methodological considerations. It will be clear that while I have duly emphasized the influence of philosophy and have been generally attentive to related extra-halakic factors (historical, social, personal), the focus remains the *Mishneh Torah* itself and its unique presentation of halakah. René Wellek's axiom, which is quoted later on, is worth recalling at the very outset: "The work of literature is the central subject matter of a theory of literature, and not the biography or psychology of the author, or the social background, or the affective response of the reader." The same is true for law: one must beware of substituting geneticism, sociology, or philosophy for the original subject—in this case a unique codification of a unique system of religious law.

Chapters II to VI—the core of this study—develop the five central features of the *Mishneh Torah* with a moderate measure of textual specificity. Chapter VI, within the inevitable constraints imposed by the structure of this study and by its being written in English, contains somewhat more *explication de texte*. As is noted, I have focused on philosophic issues and sensibilities only as they directly arose from, or impinged upon, the *Mishneh Torah*. It was important to avoid being misled by Whitehead's "fallacy of misplaced concreteness"; we are dealing with a code, and although its philosophic component is significant, its judicial-halakic aspects are paramount. The brief epilogue comments on the Code's variegated modes of influence and its historical impact—an important ramified subject for a separate volume.

In order for each chapter, which attempts to combine abstraction with perception of the particular, to retain its integrity, a small measure of overlap has been allowed. Certain central themes and problems have been presented in their several contexts. Note also that when the occasion required a review of, or reference to, previous theories, characterizations, or interpretations, polemics were deemed dispensable. Differences of approach or emphasis will be readily discernible.

I have tried to avoid modernizations of various kinds which, aside from being either suspect or sometimes even shoddy, do not

## PREFACE

enhance the relevance of Maimonides. It seemed best to describe with maximum precision Maimonides' own comprehensive reformulation of halakah, his motives and methods, and his axial conception concerning the reciprocity of law and philosophy. Students will then be guided and instructed, stimulated and provoked by him; they may find themselves reading insights into, or out of, his carefully constructed statements, but at least they will be dealing with him directly. The fact is that Maimonides, sinking so easily into the background of his own work, nevertheless reveals himself, his ideas and aspirations, to the patient and receptive reader. As Henry James has said, "The artist is present in every page of every book from which he sought so assiduously to eliminate himself." For all his overtures to anonymity, the *Mishneh Torah* does expose its author, allowing the reader to penetrate the thought and outlook of Maimonides in all its diversity and originality. He is, after all, an author and not an editor. Such a study is, in short, the best introduction to Maimonides, and through him to a large part of medieval Judaism; for I would say that the "view of the world of a particular epoch" (Whitehead, *Science and the Modern World* [New York, 1929], p. vii) is best glimpsed by a study of legal formulations and their philosophical-ethical interpretations.

This book is actually structured as a general *introduction* to Maimonides' great work, aiming to introduce and illumine the main features of the Code and to analyze the motives for its composition and the methods of its creation. It is thus an attempt to describe what the *Mishneh Torah* is, and to some extent, how it came into being. By dint of the subject and my approach to it, the book is also an introduction to select problems in the ongoing study of the work through the ages. The decision to structure this volume as a literary-historical introduction—i.e., to interpret the Yale mandate literally—firmly imposed certain obvious restraints and necessitated the omission of certain dimensions of Maimonides' total accomplishment. Extended treatment of Maimonides' *Commentary on the Mishnah* and analysis of the nature of its explanations, the sequence of commandments in the *Sefer ham-Miṣwot* and the full import of its fourteen principles, his significance as a commentator of the Palestinian Talmud and his use of it in the Code, detailed study of the fragmentary autographs of the Code and evaluation of the stylistic as well as substantive changes reflected therein—inclusion of such important topics, and related ones, would have produced an asymmetrical and multivolume work. Careful textual study of the *Mishneh Torah* (or select sections of it) as well as jurisprudential study of problems in the history of halaḵah are also high on the still long and demanding agenda of Maimonidean studies. Many biobibliographical issues—e.g., the allegedly youthful works on logic (*Millot ha-Higgayon*) and astronomy, the *'Iggeret haš-Šĕmaḏ* for which no Arabic original is extant, the whole issue of Maimonidean pseudepigrapha, aspects of his communal career—need review, clarification, or summation. There is much unfinished business in Maimonidean scholarship. My hope is that this study will contribute in some ways to pushing back the frontiers of this scholarship.

Permission has been granted to use parts of my article "The Mishneh Torah of Maimonides," which was published in Volume V of the *Proceedings* of the Israel Academy of Sciences and Humanities (Jerusalem, 1976). Alexander Altmann of the Philip W. Lown School of Near Eastern and Judaic Studies of Brandeis University and the Harvard University Press have given permission to include portions of my essays published in *Biblical and Other Studies* © 1963 by the President and Fellows of Harvard College and *Jewish Medieval and Renaissance Studies* © 1967 by the President and Fellows of Harvard College.

This book, which I was invited to write for the Yale Judaica Series a long time ago, has been in gestation for many more years than anticipated. There are, of course, routine reasons for inefficiency and procrastination. Let me record here that the delay in completion was due in great measure to existential, academic, and literary commitments or distractions, actually significant or merely unavoidable, but probably the major determinant was the endless fascination of the *Mishneh Torah* itself. Every time you turn its pages or zero in on a specific passage (even for the hundredth time), it reveals new treasures, unperceived emphases, novel explanations, stimulating allusions, and stunning insights

# PREFACE

—all of which effectively restrain attempts at hasty generalization, almost compulsively lead you to add one more reference or to refine your proposed interpretation, and most dramatically underscore the prime value of page-by-page commentary.

Maimonides has been my companion for many, many years. I have studied him, have pondered and probed his writings, have been excited and enthralled by them almost daily. I have regularly discussed his works, particularly the *Mishneh Torah,* with many friends, colleagues, and students, whose names I could not possibly assemble here, and have benefited greatly from all of them. My father-in-law, Rabbi Dr. J. B. Soloveitchik, deserves special mention. I repeatedly benefited from his immense and genuinely effervescent learning and was warmed by his unfailing devotion. He has, in short, given me so much over the years that it would be folly to assume that a formal acknowledgment would be fully expressive. May he be blessed with good health and continued vigor.

I must, at this point, mention my mother, of blessed memory, who passed away (1 Tebet, A.M. 5737—December, 1976) while I was still, sometimes compulsively, adding footnotes to this book, long after the typescript had been mailed to the editor. She was generally an extraordinary woman whose piety and wisdom, conviction and compassion affected many people; for me particularly she was an unfailing guide and a very special source of inspiration. I still hear her, in a tone combining a mild query with a firm suggestion, commenting on why in the world I was writing about the RaMBaM (i.e., Maimonides) in English!

Professor Jacob Katz was gracious enough to read most of the typescript, and made a number of important comments which I found helpful and enlightening and for which I am truly grateful. My brother-in-law, Professor Haym Soloveitchik, read the entire manuscript with very great care; his discriminating comments and suggestions led me to rephrase certain interpretations and polish or sharpen certain formulations. Professor Shlomo Pines kindly responded to my request to read Chapter VI; his general agreement was welcome and his comment concerning the need to differentiate between the various facets of the Alfarabian influence was particularly helpful. I appreciate the time and effort which they generously invested. Needless to say, I alone am responsible for errors or misinterpretations.

I wish to express my sincere appreciation to Dr. Leon Nemoy for his painstaking review of the typescript, his abundant editorial queries and suggestions, and his unfailing courtesy and helpfulness. His careful and precise reading and rereading contributed notably to the consistency and accuracy of the text. I thank Mr. C. Grench and Mr. W. Bidwell of the Yale University Press for their skillful editing of the entire manuscript. Special thanks are due Carolyn I. Cross of Harvard's Department of Near Eastern Languages and Civilizations for her great skill, steady patience, and abundant good humor in converting my frequently illegible writing into an impeccable typescript.

Happily, my children, Mosheh, Tzipporah Rachel, and Mayer, were around to preoccupy my time and attention on many occasions; they have enriched my life immeasurably and taught me very much in many spheres.

Dedication of the book to my wife, Atarah, is a pale indication of my profound, all-consuming indebtedness to her. Any attempt to articulate it, to comment on her wisdom and probity, strength and sensitivity, would inevitably ring hollow, but inasmuch as she is attuned to my silences she will understand every nuance and hear every resonance. Her very name tells the story: she has been a beautiful crown for me and our family.

I wish, in conclusion, to mention my beloved father, the illustrious Rebbe of Talne, of blessed memory (passed away 26 'Iyyar, A.M. 5732—May, 1972); his saintliness, kindness, purity, and nobility of character are unforgettable.

# I

# Introduction: The *Mishneh Torah* in the Life and Work of Maimonides

Rabbi Moses ben Maimon, known in Hebrew literature as the RaMBaM and in Western culture since the Renaissance as Maimonides, is perhaps the most famous and resplendent figure of medieval Judaism. His fame is a direct result of the quality and quantity, scope and originality, magnetism and fascination of his writings. For Maimonides—born in Cordova, Spain (1135); died in Cairo (Fustat), Egypt (1204)—was a prolific author of amazing vigor and precision, of intellectual, moral, and religious force, of analytic sharpness and aesthetic delicacy. This is well known and generally appreciated, often with a dash of gratuitous hyperbole. In truth his reputation needs no inflation or exaggeration, for his stature is nearly sui generis and his commanding influence has been almost universally recognized. His literary oeuvre was not only remarkably comprehensive but also endlessly repercussive. He wrote epoch-making works in the central areas of halakah and religious philosophy—an achievement that is unquestionably, almost overpoweringly, characterized by monumentality, using the term very literally. His works, representing an unprecedented conjunction of halakic authority and philosophic prestige, were extensively studied, meticulously annotated, frequently translated, and intensively interpreted. Their influence, direct as well as indirect, reflected through many works in various genres by a host of authors, was global. His mighty historical image assumes heroic proportions rather early in his posthumous career, and it is this heroic figure which dominates the stage.[1]

---

1. The biography by D. Yellin and I. Abrahams, *Maimonides* (Philadelphia, 1903)—reissued (New York, 1972) with bibliographical supplement by J. Dienstag—is still useful. The more popular Hebrew biography by M. Uryan, *Ham-Moreh lĕ-Doroṭ* (Jerusalem, 1956), is well written and perceptive. See also Y. Baer, *A History of the Jews in Christian Spain* (Philadelphia, 1961), I, 96–110; S. Baron, *A Social and Religious History of the Jews* (New York, 1958), VI, 97–107 (on the MT); VIII, 55–138 (on philosophy); J.

## 2 INTRODUCTION TO THE CODE OF MAIMONIDES

That his writing (with the exception of his medical works)[2] is distinctively original and trailblazing is indisputable; while he appears simultaneously in two inseparable roles—as transmitter as well as creator, as vigilant guardian of the past and visionary architect of the future—the originality of his work is salient and its center of gravity lies in its forward movement. Maimonides himself sensitively evaluated his historic position and emphatically called attention to the innovating aspects of all his writings, and this evaluation has been resoundingly endorsed by a chorus of

---

Guttmann, *Philosophies of Judaism* (New York, 1964), 150–83; B. Dinur, *Yiśra'el bag-Golah*, II, book 4 (Jerusalem, 1969); J. Ḳāfiḥ's introduction to his Hebrew translation of MN (Jerusalem, 1972); and the various bibliographical studies by J. Dienstag (listed in the bibliography, below, pp. 581–82). The following contain important biographical details: E. Ashtor-Strauss, "Saladin and the Jews," *HUCA*, XXVII (1956), 305–26; S. D. Goitein, "Maimonides as Chief Justice," *JQR*, XLIX (1959), 191–203; idem, "The Title and Office of the Nagid: a Re-Examination," *JQR*, LIII (1962), 93–120; idem, "Tiḳḳunim . . . la-RaMBaM," *Tarbiz*, XXXII (1963), 188, and XXVIII (1959), 190ff.; idem, "Ḥayye ha-RaMBaM lĕ-'Or Giluyim Ḥadaśim," *Pĕraḳim*, IV (1966), 29ff.; B. Lewis, "Maimonides, Lionheart, and Saladin," *Eretz-Israel*, VII (1964), 70–75. B. Septimus, in his unpublished doctoral dissertation "Meir Abulafia and the Maimonidean Controversy" (Harvard University, 1975), discusses the emergence of the heroic image of Maimonides. For a different use of "heroic," see H. Butterfield, *The Whig Interpretation of History* (London, 1931).

2. These works, while illustrating his vast erudition and the lofty ethical standards discernible in his approach to medicine, need to be assessed in the light of the general history of medieval medical literature, particularly Arabic medical writings and their indebtedness to Greek sources and models. The following references are useful: M. Meyerhoff, "The Medical Works of Maimonides," *Essays on Maimonides*, ed. S. Baron (New York, 1941), pp. 265–301; idem, "L'oeuvre médicale de Maimonides," *Archeion*, XI (1929), 138ff.; M. Etziony, "Apropos of Maimonides' Aphorisms," *Bulletin of the History of Medicine*, XXXV (1961), 163–68; F. Rosner, "Maimonides the Physician: a Bibliography," *Bulletin of the History of Medicine*, XLIII (1969), 221–35; H. Friedenwald, *The Jews and Medicine* (Baltimore, 1944); J. Pagel, "Maimuni als medizinischer Schriftsteller," *MbM*, I, 231–47; and the Hebrew edition of his medical works (*Pirḳe Mośeh bi-Rĕfu'ah*), ed. Z. Muntner (Jerusalem, 1959). Noteworthy is the Maimonidean polemic against Galen (ibid., pp. 321ff.); cf. O. Temkin, *Galenism: Rise and Decline of a Medical Philosophy* (Ithaca, 1973); also C. Bürgel, *Averroes contra Galenum* (Göttingen, 1968); S. D. Goitein, "The Medical Profession in the Light of the Cairo Genizah Documents," *HUCA*, XXXIV (1963), 177–94; F. Rosenthal, "The Defense of Medicine in the Medieval Muslim World," *Bulletin of the History of Medicine*, XLIII (1969), 519–32; I. M. Ullmann, *Die Medizin im Islam* (Leiden, 1970). *Dine Israel*, VII (1976), contains many articles on medicine and the halakah, with frequent references to Maimonides.

Maimonides vigorously and repeatedly defended medicine, sharply repudiating those who questioned its legitimacy on religious grounds; see especially PhM, Pes 4:10 (p. 177); *De'ot*, iv, 20, 21; and below chap. VI, nn. 28 and 320.

R. Bolgar, *The Classical Heritage and Its Beneficiaries* (New York, 1964), p. 133, writes: "Law, medicine, and theology were the three foci of medieval thought."

# INTRODUCTION

voices through the ages. No book like the *Moreh Nĕbukim* (*Guide of the Perplexed*), he asserted, had been "written in the religious community in these times of Exile."[3] With regard to the *Mishneh Torah* in particular, we note that it contains none of the conventional protestations of modesty usually found at the beginning of such a work, neither diffidence about his undertaking it nor apologies for its deficiencies. Indeed, he candidly declared, combining a confident realization of primacy with an undaunted anticipation of criticism, that a work of such scope and arrangement, of such form, style, and systematization was totally unprecedented.[4] It was his great intellectual act of daring.

That his biography is characterized by a profound paradox, relevant for his work and its message, is also clearly recognized. A philosopher by temperament and ideology, a zealous devotee of the contemplative life who eloquently portrayed and yearned for the serenity of solitude and the spiritual exuberance of meditation, he nevertheless led a relentlessly active life that regularly brought him to the brink of exhaustion. A harassed physician, subject to the pressures and whims of the Sultan, and a conscientious leader of his community, sensitive to the physical-spiritual needs of its members, he combined a nerve-racking and strength-consuming professional routine with unabated scholarship, vigorous creativity, and literary productivity. Maimonides' life was a mosaic of anxiety, tribulation, and at best incredibly strenuous work and intellectual exertion. The record is simply extraordinary, almost surrealistic. His physical infirmity and all these apparently stultifying and asphyxiating conditions notwithstanding, he continued studying, teaching, and writing.

---

3. MN, introduction (p. 16), and cf. I, 71. See also PhM, introduction (p. 47) and ShM, introduction (II, p. 361); the fourteen *šorašim* are the real *novum* of the latter work.
  Concerning the consciousness (and/or denial) of originality, see below, p. 49 and chap. II; for specific issues note, e.g., PhM, Yoma 2:1 (p. 242); Țohāroṭ, introduction (p. 37); SP, chap. IV (end). Cf., e.g., R. Saadiah Gaon, *Commentary on Psalms*, ed. J. Ḳāfiḥ (Jerusalem, 1965), p. 37.

4. *Ḳobeṣ*, I, 25b: לפסוק הלכות . . . לא קדמני אדם אחר רבנו הקדוש. This is the emphasis of R. Aaron ben Meshullam in his letter to R. Meir Abulafia, *Ḳobeṣ*, III, 11d; R. Menaḥem ham-Me'iri, *Bet hab-Bĕḥirah*, introduction, p. 25; and P. Duran, *Ma'áśeh 'Efod* (Vienna, 1865), p. 19. Also R. Menaḥem ben Zeraḥ, *Ṣedah lad-Derek* (Warsaw, 1880), p. 6. Even those who did not follow him—as will be noted in chap. VII—acknowledged that his work was sui generis.

## 4   INTRODUCTION TO THE CODE OF MAIMONIDES

Indeed, the two realities, existential and intellectual, are antithetically related, as he intimates in a letter written in 1184, after the completion of the *Mishneh Torah*, while he was working on the *Moreh:* "Were not the study of the Torah my delight, and did not the study of wisdom divert me from my grief, *I should then have perished in mine affliction* (Ps. 119:92)." When Maimonides writes to R. Jonathan "how hard have I worked day and night throughout these past ten years in order to compile" the *Mishneh Torah,* we can only marvel at the achievement as well as the measured words used to describe its preparation. The deliberate understatement has maximum effect. Even if he had enjoyed optimal conditions of comfort and security, unlimited research and secretarial assistance, the work would defy imagination. In assessing this achievement, therefore, it is particularly pertinent to recall Maimonides' graphic and pungent description of his arduous professional and communal schedule, contained in his letter of 1199 to Samuel ibn Tibbon.[5]

---

5. Letter to R. Japheth, *Kobeṣ*, II, 37b; letter to R. Jonathan, *Tešubot*, III, p. 57 (translated below, p. 39). See S. Heschel, *The Insecurity of Freedom* (New York, 1972), pp. 285ff. ("The Last Days of Maimonides"). The letter to Samuel ibn Tibbon (*Kobeṣ*, II, 28a; and ed. A. Marx, *JQR*, XXV [1935], 376ff. reads, in part, as follows: Now God knows that in order to write this to you I have escaped to a secluded spot, where people would not think to find me, sometimes leaning for support against the wall, sometimes lying down on account of my excessive weakness, for I have grown old and feeble.

With regard to your wish to come here to me, I cannot but say how greatly your visit would delight me, for I truly long to commune with you, and would anticipate our meeting with even greater joy than you. Yet I must advise you not to expose yourself to the perils of the voyage, for beyond seeing me, and my doing all I could to honor you, you would not derive any advantage from your visit. Do not expect to be able to confer with me on any scientific subject, for even one hour either by day or by night, for the following is my daily occupation. I dwell at Miṣr [Fusṭaṭ] and the Sultan resides at Ḳāhirah [Cairo]; these two places are two Sabbath days' journey [about one mile and a half] distant from each other. My duties to the Sultan are very heavy. I am obliged to visit him every day, early in the morning; and when he or any of his children, or any of the inmates of his harem, are indisposed. I dare not quit Ḳāhirah, but must stay during the greater part of the day in the palace. It also frequently happens that one or two of the royal officers fall sick, and I must attend to their healing. Hence, as a rule, I repair to Ḳāhirah very early in the day, and if nothing unusual happens, I do not return to Miṣr until the afternoon. Then I am almost dying with hunger. I find the antechamber filled with people, both Jews and Gentiles, nobles and common people, judges and bailiffs, friends and foes—a mixed multitude, who await the time of my return.

I dismount from my animal, wash my hands, go forth to my patients, and entreat them to bear with me while I partake of some slight refreshment, the only meal I take in the

## INTRODUCTION 5

Moreover, this aspect of his biography provides a concrete matrix for certain recurrent themes of his writing. Some of the most impassioned and protreptic prose of the *Mishneh Torah*, for example, expresses his opposition to the existence of an institutionalized and salaried rabbinate, dependent upon the largesse of patrons or charitable collections. He himself, of course, did not receive any financial aid or official remuneration from the Jewish community, even after he emerged as its untitled leader, combining the duties of rabbi, local judge, appellate judge, administrative chief responsible for appointing and supervising community officials, and overseer of the philanthropic foundations (to which he was especially dedicated). His advice to students mirrors the same unshakable conviction as does his critical appraisal of past practices. The religious indignation, moral pathos, and de facto inflexibility of his position become even more poignant and meaningful in the light of his own turbulent biography and its remarkable consistency in this area, in defiance of all challenges, pressures, and temptations.[6]

---

twenty-four hours. Then I attend to my patients, write prescriptions for their various ailments. Patients go in and out until nightfall, and sometimes even, I solemnly assure you, until two hours and more in the night. I converse and prescribe for them while lying down from sheer fatigue, and when night falls, I am so exhausted that I can scarcely speak.

In consequence of this, no Israelite can have any private interview with me except on the Sabbath. On this day the whole congregation, or at least the majority of the members, come to me after the morning service, when I instruct them as to their proceedings during the whole week; we study together a little until noon, when they depart. Some of them return, and read with me after the afternoon service until evening prayers. In this manner I spend that day. I have here related to you only a part of what you would see if you were to visit me. Now when you have completed for our brethren the translation you have commenced, I beg that you will come to me but not with the hope of deriving any advantage from your visit as regards your studies; for my time is, as I have shown you, excessively occupied."

The fragmentary letter published by D. Baneth in *Sefer Zikkaron lĕ-Gulaḳ wĕ-Klein* (Jerusalem, 1942), pp. 50ff., also reflects these emphases.

6. *Talmud Torah*, iii, 10; *Mattĕnot 'Aniyyim*, x, 18; *Zĕkiyyah u-Mattanah*, xii, 17; *Sanhedrin*, xxiii, 5; *'Iggĕrot*, 68; PhM, 'Ab 4:7 (pp. 441ff.); Ned 4:3 (p. 128). Note particularly that the letter to R. Japheth, written in 1184, refers to his plight during the years he was trying to complete the MT. On the question of remuneration for scholars, cf. the position of his younger contemporary, Joseph ibn Aknin, *Sefer ham-Musar: Peruš 'Abot*, ed. W. Bacher (Berlin, 1911), p. 121. Maimonides' ideal type of scholar-philosopher and compassionate sensitive leader is clearly reflected in the MT; e.g., *Yĕsode hat-Torah*, v, 11; *De'ot*, v, 13; *Talmud Torah*, i, 11, 12, and vi, 3; *Sanhedrin*, xxiv, 10; xxv, 1–2; *Mĕlakim* ii, 6; iv, 10; also *Ḳobeṣ*, I, 3b; II, 31b. See H. H. Ben-Sasson, "Ha-RaMBaM: Hanhagat 'Iš

# 6 INTRODUCTION TO THE CODE OF MAIMONIDES

## Maimonides' Literary Oeuvre: Unity and Diversity

Equally important but less prominent is the fact that Maimonides' life's work—a fastidious interpretation and thoughtful reformulation of Jewish belief and practice—seems to have been clear in his mind from an early age. All the formal-thematic heterogeneity and conceptual diversity notwithstanding, there is a conscious unity and progressive continuity in his literary career, suffused as it is with originality and virtuosity, boldness and thoroughness, in which there is no room for leisurely and discursive writing. It is as if he were following a carefully etched blueprint and as a result was never free, was never "between performances." He was always, in the literal sense, preoccupied. What is most striking is how early his ideas, ideals, and aspirations were formed, how logically they hang together, and how consistently and creatively they have been applied. For all the frenetic activity, professional and communal commitments, personal tensions, social conflicts, cultural complexities, and intellectual challenges, there is a steady momentum and rhythm to his writing and a clear focus to his activity. He began early—with zeal, almost with a sense of mission—and continued prodigiously to the end of his life. As he moved from one literary form to another, from textual explication to systematic exposition, and from one level of exposition to another, the unified, if multidimensional, themes of development shine forth, and the firm structures of his consciousness, perception, and motivation are clearly discernible. The dynamic force behind the incomparable juridical-philosophical labors of Maimonides seems to be his desire to realize a grand goal. A quick glance at Maimonides' literary biography, which we are able to reconstruct with considerable accuracy, will provide a natural organic framework in which the *Mishneh Torah* is to be seen, and this in turn will automatically underscore its centrality, both in terms of chronological symmetry as well as substantive importance.

---

ha-Ruaḥ," *Ha-'Isiyyut we-Dorah* (Jerusalem, 1964), pp. 93ff. See, generally, G. Post, "Masters' Salaries and Student Fees," *Speculum*, VII (1932), 181ff., and his note in *Archives d'histoire doctrinale*, XXI (1954), 135, concerning the adage *vere philosophantes pecuniam contemnunt;* also W. M. Watt, *Muslim Intellectual: a Study of al-Ghazālī* (Edinburgh, 1963), p. 114.

## INTRODUCTION

*Three Sources of Information*

Three sources are particularly informative: (1) a passage from the introduction to the *Commentary on the Mishnah* conjoined with a few items in the *Commentary;* (2) a responsum to R. Nehorai had-Dayyan; (3) the beginning of the introduction to the *Sefer ham-Miṣwot*.

1. Toward the end of the introduction to his *Commentary on the Mishnah*, after candidly and curtly characterizing Gaonic literary activity in the area of halakah, its achievements and shortcomings, he leaps or lapses into an autobiographical account:

> When it was our time, we undertook, in the footsteps of our predecessors, to investigate and study and exert ourselves according to our abilities to attain that which we hope will benefit us before God. I collected all that happened to come into my hand from the glosses of my father, may the memory of the righteous be for a blessing, and others, in the name of R. Joseph hal-Levi [ibn Megas]. I testify that that man's understanding of the Talmud astounds everyone who takes note of his statements and the profundity of his perception, so that it is possible for me to state about him *And like unto him was there no king [scholar] before him* (2 Kings 23:25) in his method of study. I also collected all the laws that I myself gleaned from his own commentary as well as those explanations of mine which seemed right, according to my weak ability, and whatever I attained from [the study of] science (*'ilm, ḥokmah*). I composed commentaries on three orders of the Talmud, *Moʻed, Našim* and *Nĕzikin,* with the exception of four tractates on which I am now trying to write something, but have yet to find free time for this. I also composed a commentary on the tractate *Ḥullin* as a result of the great need for it. This is what I have been busy with, together with the study of everything that I studied. Afterwards I deemed it proper to compose a work on the Mishnah, for which there was compelling need, as I shall explain. [He then proceeds to pinpoint some of the complexities of the Talmud which dissipate its usefulness as a commentary on the Mishnah.][7]

Students of Maimonides will appreciate the hurried glimpse into his workshop which this compact passage provides and what it tells us about his concerns and interests and his religious-historical motivations. It establishes, first of all, his authorship of

---

7. PhM, introduction (p. 47).

# 8 INTRODUCTION TO THE CODE OF MAIMONIDES

a Talmudic commentary on those three practical orders of the Babylonian Talmud which were regularly studied in the Spanish schools. This work, which remained rather marginal in the later history of Talmudic interpretation, represented a conventional preoccupation of Rabbinic scholars which had been shaped by utilitarian criteria, and that explains the inclusion of *Ḥullin*, for this was very practical. Second, it gives us some inkling of his procedure, his literary policies, and his interpretative principles; it also notes his point of departure, at which Maimonides is seen as conforming to traditional patterns of study and collecting whatever was available to him in the given areas. Basic genetic and literary-historical relationships are outlined. His great admiration for R. Isaac Alfasi, whose *Halakot* is unreservedly lauded just before the above-quoted passage, is already firm, and there is an implicit reliance upon his opinions and conclusions.[8] Many lauded him; many learned from him; he was the lodestar of an entire generation. The figure of R. Joseph ibn Megas,[9] prestigious successor of Alfasi in the school of Lucena, looms large—any halakic interpretation of his, whether culled from the scholia of his father and (presumably) other disciples or from

---

8. Ibid. (pp. 46–47). The resounding praise of Alfasi, that his work eclipsed all Gaonic compositions (ההלכות הספיקו במקום כולם), immediately precedes the passage; see also below, chap. IV. In his letter to Ibn Tibbon (*Kobeṣ*, II, 28b), Maimonides has identical praise for Aristotle vis-à-vis all his predecessors: ספרי אריסטו יספיקו על כל מה שחבר לפניהם. It is interesting that RABD occasionally notes—sometimes agreeing, sometimes disagreeing, and sometimes remaining neutral—Maimonides' reliance on Alfasi; see *Šabbaṭ* xxv, 13, and *Malweh wĕ-Loweh*, xxi, 3; *'Išuṭ*, xvii, 8, and *Šĕkiruṭ*, x, 11; *Gĕzelah wa-'Ăbedah*, iv, 13, and *Zĕkiyyah u-Mattanah*, iii, 5.

9. *Šĕ'elah u-Fiḳḳadon*, v, 6; *Tĕšuboṭ*, 269 (p. 516); 294 (p. 553); PhM 'Ab 4:7 (p. 446); Abraham ibn Daud, *Sefer haḳ-Ḳabbalah*, ed. G. Cohen (Philadelphia, 1967), p. 86. See the excellent bibliographic survey by I. Ta-Shema, "Yĕṣirato has-Sifrutiṭ šel Rabbenu Yosef 'ibn Megaš," *KS*, XLVI (1971), 136ff. It is not surprising that we have only his commentaries on *Baba Batra* and *Šĕbu'oṭ*, for even Maimonides' acquaintance with his literary oeuvre was limited to these two works; *Tĕšuboṭ*, 82 (p. 127), 393 (p. 671), 428 (p. 708). Even if we take into account the fact that the printed texts of Ibn Megas' commentaries are deficient and defective (see L. Ginzberg, *REJ*, LXVII [1914], 151, and I. Ta-Shema, "Yosef 'ibn Megaš," 141), his legacy remains meager. We may cite as an interesting historical parallel to this situation—widespread influence and venerable reputation vis-à-vis minimal literary output—the case of R. Isaac Canpanton (fifteenth century); see *Sĕfunoṭ*, VII (1962), 83 (the statement of R. Abraham ibn Megas).

Further illustration of his influence upon Maimonides is provided by the eight responsa recently published by I. Ta-Shema and H. Ben-Shammai, *Ḳobeṣ 'al Yad*, VIII (1976),

Maimonides' own methodical scrutiny of Ibn Megas' commentaries, is treasured. Maimonides' usual reference to him as "my teacher" illustrates that discipleship need not be based on direct personal contact—literary influence also establishes discipleship. This remarkable relationship to Ibn Megas—almost a Sphinx-like figure in Spanish-Jewish history who to the best of our knowledge had no interest or involvement in philosophy, or science, or any extra-Talmudic discipline—invites further analysis, for while Ibn Megas' literary heritage is relatively meager it was extremely influential. In the case of Maimonides, the influence was so profound that he clearly viewed himself as a pupil of Ibn Megas. This rich but not very extensive literary inheritance, which he truly esteems, lavishly praises, and helps transmit, is quite naturally combined with Maimonides' own interpretations, and this use of available sources together with his own resourcefulness is particularly crucial for appreciating the originality, value, and character of the *Mishneh Torah*. The silence concerning the Geonim in this context—they are, to be sure, mentioned summarily, almost ritualistically, in the *maqāmah*-style introduction to the entire work, and there is a lean, bare-bones enumeration of book titles immediately before the paean to R. Isaac Alfasi—suggests the difference he perceived between their methods and accomplishments and his own. Indeed, Maimonides' dissatisfaction with the Geonim is clearly mirrored in his praise of R. Isaac Alfasi, whose *Halakot,* by calculated and consistent omission or skillful use of understatement and nuances of formulation and emphasis, diminished the import and impact of Gaonic writing. Finally, the natural integration, without any trace of self-consciousness or tinge of defensiveness, of Talmud with other sciences, which will

---

167ff. See also J. Ḳāfiḥ, "Mim-Megillat Setarim le-RI Megaš," *Sefer Marğaliyyot,* ed. I. Refa'el (Jerusalem, 1973), pp. 70ff. See further S. D. Goitein, *A Mediterranean Society* (Los Angeles, 1967), I, 406, n. 31, where Ibn Megas is designated as the *yeḥid had-dor*.

For Maimonides' father, R. Maimon, see *'Iggeret han-Neḥamah,* tr. B. Klar and ed. J. Maimon (Fishman) (Jerusalem, 1945); A. Freimann, "Tešubot R. Maimon," *Tarbiz,* VI (1935), 164ff.; and A. Marmorstein, *Tarbiz,* VI, 426; PhM, introduction (p. 47); 'Ed 1:3 (p. 284); Bek 8:8 (p. 271); Shebu 6:7 (p. 270); IT, xx; *Birkat 'Abraham,* n. 29; *Tešubot,* 126 (p. 224). In the MT, see *Šeḥiṭah,* xi, 11. For Maimonides' theory on the reasons for the institution of fixed prayer (*Tefillah,* i, 4), see *'Iggeret han-Neḥamah,* pp. 22ff.

## 10 INTRODUCTION TO THE CODE OF MAIMONIDES

remain a pivot of his life and his achievement, is clearly noted.[10] Ḥokmah (wisdom, science) is pervasive and indispensable.

Other literary references found in the *Mishnah Commentary* itself also reveal to us, at the same early stage of his career, the constant intersection of halakic and philosophic preoccupations on the one hand, and the use of various forms of halakic writings on the other. There is here an early adumbration of both the multiplicity and the persistence of his interests. In addition to his commentaries on the Talmud and Mishnah, he was preparing, he informs us, a special minicode, a compendium of laws found in the Palestinian Talmud (*Talmud Yĕrušalmi*).[11] The purpose of the *Hilkot Yĕrušalmi* was significant: to extract all those sections of the rather neglected Palestinian Talmud which would shed light on the more normative and academically more popular Babylonian Talmud, illumine obscurities, fill in halakic details, or provide reasons for certain laws not explained elsewhere. In common with other scholars of North Africa (particularly Kairouan) and Spain, Maimonides was devoted to the study of the Palestinian Talmud and eager to increase its popularity and extend its influence. Maimonides' reliance upon it in his *Mishneh Torah* is unusually bold and extensive. There are parts of the Palestinian Talmud, particularly in an area such as *Zĕra'im,* which Maimonides, by his careful and persuasive use, helped raise to a level of normativeness equal to that of the Babylonian Talmud. The early preoccupation with it is thus emblematic of both an abiding interest and a far-reaching halakic influence. Any all-inclusive study of Maimonides' halakic achievement would have to identify, analyze, and fully document this theme.[12]

---

10. See, e.g., PhM, Ter 1:2 (p. 270); RH 2:7 (p. 317); Suk 1:1 (p. 269); Kel 1:5 (p. 49), and others; below, chap. VI, especially n.31. And see the parallelism of Torah and wisdom in the previously cited letter to R. Japheth (above, n.5).

11. PhM, Tam 5:1 (p. 420); and see *Hilkot Yĕrušalmi la-RaMBaM,* ed. S. Lieberman (New York, 1948), pp. 5ff.

12. See, e.g., *Tĕšubot,* 299 (p. 558); *Ḳĕri'at Šĕma',* iii, 6, and RABD; *Šĕmiṭṭah wĕ-Yobel,* ix, 8, and RaDBaZ; *Mĕkirah,* xiii, 1, and RABD; Naḥmanides, *Torat ha-'Adam,* ed. C. Chavel, *Kitbe RaMBaN* (Jerusalem, 1963), II, 169; R. Joseph Kolon, *Tĕšubot,* 100. R. Elijah Gaon of Vilna regularly underscored Maimonides' creative use of the Palestinian Talmud; e.g., *'Oraḥ Ḥayyim,* 546:5 (סמך על הירושלמי כדרכו ברוב מקומות). See generally *Hilkot Yerušalmi,* 14, and my discussion of the use of the Palestinian Talmud by the

INTRODUCTION

He also mentions plans for a special commentary which would classify, explain, and rationalize aggadah: "I hope to write a book collecting all the Sages' teachings on this subject from the Talmud and other works. I shall interpret them systematically, showing which must be understood literally and which metaphorically, and which are dreams to be interpreted by a wakeful mind. There I shall explain the many principles of our faith of which I have discussed a few here."[13] Although he later abandoned the idea of composing such a work, the *Moreh Nĕbukim,* which was devoted in great part to matters of exegesis, allegory, and prophecy, was seen as a partial substitute for it:

> We had promised in the *Commentary on the Mishnah* that we would explain strange subjects in the "Book of Prophecy" and in the "Book of Correspondence"—the latter being a book in which we promised to explain all the difficult passages in the Midrashim where the external sense manifestly contradicts the truth and departs from the intelligible. They are all parables. However, when many years ago we began these books and composed a part of them, our beginning to explain matters in this way did not commend itself to us. For we saw that if we should adhere to parables and to concealment of what ought to be concealed, we would not be deviating from the primary purpose. We would, as it were, have replaced one individual by another of the same species. If, on the other hand, we explained what ought to be explained, it would be unsuitable for the vulgar among the people. Now it was to the vulgar that we wanted to explain the import of the Midrashim and the external meanings of prophecy. . . . With regard to the meaning of prophecy, the exposition of its various degrees, and the elucidation of the parables occurring in the Prophetic Books, another manner of explanation is used in this Treatise. In view of these considerations, we have given up composing these two books in the way in which they were begun.[14]

These autobiographical-bibliographical statements not only raise the history of aggadah to a higher level than is usually accorded to it, suggestively placing the *Moreh* in an aggadic as well as in a

---

*rišonim* in my *Rabad,* pp. 206ff. Note R. Joseph ibn Megas, *Tĕšubot,* 81. In PhM, Tam 3:4 (p. 414), Maimonides added a reference to the Palestinian Talmud not found in the first version of the commentary. See also PhM, Soṭ 1:6 (p. 249).

13. PhM, Sanh, *Ḥelek* (p. 209).
14. MN, introduction (p. 9).

philosophic tradition,[15] but also help provide a rather complete version of Maimonides' bibliography. The reader realizes, moreover, that the use of aggadah and the analysis of prophecy as well as the methodological comments on exegesis and allegory are not peripheral or accidental in the *Mishneh Torah*. He may have "given up composing these two books *in the way in which they were begun*," but the themes of these abandoned compositions never became peripheral for him. We cannot dodge the conclusion that the contours of his entire literary career, its sequence and structure, its forms and themes, were clearly visible from the very outset.

2. A responsum of Maimonides adds another dimension to the structural-generic variety of his Talmudic writing by revealing the existence of a different genre: animadversions and scholia.[16] In answer to a question concerning an obvious disagreement between himself and R. Isaac Alfasi, he notes that this is not an isolated instance. In fact, we are told that he had in manuscript first drafts of tracts containing criticisms of Alfasi, some of which were initially put forward by R. Joseph ibn Megas. These were not completed and prepared for publication because of lack of time—the same reason which kept him from explaining fully the *Hilkot Yĕrušalmi* which he had collected and from editing properly another work of his referred to as "a *peruš* (explication) of difficult halakot in the entire Talmud." All the evidence favors the view that the latter is not identical with the commentary referred to in the introduction to the *Mishnah Commentary*, and that Maimonides actually wrote two kinds of commentary: (a) a commentary on three orders of the Talmud, à la Rashi or R.

15. See below, chaps. II and IV. Later commentators of the aggadah took their cue from Maimonides; e.g., R. Shem-Tob ibn Shaprut, *Sefer Pardes Rimmonim* (Sabbioneta, 1514), p. 2; R. Isaac Abarbanel, *Yĕšu'ot Mĕšiḥo* (Koenigsberg, 1861), p. 5; see my forthcoming Hebrew article, "Yĕda'yah hap-Pĕnini Paršan ha-'Aggadah," *Alexander Altmann Jubilee Volume*, ed. S. Stein (University, Alabama, 1979). Cf. L. Strauss, *Persecution and the Art of Writing* (Glencoe, 1952), p. 48.; note R. Judah Loew (MaHaRal) of Prague, *Bĕ'er hag-Golah* (Jerusalem, 1972), chap. 4, p. 49.

16. *Tĕšubot*, 251 (p. 459). Criticism of R. Isaac Alfasi started immediately, all the genuine esteem notwithstanding (see below, end of chap. II). For R. Ephraim, see B. Benedikt, "Sefer hat-Tašlum šel R. 'Efrayim," *KS*, XXVI (1949–50), 322–36; Twersky, *Rabad*, p. 248; and the important study by I. Schepansky, *Rabbenu 'Efrayim: Talmid-Ḥaber šel ha-RIF* (Jerusalem, 1976).

Hananeel; and (b) novellae or glosses, à la the Tosafot or later *ḥiddušim*, on select sections, cruxes of the whole Talmud.[17] Maimonides stands here squarely in the Spanish literary tradition of composing glosses or scholia on select themes and particularly vexing problems. Maimonides' "*peruš* of difficult halakot," parts of which were composed after the *Mishneh Torah,* thus fits into a respectable genre, and more significantly, illustrates his abiding devotion to pure Talmudic study, unrelated to "practical" needs. In sum, this ongoing preoccupation with Talmud commentary adds an important dimension to Maimonides' life's work.

3. The source that is the sturdiest link joining his three major halakic works is the introduction to *Sefer ham-Miṣwot (Book of*

---

17. See *Ḥidduše ha-RaMBaM lat-Talmud,* ed. J. L. Sacks (Jerusalem, 1963). This view, put forward by S. Eppenstein, long ignored by students of Maimonides, finally jettisoned by the late Professor S. Assaf, and recently rehabilitated by the late Rabbi Sacks, rests on the following evidence: The logic and sequence of the first statement ("I composed a commentary on three orders . . . and afterwards I saw fit" to deal with the Mishnah) suggest that both were in Arabic. This is explicitly stated by the translator (R. Jacob ben Aksai) of part of his *Mishnah Commentary (Seder Našim).* However, in his correspondence with the scholars of Lunel, Maimonides speaks of commentaries which he composed in Hebrew (or Hebrew-Aramaic, the lingua franca of Rabbinic scholarship, *lišna' dĕ-rabbanan*), and his son quotes him verbatim a number of times. Moreover, it would appear from some references that Maimonides was working on a Talmud Commentary *after* the *Mishnah Commentary.* Finally, the characterization of the work in the responsum, written *after* the MT, differs in two respects from the earlier references: (a) its scope includes the whole Talmud and not merely the three practical orders; (b) it is selective and discursive, à la the Tosafot, rather than a running commentary, à la Rashi or Rabbenu Hananeel. These four discrepancies—language, time of composition, type of commentary, and scope—sustain the separate identity and independence of these works. See also M. Hershler, "Keṭa' mip-Peruso šel ha-RaMBaM lĕ-Ḥagigah," *Sinai,* LIV (1964), 185–90. On the disputed commentary to Roš haš-Šanah, see S. Lieberman, *Hilkot Yĕrušalmi,* p. 2; E. Kupfer, "Hašlamah lĕ-Peruš RaMBaM lĕ-Roš haš-Šanah," *Sinai,* LV (1964), 230–35; and the recent comment of I. Ta-Shema, *ḲS,* XLVI (1975), 139.

A good example of his inexhaustible Talmud study is his ongoing preoccupation with a complicated problem concerning the Temple ceremonial on the Day of Atonement, which was treated in both versions of PhM, Yoma, 2:1 (p. 242), summarized at great length in the MT, *Tĕmidin u-Musafin,* iv, 3, and was still under discussion in his *Tešuḇot,* 126 (p. 223). See S. H. Kook, *'Iyyunim u-Meḥkarim* (Jerusalem, 1963), I, 304, and S. Lieberman, *Hilkot Yĕrušalmi,* p. 11. Concerning parallel and precedent in this kind of writing, note the *Mĕgillat Sĕtarim* of R. Nissim Gaon, the *Peruš Sugyot Ḥamurot* of R. Samuel han-Nagid, the *Peruš Sugyot* which R. Isaac Alfasi appended to his *Halakot,* and the *Peruš Mikṣat Halakot Ḥamurot* which R. Zeraḥiah hal-Levi mentions in the introduction to his *Sefer ham-Ma'or.* See also MT, introduction ("Those who had put the questions [to the Geonim] collected the responses which they made into books for study"); *Ḳobeṣ,* II, 16a; R. Joseph ibn Megas, *Tešuḇot,* 114; S. D. Goitein, *Sidre Ḥinnuk* (Jerusalem, 1962), pp. 156–57.

## 14 INTRODUCTION TO THE CODE OF MAIMONIDES

*Commandments*).[18] Not only was this work a model of classification and analysis and of confident originality, "self-commissioned" as it were in conjunction with the *Mishneh Torah* (its listing of the 613 commandments was intended to guarantee the comprehensiveness of the Code), but the *Mishneh Torah* itself is here presented as the logical sequel and salient finale to his previous Talmudic efforts. The basic literary traits and methodological modes of his codificatory work are already underscored. Systematization is inextricably linked with brevity and clarity. He expresses, and then maintains, his conviction that diffuseness and preoccupation with conflicting interpretations and minority opinions are serious obstacles to proper knowledge. While many of the traits which reach full maturation later may be seen germinating in the *Mishnah Commentary*—concise style, comprehensiveness, conceptualization, classification, rationalization and spiritualization of halakic precepts—and many novel Talmudic interpretations or juridical definitions already appear in the *Sefer ham-Miṣwot*, the *Mishneh Torah* is undoubtedly the crowning and consummate achievement of his rich halakic enterprise.

### *Centrality of the* Mishneh Torah

We have, in sum, an expanding variety of Rabbinic works—*Commentary on (three orders of) the Babylonian Talmud, Commentary on the Mishnah, Compendium of Laws in the Palestinian Talmud, Commentary on difficult halakot of the entire Talmud*, animadversions against R. Isaac Alfasi, *Book of Commandments*—leading up to the *Mishneh Torah*. Talmudic study which continues after the completion of the Code is to a great extent, directly or indirectly, related to it. Mention should also be made of two very important *pièces de circonstance*, the *'Iggeret haš-Šemad* (*Epistle on Conversion*) (ca. 1161–62) and the *'Iggeret Teman* (*Epistle to Yemen*) (1172), whose halakic positions, theological emphases, and aggadic interpretations are particularly relevant for the *Mishneh Torah*. The *'Iggeret Teman*, after all, was written at the very time that

---

18. ShM, introduction (II, p. 361), cited below, pp. 25ff. See Maimonides' characterization in *Tešubot*, 310 (p. 574), 447 (p. 725), and below, chap. IV. On the title of this work, see J. Neubauer, *Ha-RaMBaM 'al Dibre Soferim* (Jerusalem, 1957), pp. 91ff.

## INTRODUCTION 15

Maimonides was compiling the *Mishneh Torah*. Both epistles attempt to cope with the "problem of history": to confront the recurrent facts of catastrophe and decimation without increasing anguish and despondency, and to explain the ubiquitousness of suffering while discoursing on the tenacity of faith and the solace which a long-range theological view of history provides. Hence the thoughtful reader of these texts will be in a position to gauge the stylistic and substantive transformations that occur in a major multiplex literary oeuvre when a philosopher-jurisprudent becomes a polemicist and popularizer. These letters, eloquent and erudite, sensitive and empathetic, reveal Maimonides as a resourceful pedagogue, using literary skill, scientific knowledge, philosophical reasoning, and exegetical virtuosity in order to enlighten as well as encourage his readers.[19]

Concomitantly—for the intellectual panorama is very wide—Maimonides unceasingly pursued his philosophic-scientific studies which, by all indications, meant encyclopedic coverage of the entire field, achieving diversity without sacrificing profundity or succumbing to dilettantism. He produced the *Treatise on Logic* and the *Treatise on the Intercalation of the Calendar*, entertained plans for a philosophic work on aggadah (i.e., Jewish thought), and interpolated significant philosophic excursuses, introductions, or digressions into his Rabbinic writings. In addition to being a conscientious practicing physician, he was also an avid teacher of philosophy and science, "reading" classical texts with worthy students.[20] This facet of his work may thus be seen

---

19. The same is true for the LA; see R. Lerner, "Maimonides' Letter on Astrology," *History of Religions*, VIII (1968), 143–58. For the *'Iggeret haš-Šemad*, see the Harvard honors thesis (1958) by H. Soloveitchik. See the Hebrew introduction of A. S. Halkin to the IT, pp. ix ff. The following themes in IT are noteworthy: (1) the phenomenology of persecutions of the Jews; (2) the notion that Christianity and Islam, Judaism's "daughter religions," are only surface imitations of Judaism and bear a special animosity toward Judaism; (3) the vigorous refutation of the contention, frequently repeated by Muslim apologists, that Scripture contains veiled allusions to Islam; (4) the summary of Maimonides' fundamental doctrine that all commandments in Judaism have an inner meaning designed to lead man to perfection; (5) the plea not to calculate the advent of the Messianic era, coupled with the recording of a family tradition which nevertheless suggests a date for it.

20. See the passage from al-Qifṭī's *History of Physicians*, cited by B. Lewis, *Eretz Israel*, VII (1964), 70–71: "He earned a living by dealing in precious stones and the like and

## 16 INTRODUCTION TO THE CODE OF MAIMONIDES

as leading up, in different ways, both to the *Mishneh Torah* and particularly to the *Moreh*, his philosophic testament par excellence.

There is still another aspect to the centrality of the *Mishneh Torah*. It would appear that Maimonides was constantly reviewing his earlier works in the light of conclusions arrived at in the *Mishneh Torah* and of insights provided by it:

That which we have written in the compendium [*ḥibbur*, i.e., the *Mishneh Torah*] is indubitably correct. We have written accordingly in the *Mishnah Commentary*. That [version] which you possess is the first version which was circulated before we reached the precise interpretation. We followed in that early version the opinion of Rabbi Ḥefeṣ, the author of the *Sefer ham-Miṣwot*, and that was an error on his part; the fact that we followed him evinced lack of reflection on our part. After we had reflected upon the dicta and interpreted them precisely, that [conclusion] which we wrote in the compendium, which is the correct one, became clear and we corrected the *Mishnah Commentary*.[21]

---

*people studied philosophy under him."* Note also MN, introduction, dedicatory epistle (p. 3: "when you came to me . . . to read texts under my guidance"). In *Ḳobeṣ*, I, 25b, he talks about "reading" Rabbinic texts with select students.

21. *Tešubot*, 212 (p. 383 and n.4, concerning *Šemiṭṭah wĕ-Yobel*, ix, 22, and PhM, Shebi 10:5). For ShM, see Kāfiḥ's introduction, p. 11; ShM, negative 353, refers to PhM, Sanh 7:4, and not to MT. R. Moses ibn Tibbon remarks (in the introduction to his Hebrew rendition of the ShM) that although it was designed as an introduction to the MT, Maimonides reworked it in the light of insights and conclusions reached in the MT. Naḥmanides, in the introduction to his strictures on ShM, notes that there are errors in this work which were corrected in the MT. See also PhM, Men 4:1 (p. 121), where the revised version refers to ShM.

It is thus noteworthy that while MT clearly emerges as the pivot of his Talmud study, it does not supersede PhM. He still returns to it, revising and rectifying as need or insight arises. In other words, all the statements about MT's self-sufficiency and comprehensiveness notwithstanding, this commentary—and by implication other expansive commentatorial works as well—remains useful and relevant. MT, while providing the best codificatory summary of halakah, does not pre-empt all study. We should recall that Maimonides intended his PhM to serve simultaneously as an introduction to the Talmud—this follows from the nature of the Mishnah—and as a review of the Talmud—this follows from the nature of his commentary which summarizes different interpretations and indicates the normative conclusions. This inference must be weighed along with other statements, implications, and innuendos in determining Maimonides' complex attitude toward Talmud study. See Twersky, "Non-Halakic Aspects," p. 111, n.70.

Note the emphasis in the letter to Ibn Jābir (*Ḳobeṣ*, II, 16b) that study should be an endless, continuous process: כל המתעצל מן התוספת, ואפילו הי׳ חכם גדול, הוא מבטל עשה של ת״ת.

## INTRODUCTION

The *Mishneh Torah*, the massive intellectual effort connected with its preparation and presentation as well as its defense and dissemination, served thus as a gadfly for critical self-examination and continuous correction, refinement, or retraction.

Moreover, Maimonides kept reviewing and revising the *Mishneh Torah* itself, rethinking interpretations, reassessing inferences, introducing stylistic and substantive changes which reflect subtly varying nuances or really divergent emphases. This dynamism is reflected in various responsa concerning the *Mishneh Torah* as well as in the few extant holographs or corrected copies of the Code, which reveal the author-artist at work, erasing, adding, deleting, rectifying, and rearranging.[22] Just as there are successive editions, or rather one open-ended edition, of the *Mishnah Commentary*, there is an open-ended edition of the *Mishneh Torah*.[23] In answer to questions, Maimonides would sometimes note that the inquirer possessed a faulty text which misplaced certain marginal annotations or emendations that he had made, and that the resultant reading was hopelessly garbled. Even after the Code was widely circulated, he looked upon changes which he recorded in responsa as definitive and requested

---

22. *Tĕšubot*, 310 (p. 573), 345 (p. 618); *'Iggĕrot*, 58. Unflagging revisionism is simultaneously a methodological and ideological principle. It is, for Maimonides, the nerve center of Talmud study; it is, in fact, the hallmark of much of traditional Rabbinic literature. On the MT fragments, see S. Atlas, *A Section from Yad ha-Hazakah of Maimonides* (London, 1940), and the review by S. Assaf, *KS*, XVIII (1941–42), 150ff., who lists medieval references to Maimonidean autographs; S. Rosenthal, "'Al Derek ha-Rob," *Pĕrakim*, I (1968), 185, n. 10; the most recent note by M. Beit-Arié, *Bulletin of the John Rylands University Library*, LVII (1974), 2ff.; and below, chap. IV.

23. See S. Lieberman, *Hilkot Yĕrušalmi*, pp. 6ff.; M. Kasher, *Ha-RaMBaM wĕham-Mĕkilta de-RaSHBI* (New York, 1943), p. 36; and the introduction of J. Kāfih to his edition and translation of PhM, p. 16. Of course I do not mean to suggest that the scope of revisions of MT is comparable to that of PhM. The latter is much more extensive, for clearly a work written in youth, amidst conditions of unrelenting adversity, would be subject to more revision than a work written in maturity, attended by a measure of relative stability. Nevertheless, the literary phenomenon is the same; the MT was in no sense a sealed and closed work, thus reflecting the open and lively mind of its author.

It may be, moreover, that the revisions of PhM and MT are intertwined, and MT on occasion may possibly reflect the early version of PhM. See S. Rosenthal, "'Al Derek ha-Rob", 185.

On the debate concerning the Maimonidean autograph of PhM, published by S. Sasson (Copenhagen, 1955), see S. Stern, *Tarbiz*, XXIII (1954), 72ff.; J. Blau, *Tarbiz*, XXVII (1958), 536ff.; and Stern, *Tarbiz*, XXIX (1960), 261ff.

18 INTRODUCTION TO THE CODE OF MAIMONIDES

that these emendations be inserted in all copies of the *Mishneh Torah* text. His own *talmud Torah* (study of Torah) never ended, and the *Mishneh Torah* was the natural receptacle for the results. Indeed, the very scope, complexity, and ambitious goals of the *Mishneh Torah* necessitated unflagging alertness and scholarly dynamism. An interesting indication of the extent of ongoing revision is the fact that there are a few cases (concerning central, even volatile, halakic issues) where his son insists upon a change of text not attested by Maimonides' written legacy, but presumably on the basis of oral communications or traditions.[24]

The *Mishneh Torah* also becomes an Archimedean fulcrum in the sense that he regularly mentions it and refers correspondents and inquirers to it. The repeated references convey the impression that he wanted to establish it as a standard manual, a ready, steady, and uniform reference book for practically all issues. Even a responsum on free will directs the reader to "the great compendium which we composed concerning all the commandments"; a textual inquiry concerning a source on repentance is likewise answered with a reference to the "great compendium."[25] Many responsa, apparently written while the *Mishneh Torah* was being completed, use identical formulations—they could have been lifted lock, stock, and barrel from the *Mishneh Torah*—without mentioning it by name.[26] He also frequently correlates it with his *Moreh Nĕbukim*.[27] There is indeed a special relationship between

---

24. E.g., *Tĕšubot*, 355 (p. 633), and n.21; also 433 (p. 713); R. Aaron hak-Kohen of Lunel, *'Orḥot Ḥayyim*, I, 11b; and many others. One must allow for the possibility that the suggested changes were motivated by apologetic considerations. Note also that certain formulations in MT were finalized as a result of questions addressed to Maimonides: *Tĕšubot*, III, p. 15.

25. *Tĕšubot*, 121 (p. 217), 213 (p. 377), 436 (p. 715); also *Kobeṣ*, I, 4b, 23b; II, 15b; *Tĕšubot*, 310 (p. 573); III, p. 15; LA, 228; MTH, 4, 5, and passim; *'Iggerot*, 52. One should not base too much on Maimonides' sharp distinction, in his letter to R. Phinehas, between *ḥibbur* and *peruš*, for in MN and MTH he regularly refers to both MT and PhM as *ḥibburenu hat-Talmudiyyim; ḥibbur* is, in other words, a generic term. Note, however, that in addition to this generic reference, MT is sometimes cited, even in the Arabic text, as "the *ḥibbur*." See MTH, 5, 10 (חבורנו זה, ר״ל החבור). See Immanuel of Rome, *Maḥbĕrot 'Immanu'el*, chap. 18, ed. D. Yarden (Jerusalem, 1957), II, 311.

26. E.g., *Tĕšubot*, 373 (p. 652), and n.23; also 130 (p. 246), and note by S. Abramson in his Addenda, III, p. 158.

27. E.g., MN, introduction (p. 6), and see index, p. 658.

these two major works. In some respects, as we shall see, the *Moreh* is a conceptual-interpretative-demonstrative expansion of, and supplement to, parts of the *Mishneh Torah*. There are, to be sure, subtle divergences and clear differences between them, but many themes which are presented summarily or apodictically in the Code are elaborated and accompanied by full demonstrative apparatus in the *Moreh*. In short, these pervasive references to the *Mishneh Torah* reflect, but also further enhance and entrench, its position of centrality.

The *Mishneh Torah* may be described as central also in terms of the universalization of Maimonides' reputation. Long distinguished among Oriental Jewry—his *Epistle to Yemen* even gave him unusual charismatic-religious status as it were among the Yemenites, who not only included the name of Maimonides in the recitation of the *ḳaddiš* but also remained ardent students, copyists, and commentators of Maimonidean writings through the ages[28]—his Arabic works, including the *Mishnah Commentary*, were inaccessible to European scholars and his fame was thus automatically restricted. Linguistic confinement was more serious than the temporary isolation resulting from geographically determined difficulties of communication. Ultimately the mobility of texts and ideas prevails and borders are crossed, but linguistic barriers are sometimes insurmountable; the truncated influence of Maimonides' *Mishnah Commentary*, even after its fragmentary and belated translation into Hebrew, is a regrettable fact of Jewish intellectual history. Had it been originally composed in, or immediately translated into, Hebrew, its history and impact would most likely have been different. The *Mishneh Torah*, which was to change the entire landscape of Rabbinic literature, also pushed back the frontiers of Maimonides' sphere of influence and made his fame global as well as imperishable. It transformed him, in the course of a few decades, from the "light of the East" to "the

---

28. Abraham Zacuto, *Yuḥasin haï-Šalem* (Jerusalem, 1953); J. Sapir, *'Eben Sappir* (Lyck, 1866), I, 53, observes עיקר לימודם הוא בספר היד. See J. Ratzhaby, "Sifruṯ Yěhuḍe Teman," *ḲS*, XXVIII (1953), 255ff.; XXXIII (1957), 111ff.; XXIV (1947), 109ff. Commentaries on works of Maimonides predominate in this list over all other genres. Note Hermann Cohen's emotional comment on the inclusion of Maimonides in the *ḳaddiš*; *Daṯ hat-Těḇunah* (Jerusalem, 1971), p. 410.

## 20 INTRODUCTION TO THE CODE OF MAIMONIDES

light of the [entire] exile."[29] He almost literally became a major Jewish luminary. Indeed, as we shall see, his choice of Hebrew (rather than Arabic) expresses his determination to write for the "entire nation" instead of only for his immediate countrymen. An obvious aspiration to universality by transcending linguistic-geographic barriers, rooted in a new self-awareness, contributed to the crystallization of the most ambitious and comprehensive code of Jewish law, the climactic achievement of Jewish jurisprudence.[30]

Looking ahead, there is, of course, the position of centrality which the *Mishneh Torah* occupies in the overall development of Rabbinic literature. It is, as we shall see, unprecedented in terms of scope and structure, and although it did not have the precise impact which Maimonides envisaged, it is decidedly unique in its multifaceted influence. In one broad generalization, we may say that the *Mishneh Torah* became a prism through which reflection and analysis of virtually all subsequent Talmud study had to pass. There is hardly a book in the broad field of Rabbinic literature that does not relate in some way to the *Mishneh Torah*.

### HIS ACCOUNTS OF THE PURPOSES AND FEATURES OF THE *Mishneh Torah*

Given the general reticence and autobiographical shyness that constricts so much of medieval Jewish writing, it may be unequivocally asserted that Maimonides was unusually articulate in commenting upon the purposes, methods, and characteristics of the *Mishneh Torah*. In fact, Maimonides discussed the nature and objectives of his magnum opus (*ḥibbur gaḍol*), revealed his motives and assumptions, and exposed the implicit processes of his reasoning in many places. It is a matter of not just a well-balanced introduction to a book, common in Hebrew literature at least from the time of R. Saadiah Gaon, but of a variety of theoretical disquisitions, long and short. Some of these consist of a priori programmatic statements of intention while others are retrospective justifications and vindications in response to either friendly

---

29. *Tešubot*, 198 (p. 355); 201 (p. 357); 268 (p. 510); S. D. Goitein, *Mediterranean Society*, I, 301.
30. See below, chap. V.

interrogation or hostile criticism. Should we, therefore, ask what are the distinctive and innovating characteristics of the *Mishneh Torah* that assured it such a remarkable resonance in Jewish history, what goals did Maimonides set for himself in undertaking his massive codification of halaḵah, and what sets him apart from his predecessors, we would properly expect, in the light of his being so revelatory, self-conscious, and assertive, to elicit substantive answers from Maimonides himself, thereby reducing the need for excessive conjecture and speculation, whether psychological, sociological, or ideological.[31]

Of course the factual data and associative implications extracted from Maimonides' own pronouncements will have to be correlated with the results of independent literary-historical analysis. A person should not be allowed to determine his own place in history or to dictate the appraisal of his own work. While an author's self-perception is interesting, self-evaluation is not an objective process.[32] There may be a difference between the methods "which the scientists in fact followed in their own field" and "those which they believed that they employed." "The scientist reflecting and theorizing about his procedure is not always a reliable guide."[33] We must at least be prepared to differentiate between an author's program and its realization, without in any way minimizing the importance of the statements of intention which after all are themselves part of our study. In this context we are not addressing ourselves to the hazards of what literary critics usually label "the intentional fallacy," for the focus of our inquiry is not whether "the design or intention of the author is . . . a standard for judging the success of a work of literary art," i.e., the correlation of the historic destiny and influence of a work with

---

31. See my "Sefer MT," pp. 3ff., for a review of the major hypotheses in which psychological, sociological, and ideological explanations are interwoven.
32. See W. Jaeger, *Aristotle* (London, 1962), pp. 11–13. Note R. Isaac Canpanton, *Darke Gĕmara'* (Vienna, 1891), p. 15: "In any work of a commentator or author that you may study, always endeavor to discover first the methods adopted by that commentator in his annotations, and then read the work and see if he actually follows his method in his comments."
33. F. A. Hayek, *The Counter-Revolution of Science* (Glencoe, 1952), p. 14. On the divergence between programmatic statements and concrete achievements, see also T. S. Kuhn, "The Relations between History and History of Science," *Daedalus*, (Spring 1971), p. 275.

the author's conception of influence.[34] Historical success, its repercussions and metamorphoses, may, and frequently does, differ drastically from the directions which the author anticipated and the intentions which he fondly formulated. An important work may have one life and a different afterlife. Our interest at this stage is rather the relationship between the author's assessment of his work and its objective reality, between conscious motivation and unconscious propulsion, between self-interpretation and dispassionate analysis of the literary product. An extreme version of one approach has been formulated as follows: there are "psychological critics who maintain that the author himself often scarcely knows the sources of his own activity; that the springs of his genius are invisible to him, the process itself largely unconscious, and his own overt purpose a mere rationalization in his own mind of the true, but scarcely conscious, motives and methods involved in the act of creation."[35] This is, of course, as much a general issue of critical literary methods as a special psychologism. In any event, theoretical (sometimes dogmatic) assumptions to one side, literary-thematic analysis of a work may suggest one of three varying conclusions: that there is nearly complete disparity between intention and implementation, that there is complete identity or equivalence, or that there are various intermediate ratios of divergence and congruence. For our purposes, we need merely begin with an openness to all these options as we ponder Maimonides' statements or ruminations and examine his actual creation.

---

34. W. K. Wimsatt and M. C. Beardsley, "The Intentional Fallacy," *Sewanee Review*, LIV (1946), 468. The statement of G. B. Shaw, cited by Albert Tsugawa, "The Intention of a Work of Art," *Essays in Philosophy* (University Park, Penna., 1962), p. 46, is worth reproducing: "These works must speak for themselves: if the *Ring* [*of the Niebelung*] says one thing and a letter written afterwards says that it said something else, the *Ring* must be taken to confute the letter just as conclusively as if the two had been written by different hands."

In discovering the nature of the intention of the work of art, then, the intention of its creator, or his psychological motives (albeit unconscious), or his social origins, though all interesting and illuminating, are logically irrelevant.

35. I. Berlin, *The Hedgehog and the Fox* (New York, 1957), p. 61; see also G. Clive, *Romantic Enlightenment* (New York, 1960), p. 10; H. Hatfield, *Goethe* (Cambridge, 1964), p. x.

# INTRODUCTION

In our attempt to elicit Maimonides' own perspectives, we need not be deterred from placing them in a broad context. On the one hand, introductory statements will have to be carefully examined in order to determine, first of all, to what extent Maimonides succeeded in pinpointing precisely the major characteristics and tendencies of his work, and secondly, to what extent his a priori statements jibe with, and are verified by, the actual implementation—to what extent his "overt purpose" is a true crystallization of motives and methods. Discrepancy between promise and performance is quite common and is due to varying causes. One should not expect uniform consistency in the application of principles and directives, even those that are accurately formulated. A measure of discrepancy between formally declared intentions and actual achievements is inevitable, if only for the reason that no individual can write fourteen volumes according to a preconceived notion with complete consistency. Moreover, there is uncharted movement in the very process of implementing pre-established goals. There is an unpredictable and spontaneous factor of creativity, both conscious and unconscious. It may thus be helpful on occasion to speculate, cautiously and patiently, about *das unbewusste Schaffen* from which creativity stems or sometimes erupts. By sharpening themes, buoying up submerged motifs, detecting pale nuances, and deflating rhetorical formulae, it may be possible to put a literary creation into a more expressive context. On the other hand, the retrospective statements, epistolary epilogues as it were, must be critically examined for apologetic refractions, *captatio benevolentiae,* tendentious streaks, and ad hoc one-sided emphases. Extrapolating a single aspect from a more complex and multifaceted reality, and hence oversimplifying, is a commonplace in any theorizing. Certainly an author, straining to define or defend his work, is likely to succumb to such one-sidedness. With regard to all the formulations, prospective or retrospective, divergent stresses must be integrated or otherwise accounted for, while contradictions must be noted, and where logically possible, without stress or artificiality, explained. There is, in sum, movement, some of it spontaneous, as a mental construct becomes a creative force which eventually produces a literary reality. It may be that, at the very least or at the most, independent and empirical review of a work will illumine or flesh out an author's declarations and add a certain delicacy, depth, or precision to our understanding of his words. Already in Maimonides' lifetime a trusted correspondent reported that his intention was not grasped and his words misunderstood. There are, he says, "people who study but do not know what they study, misunderstand the subject matter of the work, and fail to comprehend your real intent." Maimonides himself observed in reply to the critics: "You have not paid attention to my works."[36]

*Seven Statements*

At this point we should, therefore, briefly describe the major Maimonidean pronouncements, citing the relevant passages in extenso, even though key sentences or fragments will be extracted and explicated in the following chapters as the special themes are unfolded. This description will provide a springboard for our discussion of the major features of the work as well as its motives and its use of sources. It will also enable the reader to confront directly these varied statements, their special emphases and nuances, harmonies and dissonances, and concomitant problems of interpretation.

1. Introduction to the *Sefer ham-Miṣwot*. This propaedeutic work, which contains an original and systematic classification and detailed enumeration of all the commandments of Judaism, should be seen in dual perspective. On the one hand, it belongs to a conventional genre of Rabbinic literature which was based on the Talmudic reference to 613 divine commandments. While there has been general agreement on the number 613,[37] there has been no agreement on which commandments deserve to be included in the enumeration. Dismissing his predecessors (the author of the *Halakot Gedolot* and the many poets who composed

---

36. *Ḳobeṣ*, I, 25b. Note also *Tešubot*, 310 (pp. 573–74), where Maimonides urges close reading of his Code. George Steiner, *After Babel* (New York, 1975), p. 302, quotes Schleiermacher's notion of a hermeneutic which "knows better than the author did." See also the stimulating study by J. H. Hexter, *More's Utopia* (New York, 1965), p. 3.

37. A significant reservation was registered by Naḥmanides, at the beginning of his strictures on the ShM, *Šoreš* I. R. Baḥya ibn Paḳuda, *Ḥobot hal-Lebabot*, introduction, I, 26, refers to "about 613"; see below, chap. IV, n.25. Baḥya's text needs study.

'Azharot) with a few lines of devastating critique,[38] Maimonides suggests fourteen guiding principles, rich in provocative assumptions as well as profound insights, which should help bring about a consensus. This ambitious attempt to add rigor and objectivity to the enumeration by classifying Jewish law, defining the differences between Biblical and Rabbinic commandments, differentiating between general exhortations and specific commands, avoiding redundancies, separating negative from positive commandments, omitting temporary injunctions as distinct from timeless laws, is the most novel and original part of the book. As a result, it was simultaneously a stimulant and an irritant.[39] On the other hand, it was considered a necessary prerequisite to his Code, designed to insure its comprehensiveness. He needed an exact and exhaustive list of commandments which provided the scaffolding for the *Mishneh Torah* and guarded against forgetfulness and omissions. It is in this context that we find the most elaborate statement concerning the scope and structure of the *Mishneh Torah*. The author registers with seismographic detail his deliberations, records the motives which stimulated and the problems which confronted him, and depicts the decision-making process which led to the final crystallization of his work. The statement is especially important for the light it casts upon the inner-organic development of Maimonides' writings—this is apparently the only place in which Maimonides establishes liaison between his three major Rabbinic works and indicates the premeditated progression in them:

After having completed our previous well-known work wherein we included a commentary to the whole Mishnah—our goal in that work having been satisfied with the explanation of the substance of each and every halakah in the Mishnah, since our intention there was not to include an exhaustive discussion of the law of every commandment which would

---

38. ShM, introduction (II, 361). See below, chap. IV. Maimonides used the occasion to decry the rampant intellectual conservatism which prevented people from undertaking a critical review of accepted principles.

39. This is clearly illustrated by Naḥmanides' critique. For one vexing issue and its long history of interpretation, see J. Neubauer, *Dibre Soferim*. See the "bio-bibliographical lexicon of scholarship pertaining" to the ShM by J. Dienstag, *'En ham-Miṣwot* (New York, 1969).

embrace all that is necessary (to know) of the prohibited and the permissible, liable and free, as will be made clear to him who studies that work—I deemed it advisable to compile a compendium which would include all the laws of the Torah and its regulations, nothing missing in it. In this compendium I would try, as I am accustomed to do, to avoid mentioning differences of opinion and rejected teachings, and include in it only the established law, so that this compendium would embrace all the laws of the Torah of Moses our teacher, whether they have bearing in the time of the exile or not.

It also appeared to me to be advisable to omit the *'asmaktot* and the proofs brought (for the various laws), by mentioning the bearers of the tradition; thus, I would not say with each and every law, "These are the words of this Rabbi," or "This Rabbi says so-and-so," but instead I would mention in a general way at the beginning of this compendium all the Sages of the Mishnah and the Talmud, peace be upon them, and I would say that all the laws of the Torah—that is, the Oral Torah—have been received and handed down from teacher to pupil (through the ages) up to Ezra (and thence) up to Moses our teacher. Together with the leader of every generation that received the tradition, I would mention also the outstanding persons in his generation, who were associated with him in the imparting of the Oral Teaching. All this (I would do) out of a desire for brevity.

Similarly, I also found it advisable not to compose (this work) in the language of the Holy Scriptures, since that sacred language is too limited for us today to write the whole complex of the law in it. Nor would I compose it in the language of the Talmud (namely, Aramaic), since only a few individuals among us understand it today, and even the erudite in the Talmud find many of its words foreign and remote. Instead, I would compose it in the language of the Mishnah, so that it should be easily understood by most of the people. And I would include in it everything of the Torah that has been established and confirmed, omitting no question which might arise, or at least I would mention the principle by means of which that question can easily be resolved without too deep reflection. Such was my goal to be in this work: brevity with completeness—so that the reader thereof might encompass all that is found in the Mishnah and Talmud, Sifra, Sifre, and Tosefta, and more than that, all decrees and ordinances of the later Geonim, of blessed memory, as well as all that they have explained and commented upon concerning the prohibited and permissible, unclean and clean, invalid and valid, liable and free, pay and not pay, swear and free from swearing. In short, outside of this work there was to be no need for another

# INTRODUCTION

book to learn anything whatsoever that is required in the whole Torah, whether it be a law of the Scriptures or of the Rabbis.

As I directed my attention toward this goal, I began thinking about how the division of this work, and the arrangement of its parts, were to be done. (I wondered:) should I divide it in accordance with the divisions of the Mishnah and follow in its footsteps, or should I divide it in some other way, arranging the subjects at the beginning or at the end of the work as logic will dictate, since this is the proper and easier way for learning? Then it became clear to me that in place of the tractates of the Mishnah, it would be best to arrange this work in groups of halaḵot (laws), so that it would read: "The Laws of the Tabernacle, the Laws of the Palm-Branch, the Laws of the Mĕzuzah, the Laws of the Fringes"; and that I should divide every group of halaḵot into chapters and paragraphs, even as the Mishnah had done, so that, for example, in the Laws of the Tefillin there would be chapters one, two, three, four, and each chapter would be (sub)divided into various laws, so that knowledge of it by heart should render it easy for one who wishes to learn something from it by memory.

With a division of this kind, it was clear that it would not be necessary to divide the laws on any specific topic—whether it concerns a positive or a negative commandment—into two general halaḵot, but that all necessary divisions could be made within the chapters of one general section.

At times one general section would contain a number of commandments, either because there is some general topic which embraces them, or because many commandments relate to one goal. For example, in speaking of idolatry, I would designate this general topic "The Laws of Idolatry," and then I would proceed to discuss under this general topic a number of commandments: (against) beguiling an individual Israelite (after the idols), leading a community astray, causing (our offspring) to pass (through the fire) in the worship of Moloch, prophesying in the name of an idol, worshiping it, and other similar commandments specifically applying to idolatry. Similarly, in the section entitled "The Laws of Things Forbidden to Be Brought on the Altar," I would mention (the commandments against offering) leaven or honey, blemished offerings, the hire of a harlot, or the price of a dog, and similar matters, since all these commandments are embraced in one general topic, namely, things forbidden to be brought (on the altar).

Now on account of this plan I deemed it advisable to enumerate first in the introduction to that work the number of all commandments, positive and negative, so that the scope of the work might embrace all of

## 28 INTRODUCTION TO THE CODE OF MAIMONIDES

them, not one commandment being left out without being fully discussed, whether singly, such as the Tabernacle, the palm-branch, the fringes, or the phylacteries, since each of these topics can be discussed by itself; or in a group of commandments, such as those mentioned above, in which case we would enumerate them, saying, "These are the laws of Idolatry, containing this number of positive commandments, which are as follows, and this number of negative commandments, which are as follows." All this (I would do) in order to guard against omitting any topic from discussion, for only by including them in the enumeration of the commandments (heading the various halakot) would I insure against such omission.[40]

2. Introduction to the *Mishneh Torah*. We find here a rather complete, if compressed, characterization of the work as well as a discussion of motivation. The introduction was most likely written after the bulk of the work had been completed (in the year 1177), and is therefore, at least formally, as much a retrospective as a programmatic statement.[41] The relative brevity or selectivity (for example, he mentions the qualities of his style but not the choice of language) is presumably attributable to the fullness of the previous statement, even though there is a marked difference of emphasis between them. As we shall see, the Maimonidean sources often have to be conflated, the explications of one grafted upon the silences of another, in order to produce a composite statement that is meaningful and comprehensive. The relative

---

40. ShM, introduction (II, 361ff.).
41. The following dates are mentioned by Maimonides: 1176, in *Šĕmiṭṭah wĕ-Yobel*, x, 4; 1177, at the end of the introduction; 1178, in *Ḳidduš ha-Ḥodeš*, xi, 16. On the date of composition, see S. Gandz, *PAAJR*, XVII (1948), 1–7, reprinted in *Studies in Hebrew Astronomy and Mathematics*, ed. S. Sternberg (New York, 1970), pp. 113ff.; E. Wiesenberg, appendix to *Code*, Book III (YJS, 14), 561.
On histories of tradition, see R. Saadiah Gaon, *Sefer hag-Galuy*, ed. A. H. Harkavy, *Haś-Śariḏ wĕhap-Paliṭ* (Petersburg, 1892), pp. 152ff., 268ff.; R. Judah hal-Levi, *Kuzari*, IV, 64; R. Samuel han-Nagid, *Diwan Šĕmu'el han-Nagiḏ*, ed. D. Yarden, pp. 89ff.; and of course, '*Iggereṯ R. Sherira Gaon*, ed. B. M. Lewin (Haifa, 1921). For R. Samuel ben Hofni Gaon, see E. Roth and S. Abramson, *Tarbiz*, XXVI (1956–57), 410, 421; S. Abramson, '*Inyanoṯ bĕ-Sifruṯ hag-Gĕ'onim*, pp. 173ff.; see generally, G. Cohen, ed., *Sefer haḳ-Ḳabbalah*, pp. lii ff. Later Talmudists, heavily influenced by Maimonides, preface their works with histories of tradition which become also rather detailed histories of Rabbinic literature; e.g., R. Moses of Coucy, *Sefer Miṣwoṯ Gaḏol*; R. Menahem ham-Me'iri, *Beṯ hab-Bĕḥirah;* R. Menahem ben Zerah, *Ṣedah lad-Dereḵ* and R. David ben Samuel, *Sefer hab-Batim*.

# INTRODUCTION

brevity may also be rooted in the structure and purpose of the entire introduction which should be studied as a conceptualization and periodization of Jewish history from the vantage point of the origin and transmission of the law, culminating of course in Maimonides' own climactic contribution and his special place in this history. Its repercussions concerning the nature and extent of communal autonomy, on the one hand, and the (in his opinion, diminished) significance of Gaonic authority, both institutional and judicial, on the other, are noteworthy. The introduction, in any event, not merely has a limited literary function but is a carefully constructed document reflecting many basic Maimonidean social, historical, and theological perceptions. To the extent that it does suggest a special view of the history of halakah, it is parallel to that passage in the introduction of the *Moreh*, supplemented by Part I, chapter 71, which may be read as a conceptualization and periodization of Jewish history from the point of view of the history of philosophy, its rise and decline in antiquity and its medieval re-emergence, again culminating in Maimonides' pivotal achievement. Also in this case the introduction and historical overview have not merely a limited literary function but also ideological-theological implications.

In any event, some symmetry, proportion, and commensurability had to be preserved in the *Mishneh Torah* introduction between the sections of the narrative depicting the redaction of the Mishnah and its unequaled authoritativeness, the composition of the Talmud and its automatic and informal "canonization," the nature of Gaonic activity and its influence, and finally Maimonides' own work and its hoped for impact:

> On these grounds, I, Moses the son of Maimon the Sefardi, bestirred myself, and relying on the help of God, blessed be He, intently studied all these works, with the view of putting together the results obtained from them in regard to what is forbidden or permitted, clean or unclean, and the other rules of the Torah—all in plain language and terse style, so that thus the entire Oral Law might become systematically known to all, without citing difficulties and solutions or differences of view, one person saying so, and another something else, but consisting of statements, clear and reasonable, and in accordance with the conclusions drawn from all these compilations and commentaries

## 30 INTRODUCTION TO THE CODE OF MAIMONIDES

that have appeared from the time of our Holy Master [R. Judah] to the present, so that all the rules shall be accessible to young and old, whether these appertain to the (Scriptural) precepts or to the institutions established by the Sages and prophets, so that no other work should be needed for ascertaining any of the laws of Israel, but that this work might serve as a compendium of the entire Oral Law, including the ordinances, customs, and decrees instituted from the days of our teacher Moses till the compilation of the Talmud, as expounded for us by the Geonim in all the works composed by them since the completion of the Talmud. Hence I have entitled this work *Mishneh Torah* (Repetition of the Law), for the reason that a person who first reads the Written Law and then this compilation, will know from it the whole of the Oral Law, without having occasion to consult any other book between them.

I have seen fit to arrange this compendium in large divisions of the laws according to their various topics. These divisions are distributed in chapters grouped according to subject matter. Each chapter is subdivided into smaller sections so that they may be systematically memorized. Among the laws on the various topics, some consist of rules in reference to a single Biblical precept. This would be the case when such a precept is rich in traditional matter and forms a single topic. Other sections include rules referring to several precepts when these all belong to one topic. For the work follows the order of topics and is not planned according to the number of precepts, as will be explained to the reader.

The total number of precepts that are obligatory for all generations is 613. Of these, 248 are positive, their mnemonic is the number of bones in the human body; 365 precepts are negative, and their mnemonic is the number of days in the solar year.

Blessed be the All-Merciful who has aided us.[42]

3. Letter to R. Phinehas ben Meshullam, judge in Alexandria. This statement, in response to an unabashedly polemical, albeit

---

42. Concerning the statement that one who reads the MT "will know from it the whole of the Oral Law," see Twersky, "Non-Halakic Aspects," p. 110.

The charge of planning to supersede the Talmud is leveled at Maimonides in the letter of R. Phinehas; for some phases of the convoluted history of this charge, which periodically exploded, see my "R. Joseph Ashkenazi," *Salo Baron Jubilee Volume* (Jerusalem, 1975), Hebrew part, pp. 183ff. The mnemonic formulation at the end, quoted by Naḥmanides in his strictures on *šoreš* I, serves to underscore that only timeless laws, intended for eternal observance, are to be counted; see below, chap. III. For the history in MN, I, 71, see H. A. Wolfson, *The Philosophy of the Kalam* (Cambridge 1975), pp. 47ff.

polite, letter containing a variety of questions, reports, and mostly methodological-procedural queries about the *Mishneh Torah*, is very revelatory of Maimonides' psychological state in the early years of its spread. There are insinuations about Maimonides' personal practices to which he reacts with pathos and wrath. Above all, the letter conveyed to Maimonides the suspicions and apprehensions of contemporaries and an explicit arraignment of the motive and putative impact of his work—the alleged, and in the eyes of critics sinister, aim of having the *Mishneh Torah* supersede the Talmud is a focal concern. Maimonides' reply is a staunch but low-keyed defense of the rationale, integrity, and benign usefulness of his work, a defense that was to be both influential and problematic through the ages. The charge of wanting to abolish the study of Talmud in favor of his own compendium is roundly and rapidly repudiated. This is followed by a lengthier analysis of the necessary characteristics of codificatory writing—anonymity, unanimity, brevity, finality, etc. While the letter clearly emphasizes the comprehensiveness of scope, the authoritativeness of form, and the novelty of classification, it fudges the originality of interpretation—both the extent and intensity of the originality. Its polemical value in the anti-Karaite campaign is also appraised, even magnified.[43] In general, one gets the impression that Maimonides did not wish to antagonize R. Phinehas, who occupied a position of power and prestige in the same country; the immediacy and urgency of the questions are thus strengthened by geographic proximity, heightened mobility of opinions, and frequency of personal contact. Burdensome distractions and physical infirmities notwithstanding, he therefore answered patiently and respectfully but firmly, and it would seem persuasively.[44] Some apologetic overtones in this detailed rebuttal are obvious and not all emphases are readily

---

43. On Karaism, see below, n. 159.
44. See, e.g., *Tēšubot*, 233 (p. 424), concerning the close contacts with Alexandria; also 355 (p. 633), and index, III, p. 217; S. D. Goitein, *A Mediterranean Society*, I, 66; M. Luzki, *Hat-Tēkufah*, XXX–XXXI (1946), 689ff. See the reference to Alexandria in *Mēlakim*, v, 7. From *Tēšubot*, 346 (p. 623) we see that Maimonides was generally sensitive and concerned lest he be accused of presumptuousness or haughtiness (*gassut ha-ruah*). See Y. M. Toledano, *Yēhude Misrayim* (Alexandria, 1936), p. 5.

integrated with earlier statements. The letter is thus as challenging as it is informative:

> . . . In your letter you also wrote as follows: "The words of your composition are surely illuminating for all the world, but solely for the person who has already studied the Talmud and knows the names of the Rabbis who had preoccupied themselves with, and engaged in, the dialectics of the Oral Law (Talmud) and Gemara; and as a result (such a person) will not preoccupy himself exclusively with the words of your composition, for this would result in the names of the Tannaim and Amoraim being blotted out from the world. And certainly this is the case for those persons who study but do not know what they are studying; who misunderstand the subject matter and the language of the composition, and fail to comprehend your real (ultimate) intent and from what source the fountain (of your wisdom) flows. Concerning such persons, the Tanna said, 'Scholars, take great care with your words . . . lest (your students) die and the name of God be thereby desecrated. . . .' " These were your words verbatim; elsewhere in your letter you also wrote the following: "It would be proper for Your Excellency to instruct everyone not to abandon their preoccupation with the study of Gemara. . . ."

Now concerning this entire matter, it is necessary for me both to rebuke you and to inform you that I promptly understood the intentions of your words though you never specified them. Know therefore that I have never said, Heaven forbid, "Do not preoccupy yourself with the study of the Gemara, of the *Halakot* of Rabbi Isaac Alfasi, or of any other text." In point of fact, God himself is my witness that for the past year and a half (the students who have come to me) have not studied my own composition with me; quite the contrary, three students came and studied various books; the majority of the students wished to study the *Halakot* of Rabbi Alfasi, and I taught it to them in its entirety several times; two other students desired to study the Gemara, and I also taught them the tractates they wished to learn. Have I ever commanded or has it ever occurred to me to burn all the books composed before my time because of my regard for my own work?

In the introduction to my composition, I explicitly wrote that my sole purpose in composing it was to alleviate the burden of those students who because of their impatience of spirit were not able to descend to the depths of the Talmud, and therefore could not understand from it the way of determining what is permissible and what is forbidden: I discussed this matter at great length there. As for your statement about the names of the Tannaim and Amoraim, I already mentioned the names of most of the Sages at the beginning of my composition. Is it in fact the case that anyone who attempts to decide the halakah and to make (out of the law) a clean fine flour is guilty of desecration of His name, just as has occurred to you? Already before me there were Geonim and other great scholars who composed works and compiled codes, in Arabic as well as in Hebrew, in which they adjudicated the halako̱t on given subjects. No one before my time, not at least since the time of Rabbi Judah and the other holy scholars of his period, adjudicated all the halako̱t in the Talmud and all the laws of the Torah. Yet that I should be held responsible for desecrating His name solely because my work is comprehensive astonishes me greatly. As for those readers who do not know how to study my composition, no author can accompany his book wherever it goes and allow only certain persons to read it.

Futhermore, in the introduction to my composition I wrote that I had composed the work according to the method of the Mishnah and in the style of the Mishnah. But you have not paid sufficient attention to my words, nor have you understood the difference between the method of the Mishnah and the method of the Talmud. Because of your ignorance of this matter, you wrote the following criticism in your letter: "Even when I study your composition, I find in it many matters which remain unclear to me because you have not given proofs for them, while my own mind is not clear enough to comprehend them." This was the gist of your criticism; permit me now to explain.

You should know that every author of a book—whether it deals with the laws of the Torah or with other kinds of wisdom, whether it was composed by one of the ancient wise men among the nations of the world or by physicians—always adopts one of two ways (structures and styles): either that of the monolithic code (ḥibbur) or that of a discursive commentary (peruš). In a monolithic code, only the correct subject matter is recorded, without any questions, without answers, and without any proofs, in the way which Rabbi Judah adopted when he composed the Mishnah. The discursive commentary, in contrast, records both the correct subject matter and other opinions which contradict it, as well as questions on it in all its aspects, answers, and proofs as to why one opinion is true and another false, or why one opinion is proper and another improper; this method, in turn, is that of the Talmud, which is a discursive commentary upon the Mishnah. Moreover, if someone should object to my distinction between the code and the commentary, and claim that because the names of the Rabbis are cited in the Mishnah—as when one Rabbi holds one opinion about a law and another Rabbi holds a contradictory one—this kind of citation of names constitutes proof, it is necessary for me to point out that this is not proof: a proof explains why one Rabbi holds a certain opinion, while another Rabbi might hold a contradictory one.

You should also understand that if I have caused the names of any Tannaim to be forgotten by recording the correct halakah without qualification and anonymously, I have only followed the style of Rabbi Judah here. He, too, did this before me, for every halakah which he recorded without qualification and anonymously was originated by other scholars; yet even these other Rabbis had not originated the halakot themselves but had received them from still others, and these others from still others, all the way back to Moses our teacher. And just as the Tannaim and Amoraim did not bother to record the names of all Sages from the time of Moses to their own day, because there would then be no end to the citations of names, so I also have not bothered to record their names. What advantage would there ever be in doing it? Indeed, it is mentioned explicitly in several places that Rabbi Judah adjudicated the law according to the opinion of a certain Rabbi which he favored and nevertheless recorded his opinion anonymously; this is clear proof that whenever Rabbi Judah recognized a law which seemed to him to be the correct halakah, and therefore worthy of being implemented, he always recorded it without qualification and anonymously. There are many statements to the effect that the correct halakah was the opinion of a single Rabbi, and Rabbi Judah still did not record his name. In fact, the sole cases in which Rabbi Judah did record the names of the scholars was when the correct halakic decision itself was not absolutely clear to him, and when he could not adjudicate one opinion over another. Moreover, he mentioned only the names of the Rabbis from whom he himself had heard the opinion, or the names of those who lived in a time most contemporaneous with his own, and never the names of their teachers, or the teachers of their teachers, and only because in Rabbi Judah's own time many people obeyed the opinion of one Rabbi and many others obeyed the opinion of his halakic opponent. The Rabbis themselves gave this same rationale for Rabbi Judah's choice in citing the names of the authors of halakot in certain cases: thus, in the controversies between the School of Hillel and the School of Shammai, Rabbi Judah mentioned the names of the halakic opponents in order to invalidate the incorrect opinion, thereby teaching future generations not to rely upon it. And why do they record the opinion of one individual against that of the majority? So that if a (later) court approves the opinion of the individual, it may rely upon him. . . .

All these cases prove that the correct halakah alone should be recorded. And when Rabbi Judah recorded two separate opinions about the same law, this was only because there were people at the time who followed both opinions, some accepting the halakah of the Rabbi from whom they heard one opinion, while others had heard and accepted the opinion of another Rabbi. I had already decided to follow the methodology of the Mishnah, and the Talmud has already adjudicated every single halakah either ad hoc or by applying the various principles of adjudication, and there are no two ways of implementing one law. What then would have been the use in citing either the name of a Rabbi whose opinion about the halakah is not followed, or what, for that matter, would have been the purpose, in the case of correct halakot, of citing either the name of the Rabbi who is mentioned in the Talmud, like the names of Abaye or Raba, if in fact he is not the author of the halakah and it had been received by many from many? Because of this, I chose not to give any possible opportunity to the heretics to prevail, for they contend that we base our observance of the law upon the opinions of individuals, which is entirely false, since we follow the laws which we received from multitudes who themselves had received the same laws from earlier multitudes. For this reason, I also described in my introduction the transmission of the law from one High Court and its chief judge to the succeeding High Court and its chief judge, in order to prove that the tradition of the law did not consist of the traditions of individuals but of the traditions of multitudes. And for the same reason my endeavor and purpose in composing my work was that every halakah should be cited unqualifiedly (anonymously), even if it is in fact the opinion of an individual, but it should not be reported in the name of So-and-so. This would destroy the position of the heretics (*minim*) who rejected the entire Oral Law because they saw it transmitted in the name of So-and-so and imagined that this law had never been formulated before, but that the individual had originated it on his own.

As for your (critical) statement that you found in my composition certain matters which appear unclear (hidden) because they are without proof, and that your own mind is not deep enough to comprehend (them), it would have been correct for you to make this criticism if there were indeed matters in my composition which I myself had deduced on the basis of my sharp reasoning (*pilpul*) and my own opinion, and then recorded them unqualifiedly, without giving proof or reason for them. However, I have never done this. Let your own wisdom reveal them, and know that every unqualified statement which I made in my composition is based upon an explicit unqualified statement either in the

Babylonian Talmud or in the Palestinian one, is drawn from Sifra or Sifre, or from an explicit unqualified statement in the Mishnah or in the Tosefta. If I derived a law from the responsa of the Geonim, I explicitly introduced it with the remark, "The Geonim have taught," "This is an ordinance of the later Rabbis," or a similar note. And anything which I myself originated (from my sharp reasoning), I introduced with the note "It appears to me that the matter is as follows"; this is the proof, inasmuch as I had announced in the introduction to the work that all the material in it is drawn from the Babylonian or Palestinian Talmuds, Sifra, Sifre, or Tosefta.

As for your statement that there were a number of matters in it which seemed unclear (hidden) because you could not recall their source, this is certainly a distinct possibility, for you as well as for any other scholar in the world. For only a great Sage like you can realize the toil that has been put into this work. Other students will imagine that it follows the order of the Talmud, removing only the questions and answers. I am willing to swear, however, that it contains several chapters which include final formulations of halakot culled from ten or more different places in the Babylonian and Palestinian Talmuds and from the Baraitas. I do not follow the order of the Talmud or of the Mishnah, but every subject in every section comprises all the laws stated with regard to it wherever they may be, so that the halakot of that subject should not be scattered and dispersed among the various places. This was my ultimate intention in composing my work, because it is beyond all human capacity to remember the whole Talmud, Babylonian and Palestinian, and the Baraitas, three works which are the major sources for the laws. . . . [Here Maimonides records an incident about his failure to cite the correct source of a law in response to a question about it.]

. . . Because of this, I regret that I did not compose along with my composition a separate volume whose content I will now explain to you and which I still hope to compose, if God will decree that I be able to do it, even though it is a very demanding task and effort—that is, a source book to my composition which will cite the source for every halakah whose origin is not evident. For example, in the case of the halakot concerning the Sabbath, there is obviously no need for me to give the source if it can be found in either of the tractates *Šabbaṭ* or *'Erubin;* however, any halakah concerning the Sabbath whose source is in the tractates *'Abodah Zarah, Pĕsaḥim,* or *Zĕbaḥim,* I will cite and say that such-and-such halakah in a given chapter is to be found in such-and-such a chapter of a given tractate. This source book would be a separate companion volume to my composition, since I obviously cannot incorporate it into the body of the work, because the nature of its subject conflicts with the structure and style of a monolithic code, as I explained to you previously. Still, if the source for any law escapes you, kindly inform me and I will answer you, because every unqualified statement in my composition has a source in one of the five major sources of the halaḵah which I have named. The real problem of finding the source arises solely when the halaḵah has been mentioned in the Talmud only in passing, or in the course of a debate (about some other matter), that is, when the law is explicated elsewhere than where it should be, and where consequently someone cannot locate it whenever he wishes.[45]

4. Letter to R. Jonathan hak-Kohen of Lunel. Here, too, we must be mindful of the personal-literary context as we assess the relevant statements and their nuances. The writings of R. Jonathan, respected head of Provençal Jewry and the prime mover in getting R. Samuel ibn Tibbon to produce a Hebrew translation of the *Moreh Nĕḇuḵim,* were generally representative of the polite but forthright criticism to which the *Mishneh Torah* was subjected in learned circles. Acting as spokesman for the scholars of southern France, whose communal leader he had been for a long time, R. Jonathan forwarded to Maimonides twenty-four questions, textual and interpretative, which had been raised against the *Mishneh Torah.* They may be seen as a quintessence of the serious critical study of the *Mishneh Torah* initiated in Provence by such Talmudists as R. Abraham ben David (RABD) and R. Moses hak-Kohen. Maimonides' detailed reply, sometimes acknowledging error or imprecision and sometimes firmly sustaining his view, sometimes chiding the critics for an excessively cavalier attitude and sometimes praising their incisiveness, was accompanied by a covering letter which, in addition to extolling R. Jonathan and inviting thorough critical review of the *Mishneh*

---

45. *Ḳobeṣ,* I, 25a–27a. The text of the letter is grammatically and syntactically exceedingly difficult; some sentences defy precise translation. Variants in manuscripts, which I checked at the Institute of Microfilmed Hebrew Manuscripts of the Jewish National-University Library in Jerusalem, are not very significant or helpful. I thank my student David Stern who helped me greatly by preparing first drafts of the translations of these letters; I appreciate his hard work and literary sensitivity.

## 38 INTRODUCTION TO THE CODE OF MAIMONIDES

Torah,[46] contains some soul-searching confessions and generalizations about the structure and purpose of this work. It also touches upon his entire scholarly orientation and intellectual scale of values. These remarks are pointed, poignant, and very informative. The emphasis upon the ancillary role of philosophy, its teleological and axiological subservience to Torah, is particularly significant, for there was no apparent need for apologetics in this context—the Provençal scholars were enthusiastic about Maimonides' philosophical activities and were requesting the last part of the *Moreh* and negotiating for its Hebrew translation. His philosophic work was not under fire. The statement thus seems spontaneous and natural, and indeed it does reflect the common assumption (both typological and axiological) about the nobility of religious science and about philosophy being the handmaiden or bondwoman of theology, which is the mistress or queen.[47] Generally, Maimonides' praise of R. Jonathan, creative scholar and gracious Maecenas, is obviously sincere, as is his respect for the Provençal scholars whom he sees as standing on the crest of Rabbinic creativity.[48] This situation contrasts sharply with the general decline in scholarship which had generated in Maimonides a mood of cultural pessimism and apprehension about the destiny of Judaism. Maimonides' gloom and sense of living in a twilight period is offset somewhat by the reports he had received concerning Provençal Rabbis and their scholarly attainments. We may also discern here an embryonic historiosophical view of shifting cultural centers and spheres of vitality and creativity, of successive phases of religious-cultural renaissance: descendancy of Oriental centers and ascendancy of Christian Europe, the sun setting in one area and rising in another. Echoes of the medieval notion of *translatio studii*, alluded to also by R. Saadiah Gaon, are discernible.[49] In any event, as far as his Code is

---

46. See also *Tešubot*, 310 (p. 578), where Maimonides invites careful critical review of every statement.
47. H. A. Wolfson, *Philo* (Cambridge, 1947), I, 151; note also *'Iggĕrot*, 16.
48. *Kobeṣ*, II, 44a; A. Kupfer, *Tarbiz*, XXXIX (1970), 182; Twersky, *Rabad*, p. 24.
49. *Kobeṣ*, II, 44a; R. Saadiah Gaon, *Sefer hag-Galuy*, p. 158; also *'Ĕmunot wĕ-De'ot*, introduction. For some relevant discussions of *translatio studii*, see E. Curtius, *European Literature and the Latin Middle Ages* (New York, 1953), p. 29; E. Gilson, "Humanisme

concerned, at least in Provence, he feels assured that it will be properly appreciated and responsibly debated (*maśśa' u-mattan*); this last phrase has significant implications vis-à-vis the sticky and tricky question of the *Mishneh Torah*'s absolute finality, a persistent and recurring theme in the study and appraisal of Maimonides' magnum opus. Here, with some enthusiasm, Maimonides welcomes debate and indicates that his work should be studied in depth. However, we should note that the invitation to criticism, undoubtedly genuine, is strikingly majestic; the respected king, the illustrious scholar, "permits" everyone to raise questions, a rather awesome writ of permission:

I, Moses, wish to tell you, Rabbi Jonathan hak-Kohen, that when your letters and questions reached me, I rejoiced deeply and said to myself, *Blessed be the Lord who hath not left thee this day without a kinsman* (Ruth 4:14). I understood that my writings had reached someone who could comprehend their contents, who could interpret their innermost meanings (*maṣpuneah*), and debate the merits of their formulations (or: engage in dialectical review of them). Because of this, I said to myself, *He shall be unto thee a restorer of thy life, and a nourisher of thine old age* (Ruth 4:15). All the questions which you asked, you have asked properly; all the difficulties which you raised, you have raised fittingly. *Fear not, for I am with thee* (Gen. 26:24). I have already replied to each one of your many questions individually; if my replies have been delayed for several years, this is solely on account of my anxiety resulting from my illness and the many disturbances. For nearly a year I was seriously ill, and even now that I have recovered, I am still in the category of "a person who is ill but not in mortal danger." For the greater part of the day, I must lie in bed, with the burden of the Gentiles upon my shoulders, sapped of all my strength because of their questions for medical advice, without a free moment the entire day and night. Yet what can I do, now that my fame has spread through many lands? Furthermore, I

---

médiéval et Renaissance," *Les idées et les lettres* (Paris, 1955), pp. 171–90; B. Smalley, *English Friars and Antiquity in the Early Fourteenth Century* (Oxford, 1960), p. 70; A. G. Jongkees, "Translatio Studii," *Miscellanea Mediaevalia in Memoriam J. F. Niermeyer* (Groningen, 1967), pp. 41–51, cited by C. Morris, *The Discovery of the Individual* (New York, 1973), p. 50. I would mention such a work as Franz Neumann, *Cultural Migration: the European Scholar in America* (Philadelphia, 1953), as a modern supplement to this theory. This idea is implicit also in the 'Iggeret haš-Šĕmad and IT, where Maimonides urges the perplexed and disconsolate Jews to flee the land of persecution at all costs and start again elsewhere. The religious motive and scholarly result are inseparable.

no longer am as I was in the time of my youth: my vigor is failing, my heart is spent, my breath is short, my tongue is heavy, my hand falters. I find myself too sluggish to write even a single letter. Do not, therefore, be angry with me if I dictated the responsa and a few of the letters, and did not write them with my own hand, because I do not have time for this on account of both my lack of strength and the disturbances of those people who continually importune me.

Moreover, I, Moses, wish to tell you, Rabbi Jonathan hak-Kohen, and your fellow scholars, who have studied my writings: Before I had been formed in the belly, the Torah knew me, and before I came forth out of the womb, she had sanctified me for her study (Jer. 1:5), and dedicated me to disperse her fountains abroad (i.e., to spread knowledge of its teachings) (Prov. 5:16). She is my loving hind, the bride of my youth, whose love has ravished me (enraptured me continuously) since I was a young man (Prov. 5:19). Many strange and foreign women have nevertheless become rival wives to her: Moabites, Edomites, Sidonites, Hittites. The Lord, may He be blessed, knows that I took these other women in the first instance only in order to serve as perfumers, cooks, and bakers for her (my true bride), and to show the peoples and the princes her beauty, for she is exceedingly fair to behold. Still, her conjugal rights were diminished (i.e., the attention paid to her suffered), because my heart was divided into many parts through its concern for all the other branches of wisdom. And yet, how hard I have worked, day and night, for these past ten years, in order to compile this composition! Great people like yourself will understand what I have accomplished; for behold, I have gathered together subjects which were scattered and dispersed among the valleys and mountains, and I have culled (literally: called) them one from a city and two from a family (Jer. 3:14). Yet who can discern (his own) errors (Ps. 19:13), and certainly when forgetfulness is so common, especially among the elderly. For all these reasons, it is therefore proper and fitting for you to search my words and to inspect and investigate after me. It is not my wish that the reader of this work of mine should ever say, *For what can the man do that cometh after the king?* (Eccles. 2:12), for I have permitted him, *The king said, 'Let him come'* (Esther 6:5). Indeed, you have done me a great kindness—you scholars, and every other person, who may find a mistake in my words and will notify me about it will have bestowed his good favor upon me—so that not a single obstacle should remain. My sole intention in composing this text was to clear the paths and remove the obstacles from before the students of the law, so that they should not become discouraged or distressed (literally: their minds become faint) by the overabundance of debate and argumentation, and consequently err in adjudicating the law correctly. May the Lord, blessed be His name, aid you as well as us to study His law and to attain knowledge of His oneness. Let us not err, and let the following verse be fulfilled in our lifetime: *I will put my law in their inward parts, and in their heart will I write it* (Jer. 31:33).[50]

5. Letter to R. Joseph ben Judah. This trusted and beloved disciple,[51] who proudly raised the Maimonidean banner in the east only to be inundated by a tidal wave of criticism and antagonism, sought guidance from his master in the art of refuting criticism. R. Joseph, who was the immediate cause for the composition of the *Moreh,* was grievously irritated by the vehement, sometimes cantankerous, anti-Maimonidean polemics generated in the school of Baghdad and was eager to retaliate in kind—his master's honor was at stake. In the course of counseling him to ignore critics and antagonists while persisting in his own constructive efforts, Maimonides commented again on the purpose and motives of the *Mishneh Torah* and its relation to the Talmud. Utilizing the categories of challenge and response, both individual and national, Maimonides dramatically reviewed his initial decision to compose the *Mishneh Torah,* pinpointed the compelling sense of need in the light of the fact that the Jewish people had no comprehensive code, and enumerated the types of critics who in his opinion would rise to lambaste him and denigrate his work. The acutely sensitive prediction, with its emphasis on jealousy, confusion engendered by the lack of sources, and unenlightened rejection of his explanation of theological principles, as three potential reasons for criticism, is obviously noteworthy, but as we shall see, these categories of criticism are by no means exhaustive.[52] While the tone of the letter is more intimate and

---

50. *Tešuḇot,* III, pp. 55ff. On his positive attitude to honest constructive debate concerning his rulings, see the responsum (to R. Joseph ham-Ma'arabi) ed. A. Freimann, *Sefer Yoḇel le-B.M. Lewin* (Jerusalem, 1940), p. 37; also *Ḳobeṣ,* II, 16b; Twersky, *Rabad,* pp. 195ff. See PhM, introduction (p. 20). For Maimonides' correspondence with the Provençal scholars, see S. M. Stern, "Ḥalifat ham-Miktaḇim ben ha-RaMBaM we-Ḥakme Provence," *Zion,* XVI (1951), 19–28. Note *'Issure Bi'ah,* xxii, 21.
51. See D. Baneth's introduction to *'Iggerot,* pp. 1ff.; MN, dedicatory epistle (to R. Joseph), pp. 3–4. See A. Scheiber, "'Iggeret bilti Yedu'ah la-RaMBaM," *Sefunot,* VIII (1964), 137ff.; and the Saadianic fragment published in *Melilah,* V (1955), 137.
52. See Twersky, "Beginnings," p. 162.

the dialogic aspect more pronounced and vibrant than in the letters cited above, and the style flows freely with a certain warmth and immediacy, the milieu of criticism which produced the correspondence should be kept in mind. To be sure, his personal relationship to his disciple Joseph is markedly different from his relationship to his colleague R. Phinehas, but this does not automatically make the emphases, insights, and confessions of this letter more authentic or more compelling. Some of the problems involved in coordinating these letters—again, the question of ongoing Talmud study is central—will be treated later. The appeal to individuals of integrity, the remnant whom the Lord calls, is a familiar and significant motif of Maimonidean writing.[53] The elaborate introspective discussion of motives for his Code of law in a letter to the disciple whom Maimonides considered his philosophic protégé par excellence is of obvious importance for the law-philosophy problem. Also noteworthy is the extent to which Maimonides advises his student of philosophy concerning the proper methods of Talmud study:

> Know that I did not compose this work in order to become great (in renown) in Israel because of it, or in order that I might acquire fame in the world; and consequently [it is not to be expected] that I should be grieved at any opposition to the purpose for which I composed it. But in the first instance I composed it—and *my Witness is in heaven* (Job 16:19)—for my own sake, in order to free myself from the burden of investigating and searching for the halakot which are needed constantly, and then for use in my old age (as my memory weakens), and for the sake of the Lord, may He be blessed. For I was most zealous for the Lord God of Israel when I saw before me a nation that does not have a comprehensive book (of laws) in the true sense nor true and accurate (theological) opinions. Therefore I have done what I did, only for the sake of heaven.
>
> I knew, and it was perfectly clear to me at the time that I composed it, that it would undoubtedly fall into the hands of a wicked and jealous person who would defame its praiseworthy features and pretend that he does not need it or is in a position to ignore it; and (that it would fall) into the hands of a foolish ignoramus who will not recognize the value of

---

53. MT, introduction; MN, I, 34, based on Joel 3:5. See B. Sanh 92a.

this project and will consider it worthless; and (that it would fall) into the hands of a deluded and confused tyro to whom many places in the book would be incomprehensible, inasmuch as he does not know their source or is unable to comprehend in full the inferences which I inferred with great precision; and (that it would fall) into the hands of a reactionary and obtuse man of piety who will assail the explanations of the fundamentals of faith included in it. They are the majority. Undoubtedly it will also come into the hands of *the remnant whom the Lord calls* (Joel 3:5), individuals of righteousness, uprightness, and good judgment, who will recognize the value of what I have done.[54]

6. *Ma'ămar Tĕḥiyyaṯ ham-Meṯim (Treatise on Resurrection)* (1191). The Maimonidean description of the incorporeity of the eternal life in the world to come and his alleged failure to formulate in the *Mishneh Torah*[55] the belief in bodily resurrection triggered an acrimonious dispute, peaking in the accusation that Maimonides really denied this religious belief because of its incompatibility with philosophic principles. The severest attack came from R. Samuel ben 'Alī, Gaon of Baghdad, who zeroed in on many individual passages of the *Mishneh Torah* and eventually faulted Maimonides for his entire eschatological scheme, which appeared to him as deviationist.[56] Contrary to his customary refusal to engage in cyclical (sometimes inevitably cynical) recriminations—he preferred a stance of neutrality vis-à-vis critics so as not to be deflected from planned constructive efforts—Maimonides was impelled this time to answer the charges and clarify his position.[57] While this provocative treatise is not a document of prime philosophic significance, it is very important for the insights into his personality, his intellectualistic posture vis-à-vis the masses, and his art of self-defense coupled with pungent criticism. It is interspersed with comments on his literary-pedagogic habits and scholarly standards in general as

---

54. *'Iggĕroṯ*, 50ff.
55. See *Tĕšuḇah*, viii, 2, and RABD, ad loc.
56. S. Assaf, "Ḳoḇeṣ šel 'Iggĕroṯ R. Šĕmu'el ben 'Alī," *Tarbiz*, I (1929), 102ff.; see *Tĕšuḇoṯ*, 310 (pp. 572ff.); *Ḳoḇeṣ*, II, 16a; and *'Iggĕroṯ*, 66.
57. MTH, 1–3; *'Iggĕroṯ*, 49, 61, 90; also *Ḳoḇeṣ*, I, 26b; II, 16b; see I. Elbogen, "Moses ben Maimons Persönlichkeit," *MGWJ*, LXXIX (1935), 76–79.

well as on aspects of the *Mishneh Torah* in particular. This codificatory achievement, with its precision of style and its classification and rationalization of halakah, is pivotal. In short, the treatise, with the *Mishneh Torah* serving as a paradigm, is more of a defense of his method and philosophic conception of religion—and hence of his life's work—than a rebuttal of criticisms concerning resurrection:

> The fact is that when we ventured forth in a pioneering effort to compose a work concerning the laws of the Torah and the elucidation of its rules, we intended thereby to fulfill the will of God, blessed be He, not to seek recompense or honor from men, but to smooth the path, interpret, and, as we thought necessary, help those who could not understand the words of the Torah scholars, of blessed memory, who preceded us, to understand them. It seems to us that we facilitated (literally, brought close or made reasonable) and simplified abstruse [apparently non-ritual] and profound subjects; we collected and compiled subjects which were scattered and dispersed; and we knew, at any rate, that we were achieving something valuable. For if the case was as we thought it to be, then by simplifying, facilitating, and compiling, in a manner that none of our predecessors had ever done, we have already achieved something by benefiting people and have earned divine recompense. But if it proves otherwise, and we have not succeeded in clarifying or simplifying the subject to any greater extent than our predecessors did in their works, then we have at least earned God's reward; as the Talmudic saying has it, "God desires the heart [i.e., the intention of the act]. . . ."
>
> And when we ventured to undertake this project (the *Mishneh Torah*), we saw that it would be wrong to aim at our goal—to interpret and facilitate details of the laws—and at the same time to neglect its foundations (*yĕsoḏot*), i.e., that I should not explain them or guide (the reader) to their truth. . . . We saw that it would be necessary for us to explain the foundations (principles) of religion in our Talmudic works in a descriptive-apodictic fashion rather than in a demonstrative one, because a demonstrative approach to these religious principles requires an intellectual facility and familiarity with many sciences which the Talmudists do not possess, as we have explained in the *Moreh Nebukim*, and we preferred that the fundamental truths at least be accepted as articles of tradition by all people. Consequently, we mentioned at the beginning of our *Commentary on the Mishnah* principles which should be be-

lieved concerning (various matters), [e.g., prophecy]. In *Pereḳ Ḥeleḳ* [chapter 10 of Sanhedrin] we explained principles. . . . We did the same also in our great work entitled the *Mishneh Torah*, whose true worth will be recognized only by those men of religion and wisdom who acknowledge the truth and are predisposed to study intelligently, who can understand how the work was composed, and who can recognize both the extent to which these laws which we have collected had been scattered and how we arranged them in order. We have also stated therein all the religious and juridical principles, and we have intended thereby that those who are called disciples of the wise (*talmiḏe ḥăḳamim*, scholars), or Geonim, or whatever you wish to call them, should build their branches [i.e., details of the laws] on juridical roots; that their Torah knowledge should be ordered in their minds and their learning should be properly grounded; that all this should be built on religious principles; and that they should not cast the knowledge of God behind them, but should direct their utmost efforts and zeal to that which will bring them perfection and enable them to draw nearer to their Creator, not to the things that the masses deem to be perfection.

At a later point, Maimonides notes: "All our works are concise and to the point. We have no intention of writing bulky books nor of spending time on that which is useless. Hence when we explain anything, we explain only what is necessary and only in the measure required to understand it, and whatever we write is in summary form. . . . You, my readers, already know that I always tend to omit disputes and debates. Were I able to condense the entire Talmud into a single chapter, I would not do so in two."[58]

7. *Quotations in an anonymous Apologia.* A friendly contemporary or disciple of R. Abraham Maimonides wrote a fervent apology for the *Mishneh Torah* which is, in essence, a mosaic of quotations from Maimonides' writings, particularly the letters.[59]

---

58. MTH, 2–4 and 24–26. On Teicher's doubts regarding the authenticity of this treatise, see his articles in *Mělilah*, I (1944), 81ff., and *JJS*, I (1948), 35ff., and the refutation by I. Sonne in *PAAJR*, XXI (1952), 101ff. See also below, chap. VI.

59. A. Halkin, "Sanegoriyah 'al Sefer Mishneh Torah," *Tarbiz*, XXV (1957), 413ff. Parts of the letters to R. Joseph, R. Phinehas, and Ibn Jābir are quoted, along with selections from MTH, *Pereḳ Ḥeleḳ*, and MN, I, 31. On the self-sufficiency of the MT, see also below, chap. II.

## 46 INTRODUCTION TO THE CODE OF MAIMONIDES

Its importance is manifold. It demonstrates, first of all, the availability and impact of these letters, at least in certain circles. There are also some variant readings in the citations which are philologically interesting. It has, in addition, preserved several hitherto unknown passages which extend and substantiate Maimonidean convictions and contentions. Furthermore, it uncompromisingly represents a certain school of Maimonideanism in its unequivocal stress of the idea that Maimonides intended the *Mishneh Torah* to have its own integrity and complete self-sufficiency: it need not, and indeed should not, be subordinated to the Talmud; it is useful and intelligible without concomitant Talmud study. That which was a vice in the eyes of many, and caused Maimonides himself more than a twinge of discomfiture, is here underscored as a virtue, as the overriding characteristic of the work. In common with the Maimonidean letters, it emphasizes the practical-functional goal of the Code, but it sees this as growing out of the practical-functional goal of Talmud study as a whole. The controversy and debate which are quantitatively so prominent in the Talmud are axiologically peripheral; the aim is normative knowledge, applied law, and not theoretical analysis. The law is concerned with practice, and there is no need to be apologetic or defensive about the *Mishneh Torah*'s practicality. There is finally an arresting assertion: an implicit goal of the *Mishneh Torah* is to prepare the reader for proper rationalistic interpretation of "strange" passages of aggadic literature. It does, in other words, have a self-transcending ideological purpose. This connection is of obvious interest in the light of Maimonides' abiding concern for the problems of aggadah, and even the few comments on it in the *Mishneh Torah* itself. The nexus of aggadah-philosophy is basic in Maimonidean thought, as indeed it is in the entire history of Jewish thought. This Maimonidean protagonist is here accentuating its importance from the viewpoint of the *Mishneh Torah*.

The following is part of a nonextant letter of Maimonides quoted by this anonymous author:

I have decreed that you slacken not your efforts until you comprehend the Code in its entirety, make it "your book" par excellence, and teach

# INTRODUCTION

it everywhere in order that its usefulness should be enhanced. For the desired goal in all (the material) which was collected in the Talmud is destroyed and lost, and the intention of scholars is a waste of time in studying the deliberations in the Talmud, if the intention and goal is exertion in matters of controversy and nothing else. Indeed, this is not the first goal. On the contrary, the deliberation and the debate (*maśśa' u-mattan*) came only accidentally, because there emerged ambiguous statements which one (scholar) explained in a certain way while his colleague came and explained it in the opposite way, and each one saw a need to elucidate his way of reasoning which supports his view, in order that his explanation may prevail. The main intention is none other than to make known that which man is obligated to do and that from which he must refrain. This is clear to someone like yourself. Therefore I have emphasized the main intention so that it may be easy to remember it.

There is no need to continue and collate the many briefer references to the *Mishneh Torah* scattered throughout Maimonides' responsa,[60] but the references to it contained in the *Moreh* deserve to be singled out because they are so plentiful and suggestive. On the one hand, the *Moreh* clearly differentiates between the "legalistic study" of the Oral Law and its philosophical-metaphysical study.[61] The normal term of reference is "our great compilation," sometimes qualified by "our great legal compilation" or "our great compilation on the legalistc study of the law."[62] The *Mishneh Torah* is primarily a legal work. On the other hand, it is clear that Maimonides looked upon it as containing a succinct outline of philosophic principles ("the foundations of religion") and serving as a compendium of beliefs as well as a manual of laws. He unflinchingly sought a union of the two realms.[63] Specifically, he refers in the *Moreh* to certain philosophic themes, love of God, knowledge of God, prophecy, reasons for commandments, which were touched upon in the *Mishneh Torah*.[64]

60. See above, n.25, and index to *Tešuḇot*, III, pp. 189ff.
61. MN, introduction (p. 5); I, 71 (pp. 175–76).
62. E.g., MN, III, 29 (p. 517); introduction (pp. 6, 10); II, 10 (p. 273).
63. See MTH, 4; MN, introduction (p. 10); ShM, *šoreš* 9; and below, chap. VI.
64. MN, I, 21 (p. 48); II, 35 (p. 367); II, 45 (p. 403); III, 28 (p. 512); III, 43 (p. 571); and many more. Concerning the date of MN, see *'Iggĕrot*, 2; and J. Ḳāfiḥ, in his introduction to the Hebrew translation of MN, who suggests a slightly revised chronology.

## 48 INTRODUCTION TO THE CODE OF MAIMONIDES

*Five Major Characteristics*

A synchronic view of all the statements cited in the above pages shows that they repeatedly focus upon five major characteristics:

- A. Codificatory form
- B. Comprehensive scope
- C. Arrangement and classification
- D. Language and style
- E. Fusion of law and philosophy

These appear to be the basic literary-conceptual categories which Maimonides himself would use in order to describe his work systematically and telescope its novelties. We shall adopt his scheme, considering each feature fully in the following chapters, and fleshing out our analysis by an empirical examination of theory in the light of reality.

It is self-evident that all these five features are intertwined, that comprehensiveness of scope, for example, is related to philosophy and law, impinges upon the scheme of classification, qualifies the rigidity of codificatory form, and requires some stylistic variation.[65] While we shall treat each feature separately, the overlap should be kept in mind. Certain emphases will be repeated in order to leave each theme fully intact and each chapter as a meaningful unit. For example, the use of aggadah in the *Mishneh Torah* needs to be mentioned with regard to codificatory form, for it seems anomalous there, but it must also be noted in the context of the comprehensiveness of the *Mishneh Torah* as well as in the discussion of philosophy and law. Inasmuch as our pri-

---

65. See below, chap. II. It is worth quoting here the pointed presentation of four of these features as found in R. Menahem ham-Me'iri's introduction to *Bet hab-Bĕḥirah, Bĕrakot* (Jerusalem, 1964), p. 25:

"והרב מורה צדק חדש בחבורו תכונות אחרות, וזה שהוא ע"ה אחז דרך המחברים לכתוב כל דבר ודבר ביחד הלכות הלכות, אבל חדש עליהם לכתוב דבריו דרך קבלה באין הודעת מחלוקת ומשא ומתן, וכן חדש עליהם לכתוב דבריו בלשון המשנה, והוסיף אומץ לכתוב בחבוריו כל עניני התלמוד הן בענינים הצריכים לנו בזה הזמן הן בשאר הענינים."

I must confess that I came to appreciate this presentation only after my own identification of the five features. Note his emphasis on *ḥiddeš*. See below, n.111.

mary goal is an analytic description of the *Mishneh Torah,* rather than of Maimonides' attitude toward aggadah or of other specific problems (the Geonim, the role of custom, the structure of the Talmud, etc.), it seemed imperative to organize our study around the structure of this work and its features. These important problems will, in any event, be discussed in various contexts.

SOURCES OF THE *Mishneh Torah*: ERUDITION AND ORIGINALITY

Before proceeding, a word about the sources of this work, their impressive range as well as Maimonides' attitude toward them, is in order. Maimonides' statements about the sources from which he drew the material for the *Mishneh Torah* are classic instances of understatement, disarming and potentially misleading in their simplicity and summariness. The first reference which emphasizes his goal of "brevity with completeness" mentions sources almost nonchalantly: "so that the reader might encompass all that is found in the Mishnah and Talmud, Sifra, Sifre, and Tosefta, and more than that, all decrees and ordinances of the later Geonim . . . as well as all that they explained and commented upon concerning the prohibited and the permissible."[66] The *Mishneh Torah* introduction is marked by the same ethos of restraint and retrenchment concerning sources. "I studied all these works, [the Talmud, Babylonian as well as Palestinian, Sifra, Sifre, and Tosefta], so that this work might serve as a compendium of the entire Oral Law, including the ordinances, customs, and decrees instituted from the days of our teacher Moses until the compilation of the Talmud, as expounded for us by the Geonim in all the works composed by them since the completion of the Talmud."[67] Listing of sources is subservient to the underscoring of the comprehensive scope. The letter to R. Phinehas also affirms routinely that everything in the Code is based on the Talmud, Babylonian or Palestinian, Sifra, Sifre, Mishnah, and Tosefta, supplemented by Gaonic works. An attempt is made to present practically everything, excepting those statements clearly marked by a personalized introductory phrase, as flowing or

---

66. ShM, introduction (II, p. 426).
67. MT, introduction; see also PhM, introduction (p. 1).

emerging directly from available sources. Anonymity is thus also of strategic significance. It is a steady subliminal reinforcement of the claim that the views of the *Mishneh Torah* are identical with those of the sources.[68] While he was not diffident about emphasizing the value and significance of his work, Maimonides did not apparently care to flaunt his erudition or his inventiveness in interpretation and inference. He spoke, in measured terms common to Rabbinic scholars, about the study of Talmudic literature and of its ever-expanding cognate corpus of commentaries and codes produced by the Geonim. He did not indicate the great variety of his sources and his selective and discriminating use of them. Furthermore, while he, almost epitaphically, appraises each individual author and indicates his attitude to these philosophic predecessors (from Aristotle to Ibn Bajjah) in his listing of philosophic sources—today we would describe it as a little bibliographical essay or at least as an annotated bibliography—in the letter to Samuel ibn Tibbon (the translator of the *Moreh* from Arabic into Hebrew, who received instruction from Maimonides concerning philosophy as well as the art of translation),[69] in the *Mishneh Torah* he does not append critical evaluations even to the summary, almost generic, description of halakic sources. They are presented as elements of a unified mosaic.[70]

Actually the reality is more complicated, impressive, and far-reaching, as if the obviously sovereign mastery of all Talmudic literature is not enough. The erudition underlying the compendium is awesome, simply extravagant. Careful literary analysis of the *Mishneh Torah,* studious review of Maimonides' responsa in which he sometimes casually mentions sources, and searching reading of pre-Maimonidean writings enable us to establish the

---

68. *Kobeṣ*, I, 25a (cited above, pp. 32–37). Identifying select statements as original by the formula "it appears to me" blurs the inventiveness and originality of interpretation which permeate the work as a whole. *Tešubot*, 121 (p. 217).

69. In his letter to R. Samuel ibn Tibbon, published by A. Marx, *JQR*, XXV (1935), 376ff. See the translation and detailed analysis by S. Pines in the translator's introduction ("The Philosophic Sources of the Guide of the Perplexed") to MN, pp. lvii ff.

70. Of course his responsa, which need to be examined very carefully, tell us something about the range of his sources as well as his critical attitudes. The summary passages in PhM, introduction (p. 46), and MT, introduction, also provide a critical perspective, even though the tone is muted and the style restrained.

phenomenal range of literature which is reflected directly or obliquely in the *Mishneh Torah*. We have no catalogue or classified listing of works and pamphlets, comparable to the book lists which are extant for other medieval authors, but it appears that practically *all* the Hebrew and Judeo-Arabic literature available at the time reached him and was in his library. His resounding declaration concerning his readings in the literature of astrology and idolatry may be applied, mutatis mutandis, to all his readings: "It seems to me that there does not remain in the world a composition on this subject, having been translated into Arabic from other languages, but that I have read it and have understood its subject matter and have plumbed the depth of its thought."[71] His statement on medicine likewise emphasizes his commitment to know and analyze the sources of everything: "For you know how long and difficult this art [medicine] is for a conscientious and exact man who does not want to state anything which he cannot support by argument and without knowing where it has been said and how it can be demonstrated."[72] How he carefully sifted this mass of data will become clear in the following chapters. That he was not merely an omnivorous reader, a master of bookish learning endowed with an extraordinary memory and an uncanny knack for learned syncretism or synthesis, is obvious. The salient feature of the Code is not just its encyclopedic coverage but also its creative systematization and interpretation; its most important source is Maimonides' fertile mind and skill of analysis and synthesis. It is, however, necessary to establish clearly his immense bookishness, the parameters of his formal-literary sources, their range and heterogeneity.

Halakic literature in the conventional sense, almost boundless in scope and consistently challenging in content, was completely assimilated by Maimonides. It forms the bedrock of his codificatory achievement. To Mishnah and Tosefta, Sifra and Sifre, Babylonian Talmud and Palestinian Talmud, which Maimonides mentions summarily and routinely, should be added all other halakic and aggadic Midrashim, medieval (particularly Yemenite)

---

71. LA, 229.
72. *'Iggĕrot*, 69–70.

compilations, minor treatises, and the like. Such works as *Masseket Soferim* or *Masseket Derek 'Ereṣ*, *Pirke de-R. Eliezer* or *'Abot de-R. Nathan*, *Pesikta* and *Mekilta* of R. Simeon, *Sifre Zuṭa*, or *Derek 'Ereṣ Zuṭa*—all are grist for Maimonides' large mill. *Mishneh Torah* commentaries, through the ages, have with unflagging vigilance pointed out sources and/or parallels for Maimonidean formulations, nuances, and allusions over the entire range of Talmudic-Midrashic literature. These sources are either direct and immediate or associative-suggestive, but the literary relationship is incontrovertible, copiously documented, and firmly anchored.[73] Sometimes, indeed, Maimonides himself parenthetically mentions in other writings the sources of some *Mishneh Torah* formulations. There can be no serious alternative to the conclusion that Maimonides "controlled" this vast literature in its totality and used it selectively and subtly, formally yet flexibly—in the colorful but concise idiom of medieval admirers, "the hidden treasures of the Torah" were revealed to him, "no secret caused him difficulty."[74] Identifying sources is thus not a case of misplaced scholarly ingenuity but genuine *Quellenforschung*, precise and compelling correlation of a Maimonidean statement with an underlying Rabbinic source or with a mosaic of sources, for Maimonides could and did skillfully fuse words, phrases, and fragments of multiple documents into one unified seamless formulation.[75] Maimonides' predilection for proofs, reasonings, and formulations found in the halakic Midrashim, Tosefta, or Palestinian Talmud is widely recognized.[76] Hence the

---

73. The following references are representative: J. L. Maimon, *RaMBaM* (Jerusalem, 1960), pp. 83–133; idem, introduction to photo-reproduction of 1480 edition of MT (Jerusalem, 1955); J. N. Epstein, *Tarbiz*, VI (1935), 99ff.; L. Finkelstein, *JQR*, XXV (1935), 469ff.; M. Guttmann, "Zur Quellenkritik der MT," *MGWJ*, LXXIX (1935), 148–59. See below, chap. II, n.21. Note the document published by A. Scheiber, "Maimuni als Bibliophile," *Studies . . . in Honor of I. Kiev*, ed. C. Berlin (New York, 1971), pp. 415ff. A classic twentieth-century example of careful *Quellenforschung* together with literary-thematic analysis is the *'Abodat ham-Melek* (Vilna, 1931), on Book I of the MT; also *Kiryat Melek* (Jerusalem, 1964), by R. S. Kanefsky.
74. These are typical phrases used in praise of Maimonides' erudition. See R. Judah Albutini, *Yesod Mishneh Torah*, in J. L. Maimon, *RaMBaM*, p. 93. For the second, see Dan. 4:6 and B. Ḥul 59a.
75. He noted this with his customary understatement, *Kobeṣ*, I, 26a.
76. See above, n.12. R. David Pardo, *Ḥasde Dawid* (Jerusalem, 1890), provides a meticulous review of the use of Tosefta by Maimonides and RABD; see also indices to S.

INTRODUCTION 53

Měkilta, Pěsikta, or Pěsikta Zutarta, and similar works, including the minor treatises (e.g., Derek 'Ereṣ or Gerim), must be steadily scrutinized even if a parallel or analogous formulation has already been found in the Babylonian Talmud. This fact of his variegated and selective approach to sources contrasts with, and further underscores, the low-keyed manner in which he summarily referred to the sources. Perhaps the main point about Maimonides' use of his sources is the way he mined them, extracting all their valuable components and rearranging everything stylistically and materially, according to a design which he conceived. The results are invariably impressive, while the process is regularly invisible.

Post-Talmudic literature absorbed in the *Mishneh Torah* included not only major Gaonic codes and responsa as well as the influential commentaries of the North African Talmudists (R. Hananeel, R. Nissim Gaon), but also minor compilations and handbooks, special manuals and monographs. A work on těfillin by R. Moses of Cordova,[77] or the Gaonic *Šimmuša Rabbah*,[78] a compilation on ṣiṣit by R. Samuel ben Ḥofni Gaon,[79] the *Sefer ham-Mafteaḥ* of R. Nissim Gaon,[80] works on the prayer book, whether the *Siddur* of R. Saadiah Gaon or a composition on prayer by Ibn al-Jasūm, the disciple of R. Nissim, early liturgical compositions (such as the *piyyuṭ* for the Day of Atonement),[81] the

---

Lieberman's *Tosefta ki-Fěšuṭah*. For his use of the Palestinian Talmud, see above, n. 12, and Twersky, *Rabad*, p. 209. For the halakic Midrashim, see, e.g., the articles of J. N. Epstein and L. Finkelstein cited above, n. 73; also M. Higger, *Šeba' Massektot Ketanot* (New York, 1930). The source of *De'ot*, iii, 1 (P. Ned) is mentioned by Maimonides in ŠP, iv. Note also R. Aaron of Lunel, *Kitāb al-Rasā'il*, ed. Y. Brill (Paris, 1871), p. 46; R. Joseph B. Soloveitchik, *Bet hal-Levi: Těšuḅot* (reprinted, New York, 1943), I, 43 (p. 137). For use of Mekilta, see, e.g., *Ḥameṣ u-Maṣṣah*, vii, 1, and MM; *Nizke Mamon*, i, 1, and *Ma'áśeh Rokeaḥ*. This predilection is especially noteworthy in the light of the fact that these sources were not always used.

77. *Těfillin*, iii, 6, and *Těšuḅot*, 289 (p. 542). The whole responsum is a model illustration of Maimonides' erudition as well as his intellectual dynamism. See also ibid., 139 (p. 268).

78. *Těfillin*, iii, 8, 10.

79. *Ṣiṣit*, i, 6, and *Těšuḅot*, 286 (p. 538). See also '*Iśuṭ*, ii, 12, and *Těšuḅot*, 66 (p. 106).

80. *Šabbat*, i, 17, and *Těšuḅot*, 301 (p. 559). See S. Abramson's important study, *Ḥamišah Sěfarim lě-R. Nissim Gaon* (Jerusalem, 1965), p. 278, and my comment in *Tarbiz*, XXXVII (1968), 326. For frequent use of the *Měgillat Sětarim*, see S. Lieberman, *Hilkot Yěrušalmi*, pp. 38, 39, and passim.

81. A. Marmorstein, "Sefer Dine Těfillah," *Tarbiz*, VI (1934–35), 426. On Ibn al-Jasūm, see *Těšuḅot*, 313 (p. 582); S. Assaf, "Keṭa' mi-Ḥibburo šel Ibn al-Jasūm," *KS*,

## 54 INTRODUCTION TO THE CODE OF MAIMONIDES

prayer book itself,[82] "treatises and compilations of the Masorites (authorities on the Masorah),"[83] the *Ši'ur Ḳomah*[84]—all were available to him. In one place, in support of his position, he notes the chain of Spanish Talmudists: R. Enoch, his son R. Moses, R. Isaac ibn Ghiyāth, R. Isaac ben Baruch (al-Balia), R. Isaac Alfasi, and R. Joseph hal-Levi (ibn Megas), his student.[85] His probable indebtedness to Spanish predecessors generally, including R. Moses ibn Ezra, R. Baḥya, R. Abraham bar Ḥiyya, R. Judah Albargeloni, and others not mentioned in this halakic list, is discernible in a variety of forms and contexts.[86] We have no compa-

---

XXVIII (1952–53), 101ff.; S. Abramson, *R. Nissim*, p. 25. For R. Saadiah, see *Siddur RaSaG*, ed. S. Assaf (Jerusalem, 1970), p. 38.

82. See the edition of Maimonides' prayer book by E. Goldschmidt, *Yĕdi'ot ham-Maḳon lĕ-Ḥeḳer haš-Širah ha-'Ibrit*, VII (1958), 183ff. Note *Mattĕnot 'Aniyyim*, x, 3, and the important comments of S. Abramson, *Lĕšonenu*, XXXVII (1973), 317, and XXXVIII (1974), 158. Ham-Me'iri quotes from the prayer book in the name of the Men of the Great Assembly; *Bet hab-Bĕḥirah*, introduction, 1. On apparent inaccuracies in Maimonides' quotation of verses, see bibliography in J. Dienstag, "Biblical Exegesis," *Samuel Mirsky Memorial Volume* (Jerusalem, 1970), pp. 159–60.

83. *Sefer Torah*, viii, 4; see *Tĕšubot*, 154 (p. 299).

84. *Tĕšubot*, 117 (p. 201); S. Lieberman, Hebrew appendix to G. Scholem, *Jewish Gnosticism* (New York, 1960), p. 124. Although not mentioned in the MT, this is obviously important for Maimonides' vigorous insistence upon the incorporeity of God; See *Tĕšubah*, iii, 7; Twersky, *Rabad*, p. 282; and cf. H. A. Wolfson, "The Jewish Kalām," *JQR Anniversary Volume* (1967), 570ff. For possible source of *Bi'at Miḳdaš*, viii, 7, in *Ši'ur Ḳomah*, see S. Lieberman, *Šeḳi'in* (Jerusalem, 1970), p. 12; for his rejection of *Alpha Beta de-Ben-Sira*, see ibid., p. 33. See *Sefer ha-Razim*, ed. M. Margaliyot (Jerusalem, 1967), p. 40, for possible use of this strange work in *'Akum*, vi, 1. S. Lieberman, *Šeḳi'in*, p. 17, illustrates the need for care in identifying sources.

85. *Tĕšubot*, 310 (p. 576); see also *Tĕšubot*, 128 (p. 230) on the Mishnah commentary of R. Isaac ibn Ghiyāth. For the development of Jewish learning in Spain, note B. Z. Benedict, in *Tarbiz*, XXII (1951), 92, n.7. For all-inclusive references to "Sages of the West," see *Tĕšubot*, 156 (p. 201); 269 (p. 516); 294 (p. 552).

86. E.g., MTH, 19, 21; *Yĕsode hat-Torah*, ix, 4, and R. Judah Albargeloni, *Peruš Sefer Yĕṣirah*, 138 (noted by E. Urbach, *Tarbiz*, XVIII [1946–47], 20–22); ShM, *šorašim;* and R. Abraham ibn Ezra, *Yĕsod Mora'* (see J. Perla, *Sefer ham-Miṣwot lĕ-RaSaG* [reprinted, New York, 1962]). Traces of, or affinities with, R. Baḥya's rationality-spirituality are plentiful: e.g., *De'ot*, iii, 1, and *Ḥobot hal-Lĕbabot*, viii, 3 (II, p. 260); *Tĕšubah*, x, 6, and *Ḥobot*, x, introduction (II, p. 338); *Lulab*, viii, 15, and *Ḥobot*, vi, 6 (II, pp. 96, 100). This relationship deserves further study. On Messianism and resurrection, see S. Schwarzfuchs, "Les Lois Royales de Maimonide," *REJ*, CXI (1951–52), 63–86; J. Finkel, "Maimonides' Treatise on Resurrection: A Comparative Study," *Essays on Maimonides*, ed. S. Baron (New York, 1941), pp. 93ff. For Abraham bar Ḥiyya, see S. Baron, *PAAJR*, VI (1935), 9–10, n.5, and J. Levinger, *Darke ham-Maḥšabah*, 142, n.155. *Ḥameṣ u-Maṣṣah*, vi, 12; and R. Isaac ibn Ghiyāth, *Me'ah Šĕ'arim*, p. 97. Also *Yĕsode hat-Torah*, v, 11, and *'Abodat ham-Meleḳ* commentary; *Mĕlaḳim*, v, 11, and Ibn Ghiyāth, *Hilḳot Sĕmaḥot*, II, 73.

rable listing for individual Gaonic authors, but identifications with responsa and compendia of many Geonim have been made.[87]

Maimonides' use of Gaonic literature provides a paradigmatic study in dependence and independence. For all his criticism, his disavowal of certain features, forms, and forces of Gaonic writing and repeated manifestations of independence, many Maimonidean motifs and tendencies may be seen as rooted in Gaonic precedent. We must of necessity differentiate between specific discrete borrowings and more general, sometimes automatic, reliance upon predecessors, just as we must on occasion differentiate between fundamental disagreement and sporadic agreement. Generally, the whole process of intellectual growth can of course be studied by pinpointing Maimonides' relation to predecessors—and here it is worth noting once again the seminal influence of R. Joseph ibn Megas—but it can be illumined also by retracing the steps of his own development. We may analyze and assess those interpretations of the *Commentary on the Mishnah* which were abandoned or changed, the hermeneutic principles or halakic definitions which carry over from earlier works to the *Mishneh Torah*, as well as refinements and reformulations within the manuscript copies of the *Mishneh Torah* itself, and expanded or supplementary views which surface for the first time in the *Mishneh Torah*. We may study whether later thought patterns change or crystallize earlier tendencies.

These references cumulatively afford us a glimpse into his workshop and an intimation of the amount of invisible paperwork which went into the finished product. When Maimonides

---

87. See, e.g., S. Assaf, "Sifre R. Hai u-Tĕšubotaw kĕ-Maḳor lĕha-RaMBaM," *Sinai*, II (1938), 522ff. Note, e.g., *Šĕḥitat 'Asor*, ii, 8, which seems to be based on the *Šĕ'eltot* of R. Ahai Gaon (and see Naḥmanides, *Torat ha-'Adam*, *Kitbe RaMBaN*, II, 24); *Tĕmidin u-Musafin*, vii, 11, and *Hălakot Gĕdolot* (ed. Hildesheimer), p. 672; *To'en wĕ-Niṭ'an*, xii, 12, and R. Hai Gaon, *Sefer Mekkaḥ u-Mimkar* (noted by Naḥmanides, *Ḥiddušim*, BB 36a); J. Rabinowitz, *Jewish Law*, (New York, 1956), p. 295 (concerning *Mĕkirah*, xi, 18). Also *Yoreḥ De'ah*, 240:7, and R. Elijah Gaon (concerning *Talmud Torah*, v, 7).

Inasmuch as the study of Gaonic literature is still in its infancy—all the remarkable progress of the last decades notwithstanding—the relation of Maimonides to the Gaonic legacy, his use as well as criticism of it, will have to be reexamined and correlated with this abundance of new material. This became crystal clear to me when Professor Shraga Abramson showed me the amount of Gaonic literature in his files. R. Hai, R. Saadiah, R. Samuel ben Hofni are emerging into the full glare of history.

incidentally opens the doors of his study, we see how a single paragraph is conceived and formulated only after exhaustive preparation and meticulous review. The burden of careful study and literary-conceptual reconstruction is clearly upon the reader. As in the case of the scientist presenting the results of a successful experiment or significant discovery, the extensive laboratory work, often marked by repeated trial and error, hypothesis and modification, is not fully exposed.

On the other hand, we must not always automatically assume that Maimonides consciously utilized every antecedent which may come to our attention as a result of philological labors. Scholarly-textual research, sometimes imaginative, sometimes plodding, may yield a plausible source for a Maimonidean statement in cases where all circumstantial considerations suggest that Maimonides did not in fact utilize this apparent source. When asked by the Lunel scholars about a provocative halakic formulation—the inclusion of "the removal of the upper jaw" in the list of *ṭĕrefah*, although the Talmudic list, which is presumed to be complete, does not contain it—Maimonides confidently replied that originality of interpretation was a fact of scholarly life. An author particularly attuned to certain problems may discern a nuance or a *novum* in well-known texts which his predecessors had missed completely. Much depends on the author's perception of the material as well as his halakic-conceptual mass of apperceptions, in the light of which traditional texts are made to yield their meaning. An apparent addition may be merely a compelling interpretation or deduction.[88] Now it happens that the very novelty about which he was asked is found in a recently published text of R. Saadiah Gaon, one of the few Geonim whom Maimonides quotes specifically by name.[89] Yet in his answer to

---

88. *Šĕḥiṭah*, viii, 16, and *Tĕšuḇot*, 315 (p. 585).
89. J. Brumer, "Minyan hag-Giḏim ha-'Asurim lĕ-RaSaG," *PAAJR*, XXX (1962), Hebrew section, 7. Another interesting case is *Tĕfillah*, x, 2, and the view attributed to *Halaḵot Gĕḏolot* (cited also in Rashi, to B. Ber 30b). I would suggest that in the MN (III, 29, 32) an interesting parallel would be whether Maimonides used—or had in the back of his mind—the Midrashic passage in Lev. Rabbah, 22:8 which later writers (e.g., R. Moses Alashkar, *Tĕšuḇot*, 117) identified as a source, or at least an antecedent, for his provocative view (discussed further in chap. VI, below) concerning the institution of sacrifices. It is the kind of quotation which he could have used strategically and effectively.

the Lunel group, he does not argue from authority or cite precedent, as he frequently does. He defends the view as an unimpeachable inference. Since there is no reason to assume deliberate omission of this source reference, we must infer either that Maimonides forgot this source when he was responding to the Lunel inquirers or that he never had access to it. Consequently the search for sources—and the same is true for the submission of hypothetical interpretations of problematic or provocative passages—must be guided and disciplined by the light of Maimonides' explicit statements concerning method or meaning, derivation or development, substance or structure.

Scripture, of course, underlies all Hebrew writing; its regular utilization, direct or indirect, by Maimonides or other medieval Rabbis can always be assumed and requires no special emphasis. From the vantage point of his codificatory goals, however, we shall have occasion to note Maimonides' extensive use of Scripture in a variety of contexts (philosophic, halakic, ethical, historical, and linguistic) as well as his creative attainments in exegesis. It is not just "knowledge" of Scripture—apt citation of verses—which we encounter, but original explication and application. Maimonides may prefer a verse cited in a Midrash or in the Palestinian Talmud, and sometimes, it would appear, may even utilize an original Scriptural citation.[90] While the motives for this undoubtedly vary, one must always weigh the possibility of anti-Karaite polemic and the desire to tighten the nexus between the Written Law and the Oral Law by making the tradition persuasive and compelling, obvious and self-evident in exegetical-interpretative terms.[91] In this context, we should also be attentive to his selective but decisive use of the Aramaic translations of the Bible (particularly Targum Onkelos, which, according to the

---

90. RaDBaZ, *Mĕlakim*, i, 1; x, 7; also *Mamrim*, v, 15. Note also *'Arakin*, vi, 31–33; *De'ot*, iv, 15; *Šĕkirut*, xiii, 7. See *'Akum*, iv. See the far-reaching generalization of R. Baruch Epstein, *Torah Tĕmimah*, Lev. 10:6.

91. *Ḥobel u-Mazzik*, i, 6; *Šĕbu'ot*, xii, 12. Maimonides' noteworthy statements on the importance of Scripture include MN, 1, 2; *'Iggĕrot*, 16. Later, Gersonides (introduction to his Bible commentary) was to suggest a very novel hermeneutical system (a series of *topoi-mĕkomot*) whereby, in his opinion, traditional halakot were more closely and compellingly related to, or derived from, Biblical verses. The nineteenth-century Malbim commentary, of course, comes to mind in this context. See also *Nĕdarim*, iii, 8; *Ma'ăśeh hak-Korbanot*, x, 15.

## 58 INTRODUCTION TO THE CODE OF MAIMONIDES

Palestinian Talmud, was equal in status to the Oral Law) not only to corroborate linguistic explanations or demonstrate etymological affinities but also to sustain theological positions, philosophical propositions, and halakic norms.[92]

To this should be added Maimonides' thorough acquaintance with the grammatical, lexicographical, and exegetical works of his predecessors; he made use not only of R. Saadiah Gaon and R. Abraham ibn Ezra but also of R. Jonah ibn Janāḥ, R. Moses ibn Gikatilia, and R. Judah ibn Bal'am. Many of these authors are mentioned by Maimonides in his *opera minora,* and there is thus no question but that he had studied their philological works.[93] While the scholar should ordinarily beware of transferring sources and references from one work to another—those mentioned, for example, in the *Sefer ham-Miṣwoṯ* or in various epistles to the *Mishneh Torah*—for the overlap or identity is by no means axiomatic, in this case there can be no question about its intellectual propriety, both because of Maimonides' explicit statements as well as because of the basically anonymous nature of the work which *ex hypothesi* is a digest and distillation of the author's erudition and creativity. Maimonides, for example, defends his allegorical explanations of certain Messianic-eschatological verses, anonymously reproduced in the *Mishneh Torah,* by pointing out that these explanations are grounded in respected exegetical traditons.[94] The same is true for his use of Targum Onkelos. All could be reflected, directly or obliquely but usually anonymously.

Not only did he read everything and learn from everything, but he was attentive and sensitive, utilizing experience and ob-

---

92. See, e.g., *'Issure Bi'ah,* xii, 13; *'Aḇel,* v, 19 (and cf. *Ṭumē'aṯ Ṣara'aṯ,* x, 6). Z. H. Chajes, *'Iggereṯ Bikkoreṯ,* in *Kol Sifre . . . Chajes* (Jerusalem, 1958), II, 505 (concerning *Tešuḇah,* v, 1); P. Churgin, *Ḥoreḇ,* IX (1946), 87, n.15; S. Lieberman, *Tosefta ki-Fěšuṭah, Šabbaṯ,* p. 203, n.6. Targum Jonathan is cited in *Kēle ham-Miḳdaš,* x, 2. In MN (e.g., I, 2, 36; II, 33, and elsewhere) Maimonides praised Onkelos. See MN, I, 48, where he allows for the possibility of error, since, he says, we do not possess an autograph copy of Onkelos.

93. *Tešuḇoṯ,* 267 (p. 509) on *paršane Sěfaraḏ; Ḳoḇeṣ,* II, 9b, 27a; MTH, 19, 21 (Ibn Gikatilia and Ibn Bal'am), 23. See also *Yěsoḏe hat-Torah,* vi, 8; *Šabbaṯ,* xxiii, 24. The work of Ibn Ḥayyuj is mentioned in PhM, Soṭ 5:5 (p. 263). Cf. W. Bacher, *Ha-RaMBaM Paršan ham-Miḳra'* (Tel Aviv, 1932), especially chap. 21. Thorough study of the subject remains a scholarly desideratum; see, e.g., H. Rabinovitz in *Šanah bē-Šanah,* ed. A. Pachenick (Jerusalem, 1967), pp. 223ff.

94. MTH, 19, 21.

servation of usages and established practices and referring to them when useful. Oral traditions ("*ḳabbalah* from the Sages") and personal observations are thus to be counted among the sources which underlie the *Mishneh Torah*. In one letter, for example, he tells Ibn Jābir about a certain custom that was widespread in Spain and France, which is indeed the authentic Talmudic law (as distinct from the erroneous custom in Egypt), and for good measure he adds, "We found all the Jews of the Land of Israel following this practice when we lived with them."[95] We must remember that he did not spend too much time in the Holy Land as he made his way from Acre, through Jerusalem, southward to Egypt. We also find references to various kinds of contemporary preachers and homilists, and to pseudo-Messiahs and their calamitous movements.[96] Ancient sources and contemporary events merged: the former were never antiquarian while the latter were clearly relevant, whether illustrating correct customs which should be upheld or deviant developments which should be uprooted.

Special mention should be made of Maimonides' use in the Code of non-Jewish sources: medical literature, works on astronomy, mathematics, and geometry, and the whole range of classical philosophy. As we shall see, this use is striking but not at all problematic for Maimonides, inasmuch as the harmony of faith and reason, which means in practical-literary terms the congruence of philosophical literature and traditional (Biblical-Talmudic) literature, is a commonplace of the medieval religious philosophy and epistemology which guided Maimonides.[97] Indeed, the universal range of references is perfectly natural for Maimonides. Even in the heat of argument, when he had to rebut an uncongenial critic who mingled specific queries with sweeping accusations, and generally in defending the legitimacy and usefulness of his Code, Maimonides refers nonchalantly to the fact

---

95. *Ḳobeṣ*, II, 16a; *Ḳidduš ha-Ḥodeš*, xi, 3; *'Edut*, vi, 4; *Mamrim*, vi, 15. See below, chap. II. See also, for halakic issues and observations in the Land of Israel, PhM, Par 3:9 (p. 428); Soṭ 2:4 (p. 253); *Tešubot*, 320 (p. 588). For Egypt, see *Tešubot*, 268 (p. 512).
96. E.g., *Tešubot*, 110 (p. 190), IT, and *Mĕlakim*, xii, 2.
97. See below, chap. III. E.g., *De'ot*, iv, 21; *Ḳidduš ha-Ḥodeš*, xvii, 25; *Gĕnebah*, viii, 1; see below, chaps. II and VI; also MN, I, 71; II, 9, and ShM, negative 40. Note O. Neugebauer, "The Astronomy of Maimonides and Its Sources," *HUCA*, XXII (1949), 322ff.

that "any author who wrote a book dealing with Torah or with other sciences, whether the author was from among the ancient nations in possession of philosophy or from among the physicians, would necessarily adopt one of two opinions."[98] The candor and spontaneity underscore the fact that the universality of reference, and of perception, was completely routine and unrehearsed.

In sum, this awesome erudition is masked not only by the decision to omit footnotes and source references, as required by the codificatory form,[99] but also by the general thrust and tenor which determined that the constructive elements be greater than the critical ones. The total gestalt, the balanced-cadenced presentation, the summary formulation of laws and ideas, frequently incorporating in compressed form their exegetical bases and conceptual connections, are more important than identifying, isolating, or criticizing sources. The fact that Maimonidean writing is so often characterized, in Ben Jonson's phrase, by "a newness of sense and antiquity of voice" is the crucial determinant, eclipsing the formalization of genetic-literary relationships. His literary and conceptual apparatuses are purposely fused. Proper study of the *Mishneh Torah* thus necessitates tireless sleuthing, a deliberate and disciplined search for sources, together with an ever-deepening empathy for the modes of abstraction and conceptualization. In the final analysis, however, the attempt to uncover and understand "Maimonides' mind" must be paramount, for the originality of the "Maimonidean mind" was ensconced in the smooth anonymous texture of the work.

We must remember that Maimonides was not codifying in the formal-technical sense of creating norms of authority or determining canons of obligation. He himself lacked the authority to do this. Nor was there any need, inasmuch as the entire problem of the nature of law, which has so agitated the minds of modern jurisprudents (e.g., Hart, Fuller, Raz), was irrelevant to medieval scholars for whom the authoritativeness of law and of its sources was clear and immutable. Hence his task was one of collecting and systematizing authoritative sources and hallowed

---

98. *Ḳobeṣ*, I, 25b.
99. The *Bet Yosef* of R. Joseph Karo is a perfectly enlightening contrast.

## INTRODUCTION

traditions, and this inevitably entailed a large measure of interpretation as well as selection. Maimonides must certainly have been aware of the fact that there is inevitable tension between the concept of codification with its attendant rigidity and the general thrust of Rabbinic literature with its intrinsic fluidity. We may say that he was seeking authority in the sense of requesting that people rely on his decision, sanction his selection, and endorse his interpretation. This goal could be best advanced by smooth integration of the constructive and critical components, the fine fusion of traditional formulations and original emphases. The literary smoothness resulting from the scarcity of references and the reassuring anonymity would suggest the unity of Talmudic source material and Maimonidean interpretation. Indeed, his remarks about theological issues imply that he saw a consensus between his interpretations and the underlying intentions of Rabbinic statements,[100] and that is why he could codify theological opinions with anonymity and certitude. This is certainly the message, explicit and implicit, of the entire work.

### MOTIVES AND GOALS OF THE *Mishneh Torah*

A review of the programmatic pronouncements also sheds light on the question of Maimonides' motives and intentions, the germination of the idea which led to the genesis of the work. The fourteen-volume *Mishneh Torah* as we have it is the literary realization of an intellectual dream and ideological impulse which are copiously described by Maimonides. Actually, the ideological impulse seems to be composed of several strands, a congeries of distinct prepossessions. Maimonides identifies three basic motives: an external historical motive nurtured by the particular circumstances and challenges, problems and pressures of his generation; an immanent typological motive flowing from basic intrinsic requirements of jurisprudence which made the production

---

100. On a number of occasions—PhM, Soṭ 3:3 (p. 257); Shebu, i, 4 (p. 250); Sanh, x, 3 (p. 218); ShM, negative 133; MTH, 16—Maimonides says that disputed theological issues, which have no practical repercussions, need not be codified, i.e., one need not choose between the conflicting views. By implication, therefore, his monolithic codificatory formulation of theological and ethical issues reflects consensus. His interpretations, in other words, did not admit of controversy.

of a code a prime literary desideratum; a rationalistic-spiritual motive deriving from pedagogical needs, intellectual goals, and philosophical convictions which impelled him to embody his dialectical conception of the ramified halakic system in a special codificatory summation. Let us comment briefly on the literary-thematic context and reverberations of each motive in a two-pronged effort to assess their significance and to determine whether these motives are distinct and mutually exclusive or cognate and mutually reenforcing.[101] An understanding of the mental processes which produced the work will deepen our insight into the finished product, its calm surface and dynamic content.

*Historical Motive: Response to Contemporary Need*

In a rather morose overview of contemporary conditions, Maimonides pinpoints one reason for composing his Code of law:

> In our days severe vicissitudes prevail, and all feel the pressure of hard times. The wisdom of our wise men has disappeared; the understanding of our prudent men is hidden (cf. Isa. 29:14). Hence the commentaries of the Geonim and their compilations of laws and responses, which they took care to make clear, have in our times become hard to understand, so that only a few individuals properly comprehend them. Needless to add, such is the case in regard to the Talmud itself—the Babylonian as well as the Palestinian—the Sifra, the Sifre, and the Tosefta, all of which works require for their comprehension a broad mind, a wise soul, and considerable study. . . .
>
> On these grounds, I, Moses the son of Maimon the Sefardi, bestirred myself . . . [to compose a work from which] the entire Oral Law might become systematically known to all.[102]

This tone of despair and cultural gloom, in the face of the decline of Torah study induced by historical vicissitudes and inexorable pressures, echoes in other Maimonidean writings. For example: "And in these difficult times there is none left to raise

---

101. The following is a condensation of material presented more fully in my article "Sefer MT." In the various letters Maimonides specifically refers to his aims and goals, e.g., to R. Phinehas: "and this was my ultimate aim (*měgammati*); to R. Jonathan: "my intention (*kawwanah*) in this work was"; to R. Joseph: "the purpose (*maṭṭarah*) for which I composed it." For the use of *měgammah*, note *Mělakim*, iv, 10; *Ma'áśer*, iv, 11.

102. MT, introduction; see *Yěsode hat-Torah*, iv, 13.

Moses' banner and to examine minutely the words of Rab Ashi.... Everywhere the Torah has perished from among them."[103] At the beginning of the *Epistle to Yemen* he pens his own self-portrait, again emphasizing the adversities of his era, particularly the erosion of learning: "I am the least of the scholars of Spain, whose glory was brought down into exile, and though I am constantly diligent in my studies, yet have I not attained to the wisdom of my ancestors. For we have come upon hard and evil days and have not abided in tranquility; we are weary and are given no rest. How then shall the halakah become clear to one who wanders from city to city and from kingdom to kingdom?"[104]

Even if the description of intellectual fatigue and frustration does not fit the author, it mirrors his perception of his contemporaries, excepting only the Provençal Rabbis to whom he was writing and whose Talmudic knowledge he was extolling. They, as we have seen, kept alive the hope of *translatio studii*, of creative continuation.[105]

Similarly, at the end of his *Commentary on the Mishnah* he writes: "... and especially since my mind is frequently troubled by the calamities of our times and the Lord's decree that we

103. *Kobeṣ*, II, 44; see A. Kupfer, *Tarbiz*, XXXIX (1970), 182. The sad words of R. Abraham ibn Daud are well known: "After the death of Rab Joseph hal-Levi, of blessed memory, the world became devoid of *yĕšibot* of learning.... They were years of crisis, evil decrees, and religious persecution for Israel, and they went into exile from their places, some to die, some to fall by the sword, some to starve, and some to be taken captive.... Consequently the sons of Rab Joseph could not establish *yĕšibot*, but went into exile, at the head of the banished ones, into the state of Toledo. And they were endeavoring to raise up disciples to the best of their ability ... and they represent the last Talmudic scholars of our time" (*Sefer hak-Kabbalah*, ed. G. Cohen [Philadelphia, 1967], p. 66).

J. Schirmann published an elegy that begins with the following melancholy verse: "How fearful! The West is destroyed, all hands are limp, Woe! Calamity has come upon Spain from Heaven" (*Kobeṣ*, 'Al Yad, n.s. III [Jerusalem, 1940], 33). For a complete analysis of the sources, see D. Corcos, *Zion*, XXXII (1967), 137–60.

104. IT, iii. It is noteworthy that his opinion about the moral position of his time accords with his view of the prevailing state of Torah learning. In *De'ot*, vi, 1, Maimonides interpolates this observation: "And if the conduct of all the countries that he knows, or of whom he has heard, is not good, as in our time."

105. See above, n.49; Twersky, *Rabad*, p. 24. See also the letter of R. Anatoli to Maimonides describing the decline of Torah in Sicily, J. Mann, *The Jews in Egypt* (reprinted, New York, 1970), II, 326.

should suffer exile and wandering in the world from one end of the heavens to the other."[106] Maimonides' response to this challenging situation in which knowledge of Torah is sadly lacking or exists very precariously—"the wisdom of our wise men" is vanishing; it is noteworthy that Maimonides' adaptation of this verse becomes a leitmotif or slogan mirroring the worrisome progressive decline in scholarship[107]—was the composition of a comprehensive Code which would facilitate halakic study in every conceivable way.

This contemporary constellation, this historical chain of cause and effect, is reminiscent of the Maimonidean description of the period of R. Judah the Patriarch, and of the motives that impelled him to compile the Mishnah: "And why did our holy master act thus [to reduce the oral tradition to writing] and not leave the matter as it was? Because he saw that the disciples were becoming fewer, and new troubles were coming upon them, and the Roman empire was expanding and growing stronger, and Jews were wandering away to the ends of the earth."[108] The chaotic and unsettled conditions of the country, the widespread social instability, the crushing confrontation with destructive historical forces brought in their wake a serious impoverishment of the people's spiritual-intellectual forces. R. Judah was stationed on the crest of a great wave of learning and, before his contemporaries and successors fell into the trough, had to act decisively. We may safely surmise that this historical parallel influenced Maimonides either consciously or unconsciously, that he saw many points of resemblance between the era of R. Judah and his own, and that he considered his task to be analogous to that of R. Judah. Both were innovators, driven by a mission and a vision, determined to safeguard the tradition.[109] Just as R. Judah for-

---

106. PhM, 'Uk, postscript, p. 737.
107. See Twersky, "The Shulḥan 'Aruk," p. 142, n.5.
108. MT, introduction. The note of Jews wandering all over the world, struck in PhM (see above, n.106), continues to reverberate.
109. Twersky, *Rabad*, pp. 133–34. Maimonides often speaks about "remnants that the Lord calls"; see, for example, *'Iggĕrot*, 51, and above, n.53. On the composition of the Mishnah, see Epstein, *Mabo'*, II, 693. One may detect hubris in a person driven by a sense of mission, or one may discern a constructive determination to take one's place in a chain of tradition, which means a balanced combination of receptivity and creativity.

sook the way of his predecessors and did not leave matters as they were in order "that the Oral Law may not be forgotten" as a result of the troubles and turbulence of the times, so likewise Maimonides, agitated by the political turmoil and demographic displacement of his era and its intellectual discontinuities, "forsook the way of all the authors that preceded him"[110] and blazed a new path, so that "all might be well versed in the entire Oral Law."

A closer examination of Maimonides' statement shows that it is actually a split-level construction: his reason is compounded of a general proposition and of a special ad hoc factor. First of all—and this point is also emphasized in the letters to R. Phinehas and to R. Jonathan hak-Kohen—the study of the Talmud is intrinsically difficult, even without the sudden complication of adventitious historical factors. Even in the most congenial and serene conditions, this study requires "intelligence and wisdom and ample time," for "its way is a profound way."[111] The many difficulties are due to both the material and the form: the mode of arguing and reasoning, wide-ranging associations, curt and allusive formulation, broad scope, as well as intermingling of themes and concepts; in contemporary scholarly jargon we would speak of the entire complicating complex of philological-historical-phenomenological problems which make the study of Talmud difficult, almost forbidding. If this description fits the Talmud in general, there are some parts, e.g., the laws of purity, that are so difficult that even great scholars are totally disoriented and stymied.[112]

---

110. The phrase was used by RABD toward the end of the MT introduction.

111. See also *Yĕsode hat-Torah*, iv, 13; vii, 1; *Talmud Torah*, i, 13. With regard to the "method of the Gemara," see *'Iiut*, xi, 13: ". . . but the method of the Gemara does not show this." Cf. here the remarks of R. Menahem ham-Me'iri on the "method of the Gemara" and on Maimonides' attitude to it in *Bet hab-Bĕḥirah, Bĕrakot* (Jerusalem, 1965), introduction, p. 27. Ham-Me'iri draws the student's attention to the historic fact that "the master, the teacher of righteousness, introduced new features" (ibid, p. 25).

112. "And if the great Sages of the Mishnah, of blessed memory, regarded them as difficult, how much more so we! . . . Today, for our many sins, if you were to make the round of the heads of Israel's academies, not to mention the synagogues, you would find that this subject is difficult for them; every halakah concerned with purity and impurity . . . and their like are difficult even for the great Rabbis, and even more so for the students" (PhM, introduction, pp. 33–34, 37).

## 66 INTRODUCTION TO THE CODE OF MAIMONIDES

Ever since its completion, the Talmud has been a perpetual academic challenge. All Geonim—which in Maimonidean parlance means all post-Talmudic Rabbis[113]—endeavored by various expository methods and through the medium of various literary genres to "elucidate its obscurities [underlying meanings]" and explain its subject matter. They were all, by definition, commentators on the Talmud seeking to disseminate its teachings, for these were the nerve center of Judaism. Now when the number of scholars who are incapable of "delving into the depths of the Talmud" grows larger, and there is reason to fear that since "they might become discouraged by the overabundance of debate . . . they may err in arriving at the law correctly," the need for thoughtful determination of the most effective method and attractive genre for study is more acute than ever. Maimonides' conclusion was that a code, with a carefully conceived architectonic structure, is obviously preferable and pedagogically more efficient than a discursive commentary, for it can be studied and even memorized without undue trouble or effort.[114] In sum, contemporary historical contingencies had accentuated the intrinsic problematics of Talmud study and sharpened the criticism of, and dissatisfaction with, the conventional methods of study and transmission.

This construction—i.e., the nexus established between political adversity and cultural decrepitude, and vice versa, between politico-social stability and intellectual élan—is not a fortuitous idea serving as a facile justification for a grandiose and far-

---

113. MT, introduction: "The Sages, however, who arose after the compilation of the Talmud, studied it deeply, and became famous for their wisdom, are called Geonim. All these Geonim who flourished in the Land of Israel, Babylonia, Spain, and France. . . ." See L. Ginzberg, *Geonica* (New York, 1909), I, 148, n.2. RaDBaZ, *Tešuḇot*, iv, 1–179, insists on definite chronological termini for the use of this title: "Scholars up to the RIF are Geonim." He also alludes to ham-Me'iri's definition; *Bet hab-Bĕḥirah, 'Aḇot* (New York, 1944), p. 65. See S. Shiloh, "Yaḥăso šel R. Joseph ibn Megas lag-Gĕ'onim," *Sinai*, LXVI (1970), 263ff.; and M. Margaliyot, *Sefer Ḥilḵot han-Naḡid* (Jerusalem, 1962), p. 26. When Jedaiah hap-Penini (*Bĕḥinaṭ 'Olam*, end) encomiastically dubs Maimonides "the last of the Geonim," he is extending Maimonides' use of the term. Cf. S. Havlin, "Mishneh Torah—Sof Gĕ'onut," *Ham-Ma'yan*, V (1965), 48ff.

114. See *Tĕfillah*, iv, 18 (cf. B. Ber 31a); and see below, chap. II. The little tract *Be'ur Šĕmot Ḳodeš wĕ-Ḥol*, ed. M. Gaster, *Devir*, I (1923), also cites as its goal "to remove doubts" (p. 194) from the hearts of students.

## INTRODUCTION

reaching project of a diligent and ambitious author. It is a basic thought pattern of Maimonides' historiosophical apparatus, as may be precisely illustrated by the following examples:

First, Maimonides regards the Messianic era as a socio-political catalyst for intellectual advancement and cultural revitalization. Just as subjection to the Gentile empires causes "desolation and spiritual depression"[115] and prevents us from studying the Torah, so will independence, tranquility, and freedom from oppression promote profound and fruitful learning. Both at the beginning and at the end of the Code Maimonides portrays this resplendently peaceful and stimulating era, pointing especially to its brilliant consequences, spiritual and intellectual, in the sphere of Torah and *ḥokmah*. "The Sages and the prophets did not long for the days of the Messiah so that Israel might exercise dominion over the world. . . . Their aspiration was that Israel be free to devote itself to the study of the Law and its wisdom."[116] The mutual influence of socio-economic conditions and cultural developments is emphatically underscored. The transition from turmoil to tranquility is reflected in a shift from stagnation to dynamic achievement.

While Jewish thinkers generally associated the cessation of prophecy with the phenomenon of exile, they did not have one uniform explanation for it. Some stressed the exclusive superiority and pre-eminence of the Land of Israel—a geographic-climatic theory—and affirmed that prophecy was impossible outside of the Holy Land. Maimonides emphasized that socio-political troubles and the attendant personal dysfunctions—sorrow, sickness, war, and famine—and not territorial-geographical change per se militated against prophecy by preventing intellectual perfection, which is the sine qua non for the attainment of prophecy. In conformity with this view, Maimonides interprets the verse *Her king*

---

115. Ibn Aknin; see A. S. Halkin, *Joshua Starr Memorial Volume* (New York, 1953), p. 105. S. Assaf, *Měḳorot lě-Tolědot ha-Ḥinnuk bě-Yiśra'el* (Tel Aviv, 1954), I, 11: "The free soul is exalted, strong, pure, and clear, and is able to acquire intelligence and knowledge because it is not enslaved to another; but the soul that is in bondage is mean and weak and is unable to acquire intelligence and knowledge." Leo Strauss dealt with this subject from his viewpoint in "The Literary Character of the *Guide of the Perplexed*," *Essays on Maimonides* (New York, 1941), p. 49 (reprinted in his *Persecution and the Art of Writing*, p. 50).

116. *Těšubah*, ix, 2; *Mělakim*, xii, 4.

*and her princes are among the nations, instruction is no more; yea, her prophets find no vision from the Lord* (Lam. 2:9): "Because of the exile among the nations, vision has come to an end. And this is undoubtedly the primary reason for the cessation of prophecy in the time of exile, namely, indolence or some grief that a person may suffer, and even worse than this is complete subjection to fools that go astray." The soaring-searing words of hope and encouragement with which Maimonides concludes are a logical corollary of this conception: "And this is likewise the reason for the return of prophecy as of old in the days of the Messiah."[117] Here we have the explicit elaboration of the restrained Messianic meditations and aspirations of the *Mishneh Torah*.

A third example can be found in the Maimonidean interpretation of an intriguing Talmudic passage. The Sages declared: "All that Ezekiel saw, Isaiah saw. What does Ezekiel resemble? A villager who saw the king. And what does Isaiah resemble? A townsman who saw the king" (B. Ḥag 13b). Maimonides suggests two different interpretations for the Rabbinic statement about the difference between the two prophets, particularly Isaiah's brevity vis-à-vis Ezekiel's verbosity. It may mean that Isaiah was more perfect than Ezekiel and that his prophetic vision and understanding were deeper and more comprehensive than those of Ezekiel. Hence he was compared to a townsman, rich in knowledge and experience, a distinguished veteran familiar with regal ceremonies, cool and composed. A pithy and apposite observation adequately conveyed all that could be known and experienced about the theophany. But a raw country bumpkin, suddenly finding himself at the royal court, is unable to control his reactions, gazes, even gawks, in wonder, and ends up relating his unprecedented and overwhelming experiences at great length. The sure touch of the expert, graceful in its succinctness and disciplined precision, seems to be lacking. However, the Talmudic text may mean—and this is the first interpretation given in the *Moreh*—that they are both equal, "and the [prophetic] conception

---

117. MN, II, 32, 36; also *Yĕsode hat-Torah*, vii, 4. Cf. the translation of S. Munk (Paris, 1856), II, 288; H. A. Wolfson, "Hallevi and Maimonides on Prophecy," *JQR*, XXXIII (1942), 65; Judah hal-Levi, *Kuzari*, II, 8–14.

INTRODUCTION                                                         69

to which Ezekiel attained is the very same as that achieved by Isaiah." The difference between them, one being brief and the other prolix, results not from any intellectual or temperamental disparity but from the nature of their audiences: Isaiah directed his words to people living serenely and prosperously in the majestic metropolis of Jerusalem, whose minds were alert and receptive to Torah and wisdom, whereas Ezekiel delivered his address to the recently dislocated émigrés, whose sensibility had become dulled and whose power of intellect comatose in their melancholy state by the River Chebar. They were no longer capable of understanding profound theological communications expressed in terse and allusive language which the listener has to elaborate or decipher independently.[118]

Maimonides' observations on the history of Jewish philosophical thought, or more precisely, on the disappearance of philosophy in ancient Israel are in a similar vein. "The many sciences . . . that have existed in our religious community have perished because of the length of the time that has passed, because of our being dominated by the pagan [ignorant]."[119] Here, too, the political situation and the cultural position are causally correlated.

This clear historiosophical conception should not be blurred or dulled by hasty identification with other views which seek, each in its own way, to explain the process of spiritual-intellectual degeneration. We have noted, for example, the "theory of climates" which suggests that territorial-ecological conditions exert a decisive influence on the human body, and in consequence also on spiritual attributes and intellectual qualities. This theory has its roots, inter alia, in the scientific-medical doctrine of Hippocrates,

---

118. MN, III, 6. See the commentary of Shem-Ṭob, who approves the second interpretation, whereas Efodi favors the first explanation and refers to the observations of R. Samuel ibn Tibbon, in *Ma'āmar Yikkawu ham-Mayim* (Pressburg, 1821), pp. 5off. See also MTH, 31: "For those who are well versed in the sciences a mere allusion is sufficient, and they have no need of repetition or of lengthy notations." H. Merhavyah, *Hat-Talmud bi-rě'i han-Naṣruṭ* (Jerusalem, 1970), p. 353, notes a possible echo of this in William of Auvergne.

119. MN, I, 71; cf. Samaw'al al-Maghribī, *Silencing the Jews*, ed. M. Perlmann (New York, 1964), p. 56; S. Pines, *Nouvelles études sur . . . Abū-l-Barakāt al-Baghdādī* (Paris, 1955), pp. 8–15, and *Scripta*, VI (1960), 124.

70 INTRODUCTION TO THE CODE OF MAIMONIDES

and is referred to in the works of R. Judah hal-Levi.[120] Maimonides, however, is unimpressed; his comment on *her king and her princes are among the nations, instruction is no more*, cited above, is an unequivocal rejection of the theory. It is noteworthy that R. Isaac Abarbanel sensed this in his commentary on the *Moreh* and therefore tried to rehabilitate R. Judah hal-Levi's view.[121] Similarly, a distinction must be drawn between Maimonides' view, which emphasizes the role of troubles and political oppression per se, and the widespread belief that sees the very fact of dispersion as contributing to the decline of Torah study. R. Saadiah Gaon writes that when our ancestors realized the extent of the dispersion and anticipated its effects on learning they collected all oral traditions and codified them in the Mishnah. In another passage from *Sefer hag-Galuy*, R. Saadiah Gaon explains that "the reason that compelled them [the Sages] to compile it [the Mishnah] was the fact that after they [Israel] had ceased to have prophets and found themselves scattered, they were afraid that the Tradition might be forgotten; so they put their trust in that which is written [in a book]."[122] The dispersion is also emphasized by R. Joseph Roš has-Seder, a contemporary of Maimonides: "Our ancestors took counsel and wrote down the fundamentals of the Torah at the time when He that formed the mountains scattered them." [123] According to Maimonides, intellectual decline is possible even when the Israelites dwell in their own land but are weak or oppressed and hence lack peace of mind. Maimonides expressly differentiates between the time "when the Israelites were exiled among the nations" and the time when "the Gentiles were dominant."[124] R. Judah hal-Levi, on

120. *Kuzari*, II, 12. See the excellent article of A. Altmann, *Mělilah*, II (1944), 1–18; also I. Heineman, *Zion*, IX (1944), 161; and cf. M. J. Tooley, "Bodin and the Medieval Theory of Climate," *Speculum*, XXVIII (1953), 64–83.
121. Abarbanel's Commentary to MN, III, 36 (end). On climate in the writings of Maimonides, see *Pirķe Mošeh bi-Rěfu'ah* (*Koḇeṣ*, II, 22–23, and ed. Z. Muntner).
122. *Haś-Śariḏ wehap-Paliṭ mis-Sifre RaSaG*, ed. A. H. Harkavy, p. 194. See also S. Schechter, *Saadyana* (Cambridge, 1903), p. 5; cf. the remarks of al-Qirqisānī, cited in the appendix to A. S. Halkin's article, *Louis Ginzberg Jubilee Volume* (New York, 1950), p. 152.
123. L. Ginzberg, *Ginze Schechter* (New York, 1928), II, 406. See S. Abramson, *ḲS*, XXVI (1950), 72–90.
124. *'Akum*, x, 7.

the other hand, syncretized all the motifs: "The length of the Exile and the dispersion of the nation and the poverty and reduction of numbers that they suffered."[125]

There is yet another explanation for spiritual decline, namely, the view that is epitomized in the well-known aphorisms: "If the earlier Sages were sons of angels, we are but sons of men, and if they were sons of men, we are like asses" (B. Shab 112b); and "Better was the fingernail of the earlier generation than the entire body of the later generation" (B. Yoma 9b), a view that approximates the Neo-Platonic doctrine concerning καταγωγή, which states that the process of decline and degeneration is a constant and irreversible phenomenon. The former generations were great and distinguished, whereas the latter are ineluctably of an inferior order and poor in achievement. The fountain of wisdom no longer gushes forth. The very intellectual potential is different. The thought is tellingly phrased in R. Sherira Gaon's letter to the community of Kairouan: "Since Rabbi [Judah the Patriarch] saw the extent of the situation . . . he felt that matters would deteriorate even further, for he saw that understanding was diminished and the fountain of wisdom was blocked and Torah knowledge had departed, as R. Johanan states in B. 'Er: 'The understanding of the former Sages was like the [wide] entrance of the *'Ulam* [Temple vestibule], and that of the latter Sages like the [narrow] entrance of the *Hekal* [The Temple proper].' "[126] In a later period, R. Joseph Karo also echoes this idea. In explaining what prompted him to compose his code of law, he refers to the unceasing difficulties of the time and to the adverse circumstances and vicissitudes of the exile, and then repeats Maimonides' adaptation of the verse *And the wisdom of their wise men shall perish* (Isa. 29:14), on account of "the troubles that come thick and fast, vying with one another." He combines this, however, with the notion of constant and irreversible decline, amounting at times to degeneration.[127] For Maimonides, in sum, the *Drang zur*

---

125. *Kuzari* III, 11.
126. *'Iggeret R. Sherira Gaon*, ed. B. M. Lewin (Haifa, 1921), p. 20; see also ibid., p. 31.
127. *Bet Yosef*, introduction; Twersky, "The Shulḥan 'Aruk," p. 142. For different views on primitivism and progress, see, e.g., A. Lovejoy and G. Boas, *Documentary History*

## 72 INTRODUCTION TO THE CODE OF MAIMONIDES

*Codification* is nourished primarily by historical adversity and pessimism.

This association between the process of codification, or the impulse toward it, and a state of decline, is noted by Arnold Toynbee: "As a rule—and this rule is inherent in the very nature of the declines and falls of civilizations—the demand for codification reaches its climax in the penultimate age before a social catastrophe, long after the peak of achievement in jurisprudence has been passed, and when the legislators of the day are irretrievably on the run in a losing battle with ungovernable forces of destruction."[128] Toynbee speaks also of the melancholy and enervating gloom that prevails in the generation of codifiers, in contrast to the preceding generations in which the cultural level was higher and the mood optimistic and energizing. He implies that the literary results of this codificatory enterprise are of a low order, devoid of any spark of originality or streak of creativity. Maimonides, on the other hand, implies that despite the negative stimulus, codification itself is an important creative achievement, a highly desirable contribution to the development of legal literature.

This implication, however, is somewhat problematic, in that Maimonides, an ardent protagonist of oral culture, believes that the oral word is preferable to the written word. Of the conditions prevalent at the time of the compilation of the Mishnah, at the threshold of a full-orbed literary culture, he states:

> This precept ["Words that I have communicated to you orally, you are not allowed to put down in writing"; B. Giṭ 60b] shows extreme wisdom with regard to the law. For it was meant to prevent what has ultimately come about in this respect. I mean the multiplicity of opinions, the variety of schools, the confusions occurring in the expression of what is put down in writing, the negligence that accompanies what is written down, the divisions of the people who are separated into sects, and the production of confusion with regard to actions.[129]

---

*of Primitivism and Related Ideas* (Baltimore, 1955); M. Taylor, "Progress and Primitivism in Lucretius," *American Journal of Philology*, LXVIII (1947), 180–94; F. G. Teggart, "The Argument of Hesiod's *Works and Days*," *Journal of the History of Ideas*, VIII (1947), 52.

128. A. Toynbee, *A Study of History* (London, 1954), VII, 279.

129. MN, I, 71. His words find an echo in those of R. Leo de Modena, *'Ari Nohem* (Jerusalem, 1929), p. 50. On the place of this idea in the teaching of R. Jonathan

He would endorse R. Judah hal-Levi's judgment that "Oral statements are superior to those that are written."[130] R. Hasdai Crescas notes the similarity between this and the Platonic view: "And this is almost the way followed by the Gentile sages. According to what is found in their compilations, Plato condemns one who writes down their words: 'Thou dost suspect thy pure thoughts, and dost trust the hides of dead beasts!' "[131] The very act of redaction is a cultural retreat; even when the codifier is able to produce a well-integrated work, suffused with originality and vitality, the undesirable consequences inherent in the evolution and crystallization of a literary tradition are not to be overlooked. It is in this context, apparently, that Maimonides from time to time continues to stress the value of oral study and oral transmission of learning. His mind was not free from the fear that his Code, instead of providing a reliable remedy, might complicate the unhappy situation still further by enhancing the value of the written word and securing its ascendancy. It is not surprising, therefore, that Maimonides enjoined his pupil R. Joseph ben Judah: "At the same time persevere in studying the work by heart."[132] The introduction to the *Mishneh Torah* states: "And I shall divide each chapter into short halakot, so that they may be learned by heart"; while the introduction to the *Sefer ham-Miṣwot* remarks: "in order that it may be easy to learn it by heart."[133]

Eybeschütz, see also A. Shohet, *'Im Ḥillufe Tĕkufot* (Jerusalem, 1961), p. 199. I plan to discuss the history and application of this concept more fully elsewhere.

130. *Kuzari*, II, 72. In PhM, 'Ab 1:6 (p. 416), Maimonides writes: ". . . for self-study is not like learning from another, for what is learned from someone else is retained better and is clearer." See also R. Moses ibn Ezra, *Siraṭ Yiśra'el*, ed. B. Halper (Leipzig, 1924; reprinted, Jerusalem, 1967), p. 117.

131. *'Or haś-Śem*, introduction. See W. Jaeger, *Paideia* (New York, 1944), III, 194; W. C. Greene, "The Spoken and the Written Word," *Harvard Studies in Classical Philology*, LX (1951), 23ff. On oral learning in Islamic culture, see *Selected Works of C. Snouck Hurgronje*, ed. G. H. Bousquet and J. Schacht (Leiden, 1957), p. 51; M. Mahdi, *Ibn Khaldūn's Philosophy of History* (Chicago, 1957), p. 114. See also the important observation concerning oral culture by ham-Me'iri, *Bet hab-Bĕḥirah*, 'Abot, introduction, 65–66.

132. *'Iggĕrot*, 68; see my article in *Tarbiz*, XXXVII (1968), 326; S. Abramson, *'Inyanot bĕ-Sifruṭ hag-Gĕ'onim* (Jerusalem, 1974), p. 266, n.1, and p. 270.

133. See also PhM, Ṭohărot, introduction (p. 33). Note Frances Yates, *The Art of Memory* (Chicago, 1966); H. Hajdu, *Das mnemotechnische Schrifttum des Mittelalters* (Amsterdam, 1961). The MT reveals traces of what was known as the *ars memoriae:* mnemonic techniques or skill in arrangement, formulation, and association which would facilitate remembering the material.

## 74 INTRODUCTION TO THE CODE OF MAIMONIDES

Maimonides chose the style and language of the Mishnah so that his work "might encompass the entire Oral Law," and so that the reader would learn "from it the whole Oral Law"; nevertheless, he was not impervious to the tradition of oral study, which was hallowed as well as helpful. While the Mishnah inevitably and irretrievably eclipsed oral study, Maimonides was still attuned to the value of the latter. His spirit surely must have been gratified when R. Ḥayyim ibn 'Aṭṭār, centuries later, testified concerning the scholars in the Land of Israel in his day that "a number of them endeavor to know Maimonides by heart."[134]

### Literary-systematic Motive: Jurisprudential Need

In the letter to R. Joseph ben Judah, and more obliquely in the introduction to *Sefer ham-Miṣwot*, Maimonides formulates a literary motive for the compilation of the *Mishneh Torah* entirely unrelated to the historical impetus described both in the introduction to this work and in the letter to R. Phinehas. The emphasis is methodological, focusing on a literary lacuna in the field of Jewish jurisprudence. In the introduction to *Sefer ham-Miṣwot*, where Maimonides described his grand plan simply and precisely, there is no reference or allusion to historical pressure or to an extraordinary stimulus resulting from the contemporary adversity. In the letter a personal aspect is added; his own juridical needs as well as the collective national needs are underscored.

The seeming contradiction between the motive of personal need and that of general benefit does not in any way undermine the value or credibility of this compact declaration. The two reasons may be seen theoretically as distinct and unrelated, a case of parallelism. The two-tiered statement may also be viewed as a literary topos. For example, R. Bahya ibn Pakuda, one of Maimonides' influential predecessors, declares that he has written *Ḥobot hal-Lĕbabot* for his own use and that he hopes others will also benefit from it. R. Judah ibn Tibbon, the Hebrew translator, elaborates R. Bahya's own words, outlining the two-fold aim of the book more pointedly: "[Perhaps he did this] because he said that he composed it as an *aide-mémoire* for himself and his friends;

---

134. A. Ya'ari, *'Iggĕrot 'Ereṣ Yiśra'el* (Tel Aviv, 1953), p. 264. It is also cited by J. Avida, *Sura*, II (Jerusalem, 1955), p. 296, n.11.

# INTRODUCTION

but . . . he subsequently said that it was also his wish to benefit thereby other people."[135] Following Maimonides, R. Jacob Anatoli says of his work *Malmaḏ hat-Talmiḏim:* "For I did this to help myself and others with me."[136] R. Shem Ṭob ibn Falaquera states at the end of the introduction to his book *Moreh ham-Moreh:* "And my intention in writing my work was that which I have mentioned above regarding the general usefulness of the commentary, and that it might serve me as an *aide-mémoire* in old age."[137] In the introduction to *Pirḳe Mošeh,* which is a kind of medical anthology, Maimonides himself again reverts to this literary stereotype: "Although I have selected these chapters as a memorandum for myself, yet whoever is like me, or has less knowledge than I, will likewise benefit from them."[138] The needs of the author or the individual and those of the public are not contradictory; they are parallel needs which can provide a joint stimulus and prove to be mutually beneficial and reenforcing.

The motif of old age is, of course, a persistent theme. Maimonides often referred to the debilities of illness and to the infirmities of age. Anxiety, trouble, weakness, and depression, compounded by social-political instability, are recurring themes in both his letters and his books. Already at the end of his *Commentary on the Mishnah,* when he was thirty-three years old, he mentioned his troubles and burdens, applying to himself the verse *[Blessed be] He [who] giveth power to the faint, and to him who has no might He increaseth strength* (Isa. 40:29).[139] At the beginning of the *'Iggereṯ Teman* he speaks of "evil days and hard times," while in a letter to R. Yefet of Acco he bemoans his "severe misfortunes, illness, and material losses." It is noteworthy that an Arabic fragment published by E. Mittwoch quotes Maimonides

---

135. *Hoḇoṯ hal-Lěḇaḇoṯ,* introduction. See the preface of the translator (Ibn Tibbon), ed. A. Zifroni (Jerusalem, 1928), p. 4.
136. *Malmaḏ hat-Talmiḏim* (Lyck, 1866), introduction, p. 12 (not numbered).
137. *Moreh ham-Moreh* (Pressburg, 1837), p. 8. On books composed for an individual, whose authors nevertheless had in mind the benefit of a larger public, see J. Reifmann, *Toleḏoṯ Rabbenu Zeraḥiah hal-Levi* (Prague, 1853), pp. 9ff. Cf. W. D. Greene, "Gentle Reader," *The Classical Tradition (In Honor of Harry Caplan)* (New York, 1966), p. 339. Concerning MN, composed for a student, see L. Strauss, *Persecution and the Art of Writing,* p. 49, and below, chap. VI.
138. *Pirḳe Mošeh bi-Rěfu'ah,* ed. Z. Muntner (Jerusalem, 1959), p. 13.
139. PhM, 'Uḳṣin, postscript, p. 737.

# 76 INTRODUCTION TO THE CODE OF MAIMONIDES

to the effect "that forgetfulness, which overpowers people, did not affect me in my youth."[140] In his letter to R. Jonathan hak-Kohen, which was written in the same period in which he wrote to R. Joseph ben Judah, he bemoans: "Furthermore, I am no longer now as I once was in the time of my youth: my vigor is failing, my heart is spent, my breath is short, my tongue is heavy, and my hand falters. . . . Yet who can discern [his own] errors (cf. Ps. 19:13) . . . and certainly when forgetfulness is so common, especially among the elderly." The problems of increasing weakness and lack of time are mentioned together at the end of another responsum: "For I am very preoccupied with a number of matters and my health is poor . . . and I have no free time at all on account of my perpetual bodily weakness and my private study of a number of subjects."[141] The strenuous rhetoric should not becloud the personal reality.

Maimonides' reflections, both *apologia* and *confessio,* are understandable also in terms of the conscious and unconscious powers and resources of an author. Karl Mannheim has noted the relationship between the insight and feeling of the genius and the historical experiences of the community to which he belongs.[142] While this is clearly not a case of complete identity, there is a significant overlap: the experiences of the group are reflected in the activities of the individual; they stimulate him and help fashion the forms of his creativity. The trail-blazer leaves his imprint on his age and on future ages, but his age leaves its imprint on him as well.

---

140. F. Mittwoch, "Ein Geniza Fragment," *Zeitschrift der Deutschen Morgenländischen Gesellschaft,* LVII (1903), 63, 65.
141. Ḳobeṣ, I, 27a. Note an echo of this in the introduction to the 'Aḇoṯ commentary by R. Mattithiah hay-Yiṣhari, published by I. Loeb, *REJ,* VII (1883–84), 155, and cf. RaDBaZ, *Tešuḇoṯ,* I, 407 (כי השכחה מצוי' כ"ש בזקנים).
142. K. Mannheim, *Ideology and Utopia,* tr. L. Wirth and E. Shils (New York, 1936), p. 269: "Underlying even the profound insight of the genius are the collective historical experiences of a group." Cf. the observations of David Hume, as cited by L. Trilling, *The Liberal Imagination* (New York, 1953), p. 185. See also J. Marias, *Generations: a Historical Method,* tr. H. Raley (University, Alabama, 1970); Y. Renouard, "La notion de génération en histoire," *Études d'histoire médiévale* (Paris, 1968), pp. 19ff. This was brought to my attention by D. Herlihy, "The Generation in Medieval History," *Viator,* V (1974), 347ff., who sums up the literature on the idea that "shared experiences at the same moment in time lent the generation a kind of unique spiritual cohesiveness" (p. 349).

## INTRODUCTION

At any rate—and this is the main thrust of his statement—Maimonides insists that there is an intrinsic, deeply felt, jurisprudential need for a code. The very nature of law—forgetting the pressure of the contemporary upheaval which imposed a premium on brevity, simplicity, ease of comprehension, and aid to memorization—calls for a *dīwān,* a systematic book of rulings which encompasses all areas of halakah. The nation requires "a compendious book" and the immediate stimulus emanates from an independent literary factor which may or may not be rooted in historical circumstances or related to other stimuli as well.

Codes of law were common in the Islamic world, and inasmuch as Maimonides was generally aware of the surrounding tendencies, this could have provided a stimulus.[143] The anti-Karaite tendency, striving to achieve and underscore unity and uniformity in halakah, should also be taken into account. Yet the motive which Maimonides pinpoints here, the independent legal-literary requirements, is quite persuasive and self-sufficient. There was a vacuum, and Maimonides sought to fill it. The sense of originality and primacy is clearly manifest in this work and was perceived by others as well.

### Philosophic-ideological Motive: Rationalistic-spiritual Need

The methodological-literary justification contains an additional, even decisive, motive: "I am most zealous for the Lord God of Israel, when I see before me a nation that does not have a comprehensive book [of laws] in the true sense nor true and accurate [theological] opinions."[144] He felt the urgent need not only for a book of statutes and rulings but also for the standardization and systematization of the "halakot of belief." The essential relationship of philosophy and law, their ongoing reciprocity and complementarity, is the touchstone here. His remarks at the beginning of *Ma'āmar Tĕḥiyyat ham-Metim* go to the root of the matter: "And we intended thereby that those who are called Scholars

---

143. See J. Schacht, *An Introdcution to Islamic Law* (Oxford, 1964); N. J. Coulson, *A History of Islamic Law* (Edinburgh, 1964). On the place of *Sefer ham-Madda'* in a code book, see F. Rosenthal, *Knowledge Triumphant—the Concept of Knowledge in Medieval Islam* (Leiden, 1970).

144. *'Iggĕrot,* 50.

# 78 INTRODUCTION TO THE CODE OF MAIMONIDES

or Geonim, or whatever you wish to call them, should build their branches [i.e., halakic constructions] on Talmudic roots and that they should not cast the knowledge of God behind them."[145] This purpose was realized not only in the distinctly speculative parts of *Sefer ham-Madda'* (*Book of Knowledge*), but also in the incidental *dicta*, the exegetical notes that sometimes appear to be digressions, in the intellectual-ethical explanations of laws as means of perfecting body and soul. Throughout the work we find an effort "to correct our opinions and to keep straight all our actions,"[146] and an emphasis upon the preeminence of theological knowledge.[147] It is clear that Maimonides intended from the outset not only to compile "rules in respect of that which is forbidden and permitted, clean and unclean," but also to elucidate "Torah principles" and "theological fundamentals," to set forth "true and exact opinion," and to indicate how each person can understand "the ultimate goal of the precepts, according to his capacity."[148] Maimonides fully realized the difference between the statute and its explanation or rationalization, between the aspect that directs and enjoins, demanding unqualified obedience, and the aspect that explains, educates, and persuades. His aim was to integrate them, to provide knowledge, understanding, and even inspiration, and not merely to summarize practical conclusions and obligatory instructions.

This characterization, which is buttressed by a close analysis of the *Mishneh Torah*, is quite explicitly underscored in the *Ma'ămar Tehiyyat ham-Metim*, where Maimonides declares: "And we intended . . . to smooth the path for, and explain and elucidate [the halakot] to, one who is unable to understand . . . and it seems to us that we facilitated and simplified [*kerabnu;* literally, "brought close" or "made reasonable"] abstruse [apparently nonrational] and profound subjects, and we collected and compiled [*kibbaṣnu*] widely scattered material."[149] This is not an instance

---
145. MTH, 4.
146. *Tēmurah*, iv, 13; see *Šĕḥiṭah*, xiv, 16.
147. *Yĕsode hat-Torah*, iv, 13; *Talmud Torah*, i, 11, 12; *'Issure Bi'ah*, xiv, 3; *Gĕzelah wa-'Ăbedah*, vi, 11; *Roṣeaḥ*, vii, 1; and see generally, chap. VI, below.
148. MT, introduction; MN, introduction (p. 6); *'Iggĕrot*, 50; *Mĕ'ilah*, viii, 8.
149. MTH, 2; see *Tĕšubot*, 252 (p. 460). In Maimonides' letter to R. Jonathan of Lunel (*Tĕšubot*, III, p. 52), in which Maimonides declares "For I have brought nigh (קרבתי)

of rhetorical parallelism or synonymy. Maimonides is calling attention to two qualities of his work, two separate achievements. "Collection and compilation" refer to the arrangement of the halakot, their sorting and classification—a major and novel achievement necessitating an overall view and total grasp of the entire legal material. "Facilitation (*ķerub*) and simplification" refer to the method of exegesis and exposition and to the motive of rationalization, of bringing the law close to reason and making it comprehensible and intelligible. This injection of a philosophic sensibility is a primary motive of the work as well as one of its basic traits.

In sum, these three motives, which appear totally distinct and unrelated, actually intersect at one identical goal, and each from its own point of departure reaches the same conclusion: the pressing need for codification. Whether the primary or immediate need is historical-external or immanent-jurisprudential or ideological-rationalistic does not change the picture. Indeed, why should we, in an excess of analytical zeal, search for a single, airtight, one-dimensional reason, free of varying nuances and impulses? Why should we strive for monolithic causation which might oversimplify and attenuate a multi-faceted reality? The historian or philosopher, in the quiet of his study, committed as he is to system and order, often underrates the fluidity and contingency of historical events, their dialectical crisscrossing and frequently volatile interaction. In our desire to reduce everything to neat schemes and tight formulae, we sometimes tend to compartmentalize too rigidly and atomize complicated but interrelated entities. It has been observed that by comparing and integrating the various comments of an author on the same subject we may achieve greater insight into, and a more balanced understanding of, his thought processes, motives, and aspirations. Kant has gone so far as to submit that "it is by no means unusual

---

matters that were scattered and separated," the reading cited in the notes is to be preferred: "I have gathered together (קבצתי) matters"; in this way the specific meaning of קרב emphasized here is preserved. It is instructive to compare Maimonides' programmatic formulation (*dĕbarim bĕrurim ķĕrobim nĕķonim*) with that of R. Joseph Karo, introduction to the *Šulḥan 'Aruķ* (*'aruķim bak-kol u-šĕmurim, sĕdurim u-bĕrurim*). Maimonides' use of *ķĕrobim* is prominent.

upon comparing the thoughts which an author has expressed in regard to his subject to find that we understand him better than he has understood himself."[150] Varying pronouncements, confessions, or explanations may complement and illumine rather than contradict and obscure. Indeed, the artificial and antiseptic separation of interlocking motives may produce misunderstanding. In our case, the common elements amidst the differing emphases are clear. Maimonides felt that it was beyond "human capacity to remember the entire Talmud," and because he was convinced that study of the Talmud should remain comprehensive and not be fragmentized by the flimsy constraints of practicality and relevance, he wanted to facilitate such study. He also believed that Rabbinic literature per se needed a code, comparable perhaps to contemporary works of this genre. Clear normative guidance, *pĕsak,* was a major desideratum. This intrinsic need was exacerbated by adverse historical circumstances. We may surmise that inasmuch as this historical factor was most obvious and pressing, and reflects his general historiosophical conceptions, it was formulated in the introduction to the *Mishneh Torah.* One other personal touch, actually an ideological affirmation, is then added: once he undertook to confront this great challenge and grapple with its enormous problems in the hope of composing a pioneering work that would serve the needs of both the present and future generations, he would express and forcefully demonstrate his unshakable conviction about the interrelatedness of law and philosophy, halakah and aggadah in the broad sense, where the latter represents the many levels of philosophic reflection and ethical theory. The historical, literary, and ideological impulses form a mosaic which reflects his criticism of the past, anxiety about the present, and hope for the future. They constitute a dialectical entity, just as the *Mishneh Torah* itself is a dialectical work. As a code, its criterion is brevity: the less, the better. In its attempt to articulate the tacit assumptions and aspirations of the law, to reveal its rationale and rationality, it is expansive. Needless to say,

150. Kant, *Critique of Pure Reason,* tr. N. K. Smith (London, 1929), p. 310, quoted by E. Cassirer, *An Essay on Man* (New Haven, 1944), p. 180. See I. Heinemann, *Zion,* IX, 154, who refers to Kant and Schleiermacher.

however, a tense dialectical entity is not the same as a contradictory one. If, as has perceptively been noted, "a culture is not a flow, nor even a confluence; . . . it is nothing if not a dialectic,"[151] the same may be said for a truly great religious-cultural work of literature and jurisprudence: it is nothing if not a dialectic.

## THE MID-TWELFTH-CENTURY SCENE: INSTITUTIONAL-RELIGIOUS-LITERARY REALITIES

The impact of these assorted motives, clearly spelled out by Maimonides, can be ascertained and assessed in an independent-complementary way by reviewing briefly the institutional, religious, and literary realities of the mid-twelfth century—realities which Maimonides confronted, to which he reacted, and upon which he acted. Even an ivory tower philosopher, attempting to contemplate eternal verities beyond the flux of time, and certainly a jurisprudent concerned with temporality and contingency, law and life, ethos and experience, could not remain impassive in the face of these realities or insensitive to the special needs which they presented. In order not to prolong generalities or rehash commonplaces, we may single out five salient features which cumulatively reflect the achievements and uncertainties, tensions and challenges, continuities and discontinuities, of the period—socio-communal as well as religious-intellectual, institutional as well as cultural, external as well as internal: (1) the Gaonate, its vested interests and attenuated influence; (2) Karaism, its ideological militancy and practical anti-Rabbinite vehemence; (3) rationalism, its premises and expectations, forms and achievements; (4) the sum total of Rabbinic literature, its basic genres, accomplishments, and lacunae; (5) the state of Talmud study, or the varieties of Torah experience and aspiration.

1. An observer of the twelfth-century scene, acquainted with the history of the previous two hundred years (the age of R. Saadiah Gaon, R. Hai Gaon, R. Samuel ben Hofni Gaon) would

---

151. L. Trilling, *The Liberal Imagination* (New York, 1953), p. 20. For an assessment of the three reasons given by Cicero for the composition of his philosophical works, see the introduction of J. M. Ross to Cicero, *The Nature of the Gods* (New York, 1972), pp. 17ff. and 22.

## 82 INTRODUCTION TO THE CODE OF MAIMONIDES

most likely be struck by two facts: the qualitative decline of the Gaonate and its proliferation. The incumbents were less distinguished and commanded less respect than their predecessors. Simultaneously, individuals of various levels of scholarship in many cities—Damascus and Fustat, for example, in addition to Baghdad, the capital of the Abbasid Caliphate which had become the seat of the two original Gaonic houses of learning (Sura and Pumbeditha)—adopted the title of Gaon. Hence, there is a real context for Maimonides' ridicule of the use of titles by people who were simply not entitled to, and not worthy of, the historic associations and honorific connotations of the titles. "All these things are but the vanities of title."[152] His wide-ranging criticism of the Gaonate notwithstanding, it is unlikely that he would use such pejorative language about R. Hai and R. Saadiah. However, in a period of decline—when, despite being de facto less authoritative and less robust and unable to extend its influence over such centers as Spain which nurtured cultural-religious-institutional independence, the Gaonate still insisted, anachronistically and artificially, upon pomp and circumstance and the formal retention of institutional prestige and primacy—Maimonides' reaction and reassessment seem quite natural. Moreover, the proliferation in the use of the term, in Syria, Palestine, and Egypt in addition to Babylonia, could have, directly or indirectly, provided the basis for the new semantics with which he invested it: "Geonim" is no longer a technical title reflecting the immense power, both academic and practical-judicial, of the "head of the academy, the pride ($g\bar{e}'on$) of Jacob," but a collective designation for all post-Talmudic scholars, wherever they may be and whatever their station, who devoted themselves to understanding the Talmud. If Palestine and Egypt could have Geonim, then why not France and Spain? "The Sages . . . who arose after the compilation of the Talmud [and] studied it deeply . . . are called Geonim. All these Geonim flourished in the Land of Israel, Babylonia, Spain, and France. . . ."[153]

152. PhM, Bek 4:4 (p. 245); also *Koḇeṣ*, I, 30, 50b. S. Poznanski, *Babylonische Geonim im nachgaonäischen Zeitalter* (Berlin, 1914), is still useful.
153. MT, introduction; PhM, introduction (p. 46); see above, n.113. The Maimonidean reinterpretation of the term Geonim notwithstanding, the term still refers

## INTRODUCTION

While the original Geonim of Sura and Pumbeditha had contributed to the entrenchment of the Oral Law as the religious authority of Judaism and concomitantly to the supremacy of the Babylonian Talmud as its normative source, they associated this contribution with their own claims to absolute supremacy in interpreting the law and their occupying the "seat of authority." Their position, they claimed, should be recognized as preeminent and their rulings as incontestable. Now Maimonides' assessment of the intellectual legacy of the Geonim was not, to say the least, routinely adulatory. He realized and exposed the limitations of their achievements—as in other areas, he feared mediocrity—but above all he questioned their exclusive or preemptive rights in the realm of explication and adjudication. Only the Mishnah and the Talmud were universally binding, the former because it was endowed with the authority of the Sanhedrin, and the latter because it reflected the consensus of the entire nation. Maimonides' halakic-historical formulations underscored a basic socio-political fact: Gaonic teachings lacked intrinsic authoritativeness and could not possibly aspire to universal recognition. In other words, while the Geonim constructed their platform upon a three-pronged supremacy—of the Oral Law, of the Babylonian Talmud, and of the Babylonian Geonim in all matters of interpretation and application—Maimonides knocked out the third prong. Simultaneously, fully conscious of the fact that his forthright criticism would be uncongenial to most scholars, he repudiated the hierarchic-dynastic structure of the Gaonate and denounced their managerial methods, i.e., the maintenance of a retinue of scholars at public expense by relentless importuning for contributions. "Oblivious of predecessors or contemporaries," he challenged the conventional proofs and values on which the system rested.[154] The existence of an institutionalized and professionalized class of scholars supported by public and often high-pressured philanthropy was antithetical to Maimonides' existential posture as well as ideological position.

---

preponderantly—even in his own usage—to the Babylonian Geonim; there are, of course, exceptions, e.g., 'Išuṭ, vi, 14 and Zĕkiyyah u-Mattanah, iii, 8.

154. PhM, 'Ab 4:7 (p. 441), and above, n.6. On the "seat of authority" see S. Assaf, "Ḳobeṣ 'Iggĕroṭ," *Tarbiz*, I (1929), 64; *Sanhedrin*, i, 3. For the background of the critical

## 84 INTRODUCTION TO THE CODE OF MAIMONIDES

2. Karaism, a persistent challenge to Rabbinic Judaism, was a pervasive reality, and a contemporary observer would probably have noted that this sectarian movement was aggressive in its attitudes, sophisticated in the formulation of its attacks, and successful in occupying positions of prominence and influence in various communities.[155] In Cairo, on the eve of Maimonides' arrival, the Rabbinite community was seriously threatened and severely demoralized. Two frequently repeated arguments against the Rabbinite Jews are noteworthy: Karaite ideologues, like Christian polemicists, contended that the Oral Law violated the commandment against adding to, or detracting from, the Torah. The authoritative oral tradition was regularly denigrated by Karaites—who were, strangely enough (with a full measure of paradox), developing their own corpus of extra-Scriptural traditions and interpretations—as a willful distortion of God's word.[156] On a theological-philosophical level, Karaites sharply denounced anthropomorphism, which they sneeringly claimed to be rampant in Rabbinite Judaism, and smugly exhibited it as a sign of theological backwardness.[157] There was no dearth of fierce

---

attitude of Spanish scholars to the Geonim, see J. Mann, *Tests and Studies in Jewish History*, I, 119; M. Margaliyot, *Sefer Hilkot han-Nagid*, pp. 9, 33; S. Abramson, *R. Nissim Gaon*, p. 20; and above nn.7–8. A major task of the writers following Alfasi was to reinstate at least partially the use and significance of Gaonic writing. Maimonides was not unique in his critical attitude to the Geonim. Actually, all medieval Talmudists moved on a common dialectical field; initial independence was qualified by the inescapable authority of tradition, while initial subservience was qualified by the pervasive impulse of creative innovation. In principle, Geonim were authoritative and their views were normative, but in practice all dissented from, or qualified, certain views on one occasion or another. The exigencies of study demanded that the authority of the Geonim be tempered by independence. See my *Rahad*, pp. 216ff

155. See, generally, L. Nemoy, *Karaite Anthology* (New Haven, 1952); Z. Ankori, *Karaites in Byzantium* (New York, 1959); Twersky, *Rabad*, p. 100; G. Cohen, ed., *Sefer hak-Kabbalah*, pp. xliii ff.; S. Assaf, "Lĕ-Tolĕdot hak-Kara'im," *Zion*, I (1936), 208ff., reprinted in *Bĕ-'ohăle Ya'ăkob* (Jerusalem, 1943), p. 181. Also J. Rosenthal, "Kara'im wĕ-Kara'ut bĕ-'Eyropah ham-Ma'ărabit," *H. Albeck Jubilee Volume* (Jerusalem, 1967), pp. 425ff. Much information is found in J. Mann's two large works: *The Jews in Egypt and Palestine under the Fatimids* (reprinted, New York, 1970); *Texts and Studies in Jewish History and Literature* (reprinted, New York, 1972). After 1099, Egypt emerged alongside of Byzantium as a bastion of Karaism (J. Mann, *Texts*, II, 291).

156. E.g., S. Pinsker, *Likkute Kadmoniyyot* (Vienna, 1860), II, 24, 26; L. Nemoy, "Al-Qirqisānī's Account of the Jewish Sects," *HUCA*, VII (1930), 372, 396; Judah Hadassi, *'Eškol hak-Kofer* (Eupatoria, 1836).

157. E.g., A. Altmann, "Moses Narboni's 'Epistle on Shi'ur Qomah'," *Jewish Medieval and Renaissance Studies*, pp. 227ff.

and freewheeling invective. Rabbinite Jews had to work out a practical policy governing social relations and a theoretical program guiding theological refutations. Now there is no need to subscribe to the "pan-Karaite" tendency[158] of a major segment of modern scholarship, which sees all serious preoccupation with Biblical literature or with the nature and authoritativeness of the Oral Law as a response to Karaite attack, in order to realize that Maimonides, in common with many predecessors (R. Saadiah Gaon or R. Samuel han-Nagid) and contemporaries (R. Abraham ibn Ezra or R. Abraham ibn Daud), was sensitive to the sociological and religious implications or hazards of the Karaite heresy and felt the need to fight back. While he counseled moderation and tact in actual relations, personal as well as communal, with Karaites, he was robust and relentless in his rejection of Karaite contentions or criticisms. Although he did not compose any explicit anti-Karaite tract—Abraham ibn Daud, for example, wrote his *Book of Tradition* in order to demonstrate the continuity of Judaism and thus bolster the normative value and regulatory authority of tradition—he utilized various exegetical or codificatory contexts to ridicule or repudiate Karaite allegations. His writings are spotted with comments, usually brief but forceful, exposing Karaite follies and foibles and suggesting that this sectarianism was actually not a new movement but a recrudescence of ancient Sadduceeism which tried to challenge the centrality of the Oral Law and the authoritativeness of its transmitters.[159] The term "Sadducees," together with *minim* (heretics) or *kĕsilim* (fools, i.e., literalists), is regularly and heatedly applied to the Karaites; sometimes they are dubbed *zedim* (wicked). Reference to the Karaites clearly excites Maimonides, who will frequently add an imprecation, such as "may they quickly perish,"

---

158. See S. Baron, *Social and Religious History of the Jews*, VI, 338, n.41.
159. MT, introduction, end; '*Akum*, x, 1; *Tĕšubah*, iii, 8; *Šabbaṭ*, ii, 3; '*Eruḥin*, ii, 16; *Milah*, ii, 1; '*Issure Bi'ah*, xi, 15; *Šĕḥiṭah*, i, 4; iv, 16; *Šĕbu'oṭ*, xii, 12; *Bi'aṭ Miḳdaš*, i, 3, where Maimonides substitutes the term "*ṣĕdukim*" for the Talmudic metaphor; '*Abodaṭ Yom haḳ-Kippurim*, i, 7; *Tĕmidin u-Musafin*, vii, 11; *Parah*, i, 14, 15; x, 5; '*Abadim*, vi, 6; *Mamrim*, iii, 3; PhM, 'Er 6:2 (p. 131); Ḥag 2:3 (p. 379); 'Ab 1:3 (p. 410); Ḥul 1:2 (p. 175, and important notes *ad loc.*); ShM, positive 153 (... המינים הנקראים כאן במזרח קראים); MN, I, 71; *Tĕšuboṭ*, 242 (p. 436), 265 (p. 503), 320 (p. 533), 351 (p. 629), 449 (p. 729); in 268 (p. 514) Maimonides is seen as counseling patience and tact in dealing with

to their name. Karaism was thus undeniably a real threat. Yet it is, in my opinion, a fallacy of misplaced concreteness to view the *Mishneh Torah*, in toto, as an anti-Karaite polemic, even though traces of challenge and response are quite visible. Maimonides explicitly noted with regard to the style of the *Mishneh Torah* that he did not wish "to give the heretics an opportunity to prevail" (to establish dominion by pressing their heretical views), and that by presenting the halakah in uniform and collective style he would contribute to the "destruction of the position of those heretics who spurned the entire Oral Law."[160] Karaism was an unavoidable concern and pressing challenge, but there is no reason to see it as the major or only catalyst of the *Mishneh Torah*.

3. The role of rationalism in twelfth-century Judaism would be underestimated if it were gauged just by its formal-literary history from the works of R. Saadiah Gaon and R. Solomon ibn Gabirol through those of R. Abraham bar Ḥiyya and R. Joseph ibn Ṣaddiḳ to R. Judah hal-Levi and R. Abraham ibn Ezra. Its impact and influence transcended these classics and must be sought in other literary genres as well as in oral discussion and oral commitment. Rationalism was a modality of thought, with its own deep structures and models of perception, as well as a spiritual-intellectual objective. There were varieties of rationalism, moderate or more radical, which co-existed within the same milieu; there were differences of emphasis and direction. R. Judah hal-Levi and R. Baḥya ibn Paḳuda, R. Joseph ibn Ṣaddiḳ and R. Abraham ibn Daud had special concerns and goals. Yet for all the diversity of religious rationalism, medieval religious philosophers shared basic principles, had common characteristics, and agreed on fundamental conceptions of metaphysics, physics,

---

error generally, not only vis-à-vis the Karaites. Also, *Ḳobeṣ*, I, 3b, using the same phrase as in *Mamrim*.

160. *Ḳobeṣ*, I, 26a (see above, p. 35) refers primarily to style. Cf. C. Tchernowitz, *Tolĕdot hap-Posḳim* (New York, 1946), I, 197–208; A. Marmorstein, "The Place of Maimonides' *Mishneh Torah* in the History and Development of the Halachah," *Moses Maimonides* (London, 1935), p. 170. Generally, one should beware of exclusively horizontal or contemporary explanations for polemical formulations; e.g., *Bĕrakot*, vi, 2, has a long history—see some of the material collected by M. Kasher, *Haggadah Šĕlemah* (Jerusalem, 1961), p. 99.

and ethics.[161] The interrelatedness of what we may, anticipating Maimonides, designate as *Torah* and *ḥokmah* was deep and widespread. For its adherents, rationalism was not merely a permissible and tolerable influence from external sources but also an indispensable component of the religious tradition and religious experience. To be sure, it was a defense mechanism, for "men were sunk in a sea of doubt and overwhelmed by the waves of confusion."[162] Rationalism often is a result of polemics or apologetics. However, it was also a positive and intrinsically significant duty—intellectual attainment was indispensable for religious perfection. It was not something alien or adventitious; it was an integral component of the tradition. There was a religious obligation to apply one's intellect to the study of the world and of Scripture, both revelations of God. Man is duty-bound to realize his intellectual potential within a broadly conceived religious framework. To be sure, Judaism was a divine, not humanly contrived, system, but it was intended to be perceived as a rational construct and every effort should be made to understand it.[163] Its opponents, very suspicious of the foreign origin, philosophical associations, and objectionable repercussions of these scientific studies and rationalistic exercises, were apprehensive and hostile: it could lead to unbelief or could be, directly and indirectly, conducive to antinomianism. The opposition, in fact, could be either to the procedure or the results, i.e., the use of rational methods of demonstrating religious beliefs, or to certain rationalized beliefs themselves.[164]

One need not go beyond Maimonides' *Commentary on the Mishnah* to gauge the impact of the rationalist legacy and to take the full measure of its constructive components as well as controversial aspects. Maimonides would not only pick up the various strands of rationalism—criticizing, refining, and extending—but

---

161. See, e.g., J. Guttmann, *Philosophies of Judaism* (New York, 1964), pp. 47–265; H. A. Wolfson, *Philo*, especially II, 439–60; and idem, "The Double Faith Theory," *JQR*, XXXII (1942), 213ff., reprinted in *Studies in the History and Philosophy of Religion*, II.
162. R. Saadiah Gaon, *'Ĕmunot wĕ-De'ot*, introduction.
163. *Tĕšubah*, x, 6; see below, chap. VI. Also, A. Altmann, "The Delphic Maxim," *Biblical and Other Studies* (Cambridge, 1963), pp. 222ff.
164. See, e.g., H. A. Wolfson, "The Jewish Kalām," *JQR Anniversary Volume* (1967), pp. 554ff.

would also emerge as its symbol, representing a type of mentality and suggesting a direction of thought concerning which neutrality was impossible. It should be emphasized—and Maimonides' philosophic posture sharply illustrates this—that medieval religious rationalism did not mean "religion within the limits of reason alone." Nor—as we have underscored, even though the outer-directed motif was very prominent and the concern with external challenges and/or internal disruptions was a conscious force—was it merely an exercise in apologetics. It was predicated upon certain axioms, a tight network of religious data and traditional directives, and sought to align them with reason. There were compelling intrinsic reasons and spiritual motives. It meant pressing the intellect into the service of religion, using reason for purposes of spirituality and self-fulfillment, to avoid religious routinization and unreflective existence. Rationalism was, historically, as much as mysticism, an "antidote to religious pragmatism."[165] In any event, protagonists and antagonists would henceforth draw the lines of their positions in relation to Maimonides. The *Mishneh Torah,* as we shall see, could serve as a microcosm for this entire saga.

4. A thoughtful historian of Rabbinic literature surveying developments from the redaction of the Talmud up to the middle of the twelfth century might well reflect upon the glaring needs, while dutifully recording existing works and even generously praising the achievements of wise authors. Even though vast resources of energy and dedication had been used in the study of the Talmud, one could find only fragmentary commentaries on the Mishnah and rudimentary commentaries on the Talmud together with some lexicographical aids. The Gaonic achievement was perceived as pioneering but not profound. The highlights of a history of Rabbinic literature in Spain starting with R. Moses ben Enoch would be the *Halakot* of R. Isaac Alfasi and the impact, more oral than literary, of R. Joseph ibn Megas. Furthermore, there were no comprehensive codes of law. There were some lim-

---

165. G. van der Leeuw, *Religion in Essence and Manifestation*, tr. J. E. Turner (New York, 1963), II, 616. For the outer-directed motif, see R. Baḥya, *Ḥobot hal-Lĕbabot*, introduction, p. 18; Judah hal-Levi, *Kuzari*, I, 1; MN, III, 31; also, R. Abraham ibn Ezra, Gen 2:11. See below, chap. VI.

ited practice-oriented monographs, but the absence of an inclusive and systematic code was conspicuous. Moreover, a mood of gloom and pessimism prevailed, sharply reflected in Ibn Daud's statement that after the death of R. Joseph ibn Megas "the world became desolate of academies of learning." There was, in other words, great latitude, and equally great need, for an imaginative creative scholar to innovate in all fields (in commentary and codification), for the areas which had been cultivated and fenced in were minuscule compared to those which were unattended. Maimonides' literary career and his pithy observations on the state of Rabbinic literature show that he was guided by such an appraisal of the needs, and of course, that he felt adequate to the challenge.[166]

5. One of the most crucial and disquieting aspects of the mid-twelfth-century scene was the fragmentation of Jewish learning, with resultant rivalries and intellectual tensions. There was apparently conflict between Bible study and Talmud study, between study of different parts of the Talmud or study of the Talmud itself versus abridgements (with some, for example, concentrating exclusively on the *Halakot* of R. Isaac Alfasi), between prolonged preoccupation with Talmud study and primary attention to science and philosophy. *Talmud Torah,* in sum, was far from monolithic or undifferentiated. There was a wide range of specialists and a great variety of dissatisfaction resulting from both the interaction of different types and their lack of rapport. There were questions of intellectualism, legalism, spirituality, professionalization, and institutionalization of scholarship—in short, the proper perception of, and approach to, the mastery of spiritual and temporal matters. It has been noted that a historical period is united not by the unanimity of thought of its representatives but by the fact that they share certain concerns and address themselves to identical problems.[167] The fragmentation in this period, the competing claims for exclusivity or at least hierarchical superiority could, from one angle, be seen as threatening to

---

166. PhM, introduction; MT, introduction; see Twersky, *Rabad,* p. 125; Ibn Daud, *Sefer hak-Kabbalah,* p. 87.
167. J. Barzun, *Romanticism and the Modern Ego* (Boston, 1943), pp. 21–22.

eclipse its unifying features. In particular, there was agitated debate concerning the correct scholastic-curricular relationship between halakah and philosophy. Some favored a curriculum built exclusively around the Talmud and oriented toward religious practice. Others feared that the halakic enterprise might become externalized and impoverished if it were not coordinated with spiritual concerns, and hence contended that religious study should begin but not end with halakah; it must include additional, meta-halakic, subjects of study. R. Abraham ibn Ezra and R. Baḥya ibn Pakuda provide typological statements which are very instructive.[168] It will be helpful to peruse R. Baḥya's description of various classes of students, seen from the vantage point of their "apprehension of the wisdom of the Torah":

> The beginner's class consists of those who have learnt the Pentateuch and the rest of the Scriptures and are satisfied with their ability to read the text without any understanding of the contents. They do not know the meaning of the words nor have they any acquaintance with the grammar of the language. They are akin to a donkey laden with books.
>
> The second class consists of those who have tried to learn to read correctly, pay heed to the vowels and specially concentrate their attention on the right position of the accent. They [may be said to] belong to the class of Punctators and Masorites.
>
> The third class consists of those who have noted the insufficiency of the aforementioned classes and have striven to know the principles of punctuation and musical accentuation (*nĕginot*). They have in addition sought to acquire knowledge of the correct use of the language and its grammar—nouns and verbs, modifying parts of speech (prepositions, conjunctions, and adverbs), absolute and construct forms (of nouns and adjectives); use of the future to express the past and of the infinitive to express the imperative; the various classes of verbs: complete (all three letters sounded), defective (one letter omitted), silent (one or two letters not sounded), duplicate (verbs with the second and third letters the same); the apparent and the hidden.
>
> The fourth class consists of those individuals who have advanced beyond the preceding classes in their ability to explain words of doubtful meaning in the Holy Scriptures, and in their understanding of the plain

---

168. Abraham ibn Ezra, *Yĕsod Mora'* (Prague, 1833), chap. 1 (p. 12); R. Baḥya, *Ḥobot hal-Lĕbabot*, I, 27, 29, 35, 221; MN, introduction (p. 5), and III, 51; I. Twersky, "Religion and Law," *Religion in a Religious Age* (Cambridge, 1974), pp. 69ff. See below, chap. III.

## INTRODUCTION

sense of the text. They have also investigated the figurative and the literal meaning of words in the Hebrew language; homonyms and synonyms; derivative nouns (derived from other words), primary nouns, foreign nouns; and so with adjectives and verbs.

The fifth class consists of those who have advanced beyond the preceding classes in their knowledge of the subject-matter of the Holy Scriptures, have sought to understand its fundamental principles and have endeavoured to investigate the metaphorical sense and the true meaning of its contents with regard, for instance, to the anthropomorphic expressions in the Bible. These are the expositors of the divinely inspired books according to the plain meaning, without reference to the traditional interpretation.

The sixth class consists of those who lean on ancient tradition as contained in the Mishnah, so that they have attained knowledge of some of the laws, commandments, and juridical rules without studying the Talmud.

The seventh class comprises those who have added to what we have just mentioned an intense study of the Talmud and devoted themselves to a knowledge of its text, reading its decisions without attempting to answer its questions and clearing up its difficulties.

The eighth class consists of those who are not satisfied with the knowledge of the Torah, which had been sufficient for the previous class, but exerted themselves to comprehend the dicta of the Talmudic authorities, resolve the doubtful points and elucidate the obscurities, with the purpose of winning a name and glory. But they ignore the duties of the heart. They pay no attention to what would be detrimental to their religious and moral activities.

The ninth class consists of those who have exerted themselves to know the duties of the heart as well as the active duties and also what is detrimental to right conduct; who understand the plain sense of the Holy Scriptures as well as their inner meaning, and have arrived at a conviction of the truth of tradition, based on Scripture and on reason; have arranged the laws into an orderly system, divided the practical duties in accordance with circumstances of time and place, as a result of their comprehension of the fundamental principles of the Pentateuch; scrupulously observe these duties and exhort others (to do likewise); cherish truth inwardly and outwardly, and follow it wherever it may lead them. They are the Talmudic teachers and the Geonim who continued their predecessors' customs.[169]

---

169. Ḥoḇot hal-Lĕḇaḇot, I, 219ff.

Here, too, much of Maimonides' life's work, particularly the *Mishneh Torah,* may be appreciated against this background. His ideal, in marked contrast to the atomization of Torah study and experience, was unification and comprehensiveness.

HISTORY AND HALAKAH: ON THE STUDY OF THE *Mishneh Torah*

Let us conclude with a few simple methodological propositions about the relevance of this historical information, both that embedded in Maimonides' observations and that extracted from contemporary materials, for our study of the *Mishneh Torah.* First of all, it alerts us to the need to extricate Maimonides from the domain of historical anonymity, where his identity is blurred and beclouded, and to delineate his individual contours: his methods and achievements, critical attitudes, and traditional convictions. While abstract typologies and phenomenological distinctions are useful, they should not spread a blanket of bland homogeneity over the creative figures of the past. This historiographical commonplace bears repetition in the light of the fact that traditional Jewish conceptions tend to blur all individuality—all great men are alike. There is a basic genus or paradigm of a Rabbinic scholar, pietist, or philosopher. This conception has particularly affected the study of the *Mishneh Torah,* the flower of Jewish jurisprudence, and of Maimonides, the darling of halakists through the ages. Likewise, modern scholarship has often been ensnared by its own categorical uniformities: analytic versus synthesizing, commentatorial versus codificatory, or Platonic versus Aristotelian. There is a typical Talmudist or rationalist. With regard to Rabbinic literature in particular, modern scholarship has to a great extent, consciously or unconsciously, by acts of omission and commission, and for different reasons, taken over this ingrained Jewish tradition which standardizes and deindividualizes Rabbinic authors and authorities. "Rabbis are Rabbis" may be a slogan of glorification and exaltation (into timelessness) or an excuse for treatment characterized by banality and superficiality; the ahistorical results in either case are skewed. For if a proper definition should contain genus and species, in defining historical figures we should not omit or constrict the species, the special individuating factors and formative influences, thoughts, and aspirations.

The goal of individuation means, above all, a striving for objective understanding of views, interpretations, and tendencies regardless of one's own subjective response and judgment. There is room for a whole gamut of reactions—endorsement or repudiation, indifference, qualification or intensification—but the first step should be an unbiased presentation of the Maimonidean view. A good example is Maimonides' concept of *talmud Torah* and his definition of its components. Some halakists may find this uncongenial, reject it as a "minority view" or "individual (and therefore not regulative) opinion," but the objective and historically-conditioned student will first of all understand it in all its complexity, its exegetical bases, innovating features, and philosophic implications. While there is room for divergence, there is no room for distortion.[170]

Related to this is the attempt to see and study the *Mishneh Torah* in the context of all his writings, and to some extent in the context of his life. The former does not mean automatic transfer from one work to another, but it does mean imposing limits upon speculation and hypothetical reconstruction when Maimonides makes explicit statements about his method, motivation, or meaning. A good example would be the answers written by Maimonides to the twenty-four halakic questions submitted to him by R. Jonathan in the name of the scholars of Lunel; some of these answers clarify and interpret, some modify or change the formulation. Halakists, who were never too enthusiastic about these answers, may insist upon treating the first formulation as normative, or they may prefer alternate ways to sustain or vindicate the Maimonidean position—they place a premium on their own conceptualization. Now in completely ahistorical and systematic study, transcending time, space, and personality, various statements of Maimonides, retractions or reformulations, may be treated as so many competing, unrelated views. The early Maimonides and the later Maimonides need not be unified, may indeed be treated as individual, halakic or philosophic, personae.

170. *Talmud Torah*, i, 11–12; Twersky, "Non-Halakic Aspects," pp. 106–18.

In the abstract and systematic categories of jurisprudence or metaphysics an earlier view may be more attractive or persuasive than the later one. Chronology or even author's preference are not binding considerations. Historically, however, the authentic and final Maimonidean view should be precisely identified,[171] for his own judgment and assent are certainly determinative.

As for history and biography, they help concretize a view or illustrate, even motivate, a position. The role of medicine in all his writings is a general, rather obvious illustration. The physician is a model of probity and precision, there are comparisons between the judge and the physician, there are unexpected references to doctors or to medical science, all in addition to his medical practice and writing and to the medical compendium which Maimonides included in *De'ot*, chapter four.[172] The traces of Maimonides' commitment to philosophy, *vestigia philosophiae*, are ubiquitous. A fine detail from his life-cycle is the statement about "some of the modes of manifesting repentance." After mentioning briefly such behavioral patterns as continuous prayer, giving charity, etc., Maimonides concludes, "and exiles himself from his former place of residence, since exile atones for iniquity, inducing as it does humility, meekness, and lowliness of spirit."[173] This explanation is not found in the Talmud, and one cannot help but hear in it the echoes of Maimonides' own experiences, a profound sense of uprootedness and exile, of the troubles and tribulations that accompany constant, particularly involuntary, travel. Maimonides' inflexible oppositon to, and condemnation of, material reward for Rabbis and teachers is fully consonant, as we have seen, with his own economic self-sufficiency.

Yet the use of biography should not result in the genetic fallacy. One should not subdue literature, any literary genre, to ex-

---

171. See *Tešubot*, III, 42–43, for a list of these responsa; RaSHBA, *Tešubot*, 4, illustrates the clear recognition of the early and late Maimonides and the deliberate choice of the former. I have it, by tradition, that R. Ḥayyim Soloveitchik did not "like" the twenty-four answers.

172. See *De'ot*, iv, 21; *Malweh wĕ-Loweh*, xv, 1; *'Abel*, xiv, 5. Of course, medical opinions could not alter halakic facts; see *Šěḥiṭah*, x, 12; cf. *Roṣeaḥ*, ii, 8.

173. *Tešubah*, ii, 4. See Judah hal-Levi, *Kuzari*, 1, 115.

traneous categories (of background, society, or ideology). Such factors are of indisputable relevance in supplying motives or stimuli for interpretations, but the resultant view must be halakically defensible and unimpeachable in its own terms. The biography of a legist is no substitute for jurisprudence, just as the biography of a philosopher is no substitute for metaphysics or phenomenology. René Wellek's apodictic-methodological statement about the study of literature is especially relevant for law: "The work of literature is the central subject matter of a theory of literature, and not the biography or psychology of the author, or the social background, or the affective response of the reader."[174]

In addition to the genetic fallacy, one must beware of a methodological error which confuses form and content. Maimonides' writings are heavily exegetical but this exegesis should not be treated lightly or pejoratively. In the realm of halakah, exegesis obviously is the touchstone of the whole system, but even in the realm of philosophy it should be clearly recognized as a hermeneutic device rather than a homiletical goal. Scriptural verses and their exegesis complement philosophic ideas and their demonstrations or provide a mold for their elaboration.

Moreover, it should be clear that when dealing with philosophical matters and speaking of the relationship between philosophy and law, our frame of reference is primarily the Code and not the *Moreh*, not philosophy in the sense of scholasticism, i.e., theory of attributes, predicables, and negative theology, ontology, essence and existence, cosmological proofs for the existence of God, atomism and materialism, etc. Nor are we concerned with an abstract conception or stereotype about what a Platonic, Aristotelian, or Alfarabian philosopher should be and to what axioms he must subscribe. This itself borders on the genetic fallacy which has particularly to be avoided here: because Maimonides used Alfarabi—as he avowedly did, with great praise for Alfarabi's philosophic achievement[175]—this does not mean

---

174. René Wellek, *History of Modern Criticism* (New Haven, 1955–65), IV, 3; cf. L. Trilling, *Liberal Imagination*, p. 180.
175. See S. Pines, Translator's Introduction, MN, p. lxxviii; L. Berman, "Maimonides, the disciple of Alfarabi," *Israel Oriental Studies*, IV (1974), 154ff.

that they are identical in all respects. The volatile complexity of a creative individual changes the tidy and convenient simplicity of ideal types. In this study, we take the *Mishneh Torah* as an axis and are concerned with the philosophic ideas developed in it, with a philosophic approach to law and a philosophic sensibility manifest therein. Other philosophic matters are introduced for purposes of comparison and contrast.

This will also help us avoid artificial reductionism: seeing Maimonides *either* as Talmudist *or* as philosopher. Students of halakah disengage Maimonides the codifier from the *Moreh* while students of philosophy belittle or ignore the *Mishneh Torah* and the central position of law. Both forms of this dichotomy are distortions, for a major part of Maimonides' achievement, and his historical significance, is the integration of both. Consequently, only an integrated-holistic approach, encompassing the Maimonidean oeuvre in its totality, without blurring its diversity and tension, will be productive.

# II

# Form

ANONYMITY AND AUTHORITY. THE PURPOSE AND VALUE OF CODIFICATION: BRIEF, UNIFORM, UNDOCUMENTED NORMS

The codificatory form of Maimonides' work was central to his purpose. He aimed to produce a *sefer kolel* (a truly all-inclusive code), a *dīwān* (collection) through which all halakic material would be sifted, pruned of associative discussion, digression, and indeterminate debate, and recast in a purified or rarefied form of uniform and normative conclusions and practical directives.[1] This literary goal was frequently and unequivocally underscored by Maimonides, presenting the massive material in crisp and concise form, unobstructed and unencumbered:

> On these grounds, I, Moses the son of Maimon the Sefardi, bestirred myself, and relying on the help of God, blessed be He, intently studied all these works, with the view of putting together the results obtained from them in regard to what is forbidden or permitted, clean or unclean, and the other rules of the Torah, all in plain language and terse style, so that thus the entire Oral Law might become systematically known to all, without citing difficulties and solutions or differences of view, one person saying so, and another something else, but consisting of statements, clear and reasonable.[2]

In the reflective and highly informative introduction to the *Sefer ham-Miṣwot*, a similar declaration is found:

> After having completed our previous well-known work, wherein we included a commentary to the whole Mishnah ... I deemed it advisable

---

1. See *'Iggĕrot*, 50. Cf. B. Cohen, "Classification of Law in the *Mishneh Torah*," *JQR*, XXV (1935), 519–20, nn. 2, 3; the old garbled Hebrew translation remains a rather accurate statement in its own right. *Dīwān* is used also in the ShM, introduction, while *kolel* is mentioned in the letter to R. Phinehas, *Ḳobeṣ*, I, 25b.
2. MT, introduction. For the meaning of *ḳĕrobim* ("reasonable"), see above, chap. I, n. 149. As noted in chap. I, this formulation deliberately attenuates the originality of interpretation.

to compile a compendium which would include all the laws of the Torah and its regulations. . . . In this compendium I will try, as I am accustomed to do, to avoid mentioning differences of opinion and rejected teachings, and include in it only the established law. . . . It also appeared to me to be advisable to omit the *'asmaktot* and the proofs brought (for the various laws) by mentioning the bearers of the tradition; thus I will not say with each and every law, "These are the words of this Rabbi," or "This Rabbi says so-and-so," but instead I will mention in a general way at the beginning of this compendium all the Sages of the Mishnah and the Talmud, peace be upon them, and I will say that all the laws of the Torah—that is, the Oral Torah—have been received and handed down from teacher to pupil (through the ages) up to Ezra (and thence) up to Moses our teacher. Together with the leader of every generation that received the tradition, I will mention also the outstanding persons in his generation, who were associated with him in the imparting of the Oral Teaching. All this (I will do) out of a desire for brevity.[3]

---

3. ShM, introduction (II, 361).
The phrase "as I am accustomed to do" suggests that the PhM already sought to minimize the role of controversy. See PhM, introduction (p. 48). See also MTH, 24. This was Maimonides' lodestar.
Ezra is a crucial link in the transmission of the Oral Law. This is reflected in the formulaic change in the MT introduction where, until Ezra, the recipient of the tradition is named individually while the transmitter's name is accompanied by "and his court." From Ezra until Hillel and Shammai the phrase "and his court" accompanies both receiver and transmitter. Starting with R. Johanan ben Zakkai, "and his court" is omitted completely; see *Mamrim,* i, 4; MN, I, 71.
The letter to R. Phinehas finds a different reason for the omission of names. While here its goal is brevity, in the letter its goal is authority, to deepen the impression of consensus and uniformity. In ŠP, introduction, Maimonides underscores the value and virtues of anonymity as a means toward intellectual integrity, explaining why the style of anonymity should not be condemned as a species of plagiarism: "I have gleaned them from the words of the wise occurring in the Midrashim, in the Talmud, and in other of their works, as well as from the words of the philosophers, ancient and recent, and also from the works of various authors, as one should accept the truth from whatever source it proceeds. Sometimes I may give a statement in full, word for word in the author's own language, but there is no harm in this, and it is not done with the intention of glorifying myself by presenting as my own something that was said by others before me, since I have just confessed (my indebtedness to others), even though I do not say "So-and-so said," which would necessitate useless prolixity. Sometimes, too, the mentioning of the name of the authority drawn upon might lead one who lacks insight to believe that the statement quoted is faulty and wrong in itself, because he does not understand it. Therefore, I prefer not to mention the authority, for my intention is only to be of service to the reader and to elucidate for him the thoughts hidden in this tractate."

Brevity, in this context, is related not to principles and models of style but rather to canons and standards of codification. Similarly, the statement that "were I able to condense the entire Talmud into a single chapter, I would not do so in two chapters"[4] is also a codificatory goal and not just a stylistic program; brevity is a sort of wide protective umbrella for the whole program. The most pungent definition of the Code is a negative one, indicating what the author will omit. The reader will not have to choose repeatedly between conflicting views, will not have to follow the dialectical and argumentative unfolding of laws, ordinances, and decrees, and will not be burdened with a listing of sources or authorities, and as a result will not have to spend time poring over commentaries and supercommentaries. The Code will speak with an anonymous-collective voice, will present rigid and unilateral decisions, completely undocumented and unelaborated, free of non-normative motifs. The elimination of debate (*maśśa' u-mattan*) and its complexities is a cardinal virtue of his work. It will in some respects restore the original state of the Oral Law which was free of "multiplicity of opinions, variety of schools . . . and the production of confusion with regard to actions." Maimonides is especially and invariably critical of controversy, which should be seen as an unavoidable by-product of the Talmud rather than as a premeditated or indispensable feature.[5] Hence there is no need to glorify or perpetuate it, and his Code will provide relief from this exhausting and unrewarding study. Indeed, this expunging of controversy is such a self-evident achievement that in the letter to R. Phinehas Maimonides felt compelled to declare that he did more than eliminate questions and answers and argument from Talmudic literature—this was clear to everyone—he created a new topical-conceptual arrangement as well.

---

4. MTH, 24–26. Maimonides uses the phrase קב ונקי (B. Yeb 49b) to mean consistently brief. He repeats there that he omits controversy and debate and does not reproduce obvious matters. On questions of select omissions from MT, see chap. III, below.

5. MN, I, 71; PhM, introduction (p. 20); A. S. Halkin, "Sanegoriyyah 'al Sefer Mishneh Torah," *Tarbiz*, XXV (1956), 418, 421. Maimonides' statement in PhM about the emergence of controversy in halakah provided a classic formulation of a problem which concerned many prominent Talmudists throughout the ages; see, e.g. RITBA, *Ḥiddušim*,

## 100 INTRODUCTION TO THE CODE OF MAIMONIDES

In essence, Maimonides establishes a basic equivalence between anonymity and authority, between frugality of discourse and finality of presentation. All diversionary motifs, the entire judicial process, the accepted insignia of Rabbinic discourse, will be excised, for these matters are totally dispensable, even undesirable, for the codifier. The presumption that the Code will be absolutely self-sufficient is echoed not only in the provocative promise—in the eyes of many, a presumptuous premise—that "a person who first reads the Written Law and then this compilation" will not have "to consult any other book between them," but also in the tenor and emphasis of all these programmatic statements. His letter to R. Phinehas had-Dayyan concludes by reiterating that the *Mishneh Torah* aimed "to mention only the correct statements without question and without answer and without any proof whatsoever"—not only the same emphasis but also the same language as in the *Mishneh Torah* introduction. Of course, theological-ethical subjects could also be presented in apodictic-codificatory form. The difference between a catechism and a codex pertains to the subject matter: theology versus positive law. Both, however, may be treated demonstratively, reflectively, and discursively, or concisely, monolithically, and authoritatively; the key determinant of the codex is the omission of "question and answer and proof" and the preparation of "clean (fine) flour" (*solet nĕkiyyah*),[6] a finely distilled product.

The reason for Maimonides' choice of the codificatory form is essentially identical with the motive for his fecund and successful experimentation with a new topical classification—his desire to

---

B. 'Er. 13a; P. Duran, *Ma'ăseh 'Efod*, p. 6; R. Solomon Luria, *Yam šel Šĕlomoh*, BK, introduction; idem, *Tĕšubot*, 98; for kabbalists, see R. Meir ibn Gabbai, *'Abodat hak-Kodeš* (Jerusalem, 1973), part III, chap. 23 (p. 169); *Tĕšubot Ḥawwot Ya'ir*, 98; R. Moses Cordovero, *Tomer Dĕborah*, chap. 7; also S. del Medigo, *Bĕḥinat had-Dat*, p. 45. At the beginning of the eighteenth century D. Nieto (*Matteh Dan: Kuzari Šeni* [Jerusalem, 1975], introduction, p. 4) referred back to the PhM passage concerning the problem of controversy in the Oral Law; note incidentally that he equated Maimonides' view with that of Abraham ibn Daud, *Sefer hak-Kabbalah*. The whole subject merits further study.

6. *Kobeṣ*, I, 25b. See *solet nĕkiyyah* in R. Solomon Luria, *Yam šel Šĕlomoh*, BK, introduction. The rhetoric of such placid phrases mirrors Maimonides' dissatisfaction with the Talmudic process in terms of codificatory goals. Concerning the statement that the reader of the *Mishneh Torah* will not have to consult any other book, see Twersky, "Non-Halakic Aspects," pp. 95–118, especially p. 110. See especially, ham-Meiri, *Bet hab-Bĕḥirah*, introduction, p. 25. See also PhM, Soṭ 5:1 (p. 261).

provide a comprehensive summary of halakah because contemporary conditions had intensified the difficulties of study and accelerated an intellectual decline. Conceptual classification, on the one hand, and judicious condensation and consolidation, on the other, each, in its own way, will facilitate study and aid the student in understanding and remembering. Both eased the burden of Talmudic dialectic and minimized distractions; both helped crystallize a concentrated and unified system in place of a diffuse and diversified tradition. We may put it this way: whereas Maimonides' attempt to rationalize the law involved him in an expansive and accretionary movement, making muffled sounds audible and blurred sights visible,[7] his choice of codificatory form led to a constrictive gesture, excising as much as possible in order to mold sharp foci and unobstructed views. One goal consisted of uncovering the warm and palpitating heart of the legal system; the other necessitated paring away whatever covers the muscle and sinew of the system.

There are two kinds of Torah study (*dibre Torah*) which Maimonides himself described parenthetically in the section of the Code dealing with mental preparation and concentration for prayer:

So, too, persons should not stand up to pray after indulging in jest, laughter, frivolity, idle talk, quarreling, or outbursts of anger, but only after engaging in study of Torah; not, however, after dealing with (the intricacies of) legal analysis, even though these constitute *dibre Torah*, for one's mind would then be preoccupied (and distracted) with halakah, but only after the study of *dibre Torah* which require no profound reflection, as for instance fixed rules (*halakot pĕsukot*).[8]

The *Mishneh Torah* belonged to the latter genre which had been initially cultivated by the Geonim: *halakot gĕdolot, halakot kĕṭu'ot, halakot pĕsukot, halakot kĕṣubot*—all variations of the same theme. Maimonides, as we shall see, was to refine this literary genre, expand and enhance it, and produce its noblest specimen. His concern was with simplification, with material restructuring, and

---

7. See chap. VI, below, especially pp. 407ff.
8. *Tĕfillah*, iv, 18. A comparison of this with the underlying Talmudic text (B. Ber 31a) shows that Maimonides changed the amorphous *dĕbar halakah* into *halakot pĕsukot*, which has associations with a well-known literary genre. Cf. *Bi'at Miḳdaš*, i, 4.

also with the practical-normative aspect, the magnified value of "fixed rules" as distinct from halaḵic disquisitions. All his letters emphasize that his work will clear away obstacles and reduce "error in the *pĕsaḵ halaḵah*," that it will make "the halaḵot which are constantly required" easily accessible, that it will help one understand "the way of that which is prohibited and permitted." Halaḵic functionality or pragmatism is paramount, inasmuch as observance is the goal and Talmudic literature per se is too intricate to serve as a guide.⁹

REACTIONS TO THE CODE: STRICTURE AND SUPPLEMENT

This characterization of the Code was sharply delineated, and it was precisely this aspect of his judicial work—excluding for the moment his uncompromising devotion to the unity and reciprocity of philosophy and law—that triggered criticism and controversy and thwarted the irenic consensus which he sought. The codificatory achievement made the *Mishneh Torah* a focus simultaneously of sustained controversy as well as of exhaustive study. Allowing for varying emphasis, two major trends are discernible in all subsequent Maimonidean studies: (1) criticism of Maimonides for omitting what we may loosely call the *apparatus criticus* from his *Mishneh Torah*, and concomitantly partial disqualification of this work as an ultimate guide in codification; (2) conversely, concerted efforts to supply the necessary sources and explanations for his statements and thus rehabilitate the *Mishneh Torah* as an authoritative code. These two approaches, apparently antithetical yet in many respects mutually complementary, are the axes around which all commentaries, supercommentaries, and critical supplements revolve. Both are articulated and to some degree implemented in the early decades of *Mishneh Torah* investigation by those very writers usually described as hypercritical and anti-Maimonidean.

A good example of the early critic-commentator foreshadowing both these aspects in theory as well as in practice is RABD of

---

9. Cf. the statement of *Seder 'Olam Zuṭa* concerning motives for codification: לעיין בהם ולסמוך על דבריהם בני אדם שאין מספיקים לסדרים [ו]למסכתות; *Medieval Jewish Chronicles*, ed. A. Neubauer (Oxford, 1887), I, 178. See below, n. 200.

Posquières. The argument concerning the lack of sources, which led to a systematic exposé of other weaknesses and errors—alleged flaws, apparent discrepancies, strained interpretations—was fully articulated by RABD in one of the early *haśśagot,* where he castigates Maimonides for "forsaking the way of all authors who preceded him."[10] Precisely because Maimonides mentions no names and adduces no proofs, because the derivation of normative judgments from hylic Talmudic debates is not traced, RABD illustrated that the *Mishneh Torah* was not the last word in codification, that some statements were erroneous, others were based on faulty inferences, and still others were merely one possible alternative, arbitrarily selected. Errors, real or apparent, serious or trivial, of various sorts—textual, stylistic, theoretical, methodological, codificatory, consuetudinary, classificatory, but mostly interpretative—evoked various critical reactions from RABD.

This critical note, once struck, reverberates throughout later literature and helps establish a major category of interpretative and critical annotations. RABD's immediate successors in Maimonidean critique, such as R. Moses hak-Kohen, shared this concern. It is expressed or implied in a host of other contemporary statements from the pens of both antagonists and protagonists, such as R. Samson of Sens, R. Joseph ben Todros Abulafia, R. Sheshet han-Naśi' of Saragossa, and an anonymous partisan of the *Mishneh Torah.*[11] R. Moses of Coucy, author of the

---

10. *Haśśagot*, MT, introduction: "He intended to improve but did not improve, for he forsook the way of all authors who preceded him. They always adduced proof for their statements and cited the proper authority for each statement; this was very useful, for sometimes the judge would be inclined to forbid or permit something, and his proof would be based on some other authority. Had he known that there was a greater authority who interpreted the law differently, he might have retracted. Now, therefore, I do not know why I should reverse my tradition or my corroborative views because of the compendium of this author. If the one who differs with me is greater than I, fine; and if I am greater than he, why should I annul my opinion in deference to his? Moreover, there are matters concerning which the Geonim disagree and this author has selected the opinion of one and incorporated it in his compendium. Why should I rely upon his choice when it is not acceptable to me, and I do not know whether the contending authority is competent to differ or not? It can only be that 'an overbearing spirit is in him.' "
See Twersky, *Rabad,* p. 131.

11. Letter of R. Samson, *Kitāb al-Rasā'il* (Paris, 1871), pp. 131–32: ואיש אל ישים R. Joseph יגיעו בספרים הסתומים . . . וכל האומר דבר בשם אומרו מביא גאולה לעולם;

*Sefer Miṣwot Gadol* which is actually based on the *Mishneh Torah* and organized in accord with Maimonidean principles of classification, mentions the lack of sources as a serious deficiency impairing the value and restricting the usefulness of the *Mishneh Torah*.[12] His own book cites sources and includes summary presentations of explanations and inferences. R. Asher ben Jehiel correlated the ability—even the possibility—to use the *Mishneh Torah* with one's knowledge of the sources: "One should not rely upon his reading in this book to judge and issue decisions unless he finds proof in the Talmud."[13] Ham-Me'iri also stresses this deficiency, even though he does not explicitly condemn it.[14] R. Joseph ibn Kaspi chides the scholars of his day for seeking proofs and explanations of the commandments rather than being content with the apodictic codified traditions of the *Mishneh Torah*.[15] R.

---

Abulafia, *Jeshurun*, VIII (1872), 39–40: היחשבו כל הספר הסתום למשה מסיני הלכה; "Letter of R. Sheshet," ed. A. Marx, *JQR*, XXV (1935), 414: ואחרי אשר איננו מביא ראיות מדברי חכמי התלמוד לדבריו, מי ישמע אליו. A. S. Halkin, "Sanegoriyyah," pp. 413–28. See also D. Kaufmann, "The Etz Chayim of Jacob ben Jehudah of London," *JQR*, V (1893), 368: ועל כי הגאון לא הביא בספרו ראיה גם לקצת דבריו חלוקין גאוני עולם האחרונים . . . ועמד הרב ר משה מקוצי וחבר חבור מכל התורה על פי ספר הגאון והביא ראיות לרוב דבריו . . .; R. Jacob Ḥazzan, *'Eṣ Ḥayyim*, ed. I. Brodie (Jerusalem, 1962), p. 2.

12. R. Moses ben Jacob of Coucy, *Sefer Miṣwot Gadol* (Venice, 1522), introduction: לא הביא הגאון שום ראיה בספריו וכל אדם שיורה מתוך ספריו ויבקשו ממנו כתב ראיה מנין אם לא למד הראיה או אפי' למדה ואינו זוכר יהא לו הדבר ההוא כחלום בלא פתרון.

13. R. Asher ben Jehiel, *Responsa* (Venice, 1595), *kĕlal* XXXI, 9.

14. R. Menahem ham-Me'iri, *Bet hab-Bĕḥirah*, introduction, 27. After giving a perceptive and laudatory evaluation of Maimonides' Code, ham-Me'iri emphasizes that Talmudists refused to abandon the Talmudic process of discursive-demonstrative study, and hence the *Mishneh Torah* was inadequate. Actually ham-Me'iri is here trying to restore the respectability and academic propriety of Talmud study in the eyes of those intellectuals who argued that codes are perfectly adequate and discursive Talmud study is unnecessary; he counters that just as rationalized understanding is superior to unexamined faith, so knowledge of the process of the law is superior to simple acquaintance with rigidly formulated normative conclusions. He is adding intellectual ballast to traditional Talmudism. See also R. Jeroḥam ben Meshullam, *Sefer Mešarim* (Kopys, 1908), p. 2.

15. Will of R. Joseph ibn Kaspi, *Hebrew Ethical Wills*, ed. I. Abrahams (Philadelphia, 1926), I, 153: כי לא יספיק לכם הקבלה מספר משנה תורה שחבר רבנו משה ואעפ"י שאמר הוא ז"ל ואינו צריך לספר אחר ביניהם. Earlier R. Jacob Anatoli had written in the introduction to *Malmad hat-Talmidim* (Lyck, 1866), fol. 6a of unpaginated introduction: אבל הדבר הגדול היום בעיני חכמינו בעלי הגמרא הוא העסק בסוגיות התלמוד ולא העסק בפסק הנברר ממנו. A Yemenite rabbi criticized R. Abraham Maimonides for failing to refer to the Talmud and apparently quoting only the MT; see document by S. D. Goitein, "Temanim. . . ," *Har'el* (Tel Aviv, 1962), pp. 135–36, and note, per contra, R. Abraham Maimonides, *Tešuḇot*, 82 (pp. 115–16).

Ḥasdai Crescas, who had contemplated a comprehensive work on law as well as dogma, practically reproduces RABD's objections.[16] R. Isaac ben Sheshet Perfet endorses R. Asher ben Jehiel's view concerning the need to trace all decisions back to original sources; people who rely exclusively on the Code are denigrated as "rendering decisions in haughtiness."[17] Faint echoes of this refrain may be heard even from R. Joseph Karo, who admits that he would have liked to pattern his book on that of Maimonides, but was compelled to alter his plans "because he brings only one opinion while I had to elaborate and write the opinions of other codifiers and their reasons."[18] This attitude—and its critical consequences—is uniformly reflected in the sustained refusal of halakists to use the name *Mishneh Torah*, which struck them as somewhat audacious in its presumption to serve as the sole companion to Scripture.[19] They quietly substituted the title *Yad ha-Ḥazakah* and used various personal references or literary circumlocutions, but almost without exception imposed a blackout on Maimonides' chosen title. Indeed, what more need be said than to call attention to the fact that Maimonides himself was conscious of this characteristic, discussed it a number of times in his correspondence, and anticipated the criticism it would provoke.[20]

16. R. Ḥasdai Crescas, *Sefer 'Or haš-Šem* (Vienna, 1860), p. 32. Del Medigo also announced his intention of composing a code which would supersede the *Mishneh Torah*; see *Sefer Noḇělot Ḥokmah* (reprinted, Jerusalem, 1970), fol. 6a of unpaginated introduction: אני בוטח בה' להוציא ספר א' גדול הערך שיועיל לרבים יותר מס' היד של הרמב"ם. Such intellectuals as Shem Ṭoḇ ibn Falaquera and Isaac Polgar also stressed the full codificatory value of the MT, e.g., *'Ezer had-Daṯ* (reprinted, Jerusalem, 1970), I, 7 (p. 26).
17. See A. Hershman, *Rabbi Isaac ben Sheshet Perfet* (New York, 1943), p. 69.
18. *Bet Yosef, Ṭur 'Oraḥ Ḥayyim*, introduction.
19. See the defensive statement of R. Solomon Duran, *Milḥemeṯ Miṣwah* (Maḵor reprint, together with *Ḳešeṯ u-Magen*, Jerusalem, 1970), fol. 38b. I have discussed and illustrated this phenomenon in great detail in my "Beginnings," p. 173, n.55, and in my "R. Joseph Ashkenazi wĕ-Sefer Mishneh Torah," *Salo Baron Jubilee Volume*, ed. S. Lieberman (Jerusalem, 1974), III, 185ff. Duran also suggests an explanation of the title MT in the light of *Tefillah*, i, 1 (*mišneh tefillah*).
20. *Ḳoḇeṣ*, I, 26a. See the well documented study by I. Kahana, "Hap-Polmos mis-Sabiḇ lĕ-Ḳĕbi'aṯ ha-Hălakah kĕha-RaMBaM," *Sinai*, XXVI (1955), 391–411, 530–37, reprinted in his *Meḥḳarim bĕ-Sifruṯ hat-Tĕšuḇoṯ* (Jerusalem, 1973), pp. 8–89. There is still the more extreme opposition of such authorities as the MaHaRaL (e.g., *Nĕṯiḇoṯ 'Olam, nĕṯiḇ hat-Torah*) or R. Solomon Luria, who avoided all "detours" and regularly went directly to the Talmud.

The second trend in Maimonidean study—corroborating and elucidating the *Mishneh Torah* by unearthing its Talmudic sources and revealing its latent processes of reasoning—also had its origin in RABD's *Haśśagot*. He was the first to emphasize the need of such work and, in part, to undertake its implementation. His *Haśśagot* contain many positive appreciatory elements, starting with a sustained quest for sources and continuing to pointed lexical annotation as well as lengthy halakic clarification. All the standard commentators, starting with R. Shem Ṭob ibn Gaon and R. Vidal of Tolosa (and before them in the *Sefer ham-Měnuḥah* of R. Manoah), through R. David ibn Abi Zimra (RaDBaZ), R. Abraham de Boton (author of *Leḥem Mishneh*), and R. Joseph Karo, and continuing until this very day, were preoccupied with this task; the center around which their commentaries revolve is the enumeration of sources and their explication in a Maimonidean vein. R. Joseph Karo provides an excellent description of the inherent difficulties and shortcomings of the *Mishneh Torah* and the attempts to resolve them: "The generations that followed him could not understand his works well . . . for the source of every decision is concealed from them. . . . One wrote a commentary *Maggid Mishneh* in which he revealed the source of every law. . . . But he illuminated only six [of the fourteen] parts. . . . So I, the youngster, arose . . . to write on the source of every decision and explain his statements."[21] To this day, the quest for *Mishneh Torah* sources in unknown Midrashim and Geonic responsa, variant readings, etc., continues unabated as one of the main forms of Rabbinic scholarship. This quest is supplemented, as we shall see, by attempts to identify or reconstruct the principles of Maimonides' interpretation, his general methods of study as well as ad hoc handling of discrete issues, the reconciliation of certain formulations with the Talmudic sources as well as the inner con-

---

21. KM, introduction. See a similar statement by R. David ibn Abi Zimra, *Yĕḳar Tif'eret*, ed. S. B. Werner (Jerusalem, 1945), p. 11; also R. Judah Albutini, ed. M. Benayahu, *Sinai*, XVIII (1955), 242. Some recent examples are A. J. Bromberg, *Mĕḳorot lĕ-Fisḳe ha-RaMBaM* (Jerusalem, 1947); A. Hilvitz, *Li-Lĕšonot ha-RaMBaM* (Jerusalem, 1950); S. Strashun, *Mĕḳore ha-RaMBaM*, ed. Z. Harkavy (Jerusalem, 1957). See also the classic commentary on *Madda'* by R. Menahem Krakowski, *'Aḇodat ham-Meleḵ* (reprinted, Jerusalem, 1971).

sistency and meaningfulness of the Maimonidean formulations per se. What more need be said than to call attention to the fact that Maimonides himself, fully cognizant that his method would invite criticism, contemplated the composition of a *Sefer hab-Be'ur*, a kind of sourcebook which would serve as a supplement to the *Mishneh Torah*.[22]

We may presume that Maimonides would not have been disarmed or confounded by RABD's (and other) criticism of his work, particularly of his conception of the proper method of codification: "He intended to improve but did not improve, for he forsook the way of all authors who preceded him. They always adduced proof for their statements and cited the proper authority for each statement." Maimonides would say in rebuttal that this is not a conflict between old-fashioned and newfangled types of writing, for he has respectable antecedents. The singularity of his work, as the discussion of classification underscores, lies in its unprecedented scope and thoroughness. He is not a literary innovator, one "who forsook the way of all authors," in a formalistic sense. Maimonides has the best of both worlds: his work *is* a breakthrough, but it has generic antecedents.

We may extend this by noting that in addition to the literary tradition, there was a practical tradition of positive evaluation of, and confident reliance upon, codificatory works. Maimonides' revered predecessor, whom he looked upon as his teacher, R. Joseph ibn Megas, though himself the writer of commentaries and responsa, unreservedly sanctioned the use of *halakot pěsukot*, especially by those judges for whom the Talmud itself presented great difficulties. The level of halakic learning was not exceptionally high, and in fact Maimonides' Code was destined to help raise the standard of knowledge among students of various kinds. Authoritative codes were useful, perhaps indispensable.[23]

---

22. R. Abraham Maimonides, *Birkat 'Abraham*, ed. B. Goldberg (Lyck, 1859), p. 8; *Kobeṣ* I, 26a; *'Iggĕrot*, 51. R. Abraham also started such a *Sefer hab-Be'ur*.

23. R. Joseph ibn Megas, *Těšubot* (Warsaw, 1870), p. 114. Twersky, "Sefer MT," pp. 3-4, n.12. I. Ta-Shema, "Šipput 'Ibri," *Šěnaton ham-Mišpat ha-'Ibri*, I (Jerusalem, 1974), 371, n.71. Note especially the references in my article to the *Sefer Minhot Kěna'ot*, where the author describes the deterioration of Torah study in Spain and the great influence exerted by the MT. The real turning point was to be the activity of R. Meir hal-Levi Abulafia, as will be documented in the forthcoming monograph of B. Septimus.

## 108 INTRODUCTION TO THE CODE OF MAIMONIDES

Maimonides may have had all this in mind when he described the intellectual decline, blaming it, as he did, on unfavorable historical circumstances. In any event, there was a widespread literary nexus as well as a practical matrix for codes and codification.

As for his plan (mentioned in his letter to R. Phinehas) to compose a source book to accompany the *Mishneh Torah*, this is by no means a retreat from his firm commitment to the codificatory form. It is perfectly clear that were this book to be written, it would remain a separate work and could never be merged with the Code. The source book, in other words, would not replace or even dilute the Code; it would literally be a companion volume for eager students, part of "Talmud," of the additional highest level of amplificatory study. There is, in sum, no need to see this unfulfilled promise as a backing away from his declarations about the self-sufficiency of the Code. The *Mishneh Torah*, a distillation of the entire halakic literature, could certainly be studied without the Talmud. One could, however, study it with the Talmud as well, and that fact, as will be noted in Chapter VII, was actually to determine its historical destiny and self-renewing vitality. The *Mishneh Torah*, after all, was written for the benefit of "small and great." Maimonides himself indicated, as we have seen, that it could be studied in depth by sensitive students who would realize its profundities.

### A SECOND LOOK: EXCEPTIONS TO THE AUSTERE CODIFICATORY FORM

Nevertheless, close study and evaluation show incontestably that what was said above is hardly adequate as a realistic literary characterization of the form and contents of the *Mishneh Torah*. It may, therefore, be useful to identify several categories of exceptions to, or infringements upon, the codificatory form as conventionally perceived;[24] we may also anticipate that the cumulative consequence of confronting these exceptions, which will be seen to be quite impressive quantitatively as well as qualitatively, will

---

24. Note the perceptive remark of R. Isaiah di Trani, *Kiryaṭ Sefer* (Warsaw, 1902), chap. 8 of introduction, p. 24: השמיט המשא ומתן ודרכי לימוד כי אם במקומות מועטים. ... אבל פרטי הדינים אינו מזכיר מאיזה מקומות נלמדו כי אם במקומות מועטים.

lead to a redefinition of the Maimonidean Code. Its sparse codificatory form will then emerge properly silhouetted against a more supple commentatorial background, and the intent of Maimonides' own seemingly austere statements will be freshly appreciated.

(1) *Attribution to original authorities, anecdotes and quotations*

All his protestations notwithstanding, Maimonides does mention names and attribute halakot directly to original authorities. This is all the more remarkable when we recall that in the major retrospective defense of his work (the letter in which he reassured R. Phinehas concerning his intentions), where the issue of his presumption in failing to discuss and demonstrate his conclusions is broached, he further minimized the importance of names. Citing names, he avers, has no connection with providing proof. Only one who fails to understand will contend that using the formula "R. So-and-so said" has demonstrative or didactic value. Reproducing reasons why one Sage maintained one view and another a conflicting view—this is proof, and it is precisely the omission of this critical-argumentative dimension, the feature characterizing Talmud as distinct from Mishnah, which aroused genuine misunderstanding and wide-ranging criticism. Maimonides readily acknowledged this and deftly defended his procedure. His omission of names, however—an elementary component of this form—was a non-issue according to Maimonides. One could even reverse the tables and contend, as Maimonides did, that anonymity was a virtue, for it bolstered the authoritativeness of the oral tradition by removing any misleading impressions of fragmentation, dissonance, and conflict. It substituted consensus for controversy, general norm for individual opinion, and was therefore a powerful anti-Karaite weapon. It was not only a literary device but also a polemical-ideological achievement.[25]

25. Note that R. Samuel han-Nagid, in the introductory poem to his halakic compendium (*Diwan Šĕmu'el han-Nagid,* ed. D. Yarden [Jerusalem, 1966], p. 92), emphasizes that he will cite names. Maimonides himself, in the *Treatise on Asthma,* ed. S. Muntner (Philadelphia, 1963), p. 3, comments: "Furthermore, I shall cite the names of the sources I relied upon, to lend greater force to my discourse." This remark is antithetical to the

Nevertheless, in the *Mishneh Torah* we find references to juridical sources, personal attributions, biographical episodes, and anecdotal reports (the equivalent of *ma'áśeh rab*). The chronological range is quite wide: from Ezra and the Great Assembly,[26] Simeon the Just and his follower Johanan the High Priest,[27] through various prominent Talmudic authorities—Hillel the Elder,[28] Rabban Gamaliel,[29] Rabban Johanan ben Zakkai,[30] Rabbi 'Akiba,[31] Rabbi Judah the Patriarch ("our holy master"),[32] Rab,[33] Abbaye, and Raba,[34] all watershed personalities in every sense—to Geonim[35] and early medieval figures, such as Ben

---

emphasis in his letters cited in chap. I, above. In medicine, apparently, the nature of authority is different. Furthermore, certain medical suggestions were in conflict with Islam and needed to be bolstered and fortified. Concerning anonymity in the Mishnah, see the strange remark of Eldad had-Dani, *Kitbe A. Epstein*, ed. A. M. Habermann (Jerusalem, 1950), p. 40.

26. *Tefillah*, iv, 4; xii, 1, 10; xiii, 1; *'Issure Bi'ah*, xii, 1, 23, 24; *Mikwa'ot*, ii, 16. See the explicit citation from the Book of Ezra in *Sanhedrin*, xxiv, 5.

27. *Tefillah*, xiv, 10; *Ma'áśer*, ix, 1. See the reason suggested for this identification in *KM*. An alternative explanation is that Maimonides wanted to indicate the historical context, a time of prosperity, for the subject (*bittul ham-mě'orěrim*). Note PhM, introduction (pp. 26, 50). See S. Abramson, *'Inyanut bě-Sifrut hag-Gě'onim* (Jerusalem, 1974), p. 53, n.3. Note also PhM, Men 13:10.

28. *Tefillin*, ii, 13; *Sanhedrin*, iv, 5. In *'Issure Bi'ah*, xxii, 3, Hillel and Shammai are cited. For the veiled reference to Hillel as woodchopper in *Talmud Torah*, i, 9, see PhM, 'Ab 4:7 (p. 442).

29. *Tefillah*, ii, 1—apparently Rabban Gamaliel the First (of Jabneh); note also the use of *bet dino*. See Rashi to B. Ber 28b.

30. *Tefillah*, xiv, 6; *Lulab*, vii, 15; *Kidduš ha-Ḥodeš*, iii, 6.

31. *Mělakim*, xi, 3; *Yěsode hat-Torah*, v, 4; *'Išut*, viii, 5. See *Mattěnot 'Aniyyim*, x, 8, for R. Hananiah ben Teradion.

32. *Tefillin*, iv, 25; *'Issure Bi'ah*, xx, 14; *Těrumot*, i, 5; *'Abel*, xiii, 10.

33. *De'ot*, iv, 2; *Tefillin*, iv, 25. Rab is identified as the "disciple of R. Judah."

34. *Kidduš ha-Ḥodeš*, v, 3; *Ṭo'en wě-Niṭ'an*, viii, 10. The phrase *hawwayot dě-Abbaye wě-Raba* in *Yěsode hat-Torah*, iv, 13, is clearly not a personal reference. For additional references to Tannaim and Amoraim, see *'Išut*, viii, 4, 5; xv, 13; *Mattěnot 'Aniyyim*, x, 8; *Šěmittah wě-Yobel*, ix, 17; *Parah 'Adumah*, xiii, 2. Just before publication, I noticed the list (which is not completely reliable) in S. Neuhausen, *Torah 'Or la-RaMBaM* (Baltimore, 1941), pp. 98ff.

35. See A. Schwarz, "Das Verhältnis Maimuni's zu den Gaonim," *MbM*, I, 332–410. See also the large work of H. Tykocinski, *Takkanot hag-Gě'onim* (Jerusalem, 1959). M. Havazelet, *Ha-RaMBaM wěhag-Gě'onim* (Jerusalem, 1967), has treated certain select themes. Sometimes supportive reference to Geonim seems to have special significance; e.g., *Šěkenim*, iv, 13, and *Těšubot*, 70 (p. 110); also *Malweh wě-Loweh*, xxv, 13; xxvi, 11. Maimonides also specifies on occasion *gě'onim 'aḥaronim*, "later Geonim," e.g., *Malweh wě-Loweh*, xi, 11; *gě'one ham-ma'arab*, "Geonim of the West," e.g., *Ma'akalot 'Asurot*, xi, 10.

Asher (whose Biblical Codex was praised as the most accurate and authoritative),[36] the "Sages of Spain,"[37] "scholars of the west,"[38] and particularly R. Joseph ibn Megas and R. Isaac Alfasi whom he for the most part designates reverentially but anonymously as "my teachers."[39] There are also collective references to Tannaim and Amoraim under the totally plastic rubric of *ḥăkamim* or *ḥăsiḏim*,[40] and such temporal or encomiastic variations as "early Sages," "the greatest among the Sages," "the pious of the Sages," "the righteous (*ṣaddiḳim*)"[41] or "the Sages of the Mishnah" and "the Sages of the Talmud."[42] Talmud (or Gemara) without further qualification is also cited.[43]

The legislative history of some basic ordinances is occasionally traced all the way back, e.g., to Moses ("Moses our teacher established the rule for Israel that they should read the Torah publicly")[44] or to Solomon ("the regulation to this effect was first made by Solomon and his legislature"),[45] while some Scribal practices are specifically described as non-Talmudic but venerable: "There are other practices which were not mentioned in the Talmud but are observed by the Scribes as a tradition (*ḳabbalah*,

---

36. *Sefer Torah*, viii, 4.
37. *Měkirah*, xi, 18; see *Těšuḇoṭ*, 269 (p. 516). Note *Ḥoḇel u-Mazziḳ*, iii, 6.
38. *Malweh wĕ-Loweh*, xi, 10; *Miḳwa'oṭ*, iv, 9. See *Těšuḇoṭ*, 154 (p. 200), 156 (p. 201).
39. *Malweh wĕ-Loweh*, xiv, 13; xxvii, 1; *Šě'elah u-Fiḳḳadon*, v, 6 (mentioned by name); *To'en wĕ-Niṭ'an*, iii, 2; in *Těšuḇoṭ*, 126 (p. 224), Maimonides refers to Ibn Megas as his father's teacher. Nahmanides on occasion refers to Maimonides as the disciple of Ibn Megas; see, e.g., *Ḥidduše RaMBaN* to B. Shebu 25b.
40. *Talmud Torah*, v, 13.
41. *Talmud Torah*, vii, 1, 13; *Těšuḇah*, x, 4; *Těfillah*, iv, 5; *Sefer Torah*, x, 11; *'Issure Bi'ah*, xxi, 24; xxii, 20; *Šabbaṭ*, xxx, 2, 10; *Sanhedrin*, iii, 10; also, *Nizḳe Mamon*, xiii, 22. Note *Zěkiyyah u-Mattanah*, xii, 17.
42. *Běrakoṭ*, i, 17; *Ṣiṣiṭ*, i, 17; *Ḳidduš ha-Ḥodeš*, v, 3; *'Issure Bi'ah*, xi, 3, 6; *Ma'ăḳaloṭ 'Asuroṭ*, iii, 13; *Šěḥiṭah*, xi, 7; *Těrumoṭ*, i, 26. Note also such a reference as *Kěle ham-Miḳdaš*, i, 11.
43. *Ḳidduš ha-Ḥodeš*, xviii, 6; *'Išuṭ*, xi, 13; xiv, 14; *Šěmiṭṭah wě-Yoḇel*, x, 5; *Malweh wě-Loweh*, vi, 7; xv, 2; *Sanhedrin*, xxi, 5; *Mattěnoṭ 'Ăniyyim*, i, 14; *Sefer Torah*, vii, 10. The reference to B. Shab in *Yěsode hat-Torah*, x, 4, is clearly an interpolation. In PhM, Ker 3:5 (p. 363), he mentions *rabbanan Sěḇora'e* (our masters the Seboraim).
44. *Těfillah*, xii, 1, and see the reference to *Masseḵet Soferim* in KM, ad loc.; also *Sanhedrin*, iv, 1 (for *sěmikah*); xii, 3; and *Šěḳalim*, i, 3. Note *Gěneḇah*, vii, 7. For Joshua, see, e.g., *Nizḳe Mamon*, v, 3.
45. *'Eruḇin*, i, 4; also *Kěle ham-Miḳdaš*, iii, 9, 10; *Nizḳe Mamon*, v, 4. For a ruling of King David, see *'Issure Bi'ah*, xii, 23.

*paradosis*) handed down orally from one to another."[46] Improper and impure motivation for religious behavior is condemned by highly charged universalized reference to "the standard set by the prophets and Sages."[47] Biblical references, in general, abound and invite special scrutiny and evaluation. Post-Biblical and post-Talmudic precedents, rather sweepingly described, for example, as "such is always the custom in the West" or "these are daily occurrences with us in the West," are also specified.[48]

The identification of oral traditions, a very important kind of source, is also significant in this context. Even with the ever-increasing dominance of written culture, oral traditions remained valuable, and Maimonides in particular was a devotee of oral culture. As we have seen, he emphasized its intrinsic superiority and harmoniousness. Concerning the specifications of a certain law, Maimonides codifies that which "we have heard from our elders";[49] another section is introduced by "all courts of law which we have seen or concerning which we have heard follow this practice."[50] Concerning the recitation of a benediction before the eating of *tĕrumah* (heave offering), Maimonides adds "we have received such a tradition and have seen them reciting this benediction."[51] In the case where a father is obligated to swear an oath to his son, Maimonides notes that "we have seen that the universal practice is. . . ."[52] Elsewhere he states "we have heard that in France, down to this day, it is customary. . . ."[53] Oral tradition remained a source of energy and information for the codifier.

While the calculated intrusion of sources thus plays a decidedly discernible role, it is difficult to discern any consistent formulary

---

46. *Sefer Torah*, vii, 10.
47. *Tĕšubah*, x, 1.
48. *Naḥalot*, vi, 12; *Sanhedrin*, vi, 9; and see above, n.38. Note PhM, Pes 2:2 (p. 166). Use of some references, anecdotal interludes, and illustrations is found in the *Šulḥan 'Aruk* also; see, e.g., *'Oraḥ Ḥayyim*, 241, 7.
49. *'Akum*, xii, 6. See IT, xv, and Halkin's important Hebrew introduction; p. xii. PhM, Bek 8:8 (p. 271).
50. *'Edut*, vi, 4; see also *Sanhedrin*, xxi, 5; and *Naḥalot*, vii, 3.
51. *Tĕrumot*, xv, 22.
52. *Mamrim*, v, 15; for similar use of oral traditions in responsa, see *Tĕšubot*, 70 (p. 110), 156 (p. 201). Note also *'Išut*, xxv, 2.
53. *'Issure Bi'ah*, xi, 7. In MN, I, 48 (p. 106), he refers to "what I had heard in the course of instruction." Note *Tĕmidin u-Musafin*, vii, 11; *Ḥobel u-Mazziḳ*, i, 6.

or rhetorical pattern in these source references—when will they appear and in what form? On the whole, this selective footnoting will substantiate a given formulation, support a special nuance, vivify or concretize it, underscore its normativeness, determine its genesis, explain its circumstances, or dramatize its scope. Let us cite just a few illustrations from Book Two.

In discussing the Eighteen Benedictions, Maimonides explains: "In Rabban Gamaliel's days, the number of heretics in Israel increased. They were wont to vex the Israelites and induce them to turn away from God. When Rabban Gamaliel realized that the most urgent need was to remove this evil, he composed a benediction which contains a petition to God to destroy the heretics, and incorporated it in the Eighteen Benedictions, so that it should be in a fixed form for all. Hence the total number of blessings in the daily service is nineteen."[54]

After recording the law that "a man who has written phylacteries with his own hand or has purchased them from an expert need never reexamine them, even after the lapse of many years," Maimonides adds: "Hillel the Elder was wont to say, 'These phylacteries belonged to my mother's father.' "[55]

After extolling the sanctity of phylacteries and the cathartic and sublimating effect of having them on one's head and arm, Maimonides concludes: "A man should therefore endeavor to wear phylacteries the whole day, this being the right way of fulfilling the precept. It is said of Rab, the disciple of our sainted teacher (R. Judah the Prince), that throughout his life no one saw him walking for four cubits without Torah, ṣiṣit (fringes on his garments), or phylacteries."[56]

The following passage from the end of the Laws Concerning Sabbath is also significant; while the names, which we can readily supply, are not mentioned, the specific references are colorful and forceful:

Even if one is a person of very high rank and does not as a rule attend to the marketing or to the other household chores, he should nevertheless himself perform one of these tasks in preparation for the Sabbath,

---

54. *Tefillah*, ii, 1.
55. *Tefillin*, ii, 11.
56. *Tefillin*, iv, 25.

for that is his way of honoring it. There were some among the Sages of old who split firewood for the cooking; others cooked or salted meat, plaited wicks, lit lamps, or went to market to buy food or drink for the Sabbath, although none of these Sages customarily performed such tasks on weekdays. Indeed, the more one does in the way of such preparation, the more praiseworthy he is.[57]

The form is highly variable: sometimes individualized, sometimes collective. A direct, and hence easily identifiable, quotation may be prefaced by the phrase '*omru ḥăḵamim* ("the Sages said") instead of the name of its author, or an anecdote or precedent will be reported in behalf of *ḥăḵamim* instead of the one individual mentioned in the sources.[58] In one context a saying of Hillel will be attributed directly to him, while in another a Hillel dictum will be introduced by '*omru ḥăḵamim*.[59] When the phrase "the Sages said" introduces more than one quotation, it is stylistically self-explanatory.[60] Of course, in keeping with Maimonides' letter, we are cognizant that an anonymous-collective reference is more impressive and more resonant than an individual one, but the rhetorical variations remain puzzling—after all, Maimonides did not completely eliminate individuality.

Even a cursory glance at any one section, for example, *Hilḵot Talmud Torah*, illustrates the extent of source references, anecdotal interludes, quotations, and expositions which, in this case, serve generally to exemplify humble and unselfish behavior, unqualified dedication to Torah, freedom from pomp and pretense, and scholarly independence, economic as well as intellectual.[61]

---

57. *Šabbaṭ*, xxx, 6.
58. *Talmud Torah*, i, 13; iii, 8; iv, 5 (both Hillel); *Sefer Torah*, x, 11 (R. Jose bar Ḥalafta in 'Ab 4:6); cf. also *Talmud Torah*, i, 9, which alludes to Hillel, R. Huna, R. Joseph (see B. Yoma 35b; Ket 105a; Pes 116b); *Měkirah*, xi, 12; *Malweh wě-Loweh*, i, 3, and 'Ab 2:12; *Mamrim*, ii, 4, and B. Yoma 5b; PhM, introduction (pp. 50–51). See MN, III, 52 (*gědole ḥaḵamenu*) for similar usage.
59. See above, n. 58; also *Talmud Torah*, iii, 10; *Naḥălot*, vi, 12.
60. E.g., *Talmud Torah*, iii, 10; see *Talmud Torah*, v, 13, which is attributed to different Tannaim in different sources: B. Ta 7a, Mak 10a.
61. E.g., *Talmud Torah*, chap. iii, particularly 1, 2, 3, 6, 8, 10, 12, 13. In PhM, introduction (pp. 50–52), Maimonides separates names mentioned in the Mishnah in connection with laws from those mentioned in connection with stories. See the appendix to this chapter, below, pp. 176–87.

As a subcategory of this rubric, mention should be made of Maimonides' digressions and/or explanations concerning textual criticism. Thus, when a ruling might appear to be strange or at odds with incontrovertible sources or explicit precedents, Maimonides may merely point out that these rest on corrupt texts while his formulation is based on the authentic version. The following passage shows the amplitude of expository-polemical-personal emphases integrated into a forceful statement concerning his painstaking quest for textual precision and the incontestable superiority of his results:

> There are versions of the Gemara in which it is written: "If a man says to his fellow, 'Do not pay me save in the presence of witnesses,' and the borrower says, 'I paid you in the presence of such-a-one and such-a-one who have since departed overseas,' he is *not to be believed.*" This is a scribal error which has misled those who have taught in accordance with these books. I have investigated the old versions and found therein that the reading is "he *is to be believed.*" There has come into my hands in Egypt part of an old Gemara written on parchments, as they were wont to write approximately five hundred years ago, and I have found two copies of this proposition in these parchments, in both of which it is written, "And if he said, 'I paid you before such-a-one and such-a-one who have since departed overseas,' he is to be believed."
>
> Because of a similar error which occurs in some books, some of the Geonim have taught. . . . This teaching of the Geonim, too, is based upon their books in which it is written. . . . This too is a scribal error, the version I have found in the parchments reading, "He went and paid him in privacy."
>
> The above teaching is therefore contrary to the rule as it appears in the Gemara, where the reading is corrected in the manner stated above.[62]

The following is a more compressed example of the same tendency: "There are some Geonim who taught that. . . . The text

---

62. *Malweh wĕ-Loweh*, xv, 2; see also ShM, negative 199; PhM, Ṭohărot, introduction (p. 31). Maimonides encouraged the critical quest for textual accuracy; see his pungent observation, *Tĕšubot*, 442 (p. 721): וכי המשנה ספר העזרה היא שאין בה אות חסירה או יתירה? As for his producing what we would call an "eclectic text" of the Mishnah, based on Spanish versions, see J. N. Epstein, *Mabo' lĕ-Nusaḥ ham-Mishnah*, p. 1276. For text-criticism of responsa, see, e.g., Ibn Megas, *Tĕšubot*, 114; R. Abraham Maimonides, *Tĕšubot*, 82 (p. 109).

of the Talmud, however, does not indicate this conclusion, and these authorities had an error in their copies of it. I have long since examined many ancient copies of the Talmud and found the matter to be as we have stated it."[63]

(2) *Original views, personal preferences, autobiographical statements*

Not only does Maimonides sometimes identify previous sources, texts, and authorities—with an occasional foray into paleography—but he also identifies personal views, private preferences, and individual inclinations. In other words, being a real, vibrant, self-conscious author, he breaks through the veneer of anonymity and impersonality and leaves a direct and immediately visible imprint, in addition to the invisible one which can be brought to the surface by patient analysis and X-ray procedures. There are, first of all, nearly two hundred original sentences, inferences, qualifications, and applications, usually identified by the formula "it would appear to me" but sometimes by such variants as "I say," "the things appear to me," "therefore I say," "it is most probable in my opinion."[64] Sometimes these original views stand alone and sometimes the introductory formula serves to mark their conflict with others (usually the Geonim, but also R. Isaac Alfasi and even Maimonides' father). For example:

There are some Geonim who disagree with the above and say that the poor can acquire title only to those things that an ordinary man can acquire, and therefore cannot acquire title to a thing not in existence.

I, however, am not inclined to agree with this opinion, because while one is not under obligation to transfer any object, he is under obligation to fulfill a promise made to give to charity or to consecrate an object to the Temple, even as he is commanded to fulfill a vow, as we have explained in the Laws Concerning Vows of Valuation.[65]

---

63. *Ĭšuṭ*, xi, 13; also *Gerušin*, ix, 31.
64. See the latest and comprehensive listing by J. Levinger, *Darke ham-Mahăšabah šel ha-RaMBaM* (Tel Aviv, 1965), appendix 3 (pp. 210ff.). Of special interest is such a short passage as *Bikkurim*, x, 17, which contains both "therefore I say" and "it appears to me."
65. *Mĕkirah*, xxii, 17. The reference ("who disagree with the above") is to the law mentioned just previously in xxii, 15. See I. Twersky, "Some Aspects of the Jewish Attitude toward the Welfare State," *Tradition*, v (1963), 155, n. 16.

Concerning a detail of ritual slaughtering, Maimonides concludes: "My revered father belonged to those who declared it forbidden, while I am of those who declare it permitted."[66]

These soft and unobtrusive formulae, speaking to us almost in a barely audible whisper, occasionally introduce fresh and innovative options with far-reaching implications. A good example is Maimonides' opinion that genuine Rabbinic ordination (*sĕmikah*) may be restored if there is a consensus among the Sages of Israel. The entire paragraph illustrates the expansive quality, expository style, and explanatory effort of Maimonides. After first stating that "No one is qualified to act as judge . . . unless he has been ordained by one who has himself been ordained. Moses our teacher ordained Joshua by laying his hands upon him . . . He likewise ordained the seventy elders. . . . The elders ordained others, who in turn ordained their successors. Hence there was an uninterrupted succession of ordained judges, reaching back to the tribunal of Joshua—indeed, to the tribunal of Moses our teacher," and after describing the "procedure throughout the generations" concerning ordination and its vicissitudes, Maimonides adds in low key:

> It seems to me that if all the wise men in the Land of Israel agreed to appoint judges and to ordain them, the ordination would be valid, empowering the ordained to adjudicate cases involving fines and to ordain others. If what we have said is true, the question arises, Why were the Rabbis disturbed over the matter of ordination, apprehending the abolition of the laws involving fines? Because Israel is scattered and agreement on the part of all is impossible. If, however, there were one ordained by a man who had himself been ordained, no unanimity would be necessary. He would have the right to adjudicate cases involving fines because he would be an ordained judge. But this matter requires careful reflection.[67]

---

66. *Šĕḥiṭah*, xi, 10. See the reference in IT, xx; also PhM, 'Eḍ 1:3 (p. 284); 4:7 (p. 312); PhM, Sheḅu 6:7 (p. 270); and see above, chap. I, n.9. Sometimes a personal reference expresses agreement, e.g., *Malweh wĕ-Loweh*, xxv, 14.

67. *Sanhedrin*, iv, 1, 2, 11; PhM, Sanh 1:3 (p. 148) supplements this by explaining Maimonides' rationale. For some halakic analyses, see A. Maimon, *Ḥidduš has-Sanhedrin* (Jerusalem, 1957). See J. Katz, "Maḥăloket has-Sĕmikah," *Zion*, XVI (1951), 28ff.; M.

This restrained paragraph provided the ideational backdrop and juridical stimulus for a colorful, significant, and quite acerbic controversy in sixteenth-century Judaism, whose essence was an abortive attempt to resuscitate traditional and fully authoritative ordination and hence revitalize judicial procedure.

Now while these personal intrusions definitely contradict the formal pronouncements and assumptions covering an anonymous monolithic code—technically they should have been inconspicuously absorbed into the texture of the work and not specially colored—Maimonides did provide a retrospective explanation for this in his letter to R. Phinehas: he identified these views in order to call attention to their originality and by implication emphasize the consensual character of the remainder of his work, which he claimed was fully based upon the Talmud. His message was that there was nothing enigmatic or inscrutable about his Code; all was clear and forthright, and completely congruent with the sources. The rule of "from the negative we implicitly derive the affirmative," and vice versa, was operative; this delimited stamp of individuality reinforced the overriding universality. While this explanation leaves the issue of selectivity beclouded—one could convincingly argue that there are many strikingly original views, some of which we shall subsequently note, not identified by this rubric—it undeniably serves a constructive purpose. The few exceptions to anonymity entrench the Code's universality.

The *Mishneh Torah,* however, goes beyond recording its author's personal interpretations or inferences. It contains pointed autobiographical pronouncements describing personal pietistic practices, halakic decisions, or experiences and observations. His statement concerning the Scroll of the Law which he himself wrote reflects fully the unabashed personal emphasis and the compelling motives (i.e., scribal chaos) for this apparent digression:

Inasmuch as in all the Scrolls that I have seen I have noticed serious incorrectness in these matters, while authorities on the Masorah, who write treatises and compilations with the aim of pointing out the sec-

---

Benayahu, in *Y. Baer Jubilee Volume* (Jerusalem, 1961), pp. 25off.; C. Dimitrovsky, *Sĕfunot,* x (1966), 113ff. Note that the assumption is reflected in *Šofar,* ii, 9.

tions that are closed and those that are open, differ according to the variations in the Scrolls on which they rely, I deemed it fit to write here a list of the sections which are closed and those which are open, as also the forms in which the songs of the Pentateuch are written, so that all the Scrolls may be corrected from, and compared with, them. The copy upon which I relied is the well-known Egyptian codex which contains the twenty-four books of Scripture and which had been in Jerusalem for several years, used as the standard text for the examination of Scrolls. Everyone relied upon it because it had been examined by Ben Asher, who closely studied it for many years and examined it again whenever it was being copied. This codex was the text upon which I relied in the Scroll of the Law that I myself wrote according to the rules.[68]

His description of the proper practice for the day preceding the fast of the Ninth of Ab is equally enthralling. After codifying the accepted law and its prevalent practice, he records the supererogatory practice of pious men and ends with a pointed but poignant personal confession:

The practice of the pious men of old, however, was as follows: On the eve of the Ninth of Ab, each man in his solitude would be served dry bread and salt, and he would dip this in water and eat it while seated between the oven and the stove. He would wash it down with a pitcher of water, drunk in sadness, desolation, and tears, like a person seated before his dead kinsman. This procedure, or one very much like it, is the one appropriate to scholars. In all my life, I have never eaten cooked food, even cooked lentils, on the eve of the Ninth of Ab, unless this day was a Sabbath.[69]

Brief personal observations are recorded. For example, after defining the basic philanthropic institutions of the community—*kuppah* (charity fund) and *tamḥuy* (charity plate)—Maimonides notes: "We have never seen or heard about a Jewish

---

68. *Sefer Torah*, viii, 4; also ix, 10. See M. Goshen-Gottstein, "The Authenticity of the Aleppo Codex," *Textus*, I (1966), 17–58. The problem persisted, as mirrored in R. Meir hal-Levi Abulafia, *Masoret Sĕyag lat-Torah* (Berlin, 1760), and R. Menahem ham-Me'iri, *Ḳiryat Sefer*, ed. M. Hershler (Jerusalem, 1956). See I. Ta-Shema, *KS*, XLV (1970), 119ff. See also I. Polgar, *'Ezer had-Dat* (reprinted, Jerusalem, 1970), p. 86.
69. *Ta'ăniyyot*, v, 9 (cf. R. Solomon Luria, *Tĕšubot*, 30). See I. Twersky, "Ḥămiššah Sĕfarim lĕ-RaN," *Tarbiz*, XXXVII (1968), 326. See for other examples *Tĕšubot*, 136 (p. 261). See PhM, Pes 10:3 (p. 202).

community that did not have a *kuppah.*"⁷⁰ Elsewhere he interjects: "All the places that I have seen . . ."⁷¹ In sum, the reader is periodically brought face to face with an author who selectively shares his experiences, family background, environment, and travels, thereby injecting fresh motifs into routine rules and generalizations.

Sometimes one has the impression that the personal emphasis is masked by a generalized reference to "the custom of my teachers." For example, Maimonides is of the opinion that on the Feast of Tabernacles the Sanctification benediction (*kiddus̆*) should be recited while standing, then one should recite the benediction *"les̆eb̲ bas-sukkah"* ("to dwell in the booth"), and sit down. "This procedure, with the Sanctification benediction recited standing as just explained, was the one customarily observed on the first night of the Feast of Tabernacles by my teachers and the other Rabbis of Spain." This practice, apparently based on a literalist understanding of the word *les̆eb̲,* was severely criticized by many medieval halakists. Maimonides presents it nonchalantly as the prevalent Spanish custom.⁷² His presentation of *'asmak̲ta* confirms this impression by illustrating concretely how he fully discusses a law, its controversial aspects, and certain guiding precedents, and indicates at the end his own practice as well: "When the Sages of Spain wished to validate a transfer by *'asmak̲ta,* they made the following arrangement. . . . *We would act* in accord with this procedure concerning all stipulations between husband and wife . . . and in all similar matters."⁷³ Note also the merger of a personal interpretation (qualification of some laws of evidence) with a reference to widespread precedent: "For we say that the strictness of the rule (applies only to the right of remarriage and not to financial matters). . . . Such is the daily practice of all the courts, and we have heard of no dissent in the

---

70. *Mattĕnot̲ 'Āniyyim,* ix, 3.
71. *Ḥanukkah,* v, 14.
72. *Sukkah,* vi, 12; R. Isaac ben Abba Mari, *Sefer ha-'Iṭṭur* (reprinted, New York, 1955), *Hilk̲ot̲ Sukkah,* beginning (p. 152), refers to it as *da'at̲ ḥiṣoni* ("heretical opinion"). See R. Joshua ibn Shu'ayb, *Dĕras̆ot̲* (Jerusalem, 1969), p. 94b.
73. *Mĕk̲irah,* xi, 18 (italics mine). Note also *Sabbat̲,* xxix, 14.

## FORM

matter."[74] The use of exempla, personal or historical, moral or intellectual, individual or collective, is a significant thread unifying these two categories.

(3) *Multiple opinions*

Another clear breach of the codificatory rigor and restraint is the fact that all his announced intentions of presenting ex cathedra unilateral norms notwithstanding, he does cite two or more opinions. Sometimes—and this may obviously reflect a lack of certitude or untypical Maimonidean diffidence—he will merely record the multiple views, thereby inviting his readers or critics to defend one or the other. The precise form of a liturgical text, the determination of the proper blessing over certain foods, aspects of Temple laws, dietary laws, oaths, and vows are treated in this pluralistic and standoff manner.[75]

On occasion there is a very low-keyed indication of preference between views, either by juxtaposition, simple statement of fact, or a mild addition. For example—and this is a three-tiered formulation—"The juice pressed out of the sweet canes . . . requires in the opinion of all the Geonim the blessing. . . . Some are of the opinion that the blessing is. . . . I say that . . . the only blessing to be said is. . . ."[76] Or "The *kidduš* may be said only over wine that would have been fit for libation upon the Temple altar. Accordingly, if honey or leaven is mixed with the wine . . . *kidduš* may not be said over it. This is the rule in all the countries of the West (Maghrib). Some authorities, however, allow it . . . because, they say. . . ."[77] On a rather crucial matter of divorce procedure, Maimonides writes: "If a scribe writes a writ of divorce, it is valid. . . . There is, however, one authority who maintains that . . . it is null and void, because. . . . This view does not seem correct to me, because. . . ."[78]

---

74. *Naḥălot*, vii, 3. The use of exempla is common in medieval moralistic literature; see, e.g., *Sefer Ḥăsidim*, and R. Baḥya ibn Paḳuda, *Sefer Ḥobot hal-Lĕbabot*.
75. *Bĕrakot*, ii, 4; viii, 14; *Šĕḳalim*, iii, 9; *Nĕḏarim*, ii, 4, 6; *Ma'ăkalot 'Ăsurot*, iii, 1; vii, 9. See the responsum attributed to RABD, edited by S. Assaf in *Ḳobeṣ ha-RaMBaM* (Jerusalem, 1935), p. 278. On multiple explanations, see also MN, I, 21.
76. *Bĕrakot*, viii, 5.
77. *Šabbat*, xxix, 14 (and see *'Issure Mizbeaḥ*, v, 1).
78. *Gerušin*, iii, 8.

A rather striking example, because of its contents as well as its form, concerns astronomical theory: "As to the solar year, there are certain Jewish Sages who have held that it consists of 365 days and one-quarter of a day, . . . while some have held that the fraction is less than a quarter of a day. And the same disagreement may be found also among the Greek and Persian scholars." After fully explaining the calculations for intercalation according to both opinions, he coolly adds: "I believe that at the time of the Supreme Court *(Sanhedrin)* . . . the court did in fact rely upon this value. . . . For this value is nearer to the truth than the other value, and agrees more closely with the propositions advanced in the science of astronomy than the other value."[79]

Maimonides may cite a novel view of the "great Sages," implicitly opposed by others, and add his personal endorsement: "Some great Sages have taught . . . and this teaching is sound in reason, and in accordance therewith judgment should be rendered in practice."[80] At the other end of the spectrum, the following passage (concerning the ritual propriety of immersion pools) is intriguing. Maimonides records that "some of the scholars of the West have taught as follows. . . . According to this teaching . . ." He proceeds to note the radical implications and then concludes: "but never have we seen anyone who carried out such a thing in practice."[81] Apparently the logic and consistency of the reasoning are beyond reproach and hence deserve to be noted. In any event, authoritativeness may be achieved by various forms of

---

79. *Ḳidduš ha-Ḥodeš*, ix, 1. For astronomy, see *Sanhedrin*, ii, 1.
80. *Malweh wĕ-Loweh*, xxi, 1 (against Alfasi); xxv, 13, 14; also *Šĕḳirut*, ii, 3 (against Ibn Megas). Sometimes he specifies that he is rejecting his masters' opinions, e.g., *Išut*, v, 15; *Zĕḳiyyah u-Mattanah*, iii, 8; *Šĕluḥin*, vi, 5; *Malweh wĕ-Loweh*, xxvii, 1.
81. *Miḳwa'ot*, iv, 9. See also *Šĕḥiṭah*, xi, 6: "On this basis it would logically follow that if a lung is found to have suspended adhesions . . . one should cut the adhesion, remove the lung, and inflate it in warm water. . . . If the water does not bubble, indicating that the lung is free from any perforation, the animal should be permitted. . . . But we have never found anyone who had rendered a decision to this effect, nor have we heard of any place where such a procedure is followed." His son R. Abraham (*Tĕšubot*, 61), recording that some people did in fact implement this view, argues that while logically their position is unassailable, they were not justified in changing the prevalent custom. R. Simeon Duran (*Tĕšubot*, iv, 31), in a discussion of judicial methodology, raises the issue of whether a codifier identifies with the first or second of the views he quotes.

gentle and simple assertion, taking the reader into his confidence and trusting the reader's judgment. While instructing, he appears as a colleague because the reader's choice is not completely eliminated.[82]

Sometimes he will use forcefully elaborate reasons for his preferential treatment of a specific position. This practice may thus contain an argumentative-interpretative dimension. The divergent view which he wishes to squash may have been a respectable or prevalent one and hence could not merely—or apodictically—be discarded. Or to alter the perspective, he may be seen as pleading a case, and since there was no authoritative structure which would automatically guarantee acceptance of his option (for as we noted in Chapter I, Maimonides did not have the power or authority to codify in the conventional sense of the term), he must be exhortatory and persuasive. The argument may be full-dress or it may be compressed in a pithy postscript: "it is not proper to do it this way" or "and this is the proper way to judge."[83] A completely peremptory decision might miss the mark in such cases, while a dash of reasoning or a heavy dose of argument, depending on the circumstances, would tip the scales in the desired direction. We can easily establish that Maimonides does not always cite in his Code all divergent views which he knew and *ex silentio* rejected.[84] Hence we are left with the phenomenon of his citing multiple opinions either in order to preserve them or in order to argue explicitly against one of them, or perhaps because he could not reach absolute certitude concerning the issue.

---

82. Cf., in a different context, the evocative formulation of E. Auerbach, *Literary Language and Its Public in Late Latin Antiquity and in the Middle Ages* (New York, 1965), pp. 297, 300, 310.

83. *Milah*, iii, 1; *Malweh wĕ-Loweh*, xxvi, 11; *'Išuṭ*, vi, 14. Also *Gerušin*, i, 16 (merely recording a dissenting Gaonic view) and iii, 8 (elaborating his reason for rejecting the Gaonic view, cited also by Alfasi, on B. Giṭ 86a); note also the gloss of RaSHBaM, ed. S. Friedman, *Ḳobeṣ 'al Yad*, VIII (1976), 215. In *Šĕluḥin*, iii, 7, Maimonides writes: "Such is the rule as it seems to me from the Gemara. The Geonim, however, have provided. . . . They have further provided. . . . These enactments are tenuous and weak, for. . . ." This argumentative aspect may be found even when the alternate view is not cited, e.g., *Ṭo'en wĕ-Niṭ'an*, viii, 10.

84. E.g., *'Išuṭ*, iii, 23; *Ḳobeṣ*, I, 3b.

Very significant also in the light of our comments on textual criticism is the case where Maimonides quietly and unceremoniously cites two versions of a Talmudic text without choosing between them. After formulating the law, he adds: "In some copies of the Talmud this rule reads as follows . . ."[85] There is no room here for theoretical subtlety or interpretative ingenuity. The issue concerns manuscript evidence and is left moot. We may note one brief passage which combines a statement in the first person, a curt critique of the alternative view, a "generous" suggestion of scribal error, and a confident conclusion: "I have seen statements by Geonim . . . and (they are so wide of the mark) that it is not worth refuting them at length. Most probably they are the result of scribal error. And as for the truth, we have already explained its way."[86]

In short, all oracular pronouncements notwithstanding, Maimonides acknowledged by his actions that total finality and absolute uniformity, undocumented and undemonstrated, were a wistful goal. There is creative tension between the program and its realization. A consistently Delphic manual was beyond reach; one might even contend that it was never unreservedly intended.

## (4) *Variant customs*

Given the fact, on the one hand, that custom wielded great influence in halakic debate, and on the other, that there was no completely uniform practice for many facets of ceremonial or ritual law, it is not surprising that Maimonides, again contravening his own directives concerning unitary and systematic formulation, cited variant customs without endorsing or rejecting one or the other. This category is basically identical with the previous one which is theoretical-interpretative while this is empirical-consuetudinary; together they provide elasticity, some relief from the steady and solid authoritativeness, and hence a measure of collegiality, real or rhetorical, between student-reader and mentor-

---

85. *Yom Ṭob*, ii, 12.
86. *Maʿăśer Šeni*, ix, 12. See also *'Issure Bi'ah*, xi, 15, concerning corrupt responsa of Geonim.

author. The common denominator is the pluralism, recording practical alternatives and consequently preserving them for possible future use.[87] It might follow, therefore, that when his reference to a custom is characterized by sustained harshness and outraged impetuosity, his aim is to repudiate this view or practice once and for all. It is hard to imagine, for example, that Maimonides would detachedly record the practice of those "who write names of angels, holy names, a Biblical text, or inscriptions within the mĕzuzah" and not pass judgment on it, for these practitioners are in his opinion "fools . . . who not only fail to fulfill" the commandment but also pervert and distort it. As a jurisprudent he could not permit such entanglement in the coils of error and superstition. Moreover, it was too crucial and widespread to be blithely or benignly overlooked. It had to be crushed stridently.[88] However, while Maimonides may condemn by acidulous stricture, energetic argument, and forceful rejection in practice, an overview of his writings shows that he also could deliver a coup de grace by silence, by calculated omission and neglect. Many customs, mentioned in his own or in contemporary writings, are excised from the Code and hence, at least in his opinion, consigned to oblivion.[89]

As in the previous category, there are instances when Maimonides gently chooses between customs, identifying his own practice, indicating mild preference, or noting softly that one of the two customs mentioned is not very widespread. Concerning the annual or triennial cycle of Torah reading, Maimonides writes: "The custom prevailing throughout all Israel is that the reading of the Torah is completed in one year. . . .

---

87. See 'Ed 1:5, 6, and PhM, ad loc. (p. 266); *Tĕšubot*, 138 (p. 266), 259 (p. 486); Twersky, *Rabad*, pp. 166–67.

88. *Mĕzuzah*, v, 4, and see PhM, Soṭ 7:4 (p. 267); MN, I, 61, 62. R. Moses hak-Kohen, in his strictures, notes the prevalence of the custom; see *Haśśaḡot ha-RaMaK*, ed. S. Atlas (Jerusalem, 1969), p. 37. See also R. Margaliyot, *Ha-RaMBaM wĕhaz-Zohar* (Jerusalem, 1954), p. 28; E. Urbach, *Ba'ăle hat-Tosafot* (Jerusalem, 1955), p. 138. For the stridency of Maimonides' formulation, see, e.g., *Tĕšubah*, v, 2; '*Akum*, xi, 12; *Talmud Torah*, iii, 10; *Sanhedrin*, xxv, 4. See also *Šĕḥiṭah*, xi, 15.

89. E.g., *Tĕfillin*, iii, 5, and *Tĕšubot*, 289 (pp. 542–45); *Šabbaṭ*, iii, 8, and *Tĕšubot*, 304 (p. 562).

126 INTRODUCTION TO THE CODE OF MAIMONIDES

Some complete the reading in three years, but this is not a prevalent custom."[90] A certain way of winding the white threads used to make ṣiṣit is described, and Maimonides notes, "this is our custom." However, he records without further comment that "some pay no attention to this point."[91] A detail of laws of šĕḥiṭah is discussed as follows: "There are also places where it is customary to inflate the lung in order to see whether it has been perforated, but in most places the custom is not to inflate it. . . . In Spain and in the Maghrib we have never inflated a lung unless . . ."[92] His description of the recitation of the Hallel illustrates his preferred prescription, together with an inevitably open-ended presentation:

Which are the passages to be omitted? . . . This is the custom accepted generally, but there are places where the omitted passages are different. . . .

There are places in which it is customary to repeat a second time every sentence. . . . If the custom of a particular locality is to repeat these verses, they should be repeated; if the local custom is not to repeat them, they should not be repeated.

The customary manner of reciting the Hallel in the time of the Sages of old was as follows. . . . This was the original custom and the one that should properly be followed. Nowadays, however, all the places that I have seen have different customs both for the reading of the Hallel and for the response of the congregation, and no two customs are alike.[93]

One may even hear an echo of exasperation here, but the heterogeneous reality remains, unhedged and untrimmed.

In the light of this, we should be particularly attentive to his unannotated recording of divergent practices, for it may be of general methodological-motivational significance. While critics of the Mishneh Torah might with firm partisanship register dissenting opinions and unqualifiedly endorse them, thereby reflect-

---

90. Tĕfillah, xiii, 1. Cf. A. Büchler, "The Reading of the Law . . . in a Triennial Cycle," JQR, V (1893), 420–68; VI (1894), 1–73; J. Mann, The Bible as Read and Preached in the Old Synagogue (Cincinnati, 1943).
91. Ṣiṣit, i, 9.
92. Šĕḥiṭah, xi, 11. Note carefully the rest of this chapter.
93. Ḥănukkah, iii, 14.

ing and refurbishing local practices and traditions,[94] Maimonides' freedom of decision in this respect was considerably hampered. Inasmuch as he envisaged his Code as fulfilling a universal role, his standards had to transcend localism or nativism. This meant leaving intact the consuetudinary diversity which inheres in such areas as prayer, liturgy, benedictions, reading of the Torah, phylacteries, circumcision, marriage ceremony, and ritual slaughter.[95]

The following comments on popular matters illustrate beautifully his noncommittal description:

It is a duty to recite these three blessings daily and then read a small portion of the words of Torah. It is the custom of the people to read the Priestly Benediction (Num. 6:24–26). In some places the section dealing with the Daily Sacrifices (Num. 28:1–8) is read. In others both these sections are read.

The early Sages lauded the one who reads every day hymns from the Psalter beginning with the Psalm of David (Ps. 145) and continuing until the end of the book. The people are also accustomed to read verses before and after these Psalms. . . .

In some places it is the custom . . . to read daily the Song of the Red Sea (Exod. 15:1–18). . . . In other places the custom is to read the Song of *Ha'ăzinu* (Deut. 32). Some individuals read both Songs. All this is governed by custom.[96]

The standoff conclusion quoted above concerning *Hallel*, "and no two customs are alike", also sums it all up very concisely. Maimonides the codifier inevitably becomes for a while the student of comparative customs, and we may recall that it is exactly during his time that the genre of "customs literature" was beginning to burgeon.[97] In Bracton's terms, one part of the *Mishneh Torah* might be entitled *"De legibus et consuetudinibus."*

94. This determines the relationship of *Haggahot Maimoniyyot* to *Mishneh Torah* or R. Moses Isserles to R. Joseph Karo. See Twersky, *Rabad*, pp. 154–55; idem., "The Shulḥan 'Aruk," pp. 141–59.

95. This does not include those cases where the Talmud recognizes and institutionalizes diversity, as in *Ḥameṣ u-Maṣṣah*, viii, 8; *Tĕfillah*, ii, 16; see *Tĕfillah*, xiii, 1; *Ta'ăniyyot*, v, 6; *Bĕrakot*, viii, 14; *Milah*, iii, 1; *Šĕbitat 'Aśor*, iii, 10 (explains both views); *'Išut*, x, 4; *'Issure Bi'ah*, xi, 5–7.

96. *Tĕfillah*, vii, 11–13; also v, 15; cf. vii, 9.

97. Twersky, *Rabad*, p. 242; see *'Išut*, xxiii, 11: "There are many customs regarding dowry."

Traditional practice often provided its own sanction—"custom causes the law to be suspended"[98]—thereby becoming practically sacrosanct, and no amount of abstract halakic reasoning or demonstration could prevail against it. Instead of focusing upon interpretation, as one would ordinarily do in questions of law, here the existing tradition is the point of departure. Hence, while "local" writers could apodictically defend their customs with zeal and verve—"we rely upon custom, and whoever changes it is at a disadvantage," or "the only guiding principle we have is the custom of the people," or simply and sturdily "our custom is"[99]—the universally geared *Mishneh Torah* had, surprisingly enough, to reflect a measure of relativism or indetermination. The *Mishneh Torah* was thus doubly vulnerable in the area of consuetudinary law. When Maimonides was monolithic, readers of the *Mishneh Torah* would undertake to give their local customs and traditions—be they Provençal, Franco-German, etc.—a fair hearing alongside of the predominantly Spanish-African-Babylonian views formulated by Maimonides. When Maimonides was pluralistic in his formulations, readers happily oblivious of the diversity would underscore their own dominant traditions.

As for Maimonides' attitude to custom (*minhaḡ*) generally, certain guidelines are discernible. Custom, generically and genetically, is characterized by multiplicity. In the *Mishneh Torah* introduction Maimonides explains in historical and juridical terms the reasons for the latitudinarianism inherent in custom as distinct from Talmudic law:

> If a court established in any country after the time of the Talmud made decrees and ordinances or introduced customs for those residing in its particular country or for residents of other countries, its enactments did not gain the acceptance of all Israel because of the remoteness of the Jewish settlements and the difficulties of travel. And as the court of any particular country consisted of individuals (whose authority was not

---

98. *Sof* 14:17 (ed. M. Higger [New York, 1937], p. 270, and bibliography in n. 103). P. BM 7:1. Also M. Margaliyot, *Ha-Ḥillukim šebben 'Anše Mizraḥ u-Bĕne 'Ereṣ Yiśra'el* (Jerusalem, 1938).

99. See these and other references in Twersky, *Rabad*, p. 241. Note the following *hassagot* on the MT: *Tĕfillah*, xii, 9; xiii, 6; *Bĕrakot*, xi, 16; *Milah*, iii, 1; *'Eruḇin*, i, 16; *Sukkah*, vi, 12; *'Issure Bi'ah*, xi, 18; *'Išut*, iii, 23.

universally recognized), while the Supreme Court of seventy-one members had, several years before the compilation of the Talmud, ceased to exist, no compulsion is exercised on those living in one country to observe the customs of another country; nor is any court directed to issue a decree that had been issued by another court in the same country. So too, if one of the Geonim taught that a certain way of judgment was correct, and it became clear to a court at a later date that this was not in accordance with the view of the Gemara, the earlier authority is not necessarily followed but that view is adopted which seems more reasonable, whether it be that of an earlier or of a later authority.

The foregoing observations refer to rules, decrees, ordinances, and customs that originated after the Talmud had been compiled. But whatever is already mentioned in the Babylonian Talmud is binding on all Israel. And every city and country is bound to observe all the customs observed by the Sages of the Gemara, promulgate their decrees, and uphold their institutions, on the ground that all the customs, decrees, and institutions mentioned in the Talmud received the assent of all Israel; and those Sages who instituted the ordinances, issued the decrees, introduced the customs, gave the decisions, and taught that a certain ruling was correct, constituted the total body or the majority of Israel's wise men. They were the leaders who received from each other the traditions concerning the fundamentals of Judaism in unbroken succession back to Moses our teacher, upon whom be peace.[100]

Negatively, there is here a measure of laissez-faire, a license to diversify; positively, there is a sturdy rationale for regionalism. A communal ordinance (*takkanat hak-kahal*) was binding even though it could not compete with Talmudic law—custom, decree, or ordinance—for universality, because it lacked *haskamah, consensus omnium*. The following statement in the *Mishneh Torah* is striking: "The Geonim have said that in Babylonia they had different customs . . . but these customs have not spread among the majority of Israel, and many great scholars in most places disagree with them. It is proper, therefore, to follow the rule of the Tal-

---

100. MT, introduction. For the universality of the Talmud, see also *Mamrim*, ii, 2 (and KM, ad loc.). On consensus (*haskamah;* Arabic *ijmā'*), see *Sanhedrin*, xxiv, 2; *Naḥalot*, x, 7. The formulation about local custom is the basis for *takkanot hak-kahal;* see *Tešubot*, 152 (p. 295). Maimonides was cognizant not only of the basic role of local custom but also of the possible conditioning of custom by external influences; see, e.g., below, n. 111, and my Hebrew article in the *Harry Wolfson Jubilee Volume* (Jerusalem, 1965), p. 179, n.64.

mud and decide accordingly."[101] Lack of acceptance is the crucial determinant; unquestioning consensus is what makes the Talmud universal, but even the validation of regional custom is contingent upon its striking deep roots.

Actually, the types of *minhāḡ* could be briefly catalogued as follows: *minhāḡ* of the prophets; *minhāḡ* of the Sages; *minhāḡ* of all Israel; *minhāḡ* of the people; *minhāḡ*, without any qualification. The first three types are clearly universal, the nature of the fourth has to be determined ad hoc, while the fifth is certainly local.[102]

These distinctions, of course, are independent of, and should not be obscured by, those cases where the Talmud itself recognizes regional diversity of practices. We are dealing with post-Talmudic heterogeneity which, in its own right, should not be taken lightly. Customs may be endowed with their own tenacity without having to claim universality. They are, moreover, not only prescriptive but also expressive of a sense of solidarity and identification. Indeed, one may be culpable just for departing from communal practice and discipline.[103]

The main import is the constraining force of custom, be it universal or local. "Tradition and practice are important and mighty pillars in judicial decision."[104] Maimonides will, therefore, on occasion specify the geographic provenance and applicability of a custom, thereby forestalling both criticism and misunderstanding while not compromising the universality of his Code. Concerning the synagogue, Maimonides writes: "Synagogues and houses of study must be treated with respect. They are swept and sprinkled to lay the dust. In Spain and in the West (Maghrib), in Babylonia and in the Holy Land, it is customary to kindle lamps in the synagogues and to spread mats on the floor on which the

---

101. *'Iśuṭ*, xiv, 14.
102. E.g., *Ḥameṣ u-Maṣṣah*, v, 17, *'Iśuṭ*, xiv, 14; *Gerušin*, i, 27; iv, 11 (citing the text of the geṭ); *Ma'ăkalōṭ 'Ăsurōṭ*, vi, 7; *Zĕkiyyah u-Mattanah*, vii, 1 (*minhāḡ pašuṭ bĕ-roḇ hammĕdīnōṭ*); *'Aḇel*, iv, 1 (*minhāḡ Yiśra'el bĕ-meṭim*). A review of Maimonidean references to widespread or univeral custom (*minhāḡ pašuṭ*) in light of other evidence would be enlightening; see, e.g., *'Issure Bi'ah*, xi, 5, and M. Zucker, '*Al Targum RaSaG lat-Torah* (New York, 1959), p. 115, n. 492; *Tĕfillah*, xi, 4, and N. Wieder, *Haśpa'ot*, p. 69.
103. *Tĕšuḇah*, iii, 11.
104. *Šĕmiṭṭah wĕ-Yoḇel*, x, 6. The implication is that tradition and practice cannot always be completely rationalized or conceptualized. See *Tĕšuḇōṭ*, 389 (p. 668).

worshipers sit. In the lands of Edom (Christian countries) they sit in synagogues on chairs (or benches)."[105] The prayer book (*siddur*), at the end of Book Two, begins with "the people are accustomed (*nahāgu*)," and the phrase is used repeatedly in the prayer book as well as in the laws pertaining to liturgy. Students of liturgy and of Maimonides' *siddur* in particular have noted the great extent to which his treatment of prayer reflects local practices; his prayer book synthesizes Babylonian traditions and local Egyptian practices. All this material is therefore punctuated by references to "the custom is."[106]

After a complex discussion of certain restrictions in marital relations, Maimonides contrasts the "widespread custom of Babylonia, Palestine, Spain, and the Maghrib" with what "we have heard concerning the practice in France," and concludes that this matter depends upon local custom."[107] In such rounded formulations the contrasts are clear and explicit. Sometimes only the local custom is described, the contrast being implicit in the territorial delimitation: "the prevailing custom in all our cities in Spain is . . .";[108] or in more inclusive terms, "nevertheless, it has long been customary in Babylonia, Spain, and all of the Maghrib . . .", "it has long been customary in Babylonia, the Land of Israel, Spain, and the cities of the Maghrib."[109] In such cases critics need not comment, for Maimonides himself, his implicit endorsement notwithstanding, had delimited the applicability of his statement and intimated regional variability.

The following is a particularly interesting instance which became the subject for heated recriminations: "The widespread custom in Spain and Babylonia is that one who has had a seminal emission may not recite prayers until he has washed all of his

---

105. *Tefillah*, xi, 5.
106. See the edition by D. Goldschmidt in *Yĕdi'ot ham-Makon lĕ-Ḥeker haś-Śirah ha-'Ibrit*, VII (1959), 158ff.; I. Elbogen, "Der Ritus im Mischne Thora," *MbM*, I, 319–31; J. Dienstag, "The Prayer Book of Maimonides," *Leo Jung Jubilee Volume*, ed. M. Kasher, N. Lamm, and L. Rosenfeld (New York, 1962), pp. 53–63. See also *Śofar*, iii, 10; *Lulaḥ*, vii, 23.
107. *'Issure Bi'ah*, xi, 5, 7; see also PhM, Pes 2:2 (p. 166), and *Ma'ăkalot 'Ăsurot*, xvii, 12.
108. *Ḥănukkah*, iv, 3.
109. *Ḥameṣ u-Maṣṣah*, v, 3, 7; also *Šĕḥitat 'Aśor*, i, 3.

body in water, in accord with the exhortation *Prepare to meet thy God* (Amos 4:12)."[110] In answer to some nameless critics who accused him of ignoring this custom, Maimonides first elaborated that this "custom obtained only in Babylonia and the Maghrib but never existed in all the cities of Rome (Italy), France, and Provence." He rebukes his correspondent (the respected *dayyan* of Alexandria) for hedging and failing to formulate the issue unequivocally by acknowledging the geographic variability of the custom: "You should have informed them . . . that (this is not a principle of Scriptural law)—the matter depends upon custom. All Israelites among the Muslims do immerse themselves while all Israelites among the Christians are not accustomed to immersing themselves." As for his own behavior, he declares with a mixture of flagrant anger and measured pride: "Heaven and earth bear witness that I have never failed to cleanse myself except as a result of sickness. How could I possibly change my custom and the custom of my ancestors without cause?"[111]

Another corollary of the force of custom is the fact that Maimonides will allow custom to overrule or subdue theory; namely, he will abandon what he considers the correct textual interpretation and bow to widespread practice. The *Mishneh Torah* has the following: "It is a widespread custom in our time that a *kohen* (person of priestly descent), even if he is an ignoramus, is the first to read in the Torah, being called even before a great scholar in Israel." Now elsewhere Maimonides argues with verve and ingenuity that a scholar takes precedence over an unlearned *kohen* and indicates how all the sources support this inference. This probably explains why he identified this particular law, which we would have read routinely, as a widespread custom to which he accommodated his interpretation.[112]

However, custom which is rooted in unmistakable error, *minhag ta'ut*, should be uprooted. Venerability and acceptance are

---

110. *Tefillah*, iv, 6 (cf. *Keri'at Šema'*, iv, 8, and *Šebitat 'Asor*, iii, 3).
111. *Kobeṣ*, I, 26a. Sickness is mentioned in *Tefillah*, iv, 6, as exempting one even from the custom. See N. Wieder, *Hašpa'ot 'Islamiyyot* (Oxford, 1947). Cf. also *'Issure Bi'ah*, xiii, 9. Also M. Havazelet, "Hištalšelut Minhag . . . Ba'äle Keri," *Talpiyyot*, VIII (1963), 531ff; and S. Lieberman, *Šeki'in*, p. 10.
112. *Tefillah*, xii, 8; PhM, Giṭ 5:8 (pp. 225–26); *Tešubot*, 135 (p. 256).

## FORM
133

not automatic and unimpeachable sanctions. In medieval terms this is the distinction between a custom *praeter legem*, which is unobjectionable, and a custom *contra legem*, which is intolerable.[113] "The people in most of our cities have the custom of reciting these blessings in the synagogue consecutively. . . . This, however, is an erroneous practice which should not be followed."[114] The custom of standing during the reading of the Ten Commandments provoked Maimonides, and he vigorously rejects the argument of precedent. The fact that there are "some sick people" does not justify spreading the disease and infecting everyone. On the contrary, we should seek to heal all the sick ones. The language is especially vehement and emotional probably because the issue had theological repercussions, i.e., the insistence upon the uniform sanctity of the entire Torah.[115] Sometimes Maimonides will not only label a practice as *minhag ṭa'ut* but will also find a heterodox origin for it: "Similarly, there is a custom which prevails in some places and which is mentioned in the responsa of some of the Geonim. . . . This, too, is not a well-founded custom, but the result of an erroneous decision in these responsa. It is a custom in the manner of the *Minim* (heretics) which is prevalent in these localities, and the inhabitants thereof had learned it from the Sadducees."[116]

Between universal custom, whether instituted by prophets or Sages, and flagrantly erroneous custom is a wide grey area of practices which may or may not appeal to Maimonides; he records them dispassionately, notes their origins, or indicates his own predilection. The *Mishneh Torah* mirrors the fact that custom was a vital religious force and a seething source of halakic energy.

---

113. See, e.g., A. Berger, *Encyclopedic Dictionary of Roman Law* (Philadelphia, 1953), p. 413. The custom concerning the *kohen* rests on another (in his opinion erroneous) interpretation, whereas *minhag ṭa'ut* apparently has no alternate interpretation on which to base itself.
114. *Tefillah*, vii, 9. For the controversial *birkat bětulim* see *Těšubot*, 207 (p. 366).
115. *Těšubot*, 263 (p. 498).
116. *'Issure Bi'ah*, xi, 15. Also see the emphatic statements of R. Abraham Maimonides, *Těšubot*, ed. A. Freimann and S. Goitein (Jerusalem, 1937), pp. 119, 126; RABD, *Haśśagot*, Pes 17a; R. Menaḥem ham-Me'iri, *Magen 'Abot* (London, 1909), pp. 6–11, 102.

## 134 INTRODUCTION TO THE CODE OF MAIMONIDES

Maimonides' statements or obiter dicta in his responsa and other writings all sustain this general approach.[117]

### (5) *Value judgments: counsels of perfection*

The treatment of, and attitude toward, custom lead directly to another trait which, clearly less of an infringement than the previous categories, is not completely congruent with the concept of straightforward and incontestable codification. Not only does the *Mishneh Torah* categorically codify that which is "permitted or prohibited, clean or unclean," but it also, as it were, exhorts and cajoles. It encourages certain behavioral patterns and frowns upon others. It uses value judgments. Certain practices are praised or damned. Even though many of these axiological terms are Talmudic, their judicial and moral import in the codificatory context needs to be appreciated. "If he does any of these things, he is, though fulfilling his duty, guilty of unbecoming conduct."[118] "Whoever . . . acts commendably."[119] "Care should always be taken. . . ."[120] The exhortation concerning *ṣiṣiṭ* is significant: "Although one is not bound . . . still it is not right for a pious man *(ḥasid)*. . . . He should be especially heedful. . . . For scholars it is particularly disgraceful. . . ."[121] A meaningful term, borrowed from Rabbinic parlance, condemns behavior which, although legally valid, "incurs the displeasure of the Sages."[122] Something may be blameworthy even though not formally prohibited.[123]

---

117. E.g., PhM, Pes 2:2 (p. 166); *Tĕšubot*, 138 (p. 266); 267 (p. 507), 304 (p. 562); *Ḳobeṣ*, I, 23b, 30a. See the general observations in I. Kahana, "Hay-Yahas ben ha-Hălaḳah wĕham-Minhag," *Mazkereṭ*, ed. S. Zevin (Jerusalem, 1962), pp. 556ff.; Y. Denari, "Ham-Minhag wĕha-Halaḳah," *Sefer Zikkaron B. de Vries* (Jerusalem, 1969), pp. 168ff. The subject, so crucial for the history of halaḳah, demands careful study and precise definition.

118. *Ḳĕri'aṭ Šĕma'*, ii, 8.

119. *Tĕfillah*, vii, 18; also *Bĕrakoṭ*, vii, 4; *Ma'ăkaloṭ 'Ăsuroṭ*, iv, 12.

120. *Tĕfillin*, iii, 19.

121. *Ṣiṣiṭ*, iii, 12. Also, *'Aḇel*, iv, 7, where the terms are clearly Talmudic. See *Tĕšubot*, 268 (p. 513) and PhM, 'Ab 1:16 (p. 417).

122. E.g., *Naḥălot*, vi, 11; *'Issure Bi'ah*, xxi, 11; cf. the mixed idiom of *Malweh wĕ-Loweh*, v, 8; also *Mĕḳirah*, vii, 8. See *Tĕšubot*, 218 (p. 386); 215 (p. 379).

123. *Naḥălot*, xi, 12. Generally, the halaḳah urges the individual to act in such a way as to avoid arousing suspicion; *Šĕḳalim*, ii, 10; *Mattĕnot 'Ăniyyim*, ix, 10. One's behavior should be not only legally unimpeachable but also sensitive, noble, and thoughtful.

# FORM

This is not just a matter of an elitist ethic[124]—there is here a more general movement from clear categorical prescriptions to evocative descriptions and ennobling counsels of perfection. It leaves a sense of elasticity and challenge, for the attentive reader will realize that the area between precise and unyielding legal directive and various modes of admonition or encouragement toward ever-spiralling improvement is broad and inviting. There are specific obligations, but there are also transcendent goals. This echoes R. Baḥya ibn Paḳuda's notion that the rational (spiritual) laws are an addition to, not a part of, the 613 prescribed commandments, and that their observance is a function of understanding God's greatness; the more profound one's perception, the more zealous one's observance.

(6) *Pedagogic devices: direct address, introductory generalization, exempla*

A decided pedagogic consciousness, concretely manifested in stylistic and substantive modes, also tended to loosen the taut fabric of the codificatory texture. Technical presentations are punctuated by apostrophes to the reader, calling his attention to fundamental rules and basic definitions, or offering guiding insights which remain relevant in many different contexts. The reader is warned against perfunctory study. He is alerted to the need for association, for carry-overs, for reflective review. He must be periodically stimulated, charged, and recharged. On occasion it would seem that the more technical the subject, the greater the use of direct address, trying to take the reader by the hand and urge him to study thoughtfully and patiently. The astronomical chapters rhythmically use "if you find," "suppose we

---

People in positions of authority or communal trust and responsibility must be especially careful; *Yĕsoḍe hat-Torah*, v, 11; *De'ot*, v, 13; *Talmuḍ Torah*, vi, 3; *Sanheḍrin*, xxiv, 10; *Mĕlaḳim*, iv, 10; see *Tĕšuḇot*, 135 (p. 256). See above, chap. I, n.6. Note, however, that not all supererogatory counsels are included. See *Tĕšuḇot*, 395 (p. 673), where Maimonides explains his omission of *diḇre ḥasiḍut*. Note the special phrase in *Gĕzelah*, v, 10.

124. See, e.g., *Gĕzelah wa-'Aḇeḍah*, xi, 17; also PhM, 'Aḇ 1:17 (p. 421); and below, chap. VI; cf. L. Fuller's discussion of the moralities of duty and aspiration, *The Morality of Law* (New York, 1964). On medieval "counsels of perfection" see *Ḥoḇot hal-Lĕḇaḇot*, introduction (p. 26); III, 3 (p. 201).

wish to know," "you proceed in similar fashion," "there are certain indications by which you may be guided," "if you wish to know," etc.[125] Other forms of apostrophe used by Maimonides include: "Thus all the terms whose meaning we have explained in these two chapters are twenty in number. . . . Keep these terms constantly before you, and let not their meanings out of your sight, so that we will have no need to explain each of these terms every time we mention it";[126] "wherever in this work we have used the expression . . . the meaning is . . .";[127] "all these coins, whose weights we have just given, are the standard coins normally alluded to. We have described them here in order to avoid the need for stating their weights on every occasion henceforth";[128] "in these matters always remember this important principle . . .";[129] and "hence you have learned that. . . ."[130]

Halakic explanations, novel and repercussive, are also very effectively introduced by direct address to the reader: "Let it not seem perplexing to you that the Sages. . . ."[131] Sometimes the direct address underscores the open-endedness of a rule: "In all these and similar cases, you should take heed of the important principle governing vows. . . . It is in accordance with the principle that you should formulate your teaching that. . . ."[132]

Unlike "appeals to the reader" in medieval literature, which are designed to gain "the sympathy of the audience," and "favor, approval, and prestige"[133] for the author, Maimonides' direct ad-

125. E.g., Kidduš ha-Ḥodeš, vi, 14; viii, 9; xi, 4, 8. Also Tĕšubah, v, 2, 4, 5; vi, 1; vii, 2. In Mĕṭamme' Miškab u-Mošab, vi, 5, direct address is used even to restate Talmudic complexities.
126. 'Išut, ii, 27. This passage illustrates several expansive features: lexicography, summary, pedagogic emphasis, direct address.
127. Gerušin, ii, 7.
128. Šĕkalim, i, 4; cf. PhM, Ber 8:8 (p. 86); introduction to Ṭohărot (pp. 9, 32); introduction to Yadayim (p. 704).
129. Mĕkirah, xxvii, 11; see R. Solomon Luria, Tĕšubot, 35 (p. 105); and see 'Erubin, i, 13.
130. E.g., Bikkurim, i, 7; also, 'Issure Bi'ah, vii, 12, 14; Šĕḥiṭah, iii, 7.
131. Gerušin, xiii, 29; see also Ma'ăkalot 'Ăsurot, iv, 8 (on the halakic identity of nĕbelah and ṭĕrefah); xv, 12. Note Ṭo'en wĕ-Niṭ'an, viii, 9.
132. Nĕdarim, ix, 13; also iii, 8; 'Išut, vi, 13; Tĕšubah, vii, 4.
133. Auerbach, Literary Language, p. 29. For the use of direct address in ShM, see positive 4, 56, 57, 75, 77, 82, 111, 159, 161, 167, 209; negative 187; and others. In MN, Maimonides frequently interpolates "and understand this."

dress is designed to emphasize and educate, and possibly provide interludes of companionship. This ad hominem writing not only helps retain some of the tonality and stress of the spoken word, making the massive Code somewhat more immediate and less impersonal, but also warns the reader against being impervious to novel concepts, special regulations, or unusual procedures. Direct address is thus a means of accentuation, a source of spontaneity, a medium for more intimate communication, a means of punctuating the monolithic discourse with rhetorical dialogue. Direct address seems to be not mere literary convention but an educational device which both flatters and fascinates the reader, who is now and then encouraged to see himself as a one-man audience receiving exclusive attention.

Introductory generalizations or concluding summaries, pedagogically very valuable, also automatically account for a measure of expansiveness and suppleness. "Thus we learn" or "to sum up" are refreshing and educating pauses. Maimonides tells us that he even tried to anticipate difficulties and obviate misinterpretations by using certain literary devices—summaries, captions, enumerations.[134]

There is also a pedagogically effective balance between judicial generalization and case law, general principles and specific applications. What Maimonides says in his *Mishnah Commentary* on *Ṭohărot* concerning the need for, and the teaching value of, abstractions and conceptualizations—they not only inform but also form one's mind—is applicable to his entire approach in the *Mishneh Torah*.[135] To be sure, these instructionally indispensable rules and generalizations transcend the details, but specific examples are still needed to concretize, vivify, or show the full range of the abstract principles. It makes no difference, of course, for our appreciation of this trait whether the cases or examples are Talmudic or Maimonidean; as a matter of fact, Maimonides regularly tries to use Talmudic examples. What counts is the skillful educative weaving of abstract generality and illustrative detail.

---

134. *Tēšubot*, 423 (p. 701); MTH, 6; see *Zĕkiyyah u-Mattanah*, viii, 18; also *'Išut*, vi, 13; *Gerušin*, x, 1–3; *Yibbum*, xii, 22.

135. PhM, Ṭoh, introduction (p. 37).

## 138 INTRODUCTION TO THE CODE OF MAIMONIDES

Often the relationship is made explicit by the word *"keṣad"* ("how is this?" or "in what way is this to be understood?"), and the rule is immediately illustrated.[136] Inductive and deductive methods alternate. Sometimes Maimonides will begin by saying "this is the rule" (*zeh hak-kĕlal*), and sometimes he will discuss one or more cases as a paradigm and imply that other similar cases should be related and compared to it (*wĕ-ken kol hay-yoṣe' baz-zeh*).[137]

A good and very interesting illustration is the impassioned summary of the prohibition cautioning the judge against accepting any gift or favor, tangible or intangible, great or trivial, even if it will not lead to a perversion of justice:

> *Thou shalt take no gift* (Exod. 23:8). The purport of this prohibition is . . . to warn him not to accept a bribe even if he proposes to acquit the innocent and condemn the guilty. . . . To him too is addressed the admonition, *Cursed be he that taketh a bribe* (Deut. 27:25).
>
> Any judge who stays at home and magnifies his greatness in order to increase the perquisites of his attendants and clerks is classed with those who turn aside after gain. The sons of Samuel did it; therefore it is written concerning them: *And . . . [they] turned aside after lucre and took bribes* (1 Sam. 8:3). Not only is a bribe of money forbidden but also a bribe of words.
>
> It happened once that a judge was crossing a river on a small fishing boat, when a man reached for his hand and helped him get ashore. But that man had a lawsuit, and the judge said to him, "I am disqualified from acting as judge in your suit."
>
> It also happened that a man once removed a bird's feather from a judge's mantle; another man once covered spittle in front of a judge. In each of these instances, the judge said, "I am barred from trying your case."
>
> There is also an incident on record of a man who presented to a priest, who was also a judge, a gift due to the priest. The judge said to the man, "I am ineligible to act as judge in your suit."
>
> There is still another incident of a tenant farmer who on Fridays used to bring to the owner (who was a judge) figs from the garden he was cultivating. On one occasion, however, he brought the figs on Thurs-

---

136. E.g., *Bĕrakot*, xi, 11, 12; *Yom Ṭob*, i, 24; see M. Zilberg, *Kak Darko šel Talmud* (Jerusalem, 1961), pp. 20, 24.
137. E.g., *Ṭo'en wĕ-Niṭ'an*, ix, 7, 8; *Kil'ayim*, v, 20.

day, because he had a lawsuit. The judge, however, said, "I am barred from acting as judge in your case," for though the figs were his, since the tenant brought them ahead of time, he was ineligible to try the case.[138]

This series of vignettes or *tableaux vivants* clearly achieves its judicial-literary purpose.

Note also Maimonides' reproduction of the following Talmudic tale, fascinating in its colorful detail:

Whosoever comes forth and declares that he is a priest is not to be believed, and may not be elevated to the status of a priest on the strength of his own statement. . . . If, however, he speaks in all innocence, he is to be believed. How so? It happened that a man said in all innocence, "I remember when I was a child and was borne on my father's shoulder, that they took me out of school and removed my shirt and immersed me, so that I could eat of the heave offering that evening; and my companions kept their distance from me and called me "Johanan, the eater of dough offering." Thereupon the saintly Rabbi Judah han-Naśi' elevated him to the status of a priest on the sole basis of his own statement.[139]

## *The Impossibility of Absolute Finality*

Many of these categories converge upon one overriding fact: Maimonides' realization that law has immanent uncertainties, that the legist regularly and unavoidably faces unimagined contingencies and new hesitations. Absolute finality is a utopian construct. Like the historical process or personal experience, law can never be purified of its mutations and individuality. A code is a rational construction which captures and freezes as much as possible of a fluid, unpredictable, sometimes recalcitrant reality, but there is always a fluctuating residuum which must be confronted openly and freshly. Maimonides was well aware of this and indicated it in various ways.

There are instances of direct address clearly intended for the judge, or more precisely, for any learned individual who may be called upon to issue a ruling or resolve doubts. For example,

---

138. *Sanhedrin*, xxiii, 1, 3.
139. *'Issure Bi'ah*, xx, 17; *Šĕkiruṭ*, v, 8.

"You must always, in all these doubtful cases, take care to be guided by these fundamental principles. . . . In this manner you must interpret and render decisions in all doubtful cases that may occur in matters touching levirate marriage . . . according as we have explained all the principles you are to rely upon."[140] These instances appear to be often technical and more specialized than the general direct address previously described.

While a code may skillfully summarize and greatly help with a conceptual schematization and generic guidelines, it cannot deprive the judge and legist of a creative-interpretative role in procedural as well as substantive matters. Sometimes he must rule on a definition and sometimes on implementation; both, although phenomenologically and jurisprudentially distinct and quite variable in terms of their creative component, are similar from the codificatory vantage point in that they generate spontaneity and flexibility in varying degrees. Judicial discretion and codificatory rigidity are incompatible. "For this is not clear proof, and the witnesses' estimate is not the judge's estimate. The judge is to be guided only by that on which he, in his own mind, is inclined to rely."[141] Similarly, with regard to the determination of the "ordinately foolish" who are ineligible to testify, Maimonides adds: "Discretionary power is vested in the judge in this matter, as it is impossible to lay down detailed rules on this subject."[142] The formula "the matter must be given ample deliberation"[143] expresses the same attitude. Furthermore, not only does the need for the jurist's ad hoc determination of proper procedure and assessment of evidence defy bland and unexceptionable prescription by legislator or codifier, but also his intuitive judgment and its spontaneity are likewise acknowledged, indeed encouraged. After one of the longest halakic presentations in the entire *Mishneh*

---

140. *Yibbum*, viii, 12–13, and *MM*, ad loc.
141. *Šě'elah u-Fiķķaḏon*, vi, 4; see an example in PhM, Giṭ 5:7 (p. 225).
142. *'Eḏuṯ*, ix, 10; J. Bazak, *'Aḥarayuṯo hap-Pělilīṯ šel hal-Laķuy bě-Nafšo* (Jerusalem, 1964), pp. 228ff. See R. Abraham Maimonides, *Těšubot*, 66 (p. 77), 144.
143. E.g., *'Išuṯ*, xvi, 9; *Malweh wě-Loweh*, ii, 4; *Sanhedrin*, xiv, 10; xxi, 11; *'Eḏuṯ*, xvi, 4. For comparative purposes, Maimonides may be seen here as a critic of *taqlīd*, the view that jurists should not rely on independent legal reasoning but should follow the teachings and precedents of recognized authorities; see *Islamic Jurisprudence: Shāfi'ī's Risāla*, tr. M. Khadduri (Baltimore, 1961), p. 43.

*Torah,* concerning relations of creditor and debtor, Maimonides adds this epilogue: "To put it generally, everything the judge does in these matters with the intention of pursuing only justice, as we have been enjoined to pursue it, and not of tampering with the law to the detriment of one of the litigants, he is permitted to do, and he will receive heavenly reward for it, provided always that his deeds are for the sake of heaven."[144] Note also the following conclusion to a chapter in which certain rights, duties, and prerogatives (some of them extraordinary) of the judge are catalogued:

> With regard to all these disciplinary measures, discretionary power is vested in the judge. He is to decide whether the offender deserves these punishments and whether the emergency of the hour demands their application. But whatever the expedient he sees fit to resort to, all his deeds should be done for the sake of heaven. Let not human dignity be light in his eyes; for the respect due to man supersedes a negative Rabbinical command. This applies with even greater force to the dignity of the children of Abraham, Isaac, and Jacob, who adhere to the True Law. The judge must be careful not to do aught calculated to destroy their self-respect. His sole concern should be to enhance the glory of God, for whosoever dishonors the Torah is himself dishonored by men, and whosoever honors the Torah is himself honored by men. To honor the Torah means to follow its statutes and laws.[145]

The judge, who is generally required to have great moral and intellectual qualities,[146] must be guided by his conscience, and this cannot be codified or quantified.

It should be clear that the formula "this matter requires due (or ample) deliberation" (*miṯyašḫin bĕ-daḫar zeh*") is double-edged. It refers, in the first instance, to the question of the finality of the *Mishneh Torah,* and it candidly affirms that Maimonides could not or would not—attribute it to modesty or to hard-headed realism, as you like—resolve every single doubt. Judicial indeterminacy, in this context, is not a sign of intellectual timidity or retreat but

---

144. *Malweh wĕ-Loweh,* ii, 4; also xxiii, 2.
145. *Sanhedrin,* xxiv, 10. Note the use and explanation of 'Ab 4:6 (and see a slightly different use in *Sefer Torah,* x, 11); cf. *Tĕšuḫot,* 1 (p. 1). Power requires sensitivity and (see above, n. 123) humility.
146. *Sanhedrin,* ii, 1–7; *Tĕšuḫot,* 135 (p. 256).

an integral component of the codificatory enterprise. Secondly, it refers to certain standard procedural aspects, to the necessarily broad and unrehearsed role of the judge, to his options and prerogatives, indeed to his responsibilities in interpreting and applying the law. In other words, it deals with the question of the finality of codification per se. To some extent, the whole problem of doubt in the halakic system itself may be reflected here; even when all the facts are in, the judicial determination may remain moot. Given these extensive areas of indeterminacy, which must be filled by wisdom and experience, interpretation and intuition, a sense of justice and compassion, can any code claim to be final and obviate the need for continuing creativity by recognized authorities? "Codes and statutes do not render the judge superfluous, nor his work perfunctory and mechanical. There are gaps to be filled. There are doubts and ambiguities to be cleared." It has been aptly said that "Justinian's prohibition of any commentary on the product of his codifiers is remembered only for its futility."[147] All his desires for finality, objectivity, and universality notwithstanding, Maimonides was sophisticated and realistic, sensitized by the very Rabbinic tradition which he was codifying. He knew that despite his major contribution to condensation and consolidation the vitality and effervescence of halakah could not be fully contained or compressed. The logic of law and the contingencies of life have always to be aligned. Halakah and reality are both multifaceted realities.

Note how Maimonides summarizes, with his own cadences and emphases, the power of the court:

> However, the court, even if it be inferior (to the former), is authorized to dispense for a time even with these measures. For these decrees are not to be invested with greater stringency than the commands of the Torah itself, which any court has the right to suspend as an emergency measure. Thus the court may inflict flagellation and other punishments, even in cases where such penalties are not warranted by the law, if in its opinion religion will thereby be strengthened and safeguarded and the people will be restrained from disregarding the words of the Torah. It must not, however, establish the measure to

---

147. B. Cardozo, *The Nature of the Judicial Process* (New Haven, 1921), pp. 14, 18.

which it resorts as a law binding upon succeeding generations, declaring, "This is the law."

So too, if in order to bring back the multitudes to religion and save them from general religious laxity, the court deems it necessary to set aside temporarily a positive or a negative commandment, it may do so, taking into account the need of the hour. Even as a physician will amputate the hand or the foot of a patient in order to save his life, so the court may advocate, when an emergency arises, the temporary disregard of some of the commandments, so that the commandments as a whole may be preserved. This is in keeping with what the early Sages have said: "Desecrate on his account one Sabbath, in order that he be able to observe many Sabbaths" (B. Yoma 85b).[148]

This carefully worded formulation, rich in suggestive metaphors and interpretations, tells the whole story.

THE CODE AS COMMENTARY: EXPOSITORY-EXEGETICAL MATERIAL

The most significant category, which by itself would necessitate a redefinition of the codificatory form, is the colorful spectrum of expository-exegetical material which imperceptibly but irreversibly converts the *Mishneh Torah* into a compendium that teaches and not only guides, that instructs while it directs. In many respects it turns out to be a suggestive and selective commentary cast as a code. The expository-exegetical range is wide and varied, including many levels of explication and even rationalization, Scriptural exegesis, aggadic commentary and halakic investigation, counsel and exhortation, even the cultivation of ontological perceptions and teleological awareness—all these definitely transcend the needs of apodictic summary and serve a primarily informative-academic-edifying purpose. The fact is that one may open any page at random and come face to face with these supra-functional facets. The *Mishneh Torah* is a richly-textured academic summary of the Oral Law as well as a normative-functional guide to halakic observance.

---

148. *Mamrim*, ii, 4; iii, 7; MN, III, 34. Cf. J. Levinger, *Tarbiz*, XXXVII (1968), 28. Maimonides' statement is striking—as noted, e.g., by RaDBaZ—but see also *Šabbaṭ*, ii, 3; *Gerušin*, ii, 20.

## 144 INTRODUCTION TO THE CODE OF MAIMONIDES

1. There is, first of all, philological-lexicographical material which presents the codifier in the limited role of *grammaticus*. The word for usury (*nešek*, literally "biting") is explained: "Why is it called *nešek*? Because he who takes it bites his fellow, causes pain to him, and eats his flesh."[149] Various terms for lamentation (*'innuy, kinah*) are defined, thereby showing that they are not completely synonymous.[150] Technical astronomical terms, *'ibbur* and *molad*, basic for understanding the calendar, are defined.[151] Arabic equivalents are provided for all the names of spices used in the preparation of the incense (*ketoret*).[152] This commentatorial strain is especially pronounced in such sections as *Hilkot Kelim*, whose subject matter abounds in lexicographical and terminological difficulties. In his restatement of a law, Maimonides will frequently substitute a lengthy expository paraphrase for the key word or *terminus technicus* of the underlying Talmudic passage. This lexicographical facet is often inconspicuous and only careful correlation with the sources will bring it into clear focus.[153] It is noteworthy that RABD sometimes speculates about the lexicography underlying a Maimonidean ruling, for he realizes that the understanding of a certain word determines the halakic formulation.[154]

Sometimes, to be sure, an excursus into lexicography has obvious practical-halakic repercussions. "So, too, they instituted a service to be recited after the afternoon service close to sunset, but only on a fast day, in order to add petitions and supplications on account of the fast. This service is called *ně'ilah* ('closing'), namely, the gates of heaven are closed to the sun." This is an effective way of rejecting the view that *ně'ilah* means the closing of the gates of the Temple, which would considerably advance the time of its recitation.[155] Similarly, *'erub, kuppah, tamhuy, tebel*, and other terms are explained or defined, so that all halakic im-

---

149. *Malweh wě-Loweh*, iv, 1; also xviii, 1 (*toref*).
150. *Yom Tob*, vi, 24.
151. *Kiddus ha-Hodeš*, vi, 1.
152. *Kěle ham-Mikdaš*, ii, 4. See ibid., viii, 2, where the Biblical *migba'at* is explained.
153. *Kěri'at Šěma'*, i, 7; ii, 9.
154. *Kelim*, x, 15; see also *Šěkalim*, ii, 10, which is a beautiful example.
155. *Těfillah*, i, 19; and see *'Orah Hayyim*, 623, 2.

plications are clear. As in other respects, this concern with lexicography, *de verborum significatione* (to borrow a title from the *Digest*), has roots and parallels in the *Mishnah Commentary*.[156]

2. Scriptural exegesis, in a variety of forms, is a paramount motif. This category starts with citation of verses for emphasis or embellishment—the Scriptural mottoes and conclusions of each book of the *Mishneh Torah* should be seen in this light. It includes new exegesis or new application of verses, as well as popularization or endorsement of certain interpretative views. It also serves an anti-Karaite purpose, as illustrated by Maimonides' use of Josh. 5:11 in the cardinal dispute concerning the date of Pentecost.[157] The providential lesson shown to be implicit in fasting is based on such exegesis.[158] The interpretation of the Song of Songs as an allegory of the soul's relation to, or communion with, God—a favorite philosophic topos substituting for the national-historical interpretation advanced in the Midrash, which sees it as a drama of God and Israel—is clearly and explicitly presented: "The entire Song of Songs is indeed an allegory descriptive of the love (of God)."[159] Generally Solomon is frequently cited; "and so said Solomon in his wisdom" is a common rhetorical trimming, for Proverbs provides numerous quotations for the *Mishneh Torah*.[160]

The insistence that natural law will continue in the Messianic era is nourished by a sweeping exegetical rule:

156. *'Eruḫin*, i, 16; *Ma'aḵalot 'Asurot*, vi, 19; *Mattĕnot 'Ăniyyim*, ix, 1, 2; *'Issure Bi'ah*, i, 10; see also *'Išut*, i, 2; *Yibbum*, introductory paragraph; *Tĕšuḇot*, 153 (p. 297); for similar explanations elsewhere, see, e.g., PhM, Ket 10:5 (p. 102) (on *pĕšarah*, compromise); PhM Men 4:4 (p. 124) (on *ḥinnuḵ*, training). RABD also, of necessity and sometimes as complementing or criticizing Maimonides, engaged in philological comment. *'Išut*, i, 4; *Na'arah Bĕtulah*, ii, 17.

157. *Tĕmiḏin u-Musafin*, vii, 11; see *Halaḵot Gĕḏolot*, ed. A. Hildesheimer (Berlin, 1892), p. 672.

158. *Ta'āniyyot*, i, 1–3.

159. *Tĕšuḇah*, x, 2; *'Aḇot hat-Ṭumĕ'ot*, ix, 6, which refers to the Song of Songs as *diḇre ḥokmah*, must reflect this view also. On the Song of Songs, see MN, III, 51. See further, Twersky, "Non-Halakic Aspects," p. 103, n. 37.

160. E.g., *Yĕsoḏe hat-Torah*, ii, 12; *De'ot*, iii, 4, 15, 19; vii, 4; *Talmuḏ Torah*, iii, 12; see also *'Issure Bi'ah*, xiii, 14; M. Roth, "He'arot," *Zikkaron*, ed. J. L. Maimon (Jerusalem, 1945), pp. 268ff.; and most recently, S. Leiman, *The Canonization of Hebrew Scripture* (Transactions of the Connecticut Academy of Arts and Sciences, 47 [1976]), p. 173, n.317.

Let no one think that in the days of the Messiah any of the laws of nature will be set aside, or any innovation will be introduced into creation. The world will follow its normal course. The words of Isaiah, *And the wolf shall dwell with the lamb, and the leopard shall lie down with the kid* (Isa. 11:6) are to be understood figuratively, meaning that Israel will live securely among the wicked of the heathens who are likened to wolves and leopards, as it is written, *A wolf of the deserts doth spoil them, a leopard watcheth over their cities* (Jer. 5:6). They will all accept the true religion, and will neither plunder nor destroy, and together with Israel earn a comfortable living in a legitimate way, as it is written, *And the lion shall eat straw like the ox* (Isa. 11:7). All similar expressions used in connection with the Messianic age are metaphorical. In the days of King Messiah the full meaning of those metaphors and their allusions will become clear to all.[161]

The summary of ideal labor-management relations is likewise capped with a Scriptural flourish:

Just as the employer is enjoined not to deprive the poor worker of his hire nor withhold it from him when it is due, so is the worker enjoined not to deprive the employer of the benefit of his work by idling away his time, a little here and a little there, thus wasting the whole day deceitfully. Indeed, the worker must be very punctual in the matter of time, seeing that the Sages were so solicitous in this matter that they exempted the worker from saying the fourth benediction of grace.

The worker must work with all his power, seeing that the just Jacob has said *And ye know that with all my power I have served your father* (Gen. 31:6), and that he received his reward therefor in this world, too, as it is said, *And the man increased exceedingly* (Gen. 30:43).[162]

Generally Maimonides makes frequent, brief, and effective reference to Biblical heroes, not only to Solomon.[163]

Maimonides' interesting typology of the moral-intellectual traits required for appointment to a court of law is avowedly based on explicit Scriptural statements, but analysis reveals that much of the exegesis is novel:

---

161. *Mĕlakim*, xii, 1. In MTH, 21, this interpretation is attributed to the Spanish school of exegesis, represented by "Moses ibn Gikatilia and Ibn Bal'am and other commentators."
162. *Sĕkirut*, xiii, 7.
163. E.g., *Ķĕri'at Šĕma'*, i, 4; *Bĕrakot*, xi, 16; *'Arakin*, vi, 33; *Sĕkirut*, xiii, 7; *Naḥălot*, vi, 13; *'Ăbadim*, ix, 8. Also, *Yĕsode hat-Torah*, v, 10 (and *Mĕlakim*, v, 11); *De'ot*, vii, 7; *'Akum*, i, 2 (and see PhM, Soṭ 3:3 [p. 256]).

In the case of a court-of-three, all the above-mentioned requirements are not insisted upon. Nevertheless, it is essential that every one of the members thereof possess the following seven qualifications: wisdom, humility, fear of God, disdain of gain, love of truth, love of his fellow men, and a good reputation. All these prerequisities are explicitly set forth in the Torah. Scripture says *wise men and understanding* (Deut. 1:13), thus stating (that those chosen) must be men of wisdom; *and beloved of your tribes* (ibid.), that is, men with whom the spirit of their fellow creatures is pleased. What will earn for them the love of others? A good eye, a lowly spirit, friendly intercourse, and gentleness in speech and dealings with others.

Elsewhere it is said *men of valor* (Exod. 18:21), that is, men strong in the performance of the commandments and strict with themselves, men who control their passions, whose character is above reproach, aye, whose youth is of unblemished repute. The phrase *men of valor* implies also stoutheartedness to rescue the oppressed from the hand of the oppressor, as it is said, *But Moses stood up and helped them* (Exod. 2:17). And just as Moses our teacher was humble, so every judge should be humble. *Such as fear God* (Exod. 18:21)—this is to be understood literally; *hating gain* (ibid.), that is, who are not anxious about their own money and do not strive to accumulate wealth, for he that hastens after riches, want shall come upon him; *men of truth* (ibid.), that is, who pursue righteousness spontaneously and of their own accord; they love truth, hate violence, and flee anything that savors of unrighteousness.[164]

Especially noteworthy are the longer excursuses which integrate Biblical themes or narratives into the halakic context, finding a Scriptural precedent or analogy for a law or interpreting the Scriptural incident in accordance with the law. For example, toward the end of a long chapter, rich in Scriptural motifs, devoted to the details of the seven Noahide commandments, Maimonides comments:

---

164. *Sanhedrin*, ii, 1–7. Comparison with pre-Maimonidean typologies of the prerequisites and traits of a judge again enhances our awareness of the special stylistic-substantive qualities of Maimonides' formulation; see, e.g., *Sefer wĕ-Hizhir*, I, 80–81; the text of R. Samuel ben Hofni Gaon, ed. A. Greenbaum, *Leo Jung Jubilee Volume*, Heb. section, p. 233; S. Abramson, *ḲS*, XXVI (1950), 82. Maimonides' formulation is quoted by N. H. Wessely, *'En Mišpaṭ* in *Dibre Šalom* (Berlin, 1782–88), p. 36. This is symptomatic of the selective enlightenment use of Maimonides, for which see most recently J. Lehmann, *Leo Baeck Year Book*, XX (1975), 87–108.

Sometimes Maimonides elaborates the Talmudic interpretation of verses, e.g., *Gĕneḇah*, vii, 9. See *Sanhedrin*, iii, 8, and the conflicting views of R. Joseph Kolon and R. Joseph

As regards the commandment incumbent upon Noahides to establish courts of justice, the duty is enjoined upon them to set up judges in each district to deal with these six commandments and to caution the people.

A Noahide who violates any of the seven commandments is executed by decapitation with the sword. Therefore all the inhabitants of Shechem were condemned to death by beheading because Shechem had been guilty of robbery. They saw it, knew it, and failed to impose sentence upon him.[165]

Maimonides clearly goes out of his way to interpolate this novel halakic comment on the Shechem adventure (a real interpretative crux) into the summary of Noahide law.

His emphatic formulation concerning the unparalleled heinousness of murder, making it worse than idolatry or immorality, and the unusually stringent measures which are justified only in punishing a putative murderer but not a suspected idolater, is mounted upon a pungent Scriptural reference:

If one has committed this crime, he is deemed wholly wicked, and all the meritorious acts he had performed during his lifetime cannot outweigh this crime or save him from judgment, as it is said, *A man that is laden with the blood of any person shall hasten his steps to the pit; none will support him* (Prov. 28:17). A lesson may be taken from Ahab, who worshiped idols and of whom it is said, *But there was none like unto Ahab* (1 Kings 21:25). Yet when his sins and his merits were set in array before the God of all spirits (cf. Num. 16:22), the one sin that brought on him the doom of extermination and the weightiest of all his crimes was the blood of Naboth. For Scripture relates, *And there came forth the spirit and stood before the Lord* (1 Kings 22:21)—this was the spirit of Naboth, who was told, *Thou shalt entice him, and shalt prevail also* (1 Kings 22:22). Now the wicked Ahab did not commit murder himself but only brought it about. How much greater then is the crime of one who commits murder with his own hand![166]

Sometimes the Scriptural interpolation is quite brief and inconspicuous, flowing along smoothly and naturally with the

---

Karo (in *KM*, ad loc.) concerning the role of "creative Midrash" in *Mishneh Torah*. Note the original application of verses in *Mamrim*, v, 15.

165. *Mĕlakim*, ix, 14; see Nahmanides, *Peruš*, Gen. 34:13; also *Mĕlakim*, viii, 8 (on Tamar and Amnon).

166. *Roṣeaḥ*, iv, 9. See the phrase in B. Sanh 7a.

halakic summation: "If a heathen asks an Israelite how far he is going, he should mention a longer distance than the true one, as Jacob did with Esau, saying to him, *Until I come unto my lord, unto Seir* (Gen. 33:14)."[167] There are Scriptural references which, in the halakic context, resolve well-known discrepancies or interpretative problems. Incorporating a theme from the Palestinian Talmud, Maimonides is able to align easily and smoothly many Scriptural references with the halakic norm:

> When you read in the prophets that the priests were girded with a linen ephod, (you should understand that) they were not High Priests, for the ephod of the High Priest was not of linen. Even Levites would gird themselves with a linen one, since Samuel the prophet was a Levite and concerning him it is said, *a child, girded with a linen ephod* (1 Sam. 2:18). Moreover, a disciple of the prophets or one who was fit that the Holy Spirit should rest upon him would gird himself with such an ephod, to make known that such as he had reached the station of a High Priest, who would speak by (the power of) the holy spirit through the means of the ephod and the breastplate.[168]

This abundance of Scriptural citation and exegesis reflects Maimonides' abiding and consuming interest, combining halakic and theological motives. In a moving elegy he had praised his brother, a merchant who drowned in the Indian Ocean on a business trip, for his profound knowledge of Scripture.[169] Maimonides assigned premium value to this. He would oppose the exclusive and monolithic Talmudism which left no room for study of Scripture, the "Book that is the guide of the first and last man," and he chided those who think that they understand this Book "while glancing through it as you would glance through a historical work or a piece of poetry."[170] He counseled his favorite student, all his other activities and intellectual pursuits notwithstanding, to study the Bible unceasingly; "from it you will see the vision of the Almighty" (cf. Num. 24:4). Philosophical and theological views are regularly related to Scripture, by

---

167. *Roṣeaḥ*, xii, 8.
168. *Kĕle ham-Miḳdaš*, x, 13. See a different case ibid., i, 11.
169. *Ḳobeṣ*, II, 37b.
170. MN, I, 2.

exegesis or eisegesis.[171] R. Abraham quotes oral-exegetical traditions which he received from his father and periodically comments on Scriptural explanations found in, or assumed by, the *Mishneh Torah*.[172] The study of Scripture and its relation to the Oral Law is a leitmotif of the *Mishneh Torah*.

3. Aggadah was a treasure trove which could be diligently searched and then creatively used to reinforce or refine a halakic formulation, to sustain a philological connection or conjecture, to exemplify an ethical trait, or to bolster a philosophic position. Maimonides, who had a sustained and life-long interest in Midrash, its hermeneutic problematics as well as its ideational potential, freely and effectively utilized nonhalakic materials throughout the *Mishneh Torah*. Aggadah and halakah had a synchronic relationship; the tendency to separate completely these two cognate areas, which often merged, should not obscure the literary-conceptual reality of Maimonides' work, or indeed of his age as a whole.[173]

The following passage from the very beginning of *Sefer 'Ahăbah* significantly illustrates not only the straightforward use of aggadic motifs but also the way they are filtered through Maimonides' intellectualistic-spiritualistic outlook:

> When reciting the *Shema'*, after concluding the first verse, one should repeat in a low tone the sentence, "blessed be the name of His glorious sovereignty for ever and ever," and then resume the reading of the first section in the regular order, from the verse, *And thou shalt love the Lord thy God* (Deut. 6:5), to the end of the section. Why is the above-

---

171. *'Iggĕrot* 16; see, e.g., his use of Jer. 10:7–8 for the history of religion (*'Akum*, i), and cf. I. Heinemann, "Tĕmunat ha-Hisṭoryah šel R. Judah hal-Levi," *Zion*, IX (1944), 171, n. 160. See above, chap. I, nn. 90ff. In the light of this, as well as other statements in his letters emphasizing his constant study of Scripture, we are led to reinterpret *Talmud Torah*, i, 12, where the study of Scripture is presented as a part-time and preliminary pursuit. Study of Scripture—Torah—is perceived on two levels: simple reading which yields knowledge or erudition and profound study which yields theological insight. This study consequently belongs to unit three as well as unit one; see below, chap. VI.

172. *Peruš R. Abraham*, ed. A. Wiesenberg and S. Sasson (London, 1959); S. Eppenstein, "Beiträge zur Pentateuchexegese Maimuni's," *MbM*, I, 411–20. There is still need to identify and appraise Maimonides' original exegesis; e.g., *De'ot*, v, 1, 8; *Yom Ṭob*, vi, 18; and many others. See above, n.164.

173. See W. Bacher, "Die Agada in Maimunis Werken," *MbM*, II, 131–97; S. Lieberman, *Hilkot Yĕrušalmi*, p. 5; and see above, chap. I, n.15.

mentioned sentence interpolated? We have a tradition that when the patriarch Jacob, residing in Egypt, gathered his sons about him in his dying hour, he earnestly charged them concerning the oneness of God and the way of the Lord in which Abraham and his father Isaac had walked. He questioned them, saying to them, "Possibly, my sons, there is some one among you who is unworthy, and is not at one with me on the doctrine of the oneness of the Creator of the world, in the same way as our teacher Moses charged the people in the words, *Lest there should be among you man or woman . . . whose heart turneth away this day* (Deut. 29:17)." They all answered, *Hear, O Israel, the Lord our God, the Lord is one* (Deut. 6:4). This means, "Our father, Israel, hear this, our (confession of faith): The Lord our God is one Lord." The aged patriarch then exclaimed, "Blessed be the name of His glorious sovereignty for ever and ever." Hence all Israelites keep the custom of reciting, after the first verse of the *Shema'*, the thanksgiving uttered by the patriarch Israel.[174]

Use of Scriptural verses and Midrashic motifs was frequently combined and the resultant passage would be so smoothly textured that it was often difficult to disentangle its composite strands. Maimonides' formulation concerning the prospective soldier's need for both physical prowess and religious fervor is a beautiful example:

*What man is there that is fearful and fainthearted?* (Deut. 20:8). This is to be understood literally, that is, the man who is not physically fit to join the ranks in battle. Once, however, he has joined the ranks, he should put his reliance upon Him who is the hope of Israel, their Savior in time of trouble. He should know that he is fighting for the oneness of God, risk his life, and neither fear nor be affrighted. Nor should he think of his wife or children, but forgetting them and all else, concentrate on the war. He who permits his attention to be diverted during a battle and becomes disturbed, transgresses a negative command, as it is said, *Let not your heart faint, fear not, nor be alarmed, neither be ye affrighted at them* (Deut. 20:3). Moreover, he is accountable for the lives of all Israel. If he does not conquer (because) he did not fight with all his heart and soul, it is as though he had shed the blood of all, as it is said, *Lest his brethren's heart melt as his heart* (Deut. 20:8). This truth is brought out with notable clearness in the injunction of the prophet, *Cursed be he that doeth the work of the Lord with a slack hand, and cursed be he that keepeth back his sword from blood* (Jer. 48:10).

174. Ḳeri'at Šema', i, 4.

He who fights with all his heart, without fear, with the sole intention of sanctifying the Name, is assured that no harm will befall him and no evil will overtake him. He will build for himself a lasting house in Israel, acquiring it for himself and his children forever, and will prove worthy of life in the world to come, as it is written, *For the Lord will certainly make my lord a sure house, because my lord fighteth the battles of the Lord; and evil is not found in thee. . . . Yet the soul of my lord shall be bound in the bundle of life with the Lord thy God* (1 Sam. 25:28–29).[175]

The literary fusion of Scriptural verses and Midrashic motifs is paralleled, often extended, by Scriptural-aggadic-halakic combinations, usually but not always perorations to sections or books. Let us note three interesting and representative examples:

Although one is not bound to purchase a garment and wear it, so as to insert fringes therein, still it is not right for a pious man (*ḥasid*) to release himself from the observance of this commandment. . . . At all times, a person should be heedful of the precept concerning fringes, since Scripture estimates it as so weighty that all the commandments are made dependent upon it, as it is said, *That ye may look upon it, and remember all the commandments of the Lord* (Num. 15:39).[176]

Mark how strictly the observance of circumcision is to be regarded. Moses, although he was on a journey, did not receive indulgence of a single hour for neglecting this duty. In connection with all the precepts of the Torah, three covenants were made with Israel; as it is said, *These are the words of the covenant which the Lord commanded . . . beside the covenant which He made with them in Horeb* (Deut. 28:69). And in the next section it is said, *Ye are standing this day, all of you, before the Lord your God . . . that thou shouldst enter into the covenant of the Lord thy God* (Deut. 29:9–11). Three covenants are here mentioned. But in connection with circumcision, thirteen covenants were made with our ancestor Abraham. *And I will make My covenant between Me and thee* (Gen. 17:2); *As for Me, behold, My covenant is with thee* (Gen 17:4); *And I will establish My covenant between Me and thee* (Gen. 17:7); *for an everlasting covenant* (ibid.); *And as for thee, thou shalt keep My covenant* (Gen. 17:9); *This is My covenant which ye shall keep* (Gen. 17:10); *And it shall be a token of a covenant* (Gen. 17:11); *And My covenant shall be in your flesh* (Gen. 17:13), *for an everlasting covenant* (ibid.); *He hath broken My covenant* (Gen. 17:14); *And I will*

---

175. *Mĕlakim*, vii, 15.
176. *Ṣiṣit*, iii, 11, 12. See R. Abraham ibn Ezra, to Num. 15:39; MN, III, 44.

*establish My covenant with him* (Gen. 17:19); *for an everlasting covenant* (ibid.); *But My covenant I will establish with Isaac* (Gen. 17:21).[177]

The site of the Altar was defined very specifically and was never to be changed. For it is said, *This is the altar of burnt offering for Israel* (1 Chron. 22:1). It was on the site of the Temple that the patriarch Isaac was bound. For it is said, *And get thee into the Land of Moriah* (Gen. 22:2), and in the Book of Chronicles it is said, *Then Solomon began to build the house of the Lord at Jerusalem in Mount Moriah, where the Lord appeared unto David his father; for which provision had been made in the Place of David, in the threshing floor of Ornan* (2 Chron. 3:1). Now there was a tradition known to all that the place where David and Solomon built the altar in the threshing floor of Ornan was the same place where Abraham had built the altar upon which he bound Isaac. This, too, was the place where Noah built an altar when he came out of the Ark. It was also the place of the altar upon which Cain and Abel offered sacrifice. There it was that Adam offered a sacrifice after he was created. Indeed Adam was created from that very ground; as the Sages have taught: Adam was created from the place where he made atonement.[178]

Maimonides' unremitting concern with aggadah is thus mirrored, from one vantage point, in the extensive role assigned to it in this codification of law and its function as a leaven causing the framework to rise and expand. Whether he quotes verses and aggadic motifs used in the Talmud or makes novel literary-exegetical-conceptual associations is of little moment for our analysis at this point. Their presence in, and lyricizing-softening effect upon, the Code is the determining consideration. The student of Maimonidean thought, following an integrative-holistic approach to the development of Maimonides' ideas, will be especially attentive to this material.

4. Evaluation of the codificatory form and appreciation of the comprehensive scope of the *Mishneh Torah* merge when we consider the inclusion of Scripture, aggadah, and, we may add, history or the historical development of certain halakic institutions. The role and organization of the Levites and Priests in the Temple is a good example:

---

177. *Milah*, iii, 9. See MN, III, 49; PhM Ned 3:10 (p. 126); *Tešubah*, iii, 6.
178. *Bet hab-Beḥirah*, ii, 2. (See Gen. Rabbah 14:9 [ed. H. Albeck, p. 132]; Pirke R. Eliezer, chap. 12; Targum Yerushalmi, Gen. 22:9); MN, III, 45.

The descendants of Levi were wholly separated (from the community of Israel) for the service of the Sanctuary, as it is said, *At that time the Lord separated the tribe of Levi* (Deut. 10:8). . . . Samuel the seer and David the king divided the Levites into twenty-four divisions. . . .

The priests were separated from the community of Levites to minister at the offerings; as it is said, *And Aaron was separated, that he should be sanctified as most holy* (1 Chron. 23:13). . . . Moses our teacher divided the priests into eight divisions. . . . They remained that way until the days of Samuel the seer, who together with King David divided them into twenty-four divisions.[179]

We see clearly how the aspects of comprehensiveness, including historical comments, and expansiveness, particularly Scriptural citations and explications, are intertwined.

5. The most important and salient feature is the large amount of halakic commentary and interpretation. This includes the reproduction of exegetical procedures, the process by which laws were crystallized, as well as the explaining of details, differences, and contents of laws, the finding of delicate nuances and edifying overtones, suggesting pathos, ethos, and logos. Such key terms as "because," "therefore," "as a result," "for it is said," "how do we know that?", "from this we learn"—which appear on almost every page of the work, sometimes very parenthetically and sometimes introducing significant explanations in compressed and epitaphic style—signal Maimonides' concern with theoretical knowledge, not just practical results, with the understanding of the process and emergence of laws, their Scriptural bases and Rabbinic elaborations, their underlying rationales and hermeneutic techniques. He moves back from legislative soliloquy to halakic dialogue. We find entire chapters structured in this way. For example, chapter five of the Laws Concerning Mourning, which enumerates all the "things that are forbidden to a mourner, on the first day by Biblical law and on the other days by Rabbinical authority," is completely exegetical. Not only is every single halakah spelled out but its derivation is also recorded: "Whence do we learn that a mourner is forbidden to cut his hair?

---

179. *Kĕle ham-Mikdaš*, iii, 19; iv, 1–3; for another kind of historical aggadah combining past recollection and future expectation, see *Sanhedrin*, xiv, 12. Note *Mĕlakim*, xi, 1 and RaDBaZ. See below, chap. III.

... Whence do we derive that a mourner is forbidden to . . . ? Whence do we learn that . . . ? Where is it intimated that . . . ? Whence do we infer that. . . . ?" Even the next chapter, which summarizes the "mourning rites which are to be observed for thirty days," continues this thrust: "What Scriptural support do the Rabbis have for this enactment?"[180]

The beginning of the Laws Concerning Divorce is noteworthy for many reasons, its lexicographical comment, its systematization and internal classification, and its exegetical structure: "A woman may be divorced only by means of a writ that reaches her, and this writ is called *get̬*. There are ten rules that are basic to divorce according to the Torah, and they are as follows: . . . The other things that are involved in the *get̬* are all of Scribal origin. *And whence do we know* that these ten rules are derived from the Torah?" The rest of the chapter is exegetical-demonstrative, marked by the repetition of such formulae as "this teaches that," "what is written in the Torah . . . implies," "and whence do we know?", "when does this apply?", etc.[181]

Rabbinic enactments are frequently explicated. For example:

According to Scriptural law, if a courtyard has many tenants, each living in a house of his own, they may all move articles throughout the whole of the courtyard. . . . For the whole courtyard is a single private domain, so that it is permitted to move articles throughout the whole of it. . . . On the authority of the Scribes, however, the rule is that if a private domain—be it a courtyard, an alley, or a city—contains separate residences, the tenants may not move articles in it unless they all prepare an *'erub̬* on Friday. The regulation to this effect was first made by Solomon and his legislature. . . . What was Solomon's reason for issuing this regulation? . . .[182]

On occasion Maimonides elaborates and argues the interpretation which underlies his codificatory formulation. A long sequence, almost a harangue, introduced by "on what evidence do I base my opinion that . . ." and punctuated by such apostrophes

---

180. *'Ab̬el*, v, 1ff.; note that v, 18 is an exception because its derivation is problematic; see *'Ab̬el*, iv, 9. See also *Ta'āniyyot̬*, ii, 3ff. for expansive use of "keṣad̬"; *Sanhed̬rin*, xv.
181. *Gerušin*, i, 1 (italics mine). See also *Kēle ham-Mik̬daš*, iii, 1–3.
182. *'Erub̬in*, i, 4, and see *MM*, ad loc. See *Ma'ăśeh hak̬-K̬orbanot̬*, x, 15.

## 156 INTRODUCTION TO THE CODE OF MAIMONIDES

as "hence you learn that . . ." and "for should you maintain the contrary. . . ," is notable.[183] Also quite significant is such argumentative-expository prose as "it would appear to me that the law . . . this may be proven by an argument a priori . . . some of the Geonim have ruled . . . but there is no basis for this view"; or "some of the Geonim have ruled . . . it would appear to me that this is a wrong decision based on an erroneous interpretation of the Scriptural verse . . . what this verse really means is . . . one should not pay any attention to this (Gaonic) ruling."[184] Finally, we may note Maimonides' lengthy contention in support of a novel distinction which he introduces with "Now it is obvious that this rule applies only. . . ."; and after several examples and qualifications he proclaims: "These are matters of common sense, and not of Scriptural decree."[185]

More often the specific interpretation, frequently arrived at by prolonged study and reflection, is implicit and must be reconstructed. Maimonides himself reminisces about spending many days studying one item while he was composing his Code, and about the reciprocity between formulating the law and explaining the underlying texts.[186] The legist, like the scientist, has his own laboratory and experimental procedure. When confronted with questions about a seemingly novel statement or illustration, Maimonides was nonplussed. While not using any of the standard metaphors in defense of originality—e.g., dwarfs standing on the shoulders of giants—he simply affirmed the fact that there is room for originality in interpretation, inference, and application. The "gates of interpretation" are open.[187] It is therefore instructive to note those cases in which Maimonides firmly responds to

---

183. *'Aḇot haṭ-Ṭumě'oṭ*, ii, 10. See also *'Issure Bi'ah*, xv, 29; *Malweh wĕ-Loweh*, vi, 7.
184. *Ma'ăḵaloṭ 'Ăsuroṭ*, x, 15, 18.
185. *'Išuṭ*, xxv, 2; see chap. VI, below, for *gĕzeraṭ hak-Kaṭuḇ*.
186. E.g., *Tĕšuḇoṭ*, 326 (p. 593); *Pĕ'er had-Dor* (Amsterdam, 1765), 27, 32.
187. *Tĕšuḇoṭ*, 315 (p. 585); MN, II, 25; see also *Tĕšuḇoṭ*, 344 (p. 616), where Maimonides answers a very weighty question (concerning *Tĕrumoṭ*, xv, 19) by revealing his exegetical approach to the problem, i.e., his novel method of interpretation. Regardless of the halakic-conceptual difficulties of his formulation, Maimonides does not retreat an inch, affirming that he consciously derived his ruling from his interpretation of a mishnah and did not feel compelled to reconcile it with a cognate Talmudic passage. See also *Tĕšuḇoṭ*, 264 (p. 501) and 326 (p. 593).

FORM 157

his critics, and regardless of apparent flaws or foibles of his formulation, does not yield. Instead, he emphasizes that a carefully conceived and consciously novel interpretation of a key passage underlies his normative summation. It follows that very often the allegation that a Maimonidean statement contradicts the Talmudic sources routinely presumes a conventional explanation of the Talmudic text or a common form of reconciliation of several texts, while in truth Maimonides operated with different explanations and different ways of handling difficult texts. This commentatorial aspect, generally undocumented, is crucial for a correct understanding of the *Mishneh Torah,* and for the most part critics and commentators alike acknowledge that Maimonides the authoritative codifier is also a versatile commentator. They are aware, moreover, that those original statements clearly labeled by the phrase "it appears to me" are a minuscule part of the *Mishneh Torah*'s all-permeating originality. It was recognized that the *Mishneh Torah* was not a mechanical scissors-and-paste compilation, that curt normative formulations reflect Maimonides' latent explanation of Talmudic texts or halakic concepts, and incorporate his inferences, deductions, and interpretative tours de force. Although Maimonides claimed to have reproduced only those Talmudic statements whose meaning is indisputable, the *Mishneh Torah* abounds with instances of originality of interpretation, harmonistic summation of disparate passages, calculated selection of variant readings, independent determination of the normative decision when the Talmudic context is inconclusive, deliberate choice of one of many possible interpretations, and the like. When Maimonides speaks of his reliance on explicit Talmudic statements (*Talmud 'aruk*),[188] one must always establish which

188. *Tešubot,* 345 (p. 618). Note the important statement of R. Isaac Alfasi on B. Yeb, 92b: ומילי דסברא נינהו דלא שבקינן תלמוד ערוך ואזלינן בתר סברא. (See Y. Weinberg, *Śeride 'Eš* (Jerusalem, 1969), IV, 132–37; H. Albeck, *Maḫo' lat-Talmuḏim* (Tel-Aviv, 1969), p. 547, n.42. The key sentence in the letter to R. Phinehas, where he also uses the phrase *Talmud 'aruk,* claiming that practically all statements of the MT are derived from Talmud sources, needs to be carefully re-examined: ודע שכל הדברים הסתם שבו תלמוד ערוך הוא בפי' בבלי או בירושלמי. It may mean the explicit Talmudic statement as determined by his interpretation (בפי' בבלי) rather than explicit (תלמוד ערוך בפי') by obvious and consensual understanding. This would recognize, even accentuate, the role of commentary. See also RaSHBA, *Tešubot,* V, 270; ham-Me'iri, *Bet hab-Beḥirah,* Meg. 4a (p. 21). See R. N. Z. Y. Berlin, *Šě'iltot* introduction (*Kiḏmat ha-'Emeḳ*).

## 158 INTRODUCTION TO THE CODE OF MAIMONIDES

explanation underlies it. *Talmud 'aruk* is not synonymous with common views or commonplace assumptions. Students of the *Mishneh Torah*, realizing fully that *Talmud 'aruk* is not a simple self-evident meaning or connotation, will regularly reconstruct how Maimonides must have interpreted the Talmudic source, and then either contest or concur with his presumed interpretation. A major task of traditional Talmudists as well as modern scholars has been to unfold or reconstruct Maimonides' interpretative processes.[189] The indirect testimony of R. Menahem ham-Me'iri is particularly relevant here. Having arrived at what seemed to be the "true explanation" of a Talmudic passage, he would consult the codes, especially the *Mishneh Torah*, in order to find the practical codificatory summation, and frequently the latter convinced him that his explanation of the Talmudic passage was defective or imprecise. He was compelled to return and review the passage. Maimonides' intention notwithstanding, the *Mishneh Torah* thus could be, and was, used as a commentary or a spur to Talmudic commentary, for it is sustained by a vast network of Talmudic interpretations.[190]

189. E.g., RABD, *Haśśagot, Nĕdarim*, i, 11; *Bikkurim*, vii, 10; *Ṭo'en wĕ-Niṭ'an*, xiv, 7. Deserving special attention is the fact that he had also to formulate rules in the realm of juridical methodology, i.e., the process of arriving at normative decisions in cases where the Talmud has left matters moot. This area of *kĕlalim*, general rules and principles of adjudication and codification, is distinct from the wide domain of original interpretations of Talmudic passages. See most recently the many articles of B. Z. Benedict, J. Levinger's book on Maimonides' techniques of codification, and the review by I. Ta-Shema, *ḲS*, XXXXI (1966), 138ff. In addition to the literature explicitly devoted to this (e.g., *Yad Mal'aki, Kĕneset hag-Gĕdolah*, and other *sifre kĕlalim*, including works on Talmudic methodology [see J. Jellinek, *Ḳuntres haḳ-Kĕlalim* (reprinted, Jerusalem, 1971)]), which frequently calls attention to Maimonidean procedures and techniques, comments of importance are strewn throughout Rabbinic literature; see, e.g., R. Nissim on B. Ned 7a (דרך הרמבם שפוסק בכל מקום אם תמצא לומר. . .); *Tĕśubot Ḥawwot Ya'ir*, 94.

190. *Bet hab-Bĕḥirah*, introduction, p. 28; *Kĕlale Šĕmu'el*, in Assaf, II, 89; RABD, *Ṭume'at Met*, xv, 5. Sometimes other Maimonidean works provide theoretical disquisitions or conceptual categorizations which underlie the MT rulings; see, e.g., PhM, Ker 3:4 (p. 359), and see *'Issure Bi'ah*, xiii, 8; *Ma'ăkalot 'Ăsurot*, xiv, 18, *Šĕgagot*, vi, 4; ShM, negative 187 (II, pp. 183–84); *Ma'ăkalot 'Ăsurot*, viii, 15, 16. As we have seen (above, nn. 187, 188), responsa frequently provide retrospective glimpses of his procedures and assumptions.

There is also an interpretative-hermeneutical dimension within the *Mishneh Torah* which needs study; see, e.g., *Šĕbitat 'Aśor*, i, 4; *'Issure Bi'ah*, ii, 6; *Ma'ăkalot 'Ăsurot*, ix, 1, 2; *Ma'ăśeh haḳ-Ḳorbanot*, xviii, 4. The idea that a verse teaches by deliberate silence is noteworthy. It is clear, moreover, that the MT contains elementary text commentary which has yet to be fully appreciated; e.g., *Ḥanukkah*, iv, 14, and B. Shab 23b.

The search for hidden, unknown, or unpublished sources—a substantive, indispensable, and certainly enlightening enterprise—must not be isolated from this attempt at meticulous and imaginative reconstruction of the submerged explanations, which could then be analyzed, correlated with other explanations, and—if and when they appeared to be erroneous, inconsistent, or unconvincing—contested. Sometimes even the cumulative resourcefulness of successive generations of scholars has failed to unravel a perplexing Maimonidean statement or propose a reasonable and credible explanation which might have been in Maimonides' mind. This is, it seems, the way in which R. Joseph Karo's statement that many animadversions of RABD require "a master artisan and son of a master artisan" to resolve and answer them, should be understood.[191] There is need to discover or intuit the Maimonidean approach. In any event, given the interpretative infrastructure, the large body of literature known as *haśśagot*—critical glosses, scholia, or animadversions—necessarily combines stricture and supplement. Open and energetic study results in reasoned corroboration, pointed criticism, or various combinations thereof. The study of the *Mishneh Torah* must combine scholarly sleuthing, finding relevant sources or special formulations within related texts, with disciplined, almost empathetic, interpretative hypothesis.

---

191. MT, introduction. (The phrase is from B. AZ 50b). One must, with empathy and erudition, penetrate the Talmudic mind of Maimonides which produced the problematic formulations. The problems are often of a twofold nature, generic-genetic and intrinsic: (1) the alignment or harmonization of Maimonidean statements with the original sources; (2) the integrity, consistency, and intelligibility of Maimonidean statements, or of one statement vis-à-vis another. R. Levi ibn Ḥabib, *Tešubot*, 12, submits that only the second kind is really challenging, for with regard to the first we must assume the existence of a special Maimonidean interpretation, even if we are unable to identify or reproduce it. Maimonidean partisans frequently assert that "perhaps some concealed source will appear in corroboration of Maimonides," a strategy of "wishful hoping." See Twersky, "Beginnings," p. 179. This is the context for Levinger's important book.

The modern method of conceptual analysis elaborated by R. Ḥayyim Soloveitchik of Brest-Litovsk (Brisk) may be seen historically as the systematic application of ham-Me'iri's insight. Note the clear statement in *KM, Bet hab-Beḥirah*, iii, 18; the student must identify the Maimonidean explanation and is not at liberty to assume that a common explanation, whether of Rashi or any other commentator, is the basis of Maimonides' summation. See also the warning of RaDBaZ, *Šebu'ot*, v, 18, against proposing far-fetched theories or solutions which are alien to the author's intention. See below p. 450.

# 160 INTRODUCTION TO THE CODE OF MAIMONIDES

Special attention should be paid in this context to Maimonides' extensive reliance on the works of his predecessors, whose explanations of specific Talmudic passages and problems he adopted and integrated into his Code. This adds another dimension to the *Mishneh Torah* and reveals it as a sturdy link in the great chain of Gaonic-Spanish Talmudic commentary. For all his actual criticism of the Geonim and his statements about his relation to them—how he increasingly emancipated himself from routine and unquestioning reliance upon their views and opinions[192]—these still are seen as the initial interpretative substratum of the *Mishneh Torah*. His use of them was pervasive. His indebtedness to Spanish scholars, most notably R. Isaac Alfasi and R. Joseph ibn Megas, remained quite profound and pervasive from beginning to end. One naturally relies upon a crystallized and respectable tradition, knowingly or unknowingly drawing upon it. There is a process, almost organic, by which the Talmudist adopts previous explanations as his own, frequently integrating them into a larger creative scheme. The fact that the majority of Maimonides' interpretations coincide with R. Hananeel's or R. Isaac Alfasi's reflects this process and his generally great reliance upon the North-African–Spanish axis. We may establish that many difficult formulations in the *Mishneh Torah* are lifted from Gaonic contexts; while this does not remove the conceptual-interpretative problem, it does show an early source. The problem for the student of the *Mishneh Torah* is then no longer why Maimonides formulated it as he did, but why he adopted a problematic Gaonic formulation or how he may have understood it.[193] The process, as indicated, may be conscious or unconscious. We may note one case, for example, where Maimonides rather emphatically informs the questioner that his decision (*Šĕkenim* i, 2) concerning a complicated Talmudic issue is based on the conclusion of Alfasi, "for his proofs are true"; R. Joseph ibn Megas also

---

192. E.g., *'Iggĕrot*, 58, and cf. *Tĕšubot*, 70 (p. 110). The same phrase is used in *Tĕšubot*, 289 (p. 542). Suffice it to recall that in the *Mishneh Torah* introduction Maimonides defined the goal of the Code as a digest of the Talmud together with the Gaonic interpretations and amplifications.

193. E.g., *Gerušin*, ix, 25, and R. Hai Gaon as cited by S. Assaf, *Sinai*, II (1938), 522. See *Kil'ayim*, ii, 9 and RABD (R. Hananeel is designated as "his teacher's teacher").

explained the issue exhaustively in his commentary on *Baba Batra*, and "everything which we have explained and elucidated" agrees with this.[194] In another instance, he reveals that he accepted the view of Alfasi because it is "the true opinion," but then qualified it with regard to one important restriction, which in his opinion had no basis whatsoever.[195] Such congruence, as a result of either routine unreflective reliance or deliberate reasoned review and critical validation of the proofs and reasoning process, is a widespread phenomenon, not always underscored. It follows naturally from being immersed in, impressed by, or dialectically involved with, this literary corpus. The *Mishneh Torah* is thus a repository of interpretations, some of which it helped preserve or disseminate. This emphasis obviously should not obscure the fact that there are many changes in the *Mishneh Torah* resulting from Maimonides' ongoing reflection and progressive precision in analysis; as his understanding of the Talmud changed, there would obviously be a corresponding change in his codificatory formulation. In short, some explication (*peruš*), often invisible, whether inherited, adapted, or totally original, is at the base of every normative formulation. This too is clearly recognized by RABD and his followers and stands as a warning against, and corrective for, glib generalization or hurried reliance upon simple characteristics. The *Mishneh Torah*, qua commentary, warrants meticulous investigation, for this aspect substantially alters the contours of the Maimonidean Code and its scholarly impact. This may indeed be the major thrust of his remarks in the introduction to the *Mishneh Torah* that his book was intended for "small and great." The unlearned will understand and benefit from a clear and comprehensive formulation, while the learned will be stimulated by its implicit interpretative insights or methodological assumptions. An halakic summation that will seem simple to an

---

194. *Tešubot*, 82 (pp. 126–27). In this context it should be noted that whenever commentators or critics relate a Maimonidean view to an "old controversy" (*maḥloket yešanah*) or find a precedent (there are "some who explain") for it, they are ipso facto underscoring Maimonides' selectivity and independence in endorsing one of many possible interpretations; see I. Twersky, *Rabad*, p. 161.

195. *Tešubot*, 122 (p. 218). He notes that criticism of this view is mere sophistry (נצוח). See also PhM, introduction (p. 23).

unscholarly or insensitive reader will strike the scholarly and sensitive reader as original, multifaceted, and suggestive.[196]

6. Our discussion of philosophy and law in Chapter VI establishes that Maimonides is most expansive, conceptually creative, and exegetically inventive, in supporting or refining, even articulating, ethical principles, spiritualistic motifs, and intellectual positions. The entire realm of *ṭa'ăme miṣwot* shows overwhelmingly how Maimonides broke the shackles of the codificatory form with its primary pragmatic purpose and focused his attention on religious impulses and spiritual consequences of laws, on the mingling of pathos and logos with ethos and pragma. Here it will be helpful to introduce a differentiation between *ṭa'ăme miṣwot* and *ṭa'ăme hălakot*, for this adds a significant interpretative dimension to the Code. While the former seeks to expose the general thrust and teleology of the law and its major categories, to identify and elaborate the purposes, goals, and stimuli of the halakic structure, its impulses and consequences, the latter seeks to explain details and nuances of certain laws, to fathom the rationale of certain technicalities, specific requirements, and details. One is macroscopic and the other is microscopic. Efforts of *ṭa'ăme hălakot* revolve around the all-important minutiae of ritual: the selection of a certain portion of the Torah to be read on the Day of Atonement, the use of spices at the *habdalah* ceremony, the symbolism of *'erub*, the permissibility of certain types of work on the intermediate days of the festivals, the monetary fine for theft, the restrictions on visiting hours of the sick.[197] The discipline of

---

[196.] See below, chap. V, nn. 61–62. The quest was for hermeneutical principles and methodological rules as well as ad hoc answers; see, e.g., *Tĕšubot Ḥawwot Ya'ir*, 94.

[197.] *Tĕfillah*, xiii, 11; *Šabbat*, xxix, 29; *'Erubin*, i, 6; and *Yom Ṭob*, vi, 2; *Yom Ṭob*, vii, 12 (cf. Rashi, B. MḲ 18b); *Gĕnebah*, i, 4, and MN, II, 41; *Ḥobel u-Mazziḳ*, iv, 8 (psychological explanation based on B. Shab 105b); *'Abel*, xiv, 5. The reason for visiting the sick, i.e., to participate in his plight and pray for him, is *ṭa'ăme miṣwah;* the reason for not visiting at certain hours is *ṭa'ăme hălakah*. *Gerušin*, ii, 20 (explained in chap. VI below). See also *'Abel*, iv, 2, and xiii, 3; *Nizḳe Mamon*, viii, 5; *Gĕnebah*, i, 10; *Ḥobel u-Mazziḳ*, v, 13; *Mĕgillah*, i, 5; *Sanhedrin*, i, 3. In PhM, Ḥag 2:3 (p. 379), he adds an original reason for a law. See also *'Ăbadim*, vi, 6 ("we have already explained *ṭa'am had-dabar* in *Gerušin*," i, 24). Cf. the Talmudic phrase להראות פנים in B. 'Er 54b; B. Ḥag 13b. For a Gaonic example, see L. Ginzberg, *Geonica* (New York, 1909), p. 82. There are also differences in this realm as in *ṭa'ăme miṣwah;* e.g., *Ta'ăniyyot*, v, 14, and *Tĕšubot*, 224 (p. 399). Awareness of this whole aspect of definitions and explanations (jurisprudential, not philosophical) illumines Maimonides' judicial mind at work. See also *Milah*, i, 18, where KM notes

*ṭaʿăme hălakot* is not an overall conceptualization of halakah as a carefully coordinated system geared to advance ethical-intellectual perfection but an informative-edifying-exhortatory appendix to specific legal norms. The following passages concerning some laws of Sabbath—the Sabbath per se is a central concern of *ṭaʿăme miṣwot*—will concretize the differences while indicating the inevitable measure of overlap:

> Some acts are forbidden on the Sabbath even though they neither resemble nor lead to prohibited work. Why then were they forbidden? Because Scripture says, *If thou turn away thy foot because of the Sabbath, from pursuing thy business on My holy day. . . . And shalt honor it, not doing thy wonted ways, nor pursuing thy business, nor speaking thereof* (Isa. 58:13). Accordingly, one is forbidden to go anywhere on the Sabbath in connection with his business, or even to talk about it. Thus one may not discuss with his partner what to sell on the next day, or what to buy, or how to construct a certain house, or what merchandise to take to such-and-such a place. All this and its like are forbidden, because Scripture says *nor speaking thereof*—speech is thus forbidden, but thinking of business is permitted.
>
> The Sages have forbidden the moving of certain articles on the Sabbath in the way they are moved on weekdays. Why did they enact such a prohibition? The Sages reasoned thus: Inasmuch as the prophets have admonished us and commanded us not to walk on the Sabbath in the way we walk on weekdays, nor to converse on the Sabbath in the way we converse on weekdays—for Scripture says *nor speaking thereof*—how much more should one refrain from moving articles on the Sabbath in the way they are moved on weekdays, in order that he should not regard the Sabbath as if it were a weekday, and so be led to lift and rearrange articles from one corner to another or from one room to another, or to put stones out of the way, or do similar things. For since one is at leisure and at home, he would look about for some occupation, and the result would be that he would not rest at all, and would disregard the Scriptural reason for the Sabbath, namely, *that thy manservant and thy maidservant may rest as well as thou* (Deut. 5:14).

---

the attempt at *ṭaʿăme hălakah*; J. Levinger, *Darke ham-Maḥăšabah*, pp. 92ff. For *Sanhedrin* xviii, 6, see N. Lamm, "The Fifth Amendment," *Judaism*, V (1956), 53ff.; and A. Kirschenbaum, *Self-Incrimination in Jewish Law* (New York, 1970). These explanations are sometimes reproduced anonymously in remote exegetical contexts; see, e.g., Abarbanel, Judges 17:1, and *Sanhedrin*, i, 3, where the semicircular seating arrangement of the court is explained in an original fashion.

Moreover, if he were to examine and move utensils used for prohibited work, he might absentmindedly handle them a little and thus be led to do prohibited work. Another reason is that there are people who have no trade or craft, but spend their whole life in idleness, such as loafers and loungers at street corners who refrain from doing work all their lives. If it were permissible to walk and talk and handle articles on the Sabbath in the ordinary weekday manner, such people would not be recognizably resting on the Sabbath at all. Accordingly, abstention from the aforementioned acts is the one form of rest which is applicable to all persons alike. It is for all these reasons that the Sages have enacted a prohibition against moving articles about, and as will be explained in subsequent chapters, forbade one to move on the Sabbath any article not actually required.[198]

Such explanation, typical of the permeating concern with *ṭaʿăme hălaḵot*, would certainly be incongruent in the context of *ṭaʿăme miṣwot*, which is by definition oriented to the totality of a law and shies away from its details.

The peroration to the entire section on the Sabbath, more exhortatory than explanatory, is also noteworthy for its quiet sublimity and forceful summation:

> Observance of the Sabbath and abstention from idolatry are each equivalent to the sum total of all other commandments of the law. Furthermore, the Sabbath is an eternal sign between the Holy One, blessed be He, and ourselves. Accordingly, if one transgresses any of the other commandments, he is merely a wicked Israelite, but if he publicly desecrates the Sabbath, he is the same as an idol worshiper, although both of these are regarded as heathens in every respect. Hence the prophet says in praise of the Sabbath observer, *Happy is the man that doeth this, and the son of man that holdeth fast by it: that keepeth the Sabbath from profaning it,* etc. (Isa. 56:2). Furthermore, with regard to him who observes the Sabbath in full accordance with the rules thereof, and honors it and delights in it to the utmost of his ability, the prophet describes explicitly his reward in this world, over and above the reward laid up for him in the world to come, in the following verse: *Then shalt thou delight thyself in the Lord, and I will make thee to ride upon the high places of the earth, and I will feed thee with the heritage of Jacob thy father; for the mouth of the Lord hath spoken it* (Isa. 58:14).[199]

---

198. *Šabbaṭ*, xxiv, 1, 12, 13. See Naḥmanides to Lev. 19:2.

199. *Šabbaṭ*, xxx, 15, and *MM;* MN, III, 43. In MN, III, 26 (p. 508) Maimonides calls attention to the fact that his attempt to elaborate a comprehensive rationalization of

## MAIMONIDES' REDEFINITION OF A CODE: ROLE OF THEORETICAL KNOWLEDGE AND EXPLICATION

These facets of the Code are too significant to be glossed over inconsequentially or dismissed as occasional inconsistencies. They demonstrate that the *Mishneh Torah* was undeniably concerned with theoretical knowledge and understanding, as is indicated also by its comprehensive scope. Indeed, at one point Maimonides sums it all up by saying: ". . . But the foregoing statements . . . have only an academic value; for our purpose was merely to enumerate all the rules governing the visibility of the new moon, in order to *make the Torah great and glorious* (Isa. 42:21)."[200] Functionality is not an adequate yardstick. Understanding for its own sake, "making the Torah great and glorious," is important.

In the light of all this we must reinterpret or broaden our definition of the codificatory form, and in so doing we may take our cue from Maimonides himself, who says that he modeled an earlier halakic compendium, a collection of the halakot in the Palestinian Talmud, on the work of R. Isaac Alfasi concerning the halakot of the Babylonian Talmud. Now this minicode, the *Hilkot Yerušalmi*, is not restricted to normative conclusions, but contains judicial explanations as well. The famous case to which Maimonides himself refers in his *Mishnah Commentary* is that concerning the reason for the Rabbinic abrogation of the ancient custom of reciting the Ten Commandments daily.[201] This practice was discontinued because of the heretical rumblings of those who said that only this part of the Torah was given to Moses at Sinai.

---

the commandments will not, and cannot, a priori, be concerned with details. Indeed, this brings to the fore a major difference between the philosophers and kabbalists in their treatment of *miṣwot:* while both seek explanations for the law, the former focus on generalities, on the specific law as a whole entity, while the latter explain each detail and assign significance to each separate component in order to sustain their conception of a mystique of the law.

200. *Kidduš ha-Ḥodeš*, xviii, 14; *Talmud Torah*, ii, 7; *Kobeṣ*, II, 23a; *Tešubot*, 310 (p. 578); PhM, Mak 3:17 (p. 247). For a good definition of "making the Torah great and glorious," see *Tešubot Ḥawwot Ya'ir*, 94; also, Maimonides' reference in *Tešubot*, 310 (p. 578).

201. PhM, Tam 5:1 (p. 420); see above, chap. I, n.11; also PhM, Meg 1:1 (p. 344) and *Megillah*, i, 5, where Maimonides interpolates the reason for the law found in the Palestinian Talmud. Also PhM, Soṭ 1:6 (p. 249).

Inasmuch as this explanation is not found in the Babylonian Talmud (Ber 12a), which merely records the fact, Maimonides felt that he should not expunge it from his codification of the Palestinian Talmud. He would not hermetically isolate the norm from its reason. A code thus, in Maimonides' conception, should teach and expound while it directs, combining prescriptions with their rationales. Fixed laws (*hălakot pěsukot*) should be studied and understood, not just obeyed. If we reread his programmatic statements about the codificatory form of his great work, we will realize that he never really repudiated expository elements. He spoke of "eliminating questions and solutions" (*bě-lo' kušyah wě-lo' peruk*) but did not say that his Code would be "without explanation" (*peruš*). Furthermore, we may latch on to his use of the word "know" (*yode'a*) in the key sentence of the *Mishneh Torah* introduction which provoked so much hostility and resentment: "a person who first reads the Written Law and then this compilation will *know* (and understand) from it the whole of the Oral Law." Actually, the model could have been the Mishnah itself, the first systematization and codification of halakah, which exhibits many of these traits: multiple views alongside of uniform rulings, names of authorities together with anonymous collective opinions, explanations and derivations of laws alongside of apodictic formulation, non-normative subject matter, and aggadic perorations. There was no antipathy between brevity and completeness, systematic summation and thorough understanding, norm and explanation. Indeed, just as the Mishnah defies simple cataloguing or categorization—law book, school text, code, commentary on Scripture, non-Midrashic summary of halakah—so also a close study of its sequel, the *Mishneh Torah*, leads one beyond literary simplicities or one-dimensional characterizations. There is something unique about both works.

Moreover, the lack of absolute finality, the recognition that some ongoing reflection, thoughtful improvisation, and inventive application would remain necessary, may also partially be read into Maimonides' introductory statement: "I would include in it everything of the Torah that has been established and confirmed, omitting no question which might arise, *or at least would mention the principle by means of which that question can easily be resolved* without too deep reflection."[202] Although this is much more restrained than the allowances and requirements for "due deliberation" made in various contexts within the work itself, its import is enhanced by our awareness of the latter. There are questions which the reader will have to grapple with independently, aided by principles and insights provided by Maimonides. In sum—and this is most important for our purpose—a measure of judicial indeterminacy is clearly acknowledged.

However, his unqualified promise to give unilateral decisions—"without differences of view, one person saying so, and another something else," "without mentioning differences of opinion and rejected teachings"—seems to remain unfulfilled, and the exceptions (multiple views, argumentation and demonstration, variant customs, tagging of personal opinions and practices, etc.) are apparently a serious breach of the codificatory form. As we have seen, controversy, i.e., "multiplicity of opinions and variety of schools," was particularly undesirable.

Maimonides' comments on why the Mishnah, committed as it is to uniformity, sometimes includes multiple opinions and cites controversies, may indirectly provide some help in understanding this matter. First, R. Judah quoted minority views in order to make it perfectly clear that these views had been considered and were rejected. If a trustworthy person will come forward and report a tradition which he received, he may be reassuringly informed that this tradition has no normative value. On the other hand, if it were not mentioned, doubt might arise about its status and value; perhaps it has been overlooked and really is authoritative. By mentioning it and repudiating it, the record is unequivocal. Second, the opinion of an individual is cited together with that of the majority in cases where the former prevailed in order to demonstrate this fact and to teach that if the reasoning is correct, clear, and convincing, we follow the individual even though he is outnumbered. Third, original opinions and later retractions are listed as a model lesson in love of truth, for this illustrates that great and pious people, perfect in knowledge, would

---

202. ShM, introduction (II, 361) (italics mine).

not hesitate to change their minds and concede error when circumstances warranted. There are no vested interests or prejudicial considerations in this area. Such insights into the process of redaction of the Mishnah may be relevant for the structuring of the *Mishneh Torah* and its periodic lapse into "multiplicity of opinions."[203]

However, it seems that the inclusion of multiple opinions can best be understood in the light of a basic attitude or modus operandi which conditions so much of Talmudic study and militates, strongly and irresistibly, against absolute finality: the admissibility of two or more equally tenable interpretations of a uniform text, and therefore of divergent conclusions—an attitude which accounts for a good measure of the controversy and polemicism in medieval halakic study. This concept of relativism—more precisely, the lack of objective determinacy, of decisive demonstration characteristic of the mathematical sciences and astronomy—was most strikingly formulated by R. Moses ben Naḥman (Naḥmanides) in his defense of Alfasi against the strictures of R. Zerahiah hal-Levi;[204] he cautions the reader about being smug or coy in trying to puncture some of his attempts to safeguard or save Alfasi's beleaguered positions. In effect he suggests that Talmud study is not for the most part based on final proofs and absolute questions; it has room for tentative hypotheses, heuristic formulations, and in the context of polemics, avowedly strained attempts to defend or rehabilitate respected views.

---

203. PhM, introduction (pp. 22–23). In *Kobeṣ*, I, 25b, Maimonides says that these literary needs of R. Judah were less compelling for him in the composition of the MT, inasmuch as the Talmud had already established all the authoritative views. It is obvious, however, that the nurturing of intellectual openness, or the need to deal with variant customs, remained. See also PhM, 'Ed 1:5, 6 (p. 285). In PhM Men 4:1 (p. 122) Maimonides refers to the Mishnah as "a book of laws" (*sefer dinim; kitāb fiqh*).

204. Naḥmanides, *Sefer Milḥāmot haŠ-Šem*, introduction:

אל תאמר בלבבך כי כל תשובותי . . . בעיני תשובות נצחות ומכריחות אותך להודות בהם . . . כי יודע כל לומד תלמודנו שאין במחלוקת מפרשיו ראיות גמורות . . . שאין בחכמה הזאת מופת ברור כגון חשבוני התשבורות.

This conception is cited, e.g., by R. Hananiah Cases, *Ḳin'at Soferim* (Livorno, 1738), introduction, in justification of his attempted refutation of Naḥmanides' criticisms. Note that R. Yom-Ṭob ben Abraham (RIṬBA) correlates Naḥmanides' intellectual stance with his temperament and personal kindness; *Ḥiddušim, Sukkah*. Joseph Ḳimḥi, *Sefer hag-Galuy*, ed. H. Mathews (Berlin, 1887), p. 4, alludes to a doctrine of relativism in exegesis.

This concept is implicit in Maimonides as well. Note the following triple-tiered situation: (1) In the introduction to the *Mishnah Commentary*, Maimonides pays homage to the excellence of Alfasi's *Hălaḵot* and declares that one would be hard put to find as many as ten errors in this monumental work, which easily eclipsed all the Gaonic compilations. (2) Yet in a responsum to an inquiry concerning a discrepancy between his view and Alfasi's, Maimonides reveals that he had prepared the first draft of a number of tracts and treatises enumerating all those places where Alfasi may be criticized. (3) There are, in fact, scores and scores of places in the *Mishneh Torah* where the normative formulation differs from that in Alfasi.[205] Now these three observations are not mutually exclusive; they mean that the *Hălaḵot* contained not more than ten glaring mistakes which were indefensible and which one was bound, regardless of partisanship or a sense of piety and reverence, to excoriate, but one could register reservations and queries, dissents and strictures, or submit alternate hypotheses and interpretative constructs with regard to many others. There were standing controversies which had never been definitely resolved, and scholars could align themselves with one side or the other. There were degrees of plausibility which had to be considered in the appraisal of divergent views, and these could not be decided on the basis of purely scientific-syllogistic criteria. One had to be resourceful, vigilant, and courageous in interpretation, but also temperate and thoughtful in criticism. A different conclusion reflected a preferred interpretation which need not unreservedly reject or brand the alternate interpretation as absolutely erroneous.

In his letter to R. Joseph ben Judah, Maimonides advises him to study the *Mishneh Torah* alongside of the *Hălaḵot* of Alfasi,

---

205. PhM, introduction (p. 47); *Těšuḇot*, 251 (p. 459). Students of the MT sometimes noted those places where the normative formulation differs from the conclusion of R. Isaac Alfasi; e.g., *Yom Ṭoḇ*, i, 14; *'Išut*, xviii, 28; *Yibbum*, vi, 27; *Zěḵiyyah u-Mattanah*, x, 2; and others. Sometimes no attempt is made to reconcile a controversy between Maimonides and RABD because the issue is recognized as an old one (אמחלוקת ישנה היא); e.g., *Šabbaṭ*, i, 7; *Yom Ṭoḇ*, iii, 8; *Ḥameṣ u-Maṣṣah*, viii, 8; *Šofar*, iii, 4; *'Išut*, xviii, 19; *Nizḵe Mamon*, xii, 8. See A. Freimann, "Těšuḇot ha-RaMBaM," *Sefer Yoḇel lě-B.M. Lewin*, pp. 30, 37. When R. Meshullam ben Moses (introduction to *Sefer ha-Hašlamah*) says that he will not take sides in the issues between Maimonides and Alfasi, he is apparently referring to *many* substantive differences.

thus incidentally emphasizing again that codificatory abridgements are, in his opinion, generally the most appropriate texts for study. Just as in the letter to R. Phinehas, so here too the work of R. Isaac Alfasi is prominent. Most significantly, however, he sensitizes the reader to the simple fact that differences between them—and the implication is that they are quite plentiful—reflect differences of Talmudic interpretation, and careful study (*'iyyun*) of the Talmud will show when and why they diverged. The statement is conspicuously reserved; rather than claims to superiority or certitude, we have a realistic avowal that interpretative-normative differences exist and the diligent student will understand them.[206]

*Maimonides' mĕleket šamayim: rigidity and resilience*

This open-ended concept—the recognition of an irreducible multiplicity—is frequently grounded on the notion of *mĕleket šamayim* (labor for the sake of heaven), which says that given the nature of Talmud study and the indispensability of hypothesis and relentless investigation, the responsible Talmudist, by definition committed to a dogmatic approach and the weightiness of tradition and precedent, will eschew misplaced dogmatism. He must be simultaneously cautious and creative, conservative and innovative. On the one hand, he will not consider himself free to desist from recording a novel interpretation or original conclusion just because no previous writer mentioned it. Inasmuch as his view *may* be the correct one, he is morally obligated to advance it, for he is engaged not in a private and optional academic enterprise but in *mĕleket šamayim*. On the other hand, the significance and solemnity of halakic study will so sensitize and humble him that he will cite views of predecessors even if opposed to his own position. Inasmuch as these opposing views *may* be correct, he is morally obligated to deflate his own authoritativeness, curb the passion of his convictions, and keep the realm of the possible and conjectural open. *Mĕleket šamayim,* in short, is concomitantly a stimulant and a depressant: a spur to originality and inventiveness but also a motive for conservatism and restraint.

206. *'Iggĕrot*, 69. See generally, *Tĕšubot*, 264 (p. 501).

# FORM

Maimonides could certainly have confronted this halakic mentality in the writing of R. Isaac Alfasi, who, for example, explained why he felt it necessary to mention a Gaonic opinion (concerning the validity of a writ of divorce) which contradicted his own view on the matter: "Even though these statements of the Gaon contradict our statements, I have seen (fit) to record them because we are engaged in *mĕleket šamayim*."[207] A younger contemporary of Maimonides, the influential R. Meir hal-Levi Abulafia, tells us why he felt free to record a totally unprecedented explanation of his own, even though it is not stated explicitly in the Talmud nor did "our teachers deal with it": "We have seen fit to write that theory (*sĕbarah*) which seemed logical to us because we are engaged in *mĕleket šamayim*."[208]

RABD of Posquières, the keen critic, also motivates his selective criticism of R. Isaac Alfasi in terms of *mĕleket šamayim*. Alfasi's greatness notwithstanding—and all concurred concerning the seminal value of the *Halakot*—his work invited critical commentary.[209] There is no inconsistency or insincerity in the fact that RABD records his deep-seated humility in the face of this Talmudic giant and then produces some serious and substantive criticisms. This situation, which is typical for the halakist, must elicit a finely calibrated response, honest and courageous, resourceful and respectful, combining diffident acceptance with deft augmentation. The intrinsic sanctity and unequaled importance of this study heightens one's sense of responsibility, which in turn leads dialectically to both rigidity and resilience, receptivity and sensitivity.

---

207. *Hălakot* (p. 48), on B. Giṭ 86a. This Gaonic view is mentioned also by Maimonides even though he rejects it: *Gerušin*, iii, 8.

208. Quoted in *Ṭur Ḥošen Mišpaṭ*, 97; see M. Elon, *Ḥeruṭ hap-Pĕraṭ* (Jerusalem, 1964), pp. 57–58. For a similar procedure, without using the term *mĕleket šamayim*, see R. Judah ben Barzilai, *Sefer ha-'Ittim*, ed. J. Shore (Berlin, 1903), p. 24. R. Jacob ben Asher (*Ṭur 'Oraḥ Ḥayyim*, introduction) cites *mĕleket šamayim* as a motive for composing his code, his young age notwithstanding; see also R. Jacob Landau, *Sefer ha-'Agur* (Venice, 1546), introduction.

209. RABD, *Hassagot* on Alfasi, Keṭ 14a. He lauds Alfasi unreservedly, but this does not inhibit him from engaging in independent and penetrating criticism. Actually, the double meaning of *hassagah*, "stricture" and "supplement," is reflected in this literary reality.

The sense of responsibility, indeed accountability, explains a cognate literary phenomenon: innovative interpretation is frequently accompanied by prayer for guidance or forgiveness (in case of error). In *mĕleket šamayim* the major determinant is divine approval, not approbation or opprobrium from critics. Hence the writer, when dealing with conceptually delicate themes, dialectically conceived presentations, or clearly innovative positions, will deem it necessary to underscore his pure, constructive intentions, regardless of the merits or shortcomings of the actual achievement.[210]

As a matter of fact, it is possible that the concept of *mĕleket šamayim* or *mĕleket haš-šem* (labor for the sake of the [Holy] Name) is found explicitly in the Maimonidean corpus. At the conclusion of his *Mishnah Commentary*, after praying that God deliver him from errors, he invites critics who will not be convinced by some of his statements, or who will come up with seemingly superior explanations for certain laws which he explained, to comment on all these matters, uninhibitedly but graciously. He acknowledges that his task was formidable to begin with, and seriously complicated further by adverse conditions, particularly wandering "from one end of heaven to the other"; the *Commentary* contains halakic explication which he wrote during his peregrinations and some matters which he jotted down while sailing the Mediterranean. In addition, he took time out for study of other sciences. A potential critic should not therefore be intimidated; God will reward him and he will be dearly beloved by Maimonides "for we are engaged in *mĕleket haš-šem*."[211]

---

210. See, e.g., Naḥmanides, *Ḥiddušim* (p. 124) on B. BB 33a (וצורנו יצילנו מכל חטא ושגיאה). Maimonides, *'Iggĕrot*, 50, makes a similar declaration; also PhM, 'Uḳ, postscript, p. 731. This attitude is, of course, discernible in philosophical-theological discourse as well; e.g., R. Saadiah Gaon, *'Emunot wĕ-De'ot*, introduction; MN, introduction (p. 16). See my "Joseph ibn Kaspi," in *Juifs et judaïsme de Languedoc*, ed. B. Blumenkranz (Toulouse, 1977), p. 201.

211. PhM, 'Uḳ, postscript, p. 731. I am assuming that *mĕleket šamayim* and *mĕleket haš-šem* are interchangeable. For *mĕleket šamayim* as teaching, see the question addressed to Maimonides in *Tĕšubot*, 469 (p. 645); in *Talmud Torah*, ii, 3, Maimonides uses *mĕleket haš-šem*, as found in Jer. 48:10; see also *mĕleket šamayim*, PhM, Sanh 1:6 (p. 152), and cf. Pirḳoi ben Baboi, in *Ginze Schechter*, ed. L. Ginzberg, II, 569. Note *Tĕšubot*, 310 (p. 578), where Maimonides seems to reject a stand-off attitude or accommodating silence, preferr-

We may note also that in the introduction to the *Mishnah Commentary* Maimonides describes in some detail the literary activities of the Geonim, with muffled but unmistakable criticism, even condescension. In the introduction to the *Mishneh Torah*, which in some respects is, as we have suggested, a periodization of Jewish history from the vantage point of the Oral Law and its study, Maimonides gives a more general, almost antiseptic, characterization of Gaonic contributions to Talmud study, identifying briefly the major genres of responsa, commentaries, and codes; then, just before describing the motives for his *Mishneh Torah*, which is of course frequently critical of Gaonic views, he adds, almost as a transitional phrase, "and this is the *mĕleket haš-šem* in which all the Geonim of Israel were engaged from the completion of the Talmud to the present day." The implication is that they were "doing their thing," but this did not acquit him of his critical-constructive task, recognizing that all were toiling in the vineyard of God.[212]

The aspect of the *mĕleket haš-šem*, whether explicit or merely implicit—and I am not at all sure that it is explicit—which is most important for understanding the *Mishneh Torah* is not the spur to originality, which is all-permeating, but the restraining impact and residual conservatism: the recognition that all customs could not be unified or standardized, that not all theoretical and interpretative controversies could be definitively resolved, his determination (critics would say, his presumption) and his codificatory goals notwithstanding. Total certitude, finality, unilateral formulation—this was a codificatory utopia never to be achieved. His attitude toward R. Isaac Alfasi—the change, as we

---

ing that every disagreement be sharply delineated. For the term *mĕḥilah* see Twersky, "Beginnings," p. 167, n.27. In any event, it is possible that Maimonides' use of *mĕleket haš-šem* differs from Naḥmanides' avowed pluralism. Maimonides may be saying that there is only one correct view, but he may have erred because of adverse conditions of study. See also PhM, introduction (p. 20) concerning the genesis of controversy among the schools of Hillel and Shammai; Maimonides sees it as a result of inadequate training. Cf., in a totally different context, Y. Baer, *Zion*, XXIII/XXIV (1958), 144.

212. See *Talmud Torah*, v, 4, concerning unqualified people, "students of small minds who have acquired an insufficient knowledge of the Torah," who presume "to judge and render decisions"; and see Maimonides' trenchant peroration: "Of such Solomon, in his wisdom, said, *Take us the foxes, the little foxes, that spoil the vineyards* (Song 2:15)."

noted, from ten loci in the *Mishnah Commentary* to thirty in his letter, and in fact uncounted differences—is not the result of a change from youthful subservience and authoritarianism to adult independence and exuberance (the process is usually inverted, in any event) but a function of discriminating between the more restricted area of egregious lapses and the expandable area of predictable and naturally tolerable divergences.

Yet when anticipating the criticism and opposition which Maimonides knew that his work would surely provoke, he failed to allow for the impact and impulse of *mĕleḵeṯ šamayim*. He predicted that (1) jealousy, (2) confusion engendered by the lack of sources and references (i.e., the essence of the codificatory form), and (3) unenlightened and unreflective rejection of his inclusion of theological principles, would provide motives and pretexts for criticism. He did not, however, allow for legitimate criticism of a less personal nature, for open-ended halakic analysis and exploration of alternatives. The fact is that probably the freest invitation to critical review and divergence of opinion, to movement from great admiration to reservation and rejection, was in the extensive area of actual Talmudic study and analysis. As we have seen, although Maimonides claimed to have codified only those Talmudic statements whose meaning is unequivocal and consensual, the indelible stamp of originality and individuality on the *Mishneh Torah* is visible to all. Students of the *Mishneh Torah*, fully aware of the concept of *mĕleḵeṯ šamayim* and its double-edged thrust, would be guided by comparable standards in their writing. They would be neither carping nor docile, even though in expressing themselves they could be caustic or complimentary. On the one hand, they would not mechanically reproduce all of their own stock views and pit them against those of Maimonides, which means of course that the argument *ex silentio* is not always valid. A critic's silence does not invariably signify concurrence. On the other hand, students of the *Mishneh Torah* would not hesitate to introduce tentative alternatives to rigid Maimonidean formulations, which means of course that they did not have to be unreservedly committed to these views. Just as Naḥmanides could weaken a view of R. Zerahiah hal-Levi in the hope of rehabilitating a view of Alfasi merely by suggesting *possible* interpretations and conjectural constructions, so also students of the

*Mishneh Torah* could at least reservedly question, if not peremptorily dismiss, a Maimonidean statement by submitting an alternative. Their purpose may be to deflate Maimonides' sense of certitude and authoritativeness when this seems very pronounced, or more generally, to stimulate further research and analysis by underscoring the existence of cogent conflicting views. Sometimes they merely reflect one's own uncertainty about the correct theory or proper practice. Needless to say, this concept could also work for the benefit of the *Mishneh Torah*. Scholars may strive to show the plausibility, if not the compelling accuracy, of Maimonidean formulations. If they contend that a dispute is inconclusive or that with regard to a certain Talmudic crux "neither of the explanations" shows exclusive compelling precision, the Maimonidean position remains defensible at least as a live option.[213]

In sum, the codificatory form and its functional goals remain central. The exceptions are significant, but it would be extravagant to speak of a conflict. All our talk about judicial indeterminacy should not be exaggerated or taken out of context. The underlying tenacity and solidity of the codificatory structure are not affected by his excursions into commentary and explication, by his recognition of a measure of pluralism, by his being swayed by interpretative desires and expository tendencies. Some Maimonidean phrases and statements of intent need to be seen in sharper perspective, and allowance must also be made for natural expansiveness, a product of Maimonides' pedagogical skills and sensibilities as well as intellectual resourcefulness and resilience. Instantaneous insertion of explanatory materials—Scriptural, aggadic, historical, biographical—in the course of collecting and codifying the halakah is an obvious factor. While "das unbewusste Schaffen," which sustains and stretches premeditated creativity in various unpremeditated ways, must be taken into account, the double-edged concept of *mĕleket šamayim* helps explain some of these Maimonidean phenomena, and more significantly, much of the post-Maimonidean literature.

213. Twersky, "Beginnings," pp. 156, 179; see R. Samson of Sens, *Kitāb al-Rasā'il*, 131; *Ṭo'en wĕ-Niṭ'an*, xiv, 7 (and *MM*, ad loc.); R. Zerahiah hal-Levi, *Sefer ham-Ma'or*, Ḥul 3b.

# Appendix: Examples of Expository-Exegetical Material

The following eight passages, each intrinsically interesting, will illustrate more fully the exegetical-expository facets of the *Mishneh Torah* and also provide some insight into the nature of Maimonides' deft paraphrase and/or skillful interpretation of underlying Talmudic sources. The fact that he includes such supple material which at first glance is incongruous with the rigid codificatory goals—material such as halakic background, aggadic embellishment, historical fact, interpretative novelty, personal emphasis, exegetical procedure, source references, and Scriptural bases or analogies—is of course what we have been elaborating in this chapter. Awareness of this sharpens our understanding of Maimonides' own definition of the Code and of what the Code is in reality. Comparison of the Maimonidean formulations with the Talmudic statements would concretize, by pointed illustration, Maimonides' modes of elaboration, stylistic variation, commentatorial insertion, and interpolation of ethical and philosophical motifs. Standard Hebrew commentaries or the notes in the YJS translation will guide the reader who wants to check the basic underlying sources or perhaps even read these in conjunction with the Maimonidean presentations.

While the demarcation line between halakic and aggadic material is obviously not firm, these passages are essentially halakic (and their expansiveness is especially striking) as distinct from the passages discussed in Chapter VI (e.g., *Mě'ilah*, viii, 8; *Těmurah*, iv, 13; *Miḵwa'ot*, xi, 12; or *Ṭumĕ'at Ṣara'at*, xvi, 10), which are primarily in the realm of *ṭa'ăme miṣwot* and therefore naturally more expansive and protreptic. In fact, I have not selected any of the concluding passages of the various books, inasmuch as students of the Code have long recognized these as edifying aggadic perorations. Careful study of some additional passages quoted in various parts of this book would further strengthen the thesis about the extent of these expansive exegetical-expository features of the Code; for example: *Těšubah*, ix, 1 (see below, chap. V, n.

50); *Ķeri'at Šĕma'*, i, 4 (see above, chap. II, n. 174); *Tĕfillah*, i, 1-4 (see below, chap. III, n. 79); *Šabbat*, xxiv, 12-13 (see above, chap. II, n. 198); *Yom Ṭob*, vi, 18 (see below, chap. VI, n. 170); *Roṣeaḥ*, iv, 9 (see below, chap. VI, n. 213); *Sanhedrin*, ii, 1-7 (see above, chap, II, n. 164); *Mamrim*, ii, 4 (see above, chap. II, n. 148); *Mĕlakim*, vii, 15 (see above, chap. II, n. 175).

I. *Talmud Torah*, iii, 1, 2, 5, 6, 8, 10, 12, 13

1. With three crowns was Israel crowned—with the crown of the Torah, with the crown of the priesthood, and with the crown of sovereignty. The crown of the priesthood was bestowed upon Aaron, as it is said, *And it shall be unto him and to his seed after him, the covenant of an everlasting priesthood* (Num. 25:13). The crown of sovereignty was conferred upon David, as it is said, *His seed shall endure forever, and his throne as the sun before Me* (Ps. 89:37). The crown of the Torah, however, is for all Israel, as it is said, *Moses commanded us a law, an inheritance of the congregation of Jacob* (Deut. 33:4). Whoever desires it can win it. Do not suppose that the other two crowns are greater than the crown of the Torah, for it is said, *By me kings reign, and princes decree justice. By me princes rule* (Prov. 8:15-16). Hence the inference that the crown of the Torah is greater than the other two crowns.

2. The Sages said, A bastard who is a scholar takes precedence over an ignorant High Priest; for it is said, *She (wisdom) is more precious than rubies* (Prov. 3:15), that is (more to be honored is the scholar) than the High Priest who enters the innermost Sanctuary.

5. At the judgment hereafter, a man will first be called to account in regard to his fulfillment of the duty of study, and afterwards concerning his other activities. Hence, the Sages said, "A person should always occupy himself with the Torah, whether for its own sake or for other reasons. For study of the Torah, even when pursued from interested motives, will lead to study for its own sake" (see B. Pes 50b).

6. He whose heart prompts him to fulfill this duty properly, and to be crowned with the crown of the Torah, must not allow his mind to be diverted to other objects. He must not aim at acquiring Torah as well as riches and honor at the same time. "This is the way for the study of the Torah. A morsel of bread with salt

you must eat, and water by measure you must drink; you must sleep upon the ground and live a life of hardship, the while you toil in the Torah" ('Ab 6:4). "It is not incumbent upon you to complete the task; but neither are you free to neglect it" (ibid. 2:21). "And if you have studied much Torah, you have earned much reward. The recompense will be proportionate to the pains" (ibid. 5:26).

8. In the Torah it is written, *It is not in heaven . . . neither is it beyond the sea* (Deut. 30:12–13). "It is not in heaven," this means that the Torah is not to be found with the arrogant; "nor beyond the sea," that is, it is not found among those who cross the ocean. Hence, our Sages said, "Nor can one who is engaged overmuch in business grow wise" ('Ab 2:6). They have also exhorted us, "Engage little in business and occupy yourself with the Torah" (ibid. 4:12).

10. One, however, who makes up his mind to study Torah and not to work but to live on charity, profanes the name of God, brings Torah into contempt, extinguishes the light of religion, brings evil upon himself, and deprives himself of life hereafter, for it is forbidden to derive any temporal advantage from the words of the Torah. The Sages said, "Whoever derives a profit for himself from the words of the Torah is helping on his own destruction" ('Ab 4:17). They have further charged us, "Make not of them a crown, wherewith to aggrandize yourself, nor a spade wherewith to dig" (ibid. 4:7). They likewise exhorted us, "Love work, hate lordship" (ibid. 1:10). "All study of the Torah not conjoined with work, must in the end be futile, and become a cause of sin" (ibid. 2:2). The end of such a person will be that he will rob his fellow creatures.

12. The words of the Torah do not abide with one who studies listlessly, nor with those who learn amid luxury and high living, but only with one who mortifies himself for the sake of the Torah, constantly enduring physical discomfort and not permitting sleep to his eyes nor slumber to his eyelids. *This is the law, when a man dieth in a tent* (Num. 19:14). The Sages explain the text metaphorically thus: "The Torah abides only with him who mortifies himself in the tents of the wise." And so Solomon, in his wisdom, said, *If thou faint in the day of adversity, thy strength is small indeed*

(Prov. 24:10). He also said, *Also my wisdom stood me in stead* (Eccles. 2:9). This is explained by our wise men thus, "The wisdom that I learned in wrath, this has remained with me." The Sages said "There is a solemn covenant that anyone who toils at his studies in the synagogue will not quickly forget." He who toils privately in learning, will become wise, as it is said, *With the lowly* (literally, *the reserved*) *is wisdom* (Prov. 11:2). If one recites aloud while studying, what he learns will remain with him. But he who reads silently soon forgets.

13. While it is a duty to study by day and by night, most of one's knowledge is acquired at night. Accordingly, when one aspires to win the crown of the Torah, he should be especially heedful of all his nights and not waste a single one of them in sleep, eating, drinking, idle talk, and so forth, but devote all of them to study of the Torah and words of wisdom. The Sages said, "That sound of the Torah has worth which is heard by night, as it is said *Arise, cry out in the night* (Lam. 2:19). And whoever occupies himself with the study of the Torah by night, a mark of spiritual grace distinguishes him by day, as it is said, *By day the Lord will command His lovingkindness, and in the night His song shall be with me, even a prayer unto the God of my life* (Ps. 42:9). A house wherein the words of the Torah are not heard at night will be consumed by fire, as it is said, *All darkness is laid up for his treasures; a fire not blown by man shall consume him* (Job 20:26). *Because he has despised the word of the Lord* (Num. 15:31)—this refers to one who has utterly neglected [the study of] the words of the Torah." And, so too, one who is able to occupy himself with the Torah and does not do so, or who had read Scripture and learned Mishnah and gave them up for worldly inanities, and abandoned and completely renounced this study, is included in the condemnation, "because he has despised the word of the Lord." The Sages said, "Whoever neglects the Torah because of wealth will, at last, be forced to neglect it owing to poverty. And whoever fulfills the Torah in poverty, will ultimately fulfill it amid wealth" ('Ab 4:11, with order of sentences reversed). And this is explicitly set forth in the Torah, as it is said, *Because thou didst not serve the Lord thy God with joyfulness and with gladness of heart, by reason of the abundance of all things, therefore shalt thou serve thine enemy* (Deut.

28:47-48). It is also said *That He might afflict thee . . . to do thee good at thy latter end.* (Deut. 8:16).

II. *Ta'ăniyyot,* iv, 1-3:

1. On each of the last seven fast days imposed on the whole community on account of deficiency of rain, the order of prayer used to be as follows: The Ark was taken out to the town's market place, and the whole population assembled attired in sackcloth. Ashes were placed upon the Ark and upon the Scroll of the Law, in order to intensify the weeping and humble the people's hearts. One of the people then took some of the ashes and placed them upon the head of the patriarch and upon the head of the chief member of the court, at the spot where the phylacteries are worn, to make them feel ashamed and cause them to repent. Then everyone else took some ashes and put them on his own head.

2. Thereupon, while everybody was seated, an elder scholar stood up among them—if there was no elder scholar present, a younger scholar stood up in his place; if there was neither an elder nor a younger scholar present, someone of imposing appearance stood up instead. Addressing words of exhortation to the gathering, he spoke as follows: "My brethren, neither sackcloth nor fasting is of any avail, only repentance and good deeds, as we find in the case of Nineveh, for Scripture does not say of the men of Nineveh, 'God saw their sackcloth and their fasting,' but *God saw their works* (Jon. 3:10), and the prophet says further, *Rend your heart and not your garments* (Joel 2:13)." The speaker then added further exhortations along these lines, to the best of his ability, until he reduced his listeners' hearts to submission and caused them to repent completely.

3. After the speaker finished his words of exhortation, they proceeded to recite the service, appointing as reader someone eligible to recite the prayers on such fast days. If the speaker who had addressed them with words of exhortation was eligible, he was deputized to act also as reader; otherwise another person was appointed.

III. *Lulab,* viii, 14, 15:

14. It was a religious duty to make this rejoicing as great as possible, but participation in it was not open to nonscholars or

anyone else who wished to take part. Only the great scholars in Israel, heads of academies, members of the Sanhedrin, elders, and men distinguished for their piety and good deeds—these only danced and clapped, made music, and rejoiced in the Temple during the Feast of Tabernacles. Everyone else, men and women, came to watch and listen.

15. Rejoicing in the fulfillment of the commandment and in love for God who had prescribed the commandment is a supreme act of divine worship. One who refrains from participation in such rejoicing deserves to be punished, as it is said, *Because thou didst not serve the Lord thy God with joyfulness, and with gladness of heart* (Deut. 28:47). If one is arrogant and stands on his own dignity, and thinks only of self-aggrandizement on such occasions, he is both a sinner and a fool. It was this that Solomon had in mind when he uttered the warning, *Glorify not thyself in the presence of the King* (Prov. 25:6). Contrariwise, one who humbles and makes light of himself on such occasions achieves greatness and honor, for he serves the Lord out of sheer love. This is the sentiment expressed by David, king of Israel, when he said, *And I will be yet more vile than thus, and will be base in mine own sight* (2 Sam. 6:22). True greatness and honor are achieved only by rejoicing before the Lord, as it is said, *King David leaping and dancing before the Lord*, etc. (2 Sam. 6:16).

IV. *Mattĕnot 'Āniyyim*, x, 1, 2, 4, 5:

1. We are obligated to be more scrupulous in fulfilling the commandment of charity than any other positive commandment, because charity is the sign of the righteous man, the seed of Abraham our father, as it is said, *For I have known him, to the end that he may command his children . . . to do righteousness* (Gen. 18:19). The throne of Israel is established and the religion of truth is upheld only through charity, as it is said, *In righteousness shalt thou be established* (Isa. 54:14). Israel is redeemed only through charity, as it is written, *Zion shall be redeemed with justice and they that return of her with righteousness* (Isa. 1:27).

2. No man has ever become impoverished by giving charity and no evil or damage has ever resulted from charity, as it is said, *and the work of righteousness shall be peace* (Isa. 32:17).

Whosoever displays mercy to others will be granted mercy himself, as it is said, *That the Lord may . . . show thee mercy, and have compassion upon thee, and multiply thee* (Deut. 13:18).

If someone is cruel and does not show mercy, there are sufficient grounds to suspect his lineage, since cruelty is found only among the other nations, as it is said, *They are cruel and have no compassion* (Jer. 50:42).

All Jews and those attached to them are like brothers, as it is said, *Ye are the children of the Lord your God* (Deut. 14:1), and if a brother will not show mercy to his brother, who will have mercy on him? And to whom can the poor of Israel look for help—to those other nations who hate and persecute them? They can look for help only to their brethren.

4. Whosoever gives charity to a poor man ill-manneredly and with downcast looks has lost all the merit of his action, even if he should give him a thousand gold pieces. He should give with good grace and with joy and should sympathize with him in his plight, as it is said, *If I have not wept for him that was in trouble? And if my soul grieved not for the poor?* (Job 30:25). He should speak to him words of consolation and sympathy, as it is said, *And I caused the widow's heart to sing for joy* (Job 29:13).

5. If a poor man requests money from you and you have nothing to give him, speak to him consolingly. It is forbidden to upbraid a poor person or to shout at him because his heart is broken and contrite, as it is said, *A broken and a contrite heart, O God, Thou wilt not despise* (Ps. 51:19), and it is written, *To revive the spirit of the humble, and to revive the heart of the contrite* (Isa. 57:15). Woe to him who shames a poor man! Rather one should be as a father to the poor man, in both compassion and speech, as it is said, *I was a father to the needy* (Job 29:16).

V. *Gĕzelah wa-'Ăḇeḏah*, xvi, 7, 8:

7. If one finds a treasure in a heap of stones or in an old wall, it belongs to him, for we assume that it belonged to the ancient Amorites; provided, that is, that he finds it deep down, as is usual with ancient treasures. But if appearances suggest that it was concealed recently, or even if he is in doubt about it, he may not touch it, for it might have been put there deliberately.

8. Now, seeing that one's courtyard can acquire title to property for its owner without his knowledge, as will be explained, why should not the owner of the courtyard acquire the treasure in the old wall even if it did belong to the Amorites, and why should not this find belong to the owner of the courtyard? Inasmuch as its existence is not known, either to him or to anyone else, this treasure is deemed lost for him and for everyone else, and consequently it belongs to the finder. For if, concerning property lost by its owner, Scripture says, *Which he hath lost and thou hast found* (Deut. 22:3)—meaning (it must be returned only if) *he* has lost it, but it is available to all other persons, thereby excluding that which has fallen into the sea and is lost for the owner and for all other persons too—how much more should this rule apply to an ancient treasure that never belonged to the owner of the courtyard and was lost for him and for all other persons too. Therefore it belongs to the finder.

VI. *Sanhedrin,* xii, 3:

3. Once the witnesses say: "We gave him due warning and we know him," the court gives them a solemn charge. How are they charged in a capital case?

The court addresses them thus: "Perhaps what you are about to say is mere conjecture or hearsay, based on secondhand information, on what you heard from a trustworthy person. Perhaps you are unaware that we will in the course of the trial subject you to inquiry and query. Know that capital cases are unlike monetary cases. In a monetary case, one may make restitution and his offense is expiated; but in a capital case (the witness) is accountable for the blood of the man and the blood of his (potential) posterity until the end of time. Thus with respect to Cain it is said: *The voice of thy brother's blood crieth* (Gen. 4:10)—that is, his blood and the blood of his (potential) descendants. For this reason but a single man was created, to teach us that if any man destroys a single life in the world, Scripture imputes it to him as though he had destroyed the whole world; and if any man preserves one life, Scripture ascribes it to him as though he had preserved the whole world. Furthermore, all human beings are fashioned after the pattern of the first man, yet no two faces are exactly alike. Therefore, every man may well say, 'For my sake the world was created.' And perhaps you will say, 'Why borrow this trouble?' It is said: *He being a witness, whether he hath seen or known, if he do not utter it, then he shall bear his iniquity* (Lev. 5:1). And perhaps you will say, 'Why should we incur guilt for the blood of this man?' It is written: *And when the wicked perish, there is joy* (Prov. 11:10)."

If the witnesses stand by their evidence, the oldest of them is called and is subjected to inquiry and query, as will be set forth in the Treatise on Evidence. If his testimony is unshaken, the second is called and examined likewise. Even if there are a hundred witnesses, each is subjected to inquiry and query. If their evidence tallies, the debate is opened with words of encouragement (to the accused), as has already been stated. He is advised not to be afraid of what the witnesses have said, if he knows that he is not guilty. Then the trial proceeds. If he is found not guilty, he is set free. If he is found guilty, he is held in custody till the following day. In the meantime the judges meet in pairs to study the case, eat but little and drink no wine at all; all night each judge discusses the case with his colleague or deliberates upon it by himself. The following day, early in the morning, they come to court. He who was in favor of acquittal says, "I was for acquittal and I hold to my opinion;" he who was for conviction says, "I was for conviction and hold to my opinion," or "I changed my opinion and am now for acquittal." Should there be any mistake as to the identity of those who were in favor of conviction or of acquittal for the same argument (deduced from two Scriptural verses), in which case the two count only as one, as has already been stated, the judges' clerks, who have a record of the reason given by each for his vote, call attention to this fact. The discussion is renewed. If (after the final vote is taken), the accused is found not guilty, he is set free. If it becomes necessary to add to the judges, the addition is made. If those for conviction are in the majority and the accused is pronounced liable, he is led forth to be executed.

The place of execution was outside the court, far away from it, as it is said: *Bring forth him that hath cursed without the camp* (Lev. 24:14). It seems to me that it was approximately six miles distant from the court, corresponding to the distance between the court of Moses, our teacher—the court located at the entrance of the Tent of Meeting—and the [outer limit of the] camp of Israel.

VII. *'Abel*, v, 1-7, 15, 19, 20:

1. The following things are forbidden to a mourner—on the first day by Biblical law and on the other days by Rabbinical authority. He is forbidden to cut his hair, to wash his clothes, to bathe, to anoint himself, to have conjugal relations, to put on shoes, to do work, to read the words of the Torah, to put up his couch, to remove the mourner's headdress, and to extend greetings—the total number of prohibitions is eleven.

2. Whence do we learn that a mourner is forbidden to cut his hair? The sons of Aaron were charged: *Let not the hair of your heads grow loose* (Lev. 10:6). We infer therefrom that any other mourner is forbidden to cut his hair, but must let it grow. Just as he is forbidden to cut the hair of his head, so he is forbidden to cut the hair of his beard or of any part of the body. This prohibition obtains whether the mourner cuts the hair of others or others cut his hair. If, while trimming the hair of another man or while another trims his hair, he learns of the death of his father, the trimming may be finished. The mourner is also forbidden to trim his upper lip or to pare his fingernails with an instrument, but he is permitted to bite them off or to remove one nail with another.

3. Whence do we derive that a mourner is forbidden to wash his clothes, to bathe, and to annoint himself? It is written: *Feign thyself to be a mourner, and put on mourning apparel, I pray thee, anoint not thyself with oil* (2 Sam. 14:2). Anointing implies bathing, for the former is preceded by the latter, as it is written: *Wash thyself therefore, and anoint thee* (Ruth 3:3). Just as the mourner is forbidden to wash his clothes, so is he forbidden to put on new white clothes that have been ironed.

4. A mourner is forbidden to anoint even part of his body. If, however, it is his purpose to remove filth, he is permitted to do it. He is also forbidden to wash even part of his body with warm water, but he may wash his face, hands, and feet, though not the entire body, with cold water.

5. Whence do we learn that a mourner is forbidden conjugal relations? It is written: *And David comforted Bath-Sheba his wife,*

*and went in unto her, and lay with her* (2 Sam. 12:24), which implies that before that time he was forbidden to do it. So too, a mourner is not permitted to take a wife, nor is a woman (in mourning) permitted to be married, even if marital relations are not contemplated. A mourner is permitted, however, to be alone with his wife, although conjugal relations are forbidden to him.

6. Whence do we learn that a mourner is forbidden to put on shoes? Ezekiel was told: *And put thy shoes upon thy feet* (Ezek. 24:17), which imples that all other mourners are forbidden to do it. If he is on the road, he may walk with his shoes on; when he enters the city he must remove them.

7. Where is it intimated that a mourner is forbidden to engage in work? It is written: *And I will turn your feasts into mourning* (Amos 8:10). Just as all are forbidden to do work during a festival, so is a mourner forbidden to engage in work. And just as he is forbidden to engage in work, so is he forbidden to buy and sell merchandise, or to go on business from city to city.

15. Whence do we infer that a mourner is forbidden to engage in the study of the Torah? Because Ezekiel was told: *Sigh in silence* (Ezek. 24:17).

19. Whence do we infer that a mourner is forbidden to remove the mourner's headdress? Ezekiel was commanded: *And cover not thy upper lip* (Ezek. 24:17). We conclude therefrom that all other mourners are bound to have the headdress on.

The cloth with which he wraps himself shall cover part of his mouth, as it is said: *And he shall cover his upper lip* (Lev. 13:45). This sentence is rendered by Onkelos, "He shall wrap himself up like a mourner."

20. Whence do we infer that a mourner is forbidden to extend greetings to others? Ezekiel was told: *Sigh in silence* (Ezek. 24:17). During the first three days he should not respond to greetings extended to him, but inform (the one who salutes him) that he is in mourning; after the third day and through the seventh, he may respond to the greetings of others; after the seventh and through the thirtieth, he may greet others, but others should not greet him. If he is in mourning for his father or his mother, others should not greet him until the expiration of twelve months.

If a mourner is forbidden to greet others, is it not an argument from the minor to the major that he is forbidden to talk much or to indulge in laughter, as it is said *in silence?* He should not hold a child in his arms, lest it lead him to levity. He should not enter a place where there is rejoicing, such as a house of feasting, or the like.

VIII.  *Mělakim*, ii, 5:

5. The king has his hair trimmed every day, pays due regard to his personal appearance, adorns himself with beautiful clothes—as it is written: *Thine eyes shall see the king in his beauty* (Isa. 33:17)—sits on his throne in his palace, sets his crown on his head. All the people come before him when he is disposed to see them, they stand in his presence, and bow down to the ground. Even the prophet stands in the presence of the king and bows down to the ground, as it is written: *"Behold Nathan the prophet." And when he was come in before the king, he bowed down before the king with his face to the ground* (1 Kings 1:23).

The High Priest, however, comes before the king only when he is disposed to do it; he does not stand in his presence, but the king stands before him, as it is said: *And he shall stand before Eleazar the priest* (Num. 27:21). Nevertheless, it is the duty of the High Priest to give honor to the king, to ask him to be seated, to rise before him when the latter comes to see him. The king therefore shall not stand in his presence save when he asks him for directions given by means of the Urim.

So too, it is incumbent upon the king to give honor to students of the Torah. When the members of the Sanhedrin and Sages of Israel visit him, he shall rise before them and seat them at his side. This is the way Jehoshaphat the king of Judah acted. When he saw even the disciple of a scholar, he rose from his throne, kissed him, called him, "my teacher, my master." This humble attitude becomes the king in the privacy of his home only, when none but he and his servants are there. He may not act thus in public, he may not rise before any man, nor be soft of speech, nor call anyone but by his name, so that his fear may be in the hearts of all.

# III

## Scope

### COMPREHENSIVENESS OF THE CODE

Maimonides invariably emphasized the encyclopedic character of his Code. The *Mishneh Torah* was designed to provide in an easy and engaging way accurate and exhaustive information concerning "what is forbidden or permitted, clean or unclean, and the other laws of the Torah . . . so that thus the *entire* Oral Law might become systematically known . . . so that *all* the laws shall be accessible to young and old . . . so that *no other work should be needed* for ascertaining any of the laws of Israel, but that this work might serve as a compendium of the *entire* Oral Law, including the ordinances, customs, and decrees instituted from the days of our teacher Moses until the compilation of the Talmud, as expounded for us by the Geonim in *all* the works composed by them since the completion of the Talmud."[1] In an earlier work Maimonides had revealed in emphatic detail that he "deemed it advisable to compile a compendium which would include *all* the laws of the Torah and its regulations, *nothing missing in it* . . . so that this compendium would embrace *all* the laws of the Torah of Moses our teacher, whether they have any bearing in the time of the exile or not . . . Such was to be my goal in this work—brevity with completeness, so that the reader thereof might encompass *all* that is found in the Mishnah and Talmud, Sifra, Sifre, and Tosefta, and more than that, *all* decrees and ordinances of the later Geonim of blessed memory, as well as *all*

---

1. MT, introduction (italics mine). Jeremy Bentham ("A General View of a Complete Code of Laws," *Works,* III [New York, 1962], chap. 31 [p. 205]) might have been speaking for Maimonides when he wrote: "It is not sufficient that a code of laws has been well digested with regard to its extent; it ought also to be complete. For the attainment of this object, it is necessary at once to embrace the whole of legislation—and this principal object has never yet been attempted. I have ventured to undertake it, and I have, so to speak, projected the sphere of the laws, that all its parts may be seen at one view."

that they have explained and commented upon concerning the prohibited and permissible, unclean and clean, invalid and valid, guilty or exempt, liable or not liable to pay, or to swear or not to swear an oath. In short, in addition to this work there was to be *no need for another book* to learn anything whatsoever that is required in the *whole* Torah, whether it be a law of Scripture or of the Rabbis."[2] This holistic conception of codification led Maimonides to "enumerate first in the introduction to that work the number of *all* commandments, positive and negative, so that the parameters of the work embrace *all* of them, not one single commandment being omitted."[3] The word "all" and variations of it occur with the rhythmic regularity of a lyrical refrain; comprehensiveness is the hallmark of these programmatic pronouncements and all-inclusiveness is their goal. Holism is another aspect of making the "Torah great and glorious,"[4] commodious and comprehensive—it helps transcend functionality.

In justifying the patient and rather fastidious review of principles of astronomical calculation which were included in Book Three of the *Mishneh Torah,* Maimonides again underscores his striving for comprehensiveness: "We have now expounded all the methods of calculation required for the determination of the visibility of the new moon and for the examination of witnesses, so that discerning students might be able to learn everything about it. Thus they will not miss this particular branch of the many

---

2. ShM, introduction (II, 361–62, 364) (italics mine). A crucial difference between the *Sefer ham-Miṣwot* and the *Mishneh Torah* is clearly underscored here. While the former lists only Scriptural commandments, the latter integrates Scriptural and Rabbinic laws. On the striving for literary self-sufficiency, see also ShM, positive 108 (I, 116–17); concerning PhM on *Ṭohărot:* it is all-inclusive and the reader need not consult any other work. Repetition of material is frequently justified in terms of completeness; see chap. IV, below. On the other hand, critics—e.g., RABD, *Haśśaḡot, Gerušin,* xii, 9, and *MM;* '*Ăḇaḏim,* vii, 6 (and *'Issure Bi'ah,* iii, 13)—sometimes add notes for this same reason. The problem of repetition in the MT still needs careful study. When Maimonides says (e.g. *Kelim,* xiii, 1), "as we have explained in many places," he shows awareness of a measure of repetitiousness which seems to be taken for granted in such a large work. See also chap. IV, below.

3. ShM, introduction (II, 364) (italics mine). While the ShM is here seen primarily as an auxiliary manual, Maimonides tended subsequently to underscore its independent value; see below, chap. V.

4. See above, chap. II, n.200.

branches of the law and will have no need to roam and ramble about in other books in search of information on matters set forth in this Treatise. *Seek ye out of the book of the Lord and read; none of these (truths) shall be missing* (Isa. 34:16)."[5]

The little peroration, applying the phrase "book of the Lord" to his own *Mishneh Torah*, is quite dramatic.[6] Nothing was to be omitted from this new "book of the Lord" which was to guide and instruct its readers in *all* religious matters. Indeed, the verse from Psalms (119:6) which serves as the motto of the introduction already strikes this keynote, which reverberates steadily: *Then should I not be ashamed, when I have regard unto all Thy commandments*. The verses—with one exception all are from Psalms—which introduce each Book of the *Mishneh Torah*, while definitely providing literary embellishment, are not merely ornamental rubrics, pietistic gestures, or rhetorical flourishes. Each verse is linked substantively to the ensuing section; if properly interpreted—and often their use is based upon unconventional exegesis which must be reconstructed—the verses appear as suggestive and evocative formulae. The verse at the beginning of the introduction heralds the aim of the *Mishneh Torah*, which is to confront the totality of the commandments.[7]

These explicit declarations are reinforced by the many curt references in his responsa emphasizing the comprehensiveness of the

5. *Kiddus̆ ha-Ḥodes̆*, xix, 13. See PhM, RH 2:7 (pp. 315–18), Suk 4:1 (p. 282). For Maimonides' work in astronomy, see the document published by S. Goitein, "Miktab 'el ha-RaMBaM," *Tarbiz*, XXXIV (1965), 235; also *Tes̆ubot*, 390 (p. 668) and n.29.

6. Naḥmanides, in the brief preface to his minicode *Hilkot Niddah* (reprinted, New York, n.d.), p. 8, applies this verse to the *Ba'ăle han-Nefes̆* of RABD (p. 89) but not to his own work. Moreover, the *Ba'ăle han-Nefes̆*, which he admired so much that he doubted the need for his own manual, purported to encompass only one subject in its entirety, not the entire law. Note that in MTH, 1–2, Maimonides also compares his work to Scripture; like the latter, his work, too, he claims, has been misunderstood. See Joseph Albo, *Sefer ha-'Ikkarim*, ed. I. Husik (Philadelphia, 1930), III, chap. 23 (p. 202); Joseph ibn Kaspi, *Mishneh Kesef*, ed. I. Last (reprinted, Jerusalem, 1970), II, 44.

7. Cf. Ibn Ezra, ad loc., where the understanding of all commandments is emphasized; *Yalkut S̆imĕ 'oni* (on '*Abot*), ed. S. Neiman (New York, 1957), p. 146. One may also see in this verse, as in Ps. 119:46, a directive emphasizing the need to remain steadfast in one's commitment and observance and immune to external pressure or ridicule. See, e.g., *Tur 'Oraḥ Ḥayyim*, 1; M. H. Luzzatto, *Mĕsillat Yĕs̆arim*, ed. M. Kaplan (Philadelphia, 1948), chap. 5 (p. 47); and Maimonides' characterization of David in *Mĕ'ilah*, viii, 8 (also *Lulab*, viii, 15). Also Isaac Abarbanel, *Naḥlat 'Abot* (New York, 1953), p. 365 (on 'Ab 5:18). For the introductory verses of each book, see chap. IV, below.

## SCOPE

*Mishneh Torah;* "a compendium (*ḥibbur*) encompassing all the laws of the Torah" is the stock phrase for referring to the *Mishneh Torah*.[8] This is its salient trait. If one were to ask why the major letters dealing with the *Mishneh Torah*, which provide so much insight into, and defense for, Maimonides' methods and motivation, ordinarily gloss over this aspect of the work, the apparent answer would be that unlike the codificatory form this was not a subject of dispute or condemnation and was not in need of vindication. It was, on the contrary, admiringly acknowledged as an intellectual act of daring, a bold shift of perspective and practice, a formidable and unprecedented venture in Rabbinic literature.[9] Maimonides freed deeper values in Talmudic culture, at least temporarily,[10] by his versatility and boldness. As Maimonides himself realized and stated with complete candor, not since R. Judah the Patriarch had an attempt been made to rework and reformulate the *entire* halaḵah, without any artificial, ephemeral, or pragmatic restrictions, without attention to historic accidents, abnormalities, or time-bound constraints. To the extent that a "summa"—a term used first by jurists and then by theologians, equivalent to the term *dīwān* or *sefer kolel* used by Maimonides himself—is "an exhaustive and systematic presentation" of the subject matter, the *Mishneh Torah* may be described as a summa of Judaism.[11] The term, however, is less important than the literary reality.

8. E.g., *Tešubot*, 121 (p. 217), 129 (p. 242), etc.
9. E.g., R. Aaron ben Meshullam in his letter to R. Meir Abulafia, *Ḳobeṣ*, III, 11d; R. Menahem ham-Me'iri, *Bet hab-Bĕḥirah*, introduction, 25; Profiat Duran, *Ma'ăśeh 'Efod* (Vienna, 1865), p. 19.
10. His vision of comprehensive Talmud study did not become a reality. See, e.g., the apology of RaDBaZ at the beginning of his commentary on MT, *Kil'ayim; Mishneh lĕ-Meleḵ*, introduction; introduction of R. Israel Lifshitz to his Mishnah commentary *Tif'eret Yiśra'el;* introduction of R. Israel of Shklov (student of the Gaon of Vilna) to his commentary on *Šĕḳalim*, and of R. Hayyim of Volozhin to the Gaon of Vilna's commentary on *Zĕra'im*. The modern revival of interest in neglected areas—e.g., the intense concern with *Ḳodašim* emanating from the schools of Radin and Brisk—owes much to Maimonides, but it is not really a continuation of his conception of comprehensiveness and simplification. The same is true for such works as the *Pĕ'at haï-Šulḥan* of R. Israel of Shklov or *Sidre Ṭohărot* of R. Gershon Enoch of Radzin. R. Joseph Karo, *Bet Yosef* on *'Oraḥ Ḥayyim*, 3, complains that no one studies the *Hilḵot Bet hab-Bĕḥirah;* and see, e.g., A. Salman, *Sefer Nĕtibot haḳ-Ḳodeš* (Jerusalem, 1955), introduction.
11. For a good description of the summa, see E. Panofsky, *Gothic Architecture and Scholasticism* (Meridian, 1951), pp. 7, 31ff.; also, E. Lesne, *Les écoles de la fin du VIIIe siècle*

## RESTRICTED SCOPE OF STUDY

The all-embracing study of the Oral Law, including laws and ideas momentarily devoid of practical value or temporarily in abeyance as a result of historical and geographic contingencies, was indeed a major innovation and a revolutionary procedure for the age of Maimonides. Study of the Oral Law was already restricted in Amoraic times (third to fifth centuries), when the first (*Zěra'im*) and the last (*Ṭohărot*) of the six orders of the Mishnah, dealing respectively with the knotty laws of Palestinian agriculture and the complex purity-impurity syndrome, went unstudied.[12] A creeping pragmatism or unimaginative philosophy of relevance, the notion that only the functional need be studied,[13] narrowed the curriculum even further, so that eventually not "four orders" but "three orders" became standard. R. Menaḥem ham-Me'iri (thirteenth century) accentuates the situation by noting, in his historical review, that everything except the "three orders" was "*totally* abandoned."[14]

Within this restrictive pattern, one must of course differentiate between various types of material and methodological abridgment, between tampering with the Talmudic text and abandoning it. There is an approach which streamlines and abridges the study of the Talmud itself by recognizing the progressive obsolescence of entire nonpractical sections and allowing them to fall into complete oblivion, but which does not result in the Talmud

---

*à la fin du XII<sup>e</sup>* (Lille, 1940), pp. 249, 251, 676. Note also L. Blau, "Das Gesetzbuch des Maimonides historisch betrachtet," *MbM*, II, 339–40, vis-à-vis B. Cohen, "Classification of Law in the Mishneh Torah," *JQR*, XXV (1935), 521. See the emphatic use of *ḥibbur* in MTH, 10. Franz Rosenzweig asserted apodictically that the MT was the summa of Judaism; see the Hebrew collection of his articles, *Nahărayim* (Jerusalem, 1960), p. 98.

12. Twersky, *Rabad*, p. 15.

13. See the statements of Maimonides and R. Moses of Coucy, below. Mutatis mutandis, it is interesting to note that for a medley of motives pragmatism or functionality was an early slogan of the modern *haśkalah* movement, which then resulted in various forms of more extreme anti-Talmudism. See such works as A. Gumperz, *Ma'ămar ham-Madda'*; N. Weisel, *Diḇre Šalom wĕ-'Emet*; early volumes of the *ham-Mĕ'assef*; and generally the articles of I. Barzilay in *PAAJR*, XXIV (1955), 39ff., and XXV (1956), 1ff. Such leading Rabbinic figures as R. Ezekiel Landau and R. David Tevele recognized and emphasized the issue of Talmudism.

14. *Bet hab-Bĕḥirah*, introduction, p. 32 (italics mine): . . . נעזבו השלשה האחרונים עזיבה מוחלטת See also ibid., p. 28, where he ridicules those who limit their study to laws of holidays, a special form of pragmatism.

being superseded by an ancillary text. There is also an approach which curtails the scope of Talmud study by outright abandonment of the Talmud and the substitution of other works, codes or compendia, for the text of the Talmud. While halakic pragmatism could manifest itself in either way, the latter practice was also a pedagogic response to the intrinsic difficulty of the Talmud, which was not only vast but intricate. Within this latter approach, furthermore, there is a fundamental distinction between bare-bones codification of results and conclusions of practical matters and full exhaustive study of these same matters. At the other end of the spectrum, there is the approach—to be adopted, as we shall see, by Maimonides—which would abandon the Talmud as a text but preserve its full scope and content by insisting on comprehensiveness of coverage. Difficulties would be eliminated but relevance and practicality would not arbitrarily dictate the order of study. Abstract theoretical study would be endorsed and greatly facilitated. Codes, in this context, were a useful and relaxing short-cut but not an unconditional surrender to pragmatism.

Perhaps the most telling illustration of the fact of increasing shrinkage, which was both a literary tendency and an educational practice, is provided by the Talmudic compendium (*Halakot*) of R. Isaac Alfasi (d. 1103), whose subject matter was radically restricted by rather inflexible considerations of practicability and applicability. By rigorously omitting all nonpractical matters—he does occasionally include an aggadic motif which is relevant—the scope of Alfasi was inevitably confined to the "three orders," with a few appendices at the end to cover such topics as *Tefillin, Ṣiṣit, Mĕzuzah, Sefer Torah*—practical topics treated in generally nonpractical tractates (e.g., *Mĕnaḥot*). The *Halakot* of Alfasi apparently embodied the tendency and filled the need of the times, for its popularity was great and in many places it superseded the Talmud as the basic text of study. It was approvingly designated as a "miniature Talmud" and earned a reputation as the best summary of laws.[15] Maimonides' encomiastic

---

15. The phrase is used by R. Menahem ben Zerah, *Ṣĕdah lad-Derek* (Warsaw, 1880), p. 6; R. Isaac ben Joseph Israeli, *Yĕsod 'Olam*, ed. B. Goldberg (Berlin, 1851), II, 34b. See also R. Aaron hal-Levi, *Pĕkudat hal-Lĕwiyim*, ed. N. Bamberger (Jerusalem, 1962), p. 1.

judgment that R. Isaac Alfasi's compendium eclipsed all Gaonic works and rendered them obsolete may mean that he perfected their tendencies and best achieved the common goal of summarizing the practical portions of the Talmud, for this was the pervasive concern of the Geonim. This pragmatism, generally, was more pronounced and more pervasive in the Spanish orbit than in the Franco-German orbit; Franco-German scholars persisted in a theoretical and comprehensive approach to the study of the Oral Law and devoted their attention to impractical themes such as Ḳodašim, while the academic habit of Spanish scholars was to study only the trilogy of Mo'ed, Našim, and Nĕzikin, and that often in abridged form.[16]

This pattern of abridged study, which we have somewhat categorically or exclusively linked with a conception of pragmatism, was actually nurtured and sustained by a variety of factors. There was, first of all, an assortment of ad hoc improvised reasons for partial limitations of Talmud study. The tractate Nĕdarim (dealing with vows) was not studied, lest expert knowledge concerning annulment of vows encourage levity and leniency in the observance of vows.[17] Some European Jews refused to study those parts of the Talmud which deal with laws and rites of mourning (Mo'ed Ḳaṭan in particular), lest preoccupation with this topic constitute a bad omen.[18]

Those sections of the Mishnah which lacked Amoraic explanation in the Talmud—the bulk of Zĕra'im and Ṭohărot—also went unstudied, even though parts were practical and relevant. In other words, parts of the Mishnah were neglected and forgotten

16. Twersky, Rabad, p. 15. One detail of R. Abraham ibn Daud's story of the four captives (Sefer haḳ-Ḳabbalah, ed. G. Cohen [Philadelphia, 1967], pp. 47–48, 65) is noteworthy: the Spanish scholars confronted by R. Moses ben Enoch were studying some nonpractical parts of Yoma; see S. Lieberman, Toseft Rišonim (Jerusalem, 1937), II, 6, and Cohen, Sefer haḳ-Ḳabbalah. On the other hand, R. Nissim Gaon, a conscientious and apparently popular pedagogue, was worried by students who lacked basic knowledge and were not oriented in all parts of the Talmud. His Sefer ham-Mafteaḥ lĕ-Man'ule hat-Talmud (reprinted, Jerusalem, 1971) was written for them, to provide cross-references easily and conveniently.

17. 'Oṣar hag-Gĕ'onim, Nĕdarim, ed. B. M. Lewin (Haifa, 1928), pp. 21–24; ham-Me'iri, Bet hab-Bĕḥirah, 'Abot, ed. S. Waxman (New York, 1944), p. 66.

18. Sefer Ḥăsidim, ed. J. Wistinetzki (Frankfurt, 1924), no. 588 (p. 160).

because their subject matter was arcane and impracticable, but in addition the Mishnah per se, because of its unusually challenging nature, limited the scope of study by forcing students to shy away from it. This was a sort of self-perpetuating neglect and therefore self-fulfilling educational program. We may cite the testimony, or confession, of R. Zerahiah hal-Levi who underscored his own diffidence, resulting from this general difficulty, in dealing with the study of *Miḳwa'ot:* "Upon entering the gate of water, my heart melted and turned to water. For the waters rose high, a stream which I am unable to cross *because we have no Talmud* for most of the *mishnayot* in it."[19] At about the same time Maimonides arraigned "a great man, a man of great speculative power, in the West (Maghrib)," for lacking knowledge of Mishnah and hence falling into error.[20] Mishnah study required assiduous labor and sleuthing, scholarly courage, interpretative resourcefulness, and powers of generalization and abstraction, and therefore was not too popular.

### HALAḲIC PRAGMATISM AND SPIRITUALITY

More substantively and more extensively, the very practice-oriented hierarchy of values which led in many quarters to absolute concentration on the study of the Talmud, to the exclusion of such "theoretical" or "scholastic" subjects as Bible, grammar, theology, etc., could be inverted in order to justify radical curtailment of the Talmud curriculum itself. The intensity could be slackened. R. Abraham ibn Ezra critically but faithfully reproduced this pragmatic rationale while describing scholars whose sole intellectual preoccupation was the Talmud. Many sections of the Bible—historical and geographic matters, for instance—are studded with difficulties and obscurities; some passages are knotty and recondite; the themes of some prophecies, e.g., on eschatological matters, are recalcitrant and defy proper interpretation. As a result, the expenditure of energy in the study of this material is unproductive, there being a gaping incommensurability between input and output, intellectual effort and tangible

---

19. *Haśśagot* on the *Ba'ăle han-Nefeš*, p. 62 (italics mine).
20. PhM, Miḳ 4:4 (p. 554).

scholarly achievement. For after all, "if we study all these (subjects) day and night, we shall not achieve knowledge of a single commandment by means of which we shall be able to inherit the life of the world to come." It follows from this that the many scholars who have studied only the Talmud from their youth onwards are all on the right track, "for from the Talmud do we know all the commandments by means of which we shall be able to inherit the world to come."[21] They plunge directly into the vast sea of the Talmud (note the parallel scholastic image of *oceanus juris*) without any preliminary or concomitant studies, because the Talmud provides the practical knowledge necessary for religious behavior. Study is the handmaiden of practice and Talmudic lore is the prerequisite for, and source of, religious performance. Inasmuch as the real desideratum is knowledge and practice of halakah, one should, these scholars contend, proceed forthwith, dispensing with propaedeutic disciplines and avoiding theoretical distractions or cosmetic additions. *Ars gratia artis,* i.e., *Torah li-šěmah,* abstract theoretical study which roams freely over *all* areas and genres, is here a victim of practice-oriented study. There is neither time nor motivation for the former.[22]

Ibn Ezra's northern French contemporary, the independent and provocative Talmudist and exegete R. Samuel ben Meir, likewise portrays this attitude very accurately, while sharply dissociating himself from it, in the famous report of his conversation-confrontation with his aging grandfather Rashi. His point of departure, and theme of his plaintiveness, is the neglect of Bible study, but his sharp delineation of the sturdy supremacy of Talmud study and the reasons for it is of far-reaching significance: "To be sure, the main objective of the Torah is to teach us (conduct) and to give us pertinent information through the various methods of ordinary as well as aggadic or halakic interpretation. For this reason the older Sages, in their great piety, immersed themselves completely in the hermeneutic teachings which are es-

---

21. R. Abraham ibn Ezra, *Yěsod Mora'* (Prague, 1833), chap. 1 (p. 12). See, most recently, A. Scheiber, "Pěrakim mis-Sefer ham-Miṣwot lě-RaSaG," *Sefer Yobel lě-Šim'on Federbush* (Jerusalem, 1961), pp. 330ff.
22. I. Twersky, "Religion and Law," *Religion in a Religious Age,* ed. S. D. Goitein (Cambridge, 1974), pp. 69ff.

sential (for practical conduct) and failed to delve into the profundities of the ordinary meaning."[23] Inasmuch as the main goal was to determine fully the practical applications of the Biblical text and those conceptual implications which were relevant to halakic norms, all other matters were derivative and ancillary. He was particularly distressed that *pĕšaṭ*, the attempt to establish philologically the *sensus litteralis*, was most easily discarded.

However, another almost antithetical corollary of this utilitarian stance, which made non-Talmudic subjects expendable, is that nonpractical Talmudic topics are equally expendable. Why, asks Ibn Ezra, the extravagant attention to *Nĕziḳin,* which would be happily anachronistic in an ideal society, free of litigation and strife? If all Jews would be righteous, laws of torts, criminal liability, fraud and deception, robbery and theft, would be superfluous. In other words, while the laws concerning sacrifices were self-evidently irrelevant in the light of a calculus of deliberately pragmatic principles, other topics could also be labelled and classified as such. Furthermore, while some laws (e.g., of prayer) are obligatory for each person individually, many commandments are not incumbent upon every single individual but are to be fulfilled collectively (e.g., sounding the shofar); consequently, in keeping with the utilitarian conception, it would suffice for one person to be informed about the details of the implementation of the latter. Universal, or even just widespread, knowledge of such matters served no practical purpose.[24]

The really universal and fully repercussive subjects of study which should command the attention of all, without exception, are, according to this, ethics and metaphysics, inasmuch as these

---

23. *Peruš*, Gen. 37:2.
24. *Yĕsod Mora'*, chap. 1 (p. 15b); the study of *Nĕziḳin* was singled out also by R. Kalonymus ben Kalonymus, *'Eḇen Boḥan*, ed. A. M. Habermann (Tel Aviv, 1936), p. 56; and R. Joseph ibn Kaspi, *Hebrew Ethical Wills*, ed. I. Abrahams (Philadelphia, 1948), I, 138. For Gaonic study limited to *Nĕziḳin*, see S. Schechter, *Saadyana* (Cambridge, 1903), p. 64, n.3; see also the poem of R. Samuel han-Nagid in his *Dīwān*, ed. D. Yarden (Jerusalem, 1966), p. 229: אבל קורין במסכת בבא. See ShM, end of listing of positive commandments (p. 258), where Maimonides concludes that of all the 613 commandments only 60 are now practical. See R. Baḥya, *Ḥoḇoṯ hal-Lĕḇaḇoṯ*, x, chap. 7 (II, 374–76), who clearly affirms, in a passage that Maimonides may have remembered while writing the ShM, that very few of the 613 commandments are actually incumbent upon the individual.

are absolutely requisite for individual perfection and cannot be achieved vicariously or collectively. Knowledge of God must be attained individually, intellectually, and experientially; the task cannot be delegated to any agent or understudy. "Man is obligated to perfect himself and to be acquainted with the commandments of God who created him, to understand His works; then will he know his Creator. Thus Moses said, *'Show me now Thy ways, that I may know Thee* (Exod. 33:13).' And David said, *'Know thou the God of thy father and serve Him* (1 Chron. 28:9)', which should be interpreted to mean 'first know Him and then serve Him.' Similarly Jeremiah exhorted *Let not the wise man glory in his wisdom,* (Jer. 9:22), whatever this wisdom may be, and irrespective of its dignity and nobility. There is only one kind of wisdom in the possession of which one may glory: *that he understandeth and knoweth Me* (Jer. 9:23)"[25] In short, this religio-intellectual emphasis could seriously, perhaps irreversibly, challenge the centrality of Talmud study and curtail its scope; the thorough and discriminating religionist, realizing this hierarchy and axiology of religious pursuits, would unquestionably rank philosophy above all other pursuits, just as kabbalists would passionately insist that the religious scholar who has not advanced to the study of kabbalah is sorely deficient.

The apparent paradox of this attitude is obvious. While protagonists of this view will endorse a utilitarian criterion for the selection of those practical parts of the Oral Law which should be studied, they will abandon it with regard to metaphysics, which by definition is concerned with knowing for its own sake. Its subject matter is the very essence, the *hyle,* of the contemplative life. The guiding principle is thus not simple practicality. The emphasis is on relevance, and this may be either practical *or* theoreti-

---

25. *Yĕsod Mora',* chap. I (p. 15b); the verses are topoi of philosophical literature, see MN, III, 51, 54; R. Judah hal-Levi, *Kuzari,* V, 22; *Hobot hal-Lĕbabot,* i, chap. 3 (I, 66); and later, e.g., J. Jabez, *'Or ha-Ḥayyim,* p. 34b. A later example of this tendency is the *Sefer he-'Agur* which was composed, as the author states, for a disciple who was passionately devoted to philosophic studies, and "time, which is very valuable, does not allow him to follow the (complex) halakic exegesis," hence the need for a summary. See *Sefer he-'Agur haš-Šalem,* ed. M. Hershler (Jerusalem, 1960), introduction, p. 15, and I. Arama, *Ḥazut Kašah* (Pressburg, 1849), p. 27b.

cal; knowledge of God is invariably and eminently relevant, for "it is the basic principle of all basic principles" (*Yĕsode hat-Torah*, i, 1), while knowledge of sacrificial law is neither practical nor relevant. Later theoreticians of Talmud study would develop the notion—reaching a crescendo or very pungent formulation in such works as the *Nefeš ha-Ḥayyim* of R. Ḥayyim of Volozhin or the *Sefer hat-Tanya'* of R. Shneur Zalman of Ladi (Liady)—that *all* Talmud study is beneficial, useful, and perennially relevant; even understanding the discarded opinion or the wrong view in a controversy is meritorious, for it is study of the word of God. Hence purely theoretical and impracticable Talmud study would be as relevant as metaphysics. It possesses an intrinsic significance, an indelible and immutable relevance.

Related to this philosophical-intellectual quest is the position which saw preoccupation with abstruse and nonpractical legal matters as vainglorious and boastful, even materialistic, and therefore serving to deflect one from the ultimate religious goal. R. Abraham ibn Ezra himself notes this parenthetically: "there is the type of scholar who meditates upon the Talmud in order to boast."[26] R. Baḥya ibn Paḳuda had also spoken disdainfully of scholars who "exert themselves . . . to resolve doubtful points and elucidate obscurities (in the dicta of the Talmudic authorities), with the purpose of winning a name and glory." In the introduction to his book, he already chided "the majority of our contemporaries" whose vision and values are askew: "And if any one of them is moved to devote himself to the study of the Torah, his motive is to be called a scholar by the masses and to gain a name among the great."[27]

Similarly R. Abraham ibn Daud emphatically differentiated between the intrinsic worthiness and necessity of legal study and the possible debasement of motive: "Like the wasting of too much time on the preparations for a journey is one's excessive devotion to the arts which are mostly of use to the material world, such as medicine and law. By this I mean to refer only to a person who wastes his time in the practice of medicine for the sake of picking

---

26. *Yĕsod Mora'*, chap. 1 (p. 15b).
27. *Ḥoḇot hal-Lĕḇaḇot*, iii, chap. 4 (I, 220); introduction (pp. 26–27).

up fees rather than for the sake of rendering merciful service, or to a person who similarly wastes his time in the practice of law in order to gain a reputation, or to amass a fortune, or to display his wit."[28]

The assumption is that dialectical skills in Talmudic analysis will bring honor and prestige, professional gain and material reward, for a person possessed of these skills will be sought as teacher and mentor. Hence the frequent correlation in these criticisms between subject and motive, i.e., as the subject is more abstruse and casuistic, there is greater likelihood of the motive being less than pure. Esoteric knowledge may be a means to boasting and popularity. In many of these criticisms, moreover, the theoretical debate or abstract polemic is leavened and fortified by allusions to a concrete and unattractive reality—a reality which in its many refractions and configurations exhibits features that betray ideal hopes and assumptions. It should be noted that this arraignment of intellectual ostentation continued, somewhat ritualistically at times, past the twelfth century and was echoed not only by rationalists convinced of the indispensability of philosophy but also by pietists fearing the crystallization of a limpid intellectualism, in which the inner religious moment would be eclipsed by the extrinsic cognitive gesture or some unworthy motive. R. Solomon al-'Ami, at the beginning of the fifteenth century, is outraged by the self-aggrandizement of certain Talmudists who distort their halakic expertise, compounded of dialectical skills and esoteric legal lore.[29] R. Joseph Jabez, a forceful antagonist of philosophic culture who analyzed the contemporary sixteenth-century socio-religious scene with passion and acumen, condemns the scholars whose commitment to, and

---

28. R. Abraham ibn Daud, *ha-'Ĕmunah ha-Ramah* (reprinted, Jerusalem, 1961), pt. II, p. 45; see H. A. Wolfson, "The Classification of Sciences in Medieval Jewish Philosophy," *Hebrew Union College Jubilee Volume* (Cincinnati, 1925), I, 315. This complaint seems to have been widespread and recurrent. Petrarch (*Epistolae de rebus familiaribus*, III, 18), for example, who found the neglect of legal history distasteful, condemns "the majority of our jurists, caring little or nothing for the origins of law and the first fathers of jurisprudence, or *anything except professional gain*" (cited by D. Kelley, *Foundations of Modern Historical Scholarship* [New York, 1970], p. 88, n.4; italics mine).

29. R. Solomon al-'Ami, *'Iggeret Musar*, ed. A. M. Habermann (Jerusalem, 1946), p. 40.

achievement in, the study of halakah were sullied by an unworthy motive, the desire to be great in the eyes of the masses.[30]

The fear that excessive or exclusive preoccupation with law, with positive and temporal matters, will erode true spirituality is quite influential, and in its own way contributes to abridgment of Talmud study. Of course, a measure of rivalry between law and theology is a historical commonplace in all religious cultures. In Judaism, it expresses itself in intermittent skirmishes, not really a war, of suspicion—suspicion that religious sensitivity will be sacrificed to legalistic expertise, that an imperious Talmudism will crowd theological insight and sensitivity out of the picture. R. Bahya ibn Pakuda articulates the spiritualistic anxiety with this kind of halakic intellectualism and expresses the religiously motivated criticism of a Talmudic pedantry which ranks farfetched impracticable legal speculation higher than theological or ethical inquiry: these same scholars, combining religious formalism and materialism,

ignore the duties of the heart. They pay no attention to what would be detrimental to their religious and moral activities. They spend their days in the study of singular deductions from the legal principles and of what is strange and difficult in the final decisions; they cite the conflicting views of the Talmudic authorities on novel points of law, while they neglect topics which they have no right to neglect—topics that affect their spiritual interests, which it is their duty to investigate, such as the truth of the prophet's signs and of tradition, and the modes by which it can be demonstrated; the obligation which the Creator has imposed upon us to adduce with our reasoning faculties proofs of His existence and to serve Him with a perfect heart, and many similar points that can be intellectually apprehended.[31]

Actually, Ibn Pakuda had already launched his criticism of this type of scholar at the beginning of his book, where he denigrates the Talmudist who "turns aside from the way of the Torah to that which will neither secure for him any special moral excellence nor

---

30. Joseph Jabez, *'Or ha-Ḥayyim* (Lublin, 1912), introduction (p. 8); chap. 1 (p. 11) להתגדל ולהתפאר.
31. *Ḥobot hal-Lĕbabot*, iii, chap. 4 (I, 220); cf. C. Haskins, *Studies in Medieval Culture* (Oxford, 1929), p. 47; S. Kuttner, *Harmony from Dissonance* (Latrobe, Pa., 1960), pp. 1–4; F. Rahman, *Islam* (New York, 1968), p. 186.

free him from spiritual stumbling, and for ignorance of which he would not be punished, while he omits to investigate the root-principles and fundamental precepts of his religion, which he should not have ignored nor neglected, and without the knowledge and practice of which no precept can be properly fulfilled." He sustains his arraignment of spiritually impoverished legalists who preoccupy themselves with "academic trifles" with a poignant anecdote, which has a striking parallel in a work of al-Ghazālī:

> A learned Rabbi, on being consulted concerning a strange case in the law of divorce, replied to the inquirer, "Thou, who askest concerning a point which will not harm anyone if he does not know it, hast thou the knowledge of duties which thou art bound to learn and art not permitted to ignore, and which it is not proper that thou shouldst transgress, that thou spendest time in speculations on curious legal problems, which will neither advance thee in knowledge or faith nor correct faults in thy character? I solemnly assure thee that for the past thirty-five years I have occupied myself with what is essential to the knowledge and practice of the duties of my religion. Thou art aware how assiduous I am in study and what an extensive library I possess. And yet I have never turned my mind to the matter to which thou has directed thy attention, and about which thou enquirest." And he continued to rebuke and shame him concerning the matter.[32]

R. Abraham ibn Daud, who like R. Baḥya excoriated improper motivation, also implied that the secondary pursuit often superseded the primary in the total intellectual-religious configuration: "It follows also that they will not acquire knowledge of the *roots* of religion and its principles, to which they should properly devote most of their speculative skill and minute attention, rather than the *branches* (of religion) for which limited study would suf-

---

32. *Ḥobot hal-Lĕbabot*, introduction (pp. 27, 29), also p. 35; see the very important Maimonidean emphasis in PhM, Nid, 6:15 (p. 617); cf. I. Goldziher, *Die Zahiriten* (Leipzig, 1884), p. 182; M. Watt, *Muslim Intellectual* (Edinburgh, 1963), p. 113. R. Baḥya's indictment (together with that of Ibn Janāḥ) is cited by R. Moses ibn Ezra, who asserts that the *Ḥobot hal-Lĕbabot* is concerned with despiritualized Talmudists; see P. Kokowtzoff, "The Date of Life of Baḥya," *Livre d'Hommage à la Mémoire de Samuel Poznanski* (Warsaw, 1927), pp. 19–20. Note S. Krauss, "Hat-Tĕlunot neḡed ha-Rabbanim," *Ṣiyyunim* (Berlin, 1929), pp. 186 ff.

fice."[33] This plaintiveness reverberates in post-Maimonidean writings, as seen in R. Isaac Aboab's introduction to his ethical compendium *Mĕnoraṭ ham-Ma'or*, where he records that "the Talmud is almost forlorn and those few who do study it engage in dialectic, preoccupying themselves with details (*pĕraṭim*) and neglecting the true generalities (*kĕlalim 'ămitiyyim*)." He becomes progressively indignant as he describes those who spend all their time learning practical conclusion (*pĕsaḳ*) in order to teach them publicly to unworthy people, while they turn their backs on aggadah and *ḥoḵmah*.[34]

The common denominator in these expressions is impatience with the possible despiritualizing effects of excessive Talmudism. Furthermore, a frequent consequence of this downgrading of monolithic Talmudism is the concrete demand that the curricular imbalance be corrected by the inclusion of specific metahalaḵic subject matter. The concept of *talmuḏ Torah* should not be excessively specialized, but instead must be sufficiently expansive and integrative so as to include specific metahalaḵic subject matter, be it philosophy or mysticism, study of Bible or aggaḏah. Legal knowledge divorced from spirituality cannot be regarded as final.

On the other hand, coming from an entirely different direction, there was apparently a species of Biblicism which contributed in its own way to the fragmentization and neglect of Talmud study. R. Judah ben Barzilai portrays Bible-centered scholars whose knowledge of Talmud is minimal and whose Scriptural interpretations are as a result frequently antitraditional.[35] This is congruent with R. Jonah ibn Janāḥ's assertion—a very significant concession from the pen of this prestigious grammarian—that

---

33. *Ha-'Ĕmunah ha-Ramah*, p. 2 (italics mine). As Dr. Nemoy reminds me, "roots" and "branches" parallel the Muslim theological terminology of *uṣūl* and *furū'*.

34. R. Isaac Aboab, *Mĕnoraṭ ham-Ma'or*, ed. J. Fries-Horeb (Jerusalem, 1961), p. 10. For critical attitudes to dialectic in northern Europe, see H. Soloveitchik, "Three Themes in the Sefer Ḥasidim," *Association of Jewish Studies Review*, I (1976), 340ff. For parallel twelfth-century criticism of the use of dialectic, see, e.g., S. Kuttner and E. Rathbone, "Anglo-Norman Canonists of the Twelfth Century," *Traditio*, VII (1949–50), 288; H. Kantorowicz and B. Smalley, "An English Theologian's Views of Roman Law," *Medieval and Renaissance Studies*, I (1941), 252.

35. R. Judah ben Barzilai, *Peruš Sefer Yĕṣirah*, ed. S. J. Halberstamm (Berlin, 1885), p. 5. See S. Lieberman, *Midrĕše Tēman*, pp. 27–31.

philologians often ignore, or are ignorant of, traditional Talmudic hermeneutics and interpretations.[36] R. Baḥya ibn Paḳuda also knows of Scripture-oriented students whose sole interest is routine and ordinary knowledge of the Biblical text.[37] Within this context we should note that tension and antipathy between grammarians and Talmudists seem to have been rather common, a particular embodiment of a general rivalry between protagonists of various disciplines who viewed other disciplines as competing and diversionary rather than complementary and supportive.[38] Whatever one's attitude to pansophism, a dichotomy, or even a wedge, between Bible and Talmud was especially insufferable, inasmuch as it could result in erosion of respect for traditon and for the absolute inviolability of the Oral Law. The specter of Karaism was always lurking in the shadows—anti-Talmudism or merely non-Talmudism was a sinister phenomenon.

Distortion of values by Talmudists or those who proclaimed themselves to be Talmudists could also discredit genuine Talmudism in the eyes of many. Exhibitionism and charlatanism are satirized by R. Samuel han-Nagid in a well-known poem. The suggestion seems to be that inasmuch as Talmud study was universally revered, the temptation to pose was great, for one could "get away with" many wrongs.[39]

MAIMONIDES' INTELLECTUAL BREAKTHROUGH

Now whatever the reasons, the decomposition of Talmud study was quite advanced in the middle of the twelfth century, especially in the Spanish orbit where legal pragmatism and metahalakic spirituality merged. Inasmuch as Maimonides was influenced by R. Baḥya ibn Paḳuda and R. Abraham ibn Ezra, the historical perspective just sketched is not merely our reconstruction of a problem but is most likely congruent with Maimonides' own perceptions and aspirations. Maimonides, in

---

36. R. Jonah ibn Janāḥ, *Sefer ha-Riḳmah*, ed. M. Wilensky (Berlin, 1929), p. 19.
37. *Ḥoḇot hal-Lĕḇaḇot*, iii, chap. 4 (I, 219).
38. See, e.g., the Hebrew translation *Mozne Ṣedeḳ* in S. Assaf, *Mĕḳorot lĕ-Tolĕdot ha-Ḥinnuḳ bĕ-Yiśra'el* (Tel Aviv, 1926), II, 43.
39. Samuel han-Nagid, *Dīwān*, p. 229. See PhM, Soṭ 3:3 (p. 256).

common with many of his predecessors and contemporaries, was also firmly convinced of the superiority and indispensability of philosophy and metaphysics. This was the ultimate and noblest subject of study, which should be pursued according to the "breadth of one's mind and the maturity of one's intellect."[40] Talmudic expertise not related to, or rooted in, philosophic knowledge was inadequate. He too was agitated by ostentation and pragmatism in the study and use of Talmud—the debasement of motive. Self-styled scholarly leaders, who seek to perpetuate devitalized or atrophied institutional forms and conform to study habits which only the masses, in flagrant error, consider conducive to perfection and lofty achievement, were a source of anguish for Maimonides.[41] He would like to puncture pretentiousness. Similarly, Maimonides had no doubts that law must be mounted on true theological conceptions and ideological imperatives, or else genuine spirituality and piety might be attenuated and the entire halakic system calcified. As we shall see, he insisted zealously upon the need for reciprocity between these two areas. Yet while sharing these unsettling concerns, Maimonides reached different conclusions with regard to Talmud study. He rose aggressively and dexterously against the disintegrative tendency, and with one heroic sweep pushed back the frontiers of Talmud study. His own development is very instructive. At first he appears as a creature of his environment, reflecting its academic tendencies and preoccupations. His youthful commentary on the Talmud covered only the usual trilogy, "in keeping with the custom of every Talmudic commentator," and the tractate Ḥullin, "for which there was great need." His orientation at this stage is thoroughly pragmatic, differentiating between the dispensable and the indispensable.[42] In the *Commentary on the Mishnah*, however, where he inevitably confronted the Oral Law in its totality, he already appears to be chafing under these intellectually and religiously stultifying restrictions and counsels his readers to transcend them. At one point he pauses to condemn

---

40. *Talmud Torah*, i, 12; MN, III, 51; PhM, Ḥag 2:1 (p. 376).
41. *'Iggĕroṭ*, 57, 63, 65; MTH, 2, 3, 4, 8; PhM, 'Ab 4:7 (p. 441).
42. See chap. I, above.

the pragmatic rationale in simple but forceful terms: "It is, therefore, proper for man to preoccupy himself with the subjects of sacrifices and to delve into them. He should not say, 'After all, these are matters for which there is no use at present,' as most people do in fact say."[43] He bemoans the fact that "even the greatest Sages" find it hard to comprehend *Zĕra'im* and *Ṭohărot*, although he readily acknowledges that they are the most difficult subjects; the themes of *Mo'ed* and *Nĕziḳin* are easy in comparison.[44] In the letter to R. Phinehas he repeats with obvious pain and regret that the laws of sacrifices are terra incognita for contemporary scholars. He suggests, moreover, that in Christian countries aspects of civil law are as alien as laws of sacrifices, because the curtailment of judicial autonomy had academic repercussions.[45] There is here another undesirable manifestation of pragmatism. The quasi-sociological observation that judicial autonomy increases the study and knowledge of parts of halakah and vice versa recurs in post-Maimonidean literature. Regional conditions also contribute to the dismantling of Talmud study. Fi-

---

43. PhM, Men 13:11 (p. 171).
44. PhM, Ṭoh, introduction (pp. 34, 37), and see *Peruš Sefer Yĕṣirah*, pp. 50–51. A comparison of this statement in PhM with a passage in MN, introduction (p. 11) illustrates how the terms "easy" and "difficult" are relative to the context. While in the former *Nĕziḳin* is "easy" compared to *Ṭohărot*, in the latter *all* Talmud study is "easy" compared to metaphysics: "You know how Solomon began his book, *To understand a proverb and a figure; the words of the wise, and their dark sayings* (Prov. 1:6). And it is said in the Midrash: 'To what were the words of the Torah to be compared before the advent of Solomon? To a well the waters of which are at a great depth and cool, yet no man could drink of them. Now what did one clever man do? He joined cord with cord and rope with rope and drew them up and drank. Thus did Solomon say one parable after another and speak one word after another until he understood the meaning of the words of the Torah.' That is literally what they say. I do not think that anyone possessing an unimpaired capacity imagines that the *words of the Torah* referred to here, which one contrives to understand through understanding the meaning of parables, are ordinances concerning the building of tabernacles, the lulab, and the law of the four trustees (*šomrim*). Rather what this text has in view here is, without any doubt, the understanding of obscure matters (i.e., philosophy)."
45. *Ḳobeṣ*, I, 26b; see S. Assaf, *Bate had-Din wĕ-Sidrehem* (Jerusalem, 1924), pp. 12–13; note the parallel observation by S. Luzzatto, *Ma'ămar 'al Yĕhude Winiṣi'ah*, ed. A. Aescoly (Jerusalem, 1951), p. 152: Jews in eastern Europe study all parts of halakah because they have judicial autonomy. Cf. S. D. Goitein, *A Mediterranean Society*, I, 258: "While the legal and moral questions created through usurious lending to Gentiles occupy enormous space in the works of the former [Rabbis of France and Germany], they play no role in the writings of the latter [the Geonim, and Moses and Abraham Maimonides]." General socioeconomic opportunities or restrictions, not merely judicial autonomy, are formative in this sphere.

nally, we may note that when repeating the praises which had been lavished upon R. Zechariah, a man of dubious achievement in Maimonides' opinion, Maimonides mentions that he had been described as a man "of great understanding, who is thoroughly conversant with the four orders of the Talmud."[46] This was the maximum that could be attributed to him.

It is in the context of these hardened but impeachable habits and undesirable limitations and constraints that the *Mishneh Torah*, without polemics or defensiveness, merely reacting to the inadequacy of existing works, presents itself as a major intellectual breakthrough, insisting that the present time, when part of the law is in abeyance, should be viewed as an historical anomaly and should not arbitrarily determine the scope of study. The real historical dimensions were to be those in which the Torah and its precepts would be fully realized (as they were in the past), that is, in the time after the restoration of the Davidic dynasty, when "all the ancient laws will be reinstituted . . . sacrifices will again be offered, the Sabbatical and Jubilee years will again be observed in accordance with the commandments set forth in the law."[47] Consequently the *Mishneh Torah* gives "equal time" to such antiquated subjects as laws pertaining to the Temple and sacrifices. There is no difference between them and the laws of prayer or holiday observance. The rigors of classification, the details of summation, the cadences of formulation, the insights of explication, are the same. The student of the *Mishneh Torah* is invariably impressed with the meticulousness and exhaustiveness which characterize Maimonides' treatment of the Temple, its sanctity, its architecture, its vessels, the duties of the priests and Levites attending to it, and the detailed regulations concerning communal and individual offerings. In a variety of contexts, laws concerning the Messianic period are treated in a nonchalant way, as halakic reality and not as esoteric eschatology.[48] Such exhaustive presentation of arcane subjects reflects the

---

46. *'Iggĕroṭ*, 59; see S. Assaf, "Ḳobeṣ šel 'Iggĕroṭ R. Šĕmu'el ben 'Ali," *Tarbiz*, I (1929), 102ff., especially 106–08.
47. *Mĕlakim*, xi, 1.
48. E.g., *Šĕmiṭṭah wĕ-Yoḇel*, xii, 16; *Beṭ hab-Bĕḥirah*, ii, 3; *Ma'ăśeh haḳ-Ḳorbanoṭ*, ii, 14; *Parah*, iii, 4; *Mĕlakim*, xiii, 8.

author's indomitable determination to destroy all barriers between the theoretical and the practical, tempestuously bursting the bounds and bonds of shrunken Spanish Talmud study. The all-embracing theoretical approach of Maimonides is fresh and energetic, a decisive, if abortive, attempt to retrieve substantial parts of the Talmud from obscurity. The codification of *Kodašim* and *Tohărot* is so new and unprecedented that one may rightly apply to Maimonides his own felicitous dictum concerning Abraham's proclamation of monotheism (*'Akum,* i, 3): "He had no teacher, no one to instruct him in anything." He calmly went into regions where his predecessors feared or failed to tread. His gesture was bold and creative, powerful and passionate. This is how he silently remonstrated with those who neglected large parts of the Talmud.

MOTIVES FOR THE UNIFICATION OF THEORETICAL AND PRACTICAL

Any attempt to reconstruct the motives for Maimonides' determination to remove the barriers between the theoretical and practical and to present the law in its entirety must take account of several factors: religious, methodological (in order to unite the Oral and Written Law), pedagogic, and a cognate motive of conceptual classification.

The desire that the study of God's laws and precepts should not be functionalized or in any way straitjacketed by ephemeral situations provided religious motivation. A Talmudic passage (B. Shab 138b) built around a verse from Amos, quoted by Maimonides in the introduction to his commentary on *Tohărot*, suggests such a motive: "When our masters entered the vineyard at Jabneh, they said, 'The Torah is destined to be forgotten in Israel, as it is said, *Behold, the days come, saith the Lord God, that I will send a famine in the land, not a famine of bread, nor a thirst for water, but of hearing the words of the Lord* (Amos 8:11).' And it is said, *And they shall wander from sea to sea, and from the north even to the east; they shall run to and fro to seek the word of the Lord and shall not find it* (Amos 8:12). And what does *they shall run to and fro to seek the word of the Lord* mean? Said they, 'A woman is destined to take a loaf of heave offering and go about in the synagogues and academies to learn whether it is unclean or clean.' "[49] Such doubt and confusion are intolerable. The "word of God" should be sought unconditionally, and knowledge of it should be readily available.

Maimonides proceeds to note rather dramatically that the study of the laws of purity is designated, without any qualification or hedging, as Torah. He then adds that this study is a ladder by which one ascends to the attainment of the "holy spirit." To omit it is therefore intellectual and religious folly. Indeed, Maimonides implies that the prevalent restriction of Talmud study eventuates in ignorance of Scripture itself. Many verses are unknown or misunderstood because their Talmudic elaboration is ignored. Hence—and it is quite plausible that Maimonides is here jabbing at the Bible-centered scholarship which some contemporaries espoused—sufficient knowledge of Scripture is also contingent upon comprehensive study of Talmud.[50] Biblicism per se is an academic dud and a religious scandal. The interrelatedness of the oral and written traditions is generally stressed not only as a theological position but also as indispensable for exegetical truth.

R. Moses of Coucy, whose Rabbinic work (*Sefer Miṣwoṯ Gaḏol*) was heavily influenced by Maimonides, repeats the Maimonidean condemnation of pragmatism and then adds: "Some of the masses say, 'What business do we have with the order of *Ḳoḏašim* and certainly with the laws of *Zĕraʿim* and the laws of *Ṭohărah,* all matters which are not practicable in this time?' You should not speak in this fashion, for the commandments which the Sovereign of the universe has decreed should be studied, and one should know their fundamentals even if they are not needed or cannot be practiced at the moment." For we are enjoined "to study them

---

49. PhM, Ṭoh, introduction (p. 33). See B. Yoma 5b (למסבר קראי). The verse from Amos (8:11) is used also in MN, I, 30.
50. PhM, Ṭoh, introduction (p. 34); cf. B. AZ 20b; see R. Moses ben Jacob of Coucy, *Sefer Miṣwoṯ Gaḏol* (Venice, 1522), introduction, p. 2; Duran, *Ma'ăśeh 'Efoḏ,* p. 15. See also PhM, Zeḇ, introduction (p. 9), where Maimonides passionately emphasizes that ignorance of the laws concerning sacrifices extends also to Scriptural verses: "the great scholar and the ignoramus from the masses are alike" in their total neglect of this subject. Note a similar emphasis in Ibn Ezra, *Yĕsoḏ Mora',* chap. 1.

with regard to *all* commandments."[51] Study per se is "practical" and need not seek to anchor itself in an external and self-transcending relevance. The "word of God" has its own enduring relevance, its own continuity and integrity. If by studying divine law one is "thinking God's thoughts," eternity and temporality meet and there is no room for a present-oriented solipsism. It is noteworthy that Maimonides does not make much of the idea of the equivalence of study and deed or the substitution of study for deed in certain areas, while R. Moses of Coucy mentions it only briefly as a final argument.[52] In their conception study is self-validating and not merely a surrogate for ritual performances which are out of reach. In sum, any dichotomy between the practical and the theoretical should be roundly repudiated for purely theoretical-religious reasons.

The special focus of the Maimonidean approach is here clear and distinct. Maimonides differentiated between *pilpul*[53]— digressive study, excessive subtlety, unrewarding exegesis, scholastic concern with highly hypothetical matters—and sovereign mastery of law in its entirety, its arcane as well as its very practical matters. In this respect he parts company with the much admired R. Baḥya ibn Paḳuda, who stressed that excessive concern with far-fetched halakic matters does not automatically enhance religious sensitivity, indeed probably detracts from it. Whereas he and his fellow spiritualists would be led to dismember the corpus of law and curtail study of nonpractical parts of the Talmud

---

51. *Sefer Miṣwot Gaḏol*, part II (*Miṣwot 'Aśeh*), introduction (italics mine).
52. Ibid.; see B. Men 110a, B. Meḡ 28b. In PhM, Men 13:11 (p. 171) Maimonides mentions B. Men 110a. Cf., e.g., R. Moses Isserles, *Toraṭ ha-'Olah* (Prague, 1871), introduction (p. 17a). For Torah study (science is treated in *Yěsoḏe hat-Torah*, ii, 1) as a means to religious experience, even ecstasy, see *Ḥăḡiḡah*, iii, especially 1, 6 (in contrast, e.g., to *Lulaḇ*, viii, 15).
53. Note, e.g., that in *Talmuḏ Torah*, v, 13, Maimonides does not use the word *pilpul*, while R. Joseph ben Judah, in a similar formulation (*Sefer Musar: Peruš 'Aḇoṯ*, ed. B. Bacher [reprinted, Jerusalem, 1957], p. 125) does. See *Beṯ hab-Běḥirah*, *Horayoṯ*, 173. Note "my pilpul" in *Ḳoḇeṣ*, I, 25a. See *'Iggěroṯ*, 56, 68–69, and cf. Shem-Ṭoḇ ibn Falaquera, in Assaf, *Měḳoroṯ*, II, 47; also ibid., II, 38. I am not here setting *pilpul* up as a whipping boy, as the opposite of logic (*higgayon*); this is a false and artificial distinction, in the same class as the artificial distinction between analysis and synthesis. Note the very apposite remarks of A. A. Kaplan, *Bě-'Iḳḇoṯ hay-Yir'ah* (Jerusalem, 1960), pp. 75–77; and before that, the writer in *Haš-Šiloaḥ*, XV (1905), 212ff. (contra Graetz and Weiss).

in order to guarantee study of ethical-theological matters, Maimonides wanted only to curtail certain kinds of apparently superfluous speculation and digressive unfruitful study, but the Talmudic corpus, recast, reformed, and reformulated, would remain intact. In his opinion, restriction of the scope of study was a major religious and intellectual discontinuity which should be avoided. It led neither to religious perfection nor to intellectual repose. Unlike the *Halakot Gedolot* or the works of R. Judah al-Bargeloni, the goal of the *Mishneh Torah* was methodological refinement, not material restriction. Just as he discounted the advocacy of material restrictions, so also was he not moved, apparently, by the counterargument that reliance upon streamlined summaries was detrimental to full-orbed study. In a word, his deft counterpoising of completeness and condensation is striking, as is his coupling of brevity and elegance. The fact that Maimonides' own interest in Talmud study continued unabated and that he even wrote commentaries and novellae, and not only responsa, on the Talmud is not at all inconsistent in this context—there were many topics for which study of the Talmudic text was indispensable. There were moot issues which necessitated repeated recourse to the Talmud, just as there were controversial interpretations whose merits could be assessed only on the basis of a review of the Talmudic text. No code or summary could achieve total finality or unanimity, and the Talmud remained the ultimate frame of reference for certain matters. Those Maimonidean partisans who criticized, with anger or sarcasm, such students as continued to study the Talmud rather than rely exclusively on the *Mishneh Torah* were not accurately representing Maimonides' views. When Maimonides says, with considerable pathos, that he has never urged the abandonment of Talmud study, there is every reason to accept and validate this declaration, within the limits which we have delineated.[54] His attitude to Talmud study was very complex and tense. According to a contemporary of Maimonides (R. Joseph Rosh has-Seder), who like Maimonides favored codificatory works, Talmud study remains the highest and therefore rather exclusive, somewhat elitist type

---

54. Twersky, "Non-Halakic Aspects," p. 110, and see above, chap. I.

of study. In terms of Maimonides' own classification, Talmud is the most difficult intellectual area. His abiding involvement in it reflects in a special way his passion for comprehensiveness.[55]

There is, furthermore, a pedagogic motive, and Maimonides was generally an effective, reflective, self-conscious pedagogue. Inasmuch as the Oral Law is an organic entity, one part moving imperceptibly into the perimeters of the other, it is often impossible to understand fully any one section in isolation. There are material as well as ideational connections between apparently unrelated topics, hence a measure of universality is necessary even for thorough and fruitful knowledge of a particular theme. A glance at the numerous cross-references in the *Mishneh Torah* readily substantiates this consideration. A point concerning festivities on the holidays receives its fullest elaboration in a section of Book Nine (Sacrifices).[56] Proper understanding of a matter concerning the Paschal offering depends upon a related formulation in the chapters dealing with conversion to Judaism.[57] The formulation in Book Six (Oaths) concerning the enormity of swearing in vain is instructive: "Although whosoever swears in vain or falsely is liable to a flogging, and whosoever swears an oath arising from testimony or from a bailment must bring an offering, the iniquity of the oath is not wholly expiated thereby. For Scripture says, *The Lord will not hold guiltless* (Exod. 20:7), i.e., this transgressor will not be free from heavenly judgment until payment has been exacted from him also for his profanation of the great Name. . . . This is one of the most grievous of sins, as we have explained in the Laws Concerning Repentance."[58] The reference to Book One (Repentance)—and the same may be said for other cross-references to the *Sefer Madda'*—is especially significant in em-

---

55. *KS*, XVIII (1941–42), 61–66, reprinted in S. D. Goitein, *Sidre Ḥinnuk* (Jerusalem, 1962), p. 148. For exceptions to the codificatory form, necessitated by this awareness of judicial indeterminacy, see above, chap. II, nn. 140ff.

56. *Yom Ṭob*, vi, 17; *Ḥagigah*, iii, 14. For universality and specialization, see G. Vico, *On the Study Methods of Our Time*, tr. E. Granturco (Indianapolis, 1965), and E. Curtius, *European Literature and the Latin Middle Ages* (New York, 1963), p. ix. For problems of cross-referencing, see F. Rosenthal, *Technique and Approach of Muslim Scholarship* (Rome, 1947), pp. 37–39.

57. *Korban Pesaḥ*, vi, 7; *'Issure Bi'ah*, xiv, 5. The reference "*bē-'inyan hag-gerut*" is clearly topical. Note also *Mĕkirah*, v, 7 (*bē-'inyan ṭumĕ'at bĕḡadim*); vii, 12 (*bĕ-din ha-'esek*).

58. *Šĕbu'ot*, xii, 2; *Tĕšubah* i, 2.

phasizing the essential interrelatedness of *all* books of the *Mishneh Torah*. There is even one very important cross-reference to the introduction of the *Mishneh Torah*.[59] The *Sefer Maddaʿ* (Book of Knowledge) is neither an afterthought nor an extraneous section but a fully integrated part of the Code. Similarly noteworthy is the following passage from the Laws Concerning Evidence: "Two men who are related to each other may not be ordained to serve in the same Sanhedrin (Supreme Court). . . . It seems to me, however, that in the case of the intercalation of the year, if it becomes necessary to appoint additional judges to form the maximum number of seven—as was set forth in the Laws Concerning the Sanctification of the New Moon—and if among those appointed are some who are related to one another, it does not matter."[60] A reference from the complex *Miḳwaʾot* (Immersion Pools) to the more popular *Bĕraḵot* (Benedictions) illustrates the interrelationship of highly technical and rather straightforward sections.[61]

A cognate motive for comprehensiveness is the striving for a conceptual classification of the entire law. In fact, rigorous classification presupposes exhaustive presentation, interpretation, and conceptualization of *all* the material. Fragmentization and conceptualization are mutually exclusive. The fragmentary nature of other codes—Maimonides implies as much for such works written before the *Mishneh Torah*, and we may apply it to those written subsequently—is responsible for their inadequacies and inconsistencies of classification. Selectivity short-circuits the process of consistent topical and conceptual classification. A massive demonstration of this integral relationship between scope and classification is provided by noting the amount of cross-references, both prospective and retrospective, in any section of the *Mishneh Torah*. In Book Nine, *Šĕḡaḡot* (Transgressions through

---

59. *Šĕḥiṭah*, i, 4. The integrative phrase *"tĕḥillaṭ ḥibbur zeh"* is significant. Other cross-references to Book One include *Tĕfillah*, v, 14 (to *ʿAkum*); *'Issure Biʾah*, xiv, 7 (to *ʿAkum*); xxi, 9 (to *Deʿot*); *Šĕḥiṭah*, iv, 14 (to *Tĕšubah*); *Šĕbuʿot*, xii, 2, and *Mĕlaḵim*, xii, 4 (to *Tĕšubah*). Also within the book, *Tĕšubah*, iv, 5 (to *Deʿot*); and vi, 5 (to *Yĕsode hat-Torah*). Cf. G. Scholem, *Major Trends in Jewish Mysticism* (New York, 1941), p. 95.

60. *ʿEdut*, xvi, 5; *Ḳidduš ha-Ḥodeš*, iv, 9. See also *'Išut*, ii, 21, which refers to *Ḳidduš ha-Ḥodeš*, vi.

61. *Miḳwaʾot*, xi, 1; also *Roṣeaḥ*, v, 4. See, e.g., similar procedure in PhM BM, 4:8 (p. 67).

Error), for example, we find this array: "as we have explained in the Laws Concerning Hallowed Things Which Become Invalid"; "we have already explained in the Laws Concerning Hallowed Things Which Become Invalid"; "we have already explained in the Laws Concerning the Manner of Making Offerings"; "as we have explained in the Laws Concerning Forbidden Intercourse"; "as we have explained many times"; "we have already explained in the Laws Concerning Oaths"; "and we have already explained in the Laws Concerning Sacrilege"; "we have already explained in the Laws Concerning Forbidden Foods"; "has been expounded in the Laws Concerning the Manner of Making Offerings"; "we have already explained in the Laws Concerning Oaths"; "and in the Laws Concerning Those Whose Atonement Is Not Complete I will explain"; and, "as we have explained in Laws Concerning Entering into the Temple."

The thoughtful student will be especially attentive to these cross-references, inasmuch as they may reveal many facets of Maimonides' methods and assumptions and, on occasion, unconscious patterns of reasoning. Sometimes they elucidate the reasons for Maimonides' classification. Sometimes they involve an interesting change of nomenclature, which may preserve alternate titles that had, at various stages, been considered by Maimonides (for as we know, Maimonides kept changing and adapting stylistic as well as substantive matters). Sometimes they appear simply as descriptive phrases rather than precise titles. The general phrase "as we have explained" or "as will be explained," without accompanying elaboration or specification, apparently indicates that Maimonides presumed a basic orientation on the part of his reader, who would be able to find the correlative passages on his own. Moreover, inasmuch as Maimonides expected the student to study the *Mishneh Torah* in the proper sequential order, this phrase may indicate Maimonides' assumption of a reasonably good memory on the part of his readers.[62] In sum, the cross-references, quantitatively and substantively, are important.

62. See, e.g., *Tĕrumot*, ix, 10 (*Mekaḥ u-Mimkar*); x, 25; xii, 2, 11; xiv, 21; *Šĕḇu'ot*, viii, 9; x, 10; xi, 6; *Kil'ayim*, x, 27; *Bet hab-Bĕḥirah*, vi, 16; *Ma'áśeh haḳ-Ḳorbanot*, v, 2; ix, 25 (and *Ḥăgigah*, ii, 10); *'Ăḇadim*, vi, 5 (*Halwa'ah*); *'Iśut*, xx, 6–7; *Malweh wĕ-Loweh*, xvi, 4. On reading the MT in order, see *Tĕśuḇot*, 332 (p. 602).

## UNITY OF ALL LEARNING

This reconstruction of motives for the comprehensive scope of the *Mishneh Torah* needs now to be integrated with the repeated Maimonidean emphasis on the unity of all learning, all branches of learning emerging from all sources of learning. The unity and indivisibility of the Oral Law is here seen also as an aspect of the unity of all human and divine learning. Comprehensiveness meant that Maimonides would not separate the theoretical from the practical, just as he would not separate the Scriptural commandments from the Rabbinic ones or the ceremonial-ritualistic from the ethical-moral. The unity of the Written Law and the Oral Law, unmistakably emphasized in the introduction to the *Mishneh Torah* and in the very fabric of the work—by constant quotation of Scriptural verses, reproduction of the derivation of halakot from verses, and new interpretations and applications of verses (a trait which may be described as creative Midrash)—is also an aspect of this overall unity, serving simultaneously as a refutation of Karaite claims and as a repudiation of those tendencies in eleventh and twelfth-century Judaism which revealed or sustained tension and friction between Biblical and Talmudic studies. The philosophical-theological component of the *Mishneh Torah* is likewise to be seen from the vantage point of comprehensiveness, as is its historical dimension. In other words, the *Mishneh Torah* includes physics, metaphysics, ethics, psychology, dietetics, astronomy, snippets of history, particularly the history of religion, everything from creation to the *eschatos;* as a result, this unique work of jurisprudence allows one to glimpse the full sweep and conceptual affluence of Judaism. For example, the relation of natural science to the ultimate religious goal of love of God is forcefully formulated by Maimonides thus:

This God, honored and revered, it is our duty to love and fear; as it is said, *Thou shalt love the Lord thy God* (Deut. 6:5), and as it is further said, *Thou shalt fear the Lord thy God* (Deut. 6:13).

And what is the way that will lead to the love of Him and the fear of Him? When a person contemplates His great and wondrous works and creatures, and from them obtains a glimpse of His wisdom which is incomparable and infinite, he will straightway love Him, praise Him, glorify Him, and long with an exceeding longing to know His great

Name; even as David said, *My soul thirsteth for God, for the living God* (Ps. 42:3). And when he ponders these matters, he will recoil frightened, and realize that he is a small creature, lowly and obscure, endowed with slight and slender intelligence, standing in the presence of Him who is perfect in knowledge. And so David said, *When I behold Thy heavens, the work of Thy fingers . . . what is man that Thou art mindful of him?* (Ps. 8:4–5). In harmony with these sentiments, I shall explain some large and general aspects of the works of the Sovereign of the universe, that they may serve the intelligent individual as a door to the love of God, even as our Sages have remarked in connection with the theme of the love of God, "Observe the universe, and hence you will realize Him who spoke and the world came into being."[63]

Much of this information, moreover, is derived from "the science of mathematical astronomy, concerning which the Greek wise men composed many treatises."[64]

The relevance of hygiene is underscored as follows: "Since by keeping the body in health and vigor one walks in the ways of God—it being impossible during sickness to have any understanding or knowledge of the Creator—it is a man's duty to avoid whatever is injurious to the body, and cultivate habits conducive to health and vigor." After a remarkable digest of hygienic rules—a physician's manual in rather miscroscopic detail—Maimonides reiterates: "Whosoever lives in accordance with the directions I have set forth has my assurance that he will never be sick until he grows old and dies; he will not be in need of a physician, and will enjoy normal health as long as he lives."[65] He then includes a summary reference to medical literature with which he

---

63. *Yĕsode hat-Torah*, ii, 1–2 (see also iv, 12). Love and fear are treated here as complementary, almost simultaneous, attitudes. Cf. ShM, positive 3 (pp. 3–4); and note Baḥya ibn Paḳuda, *Ḥoḇot hal-Lĕḇaḇot*, x, chap. 3 (II, 350); *Tĕšuḇot*, 150 (p. 286); MN, III, 28, 51. The theme of love is also treated in *Tĕšuḇah*, x (see also PhM, Sanh, *Ḥeleḳ* (p. 199); and note R. Abraham ibn Daud, *ha-'Ĕmunah ha-Ramah*, pt. III, p. 100 (the same formula concerning *de'ah* and *'ahăḇah*); G. Van Der Leeuw, *Religion in Essence and Manifestation* (New York, 1963), II, 478; ŠP, chap. V (end); PhM, Soṭ 3:3 (p. 256); Mak 3:17 (p. 247). Note also *Mĕḳirah*, vii, 12. As for the study of nature and knowledge of God, see the summary of Frank Manuel, *The Religion of Isaac Newton* (London, 1974), p. 103: Newton's studies were motivated by his desire "to know God's will through His works in the world."
64. *Yĕsode hat-Torah*, iii, 5.
65. *De'ot*, iv, 1, 20.

was thoroughly conversant and from which he presumably drew freely.

Elsewhere there is a significant reference to geometry: "There is a positive commandment to adjust balances, weights, and measures accurately and to calibrate them very carefully at the time of their manufacture, for Scripture says, *Just balances, just weights, a just 'ephah, and a just hin, shall ye have* (Lev. 19:36). Similarly, in measuring land great care must be taken to calculate the area of land according to the principles laid down in works on geometry, for even a finger's breadth of land should be regarded as if it were filled with saffron."[66]

In Book Three Maimonides inserts an extraordinary little treatise expounding all the astronomical principles necessary for the calculation of the new moon:

> From what has been stated in the preceding paragraphs (i, 6; ii, 4; vi, 1), that the court used to engage in accurate calculations in order to ascertain whether or not the new crescent could be visible (on the eve of the thirtieth day of the month), we realize that any person with an alert spirit and curiosity for these delicate and hidden matters of scientific knowledge should be eager to learn about the methods of calculation which enable one to ascertain whether the new crescent might or might not be visible on that night.
>
> As to these methods of calculation, many and great are the dissensions among the sages of the ancient peoples who used to engage in the study of astronomy and mathematics. Some great scholars blundered and overlooked certain things, and they were therefore beset by doubts. Other scholars conducted much research, yet missed the right way of performing the calculations pertaining to the visibility of the new moon—"they dived into mighty waters and came back with a potsherd in their hands."
>
> In the long run, however, and after a great deal of observation and research, some scholars did find the correct methods for these calculations. Moreover, we have traditions handed down by the Sages concerning these propositions and proofs that are not found recorded in books that are commonly accessible. Therefore I have deemed it fit to expound here the methods of these calculations in order to make them available to *every one whose heart stirred him up to come to the work to do it* (Exod. 36:2).

---

66. *Gĕneḥah*, viii, 1, 2; see also *Šabbaṯ*, xxviii, 17.

## 218 INTRODUCTION TO THE CODE OF MAIMONIDES

The importance of this extremely technical, sometimes esoteric, material is strongly emphasized:

> You should not, however, make light of these methods because of the fact that at the present age we no longer depend on them; for these methods are indeed remote and deep, and they constitute the secret of the calendar, which was known only to the great Sages and which they were not permitted to reveal to anyone except to ordained and sagacious (disciples). On the other hand, the calculations which we use (for the fixed calendar) today, when there is no court qualified to proclaim the new month according to observation, are such that even schoolchildren can learn and fully grasp them in three or four days.

Here too Maimonides calls attention to the foreign sources which he used for this part of the *Mishneh Torah:*

> As regards the logic for all these calculations, why we have to add a particular figure or deduct it, how all these rules originated, and how they were discovered and proved—all this is part of the science of astronomy and mathematics, about which many books have been composed by Greek sages, books that are still available to the scholars of our time. But the books which had been composed by the Sages of Israel of the tribe of Issachar, who lived in the time of the prophets, have not come down to us. But since all these rules have been established by sound and clear proofs, free from any flaw and irrefutable, we need not be concerned about the identity of their authors, whether they were Hebrew prophets or Gentile sages. For when we have to do with rules and propositions which have been demonstrated by good reasons and have been verified to be true by sound and flawless proofs, we rely upon the author who has discovered them or has transmitted them only because of his demonstrated proofs and verified reasoning.[67]

The relevance, indeed the indispensability, of all sources of knowledge is a crucial consideration for Maimonidean comprehensiveness and is frequently noted. These statements, scattered throughout the *Mishneh Torah,* are fully consonant with an earlier Maimonidean pronouncement affirming the same principle of the universality of knowledge and the need to remove all

---

67. *Kiddus ha-Ḥodeš*, xi, 1–3, 4; xvii, 25. See D. Gandz, "Date of the Composition of Maimonides' Code," *Studies,* ed. S. Sternberg (New York, 1970), pp. 115–16. Note S. Donnolo, *Ḥakěmoni,* introduction, ed. A. Geiger, *Mělo' Ḥofnayim* (Berlin, 1840), pp. 31–32. See above, n. 5.

barriers between seemingly disparate but actually complementary sources of knowledge: "Know, however, that the ideas presented in these chapters and in the following commentary are not of my own invention; neither did I think out the explanations contained therein, but I have gleaned them from the words of the wise occurring in the Midrashim, in the Talmud, and in other of their works, as well as from the words of the philosophers, ancient and recent, and also from the works of various authors, as one should accept the truth from whatever source it proceeds".[68] When enumerating the sources and resources upon which the entire *Commentary on the Mishnah* is based, Maimonides rather conspicuously includes *ḥokmah* ('ilm) along with the standard literary sources. He also says that during the entire turbulent decade devoted to the composition of the *Mishnah Commentary*, he regularly found time for study of "other sciences."[69] In fact, toward the end of the *Mishneh Torah*, Maimonides declares that "only those are eligible to serve as members of the Sanhedrin . . . who are wise men and understanding," and then defines the latter as those "who are experts in the Torah and versed in many other branches of learning, who possess some knowledge of the general sciences, such as medicine, mathematics, and the calculation of cycles and constellations."[70] In keeping with accepted medieval epistemology, faith and reason, or tradition and philosophy, are equal sources of knowledge. These principles were operative in Maimonides' oeuvre.

Especially significant is the extent to which Maimonides utilized aggadic materials in the *Mishneh Torah*. The problem of aggadic exegesis (i.e., the metaphorical interpretation of the non-legal sections of the Talmud, in an effort to make apparently implausible passages of aggadic literature reasonable and meaningful) was to engage Maimonides intermittently throughout his life, and his attitude toward aggadah was expressed in many different contexts. The proper interpretation of aggadah was an unrelenting challenge, sustained by internal theological needs as well as external polemical pressures. As already noted, at the time

---

68. ŠP, introduction.
69. PhM, introduction (p. 47); see above, chap. I.
70. *Sanhedrin*, ii, 1. Note the commentaries, especially the *Mirkebet ham-Mishneh*.

he was composing the *Commentary on the Mishnah*, he was planning a special commentary which would present the aggadah as a quarry from which philosophical and ethical ideas could be extracted. Since the aggadah could and should be transposed into philosophic idiom, it is not surprising that the *Guide* was seen as a partial replacement for the abandoned rationalistic commentary.[71] In the light of this, the attitude to aggadah as reflected in the selective use and varied interpretation found in the *Mishneh Torah* is revealing, for it trails clouds of meaning and *Anschauung* behind it. Aggadah, as we have seen, is used to formulate ethical directives or sustain philosophical emphases; it is used to flesh out certain halakic statements; it sometimes merges totally and inseparably with halakah; and it is a source of historical information. Appropriate quotation or original application of Scriptural verse is often intermeshed with allusion to, or exegesis of, aggadic motifs. Particularly noteworthy are the aggadic perorations in many sections which provide literary embellishments as well as conceptual flourishes. Most significantly perhaps, we realize that a clear-cut dichotomy between halakah and aggadah is a modern scholarly construct and not a reality of Jewish intellectual history, for Talmudists—and certainly philosophers, kabbalists, and ethicists—while recognizing the essential generic differences, mixed the two freely and naturally.[72] Aggadah, systematically explicated, was a fount of philosophic knowledge and generally wide-ranging insight for Maimonides, as well as a meaningful halakic source and supplement. It was a challenge and a spur to intellectual creativity.

THE HISTORICAL DIMENSION

Yet another corollary of this comprehensiveness is the notable historical dimension of the *Mishneh Torah*. Legists generally have had no patience for legal history, and as Edmund Burke put it, lawyers themselves are bad historians.[73] Nevertheless,

---

71. See above, p. 11.
72. See above, pp. 150ff.
73. See N. J. Coulson, *A History of Islamic Law* (Edinburgh, 1964), p. 1; also H. Kantorowicz, *Studies in the Glossators of the Roman Law* (Cambridge, 1938), p. 221; S. Kuttner, *Harmony*, p. 35 ("sublime disregard of history").

Maimonides, who even qua philosopher emphasized the importance of historical narrative and historical sensitivity,[74] often chronicled the historical development of laws and institutions or sketched their background. Comprehensiveness thus meant not only the inclusion of halakot momentarily devoid of practical value or temporarily in abeyance but also antiquated, adapted, or changed laws, laws which were consciously and authoritatively altered in the course of juridical development. For example, laws concerning the *soṭah*, the wayward wife, although abrogated by R. Johanan ben Zakkai in the first century, are codified in the same detail as the ever practical marriage laws. Although not unlike sacrifices inasmuch as all of these laws ceased to be practical, this seems to deserve special comment because the circumstances of its suspension are specifically recorded. All are of course equally relevant sub specie aeternitatis; the reasons for their suspension vary.

The following lengthy passage illustrates how Maimonides reviewed the evolution of a basic law from its Scriptural origin to the prevalent practice, resulting from Gaonic ordinances which take psychological realities and socio-economic contingencies into account. The formulation happens to be of intrinsic historical and juridical interest, reflecting how the relations of creditor and debtor are based on a dialectical combination of firm and impartial legal procedure with an unwavering concern for the dignity and sensitivities of the needy. While the rights of the creditor to collect his debt are uncompromisingly safeguarded, significant efforts are made to spare the debtor unnecessary humiliation:

> The rule of the Torah is that when the creditor demands the debt, an exemption is to be set apart for the debtor, if he has property, and the

---

74. MN, III, 50 (cited by R. Moses Isserles, *Toraṭ ha-'Olah* (Prague, 1871), chap. 1 [p. 20a]). Per contra, R. Baḥya ibn Paḳuda, *Ḥoḇoṭ hal-Lěḇaḇoṭ*, introduction, p. 50, sees history as the lowest part of the Torah. For some recent writing on general medieval attitudes to history, see R. W. Southern, "Aspects of the European Tradition of Historical Writing: Hugh of St. Victor and the Idea of Historical Development," *Transactions of the Royal Historical Society*, XXX (1971), 169ff.; R. Ray, "Medieval Historiography through the Twelfth Century: Problems and Progress of Research," *Viator*, V (1974), 33ff.; and cf. the older monograph by M. Schulz, *Die Lehre von der historischen Methode bei den Geschichtschreibern des Mittelalters* (Berlin, 1909); see also S. Baron, "The Historical Outlook of Maimonides," *PAAJR*, VI (1934–35), 5ff.; reprinted in his *History and Jewish Historians* (Philadelphia, 1964).

remainder is to be given to the creditor, as we have stated. If no property belonging to the debtor is found, or if only such property as is exempt is found, the debtor may go free. He is to be neither imprisoned nor told, "Produce proof that you are poor," nor subjected to an oath, as the heathen are wont to judge. For it is written, *Thou shalt not be to him as a creditor* (Exod. 22:24). The creditor is only told by the court, "If you know of any property belonging to the debtor, go and levy upon it."

If the creditor claims that the debtor has property which he is concealing, and that it is in his house, it is not lawful either for the creditor or for the court's representative to enter the debtor's house, the law being strict in this respect. For it is written, *Thou shalt stand without* (Deut. 24:11). But the creditor may have the anathema proclaimed generally against any debtor who has property and withholds it from the creditor.

When the first Geonim that arose after the compilation of the Gemara saw that deceivers had multiplied and that consequently all doors had become closed to would-be borrowers, they enacted the regulation that the debtor be subjected to a strict oath, akin to the Pentateuchal oath, while holding a sacred object, that he has nothing over and above his exemption, that he has not concealed anything in the hands of others, and that he has made no gift upon condition that it be returned to him. He is also to include in this oath a promise that whatever he may earn or whatever may come into his hands or possession as his own he will not spend on food, clothing, and maintenance of his wife and children, or give it away to any person whatsoever, but will only take therefrom thirty days' food and twelve months' clothing, that is, food which is appropriate and clothing which is appropriate, not the food of gluttons and drunkards or that which is served before kings, and not the clothing of grandees and high officers, but that to which he is accustomed. And he must continually hand over to the creditor all surplus over and above his needs until the entire debt has been paid. And at the very beginning the anathema is to be proclaimed against him who knows of property, open or concealed, belonging to the debtor and does not notify the court.

Even now, after the above regulation has been enacted, neither the creditor nor the court's representative may enter the debtor's house for the purpose of making distraint, since the enactment was not intended to abolish an essential rule of the law; the debtor himself is then allowed to keep what is properly to be kept by him, and must turn the remainder over to the creditor and take the oath provided for by the above enactment. And so the courts of Israel rule everywhere.

If the debtor is seen to be in possession of property after he has taken the above oath, and he pleads, "The property belongs to others," or, "It was entrusted to me for the purpose of engaging in an enterprise on shares," no heed is to be paid to his plea unless he produces proof. So my teachers have ruled.[75]

It is as if Maimonides applied Aristotle's insight: "Here and elsewhere we shall not obtain the best insight into things until we actually see them growing from the beginning."[76]

Maimonides gives a highly telescoped and carefully nuanced history of the festival of Hanukkah, while there is no comparable background for Purim.[77] The reason apparently is that Hanukkah is the only holiday for which there is no historical account, comparable to the Scroll of Esther, in the Scriptural canon. Hence even one who first read Scripture, and then read "this compilation"—as suggested in the *Mishneh Torah* introduction—would still be uninformed, if it were not for Maimonides' inclusion of the historical background. The laws of Purim revolve around the reading of the *Měğillah* (Scroll of Esther)—in fact, the section is entitled Laws Concerning the *Měğillah*—and this is the best history available.

Sometimes, as in the case of prayer, the historical or genetic information has practical and conceptual repercussions and not merely reportorial value. Maimonides' historical sketch of the development of the Jewish liturgy explains the origin of Rabbinic statutory prayer as distinct from Scriptural spontaneous prayer. Unlike other medieval writers who give psychological or theological reasons for the introduction of standardized and regulated prayer, in contrast to the immediacy and spontaneity of the totally fluid and unstructured prayer of Biblical times,[78] Maimonides suggests an essentially historical need:

> When the people of Israel went into exile in the days of the wicked Nebuchadnezzar, they mingled with the Persians, Greeks, and other nations. In those foreign countries children were born to them, whose language was confused. Everyone's speech was a mixture of many

---

75. *Malweh wĕ-Loweh*, ii, 1–2. See the full analysis in M. Elon, *Ḥeruṭ hap-Pĕraṭ bĕ-Darke Gĕbiyaṯ Ḥob bam-Mišpaṭ ha-'Ibri* (Jerusalem, 1964), pp. 114ff.
76. W. Jaeger, *Aristotle* (Oxford, 1950), p. 4.
77. *Ḥănukkah*, ii, 1.
78. E.g., *Kuzari*, III, 5; R. Bahya ibn Pakuda, *Ḥoboṯ hal-Lĕbaboṯ*, viii, chap. 3 (II, 210); R. Abraham ibn Ezra, *Peruš*, Eccles. 5:1.

tongues. No one was able, when he spoke, to express his thoughts adequately in any one language, otherwise than incoherently, as it is said, *And their children spoke half in the speech of Ashdod and could not speak in the Jews' language, but according to the language of each people* (Neh. 13:24).

Consequently, when any one of them prayed in Hebrew, he was unable to express adequately his needs or recount the praises of God, without mixing Hebrew with other languages. When Ezra and his council realized this condition, they ordained the Eighteen Benedictions in their present order.

The polarity of prayer is reflected as clearly and fully in this pointed description of the transition from liturgical freedom to conformity, as it is in the halakic distinctions made by Maimonides concerning the twofold status of prayer:

To pray daily is an affirmative duty, as it is said, *And ye shall serve the Lord your God* (Exod. 23:25). The service here referred to, according to the teaching of tradition, is prayer, as it is said, *And to serve Him with all your heart* (Deut. 11:13), on which the Sages commented, "What may be described as service of the heart? Prayer." The number of prayers is not prescribed in the Torah. No form of prayer is prescribed in the Torah. Nor does the Torah prescribe a fixed time for prayer. Hence women and slaves are under an obligation to pray, this being a duty the fulfillment of which is independent of set periods.

The obligation in regard to this precept is that every person should daily, according to his ability, offer up supplication and prayer; first uttering praises of God, then with humble supplication and petition asking for all that he needs, and finally offering praise and thanksgiving to the Eternal for the benefits already bestowed upon him in rich measure.

One who was fluent would offer up many prayers and supplications. If one was slow of speech, he would pray as he could and whenever he pleased. Thus also, the number of separate services depended on an individual's ability. One would pray once daily; others several times in the day. All, however, turned during prayer toward the Sanctuary, in whichever direction that might be. This was the uniform practice from the times of Moses to those of Ezra.[79]

---

79. *Tĕfillah*, i, 4. Note the following: (a) the view of prayer as a Scriptural commandment; (b) the primordial threefold structure of prayer; (c) the need for daily prayer; (d) the influence of hybrid language, based on a special interpretation of Neh. 13:24 (discussed below in chap. V). See Maimonides' father's *'Iggeret han-Nĕḥamah*, 22. While the view of

The dualism of prayer as a spontaneous and irrepressible devotional act welling up from the depths of one's soul, and as a routinized and carefully defined and concretized performance, is thus exposed, uncamouflaged and unharmonized. It has halakic and philosophical implications. It lies at the core of the practice and concept of prayer.

Maimonides' interest in the history of religion, far from being an exercise in antiquarianism, provides a ready leaven for his unremitting struggle against superstition, against any practice or belief that smacks of idolatrous perversity. Unlike the nineteenth-century evolutionary conception, which in keeping with its generally simplistic view of progress as constantly and irreversibly advancing from the inferior to the superior, saw religious belief moving slowly from polytheism to monotheism, Maimonides' scheme starts with true belief as the original state of affairs and then charts a gradual process of corruption, decline, and defection. The first stage in the process of corruption is precipitated by an error, an intellectual lapse and fallacious inference: people assume that God's will is that the cosmic forces, which appear as divine agents, should be honored and revered. This stage, which Maimonides sees as a popular response of awe and reverence, is extended by a premeditated fraud: the introduction of idolatry. False prophets claim that they were instructed to erect idols and statues and to venerate them. This cultic representation and liturgical adoration culminates in polytheism, when the idols which originally had been intermediaries and concrete symbols of God become independent objects of worship, and people begin to believe that the stars are intrinsically powerful and influential in benevolent or malevolent ways. Inasmuch as the masses pay attention to externals only, are generally incapable of abstraction and conceptualization, and are therefore easily deflected from the true goal, the meaning of God is obscured and the existence of God is forgotten. The task of Abraham, seen as an independent and rational natural philosopher, and then of

---

prayer as a Scriptural commandment is found also at the beginning of R. Saadiah's *Siddur*, it is historically Maimonides who placed it in center stage. Note the new Saadianic fragment published by M. Zucker, *PAAJR*, XLIII (1976), 29–36.

Moses—this time with the help of divine law, so that he produces a unique and unprecedented blend of belief and action—is to restore the original monotheism, to retrieve its essence and safeguard it. Maimonides' brief historical synopsis of the fate of monotheism, its successive corruptions and corrections, is streaked with contemporary allusions and ideological directives sustaining his attack on externalism and his espousal of intellectualism. His history of religion is a history of the vicissitudes of true belief, and it is in tracing this dynamic process and reconstructing reasons for its fluctuations that the parallelism and interrelationship between Maimonides' conception of religion and his perception of the history of religion are discernible, for certain kinds of challenges and errors are particularly persistent. These are foci of historical reconstruction as well as of contemporary exhortation and criticism. It also provides the framework within which the value of halaḵah is best understood, for the blend of belief and action is the most effective antidote to religious defection. Law is the *crowning* feature of Judaism, for the commandments are the indispensable means to ethical-intellectual perfection, which is the goal of man.[80]

---

80. 'Akum, i. The history of religion outlined here—for the history of religious law, see Mĕlaḵim ix, 1—should be compared with other passages, especially PhM, AZ 4:7 (p. 357) and Pes 10:4 (p. 203); MN, I, 31, 36, 63; III, 29, 32; IT, passim. For paraphrase and commentary, see, e.g., ham-Me'iri, Beṯ hab-Bĕḥirah, 'Aḇoṯ, 22–23; Joseph Albo, Sefer ha-'Iḳḳarim, III, 18. For halaḵah as the crown of Judaism (Maimonides' phrase is hiḵtiran bĕ-miṣwoṯ), see also Sefer Miṣwoṯ Gaḏol, introduction ('iṭran bĕ-miṣwoṯ). Cf. Z. Werblowsky, "Rešiṯ ham-Monote'ism," 'Iyyun, IX (1958), 152ff. Especially noteworthy is the intellectual-spiritual profile of Abraham (the convert-philosopher-teacher-builder of covenantal community) constructed from Rabbinic sources and Maimonidean emphases; see also Tĕšuḇah, x, 2; MN, I, 16; II, 39; III, 24, 51. Comparison with other "biographies" of Abraham or brief characterizations (as in Kuzari, IV, 27) projects the main motifs of Maimonides' presentation, which is more sophiography than hagiography; e.g., S. Sandmel, Philo's Place in Judaism: a Study in Conceptions of Abraham in Jewish Literature (Cincinnati, 1956); L. Feldman, "Abraham the Greek Philosopher in Josephus," Transactions of the American Philological Association, IC (1968), 143ff. Note also J. R. Jones, "From Abraham to Andrenio (Observations on the Evolution of the Abraham Legend, Its Diffusion in Spain, and Its Relation to the Theme of the Self-Taught Philosopher)," Comparative Literature Studies, VI (1969), 69ff. On Abraham as a philosopher, cf., e.g., Averroes, Faṣl al-Maqāl, ed. G. Hourani, (Leiden, 1959) chap. 1 (p. 45). See below, chap. VI, n. 81.

Generally, the brief, sometimes parenthetic, historical references incorporated into the warp and woof of halakic statements serve various purposes: to explain a law, to emphasize a point, to prove an aspect, to reconcile events of Israelite history with halakic norms. The latter is particularly noteworthy: in keeping with Midrashic technique and traditional conceptions, though often introducing original explanations, Maimonides quite naturally reviews all history from the vantage point of the Oral Law.[81]

The essentially philosophic concern with history is carried to its logical conclusion in Maimonides' eschatological reflections. Just as the history of religion is a history of the fate of monotheism, so is the Messianic vision a projection of the triumphant finale of this history. The Messianic period for Maimonides will mark the maturation of forces now operative in history, not their decomposition. Peace and normalcy, which will be the sociopolitical traits of this new phase in history, will be conducive to intellectual achievement and spiritual elevation—Israel will be "free to devote itself to the *law and its wisdom.*" Abundant and pervasive knowledge of the one true God, the goal of Abraham and Moses, will characterize the Messianic reality. *For the earth shall be full of the knowledge of the Lord, as the waters cover the sea* (Isa. 11:9) are the last words of the *Mishneh Torah.*[82]

While the all-inclusive scope of the *Mishneh Torah* is frequently mentioned, it should be clear that the real fullness and richness of this comprehensive presentation of Jewish law and thought are not immediately evident, for Maimonides skillfully incorporated many themes in compressed form, as parenthetic or tangential to the subject under discussion. He did not label all the additions and interpolations nor did he classify them by chapter headings or

---

81. *Těmidin u-Musafin,* vii, 11; *Šabbat,* ii, 24; *Mělakim,* viii, 8; ix, 1, 14; *'Issure Bi'ah,* xiii, 14. Toward the end of IT (p. xviii), when Maimonides is about to engage in "storytelling," he affirms that the use of historical narrative is pedagogically significant: "I shall now narrate to you succinctly several episodes subsequent to the rise of the Arab kingdom, *from which you will derive some benefit*" (italics mine). His Messianic teachings will be concretized and fortified. For a striking illustration of Maimonides' awareness of the simple non-Midrashic meaning, see PhM, Soṭ 3:2 (and cf. B. Shab 55b).

82. *Mělakim,* xii, 5 (italics mine). Cf. I. Baer, *Galuṭ* (New York, 1947), pp. 36–39. Note MN, III, 11.

marginal annotations. This material is so adroitly compressed and so naturally interwoven with the more usual halaḵic formulations that it has often gone unnoticed. Conventional preconceptions concerning the contents of the Code as well as firmly entrenched restrictive patterns of study have obstructed full analysis and appreciation. Comprehensiveness meant—and this will be further illustrated in Chapter VI—that Maimonides revealed himself in his Code of law not only as a jurist or legist but also as a theologian describing the triumphal age of eschatological fulfillment, a physician suggesting a regimen of health, a moralist defining the golden mean and its exceptions, a philosopher outlining principles of metaphysics and natural science, a jurisprudent seeking the rationale of the commandments, and in many other special ways. For example, in order to define the rebellious elder (*zaḵen mamreh*) precisely, Maimonides presents in the first chapters of *Mamrim* a philosophy of law, discussing such axial themes as the source and seat of authority, the transmission of halaḵah and the emergence of controversy, the role of custom and consensus, on the one hand, and the legitimacy of interpretive novelties, on the other. The reader must sensitize himself in order to realize the comprehensiveness of the *Mishneh Torah* and the fullness thereof.

Toward the end of the section on *Tĕšuḇah*, to cite just one more example, Maimonides creates the opportunity to deal with a thorny problem of Jewish thought which was also a heated polemical issue—the spiritual nature of the ultimate bliss vis-à-vis the apparent Scriptural emphasis on material, carnal, reward. The Maimonidean formulation underscores the absolute spirituality of the summum bonum by treating material reward as instrumental and transient. Note also how the interlocking of practical and intellectual virtues, the emphatic juxtaposition of knowledge and action, serve as a refrain of this lengthy passage, which deserves careful study.[83]

---

83. *Tĕšuḇah*, ix, 1. See below, beginning of chap. VI. On the issue of material versus spiritual reward, see R. Saadiah Gaon, *'Ĕmunot wĕ-Dē'ot*, chap. VIII; Naḥmanides to Deut. 11:13 (who notes also the views of hal-Levi, Abraham ibn Ezra, and Maimonides); Joseph ibn Kaspi, *Tam haḵ-Kesef* (reprinted, Jerusalem, 1970); Joseph Albo, *Sefer ha-'Iḳḳarim*, IV, chap. 40; Isaac Abarbanel to *Lev.* 26:3 (who claims that Albo followed Naḥmanides without acknowledging it); also, R. Meir Aldabi, *Šĕḇile 'Ĕmunah* (Tel Aviv, 1965), *nĕtiḇ* 8,

## Temporary Laws

While these parameters of comprehensiveness, with the selective attention to history or the historical unfolding of laws, led Maimonides to include antiquated, suspended, or modified laws, he deliberately omitted commandments which were never intended to be binding for all time. One-time laws, laws initially restricted to the exodus from Egypt, to the sojourn in the wilderness, or to the entry into Canaan were not part of the perennial Mosaic legacy (or inheritance) and were not to play any role in the enumeration of 613 commandments. This principle, the third of the fourteen guiding rules, is firmly established by Maimonides in the preface to the *Book of Commandments:* "It is not admissible to include in this classification those commandments which are not binding for all times."[84] Mosaic Torah is equated with *morašah* (inheritance) and only that which endures for all future generations is truly an inheritance. The centrality of this proposition, the need to emphasize it repeatedly, explains the concluding paragraph of the introduction to the *Mishneh Torah:* "The total number of precepts that are obligatory for all generations is 613. Of these, 248 are affirmative, and their mnemonic is the number of bones in the human body; 365 precepts are negative, and their mnemonic is the number of days in the solar year."[85] Far from being a homiletical flourish, this conclusion reinforces the principle of his enumeration and its applicability to the *Mishneh Torah*. The biological and cosmological analogies express the permanence of this number and its immutability, the salient trait of divine law.

In the light of this, the following halakic formulation would seem to be incongruous: "It is a positive commandment to destroy the seven nations, as it is said, *But thou shalt utterly destroy them* (Deut. 20:17). If one does not put to death any of them that

---

161. The statement of Aquinas, *Summa theologica*, I, II, 108, 3 and 4, is illustrative of the Christian attack. For Peter Abelard's formulation, see H. Liebeschutz, "The Significance of Judaism in Peter Abelard's Dialogus," *JJS* (1961), 1ff., especially p. 7. See references cited in chap. V, n.49, below.

84. ShM, Šoreš 3 (II, pp. 377–78); cf. *Mĕlakim*, viii, 10 (same emphasis on *morašah*).

85. MT, introduction.

falls into one's power, one transgresses a negative commandment. But their memory has long perished."[86] Does not the last assertion convert this into a law not binding for all time? Is this not a de facto limitation?

Maimonides would not be fazed by such a query, for in the *Book of Commandments* he writes at inordinate length, anticipating objections, parrying questions, and revealing himself at his pedagogic best:

By this injunction we are commanded to exterminate the seven nations that inhabited the land of Canaan, because they constituted the root and very foundation of idolatry. This injunction is contained in His words, exalted be He, *Thou shalt utterly destroy them*. It is explained in many texts that the object was to safeguard us from imitating their apostasy. There are many passages in Scripture which strongly urge and exhort us to exterminate them, and war against them is obligatory.

One might think that this commandment is not binding for all time, seeing that the seven nations have long ceased to exist; but that opinion will be entertained only by one who has not grasped the distinction between commandments which are binding for all time and those which are not. A commandment which has been completely fulfilled by the attainment of its object, but to the fulfillment of which no definite time limit has been attached, cannot be said not to be binding for all time, because it is binding in every generation in which there is a possibility of its fulfillment. If the Lord completely destroys and exterminates the Amalekites—and may this come to pass speedily in our days, in accordance with His promise, exalted be He, *For I will utterly blot out the remembrance of 'Amalek* (Exod. 17:14)—shall we then say that the injunction *Thou shalt blot out the rememberance of 'Amalek* (Deut. 25:19) is not binding for all time? We cannot say so; the injunction is binding for all time, and as long as descendants of Amalek exist, they must be exterminated. Similarly in the case of the seven nations, their destruction and extermination is binding upon us, and the war against them is obligatory: we are commanded to root them out and pursue them throughout all generations until they are destroyed completely. Thus we did until their destruction was completed by David, and this remnant was scattered and intermingled with the other nations, so that no trace of them remains. But although they have disappeared, it does not follow that the commandment to exterminate them is not binding for all time, just as

---

86. *Mĕlakim*, v, 4.

we cannot say that the war against Amalek is not binding for all time, even after they have been consumed and destroyed. No special condition of time or place is attached to this commandment, as is the case with those commandments specially designed for the desert or for Egypt. On the contrary, it applies to those on whom it is imposed, and they must fulfill it so long as (any of those against whom it is directed) exists.

Generally speaking, it is proper for you to understand and discern the difference between a commandment and the occasion for it. A commandment may be binding for all time, and yet the occasion (for its fulfillment) may be lacking at a particular time; but the lack of occasion does not make it a commandment which is not binding for all time. A commandment ceases to be binding for all time when the contrary is true: when, that is, it was at one time our duty in certain conditions to perform a certain act or carry out a certain ordinance, but this is not our duty today, although these conditions still obtain. An example is the case of the aged Levite, who was disqualified for service in the desert, but is qualified among us today, as is explained in its proper place. You should understand this principle and lay it to heart.[87]

We are here called upon to differentiate between a law which conceptually and intrinsically is limited and one which conceptually is, and was intended to be, timeless but technically, for whatever reason, has been put into the limited category. The fact that "the seven nations have long ceased to exist" as an identifiable entity makes implementation of this commandment impracticable, but the law, in its conceptual underpinnings, is not time-bound. Ideas are not to be enslaved by accidents of time. They are not abrogated by historical contingencies but merely suspended, and even if the suspension seems to be sine die, the abiding validity of the idea is unimpaired.

On occasion, in order to clarify fully the commandments which are binding for all time, Maimonides had to explain in some detail the temporary injunction valid in the wilderness. For example, "When the children of Israel were in the wilderness they were not enjoined concerning the performance of *šĕḥiṭah* upon unconsecrated animals, but were wont to stab or slaughter them,

---

87. ShM, positive 187 (I, 200–01), and reference to it in negative 48. See also *Tĕfillin*, i, 19, and PhM, Meg 2:1 (p. 348). Note *Sefer ha-Ḥinnuk*, n. 107, and commentary *Minḥat Ḥinnuk* ad loc. (concerning *Kĕle ham-Miḳdaš*, i, 1).

and then eat them like the heathens. They were commanded in the wilderness merely that whosoever wished to perform šĕḥiṭah should do so only with peace offerings. . . . This procedure was meant to apply not to subsequent generations but solely to the period when the Israelites were in the wilderness. . . . They were there commanded that upon entering the Land of Israel stabbing would become forbidden and they might eat of unconsecrated animals only after šĕḥiṭah. . . . This commandment is binding upon all generations, namely that one should first perform šĕḥiṭah and only thereafter may he eat of the flesh."[88] In this case, the detailed reference to a temporary and antiquated law is a prelude to the normative summary. The review is pedagogically necessary; contrast abets effective and precise exposition.

At this point a word about the use of the *Sefer ham-Miṣwot* for understanding the *Mishneh Torah* is in order. It is a truism that although the definitions found in the former often illumine the latter, we may not always automatically identify the two works; differing as they do in scope and intent, there are inevitable variations between them.[89] In the aforecited case, however, the relation is clear and the conceptual carry-over useful. Moreover, inasmuch as the scope of the *Mishneh Torah* is all-inclusive, even the vexed question of determining which commandments are Scriptural and which Rabbinic, so crucial for defining the contents of the *Sefer ham-Miṣwot*, is not really relevant for the *Mishneh Torah*. The identification of neither Rabbinic commandments—there are very few in any event[90]—nor Rabbinic amplifications of Scriptural commandments affects the scope of the *Mishneh Torah*, which, unlike the *Sefer ham-Miṣwot*, is intended explicitly to include everything: Rabbinic laws as well as Gaonic ordinances and interpretations or customs which have crystallized in various communities. Toward the end of the *Mishneh Torah* introduction, Maimonides affirms his goal "that all the rules shall be accessi-

---

88. *Šěḥiṭah*, iv, 17, 18. See also *Kěle ham-Miḳdaš*, iii, 8; *Ma'áśeh haḳ-Ḳorbanot*, ii, 14, 15.

89. See, e.g., introduction of J. Ḳāfiḥ to his edition of ShM (Jerusalem, 1971), pp. 12–13.

90. See the postscript to the MT introduction.

ble . . . whether these appertain to the (Scriptural) precepts or to the institutions established by the Sages and prophets." Even more interesting, and more provocative, is the following postscript (appearing right after Maimonides' enumeration of the 613 commandments), also dealing with the relation of Rabbinic and Scriptural commandments:

These are the 613 precepts which were orally imparted to Moses on Sinai, together with their general principles, detailed applications, and minute particulars. All these principles, details, particulars, and the exposition of every precept constitute the Oral Law, which each court received from its predecessor. There are other precepts which originated after the Sinaitic Revelation, were instituted by prophets and Sages, and were universally accepted by all Israel. Such are the reading of the Scroll of Esther (on Purim), the kindling of the Hanukkah lights, fasting on the Ninth of 'Ab. . . . Each of these precepts has its special interpretations and details, all of which will be expounded in this work.

All these newly established precepts we are in duty bound to accept and observe, as it is said, *Thou shalt not turn aside from the sentence which they shall declare unto thee, to the right hand, nor to the left* (Deut. 17:11). They are not an addition to the precepts of the Torah. In regard to what, then, did the Torah warn us, *Thou shalt not add thereto, nor diminish from it* (Deut. 13:1)? The purpose of this text is to teach us that a prophet is not permitted to make an innovation and declare that the Holy One, blessed be He, had commanded him to add it to the precepts of the Torah or had bidden him to abrogate one of these 613 precepts. But if the court, together with the prophet living at the time, institute an additional precept as an ordinance, judicial decision, or decree, this is not an addition (to the precepts of the Torah). For they did not assert that the Holy One, blessed be He . . . ordered the reading of the Scroll of Esther at the appointed time. Had they said this, they would have been adding to the Torah. We hold, however, that the prophets, in conjunction with the court, enacted these ordinances, and commanded that the Scroll of Esther be read at the appointed time so as to proclaim the praises of the Holy One, blessed be He, recount the salvations that He wrought for us, and that He was ever near when we cried out to Him, and that we should therefore bless and laud Him and inform future generations how true is the reassurance of the Torah in the text, *For what great nation is there that hath God so nigh unto them, as the Lord our God is (to us), whensoever we call upon Him* (Deut. 4:7). In this way every precept, affirmative or negative, instituted by the Scribes, is to be understood.

This passage deserves to be reproduced in its entirety because it is an important declaration of intent often glossed over by students of the *Mishneh Torah*. Moreover, it presents a pivotal theme of anti-Karaite polemics. A major weapon in the Karaite arsenal was the contention that the Oral Law was in fact a flagrant violation and contradiction of the Scriptural precept forbidding additions to the Torah.[91] Undoubtedly addressing himself to this accusation, Maimonides explains that there is nothing illegitimate about prophetic or Rabbinic enactments which avowedly supplement or elaborate rather than replace Scriptural precepts or claim equal status with them. Mosaic Law is a closed and inviolable entity, which no prophet may touch; there are neither pre-Mosaic residues nor post-Mosaic accretions. This purity-permanency of Torah, however, is not cause for conflict with, or censure of, clearly labeled judicial extensions or additions, which are provided for by the inner dynamics of the halakic system.[92] Furthermore, Maimonides seems to suggest that all prophetic-Rabbinic institutions are rooted in Pentateuchal precept and precedent. For example, the reading of the Scroll of Esther is a specific form of prayer and praise, and this explains the otherwise incongruous quotation of Deut. 4:7.

OMISSIONS

Our analysis of the comprehensive scope of the *Mishneh Torah* cannot be concluded without noting certain blatant lacunae. Various kinds of well-known Talmudic material are omitted. These omissions are all the more conspicuous in the light of the fact that this material is usually found in the writings of Gaonic predecessors or in later codifiers, e.g., *Ṭur, Šulḥan 'Aruk, Lĕbuš,* or in smaller more specialized collections. While the role of human fallibility, the impact of forgetfulness, and the possibility of inadvertent omission must be taken into account, an attempt should also be made to identify a few basic reasons for deliberate omis-

91. See above, chap. I, n.156.
92. See *Yĕsode hat-Torah,* ix, 1 (also *'Aḇel,* i, 1; *Mĕlaḳim,* viii, 10); *Mamrim,* i, 1; ii, 2; MN, III, 34; and R. Joseph Albo, *Sefer ha-'Iḳḳarim,* III, 23.

sion. One must be attuned to the silences as well as to the sounds of Maimonides' writing.

It is known that Maimonides systematically omitted laws and practices which he considered to be rooted in accidental, transient, nonobligatory beliefs. As part of his quest for a sensitized and rationalized view of religion and morality, he wanted to jettison certain objectionable beliefs and improper customs. This goal could be advanced by the use of divergent methods. Some statements may be reinterpreted and reclassified in order to eliminate all possible undesirable residues or accretions. Other statements may simply be dropped.[93]

It is plausible to assume that some very popular, well-known, or self-evident matters were also deliberately excluded. This happens to be a principle which Maimonides used to explain certain omissions from the Mishnah. After formulating a basic definition concerning tĕfillin, Maimonides adds:

However, laws concerning ṣiṣit, tĕfillin, and mĕzuzot, the order of making them, the benedictions appropriate to them, and all relevant laws and questions which have arisen in connection with them—it is not part of the purpose of our composition to discuss them, for (in this work), [i.e., the *Mishnah Commentary*], we play the role of commentator. Now the Mishnah has not fixed for these miṣwot special statements which include all their legal details, hence we are not obligated to explicate them (here). The reason for this (omission), in my opinion, is their great popularity at the time of the composition of the Mishnah. These matters were popular and common to all, the masses as well as select individuals [i.e., scholars]; their content was not concealed from any one. Consequently, there was no place, in his [R. Judah the Prince's] opinion, to discuss them, just as he did not fix the order of prayer, i.e., the text, or the order of appointing the reader of the prayers, because this was so

---

93. E.g., *Tĕfillah*, v, 6; *Roṣeaḥ*, xii, 5, 6; *Bi'at Miḳdaš*, ix, 13, 14; *Ma'ăśeh haḳ-Ḳorbanot*, viii, 11; *Ma'ăkalot 'Ăsurot*, i, 24. Note ham-Me'iri, *Bet hab-Bĕḥirah, Bĕrakot*, 51a (the issue of *zugot*), p. 189; see the discussion of I. H. Weiss, *Bet Talmud*, I (1881), 228, n.34; and most recently, J. Levinger, *Darke ham-Maḥšabah ha-Hilkatit šel ha-RaMBaM* (Tel Aviv, 1965), pp. 118ff. (with many good examples). A careful study of the *Mishneh Torah* and the *Šulḥan 'Aruk* with an eye to omissions and additions (as well as interpretations, both implicit and explicit) would certainly be very instructive. See also MN, III, 37 (p. 544), and the penetrating criticism of RaSHBA, *Tĕšubot*, I, 413. See below, p. 479.

popular and widespread. After all, he was not composing a prayer book but a book of laws [*fiqh*]."[94]

While this hypothesis concerning the Mishnah could not ipso facto serve as a model for limitations and omissions in the all-inclusive *Mishneh Torah*—the paradigmatic role of the Mishnah for Maimonides notwithstanding—Maimonides does note at the end of the introduction to the *Sefer ham-Miṣwot* that certain well-known halakic facts will not be repeated: "It is known that women are not qualified to act as judges or witnesses. . . . Therefore, all commandments pertaining to the court or testimony . . . it will not be necessary for me to say, 'And this is not obligatory upon women,' since this will be merely redundant and serving no purpose." Or, again: "Now since all these matters are known to most people, every positive or negative commandment pertaining to the sacrifices or the rituals (in the Sanctuary), or the death penalties. . . . it will not be necessary for me to say concerning them, 'This commandment applies only during the existence of the Sanctuary,' since this is clear on the basis of what we have mentioned."[95]

It is probably with this in mind that commentators sometimes suggest that a certain law, detail, or qualification was omitted because it is so self-evident.[96] While writing for great and small, he would not be platitudinous.

The suggestion made in a responsum attributed to RABD[97] that Maimonides might omit a law if he were not sure of the

---

94. PhM, Men 4:1 (p. 121), also Ber 7:1 (p. 81); cf. R. Margaliyot, *Yĕsod ham-Mishnah wă-'Ărikatah* (Jerusalem, 1955), pp. 22–23; and see D. Daube, "The Self-Understood in Legal History," *Juridical Review*, LXXXV (1973), 126–34. Also matters of conscience, by definition, can not be codified; *Tĕšubot*, 91 (p. 149).

95. ShM, *šoreš* 14 (II, 424–25). To some extent Maimonides is merely talking about the avoidance of repetition. See, however, *Tĕšubot*, 141 (p. 271).

96. E.g., MM, *Ma'ăkalot 'Ăsurot*, i, 24; *Mišneh lĕ-Melek, Šekirut*, xii, 2–3. KM, *Soṭah*, iv, 4, questions why Maimonides omitted a certain detail. See also *Tĕšubot*, 395 (p. 673), and above, chap. II, n.123. A characteristic comment is that of RaSHBA, *Torat hab-Bayit, Dine ta'ărubot:* הרמב״ם השמיטן ולא ידעתי למה. Students of the *Hălakot* of RIF also confronted this problem of omissions and sought to identify reasons or operative principles; see, e.g., RaZaH, *Sefer ham-Ma'or*, introduction.

97. S. Assaf in *Kobeṣ RaMBaM*, ed. J. L. Maimon (Jerusalem, 1935), p. 278: ואפשר שהיה לו בספק והניחו. Multiple views cited by R. Judah in the Mishnah are explained accordingly.

normative conclusion is puzzling in the light of the fact that Maimonides quoted multiple views and divergent customs when in doubt or when he did not care to impose a unilateral view. Another suggestion, that Maimonides omitted certain laws because he found no suitable spot for them in his scheme of organization and classification,[98] is far from convincing and is indeed somewhat cavalier. Since we shall be able to demonstrate that the *Mishneh Torah* scheme allowed, reluctantly but realistically, for associationism and, if necessary, infringements upon the conceptualization in order to include various laws,[99] it is hard to imagine that finding an appropriate place would pose an insoluble problem.

The all-inclusive scope of the *Mishneh Torah* shows that Maimonides regarded Jewish law sub specie aeternitatis. He did not readily conform to conventional views, and he protested against the widespread scholarly practice of neglecting substantial portions of the Talmud. The Torah must be studied in its entirety; its contents may be simplified and systematized but not truncated; its study is not to be approached with practical and utilitarian criteria, which impose a transient reality upon eternal values. The standard of historical reality and relevance, particularly in the abnormal conditions of exile, is a procrustean bed for the Torah in its entirety, in its wide-ranging, all-embracing scope. Such a restrictive and anemic standard must, therefore, yield to a timeless perspective, with its own values and directions—and it is precisely this contra-functional pulsating view, making the "Torah great and glorious," which determines the scope of the *Mishneh Torah*.

98. J. Levinger, *Darke ham-Maḥšabah*, p. 120.
99. See chap. IV, below.

# IV

# Classification

OPTIONS FOR CLASSIFICATION

As we shall see in the next chapter, Maimonides weighed three possible alternatives concerning the language of the *Mishneh Torah*—Biblical Hebrew, Mishnaic Hebrew, and Talmudic Aramaic—and made a carefully considered choice which he explained persuasively. Similarly he had three options with regard to the systematization, organization, and classification of the contents of the *Mishneh Torah,* and here too he arrived at a thoughtful conclusion which he justified with strenuous eloquence.

*Mishnaic-Talmudic sequence*

One obvious tradition-laden possibility was to adhere to the Mishnaic arrangement—six major divisions or "orders" (*sĕḏarim*), subdivided into sixty-one treatises[1]—which was after all the first, highly authoritative, and abidingly influential attempt at a systematic presentation of the entire Oral Law. Its merits and strengths had been enumerated by Maimonides in the *Mishnah Commentary* introduction with unreserved approbation and enthusiasm: comprehensive scope, muscular method, apodictic form, brief yet mellifluous style. Maimonides was not content with this impersonal aphoristic paean to the vitalizing power of skillful redaction, but also extolled, with intense sincerity, the unusual traits and qualifications of the Mishnah's redactor, R. Judah han-Naśi'—his nearly perfect wisdom, unexceptional piety, deep humility, personal austerity bordering on ascetic self-discipline, unrivaled mastery of Hebrew; besides, this man of saintly renown and great charm had also reached the apogee of opulence, prestige, and power, and was therefore able, with zest

---

1. This is Maimonides' count in PhM, introduction (p. 33), which unites *Baḇa Ḳamma, Mĕṣi'a,* and *Baṯra,* and separates *Makkoṯ* from *Sanhedrin.* See J. N. Epstein, *Maḇo' lĕ-Nusaḥ ham-Mishnah* (Jerusalem, 1948), pp. 982–83.

and unfailing kindness, to be a munificent and inspiring patron of scholars. His unflagging energies had been devoted to the dissemination of Torah. It is self-evident that Maimonides was fascinated by the image of R. Judah, who was for him a paragon of intellectual and moral virtue, and whose literary achievement, the Mishnah, was a genuine masterpiece—*Maidens saw and acclaimed it, queens and concubines praised it* (Song 6:9).[2]

Moreover, in everything except classification R. Judah's Mishnah served as the generic paradigm for Maimonides' *Mishneh Torah*. In his oft-quoted letter to R. Phinehas, Maimonides differentiated between two literary genres, *peruš* and *ḥibbur*, discursive or expansive commentary and monolithic or systematic code, and characterized his work as *ḥibbur*. After identifying *ḥibbur* with the "way of the Mishnah" and *peruš* with the "way of the Talmud," thus delineating two alternate approaches to the same subject matter, Maimonides emphasized the affinity of his own work with Mishnah and the "way of the Mishnah."[3]

There is further the formidable precedent of R. Isaac Alfasi's *Halakot*, an excellent compendium of law which in Maimonides' enthusiastic opinion superseded *all* previous codes and which speedily became known as the "miniature Talmud." It was an immensely popular text, generally acclaimed and extensively studied, which stimulated a rash of expository works of all kinds, commentaries, critiques, supplements. Maimonides was not alone in affirming the centrality of the *Halakot* of Alfasi: all contemporaries and successors, protagonists as well as antagonists, poets as well as Talmudists, Spanish as well as French scholars,

---

2. PhM, introduction (p. 34). Earlier characterizations of the Mishnah were brief and fragmentary but pointed to these same features; e.g., R. Nissim Gaon, *Sefer ham-Mafteaḥ*, 3b; Samuel han-Nagid, *Diwan*, ed. D. Yarden (Jerusalem, 1966), p. 90; R. Judah hal-Levi, *Kuzari*, III, 67. The qualities attributed to R. Judah are reminiscent of those enumerated by Maimonides as prerequisites for prophecy. See *Yĕsode hat-Torah*, vii, 1; MN, II, 32ff.; cf. *Sefer ham-Mafteaḥ*, 2b. In 'Aḇel, xiii, 10, Maimonides notes that "none was greater in wisdom than was our teacher, the Saint (R. Judah)." See *Tĕšuḇah*, v, 2, where Moses is the model of the "righteous person." Also, *Mĕlakim*, ii, 6.

3. *Koḇeṣ*, I, 25b. See above, chap. I, and my article "Non-Halakic Aspects," p. 109. His son invariably refers to the *Mishneh Torah* as al-ḥibbur; e.g., *Tĕšuḇot R. Abraham Maimonides*, ed. A. Freimann (Jerusalem, 1937), p. 123 and passim. See S. D. Goitein, "Abraham Maimonides and His Circle," *Jewish Medieval and Renaissance Studies*, ed. A. Altmann (Cambridge, 1967), p. 147. See above, chap. I, n. 25.

## 240 INTRODUCTION TO THE CODE OF MAIMONIDES

acknowledged that R. Isaac was a pivotal personality and that his work exerted seminal influence. This epochal work, which achieved codificatory results by abridging the Talmudic corpus, excising nonpractical material, omitting repetitions and digressions, and eliminating aggadic themes unless they had halakic implications, was characterized by fidelity to the Mishnaic sequence.[4] There is occasional rearrangement of small amounts of material, even isolated sentences, from one tractate to another, and the relevant subject matter from the mostly arcane Zĕra'im, Ḳŏdašim, and Ṭohărot is grouped together under the plastic rubric "Halakot Kĕṭanot," but the structure remains Mishnaic-Talmudic.[5]

All these plaudits and precedents notwithstanding, Maimonides unequivocally repudiated the Mishnaic sequence. In the introduction to the Sefer ham-Miṣwot he invites us to eavesdrop as he reconstructs his thoughts on this subject:

As I directed my attention toward this goal [i.e., the composition of an all-inclusive compendium of law], I searched in my heart as to what would be the proper way for the division of this work, and the arrangement of its parts. (I wondered:) should I divide it in accordance with the divisions of the Mishnah and follow in its footsteps, or should I divide it in some other way, arranging the subjects at the beginning or at the end of the work as logic [or conceptual analysis] will dictate, since this is the proper and easier way for learning. Then it became clear to me that in place of the tractates of the Mishnah, it would be best to arrange this work in groups of laws, so that it would read: 'Laws Concerning the Tabernacle, Laws Concerning the Palm Branch, Laws Concerning the Mĕzuzah, Laws Concerning the Fringes,' and that I should divide every group of laws into chapters and paragraphs, even as the Mishnah had done . . . in order to facilitate the knowledge of it by heart for one who may wish to learn some part of it by heart.[6]

---

4. PhM, introduction (p. 47); Ḳobeṣ, I, 25b; 'Iggĕrot, 69. Maimonides' evaluation coincides with that of his younger contemporary, R. Joseph Rosh has-Seder (ḲS, XVIII [1941/42], 65). See the statements collected in my Rabad of Posquières, pp. 230–31.

5. E.g., Sefer Torah, Mĕzuzah, Tĕfillin. The laws of Hallel are taken from B. 'Ar and conjoined to Ḥanukkah in B. Shab, chap. 2. See also Mĕgillah, iii. Some examples can be found in S. Shefer, Ha-RIF u-Mišnato (Jerusalem, 1967), pp. 30ff. See the transfer from B. Soṭ 40a to B. Sanh 8a.

6. ShM, introduction (II, 361). Concerning his treatise On Asthma, Maimonides says: "I thought it best to divide this treatise into several chapters, so that the reader may re-

Fidelity and conformity yielded; logical-pedagogical criteria prevailed and produced a topical arrangement.

It should be added here that whatever the initial inadequacies or inconstancies of the Mishnah arrangement from a logical-pedagogical viewpoint—and this was Maimonides' lodestar—they were compounded tenfold by the stream-of-consciousness technique of the Talmud, a scholastic method of free association and necessary, even premeditated, digression. Sometimes, in order to clarify a compact Mishnaic statement, the Talmudic analysis will roam freely over a large number of discrete topics together with their discordant interpretations, and only then, equipped with logical distinctions, halakic subtleties, and comparative data, will the analysis return to its point of departure; difficulties will be dissolved, obscurities resolved, ambiguities clarified. There is nothing haphazard about this; it is all logical, meticulously reasoned, and interconnected, but just diffuse, complicated, and even cumbersome. Lively dialectic, encyclopedic range, austere form, strenuous but discursive reasoning, exhaustive but digressive commentary, a hypothetical-deductive method of textual analysis—these are the essential traits of the Talmudic method. The Mishnaic sequence and the Talmudic method together created ruffling challenges for the student and posed nearly insurmountable problems for the codifier. Maimonides' awareness of this medley of philological, methodological, and phenomenological problems was not new or sudden. It would appear that the difficulty of Mishnah study, magnified by the complexity of Talmudic amplification, was on Maimonides' mind throughout his adult life.[7] Consequently, in structuring his great Code, he decided to give absolute priority to the rigorous needs of a succinct, systematic, and topical reordering of this massive and intrinsically difficult material. Hence in the letter to R. Phinehas—a document which records so much of

---

member it well and also find, with the help of God, the subject he is looking for without undue loss of time." The examples cited by Maimonides are found in the Halakot Gĕdolot. See PhM, introduction (pp. 27, 33) for higgayon. On learning the book by heart, see my comment in Tarbiz, XXXVII (1968), 326; also above, chap. 1.

[7]. MT, introduction; 'Iŝut, xi, 13; PhM, introduction (p. 47); PhM, Shab 4:1 (p. 32); 'Iggĕrot, 69. Also R. Menaḥem ham-Me'iri, Bĕ hab-Bĕḥirah, introduction, p. 27.

Maimonides' thoughts and feelings in the initial stages of the dissemination and reception of the *Mishneh Torah*—Maimonides conspicuously and explicitly emphasizes the novelty and originality of his classification. He suggests that some students of the Code will erroneously imagine that his achievement consists merely in having perfected the codificatory form, expunging tedious debate and conflicting interpretations: "It follows the order of the Talmud, [they will say,] but only eliminates the question and solution," i.e., it extricates itself from the dialectical-argumentative pattern. Maimonides forcefully repudiates this lopsided evaluation and demands total appreciation of his achievement, recognition of the fact that he unflinchingly abandoned the Talmudic sequence and opted for an autonomous topical-conceptual arrangement. His own verdict, neither self-congratulatory nor self-deprecatory, was forthright: "I follow neither the order of the Talmud nor the order of the Mishnah, but collect all the laws, wherever they have been formulated, relating to every single subject."[8]

This rejection of the Mishnaic sequence becomes even more striking if we remember that in the introduction to his *Commentary on the Mishnah* Maimonides investigated this arrangement and painstakingly tried to uncover the latent processes of R. Judah's reasoning. Unlike R. Sherira Gaon,[9] who posited that R. Judah never determined a precise sequence for the tractates within each division, merely fixing the order of the six divisions, and unlike R. Menahem ham-Me'iri,[10] who was ready to entertain the idea that the arrangement of the Mishnah may have been inadvertent and haphazard, Maimonides assumed that a serious and preconceived classification underlies the Mishnah.[11] With

---

8. *Koḇeṣ*, I, 26a, and see below, n.85. RABD, *Hilḵot Lulaḇ* (in *Tešuḇot ha-RaMBaN*, ed. C. Chavel [Jerusalem, 1975]), p. 206, also notes that he changes the sequence of the Mishnah. His reason is literary-structural—i.e., saving the matter which requires lengthy exposition for the end—while Maimonides' reason is logical-conceptual.
9. *'Iggeret*, ed. B. M. Lewin (Haifa, 1921), p. 32.
10. *Bet hab-Bĕḥirah*, introduction, p. 33.
11. There are, of course, Talmudic antecedents for this assumption and for the attempt to account for the juxtaposition of certain tractates; e.g., B. Ta 2a; Soṭ 2a; Sheḇu 2a; Mak 2a. See Epstein, *Maḇo'*, p. 983. The prevailing modern view is that the tractates within each order are arranged by size, the longest coming first; see *Wissenschaftliche Zeitschrift*

great ingenuity and imaginativeness he constructs principles or reconstructs reasons for the sequence of tractates: *Ta'ănit* follows *Roš haš-Šanah* as a result of chronological considerations, for the days of fasting are mentioned in the Prophetic Writings while the major festivals are recorded in the Pentateuch; similarly, *Mĕgillah* follows *Ta'ănit*, for Purim was established by the latter prophets. *Mĕgillah*, in turn, is followed by *Mo'ed Katan* (which begins with the laws concerning the intermediate days of the festivals), for there is a common denominator to Purim and the intermediate days of the festivals—the prohibition of fasting and of certain mourning practices. *'Ăbodah Zarah* comes toward the end of the fourth order of *Nĕziḳin* because it is not too practical and relevant—its subject matter is quite arcane. Scriptural sequence is responsible for the fact that *Šĕḳalim* follows *Pĕsaḥim* or that *Kil'ayim* follows *Dĕmay*. Sometimes Maimonides suggests multiple reasons for the position of a tractate: the second order of *Mo'ed* begins with *Šabbat* because (a) of its extraordinary sanctity; (b) of its frequency, recurring every seven days; and (c) Scripture lists it as the first of the festivals.[12] Everything in the arrangement of the Mishnah is explained, with great persuasiveness or with apparent perfunctoriness; certain principles, e.g., Scriptural sequence, chronology, frequency, interlocking ritual patterns or halakic traits, are used repeatedly, while some matters are explained by improvised ad hoc rationalizations. It would seem that some of the guiding principles and classificatory norms discovered by Maimonides in the Mishnah are actually lurking in the shadows of his own classification in the *Mishneh Torah*. There are some unmistakable parallels. Now and then a principle associated by Maimonides with R. Judah's scheme is hypothetically identified

---

*für Jüdische Theologie* II (1836), 488; S. D. Luzzatto, in *Kerem Ḥemed*, III (1838), 61; Z. Frankel, *Darke ham-Mishnah* (Warsaw, 1923), p. 257; Epstein, *Mabo'*, pp. 980-1006; and recently the comments of A. S. Rosenthal in *Sefer Zikkaron lĕ-Ya'aḳob Friedman* (Jerusalem, 1974), pp. 237ff., particularly p. 244, n.23. Among the medievals, note how R. Menaḥem ben Zerah, *Ṣedah lad-Derek* (Warsaw, 1880), p. 5, refers approvingly to Maimonides' explanation of the sequence of the Mishnah. A sharp monolithic explanation—like a clean surgical cut—is most effective.

12. PhM, introduction (pp. 25ff.). Multiple explanations usually weaken the case, as is seen also in the realm of *ṭa'ăme miṣwot*.

by later commentators as being operative in the *Mishneh Torah*.[13] His rejection of R. Judah's scheme consequently seems to say: the results of my lucubrations are not uniformly persuasive, or even if my explanatory insights are correct and valid, the scheme itself has too many conceptual lapses and superficial links.

Even a modified Mishnaic-Talmudic sequence, such as that adopted by the eighth-century author of the *Halakot Gĕdolot*, would not be adequate for Maimonides' conceptual purposes. The *Halakot Gĕdolot*, a pioneering Gaonic work of considerable importance and resonance, was not simply an abridgement of the Talmud, for it already moved toward an incipient breakdown and classification of laws; it introduced a fledgling topical arrangement and a number of new rubrics in order to mitigate the scholastic discursiveness of the Talmud. One finds here such captions as Hanukkah, Circumcision, Mourning, Priestly Benediction, Tĕfillin, Mĕzuzah, Fringes, Usury, Excommunication. While these are rather obvious, almost commonplace, groupings created by disengaging that which was artificially united and establishing special rubrics or subsections for certain parts of a Talmudic tractate, there are also several new and rather imaginative categories, e.g., Communal Needs. On occasion there is here a more microscopic division than one finds in the *Mishneh Torah:* the first tractate of the Talmud, for example, contains a section on *kidduš* and *habdalah*, while there is later on also a special section on Honoring of Father and Mother.[14] The existing divisions, however, seem to stem from convenience and utility, not from overall conceptual classification or analytical schematization; they

---

13. See his use of Scriptural relation and sequence at the beginning of *Bĕkorot*.

14. It has been suggested (L. Ginzberg, *Geonica* [New York, 1909], I, 112) that the author had a dual goal in mind, to provide a companion volume for the study of the Talmud as well as a manual for the judge, and as a result his work had to remain subordinated to the Talmud. One full example will concretize the extent of the incipient classification, which is often merely the obvious splitting of one treatise into two sections. Part Two, *Mo'ed*, is divided as follows: Šabbat, Ḥanukkah, Milah, 'Erubin, Pesaḥ, 'Aṣeret, Roš haš-Šanah, Yoma, Sukkah, Lulab, Yom Ṭob, Tiš'ah bĕ-'Ab, Ta'āniyyot, Mĕgillah, Mo'ed, 'Abel, Ṭum'ah, Hilkot Kohanim, Šorke Ṣibbur, Mĕzuzah, Ṣiṣit.

As we shall note later on in this chapter, excessively minute classification has its drawbacks (fragmentization of conceptual units) as well as advantages (avoidance of forced groupings; e.g., *kibbud 'ab*, which Maimonides includes in *Mamrim*, is problematic).

remain unrelated atoms in an inert atmosphere. From the vantage point of logical-pedagogical criteria, the *Halaḵot Gĕdolot*, like the other Gaonic works with which Maimonides was acquainted and the greatly admired *Halaḵot* of R. Isaac Alfasi,[15] remained within the orbit of Mishnaic-Talmudic arrangement.

In sum, while finding much in the Mishnah that accorded with his own taste for brevity, quest for eloquence, and zest for systematization, Maimonides could not comfortably submit himself to its classificatory system. While the break with this system is sharp, the tone of the prose which presents it is of course not heatedly argumentative but coolly descriptive and tranquil. As for the modifications introduced by the *Halaḵot Gĕdolot* and kindred works, Maimonides could appreciate but would not be bound in his own *Mishneh Torah* by such timid expansion or tenuous innovation.

## Listing of commandments: the Sefer ham-Miṣwot approach

A second possibility, which could be exhaustive in its coverage and of obvious functionality, was to review the corpus of halakic material by enumerating and then explicating all of the 613 commandments,[16] following either the Scriptural order or an independently conceived order. This is the format of a special genre of Rabbinic literature, the *Sefer ham-Miṣwot* or *Book of Commandments*, which may have begun sometime in the eighth century

---

15. Maimonides mentions the following works in the introduction to the PhM (pp. 46–47); *Halaḵot Gĕdolot, Halaḵot Kĕṭu'ot, Halaḵot Pĕsukot, Halaḵot* of R. Aḥa of Shabḥa (i.e., *Šĕ'eltot*), and the *Halaḵot* of Alfasi, which is the flower of all post-Talmudic Rabbinic literature.

Actually these works differ in form: some rearrange Talmudic material and some follow the Talmudic sequence but pare away unessentials. Maimonides apparently grouped them together because of their common denominator: a criterion of relevance and a concern with practical matters. In the MT introduction he refers collectively to Gaonic works and sees their authors' motivation in a desire to render the Talmud accessible to those not qualified to plumb its depths or navigate their way through its stormy seas. This pragmatic-pedagogical motive is important for Maimonides as well.

16. See M. Bloch, "Les 613 Préceptes," *REJ*, I (1880), 196–214. A. Neubauer, "Miscellanea Liturgica, II," *JQR*, VI (1894), 698–99; R. Ḥefeṣ ben Yaṣliaḥ, *Sefer ham-Miṣwot*, ed. B. Halper (Philadelphia, 1915), pp. 1–4; J. M. Guttmann, *Bĕḥinat Kiyyum ham-Miṣwot* (Breslau, 1931); Ch. Heller, ed., *Sefer ham-Miṣwot* (Jerusalem, 1946), p. 4, nn. 49, 51, 53. See 'Oh 1:8. The date of the *Halaḵot Gĕdolot* list is not clear.

with the bare and unadorned listing of commandments at the beginning of the *Halakot Gĕdolot,* a list which became increasingly influential as well as provocative during succeeding centuries. It reached its full maturation, a pinnacle of fame and influence, in two popular post-Maimonidean works, the *Sefer Miṣwot Gadol* by R. Moses of Coucy, and the *Sefer ha-Ḥinnuk* whose unidentified author claims to have innovated the use of the Scriptural sequence, i.e., fully treating each commandment where it is first mentioned in the Bible.[17] Recognizing the fact that his mighty predecessors (particularly the triumvirate R. Isaac Alfasi, Maimonides, and Naḥmanides) have "clarified everything for us," the only justification for a new book, the author of the *Sefer ha-Ḥinnuk* modestly avers, lies in its principle of arrangement: the grouping of the 613 commandments according to the sequence of the Scriptural portions. His avowed motive, moreover, is pedagogic: such a neat and functional approach, which made Talmudic material easily accessible and related to the Scriptural readings on Sabbaths and holidays, might stimulate restless and intractable youngsters and encourage them in the study of religious teachings.

As a matter of fact, the Scripturally based enumeration of precepts is adumbrated in the eighth-century *Šě'eltot,* a quasi-code in which dispersed (halakic and aggadic) material is collated and arranged in relation to a commandment mentioned in the Biblical portion. Often the Biblical text is a transparent pretext for the halakic excursus; sometimes the link between the Talmudic discussion and the Biblical base is quite shaky; moreover, only select commandments, about one-fourth of the total, are analyzed; yet all these qualifications notwithstanding, the Scriptural principle of arrangement is operative. R. Samuel ben Ḥofni reported in the eleventh century that he had heard of a work which collected all the commandments in Scriptural order.[18] More significantly, a

---

17. *Sefer ha-Ḥinnuk,* ed. C. Chavel (Jerusalem, 1952), introductory epistle (p. 29), repeated at end of introduction, p. 52. Originally, he divided the material into negative and positive precepts, and both followed the Scriptural sequence (Chavel, introduction, p. 19); see A. H. Rabinowitz, *Taryag* (Jerusalem, 1967), p. 133.

18. A. Harkavy, "Ḥelek mis-Sefer ham-Miṣwot le-Rab Šěmu'el ben Ḥofni Gaon," *Hak-Kedem,* III (1909–10), 107–10; D. Margolis, "Minyan ham-Miṣwot," *Sinai,* XL (1956), 96–102; Ginzberg, *Geonica,* p. 170.

modified Scriptural sequence *may* have been at the core of the rather original, systematic, and comprehensive *Sefer ham-Miṣwot* of R. Ḥefeṣ ben Yaṣliaḥ who "tried to follow the Bible as closely as possible," but "keeping the logical arrangement in mind, he is obliged to deviate now and again from the Biblical orders."[19] The halakic work of R. Ḥefeṣ, whose formative-educative influence Maimonides fully acknowledged and partially regretted,[20] has many affinities with that of Maimonides: both were critical of the *Halakot Gĕdolot*, both ignored accidental distinctions between practical and theoretical laws and aimed at comprehensiveness, both interspersed their normative legal formulations with fluid exegetical comments, both solidified the nexus between Scriptural verse and Rabbinic amplification, both included theological principles and ethical precepts, and both were concerned with providing reasons for laws so that experience would be deepened and intellect enlarged through their observance. Maimonides' relation to R. Ḥefeṣ is a significant tale of attraction and reaction, initial dependence and a subsequent sense of inadequacy. As in the case of R. Joseph ibn Megas, the process of intellectual growth is clearly silhouetted against the details and nuances of this dynamic relation. Nevertheless, all the affinities notwithstanding, this too was not a desirable model given Maimonides' dissatisfaction with the Scriptural sequence.

Maimonides' attitude toward the Book of Commandments genre —critical and pejorative, as we shall see—is more readily understandable if we note further that this genre was quite popular in the pre-Maimonidean period. There was a burgeoning of

---

19. Halper, *Sefer ham-Miṣwot*, pp. 57–58; S. Assaf, "Miš-šĕyare Sifruṭam šel hag-Gĕ'onim," *Tarbiz*, XV (1943), 31–33; see S. Baron, *Social and Religious History of the Jews* (Philadelphia, 1958), VI, 94–95. It is difficult to sustain the assumption that the arrangement is basically Scriptural. Note that R. Eliezer of Metz, the author of the *Sefer Yĕre'im*, explicitly rejects the Scriptural sequence, because, says he, it is preferable to group related matters together. M. Zucker has made an invaluable contribution by publishing additional sections of this work and helping clarify many moot issues, particularly its relation to the works of R. Saadiah Gaon and R. Samuel ben Ḥofni; see "Mis-Sefer ham-Miṣwot le-R. Ḥefeṣ," *PAAJR*, XXIX (1960–61), 1–68.

20. *Tĕšubot*, 217 (p. 383); *'Iggĕrot*, 58; ShM, introduction; R. Baḥya ibn Paḳuda, *Ḥobot hal-Lĕbabot*, ed. M. Hyamson (New York, 1925), I, introduction, p. 19, cites the work of R. Ḥefeṣ as an example of the literary genre which gave "accounts of the precepts in summary form"; Ibn Ezra, *Peruš*, Exod. 20:1; see Halper, *Sefer ham-Miṣwot*, p. 49.

works, best represented perhaps by the *Sefer ham-Miṣwot* (*Kitāb al-Šarā'i'*) of R. Saadiah Gaon. This work included all the commandments, practical as well as nonpractical; its method was to group related precepts together, intermingle negative and positive ones, and in each case cite·the underlying Scriptural verse.[21] R. Samuel ben Ḥofni Gaon also composed a *Book of Commandments*, in which, among other things, he reviewed the achievements of his predecessors, paying particular attention and respect to the many-faceted creativity of R. Saadiah.[22] In addition—and temporally prior—to such books, there were many poetic summaries of the 613 commandments, known as *'Azharot*, which used various literary devices and stratagems, the most prominent of which, and in the eyes of such scholars as R. Ḥefeṣ the most praiseworthy, was relating all 613 precepts to the Ten Commandments. These works were well known and widely used. Gaonic writers point repeatedly to the work of R. Saadiah, while Maimonides refers particularly to the *'Azharot* composed in Spain, presumably by such authors as R. Joseph ibn Abitur, R. Solomon ibn Gabirol, R. Isaac Gikatilia, and R. Isaac ben Reuben al-Bargeloni.[23]

Maimonides' displeasure with this entire genre was twofold. He was distressed, and had "experienced this feeling of distress for many years," with the arbitrariness, slovenliness, and erroneousness of the underlying enumeration and with the fact that there developed, consciously or unconsciously, a cult of the past, a cult of the *Halakot Gĕdolot*. All authors "followed the lead of the *Halakot Gĕdolot*," "came forward with the strangest of theories," and "counted matters which even at first thought, it would appear, should not have been included." It was "as if intellect stopped with his decision," freedom of interpretation was stifled, and the errors and phantasies of the *Halakot Gĕdolot* were enshrined. Even R. Ḥefeṣ, who registered some advances over the

---

21. A. Neubauer, "Miscellanea," pp. 698–709; H. Malter, *Saadya Gaon* (Philadelphia, 1942), pp. 400–02; D. Baneth, in *Kobeṣ R. Saadiah Gaon*, ed. J. L. Maimon (Jerusalem, 1943), pp. 365–82; *Sefer ham-Miṣwot lĕ-RaSaG*, ed. J. Perla (New York, 1962).
22. See above, n.21.
23. A. Neubauer, "Miscellanea," pp. 698–709.

*Halakot Gĕdolot*, regressed in other areas.[24] While there was general agreement on the number of 613,[25] there was no agreement on which commandments should be included in the enumeration. The tyranny of habit was so strong, however, that Maimonides was convinced that were he just to put forth his own listing of the 613 commandments, most readers would blithely dismiss it as patently erroneous and unworthy because of the fact that it contradicted the conventional listings. Even scholars do not examine a work critically with an eye to establishing its intrinsic worth and plausibility; they routinely compare it with earlier works without stopping to scrutinize the strengths and weaknesses of these works. In support of his plea for objective evaluation of the cogency and persuasiveness of arguments rather than blind reliance on whatever has already been circulated, Maimonides formulated fourteen guiding principles with which, he believed, no one could take issue. This approach demonstrates his unrelenting opposition to the pervasive mood of intellectual conservatism which usually tends to accept anything published as authoritative, anything old and familiar as correct, and anything novel as suspect. He gave forceful expression to this attitude: "The great sickness and grievous evil consist in this: that all the things that man finds written in books, he presumes to think of as true, and all the more so if the books are old."[26] Similarly, he wrote: "Man has in his nature a love of, and an inclination for, that to which he

---

24. ShM, introduction (II, 361); Maimonides postulated, with some exaggeration, the dominating and almost exclusive influence of the *Halakot Gĕdolot* on all poets; he was followed in this by R. Moses ibn Tibbon (Neubauer, "Miscellanea," p. 701) and R. Simeon Duran, *Zohar ha-Raki'a* (Vilna, 1879), p. 11. Note that even such a staunch defender of the *Halakot Gĕdolot* as Nahmanides occasionally registers his own criticism; see, e.g., his commentary on Deut. 28:14.

25. Exceptions to the use are R. Judah ibn Bal'am, R. Abraham ibn Ezra, *Yĕsod Mora'*, and later Nahmanides (beginning of his critique of the ShM, *šoreš* 1). R. Bahya refers to "about 613." Duran, *Zohar ha-Raki'a*, p. 10, speaks of "great consensus" and singles out Nahmanides as one who doubted this number. See Ibn Bal'am in L. S. Fuchs, *Studien ueber . . . Ibn Bal'am* (Berlin, 1893), chap. 30. Note also *Hobot hal-Lĕbabot*, x, chap. 7 (II, p. 375).

26. LA, 229. On the importance of the fourteen *šorašim*, see *Tĕšubot*, 355 (p. 632), 447 (p. 725). See also IT, xiv: "Do not consider a statement true because you find it in a book. . . . For the untutored and uninstructed are convinced of the veracity of a statement by the mere fact that it is written; nevertheless, its accuracy must be demonstrated in another manner." See above, chap. 1, n. 38.

is habituated. Thus you can see that the people of the desert, notwithstanding the disorderliness of their life, the lack of pleasures, and the scarcity of food, dislike the towns, do not hanker after their pleasures, and prefer the bad circumstances to which they are accustomed to good ones to which they are not accustomed. . . . In a similar way, man has love for, and the wish to defend, opinions to which he is habituated and in which he has been brought up, and has a feeling of repulsion for opinions other than those. For this reason also man is blind to the apprehension of the true realities and inclines toward the things to which he is habituated."[27]

The poetic compositions in particular aroused Maimonides' ire—*My pains are come upon me* (Dan. 10:16)—and he indiscriminately lambasted their authors. They were, in Platonic terms, poets who wrote without knowing their subject and generally sacrificed substance to style;[28] so while passing favorable judgment on their aesthetic sense, he dismissed their halakic achievement as an unredeemed failure. With a mixture of Platonic disdain and Voltairean irony, Maimonides, who had little use for poetry of any kind, even liturgical and hymnal,[29] dismissed these writers as "poets, not scholars." He was astounded and saddened by the

---

27. MN, I, 31. Also MN, I, 62 (p. 152): "These people accordingly made a secret of these writings, and the latter were found in the belongings left behind them, so that they were thought to be correct." See an interesting reference to this Maimonidean attitude in R. Moses Isserles, *Tĕšubot*, ed. A. Ziv (Jerusalem, 1971), 126 (p. 496).

28. Plato, *Republic*, X, 598ᵉ, 601ᵃ; W. Jaeger, *Paideia*, I, 35; also I, 211, 358; cf. the recent analysis by A. Gilbert, "Did Plato Banish the Poets?", *Medieval and Renaissance Studies* (Durham, 1966), pp. 35ff.

29. MN, I, 59, and RaDBaZ, *Tĕšubot* (New York, 1947), III, 645, who identifies Ibn Gabirol as the target of Maimonides' critique; *Tĕšubot*, 254 (p. 468): משוררים לא תלמידי חכמים. In his letter to R. Jonathan, Maimonides refers to the prevalence, almost ubiquitousness, of poetic writing; *Tĕšubot*, III, 56. He himself succumbs and writes part of the letter in rhymed prose even though this is not conducive to precise expression and exposition. Maimonides' criticism of unscholarly poets is repeated by his son (see *Tĕšubot*, 254, n.15) and grandson (*Tĕšubot R. Joshua han-Nagid*, 4). Actually, Maimonides evaluated poetry in the light of the criterion which he applied to all human discourse: the extent to which it contributed to the attainment of the goal of perfection. For a synoptic view of Maimonides' rather complicated attitude, see PhM, 'Ab 1:16 (p. 416); ŠP, chap. V (end); *Ta'āniyyot*, v, 14; MN, I, 5, 9, 72; III, 12, 44, 45; *Tĕšubot*, 180 (p. 328); 207 (p. 365); 208 (p. 368)—and see J. Heinemann, *Bar Ilan*, I (1963), 233 (the conclusion is noteworthy for its recognition of the hold which *piyyut* has on the people); 224 (p. 398); 254 (p. 467); 260 (p. 489); 261 (p. 490); *Millot ha-Higgayon*, chap. VIII (concerning

fact that writers with good poetic credentials but novices in Rabbinic scholarship produced inconsequential and unsubstantial works which were nevertheless popular and influential; indeed, we may note, they had been and were to remain immensely popular. R. Saadiah Gaon attested to their popularity in describing the motives for his own composition of *'Azharot:* "I have found that men of our generation customarily recite during the *Musaf* prayers [of the Festival of Weeks] the principal 613 commandments which the Lord ordained to the children of Israel. . . . I have examined them [these prayers] and found that they did not contain the complete listing of the 613 laws; I have also noted much repetition and wordiness in them . . . I have decided, therefore, to replace them by another prayer, not because it is obligatory to have such a recitation, but rather because I noticed that people had set their hearts on it."[30] The abiding popularity of R. Solomon ibn Gabirol's *'Azharot* is reflected in the numerous commentaries on it. R. Moses ibn Tibbon affirms that it is "a widespread custom to read the *'Azharot* of Gabirol on the Festival of Weeks because of their eloquence and brevity."[31] Years later R. Simeon ben Ṣemaḥ Duran (d. 1444) composed a commentary (*Zohar ha-Rakiʿa*) on the *'Azharot* of Ibn Gabirol because "it was the custom in most places to recite the *'Azharot* of the great scholar R. Solomon ibn Gabirol"; inasmuch as few people turn to the serious and profound works of Maimonides and Naḥmanides, he would engage in *haute vulgarisation* and prepare a simple compendium of the basic views and interpretations. The existing commentary of R. Moses ibn Tibbon is faulted by Duran because of its unabashed Maimonidean partisanship and failure to give

---

*hekkeš ḥamiši*, the fifth, poetic, syllogism); and see D. Pagis, *Širat ha-Ḥol we-Torat haš-Šir* (Jerusalem, 1970), p. 49. For Gaonic opposition to *piyyuṭ*, see, e.g., L. Ginzberg, *Ginze Schechter* (New York, 1928–29), II, 508; and recently E. Fleischer, "Unpublished Poems by Rav Hai Gaon," *JQR*, LXV (1974), 1. For Karaite critique, see, e.g., J. Mann, *Tarbiz*, VI (1935), 66; and A. Scheiber, *HUCA*, XXII (1948), 307. Cf. W. Bacher, "Hebraeische Verse von Maimuni," *MGWJ*, LIII (1909), 581, and H. Schirman, "Ha-RaMBaM wĕhaš-Širah," *Moznayim*, III (1935), 433ff.

30. R. Saadiah Gaon, *Siddur*, ed. I. Davidson, S. Assaf, and B. I. Joel (Jerusalem, 1941), pp. 157, 165; I have adapted the translation from Baron, *History*, VI, 92.

31. Neubauer, "Miscellanea," p. 700.

## 252 INTRODUCTION TO THE CODE OF MAIMONIDES

Naḥmanides a fair hearing.[32] In short, these poetic listings of the 613 commandments, their transparent inadequacies notwithstanding, had a lively *Nachleben,* and this irritated Maimonides.

We may assume in addition that Maimonides shared R. Abraham ibn Ezra's derisive attitude toward the whole idea of a barebones listing of precepts, such as that found at the beginning of the *Halakot Gĕdolot:* "The authors of the *'Azharot* are like a person who counts the number of herbs listed in a medical book without recognizing the function of each one; so of what use to him is a mere listing of their names?"[33] Routine and unexamined knowledge does not rank very high.

However, the erroneous listing, and its imperfect embodiment in poetic compositions or in more ambitious works like that of R. Ḥefeṣ, was not all. Beyond this substantive critique, and assuming that the methodological and conceptual impurities could be removed, it would appear that Maimonides had reservations about the usefulness of this genre as a means of codifying Jewish law. In the *Mishneh Torah* introduction he does not repeat the fact of, or rehearse the reasons for, his rejection of the Talmudic scheme, but while introducing his own conceptual arrangement he notes pointedly that the "classification (*ḥilluḳ*) of this work is in accord with topics, not with the enumeration of precepts (*minyan ham-miṣwot*)."[34] The latter, of course, was functional but not sufficiently conceptual, rigorous, or imaginative. Indeed, its method of description and narrative could be seen as antagonistic to the desired method of analysis and classification. The interrela-

---

32. *Zohar ha-Raḳi'a,* pp. 10–11. For other commentaries, see Neubauer, "Miscellanea," p. 704.

33. R. Abraham ibn Ezra, *Yĕsod Mora'* (Prague, 1833), chap. 2, p. 20b. For the influence of this work on Maimonides, see J. Perla, *Sefer ham-Miṣwot,* pp. 15ff. Many medieval writers explicitly or implicitly link Ibn Ezra and Maimonides, especially in connection with philosophy; e.g., RIṬBA, *Sefer Zikkaron,* ed. K. Kahana (Jerusalem, 1955), p. 69. Modern writers tend to overlook this connection; cf. most recently, H. Greive, *Studien zum jüdischen Neuplatonismus: Die Religionsphilosophie des Abraham ibn Ezra* (Berlin, 1973), pp. 51–52.

34. MT, introduction. On the meaning of *ḥilluḳ,* see H. A. Wolfson, "The Classification of Sciences in Medieval Jewish Philosophy," *HUCA Jubilee volume* (1925), p. 267, n. 16.

tions of laws would not emerge, and this, after all, is the very essence of classification, which should deal with implicit connections as well as explicit facts. The sporadic attempt of some to impose a topical breakdown upon the enumeration did not yield satisfactory results. The work of R. Saadiah Gaon was divided into twenty-five sections; that of R. Ḥefeṣ into at least thirty-six; but this, as we shall see, struck Maimonides as artificial and unenlightening. Maimonides wanted to balance two goals: (a) to facilitate knowledge and memorization, and (b) to aid understanding. Any device or artifice, even a rudimentary and atomistic listing of laws, would help achieve the former, but only a topical-conceptual scheme would advance the latter. It is not surprising, therefore, that his own *Sefer ham-Miṣwot* was intended merely as an exact and exhaustive checklist, preparatory to his Code and designed to insure the Code's comprehensiveness by guarding against forgetfulness and omissions: "My intention is not to explain but only to fix their number," actually to enumerate and define each commandment. This neatly differentiates his work from that of R. Ḥefeṣ, whose *Sefer ham-Miṣwot* was intended to be a full-fledged and self-sufficient code, with ample explanation and discussion.[35] In short, this form, which many Gaonic writers used rather timidly and which later scholars, such as R. Moses of Coucy, R. Isaac of Corbeille, and R. Moses di Trani, would adopt more adventurously for purposes of classifying and systematizing Jewish law, was not viable for Maimonides. Indeed, while his own *Sefer ham-Miṣwot* gave impetus to the development of these later works and substantively influenced most of them, Maimonides himself, with calm, uncompromising assurance, sought a different medium.

---

35. ShM, introduction (II, 423). See also *Tešubot*, 447 (p. 724). There are some significant exceptions in ShM where Maimonides explains substantive matters, e.g., positive 157, 187; negative 43, 365. Gersonides (*Peruš* [reprinted, New York, 1958], introduction, p. 3b) promised to produce a *Sefer ham-Miṣwot* which would cite the underlying verse of each commandment together with its roots and ramifications, so that nothing found in any branch of Rabbinic literature which was relevant to the commandment under discussion would be omitted—a balanced antithesis to Maimonides' description of his own ShM.

## Independent topical-conceptual arrangement

A third possibility, most commodious in the latitude it provided for creative experimentation, was the construction of a topical-conceptual sequence, emerging from originality of mind and boldness of perception. This method of free and composite rearrangement of Talmudic material and integrative grouping of related topics which had been treated discretely and discursively in various unrelated texts, had been tried fragmentarily by some prominent Geonim—e.g., R. Saadiah, R. Hai, and R. Samuel ben Ḥofni—and by some of Maimonides' influential Spanish predecessors, e.g., R. Isaac ibn Ghiyāth and R. Judah al-Bargeloni. They had produced monographs on various aspects of ritual and civil law, such as benedictions, prayer, *ṣiṣit*, commercial transactions, inheritance and legacy, oaths, and festivals.[36] The motivations of the authors varied. Some had purely scholarly goals in mind, desiring to abet study of difficult material, while others were more pragmatic, intending to produce compact and sinewy manuals which would be useful to jurists, who needed immediate and decisive answers to wide-ranging questions concerning halakic practice. The forms of the works also varied. They could be apodictic-codificatory, undocumented and unelaborated, uniformly omitting the complexity of Talmudic discussion as well as the diversity of post-Talmudic interpretation; or they could be more expansive, reproducing the underlying Talmudic passages, assessing alternate interpretations, validating and explaining the reasons for the resultant normative formulations, and thus providing for intellectual stimulus as well as correct guidance in religious practices. Some Geonim used both forms; the early codificatory works of R. Saadiah are, like R. Joseph Karo's *Šulḥan 'Aruk*, concise and monolithic, omitting Talmudic discussion, while other monographs of his are, like the *Bet Yosef*, more

---

36. S. Assaf, *Tĕkufat hag-Gĕ'onim wĕ-Sifrutah* (Jerusalem, 1955), pp. 154ff.; M. Margaliyot, *Sefer Hilkot han-Nagid* (Jerusalem, 1962), p. 12; S. D. Goitein, *Sidre Ḥinnuk* (Jerusalem, 1962), pp. 153–55; see the perceptive lecture of Sh. Abramson, *'Inyanot bĕ-Sifrut hag-Gĕ'onim* (Jerusalem, 1974), pp. 231ff., and index. Professor Abramson's comment about the need to balance historical information with halakic analysis is most apposite.

diffuse and excursive, proceeding from Talmudic discussion to the formulation of the codificatory upshot. There could be two objections to the first, compressed, form: (1) it is too imperious and presumptuous, countervailing the very spirit of Talmudic debate and dialectic by yielding reasoned conclusions in oracular and dogmatic fashion; (2) it is too brief and uninformative, therefore failing to satisfy the natural inquisitiveness and intellectual drive of the keen Rabbinic student, who is concerned not only with the outcome but with the process as well.[37] This is analogous to the philosophically oriented student who is not comfortable with philosophic truths presented descriptively or apodictically as articles of tradition, but seeks instead to have them elaborated demonstratively as syllogistic premises and conclusions. The latter, more supple, form, then, would remove some serious scholarly-ideological objections to codification while preserving some of its practical benefit, but its goal of brevity would be frustrated. At the very least, the pragmatic advantage of a code could be secured by regularly stating the binding regulation at the end of each subject, but the complications of over-elaboration would leave their mark.

While only the former would serve as partial precedent for Maimonides' Delphic type of code, built for the most part around staccato summaries, pointed directives, and imperious sentences,[38] both forms are significant as adumbrations of the new autonomous classification. In the introduction to the *Mishneh Torah* Maimonides takes note of these works in very general terms, ascertaining that they are significant, even if embryonic and immature, attempts at topical non-Talmudic classification. In his muted characterization of Gaonic contributions to halakic literature, he mentions without a trace of enthusiasm or commendation that "the Geonim also made compilations of fixed rules (*halakot pĕsukot*) concerning things permitted or forbidden, concerning actions which were culpable or not culpable in areas

---

[37] See the oft-quoted statement of R. Paltoi Gaon, *Tĕšubot hag-Gĕ'onim*, ed. S. Assaf (Jerusalem, 1928), p. 81. The second aspect is eloquently described by ham-Me'iri, *Bet hab-Bĕḥirah*, introduction, p. 26. See also I. Twersky, "The Shulḥan 'Aruk," pp. 141–59, especially p. 143.
[38] See the discussion of the codificatory form in chap. II, above.

which were timely and practicable." While aligning himself with this monographic approach and extolling it as the most effective and appropriate, Maimonides was fully aware that not a single predecessor had produced a *total* regrouping of halakah. They fragmentized the material in the process of producing small meaningful units, whereas he regrouped and reshaped it into a new and meaningful unity. This salient fact of *total* regrouping provides the correct perspective for assessing the many specific influences of this Gaonic literature on Maimonides; they should not, per se, be minimized or downgraded, but the radical difference between the Gaonic works and the *Mishneh Torah* in scope and structure should be sharply perceived. Omitting the stereotyped overtures to modesty, Maimonides candidly declared that the *Mishneh Torah* was absolutely unprecedented from the point of view of its scope and structure. Some Geonim produced fragmentary topical codifications of Jewish law, and he utilized their advances and insights; but not since R. Judah the Patriarch had an individual undertaken to review or rearrange systematically the entire halakah.[39] Should he be faulted or indicted, Maimonides asks his critics, simply for being more comprehensive (*kolel*) and showing greater vision than his predecessors?

The novelty of his work is that he pushed back the frontiers of this method and attempted to perfect it by being consistent and comprehensive. Authors of monographs abandoned the sequence of the Mishnah and engaged in autonomous codification but did not create an alternate scheme of total synoptic presentation. Maimonides could have the best of both worlds. The charge of literary innovation was thus, in a formal sense, not relevant, and yet he could unhesitatingly note the innovative features of his achievements. It is significant that while his critics attacked the apodictic form of his work, Maimonides defended both form and classification.

It has been truly said "that he who could perfectly classify the law would have a perfect knowledge of the law."[40] Classification

---

39. MT, introduction; *Kobeṣ*, I, 25b.
40. J. C. Gray, *The Nature and Sources of the Law* (reprinted, Boston, 1963), p. 3. Gray wryly continues: "the besetting sin of the analytic jurist is the conviction that his classification and definitions are final." For the first classification of legal concepts (by Q.

is, of course, a prerequisite for codification and necessitates interpretation, sustained conceptualization, a large measure of abstraction, and a synoptic view of the entire body of material. Classification deals not only with clear given data but also with latent assumptions and relations that must be rationally perceived; for in order to group *a* and *b* together, their common denominator, which is not always explicit, must be identified. In some respects legal classification may be said to concern itself not only with the sum total of individual laws but also with the concept of law per se, the principles underlying large areas of law and their interrelations.

The ruling passion of Maimonides' life was order, system, conceptualization, and generalization, and this received its finest expression in the *Mishneh Torah*. Maimonides repeatedly called attention to this fact. There are paragraphs in the *Mishneh Torah*, he proclaims to R. Phinehas, which are conflations of ten or more passages scattered throughout the Babylonian Talmud, Palestinian Talmud, and extra-Mishnaic Tannaitic collections. In the letter to R. Jonathan he refers to his success in "collecting" (*ḳibbuṣ*) the material for his Code. "Great persons like yourself will appreciate what I have accomplished, for I have gathered together subjects which were scattered and dispersed among the hills and mountains, and I have culled (literally, called) them one from a city and two from a family." In his *Ma'ămar Tĕḥiyyat ham-Metim* he again notes that "we collected and conjoined topics scattered and dispersed." The governing phrase in all these statements is "scattered and dispersed," and the overriding achievement is scholarly collection and creative classification.[41]

---

Scaevola) on the basis of Aristotelian logic, see H. Cairns, *Legal Philosophy from Plato to Hegel* (Baltimore, 1949), p. 124.

41. *Ḳobeṣ*, I, 25b; *Tĕšuḇot*, III, 57; MTH, 2, 4; Twersky, "Sefer MT," p. 14. Note the letter of Naḥmanides, *Kitḇe ha-RaMBaN*, ed. C. Chavel (Jerusalem, 1963), I, 343: בספר ההוא הממולא פנינים, המיוחס בספרים מבחוץ ומבפנים; and see Sh. Abramson, *Sinai*, LXX (1972), 27. See also ham-Me'iri, *Bet hab-Bĕḥirah*, introduction, p. 25; MM, *Ta'ăniyyot*, i, 14; *Mišneh lĕ-Meleḵ*, introduction: ומהפלגת רבנו בשמירת הסדר. Even a steady critic—perhaps he should be described as an avowed antagonist—such as R. Solomon Luria praises the classification of the MT; see *Yam šel Šĕlomoh, Baḇa Ḳamma*, introduction. Note also R. Judah Albutini, *Yĕsod MT*, published by M. Benayahu, *Sinai*, XXXVI (1954), 242.

## 258 INTRODUCTION TO THE CODE OF MAIMONIDES

Of course, the assumption that Maimonides was theoretically attuned to the needs and problems of classification, and predisposed to deal with them, readily suggests itself to the historian, for one of the standard preoccupations of medieval philosophy was the classification of sciences. Classification, in general, was a hallmark of philosophy ever since Aristotle.[42] Also, the Rabbis appreciated the value of systematic arrangement—R. 'Akiba was praised for his erudite collection of data followed by his careful classification and generic systematization of all this diverse learning.[43] Maimonides must have been an enthusiast of classification from the time that he composed his youthful work on logic, which "offers a clear and concise exposition of the most important logical terms," carefully systematized, and his *Mishnah Commentary,* which is distinguished by an advanced sense of systematization and many dazzling gems of classification.[44] However, it would be a case of misplaced concreteness to see the *Mishneh Torah*—a meticulous restructuring of the halakic *hylé* in a way that would not do violence to the subject matter, but would rather enhance its integrity and intrinsic rationality and also be educationally sound, i.e., conducive to retention and perhaps memorization—as resulting only from arabicized "Hellenistic" stimulation.[45] To be sure, there was a sharp contrast between the diffuse and associative Talmud and systematic works of other kinds, and the cultural milieu could sharpen one's awareness of

---

42. See Wolfson, "Classification of Sciences," p. 267.
43. *'Aḇoṯ dĕ-R. Nathan,* version A, chap. 18 (YJS, 10, 90).
44. See *Millot ha-Higgayon,* ed. I. Efros (New York, 1938), p. 3; PhM, Sanh 7:4 (p. 176); PhM, Ker 3:4 (pp. 359–60); PhM, Ṭoh, introduction (pp. 9ff.); also PhM, Shab 1:1 (pp. 7ff.). He was acutely conscious of digressions and discursive and unsystematic writing; see, e.g., PhM, Ber 9:7 (p. 92), where he justifies a theological excursus because of its overwhelming importance, and 'Ed 2:10 (p. 300), where he explains that this treatise is, by definition, a miscellany.
45. E.g., the statement of I. Goldziher in his review of an edition of *'Ĕmunot wĕ-De'ot* in *Zeitschrift der Deutschen Morgenländischen Gesellschaft,* XXXV (1881), 774–75; cf. also L. Ginzberg, *On Jewish Law and Lore* (Philadelphia, 1955), p. 169; B. Cohen, "Classification of Law in the Mishneh Torah," *JQR,* XXV (1935), 528–29; N. Wieder, *Haśpa'ot 'Islamiyyot 'al hap-Pulḥan hay-Yĕhudi* (Oxford, 1947), p. 7; and n.70, below. See generally J. Schacht, *Introduction to Islamic Law* (Oxford, 1964), especially the bibliography on classification, p. 264. In a private communication (March 27, 1978), Professor Schacht appraised Muslim authors' statements concerning classification as follows: "Those specious reasonings, however, are nothing more than private lucubrations of certain [Muslim] au-

this. In this sense, academic taste or Hellenistic stimulation, the saturation of Jewish thought in Spain and Africa with Islamic methods and modes, themselves an embodiment of the Greek spirit which placed a premium on systematization, may certainly have played a role; such intangible influences, forms of zeitgeist, are not easily quantified or delimited. They are more easily assumed than demonstrated. Trying to pinpoint them is often like trying to take hold of a goldfish in water. In any event, analysis of the work and of Maimonides' obiter dicta indicates that his combined practical-theoretical goals were the major determinants. Actually, the reason for his choice of the codificatory form is identical with that for his rearrangement and classification: accentuated and accelerated need for an authoritative, comprehensive, easily intelligible summary of law as a result of the decline in learning and the deterioration of mental capacities, for the Talmud per se was always difficult. This is his explanation of the burgeoning difficulty, if not obscurity, of Talmud study—the quantity of material in itself is not a deterrent—and of the resultant need for an easy aid. This applies equally to topical classification: a good, suggestive, and meaningful systematization aids memory in the same way that skillful abridgement facilitates memory.

## THE FOURTEEN BOOKS OF THE *Mishneh Torah*

Toward the very end of his introduction to the *Mishneh Torah*, Maimonides writes: "I have seen fit to arrange this composition in groups of laws according to various subjects, and I shall subdivide these groups of law into chapters which are appropriate for that subject. Each chapter will be divided into small paragraphs, so that they may be arranged (in such a way as to be easily learned) by memory. Among the laws in the various topics, some consist of rules in explication of a single Biblical precept, namely a precept which has much traditional matter and forms a single unified

---

thors, and cannot claim even the lowest degree of authority within their respective schools." This shows how different the study of the MT is from the study of Muslim works, inasmuch as Maimonides' statements concerning classification are quite authoritative and actually guide the student.

topic.[46] Other sections include rules in explication of several Biblical precepts if they all form a single unified topic. This is the case because the classification of this work is in accord with topics, not with the enumeration of precepts, as will become clear to the reader."

This broad declaration of intent is more or less identical with the programmatic statement at the beginning of the *Sefer ham-Miṣwot:* "It became clear to me that in place of the tractates of the Mishnah, it would be best to arrange this work in groups of paragraphs . . . in order to facilitate a knowledge of it by heart."

The elemental division of the *Mishneh Torah* into fourteen books, the real core of his classification, is mentioned for the first time, quite unobtrusively, in what looks like a postscript to the *Mishneh Torah* introduction. After listing the 613 commandments, utilizing the standard division into 248 positive and 365 negative, Maimonides notes, "I have seen fit to divide this composition into fourteen books." These fourteen divisions, which attempt to provide integrity and texture to the scheme and prevent it from being an atomized listing, may be synopsized as follows:

Book One (*Madda'*, Knowledge) contains Maimonides' summary of the essential beliefs and guiding concepts which provide the ideological and experiential substructure of Judaism. He explains that he could not compose a comprehensive work on the details of practical precepts while ignoring the fundamentals of essential beliefs, those commandments which are the "root" (*'ikkar*) of Mosaic religion and which should be known before anything else. He was, therefore, compelled to prefix an extended philosophical-theological prolegomenon to his massive Code of law, thereby underscoring the unity of the philosophical and the legal components of Judaism. Individuals distinguished by impeccable piety and Talmudic erudition ought not to be lacking in

---

46. The following sections are devoted to the elucidation of only one commandment: *Těšubah, Ķěri'aṭ Šěma', Ṣiṣiṭ, Běrakoṭ, Milah, 'Erubin, Šěḳalim, Ķidduš ha-Ḥodeš, Ta'āniyyoṭ, Ma'āśer, 'Ăbodaṭ Yom haḳ-Kippurim, Ṭumě'aṭ Meṭ, Ṭumě'aṭ 'Oklin, Miḳwa'oṭ, Ṭo'en wě-Niṭ'an, Naḥăloṭ*. Three sections of *Sefer Ḳinyan—Zěkiyyah u-Mattanah, Šěkenim, Šěluḥin*—are devoted to one topic (procedure of civil law) but do not formally include even one commandment. The same is true for *Kelim;* the subject matter is which utensils become unclean.

# CLASSIFICATION

theological sophistication and sensitivity. The systematic treatment of metaphysics and ethics, the structuring of separate sections for laws of study and laws of repentance, the devoting of a section to idolatry, which includes a history of religion and a rigorous review of superstitions or magical practices which must still be uncompromisingly rejected—all this combines to produce a new and exciting book which is an introduction to, as well as an integral part of, the entire Code. It is literally a foundation, a cornerstone of an imposing edifice.[47] Its motto is, *Continue Thy loving-kindness unto them that know Thee; and Thy righteousness unto the upright in heart* (Ps. 36:11), immediately suggesting the interrelatedness of knowledge and probity, or, even further, that knowledge is the foundation for righteousness and love. "Knowing God" is both a refrain and a leitmotif of all Maimonidean writing; it is a goal and a means.

The daily recitation of the Shema', of prayers, and of assorted benedictions, the wearing of phylacteries and fringes, and the other religious practices included in Book Two (*'Ahăḇah*, Adoration; literally, Love) are described by Maimonides as "precepts which are to be constantly observed and which we have been commanded to keep in order that we may always love God and be ever mindful of Him." The criterion for inclusion in Book Two, in other words, is the regularity, frequency, or continuity of performance, and its subject matter is ritual-liturgical in the most fundamental sense. It is the *hylé* of the religious life. The last section, on circumcision, is prima facie enigmatic and needs special comment.[48] While the first Mishnaic tractate (*Bĕrakot*) obviously supplies much material, the book as a whole is not easily correlated with any one division of the Mishnah. It thus already demonstrates why Maimonides was so proud of his having collected diverse and dispersed materials. Its motto, *How I love Thy Torah! It is my meditation all the day* (Ps. 119:97), has an obvious verbal

---

47. MTH, 3–4. On the relation of this book to the thirteen principles, see A. Hyman, "Maimonides' Thirteen Principles," *Jewish Medieval and Renaissance Studies* (Cambridge, Mass., 1967), pp. 119–45. For *'iḳḳar*, see, e.g., *Yĕsode hat-Torah*, i, 6; *Ḳĕri'at Šĕma'*, i, 2; *'Akum*, ii, 4; *Ṭumĕ'at Ṣara'at*, vi, 10; *Roṣeaḥ*, xiii, 14. For *yĕsodot* (foundations), see below, chap. VI. For "knowledge," see *Tĕšuḇah*, x, 6; *Mĕlakim*, xii, 5.

48. See below, p. 283.

connection with the book's title, but it also plays upon the themes of constancy and continuity and rather subtly links up love expressed through actions with meditation and contemplation. The reciprocity between action and reflection, deeds maintaining as well as manifesting love of God, is thus noted pithily.[49]

Unlike the precepts of Book Two, which are to be observed constantly, the precepts treated in Book Three (*Zĕmannim*, Seasons) are "fulfilled at fixed periods" only. This book therefore deals with all special days of the Jewish calendar, whether of feasting or of fasting, of celebration of religious elevation and historical success or of commemoration of national calamity, thereby illustrating also the abiding contemporaneity of historical experience and the acute historical consciousness of Judaism. The Sabbath, the Day of Atonement, and other festivals, which are of Scriptural origin, are treated first, followed by the other fast days, Purim, and Hanukkah, which are of Rabbinic origin. The Temple-oriented components of the holidays, particularly Passover and the Day of Atonement, are reserved for the books dealing with the Temple and sacrifices. Its subject matter is thus a special unit of ritual-ceremonial law, related primarily to the order *Mo'ed* in the Mishnah, separated from Book Two by its trait of periodicity rather than constancy or continuity. The inclusion of the section *Šĕkalim* (Shekel Dues), found in the Mishnaic order of *Mo'ed*, is, to be sure, problematic in terms of the Maimonidean conceptualization. The sanctification of the New Moon (*Kiddus ha-Hodeš*), i.e., the laws and principles concerning the structure and rationale of the calendar which fixes the dates of the festivals,

---

49. Book Two is the Book of Love because regular performance of commandments—uninterrupted commitment to, and involvement with, divine law—leads to love of God. Love is the culmination and goal of the intellectual process (*Tĕšubah* x, 6), but it is also the end-product of service; see, in this context, *Ḥobot hal-Lĕbabot*, x, chap. 3 (II, 350). Love, in turn, is also a stimulus to zealous and properly-motivated performance of commandments; e.g., *Tĕšubah*, x, 2; *Lulab*, viii, 15; *Šĕḥiṭah*, xiv, 16; *Bet hab-Bĕḥirah*, vii, 1; also ShM, positive 3. Love is the achievement-consummation and also the stimulus-catalyst. It is perfectly clear that love is here not a simple theological term and that the Book of Love does not, together with the Book of Knowledge, serve as an introduction to the rest of the work. Both books are integral parts of the Code. Cf. L. Ginzberg, *On Jewish Law and Lore*, p. 170; B. Cohen, "Classification of the Law," p. 534; E. Hoffmann, *Die Liebe zu Gott* (Breslau, 1937), p. 50, n.3. See also below, chap. VI.

follows *Šĕkalim;* although quite technical, it provides the theoretical-scientific underpinning of the whole *Book of Seasons,* and much of it is in any event discussed in the tractate *Roš haš-Šanah.* The inclusion of this calendrical material poignantly expresses Maimonides' desire for comprehensiveness as elucidated in Chapter III—nothing should be missing from this Code. Its motto is *Thy testimonies have I taken as a heritage for ever, for they are the rejoicing of my heart* (Ps. 119:111), taking *testimonies* ('*edot*), which is sometimes synonymous with commandments generally, as referring particularly to the holidays and other special days of the year which are a sign and a memorial to the events of history and to God's providential designs. If the emphasis is taken to be on the rejoicing, reflecting the central commandment to "honor the Sabbath and make it a delight," which "applies equally to the festivals," as well as the "duty to rejoice and be of cheerful heart" on the holidays, the verse would then relate to the major parts of this book but not its totality.[50]

Book Four (*Našim,* Women) revolves around conjugal rights, responsibilities, and restrictions. The bulk of the book details the laws of marriage and divorce, with briefer sections devoted to levirate marriage (*yibbum*) and *ḥaliṣah,* cases of seduction and rape and their consequences, and treatment of a wayward wife (*soṭah*). The comprehensiveness of the last section is significant, for testing infidelity by having the suspected woman drink the "water of bitterness"—an ordeal by water—had been abrogated by R. Johanan ben Zakkai in the first century C.E. The detailed summary of this procedure, as exhaustive as his treatment of the basic marriage laws, represents Maimonides' yearning for total coverage.[51] A comparison of the book with the third order of the Mishnah ("Women") sharply illustrates both Maimonides' dependence on, and independence from, the latter, especially as regards his omission from this book of the Laws Concerning Vows

---

50. See *Yom Ṭob,* vi, 16, 17; cf. Ibn Ezra and Ḳimḥi on Ps. 119:111; and see Naḥmanides on Deut. 6:20.

51. See *Soṭah,* iii, 19, where Maimonides attributes the abrogation to the Sanhedrin (cf. B. Soṭ 47a). The entire chapter illustrates the exegetical-expansive-explanatory features of the Code discussed in Chap. II, above. Note also the concluding verse from Job 5:24.

and Naziriteship and their inclusion in Book Six. Even when there is an obviously close relation between a book of the Code and an order of the Mishnah, as in the case of *Mo'ed* and *Našim*, this applies only to the subject matter and not to the sequence and arrangement, which bear the imprint of Maimonides' logic and originality. Book Four's motto, *The teaching of the wise is a fountain of life, to depart from the snares of death* (Prov. 13:14), is a pithy expression of the hazards and snares of sex.

Book Five (*Kědušah*, Holiness), which concerns itself with the apparently disparate themes of forbidden sexual unions (*Bi'ot 'Ăsurot*) and forbidden foods (*Ma'ăkalot 'Ăsurot, Šěḥiṭah*), is actually unified thematically because "in these two regards God sanctified us and separated us from the nations." With regard to both classes of precepts, which are the concrete expression or embodiment of holiness, it is said, *And I have set you apart from the peoples* (Lev. 20:26, 24). Its laws provide training and discipline in the art of sublime and purposive living, showing how man should strive for purity of heart and action in *all* spheres of life and allow nothing to remain perfunctory, behavioral, or purely biological. While "holiness" is the ultimate concern and goal of all laws, there is a special nexus between holiness and the laws of this book. The absence of any single parallel unit in the Mishnah is obvious. The section on Forbidden Foods, in particular, is emblematic of Maimonides' boldness and imaginativeness as well as his magisterial command of the sources. It is a microcosm of the process of collecting "subjects which hitherto were scattered and dispersed among the valleys and mountains." It also illustrates the sticky problems of conceptualization and the resultant need for repeated cross-references. Collecting and separating are complementary gestures in the art of classification. Juridically, this book is one of the most remarkable parts of the Code, a model of the entire process and achievement. Its motto, *Order my footsteps by Thy word, and let not any iniquity* ('awen) *have dominion over me* (Ps. 119:133), is a striking introductory note with unending reverberations, if we realize that *'awen* (iniquity) is taken as the negation of *kědušah*.[52]

---

52. See below, pp. 286–88, concerning the unity of this book. On *kědušah* as the goal of all laws, see ShM, *Šoreš* 4 (II, 381); *Těšubot*, 224 (p. 400). Naḥmanides, Lev. 19:2.

The common denominator of the four sections of Book Six (*Haflaʾah,* Asseveration), Oaths, Vows, Naziriteship, Valuations and Things Votive, is their concern with legal obligations and responsibilities engendered not by a person's actions but by his spoken words. The clear and unequivocal "utterance of one's lips" (*haflaʾah*) is sacred and therefore binding. A special aspect of classification, namely the sequence of the fourteen books, is alluded to by Maimonides in explaining that Book Six is conceptually associated with Book Five, because the "purpose of all this is . . . to put an end to the lusts and licentiousness manifested in seeking what is most pleasurable and to taking the desire for food and drink as an end."[53] This emphasis on vows as a means of moderation and restraint, while perfectly congruent with his philosophic stance, does not, however, cover all aspects of the book, e.g., taking an oath in God's name as a means of honoring and sanctifying Him. The stresses and strains of conceptual arrangement are here illustrated. While one may correlate major segments of the contents of Book Six with certain Talmudic tractates, there is no single overriding relationship as in the case of Book Three and *Moʿed* or Book Four and *Našim.* Indeed, this book unites material from *Našim, Nězikin,* and *Ḳodašim.* Its motto, *Accept, I beseech Thee, the freewill offerings of my mouth, O Lord, and teach me Thine ordinances* (Ps. 119:108), suggests that self-imposed obligations ("freewill offerings") should be parallel to *mišpaṭim* (ordinances). It is, in other words, a petition to bring about congruence of one's creative and spontaneous gestures and self-willed duties with God's fixed laws. Moreover, "a person is permitted . . . to swear to fulfill a commandment, in order to encourage himself, for Scripture says, *I have sworn, and have confirmed it, to observe Thy righteous ordinances* (Ps. 119:106)."[54]

The laws of Book Seven (*Zěraʿim,* Seeds) are formally concerned with agricultural matters in the broadest sense: tithing, heave offerings, first fruits, and other gifts to the priests, and Sabbatical and Jubilee years. Substantively, however, they are concerned with philanthropy, gifts to the needy, and the nurturing of a deep-seated altruism. The ultimate purpose of most of the laws in

---

53. MN, III, 35 (p. 537).
54. *Šěḥuʿot,* xi, 3. See *Nědarim,* i, 26; xiii, 23; *Něziruṭ,* x, 14.

the *Book of Seeds* is "instilling pity for the weak and the wretched, giving strength in various ways to the poor, and inciting us . . . not to afflict the hearts of the individuals who are in a weak position."[55] The juxtaposition of juridical and philosophical motifs in this case is striking, as is the medley of practical and nonpractical laws. While the title *Zĕra'im* is identical with the title of the first order of the Mishnah, the relationship between the two is not simple or one-dimensional. The underlying Talmudic material for Book Seven is very complex and quite unconventional, necessitating an inordinate reliance on Tosefta and Palestinian Talmud as well as original interpretation and integration; as late as the fifteenth century, R. David ibn Abi Zimra still records his hesitation, quite genuine by all indications, in undertaking to explicate *Sefer Zĕra'im* of the *Mishneh Torah*, for "this is a difficult enterprise: there is no Babylonian Talmud (for this), and we are not accustomed to study the Palestinian Talmud." Its motto, *Let Thy hand be ready to help me* (lĕ-'ozreni), *for I have chosen Thy precepts* (Ps. 119:173), aside from an alliterative connection between *Zĕra'im* and *'ozreni*, seems to reflect a special interpretation of *pikkudim* (precepts) as rational laws which promote social well-being.

Book Eight ('*Ăbodah*, Temple Service) addresses itself first of all to the building of the Temple, its sanctity, its architecture, its vessels, and the duties of the priests and Levites attending to it. Its second major subsection creatively synthesizes the laws concerning sacrifices per se—e.g., "things prohibited for the altar," "hallowed offerings rendered unfit," "trespass in regard to sacred objects"—together with the details governing the regular public-communal sacrifices. The meticulousness and exhaustiveness which characterize Maimonides' treatment of the Temple and of the sacrificial system are all the more impressive considering the fact that this "antiquated" and antiquarian subject was rather consistently ignored by Gaonic and Spanish Talmudists. The order *Kodašim* as a whole, the most important single source for this book, was hardly studied, while equally theoretical and impractical sections of other treatises (*Yoma*, for example)

---

55. MN, III, 39 (p. 550).

were not very popular. Scope and classification are here interwoven, helping also to put the aims of codificatory form into perspective. Its motto, *Pray for the peace of Jerusalem: May they prosper that love thee* (Ps. 122:6), emphasizes the centrality and uniqueness of Jerusalem and reflects the law that "as soon as the Sanctuary was built in Jerusalem, it became unlawful to build a house unto the Lord and to offer sacrifices at any other place. Nor will there be a temple in any future generation except in Jerusalem." Moreover, "the sanctity of the Sanctuary and of Jerusalem derives from the Divine Presence, which cannot be nullified (or banished)."[56] The Temple service, with all its details and ramifications, is inextricably linked to Jerusalem.

Book Nine (*Ḳorbanot*, Offerings), a direct continuation of the preceding, purports to describe all the sacrifices brought by private individuals, e.g., the Passover offering, festal offerings, and offerings for transgressions committed through error, as distinct from the public communal sacrifices.[57] The third section on firstborn animals and tithing of cattle is noteworthy for its integration of two seemingly disparate units.[58] Both Book Eight and Nine, frequently mingling punctilious detail with sweeping insight and ethico-theological interpretation, draw extensively upon diverse materials in unrelated sections of Talmudic literature noted for their obscurity. They end with complementary versions of the classic Maimonidean directive "to seek out the reasons for all commandments," to try to penetrate to the essence and real motive power of the laws of the Torah, coupled with the warning to obey all laws even when we fail to understand or rationalize them. Book Nine's motto, *I will offer to Thee the sacrifice of thanksgiving, and will call upon the name of the Lord* (Ps. 116:17), seems to be quite clear, and yet it has a special nuance: the *toḏah* (thanksgiving sacrifice) is the most significant and enduring of all sacrifices and is regularly accompanied by public prayer.[59]

---

56. *Beṭ hab-Bĕḥirah*, i, 3; vi, 16.
57. See *Ma'áseh haḳ-Ḳorbanot*, i, 5, 6.
58. *Bĕḳorot*, introductory caption.
59. See *Ma'áseh haḳ-Ḳorbanot*, ix, 5; *Beṭ hab-Bĕḥirah*, vi, 12; Ps. 116:17; and Ibn Ezra and R. David Ḳimḥi, on this verse.

The detailed treatment of the laws of cleanness and uncleanness in Book Ten (*Tohărah*), together with the exhaustive presentation of the laws pertaining to the Temple and its sacrifices in the two preceding books, reflects Maimonides' determination to break down all barriers between the theoretical and the practical and to codify Jewish law in its encyclopedic totality. There should be no differences between the theoretical and the practical. The book is arranged according to the various types of uncleanness, starting with the most severe, and the prescribed means of purification from the uncleanness. It contains eight sections: corpse uncleanness; the Red Heifer; the uncleanness of leprosy; those who render couch and seat unclean; other Fathers of Uncleanness; the uncleanness of foodstuffs; of utensils; immersion pools. The parameters of the book are clear but the collection and arrangement of the contents required herculean efforts, an inkling of which is foreshadowed in Maimonides' introduction to *Kŏdašim* and *Tohărot* in his *Mishnah Commentary*. Inasmuch as the subject matter of *Tohărot* is unusually complex, "bristling with fundamental difficulties which even the greatest masters find hard to comprehend,"[60] Book Ten, only roughly parallel to the last order of the Mishnah, should be seen as a highpoint in Maimonides' comprehensive interpretation and painstaking systematization of Talmudic literature. Moreover, since the subject matter embraces some of the most perplexing precepts of Judaism, Maimonides the philosopher responds to this special challenge by trying to rationalize these apparently irrational and arbitrary laws of purity and impurity and endow them with symbolic value and purposiveness. Even though human understanding may not succeed in fathoming the reasons of such ceremonial laws, the attempt should be made. In the process, it is interesting to observe the extent to which Maimonides comes up with original interpretations and creative applications of Biblical verses. Its motto, *Create me a clean heart, O God, and renew a steadfast spirit within me* (Ps. 51:12), anticipates the symbolic-spiritualizing emphasis with which the entire book concludes: "We may find some indication—*remez*—(for the moral-spiritual basis) of this proce-

---

60. PhM, Ṭoh, introduction (pp. 33–34).

dure: just as one who sets his heart on becoming clean becomes clean as soon as he has immersed himself, although nothing new has befallen his body, so, too, one who sets his heart on cleansing himself from the uncleannesses that beset men's souls, namely wrongful thoughts and false convictions, becomes clean as soon as he consents in his heart to shun those counsels and brings his soul into the waters of pure reason. Behold, Scripture says, *And I will sprinkle clean water upon you, and ye shall be clean; from all your uncleannesses and from all your idols will I cleanse you* (Ezek. 36:25). May God, in his great mercy, cleanse us from every sin, iniquity, and guilt."[61]

Book Eleven (*Nĕziķin*, Torts), which is described by Maimonides as containing precepts "concerning civil relations which cause damage to property or injury to the person," begins the last part of the *Mishneh Torah*, for Books Eleven through Fourteen may be described as the code of Jewish civil and criminal law which guided the Jewish community in all its vicissitudes and transmutations. The five sections of Book Eleven, moving in order of ascending severity from property damage through theft (including kidnaping) and robbery to bodily injury and murder, cover the whole area of torts. The title *Nĕziķin* is taken from the fourth order of the Mishnah, but again the arrangement is original and the scope transcends that of the Mishnah order. The last section ends with a medley of laws, prohibitions, and precautions aimed at safeguarding human life, thus explaining the compound title Murder and Preservation of Life. As a matter of fact, three of the five sections, Robbery and Lost Property, Wounding and Damages, Murder and Preservation of Life, have double titles—a significant trait of Maimonides' classification reflecting concurrently an attempt to link conceptually related matters as well as to prevent an open-ended proliferation of books and subsections.

---

61. *Miķwa'ot*, xi, 12. For the problem of intention here, see *Miķwa'ot*, i, 8; at the end Maimonides, seeking to spiritualize the law, applies it to all cases. He may be following the Tosefta, Ḥag. 3:2. A *perfect* act of immersion requires intention.

The proximity of this book to the laws dealing with the Temple and sacrifices may result from, on the one hand, Maimonides' emphasis that laws of purity are particularly relevant for priests, and on the other, his suggestion that these laws enhance the feeling of awe and fear toward the Holy Temple; see PhM, Ṭoh, introduction (p. 34); MN, III, 47 (p. 493).

We should pay attention to the fact that in the arrangement of the last four books, substantive law precedes procedural law (Book Fourteen), whereas in the Šulḥan 'Aruk procedural law—courts, judges, witnesses—is found at the beginning of the Ḥošen ham-Mišpaṭ.[62] The motto of Book Eleven, *Incline my heart unto Thy testimonies, and not to covetousness* (Ps. 119:36), so obviously appropriate, also impales covetousness as the major source of torts. "Desire leads to coveting, and coveting to robbery: for if the owner does not wish to sell, even when he is offered a high price and is greatly importuned, it will lead the covetor to rob him, as it is said, *And they covet houses and seize them* (Mic. 2:2). Moreover, if the owner should stand up to the robber to protect his property and prevent the robbery, this may lead to bloodshed. You can learn this from the story of Ahab and Naboth (cf. 1 Kings 21). . . . If one robs another of property worth a penny, it is regarded as if he had taken his life, for Scripture says, *So are the ways of every one that is covetous of gain, it taketh away the life of the owners thereof* (Prov. 1:19)."[63]

Book Twelve (*Ḳinyan*, Acquisition) is concerned with the modes of acquisition of property and other goods, the rights and responsibilities of ownership, the forms of relinquishing ownership, and the rights and obligations of neighbors, partners, and agents from the vantage point of joint ownership and joint responsibility. A special treatise is devoted to slaves, the modes of acquisition of various types of slaves (Jewish, female, heathen) and more briefly the methods of manumission. Inasmuch as most of the subject matter is highly practical and relevant, unaffected by the abnormality of Jewish political existence in exile, Maimonides shows himself to be especially attuned to post-Talmudic developments in the application of halakic principles. Gaonic ordinances and interpretations are carefully recorded and integrated into the discussion; significant precedents and contemporary practices are mentioned, while untenable precedents are criticized and rejected. The book's motto, *The beginning of wis-*

---

62. A. Gulak, "Gĕdarim Mišpaṭiyyim," *Tarbiz*, VI (1935), 139–51, especially p. 146.

63. *Gĕzelah*, i, 11, 13. The last part of the verse (Ps. 119:36) is presumably the key here; for *'edot* see above, on Book Three.

*dom is: Get wisdom; yea, with all thy getting* (ḳinyan) *get understanding* (Prov. 4:7), is a striking admonition to remember that all material acquisitions are transient and instrumental while intellectual acquisition is the ultimate goal and noblest perfection. Inasmuch as the halakah never negated the importance of material goods, it was especially relevant to warn subtly but strongly against a Hobbesian-like drive for wealth, power, and security.[64]

Book Thirteen (*Mišpaṭim*, Civil Laws), containing "laws of property concerned with the mutual transactions of people, such as loans, hire for wages, and deposits," completes the codification of civil laws. The subject matter of its five treatises—Hiring, Borrowing and Depositing, Creditor and Debtor, Pleading, and Inheritance—is more diffuse than that of Books Eleven and Twelve. The wide-ranging title, *Mišpaṭim*, reflects this fact and inevitably sharpens our awareness of the manifold and subtle problems which Maimonides faced in implementing his scheme of classification. None of these three books has even an approximate parallel in any single order of the Mishnah, thus illustrating again the process of collecting and arranging scattered sources. Book Thirteen's motto, *I will give thanks unto Thee with uprightness of heart, when I learn Thy righteous ordinances* (mišpaṭim) (Ps. 119:7), directly defines the book's title and indirectly emphasizes the joy of study and the continuum between study and practice.[65]

The last book (*Šofeṭim*, Judges) is concerned primarily with the procedural aspects of law, the mechanics and dynamics of the judiciary, the rules of evidence and qualifications of witnesses, as well as their rigid interrogation, the authoritative nature of the Oral Law, the special status of the Sanhedrin as its guardian and authoritative expounder, the status of those who defy it ("rebels"), and the role of authority (both judicial and monarchical), power, and discipline in the maintenance of the good society. On the one hand, Maimonides appreciated the role of power, contending that "if a criminal is not punished, injurious acts will not

---

64. See below, chap. VI.
65. Concerning *naḥălot* (inheritances), see below, p. 288. The use of *mišpaṭim* is noteworthy. It is not contrasted here with *ḥuḳḳim* (as in *Me'ilah*, viii, 8) but constitutes a special category of interpersonal and social laws; see R. David Ḳimḥi to Ps. 119:1, and cf. Naḥmanides to Deut. 11:32.

be abolished . . . and none of those who design aggression will be deterred."[66] On the other hand, he spiritualized the offices of authority in various ways. The image of the ideal judge, his moral and intellectual qualifications, his rights and responsibilities, and his creative role in administering justice, is very striking: "all judges should possess wisdom, humility, fear of God, disdain of gain, love of truth, love of fellow man, and a good reputation." He should always "concentrate his mind on matters of Torah and wisdom." Inasmuch as wide discretionary power is vested in the judge, "all his deeds should be for the sake of heaven", i.e., his actions should be purely motivated and beyond reproach. Otherwise not only will he be culpable, but "the cause of religion would suffer."[67] The king is portrayed not only as a temporal sovereign, endowed with vast powers and prerogatives, but also as a spiritual leader, charged with the duty to study Torah relentlessly, and generally committed to an exacting scale of values and ideals.[68] The conclusion of this book, and therefore of the entire Code, with a description of the Messianic age also contributes to this spiritualizing effect, for Maimonides emphasizes the value of the Messianic advent as an instrument of intellectual achievement and spiritual elevation. The book's motto, *Open thy mouth, judge righteously, and plead the cause of the poor and needy* (Prov. 31:9), underscores that all the institutions of power and authority are not final but instrumental, inducing righteousness and providing support for the downtrodden and the disadvantaged. It reflects in sharp focus the "positive command (which) enjoins upon the judge the duty to judge righteously, as it is said, *In righteousness shalt thou judge thy neighbor* (Lev. 19:15)," as well as the apparently dialectical but actually complementary obligation imposed upon the judge to assist a confused, inarticulate, or excessively agitated litigant, "in compliance with the exhortation *Open thy mouth for the dumb* (Prov. 31:8)."[69]

66. MN, III, 41; *Sanhedrin*, xx, 4.
67. *Sanhedrin*, ii, 1; iii, 7; xxiv, 10; *Mĕlakim*, iii, 7.
68. *Mĕlakim*, ii, 5, 6; iii, 5; iv, 10. We may look upon this as a Maimonidean version of the medieval *regimen principum*, constructed, of course, from Rabbinic texts and with his interpretations and emphases. Cf. L. Born, "The Perfect Prince: A Study in Thirteenth and Fourteenth Century Ideals," *Speculum*, III (1928), 470ff.
69. *Sanhedrin*, xxi, 1, 11.

## CLASSIFICATION

*Novelty of this classification*

This synoptic presentation reveals, with immediacy and force, the innovative character of Maimonides' classification. There is novelty in the grouping of laws.[70] There is novelty in the creation and delimitation of certain sections.[71] There is novelty in the nomenclature, rather imaginative and often felicitous.[72] There is novelty in the interpretations which inform and validate the juxtaposition of sections as there is in the entire sequential order, starting with the theoretical-ethical foundations of Torah, moving through the varied realms of ritual, and culminating in an imaginatively conceived presentation of civil and criminal, and we might add, constitutional, law.[73] There is novelty in the amount of extra-Talmudic material and the generally smooth integration of halakic exposition with philosophical-ethical explication. There is also, as we have seen, novelty in the scope and style—in short, in daring to undertake a work of such magnitude and structure. This many-splendored novelty must be confronted and appreciated. After our patient search for sources and influences is completed, after we have eruditely identified precedents in the Rabbinic writings of the Geonim and have conjured

---

70. E.g., *Talmud Torah, Těšubah* (see Nahmanides in *Kobeṣ*, III, 9a). Nahmanides, *Děrašah 'al Dibre Kohelet* in *Kitbe ha-RaMBaN*, ed. C. Chavel (Jerusalem, 1963), I, 208, also comments on the novelty of Maimonides' having collected the laws of charity. For suggestions concerning the origin of such a rubric as *Talmud Torah*, see B. Cohen, "Classification," p. 533; F. Rosenthal, *Knowledge Triumphant* (Leiden, 1970), p. 95. Automatic assumption of an Islamic source for original and/or difficult Maimonidean statements is, of course, shaky procedure. Note the example provided by A. Kirschenbaum, *Self-Incrimination in Jewish Law* (New York, 1970), p. 62, who thought to find an Islamic source for *Sanhedrin*, xviii, 6, until Professor Schacht wrote him that "Maimonides cannot possibly have been influenced here by Islamic thought." The explanation of the halakah in *Sanhedrin*, xviii, 6, remains challenging; see above, chap. II, n.197. For an example of Maimonides' use of Arabic terminology, see *Těšubot*, 268 (p. 512) concerning *bid'ah* (innovation).

71. E.g., *Sefer ham-Madda'* or *Sefer Kědušah. De'ot* and *Těšubah* or *Mamrim* and *Mělakim* are overwhelmingly original. In the process, such terms acquired a semantic centrality which they did not previously possess.

72. E.g., *Šebitat 'Asor*.

73. On the sequence of the fourteen books, from the foundations of Torah to ritual to civil law, see, e.g., I. Herzog, "Seder has-Sĕfarim," *Kobeṣ ha-RaMBaM*, ed. J. L. Maimon (Jerusalem, 1935), II, 257–64. See also above, concerning Books Five and Six. M. Elon, *Ham-Mišpaṭ ha-'Ibri*, III, 1315ff., has given a comparative chart of laws in the MT and the *Šulḥan 'Aruk*. The subject still awaits careful analysis.

up parallels in the codes and commentaries of Spanish Talmudists, and have, with full awareness of the sociology of learning, looked for possible external influences or stimuli emanating from the *fiqh* literature and the codification of Islamic law, we must make allowance for the author's own ingenuity and resourcefulness. Geneticism is not exhaustive; *Quellenforschung* is the first, not the last, phase of scholarship; creativity must have a place even in academic etiology. Historical context and contingency influence an individual, even the most creative and independent, but the creative individual in turn leaves his impact on the new emergent historical context. The talented, sensitive individual, working in, and committed to, a tradition, is by no means consigned to receptivity, passivity, and faithful transmission; he may be a molder and architect of ideas, and in his work we may witness the "transmutation by which the old is taken up in the new and given a fresh direction and significance."[74] If, as Aristotle said, "it is the business of the wise man to order," Maimonides displayed great wisdom in his ordering and structuring of halakah. Diderot's evaluation of Leibniz is applicable: "He combined two great qualities which are almost incompatible with one another—the spirit of discovery and that of method."

Of course, to the extent that the Mishnah itself was topical-conceptual, e.g., in parts of *Našim* or *Nĕziķin*, there are obvious similarities and affinities between it and the *Mishneh Torah*. We have noted Maimonides' avowed indebtedness to the Mishnah, whether pertaining to structure, scope, or style. The Gaonic literary achievement provided a partial precedent in the sense that there were individual halakic monographs in existence from which Maimonides benefited, but there was no synoptic presentation of all the material. There were, in addition, many standard custom-made classifications of law: positive and negative com-

---

74. E. R. Dodds, "Tradition and Personal Achievement in the Philosophy of Plotinus," *Journal of Roman Studies*, XI (1960), 1; see ham-Me'iri, *Bet hab-Běḥirah*, introduction, p. 25; and MN, III, 14. To say that the MT is merely a "compilation," a summary of Talmudic literature (see L. Strauss, *Persecution and the Art of Writing* [Glencoe, 1952]) is, first of all, to fail to appreciate the importance of such work, and second, to ignore the beguiling creativity of its classification, which is so new. The problem, in the context of belles lettres, is discussed in T. S. Eliot's classic essay on "Tradition and the Individual Talent."

mandments; laws concerning man's relation to God and those governing his relation to fellow man and to society; ceremonial, moral, and civil law, or even a reduction of this tripartite division to the two overarching rubrics of religious and civil law.[75] Another approach classified the commandments in terms of their performance by hand, mouth, or heart, i.e., deeds, words, intentions.[76] A desire to relate all 613 laws to the Ten Commandments produced decalogue-based classifications which were necessarily plastic and pliable, and very often clearly artificial.[77] An interesting scheme was proposed by R. Abraham bar Ḥiyya, who combined a threefold division of relations between man and God, man and his household, man and the rest of mankind, with a subdivision of each of these into commandments connected with thought, speech, and actions, and found them all comprised in the Ten Commandments.[78] There were other subdivisions, which could be used independently or in various combinations: practical laws which must be observed under all circumstances and at all times and places, and laws temporarily impracticable because of historical or geographical circumstances (e.g., laws concerning sacrifices or the Land of Israel); individual or private versus communal or collective precepts (e.g., building the Temple in Jerusalem); affirmative precepts which are compulsory for all people at all times (e.g., to put on phylacteries, hear the sound of the shofar on New Year's Day) in contradistinction to individual laws which are obligatory only if cognate conditions necessitate their implementation (e.g., to affix a *mĕzuzah* to the doors of a house, for there is no a priori obligation to live in a dwelling that requires a *mĕzuzah*).[79] Some writers experimented with more elaborate subdivisions, combining technical, historical, chronological, personal, and mnemonic considerations: e.g., laws

---

75. PhM, Pe 1:1 (p. 94); MT, introduction (end) and description of Book Eleven; *Bĕrakot*, xi, 2; MN, III, 35, 36. See R. Abraham ibn Ezra, *Peruš*, Exod. 20:2.
76. R. Abraham bar Ḥiyya, *Heḡyon han-Nefeš* (Jerusalem, 1966), p. 130. R. Abraham ibn Ezra, *Peruš*, Exod. 20:1; ShM, šoreš 9.
77. See E. Urbach, *ḤaZaL* (Jerusalem, 1969), pp. 301ff., especially pp. 316–20; H. A. Wolfson, *Philo* (Cambridge, 1962), II, 201.
78. R. Abraham bar Ḥiyya, *Heḡyon*, p. 131.
79. E.g., ShM, end of listing of positive commandments. See *Ḥobot hal-Lĕbabot*, x, chap. 7 (II, p. 375).

incumbent upon the priestly class but not upon commoners and vice versa; laws incumbent upon Levites; laws incumbent upon the High Priest but not upon ordinary priests; laws incumbent upon women and not upon men and vice versa; laws which are observed only during the day and not at night; etc.[80] Classifications grounded in philosophical or teleological considerations subdivided laws in terms of rational and revelational—i.e., those commandments for which clear and convincing reasons can easily be produced, as distinct from those about which reason must be silent or neutral inasmuch as they have no "clear cause" or do not seem to be of "manifest utility"—or from the point of view of their correspondence to the classification of philosophic virtues into intellectual, moral, and practical.[81] It will be obvious that some of these divisions surface in the *Mishneh Torah* while others are embedded, either transparently or inconspicuously, in certain of its groupings, but in no way do they, individually or collectively, account for the *Mishneh Torah* classification, which is a novel entity based on an intensely thoughtful reworking of the ever-expanding corpus of halakic material. The fact is that there is no antecedent, or indeed sequel, in Rabbinic literature for such a keen, energetic, and comprehensive classification, nor is there any parallel to its rigor, precision, and conceptual tidiness.

CONCEPTUALIZATION AND CLASSIFICATION: SPLITTING OF HALAKIC UNITS

In fact Maimonides never tired of emphasizing that he regularly wrote with great care and precision, that his ideas were rigorously reasoned, his perceptions of contexts and relations were not impulsive, his balanced sentences were meticulously formulated, and the sections of his various works were reflectively organized. He disclaimed anything haphazard or incidental, writing only "after reflection and deliberation and careful examination of true opinions as well as untrue ones." His general attitude was

---

80. See above, n.18, concerning R. Samuel ben Ḥofni Gaon.
81. R. Saadiah Gaon, *'Ēmunot wĕ-Dē'ot*, III, 3; R. Baḥya ibn Paḳuda, *Ḥobot hal-Lĕbabot*, iii, chap. 2; v, chap. 5; viii, chap. 3; R. Abraham ibn Daud, *Ha-'Ēmunah ha-Ramah*, III, last chapter (p. 102); MN, III, 26, 27, 28, 31, 35, and *Tĕmurah*, iv, 13.

well described in the *Epistle on Conversion:* "It is not proper to speak publicly unless one has rehearsed what he wants to say many times and studied it well. This is how the Rabbis interpreted the verse, *Then did He see it and declare it; He established it and searched it out,* and only after this punctilious preparation did He speak, *and unto men He said* (Job 28:27–28)."[82] The classification of the law in the *Mishneh Torah,* with its great self-consciousness concerning every formulation and every grouping, is a prime example of Maimonides' genius for generalization mounted on steady "reflection and deliberation." Its inner structure, particularly the premeditated splitting of laws in deference to a conceptual rather than functional or formal categorization, and the elaborate network of cross-references, attest to this.

The following illustrations vivify the extent to which Maimonides split apparently related aspects of a theme, seeking as he did accurate analysis in a logical context rather than pragmatic synthesis or instantaneous comprehensiveness. Chapter I of the section on Vows contains the following guidelines for breaking up a semantic-juridical unit (vows) which is, however, conceptually divisible:

1. "Vows may be divided into two classes. The first class covers the case of a person who forbids to himself things otherwise permitted to him. . . . Concerning this class of vows Scripture says, *to bind his soul with a bond* (Num. 30:3), i.e., to forbid to himself things otherwise permitted. This is the class which I would call vows of prohibition (*nidre 'issur*).
2. "The second class covers the case of a person who makes himself liable to a sacrifice which is not otherwise due from him. . . . Concerning this class Scripture says, *Thy vows which*

---

82. *Koḇeṣ,* II, 12b; see R. Hai Gaon, *Musar Haśkel,* ed. H. Gollancz (London, 1922), p. 34. A corollary of the care in writing is the requisite care in studying; see PhM, Yoma 2:1 (p. 242); RH 2:7 (p. 318); Ḥaḡ 3:2 (p. 383); Ṭoh, introduction (p. 37); *Tešuḇoṯ,* 310 (p. 574). Also PhM, Sanh, *Pereḳ Ḥeleḳ,* chap. 10, (p. 217): "Do not read them hurriedly, for I did not just happen to write them down. Only after careful research and introspection, when I came to see which opinions are clearly true and untrue, did I come to know what to accept"; MN, introduction. Maimonides' statements about his great care in writing were often noted; see most recently, J. Agnon, *Me'aṣmi 'el 'Aṣmi* (Jerusalem, 1976), p. 326.

*thou vowest, nor thy freewill offerings*, etc. (Deut. 12:17). This is the class which I would call vows of consecration (*niḍre heḳdeš*).
3. "The laws concerning the first class and its particulars are the ones which will be explained in the following sections, whereas the laws concerning vows of consecration and their details will all be explained in *their proper place* among the Laws Concerning Sacrificial Rites."[83]

Were Maimonides composing a Gaonic-style monograph on the Laws Concerning Vows, à la the "Laws Concerning Oaths" of R. Hai Gaon, he could have conveniently left all this material intact and ignored its conceptual divisions. Given his goal of material comprehensiveness together with juridical conceptualization, the demanding and delicate subdivisions were unavoidable. The inclusive rubric "Vows" was an inadequate binder. As we have indicated, tidy topical classification involved separation as well as fusion. Collection (*ḳibbuṣ*) did not exhaust the task of thematic arrangement.

Chapter X of the section on Forbidden Foods introduces a new and complex theme: "All the prohibitions mentioned hitherto refer to living creatures. There are, however, other interdicts in the Torah which apply to agricultural produce." The chapter mentions all such forbidden items but the details are reserved for various sections: "In the Laws Concerning Mixed Seeds it will be explained . . ."; "In the Laws Concerning the Second Tithe it will be explained . . ."; "There are other prohibitions which apply to edible holy things, all being based on the authority of the Torah; for example, the prohibition of eating the heave offerings, first fruits, dough offerings, and second tithes. There are also prohibitions of consecrated things of the altar, such as *piggul*, the remnant of sacrifices, and sacrifices which have become unclean; each of these will be explained *in its appropriate place*."[84]

---

83. *Nĕḍarim*, i, 1-2 (italics mine). The terminology, *niḍre 'issur* and *niḍre heḳdeš*, is also original. This literary phenomenon of splitting laws—putting individual components where they are most relevant—has repercussions both for Maimonides' conceptualization of the halakah as well as for the problem of repetitions (see below, n.91).

84. *Ma'ăḳalot 'Ăsurot*, x, 1, 8, 10, 23 (italics mine), is a daring act of classification with no antecedent. It is daring in its collection of disparate material and exacting in its requirements of subsequent subdivisions and cross-references.

The first chapter of *Bikkurim* (first fruits offered to the priest) is especially noteworthy, even intriguing, for like the beginning paragraphs of *Nĕḏarim* which provide a lucid explanation and justification of procedure concerning the Maimonidean treatment of the diffuse subject matter of vows, it too suggests a careful subdivision of the twenty-four priestly gifts. His fivefold grouping is sustained with special meticulousness because he then explicitly notes its divergence from the threefold Talmudic classification, which he also reproduces.[85] Such a parallel grouping is quite unique, setting up a direct "confrontation" between a conceptualization of Maimonides and a classification of the Sages (*ḥăḵamim*). In the present context we are primarily concerned with the care, thoughtfulness, and self-consciousness of the classification rather than with its challenge to, or originality vis-à-vis, the Rabbinic scheme.

Here, as in countless other instances,[86] the telling phrase is "will be explained in its proper (or, appropriate) place," propriety being conditioned conceptually and not functionally. The "proper place" is indeed a function of Maimonides' conceptualization. The numerous cross-references—"as we have explained" or "as will be explained"—are not merely didactic[87] but also methodological, serving to restrain associationism, curtail expedience, and abet topical arrangement.

This central fact that Maimonides' classification was subject to conceptual restraints, sacrificing facile functionality for tight topicality, was noted approvingly by the early *Mishneh Torah* commentators. R. Vidal of Tolosa, author of the classic *Maggiḏ Mishneh*, calls attention to this aspect of Maimonidean classification and endorses it as a stimulating corollary of Maimonides' punctilious consistency in arranging the laws. He even accuses

---

85. *Bikkurim*, i, 12. See S. Lieberman, *Tosefta Kifšuṭa, Zĕra'im* (New York, 1955), pp. 811–12. Maimonides' classification is noted by ham-Me'iri, *Bet hab-Bĕḥirah, Ḥullin*, 496. See PhM Ḥal 4:9 (p. 393) where Maimonides gives the standard classification of gifts. Another noteworthy example is *Šĕḡaḡot*, i, 4 (where Maimonides lists 43 cases compared to the 34 classes in Ker 1:1).

86. E.g., *'Issure Bi'ah*, xxii, 11; *Ma'ăḵalot 'Ăsurot*, xv, 29; *Nĕziruṭ*, ii, 11; *Yibbum*, vi, 8; *'Edut*, ix, 3; also *Mĕṭamme' Miškaḥ u-Mošaḥ*, vii, 8; *Ma'ăśeh haḵ-Ḳorbanot*, iii, 7.

87. E.g., *Šĕḵalim*, i, 4; *'Išut*, ii, 27. On Maimonides as a self-conscious pedagogue, see above, chap. II.

the great RaSHBA, R. Solomon ibn Adret, of failing to perceive that Maimonides would often present two complementary components of a law in two different contexts as a result of the rigorous requirements of his systematization.[88] On the other hand, this fact led some commentators to add glosses or scholia designed to encompass a given law in its entirety in one spot. Many times, as we have seen, Maimonides provided the necessary cross-references, but at other times he did not, without even bothering to repeat the relevant conclusions of the cognate presentations. In such cases, for example, RABD will occasionally jot down a note which anticipates a subsequent Maimonidean statement or else repeats the essence of a statement which Maimonides has already formulated but which is also pertinent in this particular context.[89] I have conjectured elsewhere that some of these glosses may have been written before RABD even read Maimonides' own elaboration or qualification, and he did not bother subsequently to delete them.[90] It now seems to me equally plausible that these notes were intended to facilitate study and augment practicality by giving all aspects of a question immediately, even though they could be collated from scattered references in Maimonides' own work. Other critics-commentators, e.g., the author of the *Sefer ham-Mĕnuḥah*, will regularly provide complete cross-references instead of fleshing out Maimonides' truncated statements by repetition and collation.[91] Still other authors, acknowledging the primacy of the *Mishneh Torah* and the

---

88. See *MM*, introduction to Book III (*Zĕmannim*). R. Jeroham, *Sefer Mešarim*, p. 2, also notes the occasional breakup of laws in the MT.
89. E.g., *Dé'ot*, iii, 2; *Tĕfillah*, iii, 7; *Yom Ṭoḇ*, vi, 22; '*Issure Bi'ah*, xi, 16; '*Aḥadim*, vii, 6. See *Bĕrakot*, vi, 1, and '*Aḇot haṭ-Ṭumē'ot*, iv, 8; and RABD (ad loc.) who is of the opinion that there are two reasons (cleanliness and impurity) for washing hands, and therefore the halakah should be mentioned in both contexts.
90. Twersky, *Rabad*, pp. 155–56; and cf. I. Herzog, *Main Institutions of Jewish Law* (London, 1965), I, 39.
91. E.g., *Sefer ham-Mĕnuḥah* on *Ḥameṣ u-Maṣṣah*, ii, 12. There are occasions when Maimonides himself repeats laws, sometimes with stylistic variations; e.g., *Bi'aṭ Miḳdaš*, iv, 2, and *Sanhedrin*, xviii, 6; *Bi'aṭ Miḳdaš*, i, 12, and *Kĕle ham-Miḳdaš*, vi, 11; *Ta'ăniyyot*, v, 3, and *Mĕlakim*, xi, 2; *Dé'ot*, vi, 8, and *Ḥoḇel u-Mazziḳ*, iii, 7 (also viii, 9). This warrants further study. Sometimes the repetition seems to result in self-contradiction or inconsistency. For example, in *Sanhedrin*, v, 1, Maimonides writes: "A king can be appointed only with the approval of the court of seventy-one." In *Mĕlakim*, i, 3, however, we

great wisdom of its author, will justify their composition of new codes in terms of their greater pragmatism. The Provençal author of the *Sefer Mešarim* (concerned with civil law), for example, claims that Maimonides' overscrupulousness in the arrangement of the *Mishneh Torah* lessened its functionality, and that his own code, while admittedly less methodical, would hopefully be more useful.[92] The subsequent history of codification, particularly the development of the *Ṭurim*, the *Šulḥan 'Aruk*, the *Lĕbuš* and cognate literature, may be seen as part of the thrust for utilitarian and totally relevant codification.[93] The topical character and conceptual refinement of Maimonides' classification and its theoretical orientation are thus acknowledged even by those who went on to construct alternate systems with halakic pragmatism as their hallmark. Excessive consistency or purity is not always marketable!

*Stresses and strains in this system*

Nevertheless, while Maimonides calls attention a priori to his determination to produce a novel classification sustained by a sophisticated juridical sensibility and insight emerging from a panoramic conception of the entire law, and goes on to structure the *Mishneh Torah* accordingly, he also indicates, directly and indirectly, explicitly and implicitly, his awareness of the stresses and strains in the system, the dilemmas of arrangement, its intricacies and challenges, and the occasional inescapable relapse

---

read that the appointment must be with the consent of the court of seventy-one and a prophet. In this case, the context apparently determined the formulation. The statement in PhM, Bek 9:3 (p. 277) shows that repetition sometimes results consciously from pedagogic purposes as well as a sense of symmetry and proportion.

92. *Sefer Mešarim*, p. 2. The arrangement of the other work of R. Jeroham, *Tolĕdot 'Adam wĕ-Ḥawwah* (Venice, 1553), is significant in this context. The first part, "Adam," contains all laws from birth to marriage, while the second, "Eve," contains all laws from marriage to death. Ease of reference and functionality are completely determinative. In the introduction (p. 2a) to the *Tolĕdot*, he reports that the *Sefer Mešarim* was acclaimed as a very useful work. See below, p. 532, n.8.

93. See, e.g., the various introductions of R. Jacob ben Asher to the *Ṭurim*. *Yoreh De'ah*, in particular, is a good example of lack of conceptualization; considerable caution is needed, consequently, in making inferences concerning, for example, the intersection of halakic classification and socio-economic contingencies. See the guarded comment of J. Katz, *Masoret u-Mašber* (Jerusalem, 1958), p. 86, n.26 (concerning laws of usury).

into expediency, functionality, or associationism. That there are problems is unmistakably evidenced by the fact that Maimonides periodically broke his customary reticence and anonymity by pausing to provide reasons for his classification and to vindicate his arrangement or juxtaposition of topics. Some explanations are found in the listing of the fourteen books at the end of the introduction, some are unobtrusively tucked away in the captions at the heads of the respective sections in the Code, some are embedded in the text itself, and some are reflected in the verses which Maimonides chose as mottoes for each of the fourteen books. These explanatory statements also vary stylistically. Some are direct causal formulations—"and for this reason I have included . . .";[94] some are descriptive in form but causal in intent; some contain a juridical definition or semantic clarification which has clear repercussions for the mechanics and dynamics of classification.[95] They again vary as to the extent of what they undertake to explain. Sometimes a single law, paragraph, or chapter is explained; sometimes the inclusion of a given section in a certain book is defended; sometimes the parameters of an entire book are explained and justified. Occasionally the opening paragraph of a section should be read as a clever and clearly premeditated explanation, while some opening paragraphs are overt programmatic pronouncements and methodological-procedural directives. Sometimes there are subtle hints that Maimonides confronted and with varying degrees of success disposed of problems of classification. Needless to say, we should be attentive to all instances where Maimonides explicates his method or reasoning processes and try to appraise these explications. There is, however, a residual problem which entices us: are we to assume that the unexplained difficulties or cruxes in classification were not troublesome to Maimonides or that he glossed over them, being unable to produce a cogent and persuasive explanation?

---

94. 'Akum, ii, 6.
95. Introduction to Bĕkorot; description of Sefer Kĕdušah; Sefer Torah, viii, 4; introduction to 'Aḇel; Šĕḥiṭah, xiii, 1; Nĕḏarim, ii, 14; Nĕziruṯ, i, 1; 'Ăraḵin, i, 1; Mattĕnoṯ 'Ăniyyim, viii, 1; Ma'ăśeh haḵ-Ḳorbanoṯ, xii, 1; Ṭumĕ'aṯ Ṣara'aṯ, xvi, 10 (šem he-'amur bĕ-šuttafuṯ). This aspect has been almost totally ignored by scholars and hence deserves to be underscored.

Should we recognize the casual, random, and parenthetical—inevitable compromises with the many exigencies of a massive task—and consequently modify, ever so slightly, the assumption of a uniformly purposive pattern? In any event, the corollary of Maimonides' frequent declarations about how carefully and thoughtfully he wrote is that the reader must study very carefully and thoughtfully, free of a priori partisanship. Only a searching analysis will yield the data with which to assess this issue.

Let us consider a few examples of each kind of Maimonidean explanation, identify what seem to be silent or subtle explanations, and then look at some apparently unexplained trouble spots.

The definition of blasphemy and laws governing the blasphemer are included in Book One in the section on Idolatry. The reason for this arrangement is explicitly stated: "Whosoever acknowledges that idolatry is true, even if he does not worship an idol, reviles and blasphemes the honored and revered name of God. The idolater and the blasphemer are in the same class, as it is said, *But the soul that doeth aught with a high hand . . . blasphemeth the Lord* (Num. 15:30). Hence the idolater is hanged, just as the blasphemer is hanged, both being first stoned. *It is for this reason* that I included the law of the blasphemer among the laws of idolatry, since both the blasphemer and the idolater deny the fundamental principle of our religion."[96]

Book Two, containing those precepts which are to be continuously observed, mostly prayers and benedictions, concludes with a section on the laws of circumcision—an apparently awkward juxtaposition or inexplicable interpolation. Anticipating potential criticism or skepticism, Maimonides explained at the beginning of the *Mishneh Torah* that "circumcision is included here because this is a sign in our flesh, serving as a constant reminder, even when phylacteries and fringes, etc., are absent." While Maimonides is undoubtedly drawing upon Rabbinic statements in Mishnah, Tosefta, and Talmud, which call attention to the permanence and omnipresent reality of circumcision, his reliance upon this insight for purposes of classification is a tour de force.

---

96. *'Akum*, ii, 6 (italics mine). See *Sanhedrin*, xxvi, 7; MN, III, 41.

Even a random sampling of codes would show that codifiers had trouble finding a suitable spot for this subject, and there is no uniformity whatsoever governing its position.[97] Maimonides solved the problem in the light of his own conceptualization, for this resourceful explanation is itself predicated on his having revealed the common denominator of all the sections in Book Two: "precepts which we have been commanded to keep in order that we may always love God." This is a good example of the kind of conceptual and suprahalakic categories which Maimonides introduced sparingly into the *Mishneh Torah*. It parallels the one general "obvious reason" which he proposes in the *Guide* for all the commandments enumerated in Book Two of the *Mishneh Torah:* "the end of these actions is the constant commemoration of God . . . the love of Him, and the fear of Him." An elliptical form of this explanation is to be found in the *Mishneh Torah* itself where Maimonides interjects: "The Sages have instituted many blessings in order that we should constantly commemorate God . . . blessings . . . the purpose of which is that we should always commemorate the Creator and fear Him."[98] Given this conceptual framework, Maimonides can deftly interpolate circumcision in the Book of Love and his explanation is quite smooth. R. Jacob ben Asher apparently used Maimonides' explanation of circumcision and its relation to tĕfillin and ṣiṣit, but refrained from discussing it in the context of the daily ritual, relegating it instead to the end of *Yoreh De'ah*, where it appears as a forlorn section related neither to that which precedes it nor to that which follows it.[99] Actually, Maimonides had to overhaul the meaning of 'ahăbah in order to accomplish and sustain this interpolation.[100] The results are conceptually invincible and the book's unity is unimpeachable.

Chapter II of the section in Book Six on vows (*Nĕdarim*) rather abruptly interpolates some paragraphs on *hefḳer* (renunciation of

---

97. E.g., R. Aaron hak-Kohen, *'Orḥot Ḥayyim*, II, 3; R. Jeroham, *Tolĕdot 'Adam wĕ-Ḥawwah*, 2a. Note also the commentary of Obadiah Sforno on Leviticus, introduction.
98. *Bĕrakot*, i, 3, 4; MN, III, 43. See *Ḥobot hal-Lĕbabot*, vii, chap. 5.
99. *Ṭur Yoreh De'ah*, 260, after the laws of charity and before the laws concerning slaves!
100. See above, n.49.

ownership). This abruptness is cushioned by a closer look at this subsection which is introduced by a brief definition: "Renunciation of ownership (*hefker*), although not a vow, is like a vow in that he who produces it is forbidden to change his mind"[101]—a definition which also explains the inclusion of the subject in this context. Later codifiers repeat the Maimonidean definition, the source of which was identified by ham-Me'iri,[102] but do not follow through conceptually vis-à-vis classification. The third section of this book, devoted to all the laws of the Nazirite and the institution of Naziriteship, begins with a similar explanation: "Naziriteship belongs to the class of vows of prohibition, for Scripture says, *Who shall clearly utter a vow, the vow of a Nazirite* (Num. 6:2)."[103] The fourth section, devoted to valuations pledged to God, also opens with a definition which relates to the substance of the section: "Valuations are vows belonging to the class of vows of consecration (*niḏre heḳdeš*)." Taking this definition into account, one would expect that valuations would be discussed in the context of sacrifices, as Maimonides had indicated at the beginning of the section on vows,[104] but since they are procedurally and substantively similar to vows of prohibition, they are included in this book.[105]

Section III of Book Nine is entitled simply Laws Concerning Firstlings but includes also the laws concerning tithing of cattle. This apparent mismatch is explained by Maimonides at the beginning of the section: "And I have included tithe of cattle with firstlings since the procedure for them both is the same, and Scripture has joined them both together, for it is said, *Thou shalt dash their blood* (Num. 18:17). From oral tradition it is learned

---

101. *Nĕḏarim*, ii, 14.
102. *Ḥošen Mišpaṭ*, 273:2; ham-Me'iri, *Beṯ hab-Bĕḥirah* on B. Neḏ 7a.
103. *Nĕzirut*, i, 1. See also PhM, introduction (p. 27). There is also philosophic justification for including it here. In MN, III, 48, Maimonides notes summarily: "The reason for Naziritism is most manifest; it consists in bringing about abstinence from drinking wine, which has caused the ruin of the ancients and the moderns." See the very end of *Nĕzirut*, x, 14; and cf. J. Levinger, " 'Al Ṭa'am han-Nĕzirut bĕ-Moreh Nĕḇukim," *Bar Ilan*, IV–V (1967), 299ff.
104. *Nĕḏarim*, i, 3. See also ibid., i, 4, where one of the verses cited relates to *ḳoḏše mizbeaḥ*.
105. *'Ărakin*, i, 1; see especially RaDBaZ, ad loc.

that this refers to the blood of the tithe and the blood of the firstling."[106] The double explanation, procedural similarity and Scriptural coupling, reveals stress and strain; a sharp and convincing reason is usually monolithic. The need and the attempt to explain are, however, unmistakable.

Maimonides' explanation of the inclusion of mourning laws in the *Book of Judges* is enigmatic and forced: "That one should mourn for deceased relatives, and that even a priest should defile himself and mourn for deceased relatives; but no mourning is to be observed for those who have been condemned to death by the court; I have nevertheless included this treatise in this book because it embodies the duty of burying the deceased on the day of death, which (as in the case of one who is executed by order of the court) is a positive commandment." This contrapuntal explanation was apparently considered a bit cloudy, for early commentators were already suggesting alternate reasons for this classification, just as post-Maimonidean codifiers could not agree on where to place this subject.[107] For our purposes, however, Maimonides' troubling statement is the best illustration of his troubled awareness of the challenges and obstacles, sometimes nearly insurmountable, to a consistently accurate and pedagogically valid classification.

Maimonides saw fit to explain his juxtaposition of two forbidden areas, forbidden foods and forbidden sexual unions, in Book Five, the *Book of Holiness:* "Because in these two regards God sanctified us and separated us from the nations, and of both classes of precepts it is said, *And I have set you apart from the peoples* (Lev. 20:26), *Who have set you apart from the peoples* (Lev. 20:24)." Many modern scholars have been agitated by this grouping and have tended not to take the explanation seriously, indeed to dismiss it—with a wry and condescending smile, one imagines—as an "afterthought."[108]

---

106. *Bĕkorot*, introduction.
107. *'Abel*, introduction. See RaDBaZ, introduction to *Sefer Šofĕṭim*. Cf. *Yoreh De'ah*, 342; also R. Aaron ha-Kohen of Lunel, *'Orḥot Ḥayyim*, II, 557.
108. E.g., B. Cohen, "Classification," p. 528; B. Ziemlich, "Plan und Anlage des Mischneh Torah," *MbM*, I, 270.

The facts, however, would seem to militate against this smug hypercriticism. Let the reader judge between the latter and the evidence that Maimonides' scheme is indeed an authentic conceptualization with ample precedent: *ḳĕdušah*, as used in early Rabbinic literature and in contemporary medieval writings, has the meaning which Maimonides attributes to it—restraint, withdrawal, separation, moderation in action, thought, and feeling.[109] Moreover, Maimonides has occasion to define *ḳĕdušah* elsewhere, and the motif of separation-sublimation emerges quite sharply: "Although it is permissible to eat unclean foodstuffs and to drink unclean liquids, the pious of former times used to eat their common food in conditions of cleanness, and all their days they were wary of every uncleanness. And it is they who were called Pharisees (*Pĕrušim*), 'separated ones.' This is an expression of special holiness (*ḳĕdušah*), and the way of piety is for a man to keep himself separate and to go apart from the rest of the people and neither touch them nor eat and drink with them. For separation leads to the cleansing of the body from evil deeds, and the cleansing of the body leads to the hallowing (*ḳĕdušat*) of the soul from evil thoughts, and the hallowing of the soul leads to striving for likeness with the Shekinah, as is written . . ."[110] Thus, both philologically and philosophically, *ḳĕdušah* is associated with separation, withdrawal, restraint, and temperance. There is a general *ḳĕdušah* which separates Israel from other nations, and there is an elitist *ḳĕdušah* which separates select individuals from larger groups within Israel.

In the light of this, the relevance of the motto of Book Five to its thematic structure is also evident: *Order my footsteps by Thy word, and let not any iniquity ('awen) have dominion over me* (Ps.

---

109. E.g., R. Abraham ibn Ezra, *Yĕsod Mora'*, chap. 10 (p. 35); Naḥmanides, *Peruš*, Lev. 19:2; MN, III, 33, 35 (the explanation of *Sefer Ḳĕdušah* in the MT). Note the following applications or definitions of *ḳĕdušah* in the MT: *Ḳĕri'at Šĕma'*, iii, 4; *Tĕfillin*, iv, 14, 25; *Ṣiṣit*, iii, 9; *Sefer Torah*, x, 2, 10, 11; *Šabbat*, ii, 22; *Yom Ṭob*, vi, 16; vii, 1; *Tĕrumot*, i, 5; *Nĕzirut*, x, 14; *Bet hab-Bĕḥirah*, vi, 13; *Kĕle ham-Miḳdaš*, iv, 2; *'Issure Mizbeaḥ*, i, 11 (and *Pĕsule ham-Muḳdašin*, iii, 18).

110. *Ṭumĕ'at 'Oklin*, xvi, 12. For likeness with Shekinah, see also *De'ot*, i, 5, vi, 2 and *Mĕgillah*, ii, 17. See MN, I, 54; III, 54.

119:133). From Maimonides' statement at the end of *Miḳwa'oṭ* we infer that *'awen* is antithetical to *ḳĕduśah:* "Just as one who sets his heart on becoming clean becomes clean as soon as he has immersed himself, although nothing new has befallen his body, so, too, one who sets his heart on cleansing himself from the uncleannesses that beset men's souls, namely thoughts of iniquity (*'awen*) and false opinions, becomes clean as soon as he consents in his heart to shun these counsels and brings his soul into the waters of pure reason."[111]

We may recall in this connection that in his *On the Special Laws* (*De Specialibus Legibus*), perhaps the first *Book of Commandments,* Philo also groups marriage laws and dietary laws together, for their common purpose is continence and temperance. Using Maimonides' terminology, R. Menahem ham-Me'iri observes that the "entire matter of forbidden sexual unions and forbidden foods" branches out from the lusting for excess pleasures. Maimonides' emphasis, however, is not so much on the underlying motive, hedonistic restraint, as on the ultimate objective, hallowed existence. *Ḳĕduśah* is a modality of existence achieved by observance of all commandments and these in particular.[112]

The last treatise of the *Book of Civil Laws* (*Mišpaṭim*) contains Laws Concerning Inheritance. Now it may be, as has been suggested, that "Maimonides did not have any more appropriate place for the laws of inheritance"[113] and put them here. However, if they do not belong here even by association, by a stream of consciousness, why not place them elsewhere? On the face of it, they would mesh beautifully with the Laws Concerning Original Acquisitions and Gifts in the *Book of Acquisition,* inasmuch as they do not involve litigation, claim and counterclaim, but only acquisition. The crucial point and major determinant is, how-

---

111. *Miḳwa'oṭ*, xi, 12. In ShM, *šoreš* 3, *remez* (hint, indication) is used as the opposite of *pešaṭ* (the literal meaning); also PhM, 'Uḳ, end (p. 737 in the Hebrew translation). For a different use of *remez*, see *Tĕšubah*, iii, 4; *Šĕ'ar 'Aḇoṭ haṭ-Ṭumĕ'oṭ*, xii, 7. Also, see the commentary of R. David Ḳimḥi to Ps. 119:133.

112. Philo, *Special Laws*, III, 4, 22; IV, 16, 97 (see Wolfson, *Philo*, II, 222, n. 170, and I. Baer, in *Zion*, XV [1950], 4, n.8); ham-Me'iri, *Beṭ hab-Bĕḥirah*, *'Aḇoṭ*, 4, 19. See ShM, *šoreš* 4.

113. Cohen, "Classification," p. 539.

ever, that the whole subject of inheritance is described as law (*mišpaṭ*). In Chapter VI, Maimonides emphasizes that "in the division of Scripture treating of inheritances it is said, *And it shall be unto the children of Israel a statute of judgment* (mišpaṭ). (Num. 27:11)." That this is a consistently sustained motif is clear from the curt assertion elsewhere: "The rule applying to lawsuits applies also to cases of inheritance, as it is said, *a statute of judgment* (mišpaṭ)." Formally, the treatise is an elaboration of "one affirmative commandment, to administer the *law* with respect to the order of inheritance (*din seḏer naḥălot*)." There is a fixed sequence and hierarchy of inheritance, and it is the function of the court to safeguard and supervise it. It seems clear that Maimonides was aware of this problem, decided upon a course of action, and scattered some allusions which help to explain his classification.[114]

Chapter XIII of the section on Murder and Preservation of Life elaborates the laws for helping a person, even one's enemy, unload his "animal which is crouching under the weight of its burden" (cf. Exod. 23:5), or helping him "raise the animal up and reload the burden onto it" (cf. Deut. 22:4). We may assume that the apparent incongruity of these laws (*ṭĕ'inah u-pĕriḳah*) in this context—other codes have these laws in widely disparate contexts—is clearly on Maimonides' mind when he adds that "one is obligated to help him load or unload, and not leave him possibly to die. For he might tarry because of his property and meet with danger, and the Torah is very solicitous for the lives of Israelites, whether of the wicked or of the righteous, since all Israelites acknowledge God and believe in the essentials of our religion. For it is said, *Say unto them: As I live, saith the Lord God, I have no pleasure in the death of the wicked, but that the wicked turn from his way and live* (Ezek. 33:11)."[115] Maimonides' new and highly sensitized interpretation of the law in this case also validates his classification. This two-tiered achievement suffices to show that

---

114. *Naḥălot*, vi, 1, and introduction; *Sanhedrin*, iii, 5; also *'Išut*, xii, 5 (italics mine). Of course, one may say that there is a certain symmetry in having five units in each of the last four books.

115. *Roṣeaḥ*, xiii, 14; cf. *Ḥošen Mišpaṭ*, 272. Note also RaDBaZ, *Tĕšuḇot*, 728.

the classification is not inadvertent or idiosyncratic; it may be seen as a thoughtful conclusion, a necessary stratagem, or an unavoidable compromise, but however it is appraised, there is no room for doubt that it was carefully planned.

Similarly, Chapter XIII of the Laws Concerning Ritual Slaughtering (*šĕḥiṭah*) deals with the halakic elaboration of Deut. 22:6, *Thou shalt not take the dam with the young,* i.e., the prohibition of taking the entire contents of the bird's nest. Now except for the fact that this subject is treated by the Rabbis at the end of the tractate *Ḥullin,* there does not seem to be any intrinsic link between this and *šĕḥiṭah*. It is perhaps with this in mind that Maimonides has added a rather conspicuous reference to *šĕḥiṭah* in the opening sentence of this chapter: "If one takes a dam with its young *and performs šĕḥiṭah* upon the dam, the flesh is permitted for consumption, but he is liable to a flogging for slaughtering the dam." The parallel formulation in the *Sefer ham-Miṣwot* makes no reference to *šĕḥiṭah:* "We are forbidden when hunting to take the entire bird's nest, mother bird and young."[116] The change seems to reflect Maimonides' awareness of the problem of classification; the solution may be strained but is not completely arbitrary—it is certainly premeditated. As Toynbee has put it, "The price of classification is, no doubt, some degree of misrepresentation. But the alternative to the payment of this price would be intellectual paralysis."[117]

However, the fourteen-volume classification is clearly not a seamless web. Some titles, programmatic and explanatory in form, apparently seek to camouflage the all too visible seams. The next to the last title in Book Seven (*Zĕra'im*), Laws Concerning First Fruits (*bikkurim*) and Other Gifts to the Priests Outside the Sanctuary, is very telling, because the laws of *bikkurim* constitute only one-third of the unit, while the bulk is devoted to the other non-agricultural gifts, such as setting apart a cake of dough for the priest, giving him parts of an animal, and redeeming a firstborn son. Yet if the unit were to bear the general title Gifts to the

---

116. *Šĕḥiṭah*, xiii, 1 (italics mine); ShM, negative 306 (II, p. 283); MN, III, 48; *Yoreh De'ah,* 292.
117. A. Toynbee, *Reconsiderations* (Oxford, 1961), p. 11.

Priests, it would be totally incongruous here; *bikkurim* had to be the prime component of the elaborate title in order to warrant its integration into the agricultural *Book of Seeds*. However, from the vantage point of the *Book of Seeds* as a whole, the ending (Other Gifts) remains conceptually awkward. Actually, the title is Janus-faced: the first part establishes a thematic link with the book in which it is found, and the second part merely unifies the section as an independent and self-contained entity. Full integration on both levels is not forthcoming.

A breakdown of the subject matter included in the section on *Kil'ayim* in the same book reveals a similar situation: the five units subsumed under *kil'ayim*, a self-contained halakic concept, whose common denominator is the forbidden junction of heterogeneous seeds, plants, etc., coexist harmoniously and meaningfully, but the subsections dealing with the "junction of heterogeneous animals by hybridization or by harnessing together" or the junction of wool and linen in the same web do not sit comfortably with the *Book of Seeds* as such. There is here a semantic connection between all these aspects and the title of the section, for *kil'ayim* is an amphibolous term, but there is no intrinsic relation between these subsections on the one hand, and the title and agricultural complexion of the book as a whole on the other.

Another illustration of this phenomenon in the same book is the section entitled Gifts to the Poor, of which the last three chapters, a real innovation in Rabbinic literature (as noted by Naḥmanides), are devoted to "giving charity according to one's means," while the earlier seven chapters deal with "agricultural gifts": leaving a corner of the field unreaped, leaving gleanings in the field and vineyard, and tithing for the poor. In this case, the title may be described as inner-directed, emphasizing the topical unity of the entire section, but it inevitably obscures the outer-directed thematic union of this section with the *Book of Seeds*, which is based on the prescribed philanthropic by-products of harvesting and reaping.

A close look at the structure of the section in Book II entitled Laws Concerning Phylacteries (*Těfillin*), Mězuzah, and Scroll of the Torah (*Sefer Torah*) reveals a similar subtle concern with the twin problems of overall macroscopic classification and internal microscopic unity. The only reason for joining these three topics is the technical aspect of scribal writing applicable to all of them, and the sanctity with which these objects are endowed. In this regard, however, the usual sequence is Scroll of Torah, Těfillin, Mězuzah, yielding the well-known acronym *sětam*. On the other hand, the strongest and clearest link to Book Two as a whole, with its emphasis on regularity, is Těfillin, and it is obviously for this reason that Maimonides ignored the acronym, changed the accepted order, and started with this subject. Mězuzah occupies second place, even though of lesser sanctity compared to the Torah Scroll, because it was possible for Maimonides to establish at least a tenuous link with the book's theme in terms of regularity and continuity of performance. Even though the discrete one-time act of affixing the mězuzah conclusively fulfills the Biblical commandment, constant awareness of it is obligatory: "A person should pay heed to the precept of the mězuzah, for it is an obligation perpetually binding upon all. Whenever one enters or leaves a home with the mězuzah on its doorpost, he will be confronted with the declaration of God's unity, blessed be His holy name; will remember the love due to God; and will be aroused from his slumbers and his foolish absorption in temporal vanities."[118] This spiritual upshot of the commandment, which is perpetually binding, serves also to integrate the section into the entire book by uncovering a dimension of constancy. Inasmuch as study of Torah, which is certainly a continuous, completely open-ended, almost infinite enterprise, is treated by Maimonides elsewhere (in Book One), there is no thematic link between these two sections and the writing of the Torah Scroll. Its presence is a result only of the technical symbiosis of these three subsections, of their being governed by common scribal rules.

There is, in short, a tension between an inner-directed unity of a given section and external integration of this section with the thematic structure and rationale of the whole book in which it is

---

118. *Mězuzah*, v, 7 (and see *Těšubot*, 334 [p. 606]); vi, 13. The first line of this paragraph is quite problematic. See, e.g., the commentaries of *Ma'ǎśeh Roḳeaḥ* and *'Or Śameaḥ*. Note A. Zaslanski, *Wě-Zot li-Yěhudah* (Jerusalem, 1946), and *Ḳobeṣ ha-RaMBaM*, p. 248. My interpretation emphasizes the word *tamid* ("always"). On being aroused from spiritual slumber, see *Těšubah*, iii, 4.

found. Various compromises between the micro- and macro-aspects of classification were forthcoming; sometimes, as we have seen, one aspect prevailed at the other's expense. The *Mishneh Torah* could not be a perfectly programmed product in which every section and every paragraph had total consistency or the same amount of rigidity uniformly distributed. Sometimes there is a limited sectional cohesion, in which all parts are fully integrated, that differs from the more inclusive topical consistency of the book as a whole, in which a few layers may not be fully integrated.

Unlike these instances of partial compromise, reflecting an immanent tension between various levels of conceptualization, where sections have inner coherence and cohesiveness but are not fully congruent with the larger framework, we find cases of outright associationism—small units, sometimes an entire chapter, sometimes a few paragraphs, grafted onto larger entities. R. Menahem ham-Me'iri, who identified this as a characteristic deeply embedded in the texture of the Talmud, already noted that this literary mode was also operative in the *Mishneh Torah*, and that Maimonides, all his rigor notwithstanding, sometimes recorded a law or a cluster of laws by a stream-of-consciousness technique.[119] The ethical prohibition of oral deception (*'ona'at dĕbarim,* verbal abuse, humiliation, hurting a person's feelings) is found in Book Twelve, Laws Concerning Acquisition, by association with the more common and blatant forms of fiscal fraud and deception (*'ona'at mamon*).[120] The Rabbinic injunction forbidding an intoxicated scholar from rendering decisions is neatly tucked away in the *Book of Temple Service* (Chapter I of Laws Concerning Entry into the Sanctuary) as an appendix to the law forbidding intoxicated *kohanim* (priests) from participating in the Temple service: "Just as a priest was forbidden to enter the Sanctuary when drunk, so is every person, whether priest or lay Israelite, forbidden to render a decision when drunk." The connecting link is Lev. 10:9–11.[121] After discussing the prohibition of cutting

---

119. Ham-Me'iri, *Bet hab-Bĕhirah,* introduction, p. 27. Additional examples could include *Kĕri'at Šĕma',* iii, 4, 5; *Tĕfillah,* xiv, 13. See also *Sanhedrin,* xv, 8; xxii, 10.
120. *Mĕkirah,* xiv, 12. See *'Abadim,* viii, 11; *Tĕšubah,* vii, 8.
121. *Bi'at Mikdaš,* i, 3, 4.

one's flesh in the heat of mourning as an expression of grief—for this was an idolatrous practice—Maimonides interpolates the following paragraph: "Included in this prohibition is the rule that in one city there shall not be two courts of law following different procedures; for such a course would lead to strife, as it is said, *Ye shall not cut yourselves (titgodĕdu)* (Deut. 14:1), which has been interpreted to mean, 'You shall not divide yourselves into factions (*'ăguddot*)'."[122] Rabbinic hermeneutics are the cementing factor in this instance of associationism. The end of Chapter IV of Laws Concerning Moral Dispositions stating that "no disciple of the wise may live in a city that does not have ten basic services," has also been included by association, for the first of the ten requirements is a physician, and this chapter deals with health and hygiene.[123] The mention of the recitation of the *Hallel* with regard to Hanukkah led to an exhaustive presentation of all laws and customs pertaining to this recitation on various festivals.[124] The presence of *Šĕkalim* (Shekel Dues) in the *Book of Seasons* is perplexing. The author of the *Maggid Mishneh* suggests that this follows from the fact that the announcement of the collection of the shekel dues was set for a specific date. A modern student of the *Mishneh Torah* has proposed the following: "the heave offering of the shekel dues was taken up three times a year, before each of the three pilgrimage festivals, so that these dues may be regarded as . . . a subsidiary feature of these festivals." We may note that in the introduction to his *Mishnah Commentary* Maimonides takes for granted that *Šĕkalim* properly belongs to *Mo'ed* and merely seeks to explain why it follows *Pĕsaḥim*. Some form of association was apparently operative here.[125]

---

122. '*Akum*, xii, 13. In this case, the context clearly reveals the Maimonidean interpretation. Many commentators, e.g., Ibn Ezra and Naḥmanides, see the verse (Deut. 14:1) as a warning against excessive mourning (note this also in '*Abel*, xiii, 11) with no idolatrous overtones.
123. *De'ot*, iv, 23.
124. *Ḥănukkah*, iii, 6ff.
125. *MM*, introduction to *Šĕkalim;* S. Gandz, in the introduction (p. xxvi) to the translation of Book Three in YJS; PhM, introduction (p. 48). Examples of single halakot whose location is noteworthy are *Gerušin*, iii, 19 (and cf. *'Eben ha-'Ezer*, 123), and *Nĕdarim* iii, 9 (the special status of the day preceding the Day of Atonement is not noted in Book Three, *Šĕbitat 'Aśor*); cf. *'Oraḥ Ḥayyim*, 604.

## CLASSIFICATION

Awareness of this literary reality tends of course to attenuate a central canon of Maimonidean study: the ability, if not the need, regularly to infer meanings and implications from the position of certain laws. There can be no doubt that Maimonides himself was conscious of the role of associationism (*gilgul*) and unavoidable, therefore to a great extent justifiable, digression in the Talmud as well as in his own writing.[126] Occasional associationism should, therefore, be recognized, as was done by R. Menahem ham-Me'iri, and careful attempts made to detect it. This would obviate the need in certain cases for strained interpretations or far-fetched inferences.

There seems to be one underlying motive for all these compromises and expediencies: the need to avoid an endless proliferation of books and subsections. There just seems to be a natural point beyond which expansiveness or atomization must cease. An uncontrolled multiplication of rubrics would reduce the benefits of conceptualization and restrict the desired perception of unnoticed relationships. While other codifiers have sometimes introduced separate sections for such themes as excommunication,[127] honoring of parents,[128] priestly benedictions,[129] and conversion to Judaism,[130] thereby avoiding the need for conceptual connections, Maimonides has dexterously interwoven them into larger units, just as he combined the unrelated laws of shofar, sukkah, and lulab into one consecutively numbered section. A more atomistic breakdown would exhibit the shortcomings of the *Sefer ham-Miṣwot* approach and neutralize the pedagogic-conceptual benefits of classification.[131] It would be a good example of intellectual timidity, if not paralysis.

126. *Kobeṣ*, I, 26a: הדבר הקשה הוא שלא יודע מקומו מפני שבא בתלמוד אגב גררא ודרך משא ומתן . . . Those phrases must have been echoing in the minds of ham-Me'iri and R. Jeroham. See above, chap. II, n.191.
127. *Talmud Torah*, vi, 12ff.; *Halakot Gedolot*, 427 (*Hilkot nidduy*).
128. *Mamrim*, v; *Halakot Gedolot*, 478 (*Hilkot kibbud 'ab wa-'em*).
129. *Tefillah*, chaps. xiv–xv; *Halakot Gedolot*, 220 (*Hilkot kohanim*).
130. *'Issure Bi'ah*, chaps. xiii–xiv; see B. Wacholder, "Attitudes Towards Proselytizing in the Classical Halakah," *Historia Judaica*, XX (1958), 77ff.
131. To claim (as does B. Cohen, "Classification," p. 539) that "the arrangement of the law in the *Yad* has its imperfections, chief of which is the insufficient number of subdivisions," misses the point. Since, as M. Radin in *Law as Logic* (New Haven, 1940), p. 96, formulates it, "classification is a logical process; it involves a consideration of genus

An explicit extension of this principle of avoiding undue atomization or uncontrolled proliferation of sections is the use of double or hyphenated titles, a stratagem which clearly and effectively prevents centrifugal acceleration. To say this is by no means to suggest that hyphenated titles should a priori be considered less rigorous or less pure than simple one-dimensional titles. As a matter of fact, the coupling of certain topics, e.g., Laws Concerning Robbery and Lost Property, shows ingenuity, fertile experimentation, and valid conceptualization. This combination is based on an halakic concept, the obligation to return stolen and lost property, as well as on a value concept, that human rights of ownership are sacred.[132] The section on Murder and the Preservation of Life is united juridically as well as metaphysically: the need to safeguard human life for metaphysical reasons—"the life of the murdered person is not the property of the avenger of blood but the property of God"—as well as for sociological reasons—"for although there are worse crimes than bloodshed, none causes such destruction to civilized society as bloodshed."[133] It follows, therefore, that "many things were forbidden by the Sages because they are dangerous to life," and these are summarized in Chapters XI and XII of this section.[134] The opening treatise of Book Fourteen is designated Sanhedrin and the Penalties Within Their Jurisdiction, for punishment is a prime responsibility of the court; as Maimonides notes in the *Mishnah Commentary*, while explaining the proximity of *Makkot* and *Sanhedrin*, "only the judges may flog and punish."[135] Laws Concerning Original Acquisitions

---

and species and differences," proliferation of independent units would be self-defeating. It is noteworthy that Maimonides' enumeration of the *miṣwot* also tends to avoid proliferation. Whenever possible, Maimonides combines rather than atomizes (e.g., *Ķĕri'aṭ Šĕma'*, i, 1; *Tĕmiḏin u-Musafin*, i, 1, 9). When he sometimes lists two separate commandments which could presumably have been combined, he addresses himself to the reader and explains what dictated the procedure (e.g., ShM, positive 13, 75, 77, 82; see also introduction, *šoreš* 9, 11, 10, 12). In order for law to become a comprehensive system, it needs, as Toynbee notes in *A Study of History*, VII, 266, "comprehensive maxims, logical principles, and imaginative vistas." The balance between consolidation and subdivision is challenging.

132. Note also *Gĕzelah*, xi, 2.
133. *Roṣeaḥ*, i, 4; iv, 9.
134. Ibid., xi, 4, 5.
135. PhM, introduction (p. 28); also, *Sanhedrin*, xiv, 2; xx, 4.

and Gifts form a unit because unlike the previous section on Sales, which involves an exchange of goods, this section provides for outright disposal or acquisition (from *hefķer*) of property. The juridical base (*da'at maknah*) unites them.[136] *Mĕḡillah* and *Ḥănukkah* are joined, for they deal with two Rabbinically ordered festivals whose essence is thanksgiving to God.[137] The practical effects of hyphenated titles, not the theoretical stimuli, tend to preserve symmetry, proportion, and interrelatedness without abandoning a conceptual scheme. It would appear, moreover, that some sections, initially separated, were joined only in Maimonides' final revision of the Code, for Maimonides was regularly revising the style as well as the substance of his Code. Just as the style shows signs of tightening and progressive Hebraization, so the double titles may be seen as increased tightening of the arrangement.[138]

The assumption that a consistent separation of "laws that were current from those that were in abeyance" served as a guiding principle for various groupings and divisions in the *Mishneh Torah* has been favored by many scholars. One may assess this as a matter of "convenience and utility," while another may emphasize that the "differentiation between matters of practice and matters

---

136. Note the introductory sentence: "Whoever takes possession of ownerless property acquires title to it." There is no specific commandment, merely aspects of civil law.
137. See *Ḥănukkah*, iii, 3. Note a similar equation in *Halaḵot Gĕdolot*, 83.
138. Concerning *Šĕ'elah u-Fiķķadon*, see S. Assaf, *ĶS*, XVIII (1941/42), 152; see *Šĕḇu'ot*, viii, 9; *Ḥoḇel u-Mazziķ*, vii, 19.
It is interesting to review the multiple titles, some of which have been explained and some of which need no explanation: Book Two: *Tĕfillah u-Birḵat Kohanim, Tĕfillin, Mĕzuzah wĕ-Sefer Torah;* Book Three: *Šofar, Sukkah, Lulaḇ, Mĕgillah wĕ-Ḥănukkah;* Book Four: *Yibbum wa-Ḥăliṣah;* Book Six: *'Araḵin wa-Ḥăramin;* Book Seven: *Ma'ăśer Šeni wĕ-Neṭa' Rĕḇa'i;* Book Eight; *Kĕle ham-Miḵdaś wĕha-'Oḇĕdim Bo, Tĕmidin u-Musafin;* Book Eleven: *Gĕzelah wa-'Aḇedah, Ḥoḇel u-Mazziķ, Roṣeaḥ u-Šĕmiraṭ Nefeš;* Book Twelve: *Zĕḵiyyah u-Mattanah, Šĕluḥin wĕ-Šutafin;* Book Thirteen: *Šĕ'elah u-Fiķķadon;* Book Fourteen: *Sanhedrin wĕha-'Onĕšin ham-Mĕsurim Lahem, Mĕlaḵim u-Milḥamoṭehem.* In addition there are the following collective or composite topics: Book Two: *Bĕraḵot;* Book Four: *Na'ărah Bĕṭulah;* Book Five: *'Issure Bi'ah, Ma'ăḵalot 'Ăsurot;* Book Seven: *Kil'ayim; Mattĕnot 'Ăniyyim;* Book Nine: *Mĕḥusre Kapparah;* Book Ten: *Mĕṭamme' Miškaḇ u-Mošaḇ, 'Aḇot haṭ-Ṭumĕ'oṭ;* Book Eleven: *Nizķe Mamon;* Book Fourteen: *Mamrim.* Sometimes, in cross-referencing, Maimonides will mention only the first part of the title, e.g. *Gĕzelah* in *Ṭo'en wĕ-Niṭ'an*, xiv, 2; *Mĕḵirah*, x, 5; and *Zĕḵiyyah u-Mattanah*, xiv, 7. Note the same with regard to *Ṭo'en wĕ-Niṭ'an* in *Šĕḇu'ot*, x, 10; *Gĕzelah*, iv, 11; and *'Edut*, v, 1.

of theory was of chief interest to Maimonides."[139] In any event, Maimonides' decomposition of such composite tractates as *Pĕsaḥim* and *Yoma*, in which practical and archaic-theoretical themes are intermingled, is explained accordingly. In fact, such an assumption is totally alien to the *Mishneh Torah*. Maimonides' conception of law was organismic, oblivious to distinctions between practicable laws and laws devoid of practical value, for these were merely anomalies that history would rectify. The very scope of the *Mishneh Torah*, a comprehensive *Corpus Juris Mosaici*, discountenanced any such artificial separation and rendered it irrelevant.[140] The separation of the Laws Concerning the Paschal Lamb from the Laws Concerning Unleavened and Leavened Bread, or the separation of the Laws Concerning Sacrifices and Temple Ritual Pertaining to the Day of Atonement from the fasting and other universal observances of that day, is conceptual, not unlike his separation of various aspects of laws concerning vows or forbidden foods. Maimonides sometimes appears to be walking a tightrope when he separates constituent elements of an halaḳic complex, whether ritual, civil, or jurisprudential, but the impulse is primarily topical-conceptual rather than utilitarian. This is further demonstrated by the actual intermingling of practical and theoretical matters in a large number of sections. *Šĕḳalim* (which is in force only during the Temple period) is in the predominantly practical *Book of Seasons,* right after the Laws Concerning Tabernacles.[141] The Sanctification of the New Moon is in the same book, even though a good part of it deals with complex methods of calculation which are currently irrelevant, impractical, and impracticable, and have been included only "to make the law great and glorious."[142] The Counting of the 'Omer is tucked away in the arcane section of Daily Offerings, even though "this obligation has remained incumbent upon every male Jew in every

---

139. E.g., B. Cohen, "Classification," pp. 521–22; L. Ginzberg, *On Jewish Law and Lore,* p. 170; B. Ziemlich, "Plan und Anlage," pp. 267 and 273ff.
140. *Mĕlaḳim,* xi, 1, 3, 4. See already A. Schwarz, *Der Mischneh Thorah* (Vienna, 1905), p. 18; J. B. Soloveitchik, " 'Iš ha-Halaḳah," *Talpiot,* I (1944), 668ff., cited in my "Shulḥan 'Aruḳ," p. 151. The apt phrase *Corpus Juris Mosaici* was used by B. Cohen.
141. See *Šĕḳalim,* i, 8.
142. *Ḳidduš ha-Ḥodeš,* xi, 4; xviii, 16.

place and at all times."[143] Laws Concerning Rebels in the *Book of Judges* treats first the totally theoretical and impracticable case of the rebellious elder who defies the ruling of the Supreme Court, and then details all the laws which flesh out the universally relevant Fifth Commandment of honoring one's father and mother.[144] Laws Concerning the Heifer Whose Neck is to be Broken ('*eglah 'ărufah*) in symbolic atonement for an unsolved murder are in the section of Murder and Preservation of Life, even though, as Maimonides himself mentions rather parenthetically, "the (ceremony of the) breaking of a heifer's neck was discontinued" already in ancient times.[145] Similarly, a section of the eminently practical *Book of Women* is devoted to Laws Concerning the Wayward Woman (suspected of infidelity, *soṭah*), who had to endure the ordeal of drinking the bitter water, even though "the Sanhedrin abolished the water of bitterness" during the period of the Second Temple.[146] The widespread ceremony of redemption of the firstborn is appended to the highly impractical section on First Fruits and Other Priestly Gifts.[147] Laws Concerning Immersion Pools, highly practical, are reviewed and synthesized together with The Red Heifer and The Uncleanness of Leprosy in Book Ten.[148] Note also the composite nature of Chapter VII of Leavened and Unleavened Bread, which describes the order of the first night of Passover at the time that the Temple existed, and then records the ritual changes which crystallized after its destruction. Indeed, the two orders form one unified mosaic.[149] Similarly, the description of the ritual for special fast days is a medley of practical and archaic procedure.[150] In short, Maimonides' quest for comprehensiveness, for the inclusion of "pure" as well as "applied" matter, did not necessitate that all this be filtered through a prism of practical-theoretical distinctions which were bland and artificial. Genuine comprehensiveness

---

143. *Tĕmiḏin u-Musafin*, vii, 22.
144. *Mamrim*, iii, 4, 5; vi, 1ff.
145. *Roṣeaḥ*, ix, 12.
146. *Soṭah*, iii, 19.
147. *Bikkurim*, ii, 1; xi, 6.
148. See, e.g., the cross-reference in '*Issure Bi'ah*, xi, 16.
149. *Ḥameṣ u-Maṣṣah*, vii, cited by J. B. Soloveitchik, "Iš ha-Halakah."
150. *Ta'ăniyyoṯ*, iv.

and valid conceptualization were not on a collision course. Conceptual-thematic considerations remained the major determinants, so that sometimes practical-theoretical subjects formed one continuum and sometimes they were separated. There is no intrinsic or doctrinaire difference between the separation of certain practical from nonpractical matters and the separation of constituent elements of completely practical topics.[151]

## DIFFERENCES BETWEEN TOPICAL-CONCEPTUAL AND PHILOSOPHIC-TELEOLOGICAL CLASSIFICATION

At this point, a crucial qualification must be registered. Maimonides' classification of the *Mishneh Torah,* which, in his footsteps, we have been describing as topical-conceptual, is not to be identified with the philosophic-teleological classification used at the end of the *Guide.* In his attempt to elaborate a philosophic rationale for the entire law, Maimonides operates with a threefold classification of the specific laws, corresponding to a similar classification of the philosophic virtues: intellectual, moral, and practical. All laws teach true beliefs, inculcate moral virtues, or else themselves constitute actions which train one in the acquisition of intellectual and moral virtues. The practical commandments also have an outer-directed social motive: to help establish a society in which "wronging each other" has been abolished and in which the individual can, therefore, flourish and devote himself to the attainment of intellectual perfection. The moral virtues are also propaedeutic: they bring about the proper social relations necessary for mankind—"through fine moral qualities human association and society are perfected." In essence, therefore, the ultimate intention of the law is a twofold one: "the welfare (*tikkun*) of the soul," which consists in the acquisiton of beliefs, and "the welfare of the body," which is achieved by practical and moral virtues.[152] *All* commandments consequently have to be interpreted in the light of this ultimate metajuridical intention and have to be re-

---

151. The exclusion of *'erub tabšilin* from *'Erubin* and its inclusion in *Yom Ṭob,* vi, is a case in point. While *'erub ḥaṣerot* and *tehumim* are Sabbath laws, *'erub tabšilin* is a holiday law—hence their separation; cf. RABD, *Yom Ṭob,* vi, 2.
152. MN, III, 27ff. See below, chap. VI.

lated teleologically to it. The contents of the fourteen books of the *Mishneh Torah* are reclassified; the "structures of the classifications" are not and could not be parallel. A new classification, based on three trans-halakic postulates reflecting the ethical-philosophical emphases of the *Guide,* was needed and created. When we compare the resultant classification with that of the *Mishneh Torah,* there is no reason whatsoever to think in terms of contradictions and inconstancies, ambiguities and obscurities, and no need to seek harmonizations; rather, we have a significantly divergent emphasis, which, of course, yields radically different groupings of the same material. The reclassification was inevitable and perfectly natural.[153] This is clearly the author's intention and is conveyed forthrightly, uncamouflaged, and without diversionary tactics. A few examples should illustrate the matter.

Circumcision, as we have seen, is classified together with basic ritual in Book Two of the *Mishneh Torah* because of the common denominator brought to the surface by Maimonides: both serve as constant reminders of, and inducements to, the love of God. These are the simple existential facts: the practice or presence of these commandments is characterized, and therefore united, by constancy. In the *Guide* circumcision is grouped together with the *Book of Women* and part of Book Five (Prohibited Sexual Relations) in the fourteenth class, which "comprises the commandments concerned with the prohibition of certain sexual unions"; the "interbreeding of beasts", part of the section *Kil'ayim* in Book Seven, is also included: "The purpose of this is to bring about a decrease of sexual intercourse and to diminish the desire for mating as far as possible, so that it should not be taken as an end, as is done by the ignorant, according to what we have explained in the *Commentary on the Tractate 'Abot.*"[154] In a later chapter Maimonides explains that the reason for circumcision is "the wish

---

153. Cf. Strauss, *Persecution,* p. 63; M. Fox, "Prolegomenon" to A. Cohen, *The Teachings of Maimonides* (New York, 1968), pp. xxvi–xxviii. There are, to be sure, a few classic instances of contradiction; e.g., *Ḥobel u-Mazziḳ,* i, 6, and MN, III, 41; *Bi'at Miḳdaš,* iii, 8 and MN, III, 41 (but see *Mělaḳim,* vi, 14, 15); *Tĕfillah,* ix, 7, and MN, III, 48; primarily, these involve the issue of Biblicism.

154. MN, III, 35; see ŠP, chap. IV (end); also PhM, 'Ab 1:5 (p. 411).

to bring about a decrease in sexual intercourse and a weakening of the organ in question, so that this activity be diminished and the organ be in as quiet a state as possible."[155] The corollary of the ascetically oriented explanation which Maimonides here proposes would be a regrouping of the subject in the *Mishneh Torah*, (e.g., in *Hilkot 'Išut*). It is clear, of course, that such a philosophic explanation could not sustain a halakic classification. Indeed, the inconstancies of purely philosophic explanation with regard to halakic classification are further illustrated by the fact that Maimonides proceeds to offer an additional "very important" reason for circumcision: it is a covenant made by our father Abraham with a view to promoting the belief in the oneness of God— "Thus everyone who is circumcised joins Abraham's covenant. This covenant imposes the obligation to believe in the oneness of God, *To be a God unto thee and to thy seed after thee* (Gen. 17:7)." Maimonides concludes, in this case, by recognizing the *multiplicity* of explanations: "This also is a strong reason, as strong as the first, which may be adduced to account for circumcision; perhaps it is even stronger than the first."[156] Self-evidently, were this "stronger reason" to prevail, still another classification would result; this result is not forthcoming, because the "structures of the classifications," the judicial and the teleological, are inherently and avowedly different.

The classification of "days of fasting" illustrates the same divergence. In the *Mishneh Torah* it is treated toward the end of Book Three, the *Book of Seasons,* together with other special days of the calendar which are characterized as precepts to be fulfilled at stated periods, i.e., intermittent rather than continuous. This is a conceptually valid grouping, even though some might separate fasts from feasts, and some might disperse the several fast days, e.g., listing the Fast of Esther with Purim.[157] In the *Guide* "days of fasting," whose essence is to call upon God in every calamity, is grouped in the very first class, together with the bulk

---

155. MN, III, 49.
156. Ibid.
157. E.g., *'Oraḥ Ḥayyim,* 549 (*Tiš'ah bĕ-'Aḇ* and other fast days), while *Ta'anit Esther* is in sec. 686, "Hilkot Mĕḡillah."

of Book One of the *Mishneh Torah,* as containing the root ideas and principal beliefs of Judaism: "The first class comprises the commandments that are fundamental opinions."[158] Crying out in prayer and sounding an alarm in a time of crisis and emergency—be it famine, pestilence, war, or sickness—has a philosophic-doctrinal rationale: it underscores the providential design in the world and uncompromisingly repudiates any theory of chance (Epicureanism). By means of this ritual action, in other words, "the correct opinion is firmly established that He, may He be exalted, apprehends our situations, and that it depends upon Him to improve them if we obey, and to make them ruinous if we disobey."[159] This metaphysical-teleological explanation is fully and clearly articulated in the *Mishneh Torah,* where Maimonides teaches that people should not see adversity, suffering, or catastrophe as accidents of nature, "that it is the way of the world for such a thing to happen to them and that their trouble is a matter of pure chance." The only legitimate, constructive, and cathartic response to torment and tribulation is to "cry out in prayer," for this induces repentance and the conviction that "his repentance will cause the trouble to be removed." To follow the Epicurean view of chance is to "choose a cruel path which will cause them to persevere in their evil deeds,"[160] for sustaining a naturalistic, immutable, and impersonal status quo anesthetizes all sensitivity in man and dampens all hope. It leaves man to be buffeted by the frosty winds of a cruel and blind fate. Prayer, with a sense of urgency and emergency, accompanied and intensified by fasting, strengthens man's belief and is therefore of great theological-pedagogical value; it is a personal lesson in the complex doctrine of providence.[161] Nevertheless, while Maimonides effectively uses this supra-halakic teleological explanation in the *Mishneh Torah,* he was not persuaded to alter the halakic classification

---

158. MN, III, 35, 36. He refers to *Hilkot Yĕsode hat-Torah* but actually includes most of *Sefer ham-Madda'*. Cf. L. Strauss, "Notes on Maimonides' Book of Knowledge," *Studies in Mysticism and Religion Presented to G. Scholem,* ed. E. E. Urbach, et al. (Jerusalem, 1967), p. 270 (concerning MN, I, 70).
159. MN, III, 36; see Ibn Ezra to Lev. 26:27–28 (the second explanation).
160. *Ta'āniyyot,* i, 3. See also MTH, 36; LA, 233.
161. See MN, III, 36.

which pays primary attention to formal-substantive considerations and semantic implications rather than teleological superstructures.

One subsection of Book Six of the *Mishneh Torah*, that concerned with oaths administered by the judges for purposes of verification and substantiation, is also grouped together with Fundamental Principles of the Torah in the first class of the *Guide*, which comprises the basic theological opinions: "To this class also belongs the commandment addressed to us to swear in His name and the prohibition addressed to us of breaking one's oath and swearing in vain. All this has a manifest reason; for it is intended to glorify Him, may He be exalted. Accordingly, these are actions necessitating a belief in His greatness."[162] In other words, swearing in God's name attests to, and concretizes, God's greatness, for this reference is the only way to anchor the oath in ultimate truth and reality.[163] Actually, the most forceful formulation of this conception is found in the *Mishneh Torah:* "Just as it is a negative commandment not to swear vainly or falsely, so is it a positive commandment that whosoever becomes subject to an oath in court should swear by the Divine Name. For the Scriptural statement, *And by His name shalt thou swear* (Deut. 6:13), is a positive commandment, and swearing by His great and holy name is one of the ways of serving God, whereby He is greatly honored and sanctified."[164] An oath of this kind is not merely a judicial technique or an indispensable instrument of justice but also a positive commandment charged with great significance, and consistent with his rationale, Maimonides included this in his enumeration of the 613 precepts—a step which provoked the critical reactions of RABD and Naḥmanides. Now the corollary of this teleological viewpoint would be to lift the judicial oath from this context into Book One, as the *Guide* suggests.

In fact, it may be further contended that this subsection does seem to be out of place in Laws Concerning Oaths, for the book is

---

162. MN, III, 36.
163. See *Šĕbu'ot*, xi, 2. Cf. S. Belkin, *Philo and the Oral Law* (Cambridge, 1940), p. 143.
164. *Šĕbu'ot*, xi, 1. RABD and Naḥmanides disagree with this formulation. The *Mišpĕṭe Šĕbu'ot* of R. Hai Gaon is limited to *šĕbu'at had-dayyanim*.

primarily concerned with obligations and commitments created by vows—hence the motto of the book: *Accept, I beseech Thee, the freewill offerings of my mouth, O Lord, and teach me Thine ordinances* (Ps. 119:108). *Freewill offerings of my mouth* applies to oaths creating new liabilities, vows of prohibition and consecration, Nazirite vows, etc., but not to the technique and practice of the judicial oath. The descriptive characterization of the book at the end of the *Mishneh Torah* introduction confirms this point: "I include in it precepts binding on one who has incurred obligation by utterances, e.g., by taking oaths or making vows." Yet in the final analysis the substantive-semantic link connecting all classes of oaths is maintained, and Book Six is constructed around it. In the *Guide,* where the metajuridical and teleological approach is basic, the judicial oath, days of fasting, and fundamental principles of the Torah are appropriately subsumed under one rubric.

The fourth class in the *Guide* classification comprises "the commandments concerned with giving alms, lending, bestowal of gifts, and matters that are connected with this, as for instance, valuations and things votive, the ordinances concerning loans and slaves, and all the commandments that we have enumerated in the *Book of Seeds,* with the exception of those treating of the mingling of diverse species and the first products of trees." In other words, Maimonides has here dismembered the topical-conceptual arrangement of Books Six, Seven, Twelve, and Thirteen of the *Mishneh Torah* and has collated parts of these books in a new grouping, whose common denominator is the nurturing of generosity and compassion: "If you consider all these commandments one by one, you will find that they are manifestly useful through instilling pity for the weak and the wretched, giving strength in various ways to the poor, and inciting us not to press hard upon those in straits and not to afflict the hearts of individuals who are in a weak position.[165] Clearly such a supercategory, forged by philosophical-ethical considerations, could not sustain the more formal-substantive grouping called for in the *Mishneh Torah.*

---

165. MN, III, 39. A by-product of the recitation of Deut. 26 upon the bringing of the first fruits is the inculcation of humility. Note again the use of multiple explanations.

Similarly, vows and Naziriteship (from Book Six) are joined in the *Guide* with forbidden foods (from Book Five) because their common denominator is training in restraining the appetite and achieving temperance. Here again this philosophical-ethical motif is found in the *Mishneh Torah*—it is of obvious rationality and utility—but is certainly not cogent enough to produce a revision of the halakic systematization.[166]

Chapters XI and XII of *Hilkot 'Akum* in Book One of the *Mishneh Torah* contain a medley of practices (certain styles of dress and haircut, divination, magic and necromancy, tattooing, etc.), which are prohibited because they imitate idolatrous mores, reflect idolatrous rites, or are motivated by idolatrous myths. The essence of these practices, philosophically, ritually, and historically, is rooted in, and is related to, idolatry, and they are therefore classified together with "the essential principle of the precepts concerning idolatry" and the laws governing personal and commercial relations between Jews and idolaters.[167] Now elsewhere in the *Mishneh Torah* Maimonides occasionally *motivates* a law by characterizing it as idolatrous.[168] For example, "It is forbidden to bury the Naśi' in a silk shroud or in gold-embroidered garments, for this is arrogance, extravagance, and an idolatrous practice (*ma'áśeh 'akum*)."[169] The essence of this paragraph is related to mourning practices—the previous paragraph deals with "the Jewish practice with respect to the dead and their interment" and various Rabbinic ordinances concerning burial—and consequently would not fit into Chapter XII of *'Akum*. However, were the classification of the *Guide* to list every single law connected with idolatry to prevail, this paragraph from *Hilkot 'Abel*, iv, 2, would certainly be included together with *Kil'ayim* in the second group, which "comprises the command-

---

166. MN, III, 48; see *Nĕdarim*, xiii, 24, 25; *Nĕzirut*, x, 14; also PhM, 'Ab 3:16 (p. 434).
167. '*Akum*, ii, 1; ix, 1ff.; xii, 1 is noteworthy for its use of historical explanation (see below, chap. VI).
168. Interesting examples are found in *Bet hab-Bĕḥirah*, i, 17; *Tĕmidin*, i, 10.
169. '*Abel*, iv, 2, and note RaDBaZ, ad loc. See the statement of Sahl ben Maṣliaḥ in S. Pinsker, *Likkute Kadmoniyyot* (Wien, 1860), appendix, p. 31. See A. Ashtour, *Korot hay-Yĕhudim bi-Sĕfarad ham-Muslemit* (Jerusalem, 1966), II, 409–10, nn. 221, 230.

ments concerned with the prohibition of idolatry." In the *Mishneh Torah* the pagan aspect is secondary and derivative. Furthermore, the pagan connection is one of *several* reasons—"arrogance, extravagance, *and* idolatrous practice"—and since for Maimonides, generally, multiple motivation or explanation usually indicates lack of certitude, it certainly could not determine the halakic classification.

As a matter of fact, the laws of mourning in toto are missing from the *Guide*. In Chapter XXXV Maimonides describes the sixth class of his classification as containing *"most* of the matters we have enumerated in the *Book of Judges,"* while in Chapter XLI, after having fleshed out the basic reasons for the various subsections, Maimonides concludes that he "has explained the reasons for *all* the commandments" (italics mine) enumerated in the *Book of Judges*. It is immediately obvious that *Hilkot 'Abel* are conspicuous by their omission, and the reason seems equally transparent. In the *Guide* Maimonides sees death as something "which in true reality is salvation from death," for one's intellectual apprehension "becomes stronger at the separation" of soul from body. This is how Maimonides understands the Rabbinic interpretation of the verse, *So Moses . . . died there in the land of Moab by the mouth of the Lord* (Deut. 34:5), indicating that he "died by a kiss." Death by a kiss (*mitat nešikah*) really means "death which is a kiss," for after the apprehension of God "increases very powerfully, joy over this apprehension and a great love for the object of apprehension become stronger, until the soul is separated from the body at that moment in this state of pleasure."[170] Clearly there is no room for grief and mourning when death is viewed from such a perspective.

While the *Mishneh Torah* classification is sustained by a philosophic as well as a juridical sensibility, the former is clearly and appropriately subservient to the latter. There is even a difference between the kinds of explanations and rationalizations offered in the *Mishneh Torah* vis-à-vis those propounded in the *Guide:* the former are essentially ethical and philosophical, seeking to enhance the spirituality and meaningfulness of the

---

170. MN, III, 51.

normative act, whereas the latter, while clearly geared to ethical and philosophical goals, include also historical and psychological explanations which render the commandments more intelligible but not necessarily more edifying or spiritually repercussive.[171] In short, while the *Mishneh Torah* has an unmistakeable philosophic flavor, contains original explanations of laws stemming from philosophic or medical conceptions,[172] and even formulates laws because of certain philosophic emphases, the latter did not impinge on the book's classification.[173]

## Internal sequence and classification

Let us note finally that the arrangement of the fourteen books seems to have been clear in Maimonides' mind from the beginning. As best as can be determined—and the state of scholarship is such that we are very far from a thorough scientific study and evaluation of all manuscripts, early printed editions, quotations, and references[174]—there is no indication that Maimonides considered alternate arrangements of the fourteen books. Unlike changes in formulation, both stylistic and substantive, or in the sequence of paragraphs and chapters, and unlike even the considerations which led to the fusion of initially separate sections (e.g., *Šĕ'elah u-Fikkadon*), the underlying fourteen-book sequence is a constant.

There is, however, some proof that Maimonides did keep rethinking and sometimes revising the sequence of chapters within treatises;[175] that very dynamism which governed his ongoing search for the mot juste or his revision of individual halakic decisions was operative here as well. This is especially significant, for

171. See below, chap. VI.
172. See, e.g., '*Akum*, iv, 6, and MN, I, 54; *Roṣeaḥ*, ii, 14 (and iii, 4); '*Aḇel*, xiv, 5; and note the divergent reactions of KM and RaDBaZ (see J. Levinger, *Darke ham-Maḥšaḇah ha-Hilḵatit šel ha-RaMBaM* [Tel Aviv, 1965], pp. 102, 110).
173. On the relationship between the respective classifications of the *Mishneh Torah* and the *Guide*, see the appendix to this chapter, below, pp. 321–24.
174. See, e.g., the introduction of S. Z. Havlin to the Maḵor reprint (Jerusalem, 1972) of the 1509 Constantinople edition of the MT and his references to some of the important studies.
175. See the note (with bibliography) by M. Beit Arie in *Bulletin of the John Rylands University Library of Manchester*, LVII (1974), 1–6.

while Maimonides, as we have seen, did sometimes explain the reasons for grouping themes within one book, and furthermore explained the sequential relationship of certain books, he did not explain the internal sequence of various treatises and chapters. This became a major concern, rife with insight and hypothesis, of *Mishneh Torah* commentators; it is almost as if they repaid Maimonides for his efforts and tried to do for the *Mishneh Torah* what Maimonides had done for the Mishnah, sometimes using similar principles, constructing similar hypotheses, or reconstructing latent assumptions. The contribution of the author of the *Maggid Mishneh* is both pioneering and paradigmatic in this respect. He identified presumed principles of arrangement of major units within the various books as well as the sequence of chapters within those units themselves. He avers, for example, that *Nĕziḳin* (Torts) begins with *Nizḳe Mamon* (Damage by Chattels) because (a) this is the order of the Mishnah, and (b) Maimonides always moved from the more common to the less common.[176] This explanation is especially significant both for its use of multiple reasons and for its assumption of selective reliance by Maimonides upon the Mishnaic arrangement. RaDBaZ also notes the operation of general principles in the internal arrangement of sections and chapters; for example, Maimonides started *Zĕra'im* with *Kil'ayim* rather than with *Pe'ah*—as the Mishnah does—because (a) it follows directly from the end of *'Araḳin,* and (b) it is very inclusive, and Maimonides regularly starts with general (inclusive) matters.[177]

There can be little doubt but that the internal sequence of treatises and chapters is not haphazard and deserves careful study. As in other cases, comparison with other codes helps sharpen the focus. For example, while the *Šulḥan 'Aruḳ* presents the *ṭerefot* in anatomical fashion, from head to toe, Maimonides presents a topical division in eight groups: "eight such categories of *ṭerefah*

---

176. MM, introduction to *Sefer Nĕziḳin;* see also *Ta'āniyyot,* i, 14. Cf. in fact what Maimonides says (PhM, introduction [p. 27]) about *Ḥāgigah* coming at end of *Mo'ed.*
177. RaDBaZ, *Kil'ayim,* i, 1. Note that the arrangement of laws in the ShM is even more baffling and still awaits thorough analysis; cf. H. Tchernovitz, *Tolĕdot hap-Posĕḳim* (New York, 1947), II, 78; M. Peritz, "Das Buch der Gesetze," *MbM,* I, 445ff.; A. Hilvitz, "Seder ham-Miṣwot bĕ-Minyan šel ha-RaMBaM," *Sinai,* XIX (1946), 258ff.

were communicated to Moses from Sinai."[178] The former grouping may seem scientifically less sophisticated but is much more functional, and quite typical therefore of the utilitarian thrust of codification. The sequence of chapters in *Tĕfillah, Šabbaṭ,* or *'Aḇel* also readily reveals their latent rationales and conceptualizations.[179] In seeking to identify and unravel these rationales, as indeed in related matters, there is need to persist in careful analysis and disciplined conjecture without yielding to an impulse which converts reflections into realities or conjectures into certainties. It is generally possible to recognize the logical patterns, with occasional exceptions, governing the internal sequence and arrangement.

We should note, finally, an internal-literary aspect of classification within the broader scheme which this chapter has been examining, namely small internal groupings and genuine nuggets of classification. For example, *Gerušin* begins with a generalization: "There are ten rules that are basic to divorce, according to the Torah, and they are as follows. . . ." Each is then explained.[180] In Laws Concerning Prayer, Maimonides groups five prerequisites, the absence of which hinders prayer and necessitates its repetition, as distinct from eight prerequisites which should be complied with but whose absence does not necessitate repetition.[181] Maimonides' original ranking of the "eight degrees of charity, one higher than the other," has become a gem of Rabbinic literature, illustrating the need for sensitivity, tact, and graciousness in the performance of intrinsically benevolent deeds; the formal objective act of giving charity is deficient and defective

---

178. *Yoreh De'ah,* 30ff.; *Šĕḥiṭah,* v–x.
179. Note that *Tĕfillah,* xi, seems to be a bit problematic. The contents of *Šabbaṭ,* iii–v—a medley of laws concerning preparation for the Sabbath, continuation of work on the Sabbath which was begun on Friday, etc.—show some conceptual strains. *'Aḇel,* v–vi, is a model of "internal classification." Even the composition of individual chapters invites study; see, e.g., *Gĕneḇah,* ix, which combines kidnaping and "entering by breaking in," and *MM,* introduction to this section, whose explanation may reflect *MN,* III, 41 (p. 562). Note also *PhM, Kel* 1:6 (p. 49), where Maimonides stops to explain the sequence and structure of the chapter.
180. *Gerušin,* i, 1, referred to in *Tĕšuḇot,* 423 (p. 701).
181. *Tĕfillah,* iv and v. The classification rests upon many interpretative novelties. Study of the following examples will illumine this aspect of internal classification: *De'ot,* v; *Tĕfillah,* xv, 1; *Tĕfillin,* i, 3; *Sefer Torah,* x, 1; *Nĕḏarim,* iii, 1; *Šĕḥiṭah,* x, 9; *Bi'aṭ Mikdaš,* vii–viii; *Sanhedrin,* xix.

if it is not characterized by kindness and sympathy. Maimonides has eloquently elaborated the Talmudic dictum (B. Suk 49b) that "the reward of charity depends entirely upon the measure of kindness in it."[182] These not only are useful pedagogic devices but also contribute significantly to the conceptualization and systematization of the material.

When additional subject matter, not immediately reducible to straightforward halakic categories, is treated, Maimonides calls attention to it. At the beginning of *Těšubah*, for example, Maimonides has the following rubric: "and the explanation of this commandment, and of the principles which are drawn in its wake, is contained in the following chapters."

Maimonides' attention to the overall classification of halakah and the arrangement of the material in his *Mishneh Torah* on all levels was indeed thorough.

PROBLEM OF CONTRADICTIONS

The knotty problem of internal contradictions, which has preempted the energy and ingenuity of *Mishneh Torah* commentators through the ages—for it is particularly serious—is most appropriately viewed in the light of all that we have seen and inferred concerning Maimonides' relentless quest for exact conceptual classification, his use of the technique of splitting laws, and his reliance upon an interlocking network of cross-references in order to achieve precision and consistency. It is further accentuated by Maimonides' repeated insistence that he wrote with great care and deliberation, and that his ideas were fastidiously reasoned and thoughtfully arranged; he claims that there is nothing haphazard or incidental in his writing. His statements about patient and painstaking interpretation and sustained and relentless review of difficult matters also reinforce the need for careful and cautious study.[183] As a result, Maimonides' work was surrounded by an aura of impeccability, bordering on infallibility; his text was studied as meticulously as was the Talmud.[184]

---

182. *Mattěnot 'Āniyyim*, x, 7. Another good example is *Šě'ar 'Abot haṭ-Ṭumě'ot*, xii, 1.
183. See n.82, above; also chap. II, n.186, above.
184. See, e.g., references cited by Ch. Heller, *Sefer ham-Miṣwot*, introduction, p. 20. See Maimonides' own statement in *Těšubot*, 310 (p. 574).

## 312 INTRODUCTION TO THE CODE OF MAIMONIDES

Yet contradictions and difficulties, real or apparent, do exist. These involve both Maimonides' implied understanding of texts as well as the inner consistency of his views. In other words, the relation of a Maimonidean law to the Talmudic sources may sometimes seem baffling, and attempts to harmonize the two will be endlessly frustrating; sometimes the problem is in the relation of one Maimonidean formulation to another, which may also seem puzzling and actually defy reconciliation or harmonization. While *Quellenforschung* has been a basic aspect of Maimonidean scholarship, and indeed identification of an out-of-the-way source may resolve interpretative problems as well, such problems of interpretation or harmonization have always been at the very center of scholarly concern. One might even say that were it not for these troublesome features, set in the matrix of Maimonides' unusual authoritativeness and heroic stature, the great upsurge of *Mishneh Torah* analysis, commentary and supercommentary as well as selective annotation or elaboration, would not have sprouted wings. *Mishneh Torah* problems have held out a powerful lure to speculative reconstruction and have made the temptation to supply original commentary almost irresistible. This has merely accentuated the tendency of some scholars to substitute their own ingenuity for the author's genius, to use the *Mishneh Torah* as a mighty oak on which to hang their own theories and hypotheses. In any event, we should remember that Maimonides himself was already confronted by this problem of contradictions, as were his son and grandson, and they handled the issue with dexterity and objectivity.[185] In fact, they indicated some basic guidelines which were often ignored by later commentators, who seemed to prefer subtlety to simplicity, complex harmonization to direct resolution.

Without becoming overly technical or cumbersome, we may illustrate the kinds of contradictions that are found, note some of the answers that have been suggested or the approaches that have

---

185. E.g., *Tĕšuḇot*, 264 (p. 500); 315 (p. 585); 332 (p. 602); 344 (p. 616); *Tĕšuḇot R. Abraham*, ed. A. Freimann and S. Goitein (Jerusalem, 1937), 81; also *Birkat Abraham* (Lyck, 1859), 19; *Tĕšuḇot R. Joshua han-Nagid*, ed. A. Freimann and J. Rivlin (reprinted, Jerusalem, 1971). Most of these responsa of R. Joshua concern MT problems; see especially 1, 3, 14, 20, 32. On the problem of contradictions in Rashi, i.e. a commentary of massive dimensions, see the recent study of J. Frankel, *Darko šel Rashi* (Jerusalem, 1975).

## CLASSIFICATION

been used, and extract from all this some fundamental methodological directives. The following examples, intrinsically interesting, have been discussed by classical commentators and thus provide the detail necessary for any valid generalization. We cite them not to endorse or question the solutions but merely to establish a typology of approaches which were used repeatedly in various contexts.

1. In *Kĕri'at Šĕma'*, i, 7, Maimonides emphasizes the immutability of the formulae of benedictions (*bĕrakot*): "These blessings as well as all the other blessings . . . were instituted by Ezra and his court, and no one is permitted to diminish or augment their wording. . . . In short, whosoever alters the form which the Sages had given to the blessings commits an error and must repeat the blessing according to its prescribed form." In *Bĕrakot*, i, 4–5, Maimonides says: "The forms of all the blessings were established by Ezra and his court. It is not proper to alter them. . . . But if the form has been changed, the duty of reciting the blessing is discharged."

2. In *Sefer Torah*, vii, 16, Maimonides writes: "None of the Holy Scriptures may be written except on ruled lines, even if they are written on paper [i.e., not on parchment]. Three words of Scripture may be written without ruling the line, but to write more is forbidden." In *Yibbum*, iv, 5, however, Maimonides says that not even three words may be written: "In writing a writ of *ḥaliṣah* . . . the lines on which the Sciptural verses contained therein are written should be ruled, because one may not write three words from Scripture without ruling the line."

3. In *Šĕbu'ot*, i, 5, Maimonides describes the second of the four types of vain oaths as "stating that a known fact which no man doubts is indeed a fact. For example, one may swear that heaven is heaven . . . or that two are two, or anything similar to this. For no normal person is in any doubt about such a thing, that he should need to substantiate it by an oath." In a later chapter (v, 22) Maimonides qualifies this rule: "It is well known to wise men endowed with understanding and knowledge that the sun is one hundred and seventy times larger than the earth. If an ordinary person swears that the sun is larger than the earth, he is not liable to a flogging. . . . For although the fact is as stated, this is not commonly known to any but the eminent scholars, and no person

is liable unless he swears about a thing well known to at least three ordinary persons, e.g., that a man is a man."

4. In *Ma'ăkalot 'Ăsurot*, ix, 4, Maimonides writes that "meat of beast . . . cooked in the milk of a beast or of an animal is not forbidden to be eaten according to the Torah . . . but is forbidden on the authority of the Scribes." In *Mamrim*, ii, 9, he cites this as forbidden according to the Torah.

5. In *Talmud Torah*, v, 1, Maimonides formulates the relationship between one's obligations to father and teacher as follows:

Just as a person is commanded to honor and revere his father, so is he under an obligation to honor and revere his teacher, even to a greater extent than his father. . . . If he sees an article that his father had lost and another article that his teacher had lost, the teacher's property should be recovered first, and then the father's. . . . But if his father is a scholar, even though not of the same rank as his teacher, he should first recover his father's lost property and then his teacher's.

In *Gĕzelah wa-'Ăbedah*, xii, 2, we read that the father must be the scholarly peer of the teacher:

If one finds his teacher's lost property and his father's lost property, the rule is as follows: If his father is the equal of his teacher, his father's property takes precedence; if not, his teacher's property takes precedence, provided that he is his preeminent teacher, from whom he has learned most of his knowledge of the law.

The first contradiction has been disposed of by R. Elijah Gaon of Vilna in the straightforward terms of a change of mind.[186] He unequivocally rejects strained attempts by predecessors to harmonize the statements. This category of change of mind is of course frequently used to explain differences between the *Commentary of the Mishnah* and the *Mishneh Torah:* the author redefined his thinking or developed a different overview of the material. Maimonides himself noted on several occasions that he had changed his mind over the years, and that the interpretation embodied in the Code is the correct one.[187] The same is now applied

---

186. *'Oraḥ Ḥayyim*, 68:1.
187. *Tĕšubot*, 217 (p. 383); *Tĕšubot R. Elijah Mizraḥi* (Salonica, 1805), 5 (p. 18); see the examples discussed by S. Lieberman, *Hilkot Yĕrušalmi la-RaMBaM* (New York,

to shifts and inconsistencies within the *Mishneh Torah* itself. There are of course two implicit assumptions in this approach: (a) that Maimonides proceeded in the present order of the books, so that we are able to pinpoint the change and adopt the last statement as definitive;[188] (b) that his editorial revisions were incomplete and he failed to align earlier formulations with later conclusions or working assumptions with final directives.[189]

The second problem was forwarded to Maimonides' grandson, R. Joshua han-Nagid, who replied that the first formulation in *Hilkot Sefer Torah* is the authoritative and reliable one, because that is the prime locus for the discussion of this law, whereas in the other it is mentioned incidentally. In other words, there is here a real contradiction, and we should let the major context prevail, without attempting artificially to attenuate the contradiction. There is no reason to assume a change of mind, and certainly not to give normative preference to the last formulation. We have, in short, a new and pliable category: the context rule.[190]

The third instance was treated by RaDBaZ as a case of *kĕlal u-fĕrat:* a general and consciously and justifiably vague proposition vis-à-vis a specific formulation spelling out all qualifying facts, details, and nuances. There is no real contradiction, inasmuch as the first chapter was a general, bare-bones, preliminary categorization, whereas the fifth chapter was intended to provide a rounded, complete, practical codification. This rule of general followed by detail may be seen as a variation of the context rule,

---

1948), introduction, pp. 6ff. See also MN, introduction (seven causes for contradictions), where the second cause is: "The author of a particular book has adopted a certain opinion that he later rejects; both his original and later statements are retained in the book." This cause is cited in the strange defense of Maimonides penned by that enigmatic Moses Botarel; see J. Zussmann, *Kobeṣ 'al Yad*, VI (1966), 311.

188. See *Tĕšubot*, 332 (p. 602).

189. On editorial revision, see *Tĕšubot*, 345 (p. 618). There are, however, oral traditions concerning changes which were not recorded by Maimonides himself.

190. *Tĕšubot* R. Joshua han-Nagid, 14, and see p. 23, n.4. The phrase דדוכתא עדיפא is cited in *KM, Sefer Torah*, vii, 16. RaDBaZ, *Tĕšubot*, II, 1, 698, rules out the easy option of attributing this to a scribal error, for all manuscripts are identical. See on this principle, *Tosafot* to B. Ta 2a, s.v. *wĕ-litne*. See also *Bĕrakot*, ii, 10, 11, and *'Iṭuṭ*, x, 3 (and *Ma'ăśeh Rokeaḥ* ad loc.). This example is also pertinent to the problem of repetitions.

for the specific detailed context, rather than the vague anticipatory statement, is the determining one.[191]

The fourth case was approached by RaDBaZ and R. Joseph Karo as a situation in which only the first statement was normative, while the second was initially intended merely as an illustration and concretization of an abstract principle, and consequently Maimonides felt free to choose the most lucid and pointed example.[192] He need not be constrained by formal considerations and juridical applicability in his quest for a clear, persuasive, and enlightening example, inasmuch as the norm was not being infringed. It is noteworthy that this approach, which may be described as a pedagogic-heuristic rule, was used by other medieval Talmudists in confronting difficulties and inconsistencies in the Talmud itself.[193] It also has great affinity with the fifth of the seven causes of contradiction identified by Maimonides in the introduction to the *Guide:*

> The fifth cause arises from the necessity of teaching and making someone understand. For there may be a certain obscure matter that is difficult to conceive. One has to mention it or to take it as a premise in explaining something that is easy to conceive and that by rights ought to be taught before the former, since one always begins with what is easier. The teacher accordingly will have to be lax, and using any means that occur to him or gross speculation, will try to make that first matter somehow understood. He will not undertake to state the matter as it truly is in exact terms, but rather will leave it so in accord with the listener's imagination that the latter will understand only what he now wants him to understand. Afterward, in the appropriate place, that obscure matter is stated in exact terms and explained as it truly is.

The fifth contradiction was resolved by the *Haggahot Maymuniyyot* as a case where the first passage was simply corrupt and should be corrected in the light of the second. RaDBaZ re-

---

191. *Šěbu'ot*, i, 4. This is clearly an attractive approach considering Maimonides' many statements concerning the exactitude of his classification. See also *Sanhedrin*, v, 1; *Mělakim*, i, 3; cf. note of B. M. Lewin in *Kobeṣ RaMBaM*, p. 101, n.1, and H. A. Wolfson, *Philo*, II, 327, n. 41. Also, *Těfillah*, xii, 5; *Běrakot*, v, 2; and *Ma'ăśeh Roḳeaḥ*, ad loc.

192. RaDBaZ and *KM*, *Mamrim*, ii, 9.

193. R. Zerahiah hal-Levi, *Sefer ham-Ma'or, Baba Batra*, cited by B. Benedict, in his important article "'Al darko šel ha-RaMBaM," *Sefer hay-Yobel lě-R. Ḥănok Albeck* (Jerusalem, 1963), p. 68.

solved the contradiction by positing that Maimonides used different Talmudic texts at various stages of his writing and did not always correlate them.[194]

By far the most prevalent approach, which is sometimes used imperiously to the exclusion of all other possibilities, is to reconcile apparent contradictions, inconsistencies, and enigmas by discovering or imposing implicit conceptual rationales or ideational patterns. An example—symptomatic of the most subtle and sophisticated kinds of textual-topical analysis which has contributed to the emergence of an advanced halaḵic phenomenology—is whether Maimonides used *rěḇi'iṯ* (a quarter-loḡ, a liquid measure equal to 549 cc.) or *kě-zayiṯ* (bulk of an olive) as the term of measurement to define the liquid quantity that must be consumed in certain legal contexts. A review of diverse formulations underscores the apparent lack of uniformity: Maimonides sometimes uses the liquid measure and sometimes the solid measure in defining liquid quantities. For example, a Nazirite who drinks a *rěḇi'iṯ* of wine or of a mixture of wine and vinegar is culpable.[195] One who drinks a *rěḇi'iṯ* of heathen wine "is liable to the flogging prescribed for disobedience." [196] With regard to juice extracted from the *ṭeḇel* fruits (which have not yet been tithed), from new produce, from sacred produce, or from the spontaneous growth of the Sabbatical year, the minimum amount is an olive's bulk.[197] This lack of uniformity is then explained, independently of any explicit Maimonidean rule or even intimation, by discerning a latent conceptual premise. If the prohibition applies primarily to eating—and drinking is a derivative prohibition—the solid measure (*kě-zayiṯ*) will be used. If, on the other hand, the prohibition applies directly to drinking—this is an independent primary prohibition and not a derivative secondary one—the liquid measure will be used.[198]

---

194. *Gězelah*, xii, 2; see G. Blidstein, *Honor Thy Father and Mother* (New York, 1975), p. 216. In another context, *KM, Beṯ hab-Běḥirah*, iii, 18, resolves a contradiction with *Bi'aṯ Miḵdaš*, v, 14, by positing that Maimonides followed two different interpretations of the underlying text.
195. *Něziruṯ*, v, 2, 3; see also *Ma'ăśer Šeni*, ii, 5.
196. *Ma'ăḵaloṯ 'Ăsuroṯ*, xi, 3.
197. Ibid., x, 9, 22, 24.
198. *Sefer ha-Ḥinnuḵ*, 148, 443, and commentary *Minḥaṯ Ḥinnuḵ*, ad loc. Rabbi J. B. Soloveitchik applied this distinction to *Šěḇu'oṯ*, iv, 3 (where no measure is mentioned), and

Now the validity, legitimacy, and cogency of these kinds of integrative-holistic conceptualizations are beyond question. They are general canons of any scholarly methodology which is determined to treat major works seriously. They oppose the arbitrariness, sometimes the whimsicality, of assuming that incongruous formulations or antithetical interpretations were mindlessly joined by a respected author. They reject the literary assumption of a hurried scissors-and-paste operation or the convenient method of resolving problems by pointing out "the interpolative character of the passages." They assume that the language of such an author is precise and purposive, not haphazard or fortuitous. Moreover, Maimonides himself suggests this general approach, in the realm of philosophy and aggadah, of interpreting parts in the light of the whole, rather than dismissing them as wayward or incomprehensible. A clearly discernible tendency should guide the understanding of an opaque detail. One needs an Archimedean point in relation to which divergent emphases or centrifugal passages may be properly and harmoniously interpreted.[199] Furthermore, with regard to the *Mishneh Torah* specifically, he handled certain alleged contradictions which were brought to his attention by indicating the existence of conceptual differences, special contexts, or divergent emphases, fully aware as he was of various degrees of tension between abstract conceptual analysis and literal textual explication, and of the need to differentiate carefully between various texts and contexts.[200] Sometimes the text has to be straitened in order to get it to conform to a logical distinction. It is noteworthy that this kind of conceptualization was taking root in Talmudic study during this period, and contemporary critics-commentators of the *Mishneh Torah* were beginning to utilize it. RABD, for example, concludes an original explanation of a text with this final word of persuasion: "The matter should be explained in this way, even though the language of the text is not clear in the light of this explanation."[201] On

---

ibid., iv, 4 (where *rěbi'it* is mentioned). The proximity of statements clearly lends urgency to the problem. See *Těšubot*, 264 (p. 500) and LM, '*Akum*, ii, 5.
199. *Těšubot*, 436 (pp. 715–16). See H. A. Wolfson, *Studies in the History of Philosophy and Religion*, ed. I. Twersky and G. Williams (Cambridge, 1973), pp. 2–3.
200. See above, n.185.
201. *Peruš Baba Kamma*, ed. S. Atlas (London, 1940), p. 57.

another occasion, cognizant that his redeeming interpretation of a seemingly erroneous statement in the *Mishneh Torah* does not dovetail with the obvious sense of Maimonides' words, he comments that "even though his language does not indicate this, reason points to it."[202] In some respects one may find here an anticipation of the modern concepts of literary criticism, which see the author's intention and the commentator's interpretation as forming one continuum, a "hermeneutic circle."

In sum, then, genuine contradictions may be acknowledged and handled by applying one of the various rules: (1) change of mind; (2) major or primary versus incidental context; (3) brief, usually preliminary, generalization vis-à-vis a full, detailed specification; (4) a normative formulation as distinct from an illustrative point; (5) textual corruption and/or use of different Talmudic texts at different times. In addition, apparent contradictions may be typologically harmonized or conceptually interpreted away. Of course this method of abstraction and conceptualization—which is utilized to deal with all kinds of difficulties and apparent innovations, deviations, or transformations—requires restraint. If it is to combine real inventiveness and creativity with faithfulness to the author's intentions and motivations, it must submit itself to the constraints of textual-conceptual reasonableness and compatibility.[203] Moreover, certain obvious, almost tangible, checks and balances for unfettered conceptualization should always be taken into account. There is the need for a horizontal perspective: Maimonides' own explanatory statements in his other writings, particularly in his responsa, should be heeded.[204] Help is also

---

202. *Sukkah*, vi, 11; *Bikkurim*, vii, 9. See also RITBA, *Sefer ha-Zikkaron*, ed. K. Kahana (Jerusalem, 1955), pp. 44, 52 (דוחק בלשון ולא בענין). R. Zerahiah hal-Levi cautions that the semantics of a word may change from one context to another; *Sefer has-Saba*, rule 2, in *Těmim De'im* (reprinted, Jerusalem, 1960), p. 110. Words of caution about the need for conformity between interpretation and text may be found, e.g., in Naḥmanides, *Ḥiddušim, Baba Baṯra*, 121. For the hermeneutic circle, see Paul de Man, *Blindness and Insight: Essays in the Rhetoric of Contemporary Criticism* (Oxford, 1971). Irene Chayes provides a useful review in "Revisionist Literary Criticism," *Commentary*, LXI (1976), pp. 65–69. Note also ham-Me'iri, BK, p. 119.

203. See *Birkaṯ Abraham*, 19.

204. E.g., *Ḥameṣ u-Maṣṣah*, vii, 1, and ShM, positive 157, where Maimonides cites the Měkilta; *Těšuḇoṯ*, 344 (p. 616). Maimonides explains explicitly the genesis of his codificatory presentation in his Talmudic interpretation. Certain halakic-conceptual difficulties of his formulation notwithstanding, he maintains his view and contends that he,

forthcoming from paleography and diplomatics—sustained attempts to determine the correct Maimonidean text in order to guarantee that one is interpreting Maimonides rather than a sloppy scribe or a careless copyist. This extends not only to the obvious area of manuscript evidence for divergent readings but even to the matter of punctuation and sentence structure; sometimes tough problems may be resolved and tantalizing formulations smoothed over by shifting the period, i.e., dividing the paragraphs differently.[205] Such considerations and guidelines will also eliminate or at least reduce the dangers of overinterpretation, which are especially acute when (a) the interpreter assumes that the author being studied is careful and precise, and (b) attempts consequently to harmonize all passages and do away with all apparent contradictions. Maimonides would certainly say that abstraction and conceptualization should supplement rather than supplant these other principles and procedures which are supportive of all interpretation. Obvious solutions should be used before resorting to hypothesis and speculative reconstruction.

---

logically and consciously, derived it from his interpretation of the Mishnah. The same often applies to contradictions. Something appears to us as a contradiction only if we presume a certain kind of explanation of a text or reconciliation of texts. In cases where Maimonides reveals his interpretation, the alleged contradiction melts away.

205. E.g., *Talmud Torah*, i, 2–3, and commentary '*Ăbodat ha-Melek*, ad loc.; *Mĕlakim*, vi, 16; vii, 1; RABD, ad loc., and Ch. Heller, *Sefer ham-Miṣwot*, positive 191 (p. 83, n.8).

## Appendix: Relationship between the Classifications of the *Mishneh Torah* and the *Guide*

It is important to remember that the fourteen classes of the MN (III, 35), which correspond only numerically to the fourteen books of the MT, are reducible to the three underlying motives or goals of the law: intellectual, moral, and practical-social. In other words, three classes would have sufficed for the *Moreh*'s philosophic classification. Maimonides himself then notes in a striking way the relationship between his threefold classification and the twofold Talmudic classification of commandments between man and his fellow man and between man and God. (See the end of the MT introduction, where Book Eleven is said to begin the commandments between man and fellow man: "Among the classes we have differentiated and enumerated, the fifth, sixth, seventh, and a portion of the third belong to the group devoted to the relation between man and his fellow man, while all the other classes deal with the relation between man and God. For every commandment, whether it be a prescription or a prohibition, whose purpose it is to bring about the achievement of a certain moral quality, or of an opinion, or the rightness of actions, which only concerns the individual himself and his becoming more perfect, is called by the Sages a commandment dealing with the relation between man and God, even though in reality it sometimes may affect relations between man and his fellow man. But this happens only after many intermediate steps and through comprehensive considerations, and it does not lead from the beginning to harming a fellow man. Understand this.")

|  | *Mishneh Torah* | *Moreh Nĕbukim* |
|---|---|---|
| Book 1. | Madda' | Class 1 |
|  | De'ot[206] | 3 |
|  | 'Ăbodah Zarah | 2 |

---

206. In MN, III, 38, Maimonides states that "certain commandments also contain prescriptions that are intended to lead to the acquisition of a useful moral quality, even if they prescribe certain actions that are deemed to be merely *decreed by Scripture* and not to

322 INTRODUCTION TO THE CODE OF MAIMONIDES

| 2. | 'Ahăḇah | 9 |
|---|---|---|
|  | Milah | 14 |
| 3. | Zĕmannim[207] | 8 |
|  | Ta'ăniyyoṯ | 1 |
| 4. | Našim | 14 |
| 5. | Ḳĕdušah | 13 |
|  | 'Issure Bi'ah | 14 |
|  | Laws Concerning Blood (Ma'ăḵaloṯ 'Ăsuroṯ, vi; Šĕḥiṭah, xiv)[208] | 11 |
| 6. | Hafla'ah | 13 |
|  | Šĕḇu'oṯ | 1 |
|  | 'Ărakin | 4 |
| 7. | Zĕra'im | 4 |
|  | Kil'ayim and 'Orlah | 2 |
|  | Kil'e Bĕhemah | 14 |
| 8. | 'Ăḇoḏah: Beṯ hab-Bĕḥirah, Kĕle ham-Miḳdaš, Bi'aṯ Miḳdaš | 10 |
|  | Remaining sections | 11 |
| 9. | Ḳorbanoṯ | 11 |
| 10. | Ṭohăroṯ | 12 |
| 11. | Nĕziḳin | 5 |
| 12. | Ḳinyan | 7 |
|  | 'Ăḇaḏim | 4 |
| 13. | Mišpaṭim | 7 |
|  | Malweh wĕ-Loweh | 4 |
| 14. | Šofĕṭim | 6 |

The fourteen classes of the MN, in turn, are subject to the following breakdown:

---

have a purpose. We will explain them one by one in their proper places" (italics mine). Were his teleological explanation to prevail, these commandments would be lifted from their contexts and placed together in class three. Even in the *Moreh* Maimonides does not operate with such a system.

207. All festivals are explained in MN, III, 43. Maimonides states that "the Biblical text gives the reasons for all of them except a few," and his explanation is taken to be an elaboration of the Biblical suggestions. It is no wonder, consequently, that no explanation is presented for Purim and Hanukkah. This "Biblicism" is crucial for many problems, e.g., "an eye for an eye" in MN, III, 48.

208. Maimonides does not give reference in class eleven of MN to these sections of the MT but does deal at length with the prohibition of the consumption of blood and the commandments concerning the sprinkling of blood or the covering of blood.

Classes 1, 2, 9, 10, 11, 12   a) intellectual
3, 13, 14                      b) moral
4, 5, 6, 7                     c) practical
8                              a) and c)

Other classes, e.g., 3, might also have a dual grouping, b and c, for they have practical repercussions as well.

## V

## Language and Style

It is not surprising that Maimonides, totally absorbed in matters of law and philosophy in connection with the most ambitious and imaginative codification and interpretation of halakah ever to be produced, deliberated at great length concerning the language and style of his work. Language was merely an instrument, a medium of communication with no self-transcending worth or metaphysical significance, and importance inhered exclusively in the subject matter being studied. In the age-old controversy concerning the nature and origin of language—is it natural or conventional?—Maimonides espoused the conventional view of language.[1] Nevertheless, a basic congruence between content and

---

1. See, e.g., *De'ot*, ii, 4; *Ķeri'at Šema'*, iii, 4, 5; *Ķobeṣ*, II, 12a, 15b; PhM, 'Ab 1:16 (p. 417). For Maimonides' nonmetaphysical view of Hebrew, see MN, III, 8 (p. 435). A Maimonidean follower, Joseph ibn Kaspi, asserts in a very positivistic manner that Hebrew is a holy tongue because it is grammatically correct; see *'Ăśarah Kĕle Ķesef*, ed. I. Last (Pressburg, 1903), II, 17. Note Judah hak-Kohen, in B. Dinur, *Yiśra'el bag-Golah* (Jerusalem, 1962), II, pt. VI, p. 19 (it is the oldest language) and P. Duran, *Ma'ăśeh 'Efod*, p. 177. Language, in Maimonides' view (MN, II, 30 [p. 357]), is conventional; see also R. Moses ibn Ezra, *Širat Yiśra'el*, ed. B. Halper (Leipzig, 1924), p. 54; and R. Abraham ibn Ezra, *Peruś*, Gen. 11:7. Cf. R. Judah hal-Levi, *Kuzari*, II, 72; Naḥmanides, *Peruś*, Exod. 30:13; and "Ma'ămar 'al Pĕnimiyyut hat-Torah," *Kitbe RaMBaN*, ed. C. Chavel (Jerusalem, 1964), II, 467; and H. A. Wolfson, *Religious Philosophy* (Cambridge, 1961), pp. 230ff. Concerning language, see the dissertations of M. Idel on R. Abraham Abulafia (Jerusalem, 1976), I, 148, and S. Rosenberg on Logic and Ontology (Jerusalem, 1974), I, 165ff. For *Ķeri'at Šema'*, ii, 10, see most recently J. Levinger, *Darke ha-Maḥšabah*, p. 187.

Maimonides' desacralization of language should be seen as an expression of his consistent opposition to hypostatized entities endowed with intrinsic sanctity; see *Mĕzuzah*, v, 4; *Sefer Torah*, x, 10, 11; *Šĕbu'ot*, xi, 14 (and RaDBaZ); MN, I, 67, Note also the analysis of *ķĕdušah*, above, chap. IV, and below, chap. VI.

Aspects of the Islamic discussion of these problems are covered by H. Loucel, "L'Origine du language d'après les grammairiens arabes," *Arabica*, X (1963), 188ff.; XI (1964), 57; L. Kopf, "Religious Influences on Medieval Arabic Philology," *Studia Islamica*, V (1956), 33ff.; R. Arnaldez, *Grammaire et Theologie chez Ibn Hazm* (Paris, 1956); M. Mahdi, "Language and Logic in Classical Islam," *Logic in Classical Islamic Culture*, ed. G. E. von Grunebaum (Wiesbaden, 1970), pp. 51ff.

form was imperative.[2] A writer conscious of the fact that the faculty of oral and written expression is a gracious gift of God, should thoughtfully choose his language and carefully determine the characteristics of his style, ever mindful of his audience and the goals of his composition.[3] There was no room or excuse for slovenliness; hasty writing, like shabby thinking, was intolerable. Inasmuch as language was inherently problematic—restrictive and deceptive, occasionally frustrating and misleading, so that ideas sometimes defied precise and meaningful expression—there was a greater imperative for care and exactitude.[4] The transition from thought or monologue to communication or dialogue was complicated, calling for constant exertion. Maimonides, as we shall see, sought a language suitable to his literary-pedagogic aims of reformulating the totality of halakah for the entire Jewish people, that (a) would be readily intelligible to the greatest number of readers; (b) would be flexible, rich, and expressive; and (c) would enable him to write with precision, brevity, and elegance.

THREE OPTIONS

There were three genuine options for Maimonides in deciding upon the language of the *Mishneh Torah:* Biblical Hebrew, Aramaic, and Mishnaic Hebrew; or the language of the Bible, the language of the Talmud, and the language of the Mishnah, the three classical, normative, and universally acknowledged texts of Judaism. He weighed these options carefully and explained curtly but clearly why he chose the latter.

The language of the Bible was dismissed because of its literary inadequacy and historical atrophy. Underlying Maimonides' pointed rejection of Biblical Hebrew—"I deemed it advisable not

---

2. B. Halper, introduction to R. Ḥefeṣ ben Yaṣliaḥ's *Sefer ham-Miṣwot*, p. 90: "The majority of post-Biblical writers were slovenly in their syntactical constructions. To them the matter was the dominant factor and the style played no important role." See also E. M. Lifshitz, *Kĕtabim* (Jerusalem, 1947), II, 144.

3. *Ma'amar Kiddus haš-Šem*, in *Kobeṣ*, II, 12a; MN, III, 8; MTH, 37.

4. ShM, *šoreš* 14 (II, 425); MN, I, 50 (p. 112): "Those who represent the truth to themselves and apprehend it, even if they do not utter it"; MN, I, 57 (p. 132): "For the bounds of expression in all languages are very narrow indeed." See R. Abraham ibn Ezra, *Peruš*, Dan. 1:4.

326 INTRODUCTION TO THE CODE OF MAIMONIDES

to compose this work in the language of the Prophetic Books, since that sacred language is too limited for us today"[5]—is the idea widespread among Jewish writers of Spain (at least from the time of R. Menahem ben Saruk) that the twenty-four books of the Bible represent only a fraction of the treasures of Biblical Hebrew.[6] Actually, there seem to be two interpretative strands interwoven here. The inadequacy of Hebrew could be explained in the light of either socio-historical contingencies or intrinsic and apparently irremediable limitations. The socio-historical explanation is suggested by R. Moses ibn Ezra, for example, who echoes the opinion that this sad linguistic situation could have been avoided had his predecessors adopted a more vigorous and fastidious attitude toward Hebrew, and he consequently feels justified in indicting "our ancestors who were indolent." Had they persisted in their efforts to sustain and develop the Hebrew language, its impoverishment and enfeeblement could have been arrested.[7] This view is causally expanded by some writers, who relate the decline and decomposition of Hebrew to the dispersion and its anomalous political conditions. R. Judah hal-Levi's well-known observation-lamentation focuses on this aspect: "[The Hebrew language] shared the fate of its bearers, degenerating and dwindling with them."[8] Somewhat earlier R. Saadiah Gaon bewailed the fact that the "nation forgot its language."[9] The second type of explanation, leaving neglect, accident, and inadvertence aside, is propounded by R. Abraham ibn Ezra who affirms that even though the holy tongue was formerly the most

---

5. ShM, introduction.
6. R. Menahem ben Saruk, *Maḥberet*, ed. Z. Filipovsky (Edinburgh, 1854), p. 12; *Tĕšubot Talmide Menahem*, ed. Z. Stern (Vienna, 1870); see generally W. Bacher, *R. Abraham ibn Ezra ham-Mĕdakdek*, tr. A. Z. Rabinovitz (Tel Aviv, 1931), pp. 28ff.; A. Halkin, "The Medieval Jewish Attitude toward Hebrew," *Biblical and Other Studies*, ed. A. Altmann (Cambridge, 1963), pp. 232–48.
7. R. Moses ibn Ezra, *Širaṭ Yiśra'el*, pp. 59–60. See also R. Joseph Ḳimḥi, *Sefer hag-Galuy* (Berlin, 1887), p. 3; R. David Ḳimḥi, *Sefer ham-Miklol* (Jerusalem, 1965), p. 1. On the linguistic decline in exile, see also Ibn Aknin as cited by A. Halkin, *Joshua Starr Memorial Volume* (New York, 1953), p. 105.
8. *Kuzari*, II, 68. This parallels the socio-historical explanation for the general intellectual decline in the face of adversity; see MN, I, 71.
9. R. Saadiah Gaon, *Sefer hag-Galuy*, ed. A. Harkavy, *Zikkaron la-Rišonim* (St. Petersburg, 1892), pp. 154–56.

commodious language of all, it is now deficient, seriously restricted, and handicapped. He does not speak of neglect on the part of those who could and should have nurtured its uninterrupted development. The fact is that the prophetic authors preserved that part of the language which happened to be relevant to, and necessary for, their purposes; other parts of classical Hebrew, once a pliant, elegant, and fully expressive medium, were forgotten, irretrievably so.[10] Given the expanded needs of communication and composition, Biblical Hebrew is a permanently pale and atrophied phenomenon.

These two explanations are sometimes fused. A good example is R. Judah ibn Tibbon's balanced introduction to his Hebrew translation of Ḥoḇoṯ hal-Lĕḇaḇoṯ. He cites the restrictive and "underdeveloped" nature of Hebrew as one of the reasons for the fact that most Spanish and Gaonic authors chose to compose their works in Arabic rather than in Hebrew; the former is "an adequate and rich language," while the latter does not enable a writer to express his thoughts "succinctly and eloquently."[11] His son Samuel repeats this evaluation of the inadequacy of Hebrew.[12] In a word, Arabic was superior simply because it continued uninterruptedly to develop, and hence its literary resilience was notable and its rhetorical powers were great, while Hebrew did not continue to grow organically. Furthermore, Hebrew is intrinsically limited because "we possess only that which is in the books of Scripture," and that does not suffice.[13] From this

---

10. R. Abraham ibn Ezra, *Peruš*, Song of Songs, end: כי לא נדע מלה"ק כי אם הכתוב במקרא שהוצרכו הנביאים לדבר; R. Moses ibn Ezra, *Širaṭ Yiśra'el*, p. 54, also records this view. See E. Fleischer in *Lĕšonenu*, XXXVI (1972), 314–15, who uses this opinion to explain Ibn Ezra's introductory poem to Job.

11. *Ḥoḇoṯ hal-Lĕḇaḇoṯ*, ed. A. Zifroni (Jerusalem, 1928), translator's introduction, p. 2; also translator's introduction to R. Jonah ibn Janāḥ, *Sefer ha-Riḳmah*, ed. M. Wilensky (Berlin, 1929), pp. 2ff.

12. Preface, *Peruš ham-Milloṭ ha-Zaroṭ*, supplement to MN, ed. J. Even Shemuel (Jerusalem, 1947), p. 11.

13. *Ḥoḇoṯ hal-Lĕḇaḇoṯ*, ed. A. Zifroni, p. 2. A similar combination of the historic-sociological explanation with the intrinsic limitation is found in R. Moses ibn Gikatilia's introduction to the Hebrew translation of Judah Ḥayyūj; see *Šĕlošah Sifre Diḳduḳ*, ed. J. W. Nutt (London, 1870), p. 1; also Judah al-Ḥarīzī, *Taḥkĕmoni*, introduction. Nethaneel ha-Rofe', translator of PhM, Ḳodašim, refers only to a sociological explanation: Hebrew was adequate but Arabic was better known.

vantage point, Arabic is superior simply because Biblical Hebrew is incomplete.

In the context of his discussion of the names of God, Maimonides says parenthetically: "Perhaps it indicates the notion of a necessary existence, according to the Hebrew language, of which we today know only a very scant portion."[14] This supplements the statement in the introduction to *Sefer ham-Miṣwot* that the "language of the Prophetic Books" is "too limited for us today."

14. MN, I, 61 (p. 148); also I, 67 (p. 162).
The conceptual-philological implication of Maimonides' position needs to be clarified. The view which characterized Biblical Hebrew as self-contained and incomplete, thereby demarcating sharply between it and post-Biblical Hebrew, is intelligible and defensible in either (1) the metaphysical or (2) the grammatical category: (1) the fact that Biblical Hebrew is the holy tongue dramatically endows it with a metaphysical status—it possesses a special quality (*sĕġulah*) which renders it unique, transcending all other languages; (2) only Biblical Hebrew is characterized by linguistic purity and grammatical consistency. Now it happens that neither of these categories is Maimonidean.
Unlike such writers as R. Menahem ben Saruḳ (*Maḥberet*, p. 10), R. Saadiah Gaon (*Sefer ha-'Egron*, p. 55), R. Solomon ibn Gabirol (*Širim*, ed. Bialik and Ravnitzky, I, 176), R. Judah hal-Levi (*Kuzari*, II, 81), R. Joseph Ḳimḥi (*Sefer hag-Galuy*, p. 3), and others, who harp upon the intrinsic sanctity, metaphysical uniqueness, and transcendental status of the language, Maimonides disavows this completely. He does not talk about the "wonderful character of our language" (hal-Levi) which was created by God or "which the angels use to sing praises to Him" (Saadiah). In the ShM introduction, he does not even use the term *lĕšon haḳ-ḳodeš* (see *Tĕfillah*, i, 4; *Kĕri'at Šĕma'* ii, 10). In fact, he suggests (MN, III, 8) a radically different criterion for evaluating the greatness and distinctiveness of Hebrew. In his opinion, Hebrew is a holy tongue because it has no words which "according to their first meaning" designate sex organs or sexual activity—an explanation, we may note, which had little resonance in Jewish thought and which was roundly repudiated by Naḥmanides, *Peruš*, Exod. 30:13. Furthermore (PhM, Ter 1: 1 [p. 269]), he defends the purity and authenticity of Mishnaic Hebrew, including apparently novel forms, and postulates an organic relationship between it and earlier forms of Hebrew. What then is meant by asserting that Biblical Hebrew is "too limited"? Why could he not consider Hebrew as a composite of its Biblical and post-Biblical strands? We may surmise that he recognized Biblical Hebrew as a linguistic type, contained in the twenty-four Prophetic Books or used in its classical form by such writers as R. Judah hal-Levi, and felt that it would be improper to mix types, for this, too, would be a kind of hybridization. As we shall see, Mishnaic Hebrew, logically and historically, incorporated parts of Biblical Hebrew. When R. Judah ibn Tibbon concludes his statement (see above, n. 11) with the remark that he innovated grammatically and morphologically by introducing new forms "not found in the Hebrew language," he is clearly referring to forms not found in Biblical Hebrew; cf. R. Abraham ibn Ezra's critique (*Peruš*, Eccles. 5:1) of R. Eleazar haḳ-Ḳalir for his undisciplined use of post-Biblical neologisms. In fact, Ibn Tibbon apologizes for actually fusing Biblical and post-Biblical Hebrew as well as for introducing foreign forms. Note R. Joseph Ṭob 'Elem, *Ṣafnat Pa'neaḥ*, ed. D. Herzog (Heidelberg, 1911), p. 7, who

Whatever the underlying reasons, Spanish-Jewish writers, including Maimonides, were unequivocally saying that Biblical Hebrew was too restricted for the expanded needs of contemporary writing. While the usual corollary was the inevitability of linguistic assimilation—i.e., of the use of Arabic, which was both adequate and well known—in this case Maimonides, as we shall see, charted an alternate course.

The language of the Talmud was deemed inappropriate because of its difficulty and unintelligibility; even dedicated students, immersed in its study and interpretation, were frequently stumped and frustrated. Aramaic was becoming increasingly arcane and esoteric, the learned jargon of Rabbinic scholars. On the one hand, it was developing and transforming itself, so that the Babylonian Aramaic of the tenth century was no longer identical with Talmudic Aramaic, which now required special philological study. Knowledge of it could no longer be assumed or routinely acquired. The study of Talmud had now to be accompanied by the study of language, a situation reminiscent of Jonah ibn Janāḥ's passionate contention that grammar and lexicography were indispensable for study of the Bible. On the other hand, Arabic, riding the crest of a triumphant empire and a sophisticated culture, was making steady inroads and was gradually but irreversibly crowding Aramaic out of the picture.[15] Maimonides is most probably alluding to these facts when in the introduction to the *Mishneh Torah* he notes the philological and conceptual difficulties of Talmud study: "Furthermore, the Talmud is composed in Aramaic mixed with other languages, this having been

---

defends Ibn Ezra's use of Biblical Hebrew, inasmuch as that "is the holy tongue and in it were the prophecies written." Moreover, the language of the Rabbis "is not Hebrew but Aramaic." On mixed Biblical-Rabbinic Hebrew in medieval poetry, see D. Pagis, *Ḥiddušī u-Masoreṯ bĕ-Šīraṯ ha-Ḥol* (Jerusalem, 1976), pp. 182ff.

15. See J. Blau in *Lěšonenu*, XXVI (1962), 281–84. It has been argued that the use of Aramaic (particularly the use of the Targum) had lost its importance and popularity not because of the ascendancy of Arabic but because of the revival of Hebrew; see H. Z. Hirschberg, "The Aramaic Targumim," *Bar Ilan Annual*, I (1963), 22. On the linguistic mutations of Aramaic, see, e.g., J. N. Epstein, *Diḳduḳ 'Āramiṯ Baḇliṯ* (Jerusalem, 1960), pp. 3ff.; B. Dinur, *Yiśra'el bag-Golah*, I, pt. IV, pp. 369–70 (and notes). Such Hebrew halaḳic works as *Hilḳoṯ Rē'u* and *Sefer wĕ-Hizhir*—early attempts to reverse the trend away from Hebrew—should be reviewed in this context. See also L. Ginzberg, *Ginze Schechter* (New York, 1928), II, 375–78 (a fragment of B. 'Er in Hebrew translation).

the vernacular of the Babylonian Jews *at the time* when it was compiled. In other countries, however, and similarly in Babylon in the days of the Geonim, no one, unless specially taught, understood that dialect" (italics mine). Even the Talmud was, with steadily increasing momentum, studied and discussed in Arabic; responsa and commentaries were composed in Arabic.[16] Maimonides could, therefore, record as a matter of unimpeachable historical fact that Babylonian Aramaic was too archaic and artificial for the purposes of an ambitious reformulation of the halakah.

His decision to compose the *Mishneh Torah* "in the language of the Mishnah, so that it should be easily understood by the greatest number of people" was thus the natural and unavoidable conclusion. Maimonides had in an earlier work, probably following the lead of Ibn Janāḥ and Moses ibn Ezra, defended the purity of Mishnaic Hebrew against grammarians (e.g., R. Menaḥem ben Saruḳ) who rather disdainfully questioned some of the morphology and vocabulary of the Mishnah. He contended vigorously and effectively that language is a living organism and its "correctness" (its "principles") is determined by the usage of the speakers of that language. The Tannaim were clearly "Hebrews in the Land of Israel"—historic-territorial continuity seems to be of the essence—and this stamps their language as authoritative.[17] Maimonides was brief but forceful. He considered his statement

16. E.g., S. D. Goitein, *Sidre Ḥinnuk mit-Tēḳufaṭ hag-Gē'onim 'ad Bēṭ ha-RaMBaM* (Jerusalem, 1962), and Blau, *Lĕšonenu*, XXVI, 281.
   Maimonides' statement about the difficulty and diversity of Aramaic also helps explain the purely lexical nature of a major part of Gaonic commentary; see Twersky, *Rabad*, pp. 60–61.

17. PhM, Ter 1: 1 (p. 269). See R. Jonah ibn Janāḥ, *Sefer ha-Riḳmah*, p. 19, and R. Moses ibn Ezra, *Širaṭ Yiśra'el*, pp. 60–61; R. Abraham ibn Ezra, *Ṣafah Bĕrurah*, p. 13. See also R. Saadiah Gaon, *ha-'Egron*, p. 32; R. Abraham ibn Ezra, *Sefer Moznayim*, introduction; R. Solomon Parḥon, *Maḥbereṭ he-'Aruḳ*, p. xxii. Maimonides' statement clearly underlies the more rambling formulation of R. Tanḥum Yerushalmi, tr. A. Halkin, "The Medieval Jewish Attitude toward Hebrew," p. 247: "There are words in the Mishnah, nouns and verbs, which are formed contrary to the known usage of the roots of the language. . . . The same method is followed in other books of law, and the words have been adopted by the community. Some modern philologans, however, reject it and call this practice an inadmissible error. . . . All this, however, is sound. . . . But the clinching reply to these arguments and to similar objections is to say that the Hebrew language was not encompassed in its entirety in the available Biblical texts, nor did those whose words

about the purity of Mishnaic Hebrew a paradigmatic retort against all "moderns" who denigrated the language of the Mishnah as unclear and incorrect. Scholars who are able to generalize about languages, Maimonides avers, will endorse his approach. Now here, in revealing his decision about the language in which the *Mishneh Torah* was to be written, Maimonides is quite restrained, almost reticent, about the potential as well as the limitations of Mishnaic Hebrew and the unhappy linguistic situation in general, restricting his hurried comment to the greater popularity and intelligibility of Mishnaic Hebrew. His reticence at this point—both his failure to echo the common laments about the sorry state of contemporary Hebrew and his silence about his own stylistic innovations and linguistic creativity—should not mislead the reader. The literary phenomenon which is the *Mishneh Torah* is not merely a stylistic mimesis, the result of following or even adapting Mishnaic Hebrew. The latter was a notable paradigm of fluent, flexible, yet precise formulation. Maimonides' Hebrew, however, was a new virtuoso creation, molded by his genius for the specific literary needs at hand.[18] He chose that form of Hebrew which was most resilient

---

are recorded in these texts intend to expound the principles of the language and to list its legitimate practices; no, they said what was needed at the time. If more words were recorded, we might perhaps find in them what we have today. Since we find these forms used by our ancients, who were nearer than we to the time of the development of the language and the spread of its practices . . . we know for sure that it was permissible." Maimonides will occasionally and quite parenthetically formulate a grammatical generalization; e.g., *Tešubot*, 214 (p. 378).

Maimonides' view suggests the notion of a linguistic Masorah, a continuous oral tradition concerning grammar and lexicography. See in this context Judah Ḥayyūj, *Šelošah Sifre Dikduk*, p. 10: ודבר זה מסורת בידינו מאבותינו . . . והעתקנוהו מזקנינו; Jonah ibn Janāḥ, *Sefer ha-Riḳmah*, 11 (בעבור שנעדרה מהם הקבלה); Joseph Ḳimḥi, *Sefer hag-Galuy*, p. 2 (מפי סופרים); and the contrary emphasis in Solomon Parḥon, *Maḥberet he-'Aruḳ*, p. 149 (לא קבלנו לשון הקודש). Also S. Poznanski, *Eine hebräische Grammatik* (Berlin, 1894), p. 11.

18. The style of the *Mishneh Torah* has elicited sustained praise from medieval commentators (see below, n.65) as well as modern scholars. E.g., E. M. Lifshitz, *Kĕtabim* (Jerusalem, 1947), I, 207; S. Federbush, "Yaḥaso šel ha-RaMBaM lal-Lašon ha-'Ibriṯ," *Ha-RaMBaM*, ed. S. Federbush (New York, 1956). A. Ben-David, *Lĕšon Miḳra' u-Lĕšon Ḥakamim* (Tel Aviv, 1967), p. 241. Concerning the neglect of Hebrew, see, e.g., the poem of Ibn Gabirol, *Širim*, ed. H. Bialik, I, 526; R. Judah hal-Levi, *Kuzari*, II, 68; Judah al-Ḥarīzī, *Tahkĕmoni*, introduction; R. Moses ibn Ezra, *Širat*, p. 54; and later Jacob ben Sheshet, *Mešib Dĕbarim Nĕkohim* (Jerusalem, 1967), p. 137.

and would allow the greatest creativity in serving the literary needs of jurisprudence, and to a great extent of philosophy.

It should be made particularly clear that the two rejected languages left their imprint, sometimes substantive, sometimes tangential, on the *Mishneh Torah*. Maimonides' selection of, and commitment to, Mishnaic Hebrew emphasized historical development and flexibility. It was meant to expand rather than constrict. It did not rule out Biblical Hebrew, but more importantly and more dramatically, it did not limit his language to the vocabulary or syntax or grammar of Biblical Hebrew. At the same time, Maimonides' selection did not mean a rigid mandate for Mishnaic purism similar to the Biblical purism of some of the Hebrew writers of the golden age in Spain. Poets such as R. Judah hal-Levi deliberately committed themselves for a variety of reasons, literary as well as polemical, to a strict classicism whose canons of style dictated that they write in a pure Biblical Hebrew with no admixture whatsoever of post-Biblical idioms. Maimonides never wanted to substitute Mishnaic purism for the Biblical purism which he deemed unfeasible and inflexible.[19] The *Mishneh Torah* is studded with felicitous Biblical idioms and metaphors which enrich its style and enhance its beauty. Biblical treasures—allusions and alliterations, constructs and concepts, rhymes and rhythms—are regularly and effectively used. There is nothing artificial or scholastic about the Hebrew of the *Mishneh Torah*. Moreover, just as he retained a good measure of Biblical Hebrew, so did he keep some Aramaic phrases, for the most part formal halakic terms which could be cumbersome or ambiguous in translation. It might even be that Maimonides originally retained numerous Aramaic terms as the path of least resistance, inasmuch as translating all such terms was challenging and some-

---

[19]. See, e.g., the attack of Shem Ṭob ibn Falaquera, *Rešit Ḥokmah* (Berlin, 1902), p. 26, on the purist-classicist Hebrew poets who used only Biblical Hebrew. Falaquera also repeats the Maimonidean view that language is conventional, not natural; W. Bacher, "Zum sprachlichen Charakter des Mischne Thora," *MbM*, II, 280ff. A study of cases where Maimonides preferred a Biblical word to a Mishnaic one—e.g., נחם to חרט in *Tešubah* i, 1 and ii, 2—would be rewarding; this should not be confused with synonymy, for which, see below, n.69.

times perplexing. Autograph fragments of parts of the *Mishneh Torah* show a progressive "Hebraization" of the text, manifest in erasures of Talmudic idioms and the substitution of Hebrew phrases.[20] As the forthcoming characterization of his style will show, there appears to be a steady refinement and purification of language consistently tempered by a strong aversion to affectation and a sustained quest for elegant brevity.

*The missing option: Arabic*

Before turning to this characterization, a comment on what seems to be a "missing language" is in order. One is struck rather forcefully by Maimonides' failure even to mention Arabic as an option for the *Mishneh Torah*—an option which at first glance would seem to be most attractive and reasonable. After all, Maimonides' other Rabbinic works, the *Commentary on the Mishnah* and the *Book of Commandments,* were composed in Arabic. In general, halakic study on all levels was hospitable to Arabic, and because of the advanced state of linguistic assimilation, major compositions in Arabic filled a genuine need. When referring to halakic works of Geonim, Maimonides sometimes specifies that they were composed in Arabic.[21] There were serious intellectuals who earned Maimonides' respect and attention and whose knowledge of Hebrew was either minimal or nil. He certainly had no intention of ignoring such people; on the contrary, there is evidence that he addressed himself sympathetically to this type of reader and was particularly desirous of encouraging these individuals, for whom Arabic was the natural medium.[22] Moreover,

---

20. See M. Luzki, *Pĕrakim mis-Sefer Mishneh Torah,* appendix to Schulsinger edition (New York, 1947), V, 1ff.; also A. N. Roth, "Kĕṭa'im mim-Mishneh Torah," *Ginze Kaufmann* (Budapest, 1948), pp. 62–71, especially p. 62, n.2, concerning *Šĕḥiṭah,* vi, 13, whether it retained an Aramaic phrase. Note *Zĕkiyyah u-Mattanah,* viii, 2; *Mĕkirah,* xi, 13. The influence of Arabisms has also been noted; see R. Samuel ibn Tibbon, translator's introduction to MN, and S. H. Kook, *'Iyyunim u-Meḥkarim* (Jerusalem, 1959), I, 320–21; M. Goshen's articles in *Tarbiz,* XXIII (1953), 210ff.; XXVI (1957), 185ff. Maimonides looked upon Arabic as "corrupted Hebrew," *Kobeṣ,* II, 27b.
21. E.g., *Kobeṣ,* I, 8a (n.28), 25b. The translations in *Kĕle ham-Miḳdaš,* ii, 4, show that Arabic was his immediate frame of reference.
22. The letter to Ibn Jābir (*Kobeṣ,* II, 15b) is most instructive in this context. It appears that R. Tanḥum Yerushalmi also composed his work for such readers.

Maimonides never tired of emphasizing that the major determinant in study and writing, in preparing for discipleship or exercising leadership, was the subject matter; language was ancillary to the contents. No "metaphysical pathos" or imperialistic flavor attached to Hebrew in the Maimonidean scheme. Like the recitation of the Šĕma‘, Torah may be studied in all languages. Comprehension and edification, rather than language per se, are the major determinants.[23]

Maimonides' attitude toward the Arabic option is illumined by attentive review of a sentence in one of his responsa. In answer to a question from the inhabitants of Tyre concerning the enumeration of commandments, Maimonides provided a very detailed characterization of his *Sefer ham-Miṣwot*, its purpose and method—a compressed anatomy of a book—and assured his correspondent that if he would only consult this work, every doubt which might arise in his mind would be dispelled. Almost as a postscript, Maimonides adds: "I deeply regret having written this work in Arabic, because all people ought to read it, and I am now awaiting the occasion to translate it into Hebrew with the help of the Almighty."[24] This comment is ambiguous, for it is not clear whether the explanatory clause ("because all people ought to read it") refers to his original motivation for writing it in Arabic or to the reason for his retrospective regret. If the former is the case, Maimonides is merely repeating parenthetically that the desire to enhance the book's accessibility and readability prompted him to write in Arabic. It would thus be analogous to the pronouncement at the beginning of the *'Iggeret Teman:* "As for the other matters concerning which you have requested a reply, I deemed it best to respond in the Arabic tongue and idiom. For then all may read it with ease, men, women, and children, for it is important that the substance of our reply altogether be understood by every member of your community."[25] Both statements would thus reflect a milieu in which the literary prevalence of Arabic was

---

23. Kĕri'at Šĕma‘, iii, 4–5. There are, of course, formal halakic considerations which determine that certain recitations must be in Hebrew; see, e.g., Soṭah, iii, 7; Šĕbu'ot, vii, 7; xi, 14; Ḥăḡiḡah, iii, 5; Ma'ăśer Šeni, xi, 5; Bĕrakot, i, 6.
24. Tĕšubot, 447 (p. 725).
25. IT, iii.

ubiquitous, thereby being reminiscent of the reasons given in an earlier period, for example, by R. Saadiah Gaon for writing in Arabic.[26] Furthermore, Maimonides' deep nostalgia for Hebrew and his poignant desire to translate this work into Hebrew may be purely romantic, as he implies elsewhere. In answer to the Provençal scholars who urged him to translate the *Moreh* into Hebrew, Maimonides confesses that he would be delighted to comply with their request, *to bring forth the precious out of the vile* (Jer. 15:19) and return the stolen object to its owners."[27] Similarly, in response to a request to translate the *Mishneh Torah* into Arabic, he affirms vigorously: "I am now seeking to return [i.e., translate] the *Commentary on the Mishnah* and the *Sefer ham-Miṣwot* into the holy tongue, so it is certainly out of the question that I should return this work into Arabic." Were he to translate it into Arabic, he notes curtly, "all its mellifluousness would be lost."[28]

However, a more plausible and enlightening interpretation of Maimonides' comment in the response to the inhabitants of Tyre emerges if we take the explanatory clause ("because all people ought to read it") as registering the reason for his regret at having composed it in Arabic. Initially, Maimonides wrote the book for a limited audience, for his immediate countrymen; the thought of a world-wide or intercontinental audience (Jews in the Christian orbit as well as in the Islamic one, in Edom and in Ishmael) never apparently crossed his mind. Arabic was, therefore, a satisfactory nearly universal means of communication, as attested, for example, in different contexts by R. Moses Gikatilia and R. Solomon Parḥon.[29] Consonant with this conception is the fact that the introduction to the *Sefer ham-Miṣwot* downgrades its importance; it is presented as a Talmudic enchiridion, a manual preparatory and auxiliary to the *Mishneh Torah*. The situation changed rather

26. See, e.g., M. Zucker, *'Al Targum R. Saadiah Gaon lat-Torah* (New York, 1959), pp. 10ff.; also R. Baḥya ibn Paḳuda, *Ḥobot hal-Lĕbabot*, p. 40: מפני שהיא קרובה להבין לרוב אנשי דורנו.
27. *Ḳobeṣ*, II, 44a.
28. *Ḳobeṣ*, II, 15b.
29. R. Moses Gikatilia, introduction to Ḥayyūj, *Šĕlošah Sifre Diḳduḳ*, observes that only those living in France (in the territory of Esau [Edom]) do not understand Arabic. R. Solomon Parḥon, *Maḥberet he-'Aruḵ*, 75a (postscript), observes that in Muslim lands Jews did not speak Hebrew because of the prevalence and unifying influence of Arabic.

## 336 INTRODUCTION TO THE CODE OF MAIMONIDES

quickly. The work achieved greater circulation than anticipated. It is not accidental, therefore, that in this letter the propaedeutic nature of the book is not mentioned at all. It now emerges as a useful, self-sufficient, and very enlightening volume, equipped throughout with the essential Talmudic references, and not merely as a necessary check-list for the *Mishneh Torah*. In this same responsum Maimonides calls attention to the fact that "many copies have reached Babylon, the extreme west, and the cities of Edom [i.e., Christian Europe]"; only then does he record his regret inasmuch as "all people ought to read it," and people in these latter places are *unable* to read it because of an insurmountable linguistic barrier. According to this interpretation it would appear that the same motive which prompted its original composition in Arabic occasioned the author's subsequent regret; his growing audience, especially in the non-Arabic west, had to be taken into account.

It follows, therefore, that the *Mishneh Torah* could not be in Arabic if it was to serve all people. In his letter to his favorite disciple Maimonides explains the motivation behind his work and his ardor as follows: "I was most zealous for the Lord God of Israel when I saw before me *a nation* that does not have a comprehensive book (of laws)."[30] A code for the entire nation, rather than for its Arabic-speaking segment, had to be in Hebrew.

---

30. *'Iggĕroṯ*, 50 (italics mine). Maimonides' judgment was resoundingly confirmed. Already at the very beginning of the thirteenth century R. Sheshet han-Naśi' of Saragossa emphasized that the accessibility of the MT was greatly increased by its being written in Hebrew. See his letter edited by A. Marx, *JQR*, XXV (1935), 406ff. See Shem Ṭob ibn Falaquera, *Sefer ham-Ma'ălot* (Berlin, 1894), p. 11: והיתה הכונה לחברו בלשון הקודש כדי שתהי תועלתו כוללת יותר.

In both the Hebrew and the Arabic letters accompanying the MN, Maimonides stresses that it was intended for a small elite—"you [i.e., his disciple] and those like you, however few they are" (MN, introduction, p. 4; see *'Iggĕroṯ*, 16). He knew (MN, p. 16) that he might "give satisfaction to a single virtuous man while displeasing ten thousand ignoramuses." Maimonides was thus fully aware of the possibilities as well as the limits of philosophical discourse and certainly had no reason to assume the existence of a high level of philosophic knowledge in Christian countries. It was R. Jonathan hak-Kohen who first suggested the idea of a translation to Maimonides. The Lunel scholars, in turn, were stimulated by Maimonides' Letter on Astrology, which contained many references to his Arabic work entitled *Guide of the Perplexed*. Their genuine interest was communicated to Maimonides and persuaded him to accede to their request: to send them either a Hebrew translation of the *Guide* or a complete copy of the Arabic original. See generally S. M. Stern, "Ḥălifaṯ ham-Miḵtaḇim ben ha-RaMBaM wĕ-Ḥaḵme Provence," *Zion*, XVI (1951), 19–28.

## LANGUAGE AND STYLE

### IN PRAISE OF BREVITY

As for the essentials of his style, Maimonides never tired of writing in praise of brevity. Although this is a rather widespread topos in medieval literature, both Hebrew and general,[31] Maimonides' formulation of the many virtues of brevity is not commonplace. The emphases, the variety of contexts and nuances, the frequent reiteration, the correlation of theory and practice are all noteworthy.[32] Implicitly, brevity represented the "style of majesty and command," and that is essential for a code whose purpose is to guide and instruct "in plain language and terse style."[33] Brevity for Maimonides is not only a sign of wisdom but also a sign of divine origin.[34] A salient feature of the Mishnah which he extols, and which contributed to its authoritativeness, is its terseness.[35] Beyond these formal-structural reasons, brevity is also a pedagogic device: it leads to clarity and precision. Brevity, like oral transmission, eliminates or minimizes confusion; a pointed and unencumbered statement is a rather safe antidote to erroneous and undisciplined interpretation. Any superfluity should be avoided; self-evident or widespread items should not be repeated; excessive speech is wasteful, if not sinful.[36] In the Bible, for example, verbosity or redundancy is only apparent; the principle that "God and nature do nothing in vain" applies to language as well. All stories are covered by the rubric *For it is no vain thing from you* (Deut. 32:47).[37] There is an

---

31. E.g., R. Jonah ibn Janāḥ, *Sefer ha-Riḳmah*, p. 26: האהבה לקצר כפי היכולת; Joseph ibn Kaspi, cited in n.33, below; R. Ezekiel Landau, *Noḍa' bi-Yĕhuḍah*, I, introduction of his son. See also E. Curtius, *European Literature and the Latin Middle Ages* (New York, 1953), pp. 478ff. ("Brevity as an Ideal for Style").

32. E.g., PhM, Ṭoh, introduction (p. 37); Kel 2: 1 (p. 54); 'Aḇ 2:5 (p. 424); ŠP, chap. V; ShM, *šoreš* 14 (II, 423); *De'ot*, ii, 5; MTH, 15, 37; *Tĕšuḇot*, 119 (p. 211); *Ḳoḇeṣ*, I, 25b.

33. H. Cairns, *Legal Philosophy from Plato to Hegel* (Baltimore, 1949), p. 242 (concerning Francis Bacon); MT, introduction. See Joseph ibn Kaspi, *Sefer has-Soḍ*, ed. I. Last, *Mišneh Kesef* (Pressburg, 1905), I, 4, who compares the brevity of the MT with the brevity of the Torah. Also Naḥmanides, *Dĕrašah 'al Diḇre Ḳohelet*, in *Kiṯḇe RaMBaN*, ed. C. Chavel, I, 208. R. Tanḥum, *Ham-Madriḵ ham-Maspiḳ*, ed. J. Toledano, p. 25.

34. ŠP, chap. V.

35. PhM, introduction (p. 34).

36. MN, I, 71; PhM, introduction (p. 48); ShM, *šoreš* 14 (II, 425); *Miškaḇ u-Mošaḇ*, vi, 1.

37. MN, III, 50.

economy of language as of nature, and this is a basic directive for study as well as for composition. With regard to his own writing, Maimonides says: "I am writing for intelligent people and am not trying to impart understanding to stones."[38] In sum, brevity simplifies reading and reduces the incidence of misinterpretation. The nexus between brevity and oral study is significant: when oral culture must yield, brevity is the most natural and desirable mode of writing.

Moreover, an unfaltering awareness of the virtues of brevity serves as a safeguard against digressions. While a sentence or even a paragraph may on occasion be digressive or parenthetical, particularly if the subject is ideologically weighty, brevity helps preserve a sense of proportion and symmetry. The straight prose line may bulge slightly but it will not be completely obstructed.[39]

Of course, if conciseness is not to produce riddles, it must be tempered by the requirements of clarity; "some authors strive to be brief as long as this does not injure the subject matter."[40] Hence there must be a suitable mean between a lifeless and antiseptic style and a prolix and flabby style. The goal was economy of language without obscurity, refinement of language without affectation. Maimonides did not strive for the greatness which Emerson characterized in his saying, "to be great is to be misunderstood," for this tempts one to indulge in calculated obscurity. Given the restrictive and deceptive nature of language—"the bounds of expression in all languages are very narrow indeed"[41]—writing was a great challenge. That inevitable "looseness of expression," inherent in the nature of language and sometimes in the imperatives of communication, had to be controlled as effectively as possible, so that the cardinal virtue of brevity should not be compromised out of existence. In sum, "in discussing Torah and wisdom, a man's words should be few but

---

38. PhM, introduction (p. 48).
39. PhM, Soṭ 5:1 (p. 261). The MT was less susceptible to digressions than the PhM, e.g., in PhM, Ber 9:7 (pp. 90–92). For the problems of classification and associationism, see chap IV, above.
40. Maimonides' introduction to Hippocrates' *Aphorisms* (*Pĕraḳim*), in *'Iggĕroṭ*, ed. J. Ḳāfiḥ (Jerusalem, 1972), p. 145.
41. MN, I, 57; also I, 50.

full of meaning. This the Sages express in their recommendation, 'A man should always teach his disciples tersely.' But where words are many and their meaning is small—that is folly, of which it is said, *For the dream cometh through much discussion, and a fool's voice through a multitude of words* (Eccles. 6:2)."[42]

Maimonides repeatedly emphasized that a bad composition is long on words and short on content. One should be more sparing of his speech than of his money; he should not augment speech and diminish subject matter. When Maimonides wants to denigrate the value of the few existing works on a given halakic subject, he affirms that they are simultaneously verbose and unedifying. His own ongoing stylistic revisions demonstrate his quest for the marriage of precision and substance.[43]

*Exceptions: cases of amplification*

In the light of the repeated statements about economy of expression and his emphatic formulations of the canon of brevity, as well as his skillful and successful development of a muscular style honed to succinct statements, precise, pertinent and persuasive, any apparent lengthiness or any infringements of the rule are problematic. The use of rhetorical strategies—in general, the relation of *brevitas* to *amplificatio*—needs to be scrutinized.[44] We must seek special reasons, and in fact we are readily able to identify certain categories—emphasis, polemical needs, particularly confrontation with entrenched authority or rejection of an erroneous, even heretical view, reflective-persuasive communication, ethical-philosophical flourishes, innovations, anticipatory avoidance of misunderstandings—which account for the spasmodic intrusion of lengthiness and sometimes repetitiousness in the otherwise uniformly crisp and concise construction.

Emphasis of fundamental ideas, usually spiritual-moral conceptions, which should be impressed upon the reader's mind so

---

42. *De'ot*, ii, 4.
43. PhM, Toh, introduction (p. 37); *Kobes*, II, 12; PhM, Sot 5:1 (p. 261). One may even compare successive formulations of the same idea, e.g., PhM, RH 4:7 (p. 327); and *Ḥanukkah*, iii, 6 (concerning the reason why the *Hallel* is not recited on New Year's Day). The MT formulation is a gem of compression.
44. See Curtius, *European Literature*, p. 478.

that they will be deeply resonant, reverberating, and refreshing, results in a measure of lengthiness. The statement about ransoming captives (*pidyon šĕbuyim*), with its repetition, stringing together halakic commands and prohibitions, and exhortation, has a deep pathos which gives the passage a rhythm of its own and almost produces a visual representation of the suffering and possible tragedy which prompt and unstinting giving of charity will prevent. One is also tempted to conclude that only a person who had traveled the Mediterranean and experienced its hazards and anxieties could have written such moving prose.[45] The long elaboration concerning the legal severity of murder illustrates similar use and effect of such passionate writing; here, however, theory alone, the abstract conception of the absolute heinousness of murder, without any empathetic relationship, is a sufficient catalyst for the poignant rhetorical impact.[46] Generally, when Maimonides combines halakic norms with aggadic props, his language will be more hortatory and emotional, frequently communicating personal feelings as well. The intensity rarely loses its simplicity and forthrightness.

Maimonides' statement about the fiscal-economic independence of the scholar combines the desire for emphasis with a sharp polemical thrust, inasmuch as Maimonides was criticizing and repudiating a deeply entrenched but highly objectionable Gaonic practice: "One . . . who makes up his mind to study Torah and not to work but to live on charity, profanes the name of God, brings the Torah into contempt, extinguishes the light of religion, brings evil upon himself, and deprives himself of life hereafter."[47] The dramatic reiteration, the staccato condemnation—and this is followed by *four* proof-texts from 'Abot—fits the situation, for the issue was highly controversial and his own position was provocative and austere. The scholar or pseudo-scholar who chooses to benefit from study by becoming a public charge is thus exposed to a stream of vilification. This follows two paragraphs in which the person who defers study because he pre-

45. *Mattĕnot 'Ăniyyim*, viii, 10.
46. *Roṣeaḥ*, iv, 9. See below, chap. VI, n. 213.
47. *Talmud Torah*, iii, 10. See above, chap. I, n.6.

fers business or worldly pleasures is condemned and repeatedly dismissed as foolish and arrogant. Indeed, all of Chapter III of *Talmud Torah* reads like a special sensitive essay, marked by careful but abundant interpolation of aggadic material,[48] overflowing with pathos and underscoring the universality of the obligation to study and its precedence over other preoccupations. It is in many respects a paean to intellectual pursuits, in which Maimonides' usual reticence and restrained formulation are slackened. The emphasis has an oral quality; the impact is powerful.

Chapter IX of *Tĕšubah* is also characterized by the reiteration of key phrases (*ma'ăśeh* and *da'at* or *ḥokmah*) which establishes the cardinal point of the section, one of the cardinal points of Maimonideanism: the reciprocity of action and study. It is worth quoting these paragraphs as an illustration, while incidentally focusing our attention on the thorny question, frequently raised against Jews by Christian polemicists, of the nature of the ultimate reward:[49]

It is known that the reward for the fulfillment of the commandments and the good to which we will attain if we have kept the way of the Lord, as prescribed in the law, is life in the world to come, as it is said, *That it may be well with thee, and that thou mayest prolong thy days* (Deut. 22:7); while the retribution exacted from the wicked who have abandoned the ways of righteousness prescribed in the Torah is excision, as it is said, *That soul shall be utterly cut off; his iniquity shall be upon him* (Num. 15:31). What then is the meaning of the statement found everywhere in the Torah that if you obey, it will happen to you thus, if you do not obey, it will be otherwise; and all these happenings will take place in this world, such as war and peace; sovereignty and subjection; residence in the Promised Land and exile; prosperity in one's activities and failure, and all the other things predicted in the words of the Covenant (Lev. 26, Deut. 28)? All those promises were once truly fulfilled and will again be

---

48. Sometimes aggadic material is imperceptibly transformed into, and identified with, halakah—e.g., *Yĕsode hat-Torah*, i–iv; *De'ot*, i, and passim; *Sanhedrin*, ii; *Mĕlakim*, xi—and sometimes, as in this case, it remains supportive, exhortatory, and edifying.

49. The materialism or "carnal exegesis" of Jews was a topos of Christian attack from Justin Martyr (*Dialogue*, chap. 14) to Aquinas (*Summa*, I, II, 108) and beyond. For Peter Abelard's formulation, see H. Liebeschutz, in *JJS*, XII (1961), 7. See Nahmanides to Deut. 11:13; Joseph Albo, *'Ikkarim*, IV, chap. 40; Abarbanel to Lev. 26:3; Ibn Kaspi, *Tam hak-Kesef*, ed. I. Last, chap. 1; J. Jabez, *'Abot* (Jerusalem, 1957), p. 3.

so. When we fulfill all the commandments of the Torah, all the good things of this world will come to us. When, however, we transgress the precepts, the evils that are written in the Torah will befall us. But nevertheless, those good things are not the final reward for the fulfillment of the commandments, nor are those evils the last penalty exacted from one who transgresses all the commandments. These matters are to be understood as follows: The Holy One, blessed be He, gave us this law—a tree of life. Whoever fulfills what is written therein and knows it with a complete and correct knowledge will attain thereby life in the world to come. According to the greatness of his deeds and abundance of his knowledge will be the measure in which he will attain that life.

The Holy One, blessed be He, has further promised us in the Torah that if we observe its behests joyously and cheerfully, and continually meditate on its wisdom, He will remove from us the obstacles that hinder us in its observance, such as sickness, war, famine, and other calamities; and will bestow upon us all the material benefits which will strengthen our ability to fulfill the law, such as plenty, peace, abundance of silver and gold. Thus we will not be engaged all our days in providing for our bodily needs, but will have leisure to study wisdom and fulfill the commandment and thus attain life in the world to come. Hence, after the assurance of material benefits, it is said in the Torah, *And it shall be righteousness unto us, if we observe to do all this commandment before the Lord our God as He hath commanded us* (Deut. 6:25). So too, He taught us in the Torah that if we deliberately forsake it and occupy ourselves with temporal follies, as the text says, *But Jeshurun waxed fat and kicked* (Deut. 32:15), the true Judge will deprive the forsakers of all those material benefits which only served to encourage them to be recalcitrant, and will send upon them all the calamities that will prevent their attaining the life hereafter, so that they will perish in their wickedness. This is expressed by the Torah in the text, *Because thou didst not serve the Lord thy God with joyfulness and with gladness of heart, by reason of the abundance of all things, therefore shalt thou serve thine enemy whom the Lord shall send against thee* (Deut. 28:47–48).

Hence all those benedictions and maledictions promised in the Torah are to be explained as follows: If you have served God with joy and observed His way, He will bestow upon you those blessings and avert from you those curses, so that you will have leisure to become wise in the Torah and occupy yourselves therewith, and thus attain life hereafter, and then it will be well with you in the world which is entirely blissful and you will enjoy length of days in an existence which is everlasting. So will you enjoy both worlds, a happy life on earth leading to the life in the world to come. For if wisdom is not acquired and good deeds are not performed here, there will be nothing meriting a recompense hereafter, as it is said, *For there is no work, no device, no knowledge, nor wisdom in the grave* (Eccles. 9:10). But if you have forsaken the Lord and have erred in eating, drinking, fornication, and similar things, He will bring upon you all those curses and withhold from you all those blessings till your days will end in confusion and terror, and you will have neither the free mind nor the healthy body requisite for the fulfillment of the commandments, so that you will suffer perdition in the life hereafter and will thus have lost both worlds—for when one is troubled here on earth with diseases, war, or famine, he does not occupy himself with the acquisition of wisdom or the performance of religious precepts by which life hereafter is gained.[50]

Lengthiness, various kinds of rhetorical amplification, in straightforward halakic contexts is usually motivated by polemical needs. A decision against a ruling of R. Isaac Alfasi, for example, warrants a measure of prolixity.[51] Similarly, when his normative conclusion is upsetting a widespread precedent, he will be relatively verbose or will add an apodictic peroration.[52] Outright repetition in the same section or in different sections is another device for polemical emphasis.[53] Sharp, sometimes acerbic, formulae of rejection obviously do not depend upon excess length for their polemical thrust; they do, however, break the stylistic rhythm, its placid brevity and anonymity, its regular ebb and flow. Concomitantly, an original view or conceptual breakthrough will be bolstered by expletives, direct address exhorting the reader to remember a certain rule or interpretative generalization, and rhetorical buoys.[54] Autobiographical references—stylistic self-mirroring in a simple sense—also rivet attention to themselves, thereby underscoring the halakah or custom that is being discussed.[55] Commentators even insisted that when Maimonides gave a long list of examples or illustrations for an

---

50. *Tĕšubah*, ix, 1.
51. E.g., *Šabbat*, xix, 20. See *Ma'ăkalot 'Ăsurot*, iii, 13, and *MM* (referring to Ibn Megas).
52. E.g., *Šĕkirut*, ii, 3; and see H. Soloveitchik, *Tarbiz*, XL (1972), 315, n.9.
53. E.g., *Šĕbu'ot*, xi, 8, 14; *Ta'ăniyyot*, v, 3; and *Mĕlakim*, xi, 3.
54. E.g., *Ma'ăkalot 'Ăsurot*, x, 18; *To'en wĕ-Nit'an*, viii, 10; ix, 1; *Šĕluhin wĕ-Šutafin*, iii, 7. Note *'Išut*, vi, 13, which sums up a real conceptual breakthrough (in defining the problem of conditional statements).
55. E.g., *Sefer Torah*, viii, 4; *Ta'ăniyyot*, v, 9.

halakic proposition, it was fruitful to analyze each specific example.[56] Various forms of rhetorical dialogue and placid dramatization—"do not wonder and say," "lest you say," "let not the notion pass though your mind"—are invariably effective.[57] It should be noted that while Maimonides generally refused to dignify criticism with countercriticism and recriminations, in the context of the *Mishneh Torah* the issues were more impersonal, exegetical, and conceptual, and as a result veiled criticism or special pleading through rhetorical effect is in order.

Anti-Karaite polemic is a unique category, combining invective (the "heretics," "erring people," and "fools" are specifically mentioned), length, and patient (often novel) Scriptural exegesis. The long section about violating the Sabbath in order to save the life of a sick person and the formulation concerning the date for the offering of the *'omer* are well known, almost classic, illustrations.[58] They are persistent and argumentative, hammering out the main theme with sharp blows.

Length is sometimes the most effective way to correct misunderstanding after it has risen or to anticipate and eliminate it a priori. Hence the simple dialectic of brevity and expansiveness: "We have already expanded and reiterated (our) words concerning that subject in order, with all our might, to remove all those doubts."[59] With regard to another issue, Maimonides says: "Even though this matter is explained, we added an explanation in the *Mishneh Torah* because of you . . . so that no one will err or find it troublesome."[60]

The occasional unevenness of style—length vis-à-vis brevity—may also be related in general to the heterogeneous audience of the book, *katon wĕ-gadol*, "small and great." Communication to masses may require expansiveness and repetition,[61] illustration and summation. There is an inverse analogue to this in his responsa: when writing to scholars, he cited sources, ex-

---

56. E.g., *Šĕbu'ot*, i, 6; and RaDBaZ, ad loc.
57. *Tĕšubah*, v, 1; also, e.g., *Tĕfillah*, xv, 7; *Gerušin*, xiii, 29; see above, chap. II.
58. *Šabbat*, ii, 1–3; *Tĕmidin u-Musafin*, vii. See also *Šĕbu'ot*, xii, 12; *'Issure Bi'ah*, xi, 15.
59. *Tĕšubot*, 119 (p. 211).
60. *Tĕšubot*, 423 (p. 700); and see *Gerušin*, viii, 4. Note also MTH, 6; and PhM, 'Ab 2:5 (p. 424).
61. MTH, 37–38.

plained reasons, and articulated theory, for they would appreciate the erudition as well as the ingenuity; when writing to unlearned inquirers, his answer was brief and to the point, sometimes consisting merely of "yes" or "no," for any display of learning or skill would be irrelevant. In any event, the difference is related to the nature of the intended audience. We may, in this context, suggest still another way in which the Code addressed itself to various types of readers. Sometimes a carefully chosen phrase or extra example may stimulate tangential strains of thought for the sensitive reader and go unnoticed by the less sophisticated reader. Such material enhances the value for one reader without disturbing or jarring the other reader. A juridical formulation that will appear simple and routine to an unscholarly reader will appear original and multifaceted to a scholarly reader. Maimonides' maxim that "it is possible for everyone to grasp them, small and great" is not a contradiction *in adjecto;* skillful and deftly nuanced writing has a multiplicity of meanings. This is a major component of the *kaṭon-gadol* syndrome.[62] It is clear that to overlook either the "great" or the "small" members of the reading audience is to distort Maimonides' intention and to dull the awareness of certain expository-analytic skills applied so effectively in his composition.

Maimonides' statements as well as actual practice in the *Ma'āmar Tĕḥiyyat ham-Metim* tell us much about rhetorical strategy as manifest in the use of invective and epithet, and repetitions—a strategy which is clearly operative in the *Mishneh*

---

62. E.g., '*Edut*, xii, 9 (together with '*Edut*, x, 2, and *Ḥobel u-Mazziḳ*, v, 13); *Mĕlakim*, iv, 4, and many others. See *Yĕsode hat-Torah*, iv, 13. Cf. how Odofredus, lecturer in jurisprudence in Italy in the thirteenth century, praised his own method of teaching: "But with me all students can profit, even the ignorant and the newcomers, for they will hear the whole book, and nothing will be omitted as was once the common practice here. For the ignorant can profit by the statement of the case and the exposition of the text, the more advanced can become adept in the subtleties of questions and opposing opinions." C. H. Haskins, *The Renaissance of the Twelfth Century* (New York, 1962), pp. 203–04.

I. A. Richards, *Interpretation in Teaching* (New York, 1938), p. vii, speaks of multiplicity of meanings and affirms that the principle of contradiction "has to do with logical relations between meanings, not with the psychological concomitance of contradictory meanings." We are here speaking of the multiplicity of interpretations, from the simple to the complex, the straightforward to the subtle; instead of a principle of contradiction, we might identify a principle of extension, of progressive denotation and connotation. See Twersky, "Sefer MT", pp. 20–22.

*Torah*. In that letter, which we have characterized in Chapter I and shall analyze further in Chapter VI, Maimonides felt that the religious integrity and philosophic consistency of his life's work had to be defended, and furthermore, that the average reader had to be influenced and safeguarded. This accounts, on the one hand, for the heavy dose of ad hominem argumentation which helps deflate myths and scholarly stereotypes as well as puncture literalist platitudes and pseudo-philosophical positions. On the other hand, it explains the use of a more popular style, repetitious and illustrative, with more than a few grains of emphasis and pathos. Length is here a result of the need for effective and, if necessary, persuasive communication. Maimonides on occasion has to walk a tightrope between brevity as a pedagogic device normally used to achieve precision, and clarity and length used now and then to emphasize as well as to clarify.[63]

PRECISION AND ELEGANCE

Now the quality of language was a major determinant in Maimonides' writing generally and his quest for brevity particularly. Maimonides was guided by the conviction that style should be elegant, not merely functional; it should be expressive, vivid, emphatic, in addition to being precise and lucid. Consequently, the Hebrew of the *Mishneh Torah* is an unusually pliant and forceful creation. One does not ordinarily expect to find lyrical qualities in a code of law, but the *Mishneh Torah* has them. The usually austere prose of a code is loosened and lyricized in various ways. The massive erudition is ennobled by linguistic virtuosity and poetic prowess. His style could become lacerating as he lashed out against befuddlement or error. It could be popular and intimate without becoming colloquial: the expression could be colorful but not jaunty; various forms of direct address, questions, evocative parables, pointed prologues or perorations, brief Scriptural references or aggadic allusions which are sure to be resonant, short philosophical meditations, anecdotal interludes, and similar flourishes are used to entice and teach as well as to add tonality and intonation. Maimonides could on occasion use

---

63. MTH, 7, 8, 12, 15; see below, chap. VI.

aphoristic prose, if not quite gnomic utterances, to summarize an important teaching or underscore an abstract principle. Maimonides wrote with verve and poignancy, lucidity and pathos, even in the essentially impersonal style which is the work's hallmark. In this sense it may be said that Maimonides was very much the disciple of Plato, who (in the *Phaedrus* and elsewhere) urged the union of eloquence and true knowledge, for the former would enhance the value of the latter and assure its influence and ascendancy.[64] As we have noted, his model was the Mishnah, and the tractate 'Aḇoṯ was a particularly significant paradigm of eloquent and profound wisdom in epigrammatic form.

Maimonides' steady practice as well as periodic pronouncements on the subject of language show conclusively that in his opinion good style should be an integral and not merely an ornamental part of a literary enterprise. Maimonides would resist being enticed by phraseology, scholastic terminology, or linguistic ornateness that did not relate to the purposes of exposition and communication. Eloquence was valuable but a disembodied eloquence was of no moment. A key concept in this context is *ṣaḥuṯ* (clear and precise expression). While Maimonides does not apply the word *ṣaḥuṯ* to his own style—many ardent admirers and important commentators do[65]—he does use it frequently in describing the language of the Mishnah, which, as we have seen, was his model for the *Mishneh Torah*. He tells us that R. Judah was a master of *ṣaḥuṯ* and an expert linguist; the Mishnah is the embodiment of *ṣaḥuṯ* par excellence; the *Baraitot* never quite attained the level and consistency of *ṣaḥuṯ* which characterizes the

---

64. See, generally, such discussions as H. Gray, "Renaissance Humanism: The Pursuit of Eloquence," in *Renaissance Essays*, ed. P. Kristeller and P. Weiner (New York, 1968), pp. 199ff.; J. E. Seigel, *Rhetoric and Philosophy in Renaissance Humanism* (Princeton, 1968). For eloquence per se, note carefully *Sanhedrin*, ii, 6 (concerning *něḇone laḥaš*) and MN, I, 34; see R. David Kimḥi to Isa. 3:3. See also *Iš́uṯ*, iv, 7.

65. E.g., R. Menahem ham-Me'iri, *Beṯ hab-Běḥirah*, introduction, p. 25 (praises Maimonides for using Mishnaic Hebrew); R. Tanḥum Yerushalmi, *Sefer ham-Maspik* (see n. 17, above), p. 25; R. Menahem ben Zerah, *Ṣedah lad-Derek*, (Warsaw, 1880), p. 6; R. Solomon Duran, *Milḥemeṯ Miṣwah*, end (unpaginated); *KM*, introduction; R. Yom Ṭob Heller, *Ma'ăḏane Yom Ṭob*, introduction; and, e.g., *Tosafoṯ Yom Ṭob* to RH 2:9. Ibn Latif (*He-Ḥaluṣ*, XII [1887], 123) speaks of "lašon 'ibrit we-śafah běrurah."

## 348 INTRODUCTION TO THE CODE OF MAIMONIDES

Mishnah.[66] Moreover, many predecessors, whose writings were known to Maimonides, sing the virtues of *ṣaḥuṭ* and single it out as the preeminent trait of good style.[67] It happens, furthermore, that Maimonides indirectly but unequivocally defines this trait in the course of explaining why fixed statutory prayer had to be introduced, even though the Torah had not prescribed a fixed form of prayer. The cause, in his opinion, is the hybridization of language:

> When the people of Israel went into exile in the days of the wicked Nebuchadnezzar, they mingled with the Persians, Greeks, and other nations. In those foreign countries children were born to them, whose language was confused. Everyone's speech was a mixture of many tongues. No one was able, when he spoke, to express his thoughts adequately in any one language, otherwise than incoherently, as it is said, *And their children spoke half in the speech of Ashdod, and they could not speak in the Jews' language, but according to the language of each people* (Neh. 13:24).
>
> Consequently, when anyone of them prayed in Hebrew, he was unable adequately to express his needs or recount the praises of God, without mixing Hebrew with other languages. When Ezra and his council realized this condition, they ordained the Eighteen Benedictions in their present order.
>
> The object aimed at was that these prayers should be in an orderly form in everyone's mouth, that all should learn them, and thus the prayer of those who are stammerers (*'illĕḡim*) would be as perfect as that of those who possess a clear (precise) language (*lašon ṣaḥaḥ*).[68]

Actually, this explanation is prima facie problematic, for if prayer is permissible in any language, why should a hybrid language be faulted? Is this not an illogical restriction? Maimonides' position is that hybridization corrupts language; the language of the "stammerers" connotes a corrupt and impure language, not just a strange idiom, or a linguistic hodgepodge, or a lack of fluency.

---

66. PhM, introduction (p. 15), also p. 34. *Ḳobeṣ*, III, 27a. See also *'Iggĕrot*, 14, in praise of his disciple.

67. E.g., R. Jonah ibn Janāḥ, *Sefer ha-Riḳmah*, pp. 12–13; R. Moses ibn Ezra, *Širaṭ Yiśra'el*, p. 55; R. Joseph Ḳimḥi, *Sefer Zikkaron*, p. 2; also R. Samuel han-Nagid, *Diwan*, ed. D. Yarden (Jerusalem, 1966), p. 81; and R. Saadiah Gaon, *Sefer hag-Galuy*, ed. A. Harkavy, p. 154. Note the comments of Moses Mendelssohn at the beginning of his *'Or li-Nĕṭibah* (1782), where Maimonides is quoted.

68. *Tĕfillah*, i, 4; see Isa. 32:4.

Hybridization per se is not the villain; it is its linguistic repercussions that are damnable. Elsewhere Maimonides equates *'illēḡim* also with those who corrupt language.[69] Hence the need for purity and precision of language, *ṣaḥut*, is the motive of liturgical standardization. The ideal style is muscular and mellifluous, correct and colorful, and *ṣaḥut* is the codeword—modest and compressed *ars dictaminis*.

### OTHER FEATURES: SYNONYMY, SYMMETRY, NEOLOGISM

This blend of brevity, eloquence, and precision helps provide a focus for viewing a few other stylistic features of the *Mishneh Torah*: synonymy, symmetry, and neologism.

The use of synonymy or rhetorical variation for literary effect is quite natural, and needless to say, does not weaken the fabric of the *Mishneh Torah*, its rigor, or its exactitude. No scholar, for example, ever tried to infer subtle distinctions from Maimonides' use of completely interchangeable terms for "maidservant."[70] Stylistic variation is deemed to be significant in cases where Maimonides clearly, and presumably consciously, alters a word or phrase in the process of reproducing his Tannaitic or Amoraic or even Gaonic source, or conspicuously changes his halakic formulation from one context to another. In those cases scholars have generally assumed that there is need to probe and analyze in order

---

69. *Nĕḡarim*, i, 16; see PhM, Nĕḡ 1:2 (p. 115). In *Tĕfillah*, xv, 1 (following B. Meḡ 24b), *'illēḡim* means inarticulate and slurred speech. Note also PhM 'Ed 1:3 (p. 284). See also *Ḳobeṣ*, II, 27b. The language of the *'aral śĕfaṭayim* (*of uncircumcised lips* [Exod. 6:12]) was pure, but stilted and not sufficiently expressive. At a later stage the difficulty of expression, compounded by linguistic assimilation, led to hybridization which corrupts language. R. Jonah ibn Janāḥ, *Sefer ha-Riḳmah*, p. 14, explicitly interprets these verses in terms of a corrupt rather than foreign language; cf., per contra, R. Saadiah Gaon, *'Egron*, p. 54. Concerning *'illēḡim*, see the text of the fourteenth-century Asher Lemlein edited by E. Kupfer, *Ḳobeṣ 'al Yad*, VIII (1976), p. 405. Maimonides' *ṣaḥut* anticipates Dante's notion of "a style that is learned and elegant and at the same time lofty, employed by the illustrious stylists" (see E. Auerbach, *Dante* [Chicago, 1961], p. 49 [quoting from *De vulgari eloquentia*, book II]).

70. *Ḳorban Pesaḥ*, v, 5; also *Ṭumĕ'at Ṣara'at*, xvi, 10; *Šĕḡaḡot*, ii, 5; *Zĕkiyyah*, vii, 4. See J. Zeidman, "Signon Mishneh Torah," *Sinai*, III (1938), 112–21. Already Bacher, "Zum Sprachlichen Charakter," listed synonyms used successively by Maimonides in the MT. See also *Tĕfillah*, vi, 7; *Šabbaṭ*, viii, 8, and x, 10. Note R. Saadiah Gaon, *Peruš*, Prov. 25:11, ed. J. Ḳāfiḥ (Jerusalem, 1963), p. 83. See L. Spitzer, *Essays in Historical Semantics* (New York, 1948), p. 303, concerning the "conceptual field," i.e., the ensemble of synonyms existing at a certain time in a certain language.

to fathom Maimonides' intent, i.e., his interpretation of the sources or his implicit harmonization of his own formulations. The awareness of synonymy as a rhetorical stratagem certainly does not militate against this assumption, which is also a methodological directive; one's conception of the role and nature of language impinges upon the axioms and goals of interpretation.

The injection of a certain literary symmetry, which begins all fourteen books with Scriptural mottoes and ends them with Scriptural or aggadic conclusions, is noteworthy. The mottoes are, of course, a literary embellishment, but as we have seen, also provide a pithy programmatic summary of the contents of the various books. The conclusions—all verses except one—are both summaries and transitions, usually serving to relax the pace somewhat. In general, these contribute both to stylistic felicity as well as to conceptual harmony, thereby underscoring the unity of these features. The ethical interpretations and philosophical insights generally have also a stylistic-literary effect in that this material loosens what would otherwise have to be relentlessly austere prose. The impression of a conscious artist at work, ever mindful of form and symmetry, is greatly strengthened by these features.[71]

Neologism, careful and creative, plays a role in Maimonides' development of an unprecedented Hebrew style. He was not vulgarizing classical Hebrew—compare the process whereby classical Latin was transformed into a common literary language and into a series of vernaculars—but following the scanty beginnings of certain predecessors,[72] he was creating a new classical Hebrew which could reach a wide public. Whereas some writers adopt deliberate archaism in order to enhance authoritativeness, Maimonides opted for an innovative and fully expressive idiom. In order to accomplish this, he significantly expanded the language by using, consciously or unconsciously, a whole array of devices, innovative, imaginative, disciplined. He transmuted the meaning of old

71. See *Těfillah*, i, 1; and *Leḥem Mishneh*.
72. E.g., R. Saadiah Gaon, R. Samuel han-Nagid, and others; see A. Ben-Ezra, "Hidduše Millim šel RaSaG," *Horeb*, VIII (1944), 135ff. D. Yarden's lexicon at the end of his edition of the *Diwan;* Z. Muntner, *Sefer 'Assaf ha-Rofe'* (Jerusalem, 1958); I. Avineri, *Gĕnazim Mĕgulim* (Tel Aviv, 1968).

Hebrew words, thereby adding flexibility and adaptability.[73] He coined some new Hebrew words by analogy with their Arabic equivalents,[74] while he also hebraized Aramaic and Arabic words. Generally he enriched his writing by avoiding artificiality or narrow formalism and by very effectively mixing Biblical and Mishnaic Hebrew. The legitimacy of this had been established by defending the purity of Mishnaic Hebrew against those pedantic grammarians who questioned certain forms used in Tannaitic writing. Of particular significance is Maimonides' original contribution to the development of a Hebrew philosophic idiom. Philosophic and scientific terminology was threadbare and Maimonides brought richness and suppleness, precision and cohesiveness, to this field. The distinctiveness of his philosophic style in Hebrew may be appraised by comparing it with earlier styles of Shabbethai Donnolo, R. Abraham bar Ḥiyya, or the anonymous French translation of parts of *'Ĕmunot wĕ-Dē'ot*, or with the contemporary achievement of the Tibbonides (particularly R. Judah ibn Tibbon and his son R. Samuel), whose translations of the classics of Judeo-Arabic philosophy became models of literalist accuracy, resolutely ranking fidelity of rendition above felicity of presentation. In comparison, Maimonides' philosophic style—as, for example, in *Yĕsode hat-Torah*, i–iv (metaphysics and physics) or vii–x (prophecy); in *Tĕšubah* v–viii, 9 (free will); or in his *Letter on Astrology*—was original, more colorful, and more creative, exhibiting all the advantages of a primary source over its translation.[75] His virtuosity is manifest even in this sphere.

73. See B. Klar, *Meḥkarim wĕ-'Iyyunim* (Tel Aviv, 1954), pp. 31–41; M. Medan, *Lĕšonenu*, XVII (1950), 110–14; S. Baron, *Social and Religious History*, VII, 4ff.
74. See nn. 73, above, and 75, below. The use of *šam* is a classic instance, already noted by Samuel ibn Tibbon, MN, introduction; also *Peruš Millot Zarot*. See S. H. Kook, *'Iyyunim* (Jerusalem, 1963), I, 320; W. Chomsky, "Hebrew during the Middle Ages," *JQR Anniversary Volume* (1967), pp. 121ff. Note the use of *'išim* in *Yĕsode hat-Torah*, ii, 7; and Samuel ibn Tibbon, *Peruš Millot Zarot; Migdal 'Oz*, ad loc.; R. Margaliyot, *Ha-RaMBaM wĕha-Zohar* (Jerusalem, 1953), p. 6.
75. See D. Baneth, "Ha-RaMBaM kĕ-Mĕtargem Dibre 'Aṣmo," *Tarbiz*, XXIII (1951–52), 170ff. The little pamphlet *Šĕmot Ḳodeš wĕ-Ḥol*, ed. M. Gaster, *Dĕvir*, I (1923), also contains some Hebrew translations from the MN. See also D. Baneth, "Lat-Terminologiyah hap-Pilosofit šel ha-RaMBaM," *Tarbiz*, VI (1935), 10ff. Even such a brief passage as *Ṭumĕ'at Ṣara'at*, xvi, 10, helps one to appreciate the special qualities of his philosophic style.

## STYLISTIC CONTINUITY AND CONSISTENCY

Throughout this large work there is a remarkable continuity of style and consistency of presentation. The reader may turn from *Tĕfillah* to *Kil'ayim* to *Ṭo'en wĕ-Niṭ'an* and sense no serious stylistic or structural disjunction. The rhythm is the same, the flow is even, the cadences are uniform, the rhetorical devices—questions, direct address, polemical streaks, literary flourishes, ethical *pensées,* Scriptural allusions or quotations—are identical. Maimonides' advice to Ibn Jābir was not misleading: if you learn enough Hebrew to start the *Mishneh Torah,* you will be able to move freely from book to book or section to section.[76] One is tempted to say that this is in keeping with another aspect of Maimonides' conception of language and his mode of literary analysis: every author has his own stylistic patterns and peculiarities. "Know that every prophet has a kind of speech peculiar to him, which is, as it were, the language of that individual."[77] Maimonides puts this principle to good use, claiming that a careful study of a prophetic author, his idioms, metaphors, and constructions results in enhanced sensitivity to, and more accurate understanding of, his message. Indeed, learning the peculiar features of an author's style is indispensable for penetrating interpretation. The principle is implicitly true for Maimonides as well.

This should not be taken to mean that his style was static. On the contrary, there is evidence of increasing hebraization in successive drafts of the *Mishneh Torah;* there are, as already noted, erasures of the original Talmudic idiom and substitution of new Hebrew phrases, so that the result is a progressive refinement and purification of language. Sometimes the original clause is condensed and sometimes it is expanded; any attempt to formulate rigid rules misses the mark here, for each case must have been handled independently with the goal of clarity and precision in mind.[78] This brings us face to face with the phenomenon of

---

76. *Ḳobeṣ,* II, 15b.

77. MN, II, 29 (p. 337); see also R. Isaac Abarbanel, introduction to *Peruš* on Jeremiah; R. Zerahiah ben Shealtiel of Barcelona, *Peruš* on Job, p. 173.

78. See M. Luzki, "Wĕ-kataḇ Mošeh," *Hat-Tĕḳufah,* XXX–XXXI (1946), 683ff., and reference in n. 20, above; E. Horovitz, "Šĕriḍim Nosafim," *Had-Darom,* XXXVIII

Maimonides' de facto translation of the Talmud from Aramaic into Hebrew, for were the parts of the *Mishneh Torah* to be rearranged according to the Talmudic sequence we would practically have a Hebrew Talmud.[79] Moreover, his occasional practice of introducing a paraphrastic translation which is also a pointed explanation reflects and illustrates his general philosophy of translation.[80] Maimonides insisted that translation should not be literal, stilted, and rigidly constrained by the order of the words or the words themselves. The translator should be proficient in both languages as well as in the subject matter, and should then produce a responsible but creative and eloquent translation. The basic principles of translation which he outlined for his translator, R. Samuel ibn Tibbon—and which were congruent, for example, with the views of R. Saadiah Gaon and R. Moses ibn Ezra—clearly governed his own writing; to the extent that this involved translation, it was interpretative and felicitous. Fidelity of rendition need not obstruct felicity of presentation.[81]

The cumulative impact of these facts is to underscore again Maimonides' conviction that language is merely an instrument while the contents are all-important. This guided his critical attitude to poetry and related genres as it shaped his constructive

---

(1974), 7ff. Concerning the MN (introduction, p. 15) Maimonides says, "For the diction of this treatise has not been chosen at haphazard, but with great exactness and exceeding precision."

79. See, e.g., *Kil'ayim*, x, 29 (reproducing B. Ber 19a). See S. Ashkenazi, "Ha-RaMBaM kĕ-Mĕtargem," *Lĕšonenu la-'Am*, XVI (1965), 139ff.

80. See, e.g., *Na'ărah Bĕtulah*, i, 13.

81. Letter to R. Samuel ibn Tibbon, *Ḳobeṣ*, II, 27b (*JQR*, XXV [1935], 374ff.); and see D. Baneth, *Tarbiz*, XXIII (1951–52), 170. For the history of this letter, see I. Sonne, *Tarbiz*, X (1939), 135ff., and S. Stern, *Zion*, XVI (1951), 18ff. For R. Saadiah Gaon, see M. Zucker, *'Al Targum RaSaG*, pp. 128–29 and passim. R. Moses ibn Ezra, *Širat Yiśra'el*, p. 32; also S. Abramson, *R. Nissim Gaon* (Jerusalem, 1965), p. 19; note RABD, *Šĕbu'ot*, vi, 9; and Twersky, *Rabad*, p. 276; E. Urbach, "Haśśagot ha-RABD," *ḲS*, XXXIII (1958), 361. In the introduction to the aphorisms of Hippocrates, Maimonides emphasizes the indispensability of maximum fidelity. For different views of the nature of translation, see R. Hai Gaon, *Tĕšubot hag-Gĕ'onim*, ed. A. Harkavy, p. 248 (who opposes interpretative and creative translation); cf. Dunash ben Labrat's critique of Saadia described by D. Herzog, "The Polemic Treatise against Saadya," *Saadya Studies*, ed. E. I. J. Rosenthal (Manchester, 1943), pp. 26ff.; and cf. the statement of aṣ-Ṣafadī cited by F. Rosenthal, *Isis*, XXXVI (1945–46), 253, and J. Seigel, *Rhetoric and Philosophy*, pp. 116ff. Note generally I. Sonne, *MGWJ*, LXXII, 67ff.; J. Teicher, "The Latin Hebrew . . . Translators," *Homenaje a Millas-Vallicrosa* (Barcelona, 1946), I, 440ff. Note KM, *Bikkurim*, i, 1.

attitude to translation.[82] It also spotlights a major difference between his own modus operandi and that of R. Judah the Patriarch, whose redaction of the Mishnah was predicated upon the principle of verbatim reproduction of authoritative sources—*mishnah lo' zazah mim-měkomah:* there was a certain sacrosanct quality to language, and it was preferable therefore not to tamper with earlier formulations. For Maimonides this dictum (*mishnah lo' zazah mim-měkomah*) could only mean that the contents were inviolable, and as a result he did not need to preserve the ipsissima verba, the very words of the sources. Priority is given to clear formulation of content rather than to verbatim reproduction.[83] We have here another way in which Maimonides differed radically from R. Judah. While exhibiting, and in fact utilizing, the Mishnah as his model, Maimonides' attitude to language was novel as was his system of classification. Dependence and independence are creatively intertwined.

THE SUCCESSFUL FUSION OF CONTENT AND FORM:
LITERARY FEATURES AND CODIFICATORY NEEDS

In sum, close, careful attention to language is definitely woven into the fabric of Maimonides' codificatory achievement. Nothing about it is haphazard. Just as there is no improvisation in his selection and arrangement of materials, so is there none in his style. He apparently knew that it was important to find the felicitous, and therefore imperishable, words in which to express eternal laws and universal truths. His initial choice of Mishnaic Hebrew, which presented itself as the most capacious and expressive medium, was prudently predicated upon the need to reach a wide public. The basic stylistic features of his composition were also substantive, not merely the result of formal rules or ornamental considerations. Literary amenities and codificatory needs are intertwined. Brevity, as noted, is both a principle of style as well as a canon of codification. Consequently, violations of this rule—verbosity, repetitions, polemical thrusts, arguments, summations, multiple views, and some of the other phenomena

---

82. ShM, introduction; PhM, 'Ab 1:16 (p. 417); MN, I, 74; III, 45.
83. B. Yeb 30a. See, e.g., MN, I, 2.

described in Chapter II—are simultaneously stylistic-rhetorical exceptions as well as substantive-codificatory exceptions and should be analyzed accordingly. We may even establish a conceptual correspondence between Maimonides' attitude to brevity and his consistent exaltation of oral culture; brief, cadenced, and unencumbered exposition is, inter alia, a means of memorization. Brevity and oral study are contiguous positions on a unified spectrum. Similarly, anonymity is a literary-stylistic principle as well as a procedural-substantive component of the *Mishneh Torah,* and exceptions—e.g., citations of authorities or personal pleading for certain views—have to be appraised bifocally. The unity of content and form, which, as we have noted at the very beginning, was Maimonides' goal, is thus an impressive accomplishment, and in common with other features of the Code, quite novel. The Maimonidean imprint is unmistakable—a work of massive erudition ennobled by poetic powers. The language was admired and its influence was great. Maimonidean idioms and metaphors, sententiae and interpretative tours de force were repeatedly reproduced, quoted, or adopted. Close study of the ways in which style and substance are interwoven drives home the point that one must be sensitive not only to the cognitive impact of formulations but to the emotive and evaluative overtones as well.

# VI

## Law and Philosophy

The significance of the fact that the *Mishneh Torah* reveals Maimonides as jurisprudent and philosopher simultaneously—the theme and thesis of this chapter—is twofold. The generations before the age of Maimonides had produced philosophers-scientists of great learning and dialectical skill as well as Talmudists-jurists of great erudition and versatility, many of them in Spain. There were even, as R. Abraham ibn Daud reports with great pride and precision in his *Sefer hak-Kabbalah*,[1] philosophically trained Talmudists such as R. Baruch ibn al-Balia—or others, such as R. Bahya ibn Pakuda or R. Joseph ibn Saddik, whom he does not mention[2]—scholars well versed in both Greek science and Rabbinic lore and thoroughly convinced of the need to maintain the peaceful coexistence of the two disciplines. Maimonides' sharp sense and unabashed claim of innovation notwithstanding—and he was not inclined to camouflage or lyricize this with any of the stereotyped overtures to modesty or perfunctory disclaimers[3]—he did not initiate a totally novel tendency. Maimonides' uniqueness is to be seen in the unusually great authority and prestige which he brought to this area, the spirited conjunction of nearly universal and widely respected Talmudic scholarship with philosophic acumen and originality,

---

1. *Sefer hak-Kabbalah*, ed. G. Cohen (Philadelphia, 1967), pp. 86–87; also p. 82, on R. Isaac ibn Ghiyāth, whose *Commentary on the Mishnah* Maimonides knew (see *Tĕšubot*, 128 [p. 230]). R. Joseph Ķimḥi, *Sefer hag-Galuy* (Berlin, 1887), p. 3, also notes the extra-Talmudic knowledge of Ibn Ghiyāth.

2. Maimonides had occasion to chronicle the names of some of these predecessors in his letter to R. Samuel ibn Tibbon, ed. A. Marx, *JQR*, XXV (1935), 374ff. R. Joseph ibn Saddik (author of the *'Olam Ķatan*) is one of those mentioned. Note also MN, I, 71, and commentary of H. A. Wolfson, *The Philosophy of the Kalām* (Cambridge, 1976), pp. 44ff. The pioneering contribution of R. Saadiah Gaon to the development of religious philosophy is widely noted; see R. Bahya ibn Pakuda, *Hobot hal-Lĕbabot*, introduction; I, 19, 52; R. Abraham ibn Daud, *ha-'Ĕmunah ha-Ramah* (reprinted, Jerusalem, 1967), p. 2; IT, xii.

3. Twersky, "Beginnings," p. 161.

## LAW AND PHILOSOPHY

also widely acclaimed, in a time of generally diminishing cultural creativity.[4] His importance is to be assessed generally in terms of the scope and profundity of his achievement, and particularly in terms of the unprecedented extent to which he amalgamated these disciplines and commitments. It is possible—because this amalgamation is so thorough—to take a good measure of Maimonides' rationalism, of his religious ideology and intellectual temper, on the basis of the *Mishneh Torah* without reference to the *Moreh*.[5] As we have stated in Chapter I, he himself spoke of his zeal "for the Lord God of Israel, when I see before me a nation that does not have a comprehensive book (of laws) in the true sense nor true and accurate (theological) opinions." This clearly underscores that the ongoing reciprocity and complementarity of law and philosophy is a key feature of the Code, which would deal with beliefs as well as actions, rationales as well as directives.

This theme, moreover, is crucial for understanding one of the most controversial issues of Maimonidean scholarship—the relationship of the sovereign master of the halakah to the zealous disciple of Aristotle. Was this marked by sincerity or by duplicity? Was the inevitable tension energizing or enervating, constructive or destructive, and did it produce an honest encounter or deft double-talk? Was Maimonides able to combine the religious *vita activa* with the philosophic *vita contemplativa?* Reflection and action, philosophical pursuit and political activity, individual perfection and social involvement—were these reconcilable? Was there a genuine incompatibility between meaningful observance of *miṣwot* and serious study and appreciation of physics and metaphysics? As a matter of fact, these questions were asked by medievals as well as moderns, partisans and antagonists, legists

---

4. See chap. I, above; also Twersky, "Sefer MT," pp. 8ff.
5. E.g., RaSHBA, *Tešubot* (Venice, 1546), 414 (esp. p. 63a); R. Simeon ben Ṣemaḥ Duran, *Magen 'Abot* (Leghorn, 1785), III, 73b; R. Menaḥem ben Zerah, *Ṣedah lad-Derek* (Warsaw, 1880), p. 34; R. Elijah Gaon, *Yoreh De'ah*, 179:13 (see J. Dienstag in *Talpiyot*, IV [1949], 255, who gives a bibliography concerning the attempt by the enlightenment writer S. J. Fuenn [*Kiryah Ne'ĕmanah*] to dismiss this comment as spurious). For an appreciative reaction, see the comment of the fifteenth-century R. Saadiah ben David, published by S. Assaf in *KS*, XXII (1946), 242. See below, n. 10.

## 358 INTRODUCTION TO THE CODE OF MAIMONIDES

and philosophers, as well as kabbalists and ethicists. Their answers were as different as their evaluations of Maimonides, tempered of course by their own ideological convictions and/or related contingencies. To a great extent the study of Maimonides is a story of "self-mirroring."[6] An open-ended study of the *Mishneh Torah* may give new direction and coherence to the investigation and resolution of this matter.

William James is reported to have said that "any author is easy if you can catch the center of his vision." The complex theme of this chapter deserves, in my opinion, to be described as the center of Maimonides' vision, the Archimedean point of Maimonideanism.

Let me emphasize again, as noted in Chapter I, that we are not primarily concerned with the peculiar problematics of the *Moreh Nĕbukim*, nor is the focus of our investigation the tension between

---

6. For premodern views, see below, n. 380. Some significant illustrations of the range of opinion and characterization in modern scholarship are provided by the works of E. Feldman, E. Goldman, I. Husik, D. Neumark, S. Pines, S. Rawidowicz, L. Strauss, G. Vajda, and H. A. Wolfson, mentioned in the bibliography, below. The shifting formulations of H. A. Wolfson demonstrate the complexity and stickiness of the issue; cf. his "Maimonides and Halevi," *JQR*, II (1912), 315, reprinted in *Studies in the History of Philosophy and Religion*, ed. I. Twersky and G. Williams (Cambridge, Mass., 1973–76), II, 138; "The Classification of Sciences in Medieval Jewish Philosophy," *Hebrew Union College Jubilee Volume* (Cincinnati, 1925), p. 313, reprinted in ibid., I; *The Philosophy of Spinoza* (Cambridge, 1934), II, 320–21. The title of G. Vajda's article, "La pensée religieuse de Moise Maimonide: unité ou dualité?", *Cahiers de Civilisation Médiévale*, IX (1966), 29–49, is emblematic. For the problem generally, see also G. Vajda, in *Tarbiz*, XXIV, 310. On "self-mirroring" see E. Auerbach, *Mimesis* (New York, 1957), pp. 289–91.

One great value of the various, probably spurious, works attributed to Maimonides is the light they shed upon the issues of the time, the attempts to assimilate Maimonides to one's own attitudes, and the countervailing tendencies (so-called left-wing and right-wing schools) in Maimonidean interpretation. *Pĕrakim bĕ-Haṣlaḥah*, ed. S. Davidowicz and D. Baneth (Jerusalem, 1939), for example, a heavily exegetical work, is very much concerned with the importance of prayer and precepts versus intellectual achievement. Prophecy, ecstasy, and symbolism are also treated. Maimonides' "will" (see *Hebrew Ethical Wills*, ed. I. Abrahams [Philadelphia, 1948], I, 115; *Kobeṣ*, II, 39b) is concerned with the specific problems of popularization and esotericism. Cf., e.g., G. Scholem, in *Tarbiz*, VI (1935), 335; A. Heschel, in *L. Ginzberg Jubilee Volume* (New York, 1946), p. 170. A review of the entire question of real or alleged Maimonidean pseudepigrapha—an issue which had already agitated medieval scholars—is a scholarly desideratum. See, e.g., Commentary of Shem Tob, MN, III, 51. Note the sharp divergence of opinion concerning the MN itself between Z. Yawitz and Rabbi A. Kook: Z. Yawitz, *Tolĕdot Yiśra'el* (Tel Aviv, 1935), XII (with special article by Rabbi Kook). See the bibliography in M. Steinschneider, *Catalogus Librorum Hebraeorum in . . . Bodleiana* (Oxford, 1852–60), columns 1932–37.

# LAW AND PHILOSOPHY

the *Moreh* and the *Mishneh Torah*. The nature of our analysis necessitates that we zero in on the real or putative manifestations of tension *within* the *Mishneh Torah* itself. All indications are that Maimonides set out to create *in his Code* a new, cohesive, organic entity. Every careful reader must therefore pause periodically to ponder whether in fact Maimonides succeeded in achieving his goal, whether this unprecedented, comprehensive, meticulously arranged Code, with its substantive philosophic component and spiritualist thrust, maintains its own harmoniousness and equilibrium or whether there are stresses and strains which ruffle its surface and content.

## COMPLEMENTARITY AND RECIPROCITY OF HALAKAH AND PHILOSOPHY

Maimonides was not only unshakably convinced of the indispensability of philosophy for religion and the general nobility of intellectual perfection but was also deeply concerned about the essential relationship or constant intersection of philosophy and halakah.[7] More precisely, he was constantly aware of the abiding need to nurture such a relationship and to demonstrate with great deliberation and emphasis the inseparability and complementarity of the two apparently discordant but intrinsically harmonious disciplines. While the jurist generally cares only about the law, the arena of actions and behavior, and considers any preamble or postscript inept and pointless, the philosopher cares primarily about the rational principle and philosophic animus, the moral standard and the intellectual objective, rather than the content of the law and its specific imperatives.[8] Maimonides as jurist and philosopher combined both interests in all his writings. His ideal

---

7. E.g., *Yĕsode hat-Torah*, iv, 13; *Tĕšubah*, x; MN, III, 51–54. I am here concerned primarily with the *Mishneh Torah*, and only to the extent that it is necessary shall I deal with the whole problem of the ideational unity of the multifaceted Maimonidean literary corpus. See Twersky, "Non-Halakic Aspects," pp. 95ff.

8. See J. W. Jones, *The Law and Legal Theory of the Greeks* (Oxford, 1956), p. 8. Plato (*Laws*, IV, 722, B) declares that unlike other legislators he will provide preambles. H. A. Wolfson, *Philo* (Cambridge, 1962), I, 131, notes that Philo was not a jurist, and this is important for the evaluation of his philosophic-homiletic interpretations. Cf. L. Berman, "Maimonides, the disciple of Alfarabi," *Israel Oriental Studies*, IV (1974), 154–78, and especially p. 169, n.51.

was a blending of that which in the *Moreh* is called "the science of the law," namely "the legalistic study of the law" (Talmud or *fiqh*), and the "science of the law in its true sense", i.e., the philosophical foundations of the Talmud.[9] The phrase "legalistic study of the law" makes us pause and ponder, as soon as we perceive that it is not an idle tautology or a clumsy formulation—as if there could be a nonlegalistic study of the law! Actually, it establishes in one bold stroke that law is two-dimensional: legal (in the restricted, positive sense) and metalegal or philosophical, two related components of the Oral Law that must not be dissociated. De facto, however, they may be separated, and as the medieval reality reflected in the introduction to the *Moreh* or in its famous palace metaphor makes clear, they have regrettably been separated; ideally of course their unity and complementarity should be maintained. Maimonides worked hard for this maintenance. His system affirmed that the halakah led from thought to habit, from belief to character, from intelligence to will, and vice versa; no fragmentation or bifurcation in study or practice is tolerable. The "science of the law in the true sense" should inform and infuse the legalistic study of the law; steady, smooth, rhythmic movement from one to the other should sustain the fusion of action and contemplation.

This theme is a central pillar of the elaborate multidimensional Maimonidean structure. His *Commentary on the Mishnah* abounds with statements favoring the process of intellectualization and stressing the ongoing reciprocity between normative action and philosophical reflection, between religious-ethical behavior and intellectual perfection, or in literary categories, between Talmudic and philosophic study. The significance of such a statement as "expounding a single principle of the principles (of religion) is more important to me than anything else that I might teach"[10] is transparent and sheds its light on the entire work.

---

9. MN, introduction; I, 71; III, 54. See, however, *'Iggĕrot*, 68.
10. PhM, Ber 9:7 (pp. 91–92). The key term is *uṣūl*, usually rendered as *yĕsodot* or principles. See also PhM, 'Ab 5:6 (p. 458); MN, I, 51. Maimonides notes on occasion that, notwithstanding their difficulty, he introduces subtle philosophic issues in his halakic works; see, e.g., PhM, 'Ab 3:20 (p. 436). In MN, I, 68, while analyzing the dictum that God is "the intellect (*ŝekel*) as well as the intellectually cognizing subject (*maśkil*) and the intellectually cognized object (*muśkal*)," he notes that this is an extremely

Concomitantly—and this of course is less surprising in a work of juridical commentary—he describes, with pride and gratification, his unremitting efforts in collecting and conceptualizing the diffuse and picayune laws of *Ṭohărot*, "bristling with fundamental difficulties even in early times . . . and which even the greatest masters find hard to comprehend."[11] Details of positive law and principles of religion—in this case, the question of reward and punishment—should be happily and necessarily intertwined; this was Maimonides' unfaltering belief.

The *Mishnah Commentary* contains one parenthetic, and I think hitherto unnoticed, statement in which Maimonides publicly told the entire story of this dialectical-symbiotic relationship. Always sensitive to matters of structure, sequence, and classification, Maimonides indirectly asks why the famous mishnah referring to the study of *ma'ăśeh bĕre'šit* (physics, according to him) and *ma'ăśeh merkabah* (metaphysics, according to him) was placed in the tractate *Ḥăḡiḡah* immediately following a highly compressed passage referring to such extremely complex halakic matters as vows, Sabbath laws, holiday sacrifices, uncleanness, etc. The question is of course typically Maimonidean and apparently quite novel. His explanation is strikingly simple: inasmuch as all these latter topics were described by the Sages as *gufe Torah* (the essentials, literally *the bodies,* of Torah), it was imperative to mention those matters which are the *yĕsoḏot gufe Torah* (the principles, roots, or foundations of these essentials). *Yĕsoḏot* are the theological foundations and premises of practical laws, their invisible core, and as we shall see, this is how *Yĕsoḏe hat-Torah* in the *Mishneh Torah* should be understood.[12] The relationship is horizontal and synchronic rather than vertical and diachronic.

---

complex concept which few will understand properly. This did not deter him from presenting the concept summarily in MT, *Yĕsoḏe hat-Torah,* ii, 10. Later R. Moses Provençalo was vehemently attacked for publicly explaining this doctrine; see E. Kupfer, *Sinai,* LXIII (1960), pp. 137ff., and R. Bonfil, *KS,* L (1975), p. 3, n.15. Such a skillful commentator as R. Moses di Trani recognized the fusion of the two fields by stating that he will regularly skip all theological and scientific matters which Maimonides included; *Kiryat Sefer,* introduction, p. 24b.

11. PhM, Ṭoh, introduction (p. 33); see Twersky, *Rabad,* p. 107.
12. PhM, Ḥaḡ 2:1 (p. 378). The crucial phrase was omitted in all printed editions, as noted by Kāfiḥ, because of haplography. Again, the key term here is *uṣūl;* see L. Berman, "Maimonides," p. 164, n.34. Note now Maimonides' use in MT, '*Akum,* ii, 5; also

The perplexed, who is described with eloquence and precision in the introduction to the *Moreh*, is perplexed by "the externals of the law,"[13] a suggestive phrase referring in the first instance to ideas and beliefs—doctrinal statements—of the law stripped of their inner allegorical meaning and true underlying essence, but also to regulations—behavioral prescriptions and proscriptions—of the law stripped of their inner motive forces and spiritual stimuli. Law per se, externalized, despiritualized, or deintellectualized, is a problem. Law properly understood and fully experienced is a means to emotional catharsis as well as to intellectual perfection. This circular-reciprocal relationship, a cornerstone of the Maimonidean system, is formulated in an adjacent passage of the *Moreh* as follows: "Do you not see the following fact? God, may His mention be exalted, wished us to be perfected and the state of our societies to be improved by the laws regarding actions (i.e., halakah). Now this can come about only after the adoption of intellectual beliefs. . . . This, in its turn, cannot come about except through divine science, and this divine science cannot become actual except after a study of natural science."[14] The effectiveness of positive law[15] is thus contingent

---

*Šabbat*, xii, 8; and cf. L. Strauss' comment in *Studies in Religion and Jewish Mysticism Presented to G. Scholem* (Jerusalem, 1967), p. 276. In the light of this, the contention of some medievals—e.g., R. Isaac Abarbanel, *Roš 'Āmanah*—that all laws are equal in worth and that it is impossible to single out thirteen basic principles, is thus completely beside the point. *Yěsodot* are synchronically related to all commandments; they permeate the entire law. See also the reference to *hilkot 'ĕmunah* in R. Nissim Gaon, ed. S. Abramson (Jerusalem, 1968), p. 333. For kabbalistic use of the mishnah in *Ḥăğiğah*, see E. Gottlieb, in *Tarbiz*, XXXVII (1968), 294ff. (reprinted in his *Meḥkarim bě-Sifrut hak-Kabbalah*, ed. J. Hacker [Tel Aviv, 1976], pp. 59ff.). For *yěsodot*, see also *Hobot hal-Lěbabot*, I, introduction (p. 20).

13. MN, introduction (p. 5): *zawāhir al-sharī'ah, pěšaṭe hat-Torah*. See also MN, I, 2 (and an interesting echo in *Peruš* to Job by R. Zerahiah ben Shealtiel of Barcelona [*Peruše Rišonim*, ed. I. Schwarz (Berlin, 1868)], p. 180); MN, I, 36, 53; III, 28, 29; and II, 47, cited further on p. 376. See the same phrase in PhM, Ber 8:8 (p. 86), and note *Těšubot*, 265 (p. 502), about Karaites who adhere to the external meaning of Scripture; MTH, 3, 9, 10; also PhM, 'Ab 4:5. See below, n.40.

14. MN, introduction (p. 9), on natural science and divine science; see also the dedicatory epistle (p. 3), I, 17, 31–34, 54; II, 1 (where all proofs of the existence of God relate to physics); III, 34, 49, 51. See S. Pines, translator's introduction, MN, p. 115. Also *Yěsode hat-Torah*, iv, 12; *Těšubah*, x, 6; and note the verse in *Těfıllah*, viii, 2.

15. For this term, see S. Kuttner, "Sur les origines du terme 'droit positif,' " *Revue Historique de Droit Français et Étranger* (1936), pp. 728ff. See also V. Mises, *Positivism* (Cambridge, 1951). I use it as the equivalent of Maimonides' "the legalistic science of the

upon some *prior* acceptance of true theological beliefs and scientific concepts. Only then will the practitioner be sensitive to the true import of the law and be exposed to the true intent of morality.

However, law, as we shall see, is also a propaedeutic and a prophylactic for true belief, i.e., laws protect and promulgate true opinions, solidify and concretize abstract notions: "You know from what I have said that opinions do not last unless they are accompanied by actions that strengthen them, make them generally known, and perpetuate them among the multitude."[16] Observance of the Sabbath is consequently explained by Maimonides as a means of concretizing and popularizing belief in God's unity and sovereignty over the world: "We are ordered by the law to exalt this day, in order that the principle of the creation of the world in time be established and universally known in the world through the fact that all people refrain from working on one and the same day."[17] Law is both cause and consequence, catalyst and crystallization, of the cognitive goal, just as it is both stimulus and sequel to love of God. Maimonides is a good teacher of the lesson that love of God fosters a dedication to, and zeal in, observance of commandments which in turn fan the flames of a more intense yearning for, and consuming love of, God.[18]

---

law," in contradistinction to metaphysics, *both* of which are components of the Maimonidean conception of the Oral Law. Note the formulation of reciprocity in MN, III, 54 (p. 633): "The Sages mention likewise that man is required first to obtain knowledge of the Torah, then to obtain wisdom, then to know what is incumbent upon him with regard to the legal science of the law—I mean the drawing of inferences concerning what one ought to do." See the balanced and judicious remarks of H. Lazarus-Yafeh, "The Place of the Religious Commandments in the Philosophy of al-Ghazālī," *Muslim World*, XI (1961), 173ff., especially pp. 178–79, concerning reciprocal influences of knowledge (*'ilm*) and action. See I. Goldziher, *Pseudo-Baḥya: Kitāb ma'āni al-nafs* (Berlin, 1907), pp. 58ff. A good example, still useful methodologically, of the question of consistency versus contradiction in an author's oeuvre is E. K. Rand, "On the Composition of Boethius' *Consolatio philosophiae*," *Harvard Studies in Classical Philology*, XV (1904), 1–28.

16. MN, II, 31; cf. III, 32 (p. 531).

17. For Maimonides' explanation of the Sabbath, cf. Naḥmanides, *Peruš*, Deut. 5:12; RIṬBA, *Sefer Zikkaron*, ed. K. Kahana (Jerusalem, 1956), pp. 63–64. See Y. Ben-Sasson's comparative study of Maimonides and hal-Levi, "Haš-Šabbat bĕ-Maḥšebet hay-Yahādut," *Ma'ăyanot* (Jerusalem, 1974), pp. 78–116.

18. ShM, positive 2; MN, III, 24 (p. 502), 27, 29 (p. 518), 52; *'Iggĕrot*, 15; Letter to Ibn Jābir, *Ḳobeṣ*, II, 16b. The goal of all commandments is fear and love of God, but the consequence of this fear and love is not only the *vita contemplativa* but a deepened, more

Indeed, the two realms *must* be inseparable, for a system that addresses itself exclusively to normative action and ignores philosophical reflection—a socio-economic behaviorism but not a theological construct—belongs to an inferior political order, in no way approximating a divine system:

> Accordingly, if you find a law the whole end of which, and the whole purpose of the chief thereof, who determined the actions required by it, are directed exclusively toward the ordering of the city and of its circumstances and the abolition in it of injustice and oppression; and if in that law attention is not at all directed toward speculative matters, no heed is given to the perfecting of the rational faculty, and no regard is accorded to opinions being correct or faulty—the whole purpose of that law being, on the contrary, the arrangement, in whatever way this may be brought about, of the circumstances of people in their relations with one another and provision for their obtaining, in accordance with the opinion of that chief, a certain something deemed to be happiness—you must know that that law is a *nomos,* and that the man who laid it down belongs, as we have mentioned, to the third class, I mean to say to those who are perfect only in their imaginative faculty.
>
> If, on the other hand, you find a law all of whose ordinances are due to attention being paid, as was stated before, to the soundness of the circumstances pertaining to the body and also to the soundness of belief—a law that takes pains to inculcate correct opinions with regard to God, may He be exalted, in the first place, and with regard to the angels, and that desires to make man wise, to give him understanding, and to awaken his attention, so that he should know the whole of that which exists in its true form—you must know that this guidance comes from Him, may He be exalted, and that this law is divine.[19]

## MAIMONIDES' CONTINUOUS PREOCCUPATION WITH RABBINICS AND METAPHYSICS

These select references to the *Mishnah Commentary* and the *Moreh* are purely representative, serving to provide a useful mold for our theme; the fact is that this dual concern is regu-

---

sensitive, highly motivated performance of laws. See also *Yĕsoḏe hat-Torah,* ii, 1; iv, 12; *Tĕšuḇah* x, 2; MN, I, 39; and above, chap. IV, n. 49; S. Rawidowicz, *'Iyyunim bĕ-Maḥšeḇet Yiśra'el* (Jerusalem, 1969), pp. 318ff. Note R. Abraham ibn Ezra, *Yĕsoḏ Mora',* chap. I (p. 15b). The concept of *'ăḇoḏah* in MN, III, 51, requires special study; it is a special form of commitment to God.

19. MN, II, 40.

larly reflected in the ongoing simultaneous preoccupation of Maimonides with the two broad genres of Rabbinics and metaphysics, from his *juvenilia* to his very last works. Textual-philological investigation, fully sustained by historical-biographical information, makes it perfectly clear that Maimonides' reputation as creative religious philosopher and enthusiastic propagator of philosophy and his identification with a lofty rationalism were widespread long before the circulation of the *Guide*. As early as in the first letter of R. Joseph ben Judah to Maimonides, a flowery and artistically constructed epistle from a trusted and devoted disciple to an admired, even venerated, master, the latter is extolled as enlightener of the bewildered, purifier of religious belief, and philosophic pedagogue par excellence.[20] Professor Baneth noted in passing that we may infer from this that Maimonides' fame as philosopher was firmly entrenched relatively early in his public career.[21] I would suggest that this reputation could have been based not only on hearsay and orally transmitted evaluations but also on thoughtful reading of "our Talmudic works" (or "our legal compilations"), as he usually designates the *Mishnah Commentary* and the Code.[22] Such a reading would reveal these characteristics, general definitions of purpose, assumptions, aspirations, and tendencies of thought. Discussion in the *Mishnah Commentary* of such problems as the authority of the Oral Law (its theoretical, historical, and doctrinal foundations),[23] prophecy,[24] the identification of physics and

---

20. *'Iggĕrot*, 5–6.
21. Ibid., 4, In the light of the references in this epistle we may with greater certitude disregard the ascription to R. Joseph ben Judah of the poem in the *Dīwān* of R. Judah hal-Levi, ed. H. Brody (Berlin, 1901), p. 105, n.72. See Brody's comments ad loc.; also J. Mann, *The Jews in Egypt and Palestine under the Fatimid Caliphs* (London, 1920), I, 234, n.8. See the poem in praise of Maimonides published by J. Toledano, *'Oṣar Gĕnuzim* (Jerusalem, 1960), pp. 29–31.
22. E.g., MN, introduction (p. 6); I, 71. There is, of course, the *Millot ha-Higgayon*, but it is difficult to gauge its immediate impact and determine the extent of its influence and popularity. Cf. D. Baneth, *KS*, XIV (1937), 330. See the annotated bibliography by J. Dienstag, *'Ărēṣet*, II (1960), 7–32.
23. PhM, introduction (pp. 4ff., 19ff.); cf. R. D. Fuerstenthal, *Das jüdische Traditionswesen* (Breslau, 1842). In the MTH, 4, Maimonides says very summarily that the introduction to the *Commentary* explored prophecy, tradition, and the Oral Law.
24. PhM, introduction (pp. 5ff.); Sanh 10, introduction, seventh principle (pp. 212ff.).

## 366 INTRODUCTION TO THE CODE OF MAIMONIDES

metaphysics with *ma'áśeh běre'šit* and *ma'áśeh merkabah*,[25] free will and predestination, together with reward and punishment,[26] history of religion,[27] magic and medicine,[28] miracles,[29] immortality and the world to come,[30] and proper use of allegory,[31] is revealing, for it is neither incidental nor accidental. Just the

25. PhM, Ḥāḡ 2:1 (p. 376); see L. Berman in *JAOS*, LXXXV (1965), 412–13. Note that Maimonides' special definition of *ḥokmah yĕwanit* in PhM Soṭ 9:15 (p. 277) helps clear the way for his exaltation of philosophy. See S. Lieberman, *Hellenism in Jewish Palestine* (New York, 1962), pp. 100–15.

26. PhM, Bĕr 9:7 (p. 91); ŠP, chap. VIII; PhM, 'Aḇ 1:3 (p. 408). See A. Altmann, "The Religion of the Thinkers: Free Will and Predestination in Maimonides," *Religion in a Religious Age*, ed. S. D. Goitein (Cambridge, 1974), pp. 25–53.

27. PhM, AZ, 4:7 (p. 357); Soṭ 7:4 (p. 267), which is a much harsher formulation than the parallel in MN, I, 61 (p. 149). Also, PhM, Pes 10:4 (p. 203).

28. PhM, Pes 4:10 (p. 177); Shab 6:2 (p. 38); Yoma, 8:4 (p. 265). Many of his letters comment on his medical career; e.g., *'Iggĕroṯ*, 69; *Tĕšuḇoṯ*, III, 56; *Ḳoḇeṣ*, II, 28b. Note *Malweh wĕ-Loweh*, xv, 1; *De'oṯ*, iv, 20 (and see Lieberman, *Šĕḳi'in*, p. 99). Also PhM Ned 4:4 (p. 129) and *Nĕḏarim*, vi, 8.

29. PhM, 'Aḇ 5:5 (p. 456); cf. MN, II, 29; and *Kuzari*, III, 73; see n.25, above, and Wolfson, *Philo*, I, 351.

30. PhM, Sanh 10, introduction [*Pereḳ Ḥeleḳ*] (pp. 200ff.). Note PhM, Ber 9:7 (p. 90).

31. PhM, Sanh 10, introduction; other significant statements on methodology include PhM, Soṭ 3:3 (p. 256); Sanh 10:3 (p. 218); Shebu 1:4 (p. 250); Neḡ 12:5 (p. 397); Mak 3:6 (p. 247). For a variety of extra-halakic references, see also Ber 1:1 (p. 60); 9:3 (p. 89); Ter 1:2 (p. 270); RH 2:7 (p. 317); Suk 1:1,4 (p. 269); BḲ 4:3 (p. 20); Sanh 3:3 (p. 158); Kel 1:5 (p. 49); and others. These concretize his statement in the introduction (see n.34, below) that his commentary is based, inter alia, on "that which I learned from wisdom (*'ilm*)."

Maimonides was very conscious of the multiple problems—general-substantive and specific—of exegesis. There was, first, the need to defend the use of allegory—particularly in aggadah—as an indispensable interpretative method. Maimonides repeatedly argues (e.g. MN, II, 30 [p. 355]) that since the rabbis freely and effectively used allegory in their interpretation of the Bible, we may—indeed must—use it in interpreting their sayings. Allegorical interpretation is of the very essence of *ḥidah* and *mašal*; it is required philologically. See, e.g., *Yĕsoḏe hat-Torah*, i, 9, 12; *Tĕšuḇah*, viii, 2, 4; MTH, 9–10.

There is also the need to anticipate the charge of arbitrariness or willful innovation in the process of such interpretation. In the introduction to the third part of the *Moreh*, Maimonides gives an elegant, carefully calibrated characterization of proper exegesis and, eo ipso, a defense of his views:

In addition to this there is the fact that in that which has occurred to me with regard to these matters, I followed conjecture and supposition; no divine revelation has come to me to teach me that the intention in the matter in question was such and such, nor did I receive what I believe in these matters from a teacher. But the texts of the prophetic books and the dicta of the sages, together with the speculative premises that I possess, showed me that things are indubitably so and so. Yet it is possible that they are different and that something else is intended. Now rightly guided reflection and divine aid in this matter have moved me to a position, which I shall describe. Namely, I shall interpret to you that which was said by Ezekiel the prophet, in such a way that anyone who heard that interpretation would think

various introductions and excursuses, especially the general introduction, the *Eight Chapters* (introduction to 'Aḇ), and the introduction to *Pereḳ Ḥeleḳ* (Sanh 10), with their philosophical, psychological, and ethical disquisitions, enable the reader to take a rather accurate measure of the Maimonidean temper.[32] Maimonides' frank declaration, to be repeated frequently, about the indispensability of non-Jewish sources of wisdom and the need to "accept the truth from whatever source it proceeds" rivets the reader's attention to itself.[33] He specifically includes *ḥokmah* (*'ilm*) among his sources and resources in the composition of the

---

that I do not say anything over and beyond what is indicated by the text, but that it is as if I translated words from one language to another or summarized the meaning of the external sense of the speech.

Allegory here in the mind of the interpreter is clearly not "a purposeful deformation of literary material," (see R. Bolgar, *The Classical Heritage*, [New York, 1964], p. 218) even though his opponents may so denigrate it; e.g. R. Meir hal-Levi Abulafia, *Yaḏ Ramah: Sanhedrin* (Warsaw, n.d.), 158 b.

Some kind of measured harmony seems to underlie the concluding paragraphs of the MT (*Mĕlakim*, xii, 1):

Let no one think that in the days of the Messiah any of the laws of nature will be set aside, or any innovation be introduced into creation. The world will follow its normal course. The words of Isaiah, *And the wolf shall dwell with the lamb, and the leopard shall lie down with the kid* (Isa. 11:6) are to be understood figuratively, meaning that Israel will live securely among the wicked of the heathens who are likened to wolves and leopards, as it is written: *A wolf of the deserts does spoil them, a leopard watches over their cities* (Jer. 5:6). They will all accept the true religion and will neither plunder nor destroy, and together with Israel earn a comfortable living in a legitimate way, as it is written: *And the lion shall eat straw like the ox* (Isa. 11:7). All similar expressions used in connection with the Messianic age are parables (*mĕšalim*). In the days of King Messiah the full meaning of those metaphors and their allusions will become clear to all.

There is here a re-affirmation of the use of figurative language and its allegorical interpretation—examples of which are given—but simultaneously Maimonides implies that not all parables can definitively be interpreted. The same hesitation echoes in the restraining counsel concerning Messianic aggaḏot. As we have seen, allegorical interpretation of aggaḏah is axiomatic and imperative for Maimonides. His concession here is that the intention of the parable may not always be transparent. The prudent interpreter will be cautious and, when necessary, suspend judgment. Allegory is thus safeguarded.

32. These were also the first sections of the commentary to be translated into Hebrew by R. Judah al-Harizi and R. Samuel ibn Tibbon; see generally A. Ya'ari, in *KS*, IX (1932), 101–09, 228–35. A sense of restraint and discipline prevented Maimonides from digressions unless there was compelling need; PhM, RH 3:6 (p. 324) and above, n. 30.

33. ŠP, introduction: "Know, however, that the ideas presented in these chapters and in the following commentary are not of my own invention; neither did I think out the explanations contained therein, but I have gleaned them from the words of the wise occurring in the Midrashim, in the Talmud, and in other of their works, as well as from the words of the philosophers, ancient and recent, and also from the works of various authors,

*Mishnah Commentary*.[34] There is a consistent juxtaposition of Torah and *ḥokmah* either as sources of his teaching and objects of his attention, or just as natural companions.[35] No comprehensive characterization of the components of Torah ever omits *ḥokmah*. One could not confront this abundant material in the *Mishnah Commentary* impassively or dismiss it as insignificant. Its uniqueness in quality and quantity was striking.

We may further combine the above reference of R. Joseph ben Judah with that of another correspondent asking Maimonides for guidance in the study of astronomy.[36] Another contemporary, R. Joseph ibn Aknin, also at a rather early date, described Maimonides in similar vein, as battling for the Torah with the "swords of syllogistic demonstration."[37] On the other hand, we have previously established that not only did Maimonides' luster as halakic authority not dim while he was preoccupied with his philosophic opus, but that he also continued to write commentaries and novellae, and of course responsa, even after the *Mishneh Torah* (which should allegedly have acquitted him of his Talmudic obligations) was in circulation and the *Moreh* was in various stages of preparation.[38] The incontrovertible fact is that the two preoccupations, not without some tension, continually

---

as one should accept the truth from whatever source it proceeds." See *Kidduš ha-Ḥodeš*, xvii, 24; *Yĕsode hat-Torah*, iii, 5; Sanhedrin, ii, 1. Note also MN, II, 8, concerning the provocative statement in B. Pes. 94b (about the superior astronomical knowledge of non-Jewish scholars), and the statement of his son R. Abraham, *Milḥamot has-Šem*, ed. R. Margaliyot (Jerusalem, 1953), pp. 86–88. I have treated the history of this passage in a forthcoming article on Joseph ibn Kaspi.

34. PhM, introduction (p. 47). For this term, see D. Baneth, "Lat-Terminologiyah hap-Pilosofit šel ha-RaMBaM," *Tarbiz*, IV (1935), 21, 23.

35. PhM, introduction (p. 39). This parallelism is already found in the introductory poem which he wrote for this commentary, A. Marx, *JQR*, XXV (1935), 389: לשום בתורתו לבד חשקו, לאכול פרי חכמה לבד חוקו. See also PhM, BM 4:10 (p. 68), and cf. *Mĕkinah*, xiv, 14, and *LM*, ad loc. Note PhM, Soṭ 9:9 (p. 276).

36. See S. D. Goitein, in *Tarbiz*, XXXIV (1965), 235–36.

37. *Hitgalut has-Sodot . . . Peruš Šir haš-Širim*, ed. A. Halkin (Jerusalem, 1964), p. 431: מופת הזמן הנלחם מלחמתה של תורה בחרבות המופת.

38. See above, chap. I. Actually, the rather remarkable letter to Ibn Jābir (*Koḇeṣ*, II, 16a) is itself a full microcosm of Maimonidean interests, emphases, and achievements. The letter moves smoothly from general remarks about the indispensability of ongoing study (regardless of the language, i.e., Hebrew or Arabic) to comments on the question of corporeal resurrection and on to clarification of certain halakic issues (Sabbath, menstruation); it then proceeds to take up the issue of immortality of the soul and concludes with halakic notes on *ta'āniyyot* and *lulab*.

existed and *both* interests were operative in *all* his writings. The literary interests mirror the ideological impulses.

In sum, the extraordinarily creative and comprehensive Maimonidean literary corpus reveals a difference of tone but a consistency of vision, an enticing variety of themes but a striking uniformity of emphasis. In spite of changes, evolution of thought, allusive presentation of certain ideas, and outright contradictions,[39] his work adds up to a judicious interpretation and systematic presentation of Jewish belief and practice. As it moves from one literary form to another, from textual explication to independent exposition, and from one level of exposition to another, the reader, moving with it, would think that Maimonides had a master plan from the very beginning to achieve his overarching objective: to bring law and philosophy, two apparently incongruous attitudes of mind, two jealous rivals, into fruitful harmony. We see him consistently espousing a sensitized view of religion and morality, demanding a full and uncompromising but inspired and sensitive observance of the law, openly disdaining the perfunctory vulgar view of the masses, searching for the ultimate religious significance of every human action, and urging a commitment to, and quest for, wisdom and perfection. He was particularly irritated by facile literalism, a source of confusion and error.[40] He wanted to unify mood and

---

39. There are, of course, numerous halakic and philosophic changes in the course of Maimonides' writing, some of which he himself noted; see, e.g., *'Iggĕroṯ*, 58; *Hilḵoṯ hay-Yĕrušalmi*, ed. S. Lieberman (New York, 1947), pp. 6ff.; also M. Guttmann, in *HUCA*, II (1925), 229ff. Concerning *ši'ur ḳomah*, see *Tĕšuḇoṯ*, 117 (p. 201), and S. Lieberman's Hebrew appendix to G. Scholem, *Jewish Gnosticism, Merkabah Mysticism, and Talmudic Tradition* (New York, 1960), pp. 118ff. Concerning charity (whether one may give more than the stipulated maximum of twenty percent), see PhM, Pe 1:1 (p. 93), and *'Ăraḵin*, viii, 13 (also *De'oṯ*, v, 12). Note the following curious instance: whether Maimonides' formulation in *Gerušin*, x, 21, concerning the reasons for divorce contradicts his statement in PhM, Giṭ 9:10 (p. 244), or in MN, III, 49, is discussed in answer to Napoleon's questions submitted to the Sanhedrin; see J. Rosenthal, *Meḥḳarim* (Jerusalem, 1967), II, 517. See below, nn. 224–30. The identification of change does not mean premeditated contradiction or shrewdly devised double standards. See below, p. 447.

40. *Siḵluṭ* (literally "ignorance")—the opposite of *ḥikmah* or *sophia* (see MN, III, 11)—is used to denote literalism. See Twersky, "Non-Halakic Aspects," p. 95, n. 1; H. A. Wolfson, "The Jewish Kalam," *JQR*, LXXV (1967), 55, n. 34; A. Altmann, "Religion of the Thinkers," p. 50, n. 124. *Saḵal* or *ṭippeš* is a literalist; see *Tĕšuḇah*, v, 1, and viii, 6; MN, II, 25; also *Tĕmidin u-Musafin*, vii, 11, where "fools" (*ṭippĕšim*) is used to designate Karaites—another type of literalist. See also *Mĕzuzah*, v, 4. For a fool or an incompetent in

medium, to integrate the thought of eternity with the life of temporality, to combine religious tradition with philosophical doctrine. He knew that this could not be done easily or indiscriminately, but he was convinced that the very attempt, though fraught with danger of vulgarization and misinterpretation, was indispensable for true religious perfection. It may be said that Maimonides allowed religious rationalization, which had led a sort of subliminal existence in earlier Rabbinic writing, to claim and obtain legitimacy and dignity.

Indeed, his reconstruction of the history of philosophy (which, as we shall see, has halakic repercussions) demonstrates most cogently that the philosophical connection of religion must be accorded legitimacy, inasmuch as philosophy had originally been an essential ingredient of the Jewish tradition. Failure to reestablish this natural unity between the legalistic science of law and law in its true sense raises the specter of illegitimacy, for unphilosophical religion is for Maimonides a historical and phenomenological aberration. His passion for philosophy is thus in a formal sense restorative rather than innovative.[41] In any event, the use of reason, as will be seen in many contexts, was not a kind of latter-day humanism or rationalism (religion within the limits of reason alone), a manifestation of hubris in the sense of "aggrandisement of man against God";[42] it did not, with smugness and illusionary conceptions, pit human reason against divine norm, but was rather an expression of love, desiring to bring man closer to God via knowledge. Human reason was to be pressed into the service of divine norm. This religious-philosophical conviction was as daring as its realization was difficult and could be misunderstood or distorted. It should, however, be understood in its own terms, in the light of its own premises, promises, and projections.

---

the usual sense, Maimonides uses *šoṭeh;* e.g., *Lulaḇ,* viii, 15; *Sanhedrin,* xx, 7 (for *gas ruaḥ,* see also *'Aḇel,* iv, 2); *'Edut,* ix, 9 (definition of *šoṭeh,* for which cf. Bazak, *'Aḥarayuto hap-Pĕlilit šel hal-Laḵuy bĕ-Nafšo* [Jerusalem, 1964], p. 228). See the special use of *tippĕšim* in *Mĕlaḵim,* iii, 6 (and note *Tĕfillah,* iv, 5). See *De'ot,* i, 7, 8.

41. See below. Any innovator, working within tradition, naturally masks his innovation by relating it to, and rooting it in, tradition. This does not, however, mean that the historical scheme is a literary fiction or a philosophical conceit. The motivation of the author must be carefully probed.

42. See W. Jaeger, *Paideia* (New York, 1965) I, 168, and below, nn. 94–97.

PHILOSOPHY AND LAW IN THE *Mishneh Torah*

Looking at the Maimonidean Code in the light of these preliminary characterizations, illustrations, and generalizations, it becomes evident that the *Mishneh Torah* itself provides a full and almost polychromatic reflection of this unified preoccupation with philosophy and law, or the philosophic-spiritualistic perception of law. The *Mishneh Torah,* anything but a cut and dried, rigorously functional code, pays attention, as we have noted, to physics, metaphysics, psychology, dietetics, astronomy, Messianism, and the hereafter. It contains many philosophical comments, theological principles and rationalistic directives, comments on the history of religion and prophecy, science and medicine, and a full ethical system. It also has frequent ethical digressions and interpolations, for as we shall see, Maimonides' systematization of the halakah included a good measure of ethicization and rationalization. Ethical assumptions and commandments are spelled out and made explicit. Ideals concretized in a particular law are articulated. Reasons for enigmatic precepts are suggested. Philosophical principles which provide the underpinning of legal details are identified. The thread of intellectualization and spiritualization, which is woven uninterruptedly and unabashedly from Maimonides' earliest writings through the *Moreh* and on through the *Ma'amar Tĕḥiyyat ham-Metim* and all his responsa, is thus especially discernible in the texture of the *Mishneh Torah.* As part of the overall unity of learning which he aspired to embody in the *Mishneh Torah,*[43] Maimonides tried to bring about the unity of practice and concept, external observance and inner meaning, visible action and invisible experience, *gufe Torah* and their foundations. This comprehensive Code takes within its purview, in other words, not only the laws but the theological stimuli and ethical underpinnings which suffuse the legal details with significance and spirituality, freshness and fullness. It was concerned not only with what Max Weber called the "methodology of sanctification," which produces a "continuous personality pattern" rather than sporadic and spasmodic action,

---

43. See above, chap. III.

but also with the religious consciousness and theological sensibility. The fixed law and the experiential component, action and reflection, were combined.[44] Awareness of this circularity and reciprocity is crucial for understanding Maimonides and medieval religious philosophy in general. Polarity recedes and yields to complementarity.

It should be emphasized, therefore, that the extra-halakic motifs and emphases explicitly or allusively incorporated into the *Mishneh Torah* are by no means concentrated exclusively in the overtly philosophic sections of the *Sefer ham-Madda'* (Book One) which briefly summarizes the metaphysical and ethical postulates of Judaism, outlines a program for the improvement of the moral qualities, and encourages learning and teaching; or more specifically, touches upon such topics as natural science and theology, sanctification of God's name, prophecy, the golden mean in ethics, history of religion, idolatry and magic, immortality of the soul, the Messianic era, proper motivation of religious behavior, and other such themes. These extra-halakic motifs are deftly sprinkled throughout all the fourteen books in prolegomena and perorations, in exegetical comments and interpretative embellishments, parenthetic explanations and assorted pretexts. By calling attention to certain emphases underscored time and again, some of them in Midrashic-exegetic garb, it is possible to obtain additional insight into the conceptions which predominated in Maimonides' mind when he was composing the *Mishneh Torah*. He aspired to produce a law code which instructs as well as commands, thereby providing an effective instrument of education and edification, for law itself is an educative force leading to ethical and intellectual perfection. Law must, therefore, be understood and appreciated as well as obeyed and implemented. The realm of law harbors an "adventure of ideas" and an odyssey of the soul. His Code, in short, would reflect his organic-philosophical conception of law.[45] To be sure, much of this escapes the atten-

---

44. See I. Twersky, "The Shulḥan 'Aruk," 153–54. Our discussion of knowledge and action is unlike the modern one, e.g., J. Dewey, *The Quest for Certainty: a Study of the Relation of Knowledge and Action* (New York, 1929). See J. Maritain, "Action and Contemplation," *Scholasticism and Politics* (New York, 1940).

45. See W. Jaeger, *Paideia* (New York, 1944), III. P. Riche, *Education et culture dans l'Occident Barbare* (Paris, 1962). Whatever one may say about Maimonides' elitism (see

tion of the reader at first because it is presented so forthrightly and unceremoniously, without emphatic preambles or declarations of intent. As a result, large bodies of material which reveal Maimonides in various guises—philosopher, moralist, physician, polemicist—are often compressed into one or two paragraphs; the scope and importance of this material have to be carefully determined.[46]

Perhaps the most significant illustration of the presence in the *Mishneh Torah* of basic philosophic ideas as well as an indication of the wide-ranging impetus they provide for a sensitized conception of halakah, is the Maimonidean system concerning the rationale of commandments, *ṭa'ăme ham-miṣwoṭ* (*ratio praeceptorum*). Attempts to provide rationalizations for the commandments, to uncover their deeper meaning or profound logic, have their roots in early Talmudic-Midrashic literature (as well as in Hellenistic Jewish writing), were notably advanced by medieval Jewish philosophy, and peak in Maimonides' rationalization, which is the most comprehensive and ambitious attempt.[47] Maimonides' system provides a paradigm for a complete conceptualization of this discipline in its various forms. Furthermore,

---

below, pp. 468–71), he was a conscious and dedicated pedagogue, eager to teach and transmit, share knowledge, and shape his reader's mind. Note particularly MN, II, 37 (p. 375). Nahmanides' characterization of the *Sefer ham-Madda'* (*Kitbe ha-RaMBaN*, ed. Chavel, I, 343), is noteworthy. He emphasizes its role as an introduction to *all* of Maimonides' works, enumerating the commandments and systematically teaching the laws of *Talmud Torah* and *Tĕšubah*. Its contents require much analysis.

46. See the examples in chap. III, above, particularly n.83.

47. See generally I. Heinemann, *Ṭa'ăme Miṣwoṭ bĕ-Sifruṭ Yiśra'el* (Jerusalem, 1949); A. Altmann, "Reasons for the Commandments," *Jewish Values* (Jerusalem, 1947), pp. 236ff.; J. Guttmann, *Philosophies of Judaism* (New York, 1964). For Maimonides, see C. Neuburger, *Das Wesen des Gesetzes in der Philosophie des Maimonides* (Danzig, 1933); Y. Ben Sasson, "Lĕ-Ḥeker Mišnaṭ Ṭa'ăme Miṣwoṭ," *Tarbiz*, XXIX (1960), 268–82; J. Faur, "Mĕkor Ḥiyyuban šel ham-Miṣwoṭ lĕ-Da'aṭ ha-RaMBaM," *Tarbiz*, XXXVIII (1969), 43ff.; for R. Bahya ibn Pakuda, see G. Golinski, *Das Wesen des Religionsgesetzes in der Philosophie des Bachja* (Würzburg, 1935); for R. Saadiah Gaon, see A. Altmann, "Saadya's Conception of the Law," *Bulletin of the John Rylands Library*, XXVIII (1944), 320ff.; I. Efros, "Gišaṭ haś-Śekel 'el ham-Musar lĕ-fi R. Sĕ'adyah wĕha-RaMBaM," *Tarbiz*, XXVIII (1959), 325ff.; Y. Elstein, "Toraṭ ham-Miṣwoṭ bĕ-Mišnaṭ R. Sĕ'adyah," *Tarbiz*, XXXVIII (1968), 120ff.; H. Ben-Shammai, "Hălukaṭ ham-Miṣwoṭ u-Muśśaḡ ha-Ḥokmah bĕ-Mišnaṭ RaSaG," *Tarbiz*, XLI (1972), 170ff. For the phrase "deeper meaning" (or "profound logic") see *Letter of Aristeas*, ed. M. Hadas (New York, 1951), sec. 143, p. 157.

components of this system are found in all his writings, *Šĕmonah Pĕraḳim, 'Iggereṯ Teman, Sefer ham-Miṣwoṯ, Ma'ămar Tĕḥiyyaṯ ham-Meṯim,* and assorted responsa,[48] and not merely in the *Mishneh Torah* or the *Moreh;*[49] a synoptic overview, centered on the *Mishneh Torah* but having also a vertical-comparative dimension, thus affords an opportunity to examine continuity and change, uniformity and divergence, concerning a basic Maimonidean theme. Finally, the Maimonidean rationalization is of methodological, and not only of substantive, importance and "of course the most important thing is to acquire a mastery not only of the contents but also of the method of philosophy."[50] For all these reasons, we must turn to a full examination of this topic.

ṬA'ĂME HAM-MIṢWOṮ IN THE MAIMONIDEAN OEUVRE

The theme may be structured in terms of a series of questions: (1) Are there reasons for the commandments? (2) Can they be discovered? (3) Should they be studied? (4) Should the results of this study be made public? (5) Is this study and its results based on certitude or conjecture? (6) What are the motives for pursuing this study? We shall outline the questions and answers on the basis of Maimonides' other writings, primarily the *Moreh,* and then correlate this structure with that found in the *Mishneh Torah.*

*Proofs that commandments have reasons*

The first question to be answered is whether or not there are reasons for the commandments, or are they perhaps to be seen as arbitrary decrees whose sole purpose is obedience—are they an expression of divine will demanding unconditional compliance

---

48. ŠP, especially chap. IV; IT, especially p. iv; ShM, negative 317, 365. MTH is a defense of his whole system; see below, p. 502; for PhM, see, e.g., Ber 9:3 (p. 88), Sanh 3:3 (p. 158), chap. 10 (*Pereḳ Ḥeleḳ*); *Tĕšuḇoṯ,* 150 (p. 286), 224 (p. 399), 252 (p. 461), 436 (p. 715); *Ḳoḇeṣ,* II, 23b; LA, 229ff.

49. Key passages, most of which will be discussed, are: *Mĕ'ilah,* viii, 8; *Tĕmurah,* iv, 13; *Miḳwa'oṯ,* xi, 12; *Ṭumĕ'aṯ Ṣara'aṯ,* xvi, 10; *Ṭumĕ'aṯ 'Oḵlin,* xvi, 12; also *Yĕsoḏe hat-Torah* iv, 13; *Talmuḏ Torah,* i, 13; *De'oṯ,* vii, 7; *Šĕḥiṭah,* xiv, 16. For *Moreh* passages, see MN, III, 26–50; also II, 40, 47.

50. See *The Fiery Brook: Selected Writings of L. Feuerbach,* ed. Z. Hanfi (New York, 1972), p. 269.

without being intended toward any end at all? Not only is Maimonides' answer resoundingly affirmative, endorsing the intellectualistic (rather than the voluntaristic) view which insists that "every commandment and prohibition in these laws is consequent upon wisdom and aims at some end,"[51] but he also adduces an ensemble of proofs for this position. A careful reading of certain key passages, particularly *Moreh*, III, 26, shows Maimonides endeavoring to prove the intellectualistic-rationalistic position, not merely propounding it as a philosophic catechism or axiom. It is important to emphasize that Maimonides is not advancing here a dogmatic assumption of ritualistic rationalism but is patiently arguing a carefully nurtured intellectualism.[52]

There are, first of all, Scriptural proofs, verses which speak of reasons for the law, of just (i.e., rational) and balanced commandments which form and inform as well as direct. With regard to this the texts of the Bible are clear: *Righteous (just) statutes and judgments* (Deut. 4:8); *The judgments of the Lord are true, they are righteous (just) altogether* (Ps. 19:10).[53] At first glance, these verses concerning just laws are enigmatic and their relevance to the issue dubious, but fortunately in an earlier chapter of the *Moreh* Maimonides has recorded his understanding of the Biblical "just":

Scripture says, *Just statutes and judgments;* now you know that the meaning of "just" is "equibalanced". For these are manners of worship in which there is no burden and excess, such as monastic life and pilgrimage and similar things, nor a deficiency necessarily leading to greed and being engrossed in the indulgence of appetites, so that in consequence the perfection of man is diminished with respect to his moral habits and to his speculation, this being the case with regard to all the other *nomoi*

---

51. MN, III, 26; also 28, 31, 49. As a matter of fact, there is some ambiguity in III, 26, concerning the universality of this position. Cf. Aristotle, *Nicomachean Ethics*, I, 18–19, concerning the agreement of the "multitude and refined few."

52. Cf. *Millot ha-Higgayon*, chap. 8, concerning matters which require no proof, and MN, I, 31, concerning matters which are impossible to prove. Here Maimonides is proving his philosophical premise that laws have reasons. Obviously, the reasons themselves are *not* proofs for the veracity or trustworthiness of the laws; acting as intellectual catalysts, they merely uncover their hidden wisdom. See below, p. 457.

53. MN, III, 26.

of the religious communities of the past. When we shall speak in this treatise about the reasons accounting for the commandments, their equibalance and wisdom will be made clear to you in so far as this is necessary. For this reason it is said with reference to them, *The law of the Lord is perfect* (Ps. 19:8).[54]

Similarly, *I said not unto the seed of Jacob: Seek ye Me in vain; I, the Lord, speak righteousness, I declare things that are right* (Isa. 45:19).[55] Seeking God through the commandments, which are just and meaningful, is not arbitrary but purposive. God's commandment is never "in vain." "Your opinions and thoughts should not become confused, so that you believe in incorrect opinions that are very remote from the truth, and you regard them as law. For the laws are absolute truth if they are understood in the way they ought to be. Accordingly, Scripture says, *Thy testimonies are righteous for ever*, and so on (Ps. 119:144), and *I, the Lord, speak righteousness* (Isa. 45:19)."[56] Toward the very end of the section on *ta'ăme ham-miṣwot* Maimonides reiterates: "Marvel exceedingly at the wisdom of His commandments, may He be exalted, just as you should marvel at the wisdom manifested in the things He had made. Scripture says, *The Rock, His work is perfect; for all His ways are judgment* (Deut. 32:4). It says that just as the things made by Him are consummately perfect, so are His commandments consummately just."[57] The firmly established equation, wise = true = just (righteous) = perfect = purposive, is crucial. The teleological motif is salient.

The *Sefer ham-Miṣwot* concludes with the following apodictic assertion: "But there is not even one commandment which has

---

54. MN, II, 39; see also III, 31, 39, 49 (p. 611); ŠP, chap. IV; *Koḇeṣ*, II, 23b. For *nomoi* of other nations, see *Millot ha-Higgayon*, chap. 14. Maimonides' anticipatory reference (in MN, II, 39) to the last section of the MN ("when we shall speak . . . about the reasons") is noteworthy in the light of a later report that he wanted to withdraw this section from circulation. See the letter of Joseph Abulafia, *Jeshurun*, VIII (1875), 36, cited by Heinemann, *Ṭa'ăme ham-Miṣwot*, p. 133, n.149; and cf. G. Scholem, *Tarbiz*, VI (1935), 97, about the assertion of fifteenth-century kabbalists. In his letters, furthermore, Maimonides refers to this section; e.g., *Koḇeṣ*, II, 23b; LA, 22. The doctrine of *ṭa'ame miṣwot* is, in sum, quite open and exoteric.

55. MN, III, 26; see *Mēlaḵim*, xi, 3. The key word is *tohu* (*in vain*).

56. MN, II, 47 (409). See also LA, 229, 233.

57. MN, III, 49 (605). On the parallelism between natural law and moral law, see MN, III, 34, and above, p. 362, n.14.

not a reason and a cause, remote or immediate. Most of these causes and reasons, however, are beyond the intelligence and understanding of the multitude; yet concerning all (the commandments) the prophet testifies, *The precepts of the Lord are right, rejoicing the heart; the commandment of the Lord is pure, enlightening the eyes* (Ps. 19:9)."[58]

There are, moreover, in addition to the prophetic pronouncements, Rabbinic proofs—Talmudic statements reflecting the belief of "the multitude of the Sages"—which affirm reasons for the law:

> About the statutes designated as *ḥukkim*—for instance, those concerning mingled stuff, meat in milk, and the sending away of the scapegoat—(the Sages) make literally the following statement: "Things which I have prescribed for you, about which you have not the permission to think, which are criticized by Satan and refuted by the Gentiles" (B. Yoma 67b). They are not believed by the multitude of the Sages to be things for which there is no cause at all and for which one must not seek an end. . . . On the contrary, the multitude of the Sages believe that there indubitably is a cause for them—I mean to say a useful end—but that it is hidden from us, either because of the incapacity of our intellects or the deficiency of our knowledge. Consequently there is, in their opinion, a cause for all the commandments; I mean to say that any particular commandment or prohibition has a useful end. In the case of some of them, it is clear to us in what way they are useful, as in the case of the prohibition of killing and stealing. In the case of others, their utility is not clear, as in the case of the interdiction of the "first products" (Lev. 19:23) (of trees) and of (sowing) "the vineyard with diverse seeds" (Deut. 22:9). Those commandments whose utility is clear to the multitude are called *mišpaṭim* (judgments), while those whose utility is not clear to the multitude are called *ḥukkim* (statutes). The Sages always say with regard to the verse *For it is no vain thing* (Deut. 32:47): "And if it is vain, it is because of you," meaning that this legislation is not a vain matter without useful end, and that if it seems to you that this is the case with regard to some of the commandments, the deficiency resides in your apprehension. You already know the tradition that is widespread among us, according to which the causes for all the commandments, with the exception of that concerning the Red Heifer, were

---

58. ShM, negative 365. Psalm 19 is pretty much of a topos for this theme. See the commentaries of R. David Ḳimḥi and ham-Me'iri on Ps. 19; P. Duran, *Ma'ăśeh 'Efod* (Vienna, 1865), p. 1.

known to Solomon; and also their dictum that God hid the causes for the commandments in order that they should not be held in little esteem, as happened to Solomon with regard to the three commandments whose causes are made clear.[59]

A major thrust of Maimonides' system is the assumption, or the attempt to make it self-evident, that the Rabbis were convinced of the rationality and purposiveness of commandments. Statements apparently contradictory of this thesis must be interpreted in accord with the predominant view: a wayward part should always be anchored in the whole. Maimonides on a number of occasions focuses our attention on the need for an integrative method which lets a prevalent tendency direct seemingly eccentric dicta.[60] The whole lends stability and coherence to its parts.

PHILOSOPHIC PROOF: WISE = GOOD = PURPOSIVE

In addition to these proofs from authority, the Written Law and the Oral Law, there is a proof from philosophic reasoning. One argument for the unqualified rejection of the antirationalistic hypothesis that *ḥukkim* "are believed by the multitude of Sages to be things for which there is no cause at all" is that "this would lead, according to what we have explained, to their being considered as frivolous actions."[61] "Frivolous actions" had been defined in the immediately preceding chapter of the *Moreh*, which contains a fourfold classification of actions as futile, frivolous, vain, and good or excellent: "A man endowed with intellect is incapable of saying that any action of God is vain, futile, or frivolous.... All His actions are good and excellent." Again, "none of them is futile, or frivolous, or vain, being acts of perfect wisdom." The following juxtaposition of verses is particularly telling: "It is upon this opinion [i.e., that all these acts are consequent upon His wisdom] that the whole of the Torah of Moses

---

59. MN, III, 26. For sources on Solomon, see M. Berlin, *Ḳobeṣ ha-RaMBaM*, p. 248. Note that Maimonides quotes "Satan" in the Talmudic statement, whereas in *Mĕ'ilah*, viii, 8, he substitutes "a man's impulse"; see below, p. 413.
60. E.g., MN, II, 38; *Tĕšubot*, 436 (p. 715), and see above, chap. II, nn. 187–91; in this context, Maimonides' interpretation of the famous saying, "The commandments were given only to purify the people," is a good example of his determination to relate difficult parts to a harmonious conception.
61. MN, III, 26.

our Master is founded; it opens with it, *And God saw every thing that He had made, and behold, it was very good* (Gen. 1:31); and it concludes with it, *The Rock, His work is perfect* (Deut. 32:4)."[62] First of all, this extends the earlier equation by interposing "good"; hence we now have a resonant sixfold sequence: wise = true = just = perfect = good = purposive. Moreover, the parallelism between God's law for nature and God's law for man, a concept used subtly and allusively in various contexts, is explicitly affirmed by applying the same verse (*The Rock, His work is perfect*) to both.[63] This reminds us forcefully that exegesis is a major aspect of all Maimonidean writing.

In sum, the attribution of nonpurposive and nonrational actions to God, arbitrary results of His will, would be blasphemous, for frivolous actions are most demeaning. As a matter of fact, this philosophic proof may be seen to underly another passage in the *Moreh* where Maimonides polemicizes against those innocents, intellectually naive and misguided people, who presume to laud God while they actually demean Him:

There is a group of human beings who consider it a grievous thing that causes should be given for any law; what would please them most is that the intellect would not find a meaning for the commandments and prohibitions. What compels them to feel thus is a sickness that they find in their souls, a sickness to which they are unable to give utterance and of which they cannot furnish a satisfactory account. For they think that if those laws were useful in this existence and had been given to us for this or that reason, it would be as if they derived from the reflection and the understanding of some intelligent being. If, however, there is a thing for which the intellect could not find any meaning at all and that does not lead to something useful, it indubitably derives from God; for the reflection of man would not lead to such a thing. It is as if, according to these people of weak intellects, man were more perfect than his Maker; for man speaks and acts in a manner that leads to some intended end, whereas the Deity does not act thus, but commands us to do things

---

62. MN, III, 25. See, e.g., R. Immanuel Benevento, *Liwyat Ḥen* (Mantua, 1557), p. 3b, who explicitly refers to the four classes of actions as proof that *miṣwot* have reasons.
63. See n.57, above. Also, *Šĕmiṭṭah wĕ-Yoḇel*, xiii, 12; and J. Schacht and M. Meyerhof, "Maimonides against Galen, on Philosophy and Cosmogony," *Bulletin of the Faculty of Arts of the University of Egypt*, V (1937), 72: "but Moses . . . has plainly stated that God does not do anything without purpose and by chance, but that he creates very well with justice and equity all which he creates." MTH, 6, 18.

that are not useful to us and forbids us to do things that are not harmful to us. But He is far exalted above this; the contrary is the case, the whole purpose consisting in what is useful for us, as we have explained on the basis of the (Scriptural) dictum, *For our good always, that He might preserve us alive, as it is at this day* (Deut. 6:24).[64]

Such people assume that only inscrutability—absence of demonstrable wisdom and purposiveness—exalts God, and consequently eschew all explanation. This is folly. Indeed, the most poignant contrast between divine precepts and pagan practices is the reason and wisdom of the former versus the uselessness and futility of the latter: "For I for one do not doubt that all this was intended to efface those untrue opinions from the mind and to abolish those useless practices which brought about a waste of lives in *vain and futile things* [see Isa. 49:4]. Those opinions turned any human thought from concern with the conception of an intelligible and from [rather: from investigation into rational conception or into] useful actions, as our prophets have explained to us and have said: *They walked after [vain] things that do not profit* (Jer. 2:8). Jeremiah says, *Our fathers have inherited nought but lies, vanity, and things wherein there is no profit* (Jer. 16:19)."[65] The law in its totality delivers one "from those unhealthy opinions that turn one's attention away from all that is useful . . . toward the crazy notions. . . . It is about these notions that the truthful prophets have said, *For they walked after vain things that do not profit* (1 Sam. 12:21; Jer. 2:8)."[66] The polemical strategy and literary symmetry of these Maimonidean fulminations against futility, coming as they do at the beginning (chap. 29) and end (chap. 49) of this entire section of the *Moreh*, should not be ignored.

EXEGETICAL-HISTORICAL PROOF

There is still another kind of proof which I would describe as exegetical-historical. Although taking off from a Scriptural verse,

---

64. MN, III, 31. For Deut. 6:24 see MN, III, 28, and note *Tĕšubah*, ix, 1. See also PhM, Sanh, chap. 10 (*Pereḳ Ḥeleḳ*) (p. 201); and ŠP, chap. VI, with special attention to the term "sickness." Note, in this context, the example cited by R. Moses Taku, *Kĕtab Tamim*, in *'Oṣar Neḥmad*, III (1860), 93.
65. MN, III, 49 (p. 612).
66. MN, III, 29 (p. 518).

this deserves separate treatment inasmuch as (a) the relevance of the verse depends upon a special, novel, almost revolutionary interpretation; and (b) it has repercussions for the kind and quality of explanation which must be sought. It is, in other words, not a mere addition of another Scriptural proof; it injects a totally new motif by helping to chart the course of investigation and prescribing the universal and outer-directed nature of the reasons to be adduced for the commandments. This proof, as we shall see, demands a special kind of rationality and intelligibility:

> *Behold, I have taught you statutes and ordinances . . . that ye should do so in the midst of the Land whither ye go in to possess it. Observe therefore and do them; for this is your wisdom and your understanding in the sight of the peoples, that, when they hear all these statutes, shall say: "Surely this great nation is a wise and understanding people." For what great nation is there that hath God so nigh to them, as the Lord our God is whensoever we call upon Him? And what great nation is there, that hath statutes and ordinances so righteous as all this law, which I set before you this day?* (Deut. 4:5–8)

This Scriptural statement is striking and ambiguous. It is striking in that it rivets attention rather dramatically on the attitude of the nations of the world. Their esteem of the Jews and Judaism is a factor to be reckoned with, and a conscious effort should be made to elicit universal acclaim and admiration. A positive and admiring posture of other peoples is part of the religious axiology of Judaism—to be sure, a unique reason for observance. Its ambiguity lies in the grammar and syntax: precisely what is it that constitutes the Jewish "wisdom and understanding" in universal terms, what is the antecedent or referent? In other words, how is the outer-directed orientation to be sustained? What will command the admiration and respect of the nations of the world?

In order to appreciate the novel tone and strong reverberations of Maimonides' interpretation, it is helpful to catalogue briefly the main pre-Maimonidean interpretations. One Talmudic view finds the antecedent in an unexpressed concept: "How do we know that it is one's duty to calculate the cycles and planetary courses? Because it is written, *For this is your wisdom and your understanding in the sight of the peoples.* What wisdom and understanding is in the sight of the peoples? Say, then, that it is the science of cycles and planets."[67] The rationale of this interpretation is clearly predicated on the attempt to identify a universal subject of study where Jews and Gentiles meet on common ground and are united in scientific achievement. Even though the study of astronomy has religious repercussions and even a religious motivation,[68] it still is primarily the kernel of a universal intellectual preoccupation which transcends restrictive religious barriers. Jewish excellence in it will, therefore, elicit esteem.

A second Rabbinic interpretation emphasizes the unique man-God relationship achieved by a posture of faith and obedience. R. Joshua ben Levi said: "All the good deeds which the Israelites do in their world will come and strike vehemently before the faces of the idolaters in the world to come, as it is said, *Observe therefore and do them, for this is your wisdom and your understanding in the sight of the peoples*. It does not say 'in the presence (lĕ-neḡeḏ) of the peoples,' but *in the sight of the peoples;* this teaches you that they will come and strike vehemently before the faces of the idolaters in the world to come."[69] Based on a subtle differentiation between *in the sight* (suggesting direct and unmediated confrontation) and "in the presence" (connoting greater detachment and distance)—almost opposite stances—this interpretation contends that Israel's unshakable commitment to God's law, recognizing no distinction between ḥukkim and mišpaṭim, characterizes the Jews and individuates them. They withstand the criticism and ridicule of the nations, for ultimately their allegiance will be vindicated and the ugly criticism will be answered decisively. If history is persistently hostile, the eschatological phase will be triumphal. It is, in any event, a unique religious regimen which intuitively, without elaboration or rationalization, endows the

---

67. B. Shab 75a.
68. Note such emphasis in *Yĕsoḏe hat-Torah*, iii, 5; *Kidduš ha-Ḥodeš*, xvii, 25; *Tĕšuḇoṯ*, 150 (p. 268); *Koḇeṣ*, II, 23b; LA, 230. R. Elijah Mizrahi, *Tĕšuḇoṯ* (Jerusalem, 1937), 5 (p. 18), reports that he wrote a commentary on the *Almagest* because of this verse. The text in *Minḥaṯ Kĕna'oṯ* (Pressburg, 1838), chap. 17, p. 19, ignores the key phrase "in the eyes of the nations." See the interesting use in *Maḥzor Vitry*, ed. S. Hurwitz (Berlin, 1893), p. 520. For a sharp kabbalistic application by R. Todros, see the text edited by L. Feldman, " 'Oṣar hak-Kaboḏ haš-Šalem," *Salo Baron Jubilee Volume* (Jerusalem, 1975), Heb. section, pp. 309–10. See below, n. 365.
69. B. AZ 4a.

Jewish people with uniqueness. The adjacent dictum of R. Joshua ben Levi supports this interpretation: "All the good deeds which Israel does in this world will bear testimony for them in the world to come, as it is said, *Let them bring their witness, that they may be justified; let them hear, and say it is truth* (Isa. 43:9): *Let them bring their witnesses, that they may be justified*—that is Israel; *let them hear, and say it is truth*—these are the idolaters."[70]

An interpretation advanced by R. Baḥya ibn Paḳuda and R. Abraham ibn Daud finds the esteem originating primarily in the systematic study of theology and in the foundations of principles of belief, for there is certainly no demonstrable impressive wisdom in suprarational laws. Moreover, the theological notions must be rationally demonstrable—only then will the nations acknowledge the greatness of the people propounding them:

> On the question whether we are under an obligation to investigate the doctrine of God's oneness or not, I assert that anyone capable of investigating this and similar philosophical themes by rational methods, is bound to do so according to his powers and capacities. In the introduction to this book, I have already furnished sufficient arguments to prove this point. Anyone who neglects to institute such an inquiry is blameworthy and is accounted as belonging to the class of those who fall short in wisdom and conduct. He is like a sick man who, though knowing well the nature of his disease and its correct treatment, relies on a physician who applies various remedies, while he himself is too indolent to use his knowledge and reasoning powers to test the physician's remedies and ascertain whether the latter is treating the case correctly or not, when he might easily have done so, there being nothing to hinder him. This duty of investigation has indeed been imposed upon us by the Torah in the verse, *Know this day, and lay it to thy heart* (Deut. 4:39). That the phrase *lay it to thy heart* means rational enquiry, is clear from the verse, *And none layeth it to heart, neither is there knowledge nor understanding* (Isa. 44:19). So too David exhorted his son, *And thou, Solomon, my son, know thou the God of thy father and serve Him with a whole heart and a willing soul, for all hearts doth the Lord search* (1 Chron. 28:9). . . . Our wise teachers have exhorted us, "Be sedulous in the study of the Torah, and know what answer to give to the unbeliever ('Ab 2:14)." The Torah

---

70. Ibid.

says, *observe therefore and do them, for this is your wisdom and your understanding in the sight of the peoples* (Deut. 4:6). It is impossible, however, that the peoples should concede our claims to a superior degree of wisdom and understanding, unless there are proofs and reasonable evidence of the truth of our Torah and the verity of our faith. . . . It has thus been demonstrated by arguments drawn from reason, Scripture, and tradition that it is our duty to investigate rationally every topic on which we can, by the exercise of our mental faculties, attain clearness.[71]

While at one point this statement may refer to the entire Torah[72]—and indeed the author's insistence upon rationalism and the indispensable role of the intellect in achieving religious perfection is thoroughgoing—the general context, quotations, and emphasis clearly concern metaphysics, the "doctrine of God's oneness" and "similar philosophical themes." As in the first Talmudic explanation, the emphasis here also is on universality, but the universality is of method (i.e., rational argument, syllogism, proofs) rather than of subject (i.e., astronomy).

Ibn Daud sustains this argument and spells out the concomitant interpretation fully: traditional laws certainly will not arouse wonder and admiration among non-Jews. Even political rules and ethical virtues cannot provide the frame of reference here, for any rational person, even without religious commitment, may elect to abide by them. The verse can only refer to the "roots of Jewish belief," which are shown on the whole to be perfectly congruent with those demonstrative truths which philosophers painstakingly elaborated in the course of thousands of years. The remarkable thing, which irresistibly attracts attention, is that God gave this corpus of truth "to us without toil or speculation, rather we took it as tradition from the true prophet." In other words, the pivot is the harmony of reason and faith, the congruence of religious tradition and philosophical speculation.[73]

---

71. R. Baḥya ibn Paḳuda, *Ḥoḇoṯ hal-Lĕḇaḇoṯ*, I, chap. 3 (p. 67); see also II, chap. 2 (p. 135).
72. See Ḳāfiḥ's note 72, in his edition of *Ḥoḇoṯ hal-Lĕḇaḇoṯ* (Jerusalem, 1973), p. 51.
73. R. Abraham ibn Daud, *Ha-'Ĕmunah ha-Ramah*, introduction, p. 4. Note R. Abraham ibn Megas, *Kĕḇoḏ 'Ĕlohim* (Constantinople, 1583), chap. 27 (p. 58b): כי היא חכמתכם . . . ועל כרחך אינו מדבר על דברי תורה, כי מי שלא ידע הדבר על אמתו, מה תועלת יש בעדותו, ומה מעלה וגדולה ויקר יושג לישראל באמרם רק עם חכם ונבון . . . Also note A. אם לא שיהיו שום בידיעה ושידעו אלה מה שידעו אלה בפתוח ויותר. Shalom, *Nĕḇe Salom* (Venice, 1575), introduction; and R. Joseph Gikatilia, *Ginaṯ 'Egoz*

### NOVEL MAIMONIDEAN INTERPRETATION OF DEUT. 4:6

Maimonides—foreshadowed by R. Abraham ibn Ezra[74] and immediately followed by R. David Ḳimḥi[75]—sees the antecedent of "wisdom and understanding" in *ḥuḳḳim:* it is precisely the *statutes*, those troublesome, tantalizing, rationally recalcitrant laws, which are a source and a sign of wisdom.[76] The apparent paradoxicality of this interpretation quickly gives way to a refreshing inference: the *ḥuḳḳim must* be intelligible and rational; otherwise they could not prove that the Torah as a whole is grounded in reason and wisdom:

> And Scripture says, *That, when they hear all these statutes, shall say: Surely this great nation is a wise and understanding people* (Deut. 4:6). Thus it states explicitly that even all the statutes will show to all the nations that they have been given with wisdom and understanding. Now if there is a thing for which no reason is known and that does not either procure something useful or ward off something harmful, why should one say of one who believes in it or practices it that he is wise and understanding and of great worth? And why should the religious communities think it a wonder? Rather things are indubitably as we have mentioned: every commandment from among these 613 commandments. . . .[77]

---

(Hanau, 1615), p. 55a. Cf. *Kuzari,* III, 39 (with reference to Mishnah); *Bet ha-Midrash,* ed. A. Jellinek (reprinted, Jerusalem, 1967), V, 67; ham-Me'iri, quoted by Simeon En-Duran, *Ḥošen Mišpaṭ,* in *Zunz Jubelschrift* (Berlin, 1884), p. 162. Note that R. Jacob ibn Gabbai, *'Abodat haḳ-Ḳodeš* (Jerusalem, 1973), p. 151, refers only to MN, II, 11 (where the verse is used for science), but does not comment on Maimonides' application of the verse to *ḥuḳḳim.* Also R. Moses Met, *Maṭṭeh Mosheh* (Warsaw, 1876), p. 28.

74. R. Abraham ibn Ezra, *Yĕsod Mora'* (Prague, 1833), chap. 8 (p. 30b). Cf., however, Gen. 2:11 and R. Samuel ibn Tibbon, *Yiḳḳawu ham-Mayim* (Pressburg, 1837), p. 173.

75. R. David Ḳimḥi, *Peruš,* Joshua, introduction: כי אין צורך לומד התורה והמצוה שהם בנויים על דרך השכל. For "outer-directed" awareness, or polemical motivation, see, e.g., *Ḥobot hal-Lĕbabot,* introduction (pp. 19–20); RaSHBaM, to Lev. 11:3; and D. Rosin, *R. Samuel ben Meir als Schriftërklärer* (Breslau, 1880), pp. 84–86; S. Poznanski, *Mabo' 'al Ḥakme Ṣarfaṭ* (Warsaw, 1913), pp. 34ff. See above, chap. I, n. 165.

76. Abarbanel, to Deut. 4:6, says that this is the only reasonable interpretation of the verse. See also R. Nissim Gerondi, *Dĕrašoṭ ha-RaN* (Jerusalem, 1959), I (p. 10) and IX (p. 63). Cf. MN, II, 11. Note how R. David Gans, *Neḥmad wĕ-Na'im* (Jessnitz, 1743), end of introduction (10a), utilizes the Maimonidean emphasis but limits it to astronomy (which was his specialty). R. Joseph Jabez, *'Or ha-Ḥayyim* (Lublin, 1912), p. 114, applies it to philosophy.

77. MN, III, 31. The last part of this paragraph, which recapitulates Maimonides' position, is discussed below, p. 388, n.80. For the first part, see above, p. 379.

*Ḥuḳḳim* are messages which must be deciphered and decoded; they appear undecipherable only for lack of knowledge, insight, and sensitivity. There may be setbacks along the road, and one may reach impasses in analysis, but the cumulative trouble and frustration should not discourage the inquirer. In sum, the Torah has stated unequivocally that statutes are purposive and must be properly interpreted, temporary confusions and uncertainties notwithstanding. This passage insists, furthermore, that the interpretation must be of such a nature that it will have a universal resonance and impress all the nations. It is not merely another Scriptural proof but it provides basic directives for the unfolding of the entire intellectual enterprise. The reasons must be universally intelligible and persuasive.

This compelling need to rationalize apparently unintelligible matters is reinforced by Maimonides when he applies the same verse to the problem of aggadic interpretation; seemingly implausible passages of aggadic literature had to be made reasonable and meaningful. Those who "accept the teachings of the Sages in their simple literal sense and do not think that these teachings contain any hidden meaning at all" are woefully ignorant and imperfect:

> The members of this group are poor in knowledge. One can only regret their folly. Their very effort to honor and to exalt the Sages in accordance with their own meager understanding actually humiliates them. As God lives, this group destroys the glory of the Torah and extinguishes its light, for they make the Torah of God say the opposite of what it intended. For He said in His perfect Torah, *The peoples . . . when they hear all these statutes, shall say: Surely this great nation is a wise and understanding people* (Deut. 4:6). But this group expounds the laws and the teachings of our Sages in such a way that when the other peoples hear them they say that this little people is foolish and ignoble.[78]

---

78. PhM, Sanh, chap. 10 (*Pereḳ Ḥeleḳ*); MTH, 9, 14, 26. For Maimonides' plan to write a book on aggadah, see chap. I, above, and my article on the *Peruš 'Aggadot* of R. Jedaiah hap-Penini in the forthcoming *Alexander Altmann Festschrift*. PhM, 'Ab 2:17 (p. 429) also has an outer-directed emphasis. For an extension of this outer-directed emphasis, utilizing the same verse, see *Peruš R. Abraham ben ha-RaMBaM* (London, 1958), p. 302. The need to go beyond the literal is a leitmotif of Maimonideanism.

The common denominator of aggadah and *ḥukkim* underscored by Maimonides is their "strangeness," their apparent remoteness from rationality. The outer-directed Scriptural imperative concerning the need to project an attractive image and maintain a respectable intellectual profile in the eyes of the world leads to a discriminating rationalistic or allegorical interpretation of both of these realms. Maimonides' contention, of course, is that the rationality is not contrived or artificially conjoined but is immanent and intentional. Only intellectual failing or fatigue stands in the way of bringing it to the surface.

*Are the reasons for the commandments knowable?*

Having seen how Maimonides answered the question of whether the commandments have reasons, and how he marshaled proofs and arguments in support of his answer, we may move to the next composite question: Is it possible for man to know the reasons, and if so, how? What method or what kind of interpretation should be used and what reasons are forthcoming? Maimonides' primary answer is that philosophic allegory or teleology will show that "all laws have causes and were given with a view to some utility."[79] Every law has a pedagogic function, and should be interpreted accordingly. As in any allegorical interpretation, one has to penetrate beneath the external behavioral pattern and surface meaning in order to identify the latent purpose or ultimate goal.

The process of identification, of course, is directed by certain presuppositions, postulates, or premises and moves from the general to the particular. The philosophic analyst has specific guidelines or coordinates along which the interpretative goal is pursued. Maimonides operates with a threefold classification of the laws, corresponding to a similar classification of the philosophic virtues: intellectual, moral, and practical. All laws teach true beliefs and inculcate moral virtues, or else themselves constitute actions which train one in the acquisition of intellectual and moral virtues. The practical commandments also have an outer-directed social motive: to help establish a society in

---

79. MN, III, 26.

which "wronging each other" has been abolished and in which the individual can, therefore, flourish and devote himself to the attainment of intellectual perfection. The moral virtues are also propaedeutic: they bring about the proper social relations necessary for mankind, "moral qualities useful for life in society." In essence, therefore, the intention of the law is a twofold one: "the welfare (*tiḳḳun*) of the soul" (which consists of the acquisition of true beliefs) and "the welfare of the body" (which is achieved by practical and moral virtues). All law, in sum, is a delicate instrument for the acquisition of moral and intellectual virtue, a goal pursued by philosophers as well, but not as effectively.[80] This fact is incontrovertible; to understand it fully requires philosophic insight and exegetical resourcefulness.

Given these guidelines, established at the beginning of this section in chapter 27 of the *Moreh*, the remaining task is completely deductive. One has to relate each of the 613 commandments to one of three goals: (a) establishment of civilized society—principles of social utility and justice; (b) development of the ethical personality—principles of goodness and love of fellow man; or (c) intellectual perfection—true knowledge and experience of God. Had the remaining chapters of the *Moreh* been lost, we could have undertaken to reconstruct the correlation between each commandment and these three goals.

80. MN, III, 27, also 28, 31, 35; ŠP, chap. IV; and PhM, 'Ab 1:17 (p. 421). The equation of divine laws and philosophic virtues is parenthetically but very effectively formulated in PhM, Sanh, chap. 10 (*Pereḳ Ḥeleḳ*) (p. 199): "The truth has no other purpose than knowing that it is truth. Since the Torah is truth, the purpose of knowing it is to do it. A good man must not wonder, 'If I perform these commandments, which are virtues, and if I refrain from these transgressions, which are vices that God commanded us not to do, what will I get out of it?' " H. A. Wolfson ("Spinoza and the Religion of the Past," *Religious Philosophy* [Cambridge, 1961], pp. 260–61) has stated it very clearly in a succinct characterization of religious philosophy prior to Spinoza: "Religion, to religious philosophers, was not only a truth, a way of knowing, but also a good, a way of living. To them, God in His governance of the world, by His individual providence, has in His infinite wisdom not only endowed men with freedom but has also revealed to them laws of conduct by which, through the exercise of their freedom, they are guided to their destined good. These divinely revealed laws, it was insisted upon by the religious philosophers, were not the prescripts of an arbitrary ruler; they were based upon reason. In fact, they were the virtues which philosophers, in their fumbling way, were trying to discover by their own faulty reason as rules of conduct whereby men were to attain their highest good." See R. Abraham ibn Daud, *Ha-'Ĕmunah ha-Ramah*, III, 101; also H. A. Wolfson, *Philo*, II, 208, 305, and 312.

## LAW AND PHILOSOPHY

A second method of interpretation, quite novel and highly controversial in the opinion of most Maimonidean successors, is that of historical causation—applying the principles of teleology to history. This can be summarily explained as follows:[81] The historical-religious background of the Torah is Sabian culture, a kind of polytheistic idolatry which denied creation of the world, transcendence of God, and the possibility of miracles. The Israelites, together with all other contemporaries, were steeped in this polytheism which was pervaded by myth and magic and placed a premium on a ramified network of sacrifices: "It is well known that Abraham . . . was brought up in the religious community of the Sabians, whose doctrine it is that there is no deity but the stars." At the time of Moses this astrocentric paganism was still rampant, almost sovereign, so that the Torah had to serve as an antidote to Sabianism: the "first intention of the law as a whole is to put an end to idolatry, to wipe out its traces and all that is bound up with it."[82] The implementation of this intention was, for many intersecting reasons, quite complicated, requiring "wily graciousness and wisdom (or cunning)" on the part of God.[83] First of all, human nature is immutable. Nature does not tolerate mercurial transitions from one extreme to another. "Man, according to his nature, is not capable of abandoning suddenly all to which he was accustomed." To violate this axiom would, therefore, require recourse to a miracle which would itself run counter to nature (*contra naturam*) and also to accepted philosophic principles concerning the sparsity of miracles as well as their tentative nature—Maimonides unequivocally taught, first of all, that miracles are very rare, and second, that they are never permanent infringements upon the law of nature but merely temporary aberrations for a specific ad hoc purpose. If there were to be a radical mutation of human nature, God would have to decree such a

---

81. The main sources are MN, III, 29, 32, 37, 45, 46; '*Akum*, i; PhM, AZ 4:7 (pp. 357ff.); MTH, 31ff.; also MN, I, 63, and see above, chap. III, n.80. I have prepared a separate monograph on Maimonides as a historian of religion.

82. MN, III, 29 (pp. 514, 517); also 30 (p. 523); 49 (p. 612).

83. MN, III, 32 (p. 525). See Pines, translator's introduction to *Guide of the Perplexed*, pp. lxxii ff. For a related kind of strategy, cunning, or pedagogic planning used by the Rabbis, note carefully PhM, AZ 2:5 (p. 345); also MTH, 33.

change, and that would nullify human freedom.[84] The only alternative was to let human nature adjust slowly, just as the human organism develops slowly. Hence the doctrine of gradualism—the idea of premeditated accommodation, or in Hegelian terms, "the cunning of reason" (*List der Vernunft*)—had to prevail. Maimonides insists that just as there is gradation and purposiveness in the processes of nature and biology, so there is in history and religion. The laws of nature, cosmic as well as human, remain immutable. The change from crass idolatry to rarefied monotheism, the transformation of an idol-worshiping community habituated to false and deceptive practices to "a kingdom of priests and a holy nation" had to be skillfully engineered in accord with the principle of accommodation: a continuum of familiar practice, but redirected and remotivated, purged and sublimated.[85] Sacrifices, which constituted the "universal service upon which we were brought up," were not abandoned; we were commanded to offer them only to God: "Through this divine ruse it came about that the memory of idolatry was effaced and that the grandest and true foundation of our belief—namely, the existence and oneness of the Deity—was firmly established, while at the same time the souls had no feeling of repugnance and were not repelled because of the abolition of modes of worship to which they were accustomed." As a result, the Torah may be viewed historically as a pedagogic-therapeutic instrument

84. MN, III, 32 (p. 529). Maimonides builds his position on (1) the general reluctance to use miracles, since an excess would virtually destroy natural law; (2) the fact that such a miracle would undo human freedom of the will; and (3) that this miracle would have to be permanent, while miracles not only are rare but also constitute temporary aberrations and not permanent changes in nature. He bases this on Deut. 5:26, *O that they had such an heart as this!*—God uses the optative rather than the imperative. Note the same in Teŝubah, v, 3. On miracles, see MN, II, 29 (p. 345); PhM, 'Ab 5:5 (p. 456); and *Kuzari*, III, 73.

85. The Biblical paradigm for this is Exod. 13:17–18; see also MTH, 32ff.; and R. Abraham ibn Ezra, *Peruš*, Exod. 7:3. The best example is the institution of sacrifices. This was so widespread and deep-rooted that it could not, by nature, be eliminated. Hence it had to be rerouted and endowed with new meaning. See most recently, A. Funkenstein, "Gesetz und Geschichte: zur historisierenden Hermeneutik bei Moses Maimonides und Thomas von Aquin," *Viator*, I (1970), 147ff., and his Hebrew article in *Zion*, XXXIII (1968), 136; also S. Pines, "Ibn Khaldūn and Maimonides," *Studia Islamica*, XXXII (1970), 265ff; and below, n. 322. There is need to note and differentiate between adaptation, necessitated by the doctrine of gradualism, and outright rejection of certain practices. See, e.g., MN, III, 45 (concerning structure of the altar), 46 (the offering of certain kinds of animals), and others.

# LAW AND PHILOSOPHY

which uses a shaded spectrum of devices to uproot all vested or vestigial pagan beliefs and practices. The Torah consciously and energetically confronted Sabianism and with wisdom and cunning eradicated it. Consequently Maimonides frequently emphasizes the value of historical information and insight: "The meaning of many of the laws became clear to me and their causes became known to me through my study of the doctrines, opinions, practices, and cult of the Sabians, as you will hear when I explain the reasons for the commandments that are considered to be without cause." After describing some of their temple ritual, he repeats: "The knowledge of these opinions and practices is a very important chapter in the exposition of the reasons for the commandments."[86] Finally Maimonides declares: "If we knew the particulars of those practices and heard details concerning those opinions, we would become clear regarding the wisdom manifested in the details of the practices prescribed in the commandments concerning the sacrifices and the forms of uncleanness and other matters whose reason cannot, to my mind, be easily grasped."[87] His quest for historical knowledge is not antiquarian; it is indispensable for exegetical penetration and theological comprehension.

It is important for our forthcoming characterization of the *Mishneh Torah* to note here that the method of sociological-historical explanation, of understanding divine laws in the light of specific temporal situations and challenges, is limited to the *ḥukkim*—e.g., sacrifices and laws of uncleanness—and is never applied to *mišpaṭim*.

*Should the reasons be investigated and discovered? —dangers of antinomianism*

Having answered that man is capable of fathoming the mind of the Lawgiver and having suggested the methods by which the

---

86. MN, III, 29 (p. 518, 521).
87. MN, III, 49 (p. 612). In LA, 229, he says that he read everything, "so that it seems to me there does not remain in the world a composition on this subject, having been translated into Arabic from other languages, but that I have read it and have understood its subject matter and have plumbed the depth of its thought. From these books it became clear to me what the reason is for all those commandments that everyone comes to think of as having no reason at all other than the decree of Scripture." See below, n. 285.

reasons for the commandments may be uncovered, Maimonides must now determine whether or not man should utilize this potential and in fact study the *ṭa'ăme ham-miṣwoṭ*. Even if one is convinced that there are underlying causes and overriding objectives which are discoverable, perhaps one should abstain from studying them for prudential-tactical reasons, inasmuch as the Lawgiver had concealed them. The danger of antinomianism is real and was clearly anticipated: "You already know the tradition that is widespread among us, according to which the causes for all the commandments, with the exception of that concerning the Red Heifer, were known to Solomon; and also the [Sages'] dictum that God hid the causes for the commandments in order that they should not be held in little esteem, as happened to Solomon with regard to the three commandments whose causes are made clear."[88] A fuller statement concerning the logic and logistics of not searching and studying the reasons for the laws had already been given at the end of the *Sefer ham-Miṣwoṭ*:

> The Exalted One explains in Scripture the reason for these three commandments, namely, *Only he shall not multiply horses to himself . . . neither shall he multiply wives to himself . . . neither shall he greatly multiply to himself silver and gold* (Deut. 17:16–17); and the knowledge of the reasons for them led to their being disobeyed, as in the notorious case of Solomon, peace be upon him, notwithstanding his preeminence in knowledge and wisdom, and his being *the beloved of the Lord* (2 Sam. 12:24).
>
> Our Sages learned from this that if men knew the reasons for all the commandments, they would find ways to disobey them. For if a man so perfect (as Solomon) wrongly supposed that his action (in taking many wives) would in no wise lead him into transgression, how much more would the weak-minded multitude (if they knew the reasons for the commandments) be led to disregard them, arguing thus: He forbade this, and ordered that, only for such-and-such reason; so we will carefully avoid the sin to prevent that for which this commandment was laid down, but will not be particular about the commandment itself; and this would destroy the very basis of religion. For this reason the Exalted One has withheld the reasons.[89]

---

88. MN, III, 26.
89. ShM, negative 365.

## LAW AND PHILOSOPHY

This is a classic formulation, based on Rabbinic data, of what may be labeled philosophic antinomianism: knowledge of the goal deludes or seduces the person into thinking that the prescribed action is dispensable. If he has reached the destination, he may assume that he has license to bypass the intermediate steps. If he should erroneously perceive the prescriptions and proscriptions as *merely* instrumental, with no intrinsic authentication or self-validating worth, the philosophically attuned person may end up ignoring them, completely substituting the ultimate goal for the normative performance. R. Judah hal-Levi expressed the view of philosophic antinomianism pointedly: "Human actions are but instruments which lead up to spiritual heights. Having reached these I care not for religious ceremonies."[90] In fact, the Christian stance that Christian allegory nullified the law or that Christianity superseded it completely, is similar in certain respects, and Maimonides briefly describes it at the very end of the Code: "Others declare that the commandments had an esoteric meaning and were not intended to be taken literally; that the Messiah has already come and has revealed their occult significance".[91] In brief, just as philosophic allegory may threaten the historicity of Scriptural narrative, so may it destroy the practical normativeness of Scriptural commandments. The issue is simple and standard: does allegory supplement or supplant the text's literal meaning?

There is also, as we shall see,[92] a second brand of antinomianism which may be characterized as agnostic or sceptical. In this case, not knowledge but ignorance of the reasons leads to nonobservance. Failure to relate the action to a noble goal inclines the inquirer to regard it as frivolous or worthless.

This potential and predictable danger—which in the eyes of the antirationalists could lead to a reduction of the law to

---

90. *Kuzari*, III, 65.

91. *Mĕlakim*, xi, 4 (in the uncensored version). Of course, the difference should not be blurred. The Christian argument totally invalidates the commandments: circumcision or holiday observance ceases to exist. The philosophic approach posits that the actual deed becomes superfluous for the individual who understands the ultimate meaning of the commandments.

92. See below, n.133.

pragmatic-utilitarian categories, and hence to its erosion[93]—is, however, overshadowed by the more immediate and ubiquitous need to satisfy one's rational faculty and involve the logos in the religious ethos. Intellectual apprehension, after all, is man's *proprium* and his "ultimate perfection is to become fully rational";[94] its religious use should be maximized. "Contemplation (i.e., deep study) of God's commandments," together with study of His works (i.e., nature), enables one to comprehend God and hence fulfill the commandment of love of God: "We have thus made it clear to you that through this act of contemplation you will attain a conception of God and reach that stage of joy in which love of Him will follow of necessity."[95] The highest stage of wisdom is that "which teaches us to demonstrate the opinions of the Torah."[96] Maimonides finds occasion to repeat this basic premise of his entire system, embracing law and metaphysics, toward the end of the *Moreh* in connection with a stunning interpretation of a Talmudic statement:

The Sages mention likewise that man is required first to obtain knowledge of the Torah, then to obtain wisdom, then to know what is incumbent upon him with regard to the legal science of the law—I mean the drawing of inferences concerning what one ought to do. And this should be the order observed: the opinions in question should first be known as being received through tradition; then they should be demonstrated; then the actions through which one's way of life may be ennobled should be precisely defined. This is what they literally say regarding man's being required to give an account with respect to these three matters in this order. They say: "When man comes to judgment, he is first asked: Have you fixed certain seasons for the study of the Torah? Have you ratiocinated concerning wisdom? Have you inferred one thing from another?" (B. Shab 31a). It has thus become clear to you that according

---

93. E.g., ham-Me'iri, *Bet hab-Beḥirah*, 'Aḇot, (New York, 1944), 3:14 (pp. 129–30); also R. Jacob ben Sheshet, *Ša'ar haš-Šamayim*, in *'Oṣar Neḥmad*, III (1860), pp. 153ff.
94. MN, III, 27; also III, 28, and I, 2.
95. ShM, positive 3. There is the same emphasis as in *Mě'ilah*, viii, 8 (see below, pp. 407–15). For love, see *Yĕsode hat-Torah*, ii, 1; *Těšubah*, x, 6; *Kěri'aṭ Šěma'*, i, 2; and above, chap. IV, n. 49. The need to incorporate some contemplative dimension in this commandment usually expresses itself by including natural science; see, however, R. Moses of Coucy, *Sefer Miṣwoṭ Gadol*, positive 3.
96. MN, III, 54.

to them, the science of the Torah is one species and wisdom is a different species, being the verification of the opinions of the Torah through correct speculation.[97]

Furthermore, only contemplation and meditation—sustained reflection on the significance and objectives of every commandment—will safeguard against perfunctory performance:

> Know that all the practices of the worship, such as reading the Torah, prayer, and the performance of the other commandments, have only the end of training you to occupy yourself with His commandments, may He be exalted, and not with that which is other than He. If, however, you pray merely by moving your lips while facing a wall, and at the same time think about your buying and selling, or if you read the Torah with your tongue while your heart is set upon the building of your habitation and does not consider what you read; and similarly in all cases in which you perform a commandment merely with your limbs, as if you were digging a hole in the ground or hewing wood in the forest, without reflecting either upon the meaning of that action, or upon Him from whom the commandment proceeds, or upon the end of the action, you should not think that you have achieved the end. Rather you will then be similar to those of whom it is said, *Thou art near in their mouth, and far from their reins* (Jer. 12:2).[98]

This is the motto of spirituality, a goal common to mysticism and philosophy, based on belief in the regenerative power of understanding and/or inwardness. Unreflective performance, without attention to the meaning and the end of the action, falls short of the desired goal. Rationalism sought to forge a holy alliance

---

97. Ibid., based on B. Shab 31a. See *Talmud Torah*, i, 11, 12; also PhM, 'Ab 4:4 (p. 438); BM 2:8 (p. 56). See also Abarbanel, *Naḥălaṭ 'Aḇoṯ* (New York, 1953), p. 205 (on 'Ab 3:22). When only *Torah* appears in the text, Maimonides interprets it to include *ḥokmah* (wisdom) as well ('Ab 1:2). When *Torah* and *ḥokmah* both appear, their separate identity or autonomy is maintained; *ḥokmah* is a necessary supplement to Torah. Note *Roṣeaḥ*, v, 5, and vii, 1. Medieval writers often observed that Maimonides introduced strained interpretations in order to reinforce his theses; e.g., S. Duran, *Magen 'Aḇoṯ* (New York, 1946), to 'Ab 1:2 (p. 408), 3:13 (p. 502); D. Ḳimḥi (printed in *Kerem Ḥemed*, V [1841], 31): והרב מורה צדק פירש . . . ואין זה מעניין המזמור; also Jer. 9:23 (and Ḳimḥi, ad loc., citing MN, III, 54; see F. Talmage, *David Ḳimḥi* [Cambridge, 1975], p. 124). R. Baḥya ben Asher, *Peruš hat-Torah*, ed. C. Chavel (Jerusalem, 1968), to Deut. 29:28, III, 435: והפירוש הזה בעצמו . . . יקר וספיר, אבל אינו בעניין הפרשה.

98. MN, III, 51 (p. 622). See the use of Jer. 12:2 also in *Koḇeṣ*, II, 24a. It is Maimonides' battle cry for introspection, sensitivity, and spirituality.

between Torah and wisdom, and thereby to preclude religious routinization and spiritual atrophy. Wisdom demonstrates "the rational matter that we receive from the law through tradition."[99]

Moreover, only knowledge of the goals of the law will enable man to achieve or approximate the desired perfection. If one is unaware of the ultimate objective and behaves mechanically, he is legally unassailable but nothing will rub off on him.[100] In addition, ignorance of the true goals may also result in perversion, not only vulgarization or mechanization, of the commandments: "For these fools not only fail to fulfill the commandment but also treat an important precept that expresses the oneness of God, the love of Him, and His worship, as if it were an amulet to promote their own personal interests; for according to their foolish minds, the mĕzuzah is something that will secure for them advantage in the vanities of the world."[101] Indeed, the most forceful argument is that only awareness of the loftier intellectual goals of the law, transcending political-material interests, underscores its divine provenance. As Maimonides asserted in a key passage cited earlier,[102] only if you find a law concerned with the "soundness of belief" as well as "circumstances pertaining to the body," do you know that "the law is divine."

The fact is that "a person ignorant of the secret meaning of Scripture and the deeper significance of the law" would not be able to withstand criticism of Judaism, for his perception of the uniqueness of Judaism would be blurred and his convictions would be shaky. The only way to strengthen his convictions is by underscoring the noble and all-encompassing purposiveness of the law. "If he could only fathom the inner intent of the law, he would realize that the essence of the true divine religion lies in the deeper meaning of its positive and negative precepts"[103]—it

99. MN, III, 54 (p. 633). See the position of his son, R. Abraham, as sketched by G. Cohen "The Soteriology of R. Abraham Maimuni," *PAAJR*, XXXV (1968), 79.
100. See *De'ot*, vii, 7. Note the following statement in a purely halakic context—R. Manoaḥ, *Sefer ham-Mĕnuḥah, Ḥameṣ u-Maṣṣah*, vii, 5: צריך לאמרן ולפרש טעמן כי לכל המצות יש טעם וידיעת טעם המצות עיקר גדול אחר עשייתן.
101. *Mĕzuzah*, v, 4.
102. MN, II, 40, quoted above, p. 364.
103. IT, iv; see below, p. 418.

would be difficult to compose a clearer statement which emphasizes both the instrumentality of the commandments and the absolute need to publicize this notion and disseminate it among all people, simple or learned.

REASONS FOR THE LAW AND MYSTERIES OF THE TORAH

Maimonides' tactical decisions concerning the quest for reasons for the law will be better understood in the context of his similar approach to the mysteries of the Torah. They have much in common, or more precisely, they are cognate phenomena.

Reasons for the law, like the mysteries of the Torah generally, are esoteric by the a priori decision of the Lawgiver; yet they must be made exoteric because of compelling religious-intellectual need. Perfunctory performance or perfunctory recitation will fall short of the mark. Such a promise as "I shall inform you of the cause of every one of these classes . . . I shall return to each of the commandments . . . and shall explain to you the cause of it"[104] is reminiscent of the promise to interpret Ezekiel's "account of the Divine Chariot" in terms of "that which is indubitably clear, manifest, and evident in my opinion," the halakic counsel about not divulging these matters notwithstanding. The esoteric-exoteric axis in both cases does not relieve the inexorable pressure of the religious-intellectual need. The interrelatedness or overlapping of those areas of *ta'ăme miṣwot* and *sitre Torah* is clear. As a matter of fact, the underlying Talmudic text used by Maimonides refers explicitly to "mysteries of the Torah" as well as "reasons of the Torah" (*ṭa'ăme Torah*).[105] Furthermore, Maimonides subsumes Scriptural stories under the rubric of "mysteries of the Torah"—and unless reasons for the stories showing "a necessary utility for the law" can be suggested, they are "thought to be useless"—just as he does with regard to the commandments themselves. Maimonides concludes his programmatic-illustrative chapter on interpreting Biblical narrative with the same motto with which he began the entire section on interpreting Biblical law: "Apply to the whole matter the principle to which the Sages . . . have drawn our attention, *For it is no vain thing for you*

---

104. MN, III, 27.
105. MN, III, introduction. See B. Pes 119a.

(Deut. 32:47); and *if it is vain, it is so because of you*."[106] This principle fortifies the inquirer, perhaps forces him to persist. The secret meanings of stories, commandments, and mysteries—complementary components of Torah—must be uncovered. Again, the polemical-literary symmetry should be appreciated.

At this point a methodological parallel between *ta'ăme miṣwot* and *sitre Torah* may be established. A key component of Maimonides' system (as elaborated in *Moreh*, III, 26) is that "the generalities of the commandments necessarily have a cause and have been given because of a certain utility; their details are that in regard to which it was said of the commandments that they were given merely for the sake of commanding something." This fact—"wisdom rendered it necessary . . . that there should be particulars for which no cause can be found"—is explained en passant in terms of the Maimonidean theory of contingency: "This resembles the nature of the possible (contingent), for it is certain that one of the possibilities will come to pass. And no question should be put why one particular possibility and not another comes to pass, for a similar question would become necessary if another possibility instead of this particular one had come to pass." Contingency must be recognized. We remember that already in the *Mishnah Commentary* Maimonides inversely used contingency to explain a certain puzzling law.[107] In any event, "those who imagine that a cause may be found for suchlike things (particulars) are as far from truth as those who imagine that the generalities of a commandment are not designed with a view to some real utility."[108] Both extremes are distortions.

In the introduction to the *Moreh*, Maimonides emphasizes that most prophetic parables should be interpreted in general—"the

---

106. MN, III, 50 (pp. 613, 617), see MN, III, 26.
107. Note carefully PhM, Ber 9:3 (p. 88); also ShM, negative 290; and *Sanhedrin*, xx, 1.
108. MN, III, 26. See J. Guttmann, "Das Problem der Kontingenz in der Philosophie des Maimonides," *MGWJ*, LXXXIII (1939), 406ff. On contingency, see also MN, II, introduction, propositions 23–24 (p. 239); N. L. Rabinovitch, *Probability and Statistical Inference in Ancient and Medieval Jewish Literature* (Toronto, 1973), p. 74; idem, *Tarbiz*, XLIV (1975), 159ff. The Maimonidean principle of contingency is extended by Ibn Kaspi, *Mishneh Kesef*, ed. I. Last (Jerusalem, 1970), I, 81.

parable as a whole indicates the whole of the intended meaning"—and "you should not inquire into all the details occurring in the parable, nor should you wish to find significations corresponding to them. For doing so would lead you into one of two ways: either into turning aside from the parable's intended subject, or into assuming an obligation to interpret things not susceptible of interpretation and that have not been inserted with a view to interpretation." It would seem that words, too, have the "nature of the possible" or contingent, in the sense that certain words must be used for the "consistent development of the parable's external meaning," but they do not affect or alter the basic meaning of the parable as a whole.[109] Overzealous and unwarranted extension of the interpretation of parables results in artificiality and distortion.

Both generalizations, however, have exceptions. There are some parables in which "each word has a meaning." There are likewise some commandments concerning which "the particulars of, and conditions for, them have become clear." As a matter of fact, Maimonides suggests that more particulars could be understood if he had more historical information; specifically, particulars concerning sacrifices and uncleanness. Furthermore, he completes the parallel by applying the same thesis to stories: "Just as, according to what I have told you, the doctrines of the Sabians are remote from us today, the chronicles of those times are likewise hidden from us today. Hence if we knew them and were cognizant of the events that happened in those days, we would know *in detail* the reasons of many things mentioned in the Torah."[110]

In short, sound philosophic-literary procedure determined that details of laws and parables should not ordinarily be investigated. Sometimes, however, they may, or must, be examined in order to complete one's insight into the entity as a whole. Generally, with regard to commandments, this careful, balanced interpretative

---

109. MN, introduction (pp. 12, 14). Note that at first (p. 12) Maimonides merely mentions two kinds of parable, but then (p. 14) says that *most* are of this kind. See C. Neuburger, *Das Wesen*, p. 33.

110. MN, III, 26 (p. 510); III, 49 (p. 612); III, 50 (p. 615) (italics mine).

approach has additional significance: it preserves the inner dialectic of the religious act, inasmuch as explaining the generalities provides a measure of rationalization or intellectualization, while recognizing the contingent (unexplainable) details preserves a dimension of authoritativeness—ultimate and impenetrable.

*Should knowledge of the reasons remain esoteric?*

Having concluded that combined religious-philosophic considerations resolutely affirm the study of *ṭa'ăme ham-miṣwoṯ*, the inquirer must next determine whether the results of this study should be revealed to, and shared with, others, or whether, even after they have been discovered, they should be guarded as esoteric lore. Is rationalization of the law, like religious rationalization generally, permissible only to those who are properly qualified? The prerequisites for the study of metaphysics are many and rigorous; it demands multiple skills and extraordinary tenacity. Maimonides repeatedly emphasizes that one should not rush into this study without patient and prolonged preparation or the results will be disastrous: "One of the parables generally known in our community is that comparing knowledge to water. Now the Sages, peace be upon them, explained several notions by means of this parable; one of them being that he who knows how to swim brings up pearls from the bottom of the sea, whereas he who does not know drowns. For this reason no one should expose himself to the risks of swimming unless he has been trained in learning to swim."[111]

Whenever he talks about finding reasons for the law, Maimonides stipulates, "to the extent of his ability," "so far as we are able to give them a reason";[112] the "clear cause" or "manifest utility" of certain commandments "is hidden from us either because of the incapacity of our intellects or because of the deficiency of our knowledge";[113] "You will never cease dis-

---

111. MN, I, 34, and, generally, 31–34; see PhM, introduction (p. 38), which compresses this entire teaching concerning the problems of philosophic study: חולשת
השכל, והתגברות התאוות, והעצלות מללמוד והחריצות לרדיפת עניני העולם הזה. Also,
PhM, Ḥag̱, 2:1 (p. 378), and 'Ab̲ 2:15 (p. 428).
112. *Mĕ'ilah*, viii, 8; *Tĕmurah*, iv, 13.
113. MN, III, 26, 28.

covering the clear and evident manifestation of justice in all the commandments of this law, if you consider them carefully"; "This is what should be believed by one who is endowed with perfection and knows the true meaning of . . .";[114] "Thus it has already become clear to you, you who engage in speculation, what Scripture intended in these particulars . . .";[115] etc. While it is thus self-evident that not everyone is psychologically and ideologically qualified to uncover the reasons, Maimonides seems to share them rather freely, for awareness of the reasons is itself a prerequisite for attaining perfection. Sensitizing one to the reasons is part of the pedagogic purpose of Maimonides. The view concerning the instrumental or teleological role of commandments is a completely exoteric doctrine. Moreover, just as philosophic truths may be presented descriptively or apodictically as articles of tradition, instead of being elaborated demonstratively as syllogistic premises and conclusions, so also may *ṭa'ăme ham-miṣwot* be popularized so that their intent is known but their intricacies reduced.[116]

## Reasons—absolute or relative?

Toward the end of his quest, the rationalizing student of the law, having utilized certain historical-philosophical-philological tools, must assess whether the reasons advanced for the commandments are absolute or relative. Does the law lend itself to multiple explanation—and each inquirer may subjectively construct reasons which are meaningful to him and which enhance his appreciation of the law—or is there actually a monolithic causal scheme which can be objectively reconstructed by assiduous study and rigorous research?

While most interpreters would agree that every wise person is free to find a different reason or taste in the law which would embellish and spiritualize the bald halakic directives—for these can be integrated with, and invigorated by, disparate metahalakic systems—Maimonides seems to suggest in certain places that the

---

114. MN, III, 49 (pp. 605, 612).
115. MN, III, 37 (p. 543).
116. See MTH, 2, 4; LA, 229. See below, p. 500.

## 402 INTRODUCTION TO THE CODE OF MAIMONIDES

discipline of *ṭa'ăme ham-miṣwot*, at least in part, is as precise and objective as any scientific discipline. Ample knowledge, judiciously interpreted and applied, yields precise reasons. This is not hubris or bumptious reliance on one's opinions, but disciplined and constructive use of intellect and insight. His introductory chapter of the *Moreh* states: "This being so, I have seen fit to divide the 613 commandments into a number of classes, every one of which comprises a number of commandments belonging to one kind or akin in meaning. I shall inform you of the cause of every one of these classes, and I shall show their utility, about which there can be no objection."[117] Concerning the *ḥuḳḳim*, brimful of enigma, Maimonides confidently promises: "However, you will hear my explanation for all of them and my exposition of the correct and demonstrated causes for them all. . . . I shall explain that all these and others of the same kind are indubitably related to one of the three notions referred to . . ."[118] Again, "thus it has been made clear to you, so that there can be no doubt about it . . ."[119] In one place Maimonides reveals a major source of the information which gives him such a sense of assurance: "I shall now return to my purpose and say that the meaning of many of the laws became clear to me, and their causes became known to me, through my study of the doctrines, opinions, practices, and cult of the Sabians, as you will hear when I explain the reasons for the commandments that are considered to be without cause. I shall mention to you the books from which all that I know about the doctrines and opinions of the Sabians will become clear to you, so that you will know for certain that what I say about the reasons for these laws is correct."[120] On the other hand, this monolithic approach is sometimes punctuated by multiple explanations of the same law: "Similarly with regard to circumcision, one of the reasons for it is, in my opinion . . ."[121] By definition,

---

117. MN, III, 26 (pp. 509–10). The general issue is discussed in Twersky, "The Shulḥan 'Aruk," pp. 155ff. For Maimonides in particular, see Y. Ben-Sasson in *Tarbiz*, XXIX (1960), 268ff.
118. MN, III, 28 (p. 513).
119. MN, III, 37 (p. 550).
120. MN, III, 29 (p. 518).
121. MN, III, 49 (p. 609); also III, 37. In MN, III, 48 (p. 599), Maimonides conjectures—"it is in my opinion not improbable"—that the reason for not eating meat

this would suggest a certain suppleness of approach, less apodictic, more tentative and open-ended. The question of certitude and conjecture in this system exercised the minds of many post-Maimonidean writers, partisans as well as antagonists. We should note particularly that many Maimonidean protagonists, eager to defend their master's system, insisted upon the relative nature of the explanations. There was in the Maimonidean system no presumption of absolute explanation, they contended, merely one possible scheme which was useful and meaningful.[122]

## Ṭaʿăme miṣwot and polemics

A cognate question, which anchors the quest for *ṭaʿăme hammiṣwot* in time-bound historical situations, is: Does all this have any practical-polemical value vis-à-vis contemporary contingencies, or is it really pure theory, an attempt to explain, motivate, and spiritualize the law sub specie aeternitatis? Did contemporary intellectual pressures and philosophical challenges contribute to Maimonides' determination to be expansive where the sources were laconic or elliptical? We should recall that medieval Rabbis were already cognizant of historical influences or stimuli. For example, R. Isaac Abarbanel assumed that Maimonides' enumeration of dogma was a response to contemporary modes—Muslim creeds (*ʿaqāʾid*) and Christian catechism. R. Simeon Duran claimed that Maimonides exaggerated certain formulations for religious reasons.[123]

---

boiled in milk is rooted in Sabian practice, but, he declares, "I have not seen this set down in any of the books of the Sabians that I have read." Note also the seesaw assertion in MN, III, introduction (p. 416): "In addition to this there is the fact that in that which has occurred to me with regard to these matters I followed conjecture and supposition. . . . But the texts . . . together with the speculative premises that I possess showed me that things are indubitably so-and-so. Yet it is possible that they are different." PhM, Ḥag 2:1 (p. 377).

122. E.g., R. Shem Tob, *Sefer ha-ʾĔmunot*, I, 1, accused Maimonides of claiming absolute certitude for his explanations; see per contra the strong demurral by R. Abraham Maimonides, *Kobeṣ*, III, 19a; RIṬBA, *Sefer ha-Zikkaron*, p. 54; R. Hillel of Verona, *Tagmule han-Nefeš* (Lyck, 1874), 25a (describing it as *mĕleket šamayim*); Leo de Modena, *ʾĂri Nohem* (Jerusalem, 1929), chap. 8; see Gersonides, *Peruš*, end of *Pārašat Ṣaw* (p. 132b); *Sefer ha-Ḥinnuk*, n.611, where the author effectively notes that other reasons may be forthcoming (קבל זה ממני עד שמעך טוב ממנו).

123. R. Isaac Abarbanel, *Roš ʾĂmanah* (Tel Aviv, 1958), chap. 23 (p. 136); R. Simeon Duran, *Tĕšubot*, I, 63. For the anti-Karaite polemic, quite clearly contemporary, see

The law had, of course, been under attack from many quarters. Of special relevance is the fact that it was frequently denounced as being an oppressive burden which must thwart rather than trigger excellence; this not only was an old Christian topos but also had contemporary echoes in the Islamic world.[124] Both the philosophical and historical components of Maimonides' approach could be used in effective rebuttal of this attack. Compared to the absurd mythological practices of idolatry—difficult, demanding, and demeaning but totally useless—the commandments of the Torah are pleasant, both palatable and productive: "Now inasmuch as these notions were generally accepted, so that they were regarded as certain, and as God, may He be exalted, wished, in His pity for us, to efface this error from our minds and to take away fatigue from our bodies, through the abolition of these tiring and useless practices, and to give us laws through the instrumentality of Moses our teacher. . . ."[125] With regard to the laws of purity, Maimonides mentions that "all the things in the law that you may perhaps imagine to involve unpleasantness or a heavy burden, appear so to you only because you do not know the usages and teachings that existed in those days."[126] Also, "most of the commandments serve . . . to lighten the great and oppressive burdens, the toil and fatigue, that those people imposed upon themselves in their cult."[127] Paganism trivializes human endeavor; the Torah elevates it. In a word, the Torah is immeasurably easier in comparison with an oppressive pagan ritual.

Elsewhere Maimonides explicitly declares, as if he were addressing himself to a critic, that the ritual law is not a heavy burden: "For these are manners of worship in which there is no

---

Maimonides' statement in *Kobeṣ*, I, 26a, and above, chap. I, nn. 159–60. Maimonides was also concerned with the theological status of Christianity and Islam; see, e.g., '*Akum*, ix, 4; *Ma'ăkalot 'Ăsurot*, xi, 7. Also PhM AZ 1:1 (p. 338). See the observations of M. Steinschneider, *Polemische und Apologetische Literatur* (Leipzig, 1877), pp. 354ff.; N. Brüll, *Jahrbücher für jüdische Geschichte*, 1 (1876), 195; and cf. Y. Shamir, "Allusions to Muhammed in Maimonides' Theory of Prophecy in his *Guide*," *JQR*, LXIV (1974), 212ff.

124. Justin Martyr, *Dialogue with Trypho*, chap. 18; Samuel al-Maghribī, *Silencing the Jews*, ed. M. Perlmann, *PAAJR*, XXXII (1964), 69.
125. MN, III, 30.
126. MN, III, 47 (p. 592).
127. MN, III, 49, (p. 612).

burden and excess—such as monastic life, pilgrimage, and similar things—nor a deficiency necessarily leading to greed and to being engrossed in the indulgence of appetites, so that in consequence the perfection of man is diminished with respect to his moral habits and to his speculation, this being the case with regard to all the other *nomoi* of the religious communities of the past."[128] It repudiates asceticism and other forms of extremism, for it has its own road to perfection: "The perfect law which leads us to perfection—as one who knew it well testifies by the words, *The law of the Lord is perfect, restoring the soul; the testimony of the Lord is sure, making wise the simple* (Ps. 19:8)—recommends none of these things (such as self-torture, flight from society, etc.). On the contrary, it aims at man's following the path of moderation and living among people in honesty and uprightness, but not dwelling in the wilderness or in the mountains, or clothing oneself in garments of hair and wool, or afflicting the body."[129] Its immediate aim is to eliminate idolatrous practices and its long-range aim is to endow one with perfection. Its system is so precise and its impact so efficacious that it can dispense with extremism. As we shall see, this repudiation of asceticism is a theoretical stance which has practical, immediate repercussions.

Furthermore, if the law is perceived as an indispensable *means* to the goal of perfection—the crowning feature of Judaism—the exertion it demands and the limitations it imposes are benignly accepted:

As for those who deem its burdens grievous, heavy, and difficult to bear—all of this is due to an error in considering them. I shall explain later on how easy they are in true reality, according to the opinion of the perfect. For this reason Scripture says, *What does the Lord thy God require of thee* (Deut. 10:12), and so on. And it says, *Have I been a wilderness unto*

---

128. MN, II, 39 (p. 380). In *'Issure Bi'ah*, xiii, 14, Maimonides does speak of the burden (טורח) of the law, but there it is an indispensable part of the admonition and instruction to the prospective convert. It helps test the latter's sincerity and determination—see ibid., xiv, 2, 3—but nevertheless should not be exaggerated. The burden becomes meaningful and pleasant. See R. Judah hal-Levi, *Kuzari*, I, 95, 115. Note also concerning the burden of the law R. David Ḳimḥi, to Hos. 11:3; ham-Me'iri, *Beṭ hab-Bĕḥirah* (Jerusalem, 1965), introduction, p. 9; R. Joseph Albo, *'Iḳḳarim*, III, 29 (pp. 272ff.). See also *De'ot* i, 6.

129. SP, chap. IV. See *Kuzari*, II, 50; III, 1–7.

*Israel?* (Jer. 2:31), and so on. However, all this refers to the virtuous, whereas in the opinion of those who are unjust, violent, and tyrannical, the existence of a judge who renders tyranny impossible is a most harmful and grievous thing. As for the greedy and the vile, the most grievous thing in their opinion is that which hinders their abandoning themselves to debauchery and punishes those who indulge in it. Similarly everyone who is deficient in any respect considers that a hindrance in the way of the vice that he prefers, because of his moral corruption, is a great burden. Accordingly, the facility or difficulty of the law should not be estimated with reference to the passions of all the wicked, vile, and morally corrupt men, but should be considered with reference to the man who is perfect among the people. For it is the aim of this law that everyone should be such a man.[130]

While paganism is linked to frustration and futility, the Torah is geared to purposiveness and perfection. Given the nobility of its goals, the means are not that stringent after all. The sensitized person will welcome its directives and abide by its imperatives, for the ultimate reward is very great.

Finally, this rationalization of law would also help bridge the gap between traditional religion, with its insistence upon the necessity and value of action, and philosophy, with its insistence upon the excellence and superiority of contemplation. A philosophic view of the instrumental or teleological role of traditional Jewish practices ruled out contempt or condescension for action and cleared the way for reconciliation. Actions which are carriers of ideas are significant even for individuals committed to the theoretical life. As a special dividend, the philosophic approach combined the necessary and untiring accumulation of minute detail with the exhilaration of insight and understanding. It was a meaningful bridge between action and reflection. We are back again to the reciprocity of the *vita contemplativa* and *vita activa*.[131]

130. MN, II, 39. See *Yĕsodē hat-Torah*, iv, 13; in '*Akum*, i, 3 (end), and IT, v, Maimonides underscores the fact that the commandments "crown" the Jews and Judaism; they preserve true belief and fortify it. See also *Kuzari*, I, 83; *Hobot hal-Lĕbabot*, ix, 7.

131. See the emphasis in MN, III, 8 (pp. 432–33). The careful formulation of S. Pines concerning the *Moreh* (translator's introduction to *Guide of the Perplexed*, p. cxvi, n.96) is applicable to our entire discussion.

## LAW AND PHILOSOPHY

REASONS OF THE LAW IN THE *Mishneh Torah*

An examination of the *Mishneh Torah* shows that Maimonides is as articulate and apodictic there about the permissibility, indeed the desirability, of a sustained inquiry into the reasons for the ceremonial and moral law as he is in the *Moreh*. Moreover, the *Mishneh Torah* not only issues a general mandate for such speculation but also intimates the guidelines and theorems. Its philosophic sensibility is unmistakable. For all their differences, both obvious and subtle, there is a remarkable, if not total, correlation between these works. Two statements which we shall examine presently summarize the Maimonidean position in all its nuances, which is as follows: (1) there are reasons, (2) which can be known by man through proper study; (3) he should investigate them, the danger of antinomianism notwithstanding, and (4) be prepared to share the knowledge with others. Answers to the last two questions concerning (5) the absoluteness or relativism of the reasons and (6) the role of contemporary pressures and polemic challenges are oblique or inferential, as we shall see.

Mĕʻilah, *viii*, 8: *a mandate for inquiry*

The first passage serves as the finale to *Hilkot Mĕʻilah* and to the entire *Sefer ʻAbodah*:

It is fitting for man to meditate upon the laws of the holy Torah and to comprehend their full meaning to the extent of his ability. Nevertheless, a law for which he finds no reason and understands no cause should not be trivial in his eyes. (1) Let him not *break through (hāros) to come up against the Lord, lest the Lord break forth upon him* (Exod. 19:24); (2) nor should his thoughts concerning these things be like his thoughts concerning profane matters. Come and consider how strict the Torah was in the law of trespass! Now if sticks and stones and earth and ashes became hallowed by words alone, as soon as the name of the Master of the universe was invoked upon them, and anyone who comported with them as with a profane thing committed trespass and required atonement even if he had acted unwittingly, how much more should man be on guard not to rebel (*baʻot*) against a commandment decreed for us by the Holy One, blessed be He, only because he does not understand its reason; (1) or to heap words (*lĕ-ḥappot dĕbarim*) that are not right against the Lord; (2) or to regard the commandments in the manner in which he regards ordinary affairs.[132]

Contained in this passage is a clear exposition of the notion of sceptical or agnostic antinomianism: rejection of religious law because it has become trivial in man's eyes after he was unable to motivate or spiritualize it. Unlike the case of philosophic antinomianism, where knowledge may lead to laxity—the idea of an intellectualist bypass of performance—in this context intellectual failure rather than intellectual attainment results in neglect. The presence of this notion in the *Mishneh Torah* is noteworthy, for it is a most potent argument in behalf of rationalization. While philosophic "activism" *may* harbor the peril of relativism and result in making light of the laws, intellectual passivity or resignation is a definite unavoidable hazard for halakic observance and will result in actual ridicule of the laws.[133] The law is of course self-validating and should never be contingent upon human reason, but proper disciplined intellectualization is its most effective prop.

We should note the careful symmetrical structure of this close-textured paragraph. After exhorting man to seek out the rationale of the law, it warns against *two* possible pitfalls. First, one may impetuously assign to the commandments reasons which are inadequate, platitudinous, or false—this is the thrust of Maimonides' use of the Biblical idiom *break through (hăros) to come up against the Lord. La-hăros,* a key word which he uses frequently

---

132. *Mĕ'ilah,* viii, 8. The numbers (1) and (2) which I inserted in the text are to underscore the parallelism of the *two* warnings which I discern in Maimonides' statement. For "regarding the commandments in the manner in which he regards ordinary affairs," see *Yĕsoḏe hat-Torah,* vi, 8; "Šemot Ḳodeš wĕ-Ḥol," *Dĕvir,* I (1923), 191ff. For use of *ba'ot* as ridicule while nevertheless observing the law, see *Šĕḡaḡot,* iii, 10. Cf. Jonah ibn Janāḥ's definition of *ba'ot in Sefer ha-Riḳmah.* The standard commentaries on this passage are paradigmatic of how Maimonidean innovations were glossed over or neutralized; e.g., *KM, Mĕ'ilah,* viii, 8: דברי רבנו ודרכיו אמונה והם ראוים אליו.

133. See *Tĕšubah,* iv, 2 (*mal'iḡ 'al ham-miṣwot*). Note R. Meir Aldabi, *Šĕḇile 'Ĕmunah* (Tel Aviv, 1965), 8th *netib,* p. 161; R. Joshua ibn Shu'ayb, *Dĕrašot* (reprinted, Jerusalem, 1969), p. 39a. R. David Ḳimḥi, *Peruš,* Ps. 119:129, emphasizes that he who does not understand a commandment will not observe it properly. See above, n. 100. I have treated this notion of agnostic antinomianism or, at best, the reduction of halakah to a form of bland behaviorism, as developed by these writers (with a common source in RaSHBA), in a separate article.

in the *Moreh* and concerning which he corresponded with Ibn Tibbon, suggests "to destroy by being overhasty, reckless, and undisciplined"; we must rather "engage in perfecting knowledge of preparatory matters and in achieving those premises that purify apprehension of its taint, which is error." One who speculates without proper preparation and prudence is a *hores,* a "wrecker."[134] To heap words (*le-ḥappoṭ dĕḇarim*) that are not right—to impute erroneous notions—means to make loose, sophistical, and ultimately blasphemous allegations about God and His law. This reading of the passage is substantiated by the following peroration to the Laws Concerning Leprosy, particularly its citation of 2 Kings 17:9:

> Now the way of the company of the scornful and wicked is this:
> In the beginning they are profuse with vain words, as in the matter whereof it is said, *A fool's voice cometh through a multitude of words* (Eccles. 5:2). Then they go on to speak to the discredit of the righteous, as in the matter whereof it is said, *Let the lying lips be dumb, which speak arrogantly against the righteous* (Ps. 31:19). Then they become accustomed to speak against the prophets and to discredit their words, as in the matter whereof it is said, *But they mocked the messengers of God, and despised His words, and scoffed at His prophets* (2 Chron. 36:16). Then they go on to speak against God and to deny the very root of religion, as in the matter whereof it is said, *And the children of Israel did impute things (wayḥappĕ'u dĕḇarim) that were not right unto the Lord their God* (2 Kings 17:9); moreover it is said, *They have set their mouth against the heavens, and their tongue walketh through the earth* (Ps. 73:9). What brought it to pass that they set their mouth against heaven? Their tongue, which first walked through the earth.[135]

*Lĕ-ḥappoṭ,* willful allegation, is a central phenomenon in this resonant indictment of slovenly-sinful speech which spreads

---

134. MN, I, 5 (p. 30); MTH, 14 and 39 (*Be'ur Millot*).
135. *Ṭumĕ'aṭ Ṣara'aṭ*, xvi, 10. See *Talmud Torah*, vi, 11; and *Tĕšuḇah*, iv, 2 (*meḥazzeh rabbotaw*); and cf. PhM, 'Aḇ 4:4 (p. 440), where Maimonides cites a different explanation of leprosy; and Neḡ 12:5 (p. 397). On the virtue of careful speech generally, see *De'oṭ*, ii, 4; *Talmud Torah*, iii, 13; *Tĕfillin*, iv, 25. One of the reasons for the vehement Maimonidean indictment of liturgical poetry is its, at worst, slovenly and sinful, and at best, inconsequential, use of language; see MN, I, 59 (p. 142), where Maimonides quotes 2 Kings 17:9 about "imputing things that were not right"—the key phrase of *Mĕ'ilah*, viii, 8, and *Ṭumĕ'aṭ Ṣara'aṭ*, xvi, 10; PhM, 'Aḇ 1:16 (pp. 416ff.); *Tĕšuḇot*, 254 (p. 467).

gradually like an uncontrollable malignancy. While Maimonides is here concerned with loose talk in general—and silence cannot be sinful—in the *Mĕʿilah* passage he is concerned only with rationalization of the commandments and insists that the absence of reason (silence) is better than a bad reason (loose talk).

This insistence is completely congruent with his general philosophic posture vis-à-vis perplexing problems or even antinomies: honest suspension of judgment—silence—resulting in traditional acceptance of a certain view is preferable to specious demonstration. Creation versus eternity of the world is such an issue:

> If a man claims that he sets out to demonstrate a certain point by means of sophistical arguments, he does not, in my opinion, strengthen assent to the point he intends to prove, but rather weakens it and opens the way for attacks against it. For when it becomes clear that those proofs are not valid, the soul weakens in its assent to what is being proved. It is preferable that a point for which there is no demonstration remain a problem, or that one of the two contradictory propositions simply be accepted.[136]

Free will versus divine foreknowledge is another, perhaps the classic, antinomy. After a candid exposition of the problem, Maimonides declares: "This being the case, we lack the capacity to know how God knows all creatures and their activities. Yet we do know beyond doubt that a human being's activities are in his own hands."[137] Maimonides' theory concerning prudence and patience in *ṭaʿăme ham-miṣwot* fits into this methodological framework of rigor and integrity. He does not want to camouflage complexities or exorcise problems by using impressive-sounding but imprecise or inadequate formulae. Such "breaking through" is self-defeating. Silent acceptance is preferable. Impulsive and undisciplined reasoning, which is woefully misleading, is to be shunned.

The second pitfall warned against in the *Mĕʿilah* passage is that of "regarding the commandments in the manner in which he regards ordinary affairs," i.e., dismissing as worthless the laws for

---

136. MN, II, 16.
137. *Tĕṣubah*, v, 5.

which one understands no cause. Human laws or narratives may be discarded as mere fables and mythological constructs if they cannot be rationalized, just as certain Greek philosophers in fact dismissed their ancient mythopoeic lore as purely legendary if they were unable to allegorize it and find in it underlying philosophic truths. All was subordinated to their philosophic perceptions—or venturesomeness; if they succeeded, fables became a *philosophia moralis,* and if not, they were vulgar mythology.[138] However, divinely revealed laws are, by definition, rooted in reason and geared to advancing perfection; they are intrinsically true and valuable. Hence, failure to find their underlying philosophic truths is a temporary setback and not an irreversible censure. It is the result of the fact that "the intellects of human beings have a limit at which they stop."[139] Tradition—i.e., the conviction that law is purposive—prevails while reason is in abeyance or in flux. Only the excessively proud or the pusillanimous will err in either direction. Eminent halakist that he is, Maimonides introduces a *ḳal wa-ḥomer* (from the minor to the major) argument: mundane objects are sanctified by man's uttering a formula which includes God's name—"this is consecrated to God"—and may no longer be treated as ordinary or profane. Words consecrate sticks and stones. It is self-evident, therefore, that anything issued by God Himself is immanently sacred, immeasurably superior to that concerning which God's name has merely been invoked, and not to be treated as ordinary or profane. This would be desecration.

Before leaving this passage we should briefly consider an alternate interpretation which finds a warning against a triple (rather than a double) distortion by viewing the phrase "a law for which he finds no reason and understands no cause should not be trivial" as one *specific* reaction rather than as a general caption introducing two possible pitfalls. According to this three-fold construction, Maimonides admonishes the searching interpreter (1) not to

---

138. See, e.g., Wolfson, *Philo,* I, 132–33, 138ff.; idem, *Religious Philosophy,* p. 243; J. Seznec, *The Survival of the Pagan Gods* (Princeton, 1972), p. 84.

139. MN, I, 32 (p. 10), and see PhM, introduction (p. 38), concerning the intellectual impasse in interpretation of aggadah; note R. Abraham ibn Daud, *Ha-'Ĕmunah ha-Ramah,* III, 103.

adopt an antinomistic stance, flouting and ignoring the law because it seems trivial as a result of his failure to rationalize it; (2) not to approach the law in a reckless, intellectually undisciplined way, suggesting indiscriminately explanations which are inadequate, erroneous, or blasphemous; (3) not to have a contemptuous attitude towards the law as one does towards profane matters (i.e., to let "his thoughts concerning these things be like his thoughts concerning profane matters"), continuing to observe the law routinely even though he lacks conviction and commitment or actually thinks that the commandments are worthless. This third possibility echoes the sentiment forcefully expressed by Maimonides in '*Ăbodah Zarah* xi, 16, where after condemning idolatrous practices as "false and deceptive," he states: "Whoever believes in these and similar things and in his heart holds them to be true and scientific and only forbidden by the Torah, is nothing but a fool, deficient in understanding"; observance should be accompanied by commitment and insight, should, in short, be congruent with one's mind and heart. Note that the symmetry of the passage, with its carefully nuanced repetition, is preserved even according to this threefold interpretation. The thrust of the sentence about a law not being trivial in his eyes—i.e., antinomianism or open rebelliousness—is sustained and strengthened by the concluding remark that "man should be on guard not to rebel against a commandment . . . because he does not understand its reason." The idea of regarding the commandments as one regards ordinary or profane matters—i.e., uninspired, sterile observance totally incongruous with one's intellectual and spiritual postulates—is explicitly repeated in practically identical terms. The pungent use of the Biblical idioms of "breaking through" in the first part and "heaping words that are not right" at the end—i.e., intellectual slovenliness and irresponsibility which result in theological error—complete the parallelism. According to both the double and triple interpretation this passage is pivotal for the Maimonidean system.

Let us now return to the concluding paragraph of the Laws Concerning Trespass (*Mě'ilah*) which continues with an elaborate affirmation of the worth of all commandments, including the apparently troublesome *ḥukkim:*

## LAW AND PHILOSOPHY

Behold, it is said in Scripture, *Ye shall therefore keep all My statutes, and all Mine ordinances, and do them* (Lev. 20:22); whereupon our Sages have commented that "keeping" (šĕmirah) and "doing" refer to the "statutes" as well as to the "ordinances." "Doing" is well known; namely, performing the statutes. And "keeping" means that one should be careful concerning them and not imagine that they are less important than the ordinances. Now the "ordinances" are commandments whose reason is obvious, and the benefit derived in this world from doing them is well known; for example, the prohibition against robbery and murder, or the commandment of honoring one's father and mother. The "statutes," on the other hand, are commandments whose reason is not known. Our Sages have said: "*My statutes* are the decrees that I have decreed for you, and you are not permitted to question them." A man's impulse pricks him concerning them, and the Gentiles reprove us about them, such as the statutes concerning the prohibition against the flesh of the pig and that against meat seethed with milk, the law of the heifer whose neck is broken, of the Red Heifer, or of the scapegoat.

How much was King David distressed by heretics and pagans who disputed the statutes! Yet the more they pursued him with false questions, which they plied according to the narrowness of men's minds, the more he increased his cleaving to the Torah; as it is said, *The proud have forged a lie against me; but I with my whole heart will keep Thy precepts* (Ps. 119:69). It is also said there concerning this, *All Thy commandments are faithful; they persecute me for nought; help Thou me* (Ps. 119:86).

All the (laws concerning the) offerings are in the category of statutes. The Sages ('Ab 1:2) have said that the world stands because of the service of the offerings; for through the performance of the statutes and the ordinances the righteous merit life in the world to come. Indeed, the Torah puts the commandment concerning the statutes first; as it is said, *Ye shall therefore keep My statutes, and Mine ordinances, which if a man do, he shall live by them* (Lev. 18:5).

This exposition of *ḥukkim* contains a number of interpretative novelties which should be noted briefly: (1) The paraphrastic substitution of one's impulse or conscience arousing a person for the original Rabbinic reference to "Satan," an overtly rationalistic change that is continued by many later writers, is consistently Maimonidean and was discussed and explained in the *Moreh*.[140] (2) The use of Ps. 119:69 as a proof-text depends upon seeing the

---

140. MN, III, 17. See Rashi, to B. Yoma 67b; P. Duran, *Ma'ăśeh 'Efod*, p. 1.

second clause in causal relationship to the first—because they maliciously increased their accusations against me, I intensified my commitment. David is thus paradigmatic of a principled defense of *ḥukkim*.[141] (3) Equally significant is the emphasis on the *outer-directed* motive, which is so paramount in the *Moreh*. While there is no overt reference to Deut. 4:6, the key proof-text of the *Moreh*, vindication of the statutes in the eyes of non-Jewish maligners is a prominent theme.[142] The common denominator is the insistence upon rationality; arguments against the law are patently false and vicious. However, it should be clear that the resultant emphasis here revolves around piety and firmness of commitment regardless of what the outsiders think, even if it *appears* that there are limits to rationality. (4) "Keeping" is not synonymous with "doing," but involves a value judgment—esteem of the *ḥukkim*. This means not just axiomatic reverence or pietistic exaltation but intellectual appraisal and rational conviction. Such an interpretation is further proof that the Torah saw the *ḥukkim* as rational and purposive, even if not transparently utilitarian or rational. The current of intellectualism that pulses through the *ḥukkim* is as strong, if less obvious, than the one in *mišpaṭim*.[143] (5) *He shall live by them* refers to life in the world to come; as a result of observance, one merits this future life.[144] (6) Needless to say, in the light of the hierarchy established in the *Moreh*, the pride of place and purpose awarded to sacrifices is puzzling. It should, however, be noted that no explanation whatsoever is here attempted for sacrifices. We have a general affirmation concerning the implicit worth of a legal genre, *ḥukkim*, but we are not given a specific rationalization for sacrifices. The

---

141. On David as a model of piety, see *Lulaḇ*, viii, 15 (and R. Baḥya ibn Paḳuda, *Ḥoḇot hal-Lěḇaḇot*, vi, 6; ed. Hyamson, II, 96 and 100); *Mělaḵim*, xi, 4; IT, xviii; PhM, 'Aḇ 4:4 (p. 439); MN, I, 40; II, 45.

142. See MN, III, 31; and PhM, Sanh, *Pereḳ Ḥeleḳ*, cited above, n.78; *Těšuḇot*, III, 57 (להראות העמים והשרים את יופי . . .). For Maimonides' awareness of contemporary conditions in general, see *Těšuḇah*, v, 1; viii, 6; *Ḳidduš ha-Ḥodeš*, xi, 5 (the possibility that a non-Jewish scholar would read this text); *'Išuṭ*, xxv, 2; *Těšuḇot*, 149 (p. 284), 448 (pp. 726–27); *Mělaḵim*, xi, 4; and IT, passim. See *Nizḵe Mamon*, viii, 5, and *Migdal 'Oz*.

143. See, e.g., *Sefer Miṣwoṭ Gaḏol*, II, introduction.

144. See Naḥmanides to Lev. 18:15, and G. Cohen, "Soteriology," *PAAJR*, XXXVI (1968), 42–43.

statement about putting the commandment concerning sacrifices first may therefore stand simply as a parallel to the Rabbinic statement in 'Abot—both re-establish the equivalence of statutes and ordinances. It may also contain the following nuance: when all is said, people will still consider the apparently nonrational *ḥuḳḳim* as less important, and therefore the Torah felt that there was an educational need to put them first.[145] It is clear, nevertheless, that the *Moreh*'s socio-historical explanation—and explicit statements that sacrifices are of secondary-ancillary worth, compared to the Sabbath which is of primary-intrinsic worth—is not easily integrated here.

Těmurah, iv, 13: *the mandate repeated and applied*

The second passage which neatly summarizes the Maimonidean position serves as the finale to *Hilḳot Těmurah* and the entire *Sefer Ḳorbanot*. It begins by reiterating the mandate to investigate and intellectualize, and summarily mentions one of the key Rabbinic proofs (elaborated in the *Sefer ham-Miṣwot*) that reasons for the law indeed exist. There is no trace of esotericism here; it is proper for all to give reasons for them. Then, unlike the previous passage which never becomes specific—it merely reiterates forcefully the

---

145. This may also explain a flagrant difficulty (see below, p. 453) in ŠP, chap. VI (cf. E. Schweid, *'Iyyunim bi-Šěmonah Pěraḳim* [Jerusalem, 1969], pp. 113ff.). Maimonides' final distinction between the motives for observing *ḥuḳḳim* and *mišpaṭim*—the former (which are beyond reason) are observed because one submits to the divine will and recognizes the heteronomous character of law, while the latter (which are eminently reasonable) should be observed freely by identifying with the divine will and spontaneously merging one's autonomous desire with the legal-ethical norm—is really self-defeating, inasmuch as he himself has argued that these two classes of commandments are ultimately alike in terms of their being intelligible. His distinction concerning autonomy and heteronomy seems to be based on the Saadianic premise which differentiates between "rational laws" and "revealed (traditional) laws"—a premise he so wrathfully denies. However, it may be that since the reasons for *ḥuḳḳim* are, when all is said, much more difficult to establish, the heteronomous stance of obedience and submission is nevertheless more appropriate. This difficulty puts them beyond the average person's reach, and hence the result is heteronomous observance. It is noteworthy in this context that Maimonides solves the stock halakic problem (concerning which religious acts are to be preceded by a benediction) almost nonchalantly: "Every duty to God, whether permissive or obligatory, requires a blessing to be said before its fulfillment" (*Běraḳot*, xi, 2). Duties to fellow men—*mišpaṭim* par excellence—are not preceded by the formula which emphasizes "who has sanctified us and commanded us." The problem of *běraḳot* is an old one: see, e.g., the responsum of R. Joseph ibn Plat in S. Assaf, *Sifran šel Rišonim* (Jerusalem, 1935), pp. 200ff. and R. David ben Joseph, *Sefer Abudarham* (Warsaw, 1878), pp. 15–17.

existence of reasons and the need to discover them—Maimonides proceeds to suggest an explanation of the law under discussion: The Torah is concerned with the intricacy and instability of the human temperament, which ultimately inclines toward material self-interest. Man may dedicate an object to God and then, yielding to fickleness and fluidity of motive, may be tempted to shortchange Him. Character training is a major goal of the law, frequently emphasized by Maimonides:

> Although the statutes in the law are all of them divine edicts, as we have explained at the close of the Laws Concerning Trespass, yet it is proper to ponder over them and to give a reason for them, so far as we are able to give them a reason. The Sages of former times have said that King Solomon understood most of the reasons for all the statutes of the law. It seems to me that in so far as Scripture has said, *Both it and that for which it is changed shall be holy* (Lev. 27:10)—as also in that matter whereof it has said, *And if he that sanctified it will redeem his house, then he shall add the fifth part of the money of thy valuation* (Lev. 27:15)—the law has plumbed the depths of man's mind and the extremity of his evil impulse. For it is man's nature to increase his possessions and to be sparing of his wealth. Even though a man had made a vow and dedicated something, it may be that later he drew back and repented and would now redeem it with something less than its value. But the law has said, "If he redeems it for himself, he shall add the fifth." So, too, if a man dedicated a beast to a sanctity of its body, perchance he would draw back, and since he cannot redeem it, would change it for something of less worth. And if the right was given to him to change the bad for the good, he would change the good for the bad and say, "It is good." Therefore Scripture has stopped the way against him so that he should not change it, and has penalized him if he should change it, and has said, *Both it and that for which it is changed shall be holy*. And both these laws serve to suppress man's natural tendency and correct his moral-intellectual qualities (*de'ot*).[146]

This illustrates the following hermeneutic generalization: "If you should test most of the commandments from this point of view, you will find that they are all for the discipline and guidance of the faculties of the soul."[147]

---

146. *Těmurah,* iv, 13. See MN, III, 41. Note that this is one of the few cases where a reason for the commandment is labeled by "it seems to me."
147. ŠP, chap. IV.

The passage ends with an artfully compressed restatement of the entire rationale of the law: "And the greater part of the rules in the law are but *counsels of old* (Isa. 25:1), from Him who is *great in counsel* (Jer. 32:19), to correct our moral-intellectual qualities (*de'ot*) and to keep straight all our doings. And so He says, *Have not I written unto thee excellent things of counsels and knowledge, that I might make thee know the certainty of the words of truth, that thou mightest bring back words of truth to them that sent thee?* (Prov. 22:20–21)."[148] Commandments are often cathartic or purgative in the literal sense, for the law takes a realistic view of human foibles and fallibilities. Laws are, in sum, politically constructive as well as ethically and intellectually edifying; they contain, and convey, counsel and knowledge, which seem to be analogous to "peace" and "truth" as code words for moral virtues and intellectual virtues, *tiḳḳun hag-guf* and *tiḳḳun han-nefeš*, respectively.

It will be helpful at this point to introduce Maimonides' summary of his teachings on this subject as formulated in the *Epistle to Yemen*. This not only is an avowedly popular work—he urges that a copy of it be sent to "every community in the cities and hamlets"—but was written at the exact time (1172) that he was

---

148. *Těmurah*, iv, 13. The use of Prov. 22:20–21 is novel. Gersonides, in his commentary, ad loc., cites this interpretation of counsel and knowledge as the intended meaning. See the use of this by R. Baḥya ibn Paḳuda, *Ḥobot hal-Lěbabot*, III, 3 (I, 202), and the letter of R. Jonathan to Maimonides, *Těšubot*, III, p. 53. The key word, *de'ot*, which is here translated "moral-intellectual," is elusive, referring both to moral as well as intellectual traits. The following passages have to be studied and correlated: *Yěsode hat-Torah*, iv, 13; *De'ot*, i, 7; v, 5 (see also v, 11 [*ba'ale de'ah* as opposed to *tippěšim*]); vii, 7; 'Akum, xi, 1; *Těšubah*, iv, 5; v, 2; vii, 7; viii, 8; ix, 1; *Gerušin*, ii, 20; *'Issure Bi'ah*, xxii, 20, 21; *Něḏarim*, xiii, 23; *'Araḳin*, viii, 13; *'Issure Mizbeaḥ*, vii, 11; note the extension of the Talmudic principle (B. BM 32b) לכוף את יצרו; note R. Hananeel, ad. loc.; and see *Ḳobeṣ*, III, 29a; *Miḳwa'ot*, xi, 12; also MN, III, 41. Since in most cases *de'ot* has a moral connotation, Maimonides' reference (in *Těmurah*, iv) to the "greater part of the law" is very careful. See I. Efros, *Philosophical Terms in the Moreh Nebukim* (New York, 1924), p. 131; and H. A. Wolfson, "Maimonides on the Unity and Incorporeality of God," *JQR*, LVI (1965), 117, n.24, and idem, "The Jewish Kalam," *JQR* 75th Anniversary Volume (1967), p. 570. Note the title of R. Saadiah's opus—*'Ěmunot wě-De'ot*—and discussion, e.g., by B. Klar, *Meḥḳarim wě-'Iyyunim* (Tel Aviv, 1953), reprinted from *ḲS*, XVI (1939–40), 242ff.; M. Zucker, in *Bitzaron*, VII (1943), 247; I. Efros, "'Iyyunim," *Sefer Yobel le-Šim'on Federbush* (Jerusalem, 1961), pp. 70ff.

## 418 INTRODUCTION TO THE CODE OF MAIMONIDES

composing the Code (1168–1178). The statement (with its assertion of the existence of a "deeper meaning" for all commandments, of the twofold perfection and the necessary progression in its acquisition, and of the key notion that each individual moves according to his ability) is thus pertinent in all respects:

> If he could only fathom the inner intent of the law, he would realize that the essence of the true divine religion lies in the deeper meaning of its positive and negative precepts, every one of which will aid man in his striving after perfection, and remove every impediment to the attainment of excellence. These commands will enable the masses and the elite to acquire moral and intellectual qualities, each according to his ability. Thus the godly community becomes preeminent, reaching a twofold perfection. By the first perfection I mean man's spending his life in this world under the most agreeable and congenial conditions. The second perfection would constitute the achievement of intellectual objectives, each in accordance with his native powers.[149]

### WIDESPREAD EMPHASIS UPON TELEOLOGICAL ROLE OF *Miṣwoṯ*

Having clearly identified this view, the student of the *Mishneh Torah* now realizes that the instrumental or teleological role of *miṣwoṯ*, so pivotal in Maimonides' philosophy of law, is explicitly noted a number of times in this Code and that explanations commensurate with this principle are freely forthcoming. Here are a few examples: (a) "For the knowledge of these things (Talmudic law) gives preliminary composure to the mind. They are the precious boon bestowed by God to promote social well-being on earth."[150] (b) "Honor is due not to the commandments themselves but to Him who ordained them . . . and therewith saved us from groping in the dark. He prepared for us a candle to make straight the perversities and a light to teach us the paths of righteousness. As it is said, *Thy word is a lamp unto my feet, and a light unto my path* (Ps. 119:105)."[151] (c) "This is the right moral prin-

---

149. IT, iv.
150. *Yĕsoḏe hat-Torah*, iv, 13. See *'Aḇoḏaṯ ham-Meleḵ*, ad loc., who submits that it was this statement rather than the designation of Talmud as a "small matter" which provoked Maimonides' critics.
151. *Šĕḥiṭah*, xiv, 15.

ciple. It alone makes civilized life and social intercourse possible."[152] (d) The words of the Torah should not be used to "cure the body, for they are only medicine for the soul, as it is said, *They shall be life unto thy soul* (Prov. 3:22)." Indeed, people who use the Torah so improperly are not only in "the category of sorcerers and soothsayers, but are also included among those who deny the Torah."[153]

We may proceed a step further and note that commandments are generally presented as the antithesis of, and antidote to, *hebel* (vanity, folly, and futility, or mechanical and compulsively repetitive behavior). This presentation in the *Mishneh Torah* is positive and emphatic, apparently free of the polemical motives and overtones which, as we have seen, accompany the *Moreh's* insistence upon purposiveness. The contrast with the fatuity of other systems is never articulated. The call to repentance is a pithy summary of halakah's role and impetus: "Those of you who forget the truth in the follies of the times (*hable haz-zěman*) and go astray the whole year in vanity (*hebel*) and emptiness which neither profit nor save, look to your souls, improve your ways and works."[154] The study of Torah is contrasted with the preoccupation with that which is accidental and transitory, with worldly inanities (*hable 'olam*)[155]—"if we deliberately forsake the Torah and occupy ourselves with the follies of the times (*hable haz-zěman*)."[156] The wise understand that mundane matters are vanity and folly (*hebel wahǎbay*), and will not, as a result, value them highly.[157] It should be clear from this that *hebel* has a dual meaning: it refers of course

---

152. *De'ot*, vii, 8; and see MN, III, 27 and 35 (class 3).
153. *'Akum*, xi, 12. The Maimonidean emphasis is sharpened when compared with the underlying passage in B. Shebu 15b, and commentaries, ad loc. See also R. Jonathan hak-Kohen of Lunel on Alfasi, Ber 5a (ed. J. Blau [New York, 1957], p. 6). See also *Těfillin*, v, 4; and cf. A. Hilvitz, *Li-lěšonot ha-RaMBaM* (Jerusalem, 1950), p. 64. Note R. Abraham Maimonides, *Peruš*, Exod. 15:26, ed. S. Sassoon and E. Wiesenberg (London, 1959), p. 278. Maimonides' "רפואת הנפש" is obviously reminiscent of "תקון הנפש". Note also *Kobeṣ*, II, 23 (נימוסין ומשמרות לנפש); II, 24: (תקון הנפש); ŠP, chap. IV; and IT, xvii–xix. See MN, I, 51.
154. *Těšubah*, iii, 4, and viii, 6.
155. *Talmud Torah*, iii, 13.
156. *Těšubah*, ix, 1.
157. *De'ot*, vii, 7. For *hǎbay*, see *'Issure Bi'ah*, xxi, 19, 24; *Ṭumě'at Ṣara'at*, xvi, 10. Also PhM, Soṭ 3:3 (p. 254); MN, III, 47; MTH, 23; *'Eben ha-'Ezer*, 23:7.

to theological inanities, to false and deceptive idolatrous practices, to which the Torah is completely antithetical;[158] in addition, *hebel* refers to moral vacuity and practical futility which the Torah seeks to eliminate. The two may even be fused, as when Maimonides asserts that believers in astrology, aside from being indictable for idolatry, are guilty of sheer folly. Astrology is a stupid distraction from useful and necessary actions.[159] Laws are a propaedeutic for meaningful nonmechanical behavior which leads to purity and integrity. Indeed, all actions—business transactions, hygienic measures, everything aimed at maintaining "physical health and vigor"—are properly seen as teleological, "in order that his soul may be upright" and that he "have a sound body with which to serve God." The law teaches man to avoid routinization—even axiological neutrality is frowned upon—and strives to make everything conscious and purposive in a God-oriented universe: "Even when he sleeps and seeks repose to calm his mind and rest his body, so as not to fall sick and be incapacitated from serving God, his sleep is service of the Almighty. In this sense our wise men charged us, 'Let all your deeds be for the sake of God' ('Ab 2:17). And Solomon in his wisdom said, *In all thy ways acknowledge Him, and He will make direct thy paths* (Prov. 3:6)."[160]

This teleological-spiritualistic conception is placed in even sharper focus if we note that ritual in particular is regularly seen as instrumental or self-transcending. The statement of the *Moreh*, "Know that all the practices of the worship, such as reading the Torah, prayer, and the performance of the other commandments,

---

158. *'Akum*, xi, 16; see *Ḥameṣ u-Maṣṣah*, vii, 2; also *Sanhedrin*, xi, 5.

159. LA, 229: "This is why our kingdom was lost and our Temple was destroyed and we were brought to this: for our fathers sinned and are no more because they found many books dealing with these themes of the stargazers, these things being the root of idolatry, as we have made clear in the Laws Concerning Idolatry. They erred and were drawn after them, imagining them to be glorious science and to be of great utility. They did not busy themselves with the art of war or with the conquest of lands, but imagined that those studies would help them. Therefore the prophets called them fools and dolts [cf. Jer. 4:22]. And truly fools they were, 'for they walked after vain things that do not profit' [cf. 1 Sam. 12:21 and Jer. 2:8]." See, generally, R. Lerner, "Maimonides' Letter on Astrology," *History of Religion*, VIII (1968), 143ff. Cf. I. Baer, *Galuṭ*, p. 36.

160. *Dē'oṭ*, iii, 3. For a striking application of this principle (*lĕ-šem šamayim*), see *Sefer ha-Ḥinnuk*, 488.

## LAW AND PHILOSOPHY

have only the end of training you to occupy yourself with His commandments, may He be exalted, and not with that which is other than He,"[161] may be read as a condensation of various formulations in the Code which see ritual as a divinely prescribed training ground for spirituality. Concerning těfillin, for example, "The sanctity of phylacteries is a high degree of sanctity. As long as phylacteries are on a man's head and arm, he is humble and God-fearing, is not drawn into frivolity and idle talk, does not dwell on evil thoughts but occupies his mind with thoughts of truth and righteousness. A man should therefore endeavor to wear phylacteries the whole day."[162] The mězuzah is not a magical amulet but a constant reminder of God's presence and a catalyst for man to rise above mundane concerns and sharpen his spiritual sensibilities as well as aspirations: "Whenever one enters or leaves a home with the mězuzah on the doorpost, he will be confronted with the declaration of God's oneness, blessed be His holy name, and will remember the love due to God, and will be aroused from his slumbers and his foolish absorption in temporal vanities (*hable haz-zěman*). He will realize that nothing endures to all eternity save knowledge of the Ruler of the universe. This thought will immediately restore him to his right senses and he will walk in the paths of righteousness."[163] The laws governing the "extreme honor and courtesy" due the Scroll of the Torah were instituted because the Scroll is a perennial reminder of the divine-human encounter: "Anyone sitting before a Scroll of the Law should be inspired with a sense of earnestness, awe, and reverence, for it is a faithful witness concerning all who come into the world, as it is said, *It shall be there for a witness against you* (Deut. 31:26)."[164] Various blessings (*běrakot*) are also divine mnemonics: "The Sages have instituted many blessings of praise and thanksgiving and petition, in order that when not partaking of material enjoyments or engaged in the fulfillment of religious duties we should constantly have God in mind. All blessings . . . the purpose of

---

161. MN, III, 51.
162. *Těfillin*, iv, 25. Note *Těfillah* vi, 1.
163. *Mězuzah*, vi, 13. See '*Edut*, xi, 3.
164. *Sefer Torah*, x, 11. The interpretation of Deut. 31:26 is new; cf. its use in MT, introduction; also *Těšubot*, 136 (p. 260). See *Ḥăgigah*, iii, 6.

which is that we should always commemorate the Creator and fear Him."[165] This is parallel to the generalization of the *Moreh* that all the commandments (prayer and benedictions) codified in Book Two of the *Mishneh Torah* have one "obvious reason": "the end of these actions . . . is the constant commemoration of God . . . the love of Him and the fear of Him." The rite of circumcision is also explained in these terms.[166] Finally, we may note that "rejoicing in the fulfilling of the commandment" is related to "love for God who had prescribed the commandment . . . True greatness and honor are achieved only by rejoicing before the Lord . . ."[167]

Fasting and praying in time of crisis and adversity is a means of impressing upon the individual the providential design in all events and reminding him of his absolute dependence on God.[168] Maimonides interprets Lev. 26:27–28, *If ye will . . . walk contrary (ķeri) unto Me, then I will walk contrary unto you in fury*, as a doctrinal statement concerning the theory of providence and as an unqualified repudiation of the Epicurean theory of chance (*miķreh*).[169] Adversity must not be seen as merely accidental, that "it is the way of the world for such a thing to happen to them and that their trouble is a matter of pure chance." This is a cruel way, for it anesthetizes all sensitivity in man and dampens all hope, leaving him to be buffeted by the frosty winds of a cruel and blind fate. The only meaningful response is to "cry out in prayer and sound an alarm," for this acknowledges design and purpose. Fasting, which endows what may be a routinized ritual performance (prayer) with a sense of urgency and emergency, strengthens man's belief and is thus of great theological-pedagogical value. It is almost a private lesson in the complex but crucial doctrine of providence.

---

165. *Bĕraķot*, i, 3; MN, III, 44. See the criticism by R. Meir ibn Gabbai, *Tola'at Ya'āķob* (Warsaw, 1876), introduction (p. 5). He focuses sharply on the tension between intrinsic-substantive and extrinsic-teleological explanation. The latter contradicts the special nature (*sĕgullah*) of the law.

166. See above, chap. IV.

167. *Lulab*, viii, 15.

168. *Ta'āniyyot*, i, 1–3; v, 1; MN, III, 36; ShM, positive 5, and Nahmanides' strictures against this formulation (quoted partially in *KM*, *Tĕfillah*, i, 1).

169. On the Epicurean theory of chance, note MN, II, 20; LA, 233; R. Saadiah, *'Ĕmunot wĕ-De'ot*, I, 3; R. Bahya, *Hobot hal-Lĕbabot*, I, 6; *Kuzari*, V, 20. See H. A.

Maimonides' treatment of holiday observance further rivets attention on this metajuridical aspect of the *Mishneh Torah*, especially in dealing with ritual; it appears that a special attempt is being made, in accord with the goal enunciated in *'Iggeret Teman*, to "fathom the intent of the law," particularly the philosophically unpalatable ritual, so as to "enable the masses and the elite to acquire moral and intellectual qualities." A Jew is commanded to rejoice on the festivals in honor of God, *and call the Sabbath a delight, and the holy (day) of the Lord honorable* (Isa. 58:13). The primary fulfillment of this commandment was originally accomplished by a special sacrifice, the peace offering, brought on the festivals. The commandment included also making one's family rejoice in the appropriate manner: "Thus children should be given parched ears of corn, nuts, and other dainties; women should have clothes and pretty trinkets bought for them, according to one's means," etc. However, this formal, material, self-centered celebration is woefully inadequate, for as Maimonides has it in his striking and poignant formulation:

... while one eats and drinks himself, it is his duty to feed the stranger, the orphan, the widow, and other poor and unfortunate people, for he who locks the doors to his courtyard and eats and drinks with his wife and family, without giving anything to eat and drink to the poor and the bitter in soul—his meal is not a rejoicing in a divine commandment but a rejoicing in his own stomach. It is of such persons that Scripture says, *Their sacrifices shall be to them as the bread of mourners, all that eat thereof shall be polluted; for their bread shall be for their own appetite* (Hos. 9:4). Rejoicing of this kind is a disgrace to those who indulge in it, as Scripture says, *And I will spread dung upon your faces, even the dung of your sacrifices* (Mal. 2:3).[170]

This is a particularly clear illustration of how moral insights and imperatives may be *elicited* from formal law. It would be preposterous to claim this as a new Maimonidean idea, for it is too indigenous and firmly rooted in Biblical verses as well as in

---

Wolfson, "Philo on Free Will," *HTR*, XXXV (1942), 131–69; idem, "Hallevi and Maimonides on Design, Chance, and Necessity," *PAAJR*, XI (1941), 105ff. In MN, III, 51 (p. 624), providence is related to intellectual achievement.

170. *Yom Ṭob*, vi, 18; *Ḥăgigah*, ii, 14.

Talmudic references.[171] Nevertheless, the fact remains that Maimonides concretized and elaborated it with persuasive eloquence and moral pathos. His formulation spells out the spirituality and ethical sensitivity which the law aims to inculcate. In addition, he provides a new proof-text, actually a new interpretation and application of a verse. Mal. 2:3 had been interpreted by the Rabbis, and repeated by Maimonides, as referring to people who gorge themselves with food and drink until the body swells; *dung of your sacrifices* (or *of your holidays, ḥaggekem*) is applied to those simple-minded and crude voluptuaries who eat and drink and spend all their days as if they were holidays. It is noteworthy, therefore, that in our context he relies on a new exegetical turn, implying very forcefully that the sacrifice is rejected and the ritualistic holiday observance vitiated if it remains hollow and meretricious, lacking the redeeming moment of genuine compassion and communion. Selfish rejoicing is a contradiction *in adjecto*.[172]

Furthermore, this is not an isolated interpretation; compassion, as an ethical objective to be pursued as well as an indigenous and almost genetic trait to be guarded and expressed, is a leitmotif of the *Mishneh Torah,* systematizing in its own way diffuse Rabbinic materials:

1. Compassion is a clue to one's genealogy:

All families are presumed to be of valid descent, and it is permitted to intermarry with them in the first instance. Nevertheless, should you see

---

171. E.g., Deut. 16:14; B. Pes 109a; MḲ 27a. Peter Berger (*A Rumor of Angels* [New York, 1969], p. 20) has discussed very pointedly the benefits as well as hazards of the process of translating traditional categories into "terms appropriate to the new frame of reference." In the MT examples being discussed here, Maimonides did not translate as much as he tried to bring to the surface latent spiritual and ethical motifs. The interplay between one's philosophic preconceptions and the exegetical process is, of course, very delicate. Concerning metaphysical problems, Maimonides himself states that "the texts of the prophetic books . . . *together with the speculative premises that I possess,* showed me that . . ." (MN, III, introduction [p. 416]) (italics mine).

172. *De'ot,* v, 1 (and cf. B. Shab 151b). See *Piske Halakah šel R. Ḥayyim 'Or Zaru'a* (Jerusalem, 1972), p. 8; M. Benayahu, *Sefer Tolědot ha-'Āri* (Jerusalem, 1967), p. 348. To call this kind of halakic formulation a humanistic approach—cf. I. Epstein, "The Distinctiveness of Maimonides' Halakah," *Leo Jung Jubilee Volume,* ed. M. Kasher, N. Lamm, and L. Rosenfeld (New York, 1962), p. 65—is misleading.

two families continually striving with one another, or a family which is constantly engaged in quarrels and altercations, or an individual who is exceedingly contentious with everyone, or is excessively impudent, apprehension should be felt concerning them, and it is advisable to keep one's distance from them, for these traits are indicative of invalid descent. . . . Similarly, if a person exhibit impudence, cruelty, or misanthropy, and never performs an act of kindness, one should strongly suspect that he is of Gibeonite descent, since the distinctive traits of Israel, the holy nation, are modesty, mercy, and loving-kindness.[173]

2. For this reason, the prospective convert to Judaism requires special instruction concerning charity and concern for the poor. After being taught the principles of the faith and the details of halakah, "he should be informed of the transgressions involved in the laws of gleanings, forgotten sheaves, the corner of the field, and the poor man's tithe." The laws of charity are underscored.[174]

3. The last chapter concerning the laws of charity illustrates Maimonides' rhetorical stratagems for emphasis and force: repetition, lyricism, exegetical flourishes. The theme of kindness is paramount: "Charity is the sign of the righteous man, the seed of Abraham our father, as it is said, *For I have known him, to the end that he may command his children . . . to do righteousness* (Gen. 18:19);" "If someone is cruel and does not show mercy, there are sufficient grounds to suspect his lineage, since cruelty is found only among the other nations." Moreover, the formal act of giving charity must be saturated with sensitivity, sympathy, and graciousness. An objectively benevolent act is easily vitiated by rudeness:

Whosoever gives charity to a poor man ill-manneredly and with downcast looks has lost all the merit of his action, even if he should give him a thousand gold pieces. He should give with good grace and with joy, and should sympathize with him in his plight, as it is said, *Did I not weep for him that was in trouble? Was not my soul grieved for the poor?* (Job

---

173. *'Issure Bi'ah*, xix, 17, and xii, 24. Also *Tĕšubah*, ii, 10; and *Ḥobel u-Mazziḳ*, v, 10.
174. *'Issure Bi'ah*, xiv, 2 (see B. Yeḇ 47b; and Rashi, ad loc.). These laws are sui generis, illustrating neither the less weighty nor the more weighty commandments. Their study is a separate requirement.

30:25). He should speak to him words of consolation and sympathy, as it is said, *And I caused the widow's heart to sing for joy* (Job 29:13).[175]

4. The phrase, *I have done according to all that Thou hast commanded me* (Deut. 26:14), part of the declaration (*widduy*) made by one who has completed tithing, is interpreted to mean that "he rejoiced and *caused others to rejoice* with it," for it is written, *And thou shalt rejoice in all the good* [*which . . . God hath given unto thee*] (Deut. 26:11). It is axiomatic that rejoicing must be shared; otherwise it would be a hedonistic indulgence and not a religious performance.[176]

5. Of all the commandments subsumed under the rubric of *Thou shalt love thy neighbor as thyself* (Lev. 19:18)—e.g., visiting the sick, comforting the mourners, dowering a bride, etc.—one act, which at first glance seems to be the least substantive, merely a symbolic gesture, towers above all the rest: "The reward for escorting strangers is greater than the reward for all the other commandments. It is a practice which Abraham our father instituted and an act of kindness which he exercised." A symbolic act, indeed, but very repercussive.[177]

6. The highlight of the Purim festivities is an act of kindness: "It is preferable to spend more on gifts to the poor than on the Purim meal or on presents to friends. For no joy is greater or more glorious than the joy of gladdening the hearts of the poor, the orphans, the widows, and the strangers. Indeed, he who causes the hearts of these unfortunates to rejoice, emulates the Divine Presence, of whom Scripture says, *To revive the spirit of the humble, and to revive the heart of the contrite ones* (Isa. 57:15)." Lest one should think that this formulation of *imitatio Dei* is a homiletical flourish, the cognate formulation of the *Moreh* should be collated with it: "In this verse he makes it clear to us that those actions (of God) that ought to be known and imitated are loving-kindness, judgment, and righteousness." Also, "for the 'thirteen charac-

---

175. *Mattĕnot 'Āniyyim*, x, 1, 2, 4. See *'Issure Mizbeaḥ*, vii, 11.
176. *Ma'ăśer Šeni*, xi, 15.
177. *'Abel*, xiv, 2. Maimonides quotes verses and Rabbinic dicta (e.g., B. Soṭ 46b). See also *De'ot*, i, 7.

teristics' (of God) [which should be imitated by man] are all of them, with one exception, 'characteristics of mercy.' "[178]

7. The full force of this emphasis is most evident in the following passage, which requires special comment:

> It is permitted to work a heathen slave with rigor. Though such is the rule, it is the quality of supralegal piety (*ḥăsidut*) and the way of wisdom (*ḥokmah*) that a man be merciful and pursue justice and not make his yoke heavy upon the slave or distress him, but give him to eat and to drink of all foods and drinks.
>
> So is it also explained in the good (virtuous) ways of Job, in which he prided himself: *If I did despise the cause of my manservant, or of my maidservant, when they contended with me. . . . Did not He that made me in the womb make him? And did not One fashion us in the womb?* (Job 31:13, 15).
>
> Cruelty and effrontery are not frequent except with the heathen who worship idols. The children of our father Abraham, however—i.e., the Israelites—upon whom the Holy One, blessed be He, bestowed the favor of the law and laid upon them statutes and judgments, are merciful people who have mercy upon all.
>
> Thus also is it declared by the attributes of the Holy One, blessed be He, which we are enjoined to imitate: *And His tender mercies are over all His works* (Ps. 145:9).[179]

Inasmuch as the mercy shown in this case is supererogatory rather than mandatory—it is avowedly *not* legislated—why refer to the laws of the Torah? The mention of "statutes and judgments" would seem to be gratuitous, inasmuch as they do not prescribe

---

178. *Mĕgillah*, ii, 17; MN, III, 54; I, 54. The correlation of MT and MN in this case is particularly useful and instructive; cf. L. Berman, "The Political Interpretation of the Maxim: The Purpose of Philosophy is the Imitation of God," *Studia Islamica*, XV (1961), 53–61; and A. Altmann, "Maimonides' 'Four Perfections'," *Israel Oriental Studies*, II (1972), 15–24 (pointing out Maimonides' indebtedness to Ibn Bajjah).

179. *'Ăbadim*, ix, 8. In *Mĕlakim*, x, 12, Ps. 145:9 is taken to mean that we must imitate God in spreading kindness and mercy; see B. Ber 7a. The reference to the "good (virtuous) ways of Job" is suggestive of, and of course fully congruent with, his intellectualistic interpretation of that story. Job was a righteous person, but "knowledge is not attributed to him"; MN, III, 22 (p. 487). Hence, while citations from Proverbs are introduced by reference to "Solomon in his wisdom," only "good ways" are associated with Job. Cf. E. Urbach, "Laws Regarding Slavery," *Annual of Jewish Studies*, I, n.213. My emphasis does not relate to Maimonides' simple restatement of Talmudic law but rather to the underlying conception that the law is a springboard for supererogatory aspiration and action.

the "way of wisdom" and piety being recommended. The clear inference, however, is that all the laws are a springboard for the highest morality and perfection which emanate slowly and steadily from them. Just as one embraces reality in order to transcend it, one adheres to the law in order that it may enhance one's perception of the good and the true and induce behavior which transcends the letter of the law. In short, law alone, in a formal sense, is not the exclusive criterion of ideal religious behavior, either positive or negative. It does not exhaust religious-moral requirements. There is rather a continuum from clearly prescribed legislation to open-ended supererogatory performance, for the goal of the Torah is the maximum sanctification of life.

The clinching illustration of this is that the ultimate religious evil, profanation of God's name, can result from lack of sensitivity or delicacy, independent of any formal transgression: "There are other things that are a profanation of the name of God. When a man great in the knowledge of the Torah and reputed for his piety does things which cause people to talk about him, even if the acts are not express violations, he profanes the name of God."[180] The entire well-known concept of *lifnim miš-šurat haddin*, frequently belabored by serious students and more often by apologists, is quietly introduced by Maimonides toward the end of this same paragraph, where ritual and human relations merge with the emphasis decidedly on the latter:

And if a man has been scrupulous in his conduct, gentle in his conversation, pleasant toward his fellow creatures, affable in manner when receiving them, not retorting, even when affronted, but showing courtesy to all, even to those who treat him with disdain, conducting his commercial affairs with integrity, not readily accepting the hospitality of the ignorant nor frequenting their company, not seen at all times, but devoting himself to study of the Torah, wrapped in the ṭallit and crowned with phylacteries, and doing more than his duty in all things, but avoiding extremes and exaggerations—such a man has sanctified

---

180. *Yĕsode hat-Torah*, v, 11; see *Deʿot*, v, 13, and *Sanhedrin*, ii, 7; also *Sanhedrin*, xxiv, 5. Note the equivalence in *Tĕfillah*, v, 6, and the emphasis in *Tĕrumot*, xii, 18, 19 (based on B. Bek 26b, but significantly expanded).

God, and concerning him Scripture says, *And He said unto me, Thou art My servant, Israel, in whom I will be glorified* (Isa. 49:3).[181]

"Doing more than his duty in all things" is a natural concomitant or spontaneous extension of being "wrapped in ṭallit̠ and crowned with phylacteries"! In any event, "statutes and judgments" and the "quality of *ḥăsid̠ut̠* and way of wisdom" are positioned contiguously on one colorful spectrum. This is the thrust of Maimonides' careful treatment of ritual.

Many other commandments are explained in the *Mishneh Torah*, sometimes explicitly, sometimes allusively. The explanation may be lengthy or it may be compressed into a parenthetic word or incidental phrase. Some of these explanations are so apposite and grafted so naturally and smoothly onto the purely juridical formulation that commentators have often failed to notice the penumbra of original insights and ideas. This is surely a measure of Maimonidean skill as well as success. Only a careful commentary attuned to this particular aspect would reveal the unexpected extent of these explanations.[182] Certain protean and pathos-laden concepts should be carefully reviewed in order to detect modes

---

181. *Yĕsod̠e hat-Torah*, v, 11. For "doing more than one's duty," see Naḥmanides, *Peruš*, Deut. 6:18; *Sefer Ḥăsid̠im* (Berlin, 1891), introduction (concerning '*arum bĕ-yir'ah* [being cunning in the fear of the Lord] and the need to recover and uncover *rĕṣon hab-Bore'* [the will of God]); and the penetrating analysis by H. Soloveitchik, "Three Themes in the *Sefer Ḥăsid̠im*," *AJS Review*, I (1976), 311ff, where he underscores the uniqueness of the *Sefer Ḥăsid̠im* in actually legislating new sets of laws. The idea of expanding the realm of religious obligation and performance, of identifying and adding new commandments (the duties of the heart) is also found in R. Baḥya, *Ḥob̠ot hal-Lĕb̠ab̠ot̠*, introduction, p. 26. On "avoiding extremes and exaggerations," see *De'ot̠*, iii, 1; R. Baḥya, *Ḥob̠ot hal-Lĕb̠ab̠ot̠*, viii, 3 (II, p. 260); R. Abraham ibn Ezra, to Eccles. 7:16. For *lifnim miš-šurat̠ had-din*, see most recently, A. Lichtenstein, "Does Jewish Tradition Recognize an Ethic Independent of Halakha," *Modern Jewish Ethics*, ed. M. Fox (Ohio, 1975), pp. 62ff.

182. The following few examples, both of Maimonidean explanation and frequently of absence or blandness of the commentators' reactions, are illustrative: *Yĕsod̠e hat-Torah*, vi, 8, and *Tĕfillin*, i, 13; *Talmud̠ Torah*, i, 13 and LM; *Tĕfillah*, xiii, 5; xv, 6; *'Erub̠in*, i, 4; *Ta'ăniyyot̠*, v, 2; *Mĕğillah*, ii, 12 (even though the phrase, *lĕ-har'ot̠ han-nes*, is missing in some texts); *Nizke Mamon*, viii, 5; *Gĕneb̠ah*, i, 10; vii, 12; *Roṣeaḥ*, i, 4; *Mamrim*, v, 15 (a very significant halak̠ic extension); *'Ab̠el*, xiv, 5 (and see J. Levinger, *Darke ham-Maḥšab̠ah*, pp. 102, 110). Also MM, *Šĕkirut̠*, xiii, 7; KM, *'Issure Bi'ah*, vii, 11; *'Issure Mizbeaḥ*, vii, 11; *Sanhedrin*, iii, 8–9; iv, 15; xxiv, 6; RaDBaZ, *Šĕmiṭṭah wĕ-Yob̠el*, xiii, 12 (and cf. *Mĕlak̠im*, vii, 15; xi, 3); *LM, Sanhed̠rin*, ii, 7; emblematic phrases are: זה מבואר; הכל כלשון רבינו; סברא דנפשי׳ וראויים הדברים לאומרם. Note *Tĕfillah*, v, 5,

and mutations of explanation; one could, in fact, undertake a series of word studies in the *Mishneh Torah* which would vivify this aspect.[183] It would, of course, be gratuitous to point out, or wonder about, the fact that so many commandments remain unexplained; this is, after all, a Code which initially promised to be crisp and concise, sans phrase and sans explication. What is relevant is the large number of commandments that are explained, the repeated emphasis on sparse and astringent codificatory form notwithstanding. These weighty exceptions and additions to the codificatory goals need to be underscored. It is significant that Maimonides did not ordinarily label these by such a phrase as "it seems to me", which, as we have seen above in Chapter II, is used about two hundred times to identify novel halakic views. Any other perspective would be warped by Whitehead's "fallacy of misplaced concreteness" or the Talmudic "barley and wheat" syndrome.[184]

DIFFERENCES BETWEEN *Mishneh Torah* AND THE *Guide*

Having seen the rather extensive role of *ṭa'ăme miṣwot* in the *Mishneh Torah*, against the background of Maimonides' general structuring of the theme, we must now direct our attention to a major methodological difference between the various essentially

---

and *Bet Yosef, Ṭur, 'Oraḥ Ḥayyim*, 95. Sometimes there is puzzled awareness of a novelty; see, e.g., KM, *'Ăbodah Zarah*, xii, 11, and note S. Belkin, *Philo and the Oral Law*, p. 39, n. 33. Note, on the other hand, that commentators will underscore a Maimonidean novelty without questioning why it is not signaled by the phrase "it seems to me" (see above, chap. IV); e.g., KM, *Mamrim*, vi, 8; *Mĕlakim*, viii, 11. All explanations introduced by "it seems to me" require careful study; e.g., *Roṣeaḥ*, ii, 14, and S. Belkin, *Philo*, p. 96; idem., *Joshua Finkel Festschrift* (New York, 1974), p. 41.

183. E.g., "'Epiḳoros"—'*Akum*, ii, 5; *Tĕšubah*, iii, 8; *Tĕfillah*, vii, 15; *Tĕfillin*, i, 13; *Bĕrakot*, i, 13; *Šabbat*, ii, 3; *'Issure Bi'ah*, xi, 15; *Šĕḥiṭah*, iv, 14; *Gĕzelah*, xi, 2; *Mamrin*, iii, 1; *Mĕlakim*, xi, 3. "'Olam hab-ba"—*Yĕsode hat-Torah*, iv, 13; *De'ot*, vi, 4; *Talmud Torah*, iii, 11; *'Akum*, ii, 3; *Tĕšubah*, iii, 5; viii, 1; ix, 1; *'Issure Bi'ah*, xiv, 3; *Mĕ'ilah*, viii, 8; *Mĕlakim*, vii, 15; PhM, Sanh, *Pereḳ Ḥeleḳ*; Mak 3:17 (p. 247); 'Ab 4:22 (p. 449); MN, III, 27; *Ḳobeṣ*, II, 54b. "*Daṭ ha-'emet*"—*Mattĕnot 'Ăniyyim*, x, 1; *Mĕlakim*, v, 10. "*Minhago* (or *ṭibĕ'o) šel 'olam*"—'*Akum*, i, 1; *Tĕšubah*, ix, 2; *Ta'ăniyyot*, i, 3; *Ṭumĕ'aṭ Ṣara'aṭ*, xvi, 10; *Roṣeaḥ*, i, 9; '*Abel*, xiii, 11. For the equation of religious and natural categories, see MN, II, 28, 48; III, 32.

184. See above, chap. II, n. 197, particularly the distinction suggested there between *ṭa'amĕ miṣwot* and *ṭa'ăme halakot*.

complementary presentations. While the *Moreh* introduces historical causation and boldly utilizes a theory of accommodation, the *Mishneh Torah* does not rely upon historical motivation of laws. The entire conception of Sabianism as the system which the Torah aimed to demolish is conspicuously absent from the *Mishneh Torah*. Aspects of the history of religion summarized in the *Mishneh Torah* are identical with the *Moreh*'s history of Sabianism; idolatry is, to be sure, seen as the opposite of Judaic belief and practice.[185] There is even a stray explanation of a law—e.g., the prohibition of certain forms of shaving—in terms of their similarity to, and occasional imitation of, pagan practice.[186] However, the notion that the Torah is a pedagogic device using a variety of stratagems—condemnation, compromise, and co-optation—which is so central in the *Moreh*, cannot even be described as peripheral in the *Mishneh Torah*; it is, for all practical purposes, missing.

The reason for this divergence is quite clear. There are two distinct kinds of intelligibility and purposiveness, and they have different reverberations. Historical explanations demonstrate adequately enough, but rather astringently, that the law is "consequent upon wisdom" and does not contain frivolous actions, and demonstrating this is the goal of the religious philosopher. Teleology in history, modeled after its role in nature or biology, is an effective component of rationalization; knowing certain antecedent facts, and in the light of them interpreting later developments, helps eliminate arbitrariness or accident and fashion instead an "intelligible whole" out of events. Historical science, like genetic sciences, looks for some kind of continuity between temporally prior happenings and subsequent events.[187] This,

---

185. *'Akum*, i; ii, 4; xi, 15; *Šabbaṭ*, xxx, 15.
186. *'Akum*, xii, 1 (which serves to explain the classification as well). Also *De'ot*, iii, 1; *'Akum*, vi, 6; *Šabbaṭ*, ii, 4; *'Aḇel*, iv, 2. Note especially *Beṭ hab-Běḥirah*, i, 17 (the joining of 'building steps leading up to the altar' with 'breaking even one stone from the altar'— a fact which puzzled *KM*—is intelligible only in the light of MN, III, 45 [p. 578]) and *Těmiḏin*, i, 10 (and RABD, ad loc.). There is, of course, a basic concept of *darke 'Ěmori* which is a central and repercussive theme; see *'Akum*, xi, 1 (and S. Lieberman, *Tosefta ki-Fěšuṭah*, Shab 6:1 [pp. 79–80]).
187. There is no indication that Maimonides confronted the problem of relativization; cf. RIṬBA, *Sefer Zikkaron*, pp. 53–55, 64. Note carefully the geographic relativism in

however, all its rationality notwithstanding, has no spiritual-ethical consequences. The *Mishneh Torah* is primarily concerned with bringing to the surface those underlying motives and overarching goals which discipline the human faculties, quell evil impulses, subdue inclination to vices, discipline the moral disposition, and advance the individual toward ethical-intellectual perfection.[188] The ethicization and intellectualization of laws in this sense, leading to "unbounded sanctity, pure thought, and disciplined moral disposition,"[189] will not be fructified by historical analysis or by excessive theoretical and psychological explanation. Outer-directed explanations are also less significant.[190] The primary concern of the *Mishneh Torah* with explanations that revolve around ethical-intellectual motifs—law as an educating-edifying force—as distinct from the *Moreh*'s concern with all kinds of intelligibility and rationality, is the crux of the issue.

The most prominent use of socio-historical causation in the *Moreh* concerned the institution of sacrifices—as we have seen, an inevitable concession to ubiquitous pagan practices—and this has no parallels or echoes in the *Mishneh Torah*, which instead focuses on certain ethical repercussions. The laws concerning exchange of

---

PhM, Ned 8:6 (p. 143); *Ma'ăkalot 'Ăsurot*, xvi, 9. For a modern formulation of the issue, see S. Leavy, *Psychological Understanding of Religious Experience* (New York, n.d.), pp. 15–16. Note also *Iṣut*, xxv, 2.

188. Such phrases are recurrent: e.g., *Nĕdarim*, xiii, 23; *'Ărakin*, viii, 12; *'Issure Mizbeaḥ*, vii, 11 (and see n.148, above); ŠP, chap. IV.

189. *'Issure Bi'ah*, xxii, 20.

190. The assumption that Maimonides' philosophy of law is not adequate to the needs and claims of halakah underlies the modern scholarly "criticism" of Maimonides; e.g., J. Guttmann, *Dat u-Madda'* (Jerusalem, 1955), pp. 100–01; G. Scholem, *Major Trends in Jewish Mysticism* (New York, 1941), p. 95; I. Baer, *History of the Jews in Christian Spain*, I (Philadelphia, 1951), p. 96; H. Graetz, *Darke ha-Hiṣṭoriyah ha-Yĕhudit* (Jerusalem, 1969), p. 58; see also, from an earlier period, R. Jacob Emden, *Mitpaḥat Sĕfarim* (Lvov, 1870; reprinted, Jerusalem, 1969/70), p. 56; R. Azariah dei Rossi, *Mĕ'or 'Enayim, 'Imre Binah*, chap. 14 (p. 199). R. Samson R. Hirsch, *Nineteen Letters*, repeats the same criticism for different reasons. It is, therefore, especially important to note that the historical and outer-directed orientation is not part of the methodological apparatus of the *Mishneh Torah;* the references in n. 186, above, contain some oblique reflections, as does *Mĕ'ilah*, viii, 8. The reference in *Šabbat*, ii, 3 (particularly the phrase "'enam nĕkamah") deserves careful study; it may be an anti-Christian polemic (see below, n.322). For psychological insights in the Code, see, e.g., *Roṣeaḥ*, xii, 12. For selective use of Maimonides' historical approach, see, e.g., Naḥmanides, to Lev. 2:11; R. Menaḥem ben Zeraḥ, *Ṣedah lad-Derek*, p. 91; RIṬBA, *Sefer haz-Zikkaron*, p. 64.

animals consecrated for sacrifice were fashioned not merely in order to insure that "the sacrifice be held in great esteem" but also in order to inculcate magnanimity. Knowing that these laws came from a different historical and religious ambiance is not too pertinent here. In this context, the jurisprudent must bring to consciousness and clarity those abiding ideals which he believes lurk behind the apparently dry directives and limpid laws. This principle, mentioned also in the *Moreh*, should motivate one's whole approach to Temple offerings. There is even the implication that the Temple ritual provides the setting for a special kind of man-God relationship:

> If all kinds (of oil) were valid for meal offerings, why did the Sages rank their quality? So that one would know which was the very best, which were equal in value, and which was the least valuable. Thus he who wished to earn merit for himself might bend his greedy inclination and make broad his generosity, and bring an offering from the finest, from the very best of the species that he was bringing. Behold, it is said in the Torah, *And Abel, he also brought of the firstlings of his flock and of the fat thereof. And the Lord had respect unto Abel and to his offering* (Gen. 4:4).[191]

The sequel, almost a little postscript to the entire section, is notable:

> The same principle applies to everything which is done for the sake of the good God; namely, that it be of the finest and the best. If one builds a house of prayer, it should be finer than his private dwelling. If he feeds the hungry, he should give him of the best and the sweetest of his table. If he clothes the naked, he should give him of the finest of his garments. Hence if he consecrated something to God, he ought to give of the best of his possessions. Thus Scripture says, *All the fat is the Lord's* (Lev. 3:16).

"Feeding the hungry" and "clothing the naked" are mentioned in the same breath with consecrating objects to God. Halakic terminology and conceptualization depict God as the "recipient" or "beneficiary" of all priestly gifts (e.g., tithes), donations to the Temple, etc. God is the juridical person that is the "owner,"

---

191. *'Issure Mizbeaḥ*, vii, 11; MN, III, 46 (p. 584). See *Yoreh De'ah*, 248:8.

agent, or trustee, and the legal procedures are based on this juridical fact. Here the scene shifts from the Sanctuary to the street, and God still appears as the ultimate "beneficiary" of gifts to the poor. Halakah, and its rationalization, put philanthropy in a new perspective, revealing its real "deep structures."[192]

Related to sacrifices is the cluster of laws, technically complex and conceptually perplexing, concerning cleanness and uncleanness. These are explained rather practically in the *Moreh* as "concerning only the Holy Place and holy things," helping to "safeguard the Sanctuary" by keeping most people away from it; inasmuch as there were so "many species of uncleanness," it was difficult to "find a clean individual," and few would be qualified to approach the Temple. On the other hand, uncleanness was no excessive burden, inasmuch as it did not impede routine preoccupations, for "there is no sin if one remains unclean, as long as one washes and eats, as one wishes, ordinary food that has become unclean." Its goal was to sustain a "feeling of awe and fear" vis-à-vis the Sanctuary, isolated and insulated, majestic and inaccessible. Now while the majesty and resultant remoteness of the Sanctuary is a clear halakic motif fully developed also in the Code,[193] the attempt of the *Mishneh Torah* to spiritualize this ritualistic syndrome and endow it with symbolic value is not even opaquely reflected in the *Moreh*:

It is plain and manifest that the laws about uncleanness and cleanness are decrees laid down by Scripture and not matters about which human understanding is capable of forming a judgment; for behold, they are included among the divine statutes. So, too, immersion as a means of freeing oneself from uncleanness is included among the divine statutes. Now "uncleanness" is not mud or filth which water can remove, but is a matter of Scriptural decree and dependent on the intention of the heart. Therefore the Sages have said, "If a man immerses himself, but without special intention, it is as though he has not immersed himself at all."

Nevertheless we may find some indication (for the moral basis) of this: just as one who sets his heart on becoming clean becomes clean as

---

192. See also *Mĕkirah*, xxii, 15; M. Zilberg, *Kak Darko šel Talmud* (Jerusalem, 1961), p. 11; I. Twersky, "Some Aspects of the Jewish Attitude Toward the Welfare State," *Tradition*, V (1963), 141.
193. MN, III, 47 (pp. 593-94); *Bet hab-Bĕḥirah*, vii and viii.

soon as he has immersed himself, although nothing new has befallen his body, so, too, one who sets his heart on cleansing himself from the uncleannesses that beset men's souls—namely, wrongful thoughts and false convictions—becomes clean as soon as he consents in his heart to shun those counsels and brings his soul into the waters of pure reason. Behold, Scripture says, *And I will sprinkle clean water upon you, and ye shall be clean; from all your uncleannesses and from all your idols, will I cleanse you* (Ezek. 36:25).

May God, in His great mercy, cleanse us from every sin, iniquity, and guilt. Amen.[194]

This kind of spiritualizing is congruent with the specific metajuridical goals of the *Mishneh Torah*.

Carrying this a step further, the *Mishneh Torah* suggests that maximum avoidance of impurity, without any connection whatsoever with the Sanctuary, is a desirable goal:

Although it is permissible to eat unclean foodstuffs and to drink unclean liquids, the pious of former times used to eat their common food in conditions of cleanness, and all their days they were wary of every uncleanness. And it is they who were called Pharisees, "separated ones," and this is a higher holiness. It is the way of piety that a man keep himself separate and go apart from the rest of the people and neither touch them nor eat and drink with them. For separation leads to the cleansing of the body from evil deeds, and the cleansing of the body leads to the hallowing of the soul from evil thoughts, and the hallowing of the soul leads to striving for likeness with the Shekhinah; for it is said, *Sanctify yourselves therefore, and be ye holy* (Lev. 11:44), *For I the Lord, who sanctify you, am holy* (Lev. 21:8).[195]

Such a supererogatory extension, in which ritual cleanness is not just a practical-psychological safeguard but a positive and repercussive "way of piety," is not even alluded to in the *Moreh*.

Many differences of emphasis and outlook, which produce divergent but not necessarily contradictory formulations, may be

---

194. *Miḵwa'oṯ*, xi, 12. This attempt to rationalize the Scriptural decree entangles Maimonides in a halaḵic problem; cf. ibid., i, 8 (and B. Ḥaḡ 19a). He may be using Tos Ḥaḡ, 3:2. See above, chap. iv, n.61.

195. *Ṭumě'aṯ 'Oḵlin*, xvi, 12. On *ḵěduš̌ah*, with its motifs of separation, restraint, and retreat, see *De'oṯ*, v, 4–5; *'Išuṯ*, xv, 20; *'Issure Bi'ah*, xxi, xxii; *Ma'aḵaloṯ 'Ăsuroṯ*, xvii, 28, 32; *'Aḇel*, iii, 12; *Mělaḵim*, vi, 15; as a prerequisite for intellectual perfection, *Yěsoḏe haT-orah*, vii, 1; MN, I, 34; II, 36; III, 27, 33; PhM, 'Aḇ 3:11 (p. 432).

understood from this perspective. The commandment to cover up the blood of animals that have been slaughtered for personal consumption is almost perfunctorily explained in the *Moreh* against the backdrop of the pagans' exaltation of blood and their investing it with magical properties: "Its blood should be covered up with dust, so that people should not gather to eat around it." While the *Mishneh Torah* does not explain the commandment per se, it does attempt to spiritualize it by taking the legal minutiae into account: "When one performs the commandment of covering up the blood, he should do it not with his foot but with his hand, or with a knife or utensil, so as not to conduct the performance of the commandments in a contemptuous manner, thus treating God's commandments with scorn. For reverence is due not to the commandments themselves, but to Him who has issued them."[196]

Similarly, the prohibition against hewing the stones of the altar is explained historically in the *Moreh:* "The reason for this is manifest, for the idolaters used to build altars with hewn stones. Accordingly, assimilation to them was prohibited, and in order to avoid this assimilation to them it was commanded that the altar be of earth. Scripture says, *An altar of earth thou shalt make unto Me* (Exod. 20:21)." The *Mishneh Torah,* which obviously does not prohibit stone altars, reads as follows: "The altar was to be made as a structure of stones only; for that which is said, *An altar of earth thou shalt make unto Me,* only means that the altar should be attached to the earth; that is, it should not be built on top of arches or on top of caves. Furthermore, the Sages have learned from oral tradition that the command, *And if thou make Me an altar of stone* (Exod. 20:22), was not a matter of choice but a definite obligation."[197]

This dissonant juxtaposition of the *Mishneh Torah* formulation and the *Moreh* explanation raises a number of important problems

---

196. MN, III, 46 (pp. 587, 585), *Šĕḥiṭah,* xiv, 6. We may assume that the explanation of the role of incense (*ḳĕṭoret*) in the Temple given by Maimonides in MN, III, 45 (p. 579) could never find its way into MT. Generally, cf. Philo, *De Specialibus Legibus,* I, 171, and S. Belkin, *J. Finkel Festschrift,* pp. 49–51.

197. MN, III, 45 (p. 578); *Bet hab-Bĕḥirah,* i, 13. See R. Abraham Maimonides, *Peruš,* pp. 326, 573.

for the total study of Maimonides,[198] only one of which is directly relevant to the *Mishneh Torah*. In suggesting reasons for laws, both in the *Mishneh Torah* and in the *Moreh,* Maimonides is not constrained by Midrashic explanations; he ranges freely and imaginatively in aligning laws with the ethical-intellectual goals he has defined or in correlating them with the historical-sociological conditions he has reconstructed. Needless to say, not only does he uninhibitedly reject Midrashic explanations, but he resourcefully provides reasons in cases where the Midrash is silent.[199] Aside from helping define Maimonides' attitude to Midrash, this sheds some light on the question of certitude or conjecture in the rationalization of the law and also on the significance of the entire enterprise. Halakah, of course, is uniform in its objective determinacy, but the experience accompanying its implementation is quite variable in its subjective understanding. Maimonides' *Mishneh Torah* explanation in ethical or intellectual categories, rather than purely Midrashic flourishes on the one hand, or archaizing historical causes on the other, is intended to contribute to this subjective concomitant. Mention of the contrary thrust of the literature of mysticism may further illumine this dialectical relationship. Just as mystical literature is an attempted objectification of subjective, almost ineffable and incommunicable, experiences, so the philosophic interpretation of halakah may be seen as an attempted subjectification of objective, fully described, and carefully prescribed performance. In this context, the two kinds of rationality and intelligibility, with their different levels of meaningfulness and impact, historical and

---

198. The most striking is the question of apparent literalism in the interpretation of certain Biblical laws, e.g., MN, III, 49 (concerning *yibbum*), and R. Abraham Maimonides, *Peruš*, p. 144; MN, III, 46 (concerning "eating of blood"). The most famous is the *lex talionis* (MN, III, 41 [p. 558]; and *Ḥobel u-Mazziḳ*, i, 6), a problem which still needs further study; cf. J. Levinger, "'Al Torah šebbě-'al-Peh," *Tarbiz*, XXXVII (1968), 282. While there are thus many instances in which Maimonides quietly bypasses the Talmudic interpretation and actually presents the literal Biblical view, only with regard to the *lex talionis* and the case of nocturnal emission (MN, III, 41) does he explicitly state that his goal is to confront the Biblical text. See above, chap. iv, n.153.

199. See the explicit statements in MN, III, 43 (p. 573), 45 (p. 578), 47 (p. 597); *Těšubot*, 458 (p. 739)—a most direct, even curt, statement about *dibre 'aggadah* and freedom of interpretation; *Mělakim*, xii, 2. Cf. W. Braude, "Maimonides' Attitude to Midrash," *Studies . . . in Honor of I. Kiev,* ed. C. Berlin (New York, 1971), pp. 75ff.

abstract or experiential and immediate, are clearly perceived. Historical-psychological explanations demonstrate wisdom and rationality; ethical-intellectual explanations nurture the subjective-spiritual component and are therefore preferable in the Code. What has been described as the "ethically-oriented mysticism" of R. Abraham Maimonides is not unlike what may be described as the spiritually-oriented rationalism of R. Moses Maimonides. The common denominator of all explanations, whether historical and abstract or experiential and immediate, about which Maimonides never expresses doubt, is the formula that all laws are rational and lead to moral and/or intellectual perfection.

A particularly poignant example of the divergent emphasis is the attitude toward death. From the philosopher's vantage point, death is not only inevitable but is the "consummation devoutly to be wished": "The result is that when a perfect man is stricken with years and approaches death, this apprehension (of God) increases very powerfully, joy over this apprehension and a great love for the object of apprehension become stronger, until the soul is separated from the body at that moment in this state of pleasure. Because of this the Sages have indicated with reference to the deaths of Moses, Aaron, and Miriam that the three of them died by a kiss. . . . Their purpose was to indicate that the three of them died in the pleasure of this apprehension due to the intensity of passionate love. . . . This kind of death, which in true reality is salvation from death. . . ."[200] Death is spiritual fulfillment, not physical destruction. It would be difficult to integrate the Laws Concerning Mourning into this Socratic-Platonic perspective concerning the happy liberation of the soul from its bodily incarceration. Indeed, this probably explains a uniquely flagrant omission. This is apparently the only section of the *Mishneh Torah* to which there is absolutely no cross-reference

---

200. MN, III, 51 (pp. 627–28). See also PhM, introduction (p. 4); and note *Tĕfillah*, xiii, 6. See Gersonides, *Peruš Šir haš-Širim* 1:2. This idea of death (as liberation and fulfillment) is a philosophic commonplace; see, e.g., F. Rosenthal, *The Muslim Concept of Freedom* (Leiden, 1960).

in the third part of the *Moreh*.[201] In the Code, of course, the laws of mourning are duly emphasized: "Whoever does not mourn the dead in the manner enjoined by the Rabbis is cruel. If one suffers bereavement, one should be apprehensive, troubled, investigate his conduct, and repent." Excessive grief over one's dead is unwise and unwarranted, not because death is happy liberation, but because it is sadly inevitable: "One should not indulge in excessive grief over one's dead, for it is said: *Weep not for the dead, neither bemoan him* (Jer. 22:10), that is to say, (weep not for him) too much, for that is the way of the world, and he who frets over the way of the world is a fool. What rule should one follow in case of bereavement? (The rule is:) Three days for weeping, seven days for lamenting, and thirty days for (abstaining) from cutting the hair and the other four things (forbidden to a mourner)."[202]

Occasional omission of halakic detail also sheds light on the tenor and tendency of the *Moreh* as compared with the *Mishneh Torah*. The law prohibiting the return of a fugitive slave to his master (Deut. 23:16) applies, according to the Talmudic interpretation, to a slave who has escaped to the Land of Israel. Maimonides, needless to say, includes this in the *Mishneh Torah*, and in the *Sefer ham-Miṣwot* comments: "In no circumstances is (the bondman) to return to his serfdom, seeing that he has come to dwell in the clean land which has been chosen for the exalted people." This patently restrictive detail is omitted from the *Moreh* where this law is explained in universal terms of "manifesting pity . . . it makes us protect and defend those who seek our protection." There is a further moral to this commandment: "If this law is imposed upon us with regard to the least of men . . . the slave, how must you act when a man of great worth seeks your protection?" The more inclusive emphasis of the *Moreh* is clearly more congenial to an outer-directed explanation.[203]

---

201. MN, III, 35 (p. 536), 41 (p. 568); on various modes of cross-reference, see L. Strauss, *Persecution and the Art of Writing* (Glencoe, 1952), p. 62; Y. Ben-Sasson, *Tarbiz*, XXIX (1960), 268–82. See above, chap. iv, n. 170.

202. *'Abel*, xiii, 11, 12; see Naḥmanides, *Torat ha-'Adam*. The firmness of one's belief in immortality notwithstanding, death is alien to the halakic religious experience.

203. *'Abadim*, viii, 10; ShM, negative 254 (and see *Mĕlakim*, v, 11, 12, on the merits of the Land of Israel); MN, III, 39 (p. 554).

## Concern with ethical perfection

Analogously, the *Moreh* uses another method of explanation which has no place in the *Mishneh Torah*. The gist of this method, used very sparingly by Maimonides and radically extended by such later Maimonideans as R. Joseph ibn Kaspi, is that the Torah takes into account erroneous, not merely unsophisticated or unrationalized, views of the masses. Laws will consequently be perceived as intentionally reflecting widespread vulgar, although invalid, conceptions. An example of this is the prohibition against cursing any person. Although this belongs to the class of "transgressions in which there is no action" and which are therefore not punishable even by flogging, this is treated more stringently by the halakah "for *in the opinion of the multitude* the injury resulting from curses is greater than that which may befall the body." The "opinion of the multitude" is thus a rationalization of the law, at least of its prescribed punishment.[204]

Now in an earlier work—and this is most likely reflected in the *Mishneh Torah* as well—Maimonides characterizes cursing as a desire for revenge, which expresses itself in various forms of intensity: killing, wounding, hitting, and least of all cursing and reviling. Its essence is a violent and malevolent emotion, even if the result does not inflict damage:

> Now we might suppose that the Torah, in forbidding us to curse an Israelite, (was moved by) the shame and the pain that the curse would cause him when he heard it, but that there is no sin in cursing the deaf, who cannot hear and therefore cannot feel hurt. For this reason He tells us that cursing is forbidden by prohibiting it in the case of the deaf, since the Torah is concerned not only with the one who is cursed, but also with the curser, who is told not to be vindictive and hot-tempered. Thus, we find, do the bearers of the tradition deduce the prohibition against cursing an Israelite from the words of Scripture, *Thou shalt not curse the deaf* (Lev. 19:14).[205]

---

204. MN, III, 41 (italics mine). For Joseph ibn Kaspi, see *Tam hak-Kesef*, ed. I. Last (reprinted, Jerusalem, 1970), pp. 32–33; and *Dĕrašot ha-RaN* (Jerusalem, 1959), p. 85. Many medieval halakists insisted upon the efficacy of blessings and curses; see RaSHBA, *Tĕšubot*, 408; *Sefer ha-Ḥinnuk*, 231.

205. ShM, negative 317; *Sanhedrin*, xxvi, 1, 2, and *'Or Sameaḥ* commentary, ad loc.; see PhM, BM 4:2 (p. 65).

The law's concern is ethical, control and catharsis of one's emotions, rather than practical, prevention of harm to fellow man; it is, therefore, concerned with the curser as well as the cursed.

It is along such lines—and this connection had yet to be made—that Maimonides explains the general prohibition of seeking revenge: "He who takes revenge violates a prohibition, as it is said, *Thou shalt not take vengeance* (Lev. 19:18). And although he is not punished with flogging, still such conduct indicates an exceedingly bad disposition. One should rather practice forbearance in all secular matters. For the intelligent realize that these are vain things and not worth taking vengeance for."[206] This prohibition is thus designed not to promote courtesy or civility to others—to guarantee that Reuben will do favors for Simeon—but to cultivate moral perfection, to develop a transcendent perspective which makes pettiness and pusillanimity self-evidently foolish. Again, the law's orientation is ethical in an inner-directed way rather than equitable in an outer-directed way.

The desire for this perfection, inner fortitude and serenity, can be extended in the direction of a spiritual aspiration which puts all worldly needs into focus and presents itself as a utopian goal for all men. Maimonides depicts such an ideal type:

> Why did the tribe of Levi not acquire a share in the Land of Israel and in its spoils together with their brothers? Because this tribe was set apart to serve God and to minister to Him, to teach His straight ways and righteous ordinances to the multitudes, as is written, *They shall teach Jacob Thine ordinances, and Israel Thy law* (Deut. 33:10). Therefore they are set apart from the ways of the world; they do not wage war like the rest of Israel, nor do they inherit land or acquire anything for themselves by their physical prowess. They are rather the army of God, as is written, *Bless, Lord, his substance* (Deut. 33:11). He, blessed be He, acquires (goods) for them, as is written: *I am thy portion and thy inheritance* (Num. 18:20).

Not only the tribe of Levi but every single individual from among the world's inhabitants, whose spirit moved him and whose intelligence

---

206. *De'ot*, vii, 7. In the very next halakah, *nĕṭirah* is explained as a prelude to revenge. In ShM, šoreš 9, prohibition of revenge is an example of the purely moral commandments, with no intellectual-philosophic dimension. See the criticism of S. D. Luzzatto, *Yĕsodĕ hat-Torah*, chap. 38.

gave him the understanding to withdraw from the world in order to stand before God to serve and minister to Him, and to know God, and who walked upright in the manner in which God made him, shaking off from his neck the yoke of the manifold contrivances which men seek—behold, this person has been totally consecrated, and God will be his portion and inheritance forever and ever. God will acquire for him sufficient goods in this world just as He did for the priests and the Levites. Behold, David, may he rest in peace, says, *O Lord, the portion of mine inheritance and of my cup, Thou maintainest my lot* (Ps. 16:5).[207]

Positioning this ideal declaration at the end of the Laws Concerning the Sabbatical Year and Jubilee is additionally significant; it subtly provides a different perspective for viewing the reasons for all these laws. In the *Moreh* their apparently heterogeneous motivations have a common denominator, a basic practicality: social-philanthropic benefit (benevolence towards all men) or ecological-agricultural benefit ("make the earth more fertile and stronger through letting it lie fallow").[208] The section's epilogue in the *Mishneh Torah,* while not denying philanthropy or ecology, suggests again a motive of inwardness, training in withdrawal, renunciation, and dedication. We may consequently speak not only of commandments devoted to the relation between man and his fellow man, and those devoted to the relation between man and God, but also of those devoted to man and himself, his inner moral perfection, a catharsis of emotions and attitudes. Needless to say, these goals are not mutually exclusive: laws may make man "acquire this noble moral quality (pity) and also benefit the recipient." All laws between man and God are concerned with man's perfection.[209]

---

207. *Šĕmiṭṭah wĕ-Yobel,* xiii, 12, 13. Note that (a) *ḥayil,* translated as substance, also means money and army; (b) Maimonides has a special interpretation of Num. 18:20; (c) this state is universal, open to "every single individual from among the world's inhabitants"; (d) the description of this individual "whose spirit moved him" might support autonomy vis-à-vis heteronomy in the realm of ethical motivation. These points must be considered in any evaluation of the status of the "righteous Gentile." Note also *Bikkurim,* x, 5.

208. MN, III, 39 (p. 553).

209. MN, III, 35 (p. 358); III, 39 (p. 554). PhM, Pe 1:1 (p. 94). This may shed light on the moot question of the goal of the law, anthropocentric (i.e., to perfect man) or theocentric (i.e., to instill love and fear of God); see, e.g., Y. Ben-Sasson, *Tarbiz,* XXIX (1960), 279. They are clearly interrelated. On *ḳĕdušah* as the goal of the law, see ShM, *šoreš*

Generally, the varied treatment of "transgressions in which there is no action"—cursing, as noted above, belongs to this category—mirrors the different emphasis. From the point of view of criminology and penology, such transgressions are at the bottom of the ladder; they do "not even entail flogging." In accord with his premise that there is a correlation between the resulting harm of a crime and the severity of the penalty, Maimonides explains: "All transgressions in which there is no action can only result in little damage, and it is also impossible to take care not to commit them, for they consist of words only." However, from the point of view of ethical perfection or moral turpitude, the parameters of concern are entirely different. Such transgressions are repeatedly emphasized as being *very severe*, "even though there is no action" in them. One should discipline and sensitize oneself so as to avoid a "great sin" even though it is not punishable by flogging. Not everything is measurable by the *forum externum*.[210]

*Socially-oriented explanations*

The extent of socially-oriented explanations in the various works of Maimonides is also revealing. Again, to start with, it must be made clear that the *Mishneh Torah* repeatedly emphasizes the social benefit of law as a whole. Commandments are "the precious boon bestowed by God to promote social well-being on earth."[211] Concerning the prohibition of bearing a grudge, Maimonides interjects: "This is the right principle. It alone makes civilized life and social intercourse possible."[212] Actions which jeopardize the civility and stability of society are the most objectionable, worse than purely theological (or ritual) transgressions. The following halakah concerning murder speaks eloquently:

If one commits murder without being seen by two witnesses at the same time, although they did see him one after the other; or if one

---

4; R. Abraham Maimonides, *Tĕšubot*, ed. H. Freimann (Jerusalem, 1937), n.63; and MN, III, 51, as well as I, 15.
210. MN, III, 41 (560). See *De'ot*, vi, 8, 10; vii, 1, 7; *'Issure Bi'ah*, xii, 7, 13; *Šĕbu'ot*, xii, 2; *Ḥobel u-Mazziḳ*, iii, 7; *Roṣeaḥ*, i, 16.
211. *Yĕsode hat-Torah*, iv, 13.
212. *De'ot*, vii, 7. Note carefully *'Edut*, xi, 1–5.

commits murder in the presence of witnesses without first receiving a warning; or if the witnesses contradict each other in the cross-examination but not in the primary investigation—the rule in all such cases is that the murderer is put into a cell and fed on a minimum of bread and water until his stomach contracts, and then he is given barley so that his stomach splits under the stress of sickness.

This, however, is not done to other persons guilty of crimes involving the death penalty at the hand of the court; rather, if one is condemned to death, he is put to death, and if he is not liable, he is allowed to go free. For although there are worse crimes than bloodshed, none causes such destruction to civilized society as bloodshed. Not even idolatry, nor immorality, nor desecration of the Sabbath, is the equal of bloodshed. For these are crimes between man and God, while bloodshed is a crime between man and man. If one has committed this crime, he is deemed wholly wicked, and all the meritorious acts he has performed during his lifetime cannot outweigh this crime or save him from judgment, as it is said, *A man that is laden with the blood of any person shall hasten his steps to the pit; none will support him* (Prov. 28:17).

This powerful formulation is even powdered with an original exegetical flourish.[213]

Similarly, the need for total honesty in business transactions, which is surely a commonplace of Rabbinic literature, is particularly pronounced, echoing the bracing note concerning the ultimate importance of human-social relations. Maimonides' formulation concerning the commandment *Ye shall do no unrighteousness in judgment, in meteyard, in weight, or in measure* (Lev. 19:35) has its own cadences and overtones: "The punishment for unjust measures is more severe than the punishment for immorality, for the latter is a sin against God only, the former against one's fellow man. If one denies the binding character of the commandment relating to measures, he denies in effect the exodus from Egypt, which was the basis of the commandments; but if one acknowledges the commandment relating to measures, he thereby acknowledges the exodus from Egypt, which rendered all the

---

213. *Roṣeaḥ*, iv, 8, 9 (see also *Mĕlakim*, iii, 10). The phrase "crimes worse than bloodshed" (e.g., idolatry) must mean "theologically worse," unless we take it to refer to the severity of punishment: idolatry—death by stoning; murder—death by sword. The reference to Ahab being judged by the "God of spirits" ('*Ĕlohe ha-ruḥot*) needs to be read in the light of *Tĕšubah*, iii, 1, 2 ('*El de'ot*). See above, p. 148.

## LAW AND PHILOSOPHY

commandments possible."[214] The determination "to rescue the oppressed from the hand of the oppressor," one of the prerequisites for being a judge, may also be mentioned in this context.[215] The king is similarly charged with special concern for social justice and human relations—"abolition of wrong-doing" and amelioration of "life in society" in terms of the *Moreh*.[216]

Yet when we turn to the *Moreh*, we are at first unprepared to realize the extent to which the alleged social benefit or social objective of specific laws is suggested as the rationale of laws. For when Maimonides' personality does intrude in the *Mishneh Torah*, the philosophic theme of individual moral and intellectual perfection is most prominent. In this sense, the Maimonidean Code of law is not an excessively socially oriented document. Social concern and socially determined modes of abstraction and rationalization are far greater in the *Moreh*. For example, the "breaking of the neck of the heifer" (*'eglah 'arufah*, Deut. 21) is seen not as a ritual of atonement, as the verses suggest,[217] but as a means of finding the murderer. The hustle and bustle, the actions and declarations of the elders of the city, etc., will arouse people to investigate and search for relevant information:

Then necessarily, in most cases, there will be many stories and discussions among the people because of the investigation, the going forth of the elders, the measurements, and the fact that the heifer is brought there. Thus, because of the latter being universally known, the killer could perhaps be recognized. For he who knows the killer, has heard about him, or has been led to him by certain conjunctures, will say, "such-and-such a one is the killer." Now when some individual, be it only a woman or a female slave, says, "Such-and-such has killed him," the neck of the heifer is not broken. For it is established that if the killer were known and silence were kept about him while they called upon God to bear witness that they do not know the killer, there would be in this great foolhardiness and a great sin. Accordingly, even a woman will tell about him if she knows. As soon as he is known, a useful purpose will be achieved. For even if the court does not sentence him to death,

---

214. *Genebah*, vii, 12.
215. *Sanhedrin*, ii, 7; see R. Obadiah Sforno, *Peruš*, Exod. 2:17.
216. *Melakim*, ii, 6; iii, 10; iv, 10; MN, III, 27.
217. Note *Roṣeaḥ*, x, 2, where Maimonides speaks of *kapparah*.

the ruler will kill him; for he may kill on the grounds of a presumption. And if the ruler does not kill him, the "revenger of blood" will do it; for he will use stratagems in order to take him by surprise and kill him. Accordingly, it is clear that the utility of the commandment . . . is to be found in the fact that in this way the killer becomes generally known. This notion is corroborated by the fact that the place in which the heifer has her neck broken *may neither be plowed nor sown* (Deut. 21:4). Consequently the owner of that land will use all stratagems and will investigate in order that the killer be known and that thus the heifer not have her neck broken, and that consequently his land will not be prohibited to him forever.

This explanation, so novel in its pragmatism, had an interesting history in Rabbinic literature.[218]

The prohibition of prostitution is likewise explained primarily in social, not sacral, terms. After a quotation from the *Nicomachean Ethics* concerning the value of friendship—and by natural extension, family cohesiveness and social solidarity—Maimonides interjects: "Accordingly, a single tribe that is united through a common ancestor, even if he is remote, because of this love one another, help one another, and have pity on one another; *and the attainment of these things is the greatest purpose of the law.*" He then concludes: "Hence harlots are prohibited, because through them lines of ancestry are destroyed."[219]

Leprosy is, as we have seen, a miraculous punishment for slander, and the leper is to be isolated. Maimonides notes: "The utility of this belief is manifest, there being also the fact that

---

218. MN, III, 40 (p. 557). For the assertion that the ruler may inflict capital punishment on the ground of presumption, see *Mĕlakim*, iii, 10. This is cited in the *Sefer ha-Ḥinnuk*, 530, in the name of Maimonides; it was apparently so novel that it warranted identification. On the other hand, see *KM, Roṣeaḥ*, x, 6, where this is cited in the name of "some commentators." This explanation is one of the views singled out for attack by S. D. Luzzatto, *Yĕsode hat-Torah*, chap. 32; in chap. 49 he challenges the very premises of the Maimonidean system.

219. MN, III, 49 (p. 601) (italics mine); *'Issure Bi'ah*, xviii, 1. To be sure, in this chapter of the *Moreh*, Maimonides gives other reasons for the prohibition of prostitution. One is reminded in this context of *'Ĕmunot wĕ-De'ot*, III, 1, where R. Saadiah explains that homosexuality is condemned because it disrupts the family structure; *'Issure Bi'ah*, xxi, 8, has no explanation, while MN, III, 49 (p. 606)—and see *Sefer ha-Ḥinnuk*, 209—has a different reason. For another example concerning the *yĕfat to'ar* (beautiful [captive] woman, Deut. 21:10–14), see *Mĕlakim*, viii, 5; and MN, III, 41 (p. 567), where the "exhortation to noble moral qualities" is stressed.

leprosy is contagious and that almost by nature all men find it disgusting."[220]

Laws concerning alms, gifts, loans, etc., are intended not only to inculcate pity—"the reason for all these is manifest, for they are equally useful in turn to all men. For one who is rich today will be poor tomorrow, or his descendants will be poor; whereas one who is poor today will be rich tomorrow, or his son will be rich." Recognizing the wheel of fortune is useful socially.[221]

The social-ecological benefit of the Laws Concerning the Sabbatical Year and Jubilee has already been noted.

According to Maimonides, there are two causes for Sabbath observance, one ideological (belief in a true opinion concerning creation of the world) and one social (voluntary inactivity and rest, in contradistinction to slavery): "Accordingly the Sabbath is, as it were, of universal benefit, both with reference to a true speculative opinion and to the well-being of the state of the body."[222]

In sum, social explanations, like historical ones, seem to be more congruent with the outer-directed emphasis. They prove rationality and intelligibility of a special kind.

### THE UNITY OR DUALITY OF MAIMONIDES' TEACHING: CONTRADICTIONS OR DIVERGENT EMPHASES

We dare not end this discussion without noting again the extent to which the question of contradictions, real or alleged, central or peripheral, has been a pivot of modern Maimonidean scholarship. The unity or duality of Maimonides, the esoteric versus the exoteric teaching, the Talmudist versus the philosopher or the Rabbi versus the Aristotelian, the native and traditional authentic doctrine vis-à-vis the extraneous, foreign, spurious doctrine, the author of "intentional perplexities" or the constructor

---

220. MN, III, 47 (p. 597). Note the emphasis on the miraculous nature of leprosy (and *soṭah* is cited as an analogous miracle), as in *Ṭumĕ'at Ṣara'at*, xvi, 10. See MN, II, 29. However, the isolation of the leper in the MT (*Ṭumĕ'at Ṣara'at*, x, 7) is more of a punishment for slander, hence the impossibility of repeating it; see R. Judah hal-Levi, *Kuzari*, II, 58–60; R. Abraham ibn Ezra, to Lev. 13:2; PhM, Neḡ 12:5 (p. 397).

221. MN, III, 35 (p. 536). See PhM, 'Ab 2:7 (p. 425) for another kind of wheel of fortune, and cf. B. Shab 151b.

222. MN, II, 31 (p. 360). R. Saadiah Gaon also utilizes social explanations, e.g., in his *'Ĕmunoṭ wĕ-De'oṭ;* see above, n. 219, for an example.

of a tense yet unified system—such formulations and/or evaluations continue to bestir or to bedevil scholars. It is not within the scope of our analysis of the theme of philosophy and law in the *Mishneh Torah* even to attempt an overall solution to this problem. I would submit, however, that two advances may be registered. First of all, the attention to the philosophic emphases in the Code as well as in other popular and mass-directed writings —emphases which are unelaborated but also uncamouflaged and quite abundant—reveals a vigorous intellectualistic posture usually associated exclusively with the *Moreh*. If this does not overturn the barriers, artful or artificial, that have been erected, it should at least contribute to a more balanced approach and open-ended assessment. The implication that the *Mishneh Torah* can suggest nothing of the typically intellectualistic stance of Maimonides, inasmuch as it "deals with beliefs and opinions only insofar as they are implied in prohibitions and commands," is simply untenable. The assertion that the *Mishneh Torah* is intended for the masses and does not consequently contain *ṭa'ăme ham-miṣwoṭ* is hardly defensible.[223]

Secondly, the very problem should be defined much more expansively, and the perspective should be widened, in order not to be straitjacketed into the scenario, and ultimately the snare, set by those who look only to the supposed esoteric-exoteric, naturalist-supernaturalist axis of the *Moreh* vis-à-vis the *Mishneh Torah*. We need to consider not only the relationship between these two major works but the interrelationship of the other writings as well. Only such a broad view will enable us to appraise properly the tricky theme of presumed contradictions and really irreducible problems.

It is imperative to differentiate between apparently blatant contradictions[224]—irreconcilable discrepancies of fact, approach,

---

223. E.g., Z. Jawitz, *Tolĕdoṭ Yiśra'el* (Tel Aviv, 1935), X, 41, 42, 47; L. Strauss, *Persecution and the Art of Writing*: J. Levinger, " 'Al Ṭa'am han-Nĕziruṭ," *Bar-Ilan*, IV/V (1967), 299ff.; cf. Twersky, "Non-Halakic Aspects," pp. 97–98. See above, n.6.

224. MN, III, 48 (cf. *Tĕfillah*, ix, 7), may be such a case; also III, 41 (cf. *Ḥoḇel u-Mazziḳ*, i, 6), and S. Belkin, *Philo and the Oral Law* (Cambridge, 1940), p. 101. Note, per contra, that in the MT (*Yĕsoḏe haṭ-Torah*, i, 5) Maimonides rather boldly operates with the eternity of the world as a basis for his proofs of the existence of God; see MN, I, 71 (p. 180). Maimonides' views on creation (whether he believed in a created or eternal world)

or evaluation—and differences of exposition and expostulation, pedagogical or tactical variations due to textual suggestions and contextual considerations. Maimonides himself noted that "it is proper that each group be addressed in accord with its capacity."[225] Not inadvertently, I think, does Maimonides, in describing the zealous and inspired teaching of Abraham, attribute to him this basic skill: "When the people flocked to him and questioned him regarding his assertions, he would instruct each one according to his capacity till he had brought him to the way of truth."[226] Historical evaluations, of course, usually involve autobiographical reflections.[227] There is no doubt that Maimonides was a gifted, self-conscious, and self-confident pedagogue, and one who would also instruct various groups according to their capacity. Must skillful communication with different audiences inevitably involve self-contradiction? How are we to appraise shifting emphases, divergent motivations, judicious emphasis of an idea or explanation and prudent suppression of a hypothesis or concept?

A few examples, working out of the *Mishneh Torah*, should help us achieve the widened perspective. Let us also remember in any event that there are straightforward halakic contradictions

---

were most recently debated by A. Nuriel and A. Ravitsky, *Tarbiz*, XXXIII (1964), 372ff., and XXXV (1966), 333ff.; see the important article by M. Allard, "Le rationalisme d'Averroes d'après une étude sur la création," *Bulletin d'Études Orientales*, XIV (1952–54), 7–59, who uses the measure of independence from Aristotle as a criterion for determining the religious sincerity of Averroes. See also *Averroes on the Harmony of Religion and Philosophy*, tr. G. Hourani (London, 1961), p. 25. Historically the religious critique of the theory of the eternity of the universe is very central. See J. Kraemer, "A Lost Passage from Philoponus' Contra Aristotelem" *JAOS*, LXXXV (1965), 320, who emphasizes that this is the "first philosophical confrontation of monotheism with the scientific cosmology of paganism." Note that the implacable anti-Maimonidean R. Shem-Ṭob ben Shem Ṭob (*Sefer 'Ĕmunot*, 14b) claims that Maimonides "deviated somewhat" from Aristotle in order to demonstrate that he believed in the Torah (!). See also the phrase "holy bodies" in *Yĕsode hat-Torah*, iv, 12; and the comment of L. Strauss, introduction to MN, p. xx. For another aspect of Maimonides' criticism of Aristotle, see Z. Bechler, "Haṭkafaṭo šel ha-RaMBaM," *'Iyyun*, XVII (1966), 34ff.; note also J. Eḇen Shemuel, *Sinai Sefer Yoḇel*, ed. J. L. Maimon (Jerusalem, 1958), pp. 126–41.

225. MTH, 38.
226. *'Akum*, i, 2.
227. Note the beautiful formulation of I. Berlin, *The Hedgehog and the Fox* (New York, 1957), p. 9. See IT, xii (concerning R. Saadiah Gaon).

due to changed interpretations,[228] to the giving of priority to widespread custom over Maimonides' own correct but unaccepted view,[229] and similar reasons which are not particularly provocative. Not every contradiction automatically signals calculated confusion or esoteric teaching. Throughout the ages even the great traditional scholars, dedicated exclusively to the study of the *Mishneh Torah*, have not shied away from occasionally acknowledging certain contradictions within the work itself. To be sure, boundless energy and ingenuity were expended in an effort to resolve all apparent contradictions and to reconcile every difficult passage—the phrase "a difficult RaMBaM" is one of the most popular idioms of Rabbinic parlance; a voluminous literature devoted to resolving such difficulties, real or apparent, has developed and continues to grow. Yet it should be noted that some Talmudists were not dismayed by an occasional inconsistency. Such a perspective on halakic matters will make it easier to achieve a more flexible view of matters in which law and philosophy interact.[230]

1. In the *'Iggeret Teman* Maimonides shows much greater enthusiasm and a heightened sense of expectation for the Messianic era than is discernible in the *Mishneh Torah*. He even reveals a family tradition concerning the imminent date of the Messianic era, thereby placing himself in the condemned camp of "calculators of the Messianic era." All this, however, does not really change the antiapocalyptic nature of the Messianic period as he depicts it in his various writings: Messianism is the completion and culmination, not the interruption or rupture, of the historic process. There will be neither miraculous changes in the law of

---

228. Medieval commentators and Talmudists frequently noted the changes between the *Commentary on the Mishnah* and the MT or even changes within various recensions of these works. See R. Elijah Mizraḥi, *Tešubot*, 5.

229. See above, chap II.

230. See above, chap. II, on the way Maimonides and his descendants handled the problem of contradictions. R. Hayyim of Brest-Litovsk (Brisk) used to say that he did not feel obligated to answer every question or resolve every problem in the *Mishneh Torah*. I wish to emphasize that the methodological value of ad hoc explanations may be very great. This should not be understood as suggesting any constraint upon the search for all-inclusive rules which may reveal Maimonides' methods; see the pioneering study of J. Levinger, *Darke ham-Maḥšabah*, and the review by I. Ta-Shema, *ḲS*, XXXXI (1966), 138–44.

# LAW AND PHILOSOPHY

nature nor substantive changes in the law of Judaism, not even methodological changes in its study.[231] Actually, Messianism may be described as the ultimate triumph of Abraham, when true belief will be universally restored. The beginning and end of history are interwoven. The task of Abraham was to form a nation that knows God, and the ultimate Messianic reality will be characterized by abundant and pervasive knowledge of God. Concerning the beginning of history and Abraham's undaunted struggle against polytheism, Maimonides records: "And so it (the transmission of Abraham's teaching) went on with ever increasing vigor among Jacob's children and their adherents till *they became a people that knew God.*" Concerning the end of history and the ultimate vindication and victory of Abraham's struggle, Maimonides predicts: "The one preoccupation of the whole world *will be to know God . . . For the earth shall be full of the knowledge of the Lord, as the waters cover the sea* (Isa. 11:9)."[232] The air of expectancy which is so natural, perhaps even necessary, in the context of the *Epistle* could not be easily integrated into the measured, restrained, in some cases agnostic,[233] formulations at the end of the Code.

231. IT, xii, xv (and A. Halkin's introduction, p. xii); *Mĕlakim,* xi and xii, particularly xi, 3, xii, 1; *Tĕšubah,* ix, 2. See the pithy presentations in PhM 'Ed 8:7 (p. 336); Sanh 1:3 (p. 148). Professor E. Urbach reminded me of R. Hai Gaon's detailed apocalyptic forecast (cited by R. Abraham ben 'Azriel, *'Ărugat hab-Bośem,* ed. E. Urbach [Jerusalem, 1939], I, 256ff.) which could be the likely target of Maimonides' polemic. Clearly, in these chapters on Messianism, Maimonides is bold and vigorous, striking a major blow for the antiapocalyptic conception. It should be noted, however, that relying on a single Talmudic statement while ignoring a host of other statements is consonant with his approach of subordinating details to one overriding, formative principle; see above, n.60. See G. Scholem, *The Messianic Idea in Judaism* (New York, 1971), pp. 27ff. Actually, by codifying the Talmudic view of Samuel, Maimonides ruled out changes, for in the Talmud (B. Shab, 151b) Samuel's view is opposed to those views which foresee natural-historical mutations. Maimonides' approach to the problems of Messianic theory—his polemic with predecessors and the criticism, in turn, directed against him—is paradigmatic for the entire history of Messianic thought which may be seen as a history of conflicting interpretations (literal versus metaphorical) of key Scriptural verses.

232. *'Akum,* i, 3; *Mĕlakim,* xii, 5 (italics mine).

233. Maimonides does not categorically reject the possibility of miracles; he suspends judgment, advocating a "wait and see" attitude. It should be noted that Maimonides treats Messianism throughout the Code very nonchalantly; laws pertaining to the King Messiah and the Messianic era are routinely and unceremoniously formulated, e.g., *Šĕmiṭṭah wĕ-Yobel,* xii, 16; *Parah,* iii, 4; *Mĕlakim,* iv, 8.

## INTRODUCTION TO THE CODE OF MAIMONIDES

2. Maimonides' attitude to Judaism's daughter religions is another case in point. On the whole, his criteria for assessing them are theological, and any differentiation between them follows from this. For example, Christianity is considered to be not monotheistic by reason of its Trinitarianism, while Islam is monotheistic. In terms of their attitude to the Bible, Christianity is presented as recognizing the integrity and authenticity of the Bible, whereas Islam is further censured for denying the absolute authority of the Bible, because it accuses the Jews of forgery and malicious "editing," primarily in order to eliminate "allusions" to Muḥammad.[234] Yet in the concluding paragraphs of the *Mishneh Torah*, he accords both Christianity and Islam a limited but decidedly positive historical function, to prepare the world for true monotheism and genuine acceptance of the Torah:

> But it is beyond the human mind to fathom the designs of the Creator; for our ways are not His ways, neither are our thoughts His thoughts. All these matters relating to Jesus of Nazareth and the Ishmaelite (Muḥammad) who came after him only served to clear the way for King Messiah, to prepare the whole world to worship God with one accord, as it is written, *For then will I turn to the peoples a pure language, that they may all call upon the name of the Lord, to serve Him with one consent* (Zeph. 3:9). Thus the Messianic hope, the Torah, and the commandments have become familiar topics—topics of conversation (among the inhabitants) of the far isles and many peoples, uncircumcised of heart and flesh. They are discussing these matters and the commandments of the Torah. Some say, "Those commandments were true, but have lost their validity and are no longer binding". Others declare that they had an esoteric meaning and were not intended to be taken literally; that the Messiah has already come and revealed their occult significance. But when the true King Messiah will appear and succeed, be exalted and lifted up, they will forthwith recant and realize that they have inherited naught but lies from their fathers, that their prophets and forebears led them astray.[235]

---

234. *Tĕshubot*, 149 (p. 284), 448 (p. 726). J. Katz, "Sublanut Datit," *Zion*, XVIII (1953), 15ff.; and idem, *Exclusiveness and Tolerance* (Oxford, 1961), pp. 114ff.

235. *Mĕlakim*, xi, 4 (uncensored version). For "our ways are not His ways," see *Tĕshubah*, v, 5, and MN, I, 33; for Zeph. 3:9, see Wolfson, *Philo*, II, 417. Maimonides' view on Christianity spreading knowledge of the Torah is echoed in the sixteenth century by R. Abraham Farissol and R. Abraham ibn Megas and in the seventeenth century by R.

By spreading knowledge of the Bible and the idea of commandments, even though they willfully misinterpret and corrupt, they plant seeds which will reach full fruition at some future, eschatological, date.

Consciously or unconsciously, Maimonides is here echoing the view of R. Judah hal-Levi that, all their inadequacies and all their animosity to Judaism notwithstanding, Christianity and Islam have been assigned a significant role in the divine economy and historical design.[236] There is nothing comparable in the 'Iggeret Teman, which as expected concentrates on the antitheses and antipathies between the religions, and whose entire polemical fabric would be weakened by such a historic appraisal. The latter, in turn, suggesting one possible way "to fathom the designs of the Creator," fits nicely into the historiosophical conception of the Mishneh Torah.

3. An aspect of ethical theory is also moot. In the Šěmonah Pěraķim Maimonides discusses a special conflict—like most such conflicts, only apparent—between the religious view and the philosophic view concerning motivation of morality. The philosophic view extols spontaneous, voluntary, natural virtue,

---

Judah del Bene; see H. H. Ben-Sasson, "The Reformation in Contemporary Jewish Eyes," *Proceedings of Israel Academy of Sciences*, IV (1970), 241, n. 9, and I. Barzilay, *Between Reason and Faith* (The Hague, 1967), p. 215.

236. *Kuzari*, IV, 23; see I. Heinemann, "Těmunat ha-Hisṭoriyah šel R. Judah hal-Levi," *Zion*, IX (1944), 147ff.; H. H. Ben-Sasson, "Yiḥud 'Am Yiśra'el," *Pěraķim*, II (1971), 155ff. There is no connection between hal-Levi's view and the theory of a special "Messiah for the nations" espoused by some tenth-century Islamic writers or by Franz Rosenzweig. Concerning the 'Īsawīyah of Iṣfāhān, see R. Brunschvig, "L'argumentation d'un théologien musulman du Xe siècle contre le Judaisme," *Homenaje a Millas-Vallicrosa* (Barcelona, 1946), I, 225–42.

Note the following two cases as well: (a) in the MT, *Tĕfillah*, i, Maimonides gives a brief history of prayer, noting the reasons for its standardization, but does not discuss the paradox of prayer, the essential question of whether prayer is even conceivable, as he does in MN, I, 59. In the MT context, prayer is taken for granted, and the main problem is not its philosophical impossibility but the reconciling of subjectivity and spontaneity with objective norms and carefully regulated forms; hence the full-orbed and original discussion of *kawwanah*—intention, attention, and inwardness—in *Tĕfillah*, iv, 15–19.

(b) Maimonides repeatedly expresses his conviction that a scholar or teacher should not be a salaried functionary. In PhM and in various epistles, he specifically criticizes the Geonim for their fund-raising machinery and ideology. In the MT we have a forceful and resounding statement, *Talmud Torah*, iii, 10, but it is anonymous. Is this lack of candor, or a proper adaptation of the message to the context?

while the religious view acclaims virtue resulting from struggle, conquest, and extirpation of evil impulses. Which is superior? Is the innately righteous person who never desires to sin superior to the one who achieves righteousness by arduous and prolonged discipline and self-control? The question, standard in Maimonides' philosophic milieu, has often been paraphrased into modern (Kantian) motivational terms: autonomy versus heteronomy. He solves the conflict by suggesting that the philosophic view refers to *mišpaṭim,* those things which all people commonly agree are evils. Clearly "a noble soul has absolutely no desire for any such crimes and experiences, no struggle in refraining from them." The Rabbinic view refers only to "ceremonial prohibitions," to those things which "were it not for the law . . . would not at all be considered transgressions." The Maimonidean compromise suggests that since the latter are not easily rationalized or motivated, the motif of serious struggle and subsequent submission to religious authority is properly paramount. Inasmuch as the other laws are universally appreciated, an autonomous observance, expressing total congruence between the norm and one's own inclination, is most appropriate.[237] Whatever the logistics and problems of his solution,[238] there is no doubt that he favors autonomy—the philosophic view. In fact, his solution is predicated on a limitation of the Rabbinic view, while the philosophic view, which only concerned universal laws in any event, is left intact. The purity and naturalness of the motivation is a moral desideratum for Maimonides.

In contrast to the above attitude, in the *Mishneh Torah* Maimonides comes down on the side of heteronomy. One relevant—and intrinsically important, and repercussive—passage should be studied in its entirety:

---

237. ŠP, chap. VI (and note R. Saadiah, *'Ĕmunoṯ wĕ-Deʿoṯ,* III, 1). The description of *mišpaṭim* reflects Aristotelian categories. See H. Davidson, "Maimonides' Shemonah Peraḳim and Alfārābī's Fuṣūl al-Madanī," *PAAJR,* XXXI (1963), 33ff.; Wolfson, *Philo,* II, 174, 258–59. See above, n. 145.
238. Two items are particularly noteworthy: (1) The conflicting religious view is Rabbinic, whereas the Scriptural is assumed by Maimonides to be in accord with the philosophic view. (2) His Rabbinic proofs are relevant only if interpreted in a certain, apparently forced, way; he himself, elsewhere, interprets the same sayings differently; e.g., *Talmuḏ Torah,* iii, 6.

Moses our teacher bequeathed the law and commandments to Israel, as it is said, *An inheritance of the congregation of Jacob* (Deut. 33:4), and to those of other nations who are willing to be converted (to Judaism), as it is said, *One law and one ordinance shall be both for you and for the resident alien* (Num. 15:16). But no coercion to accept the law and commandments is practiced on those who are unwilling to do so. Moreover, Moses our teacher was commanded by God to compel all human beings to accept the commandments enjoined upon the descendants of Noah. . . .

A heathen who accepts the seven commandments and observes them scrupulously is a "righteous heathen," and will have a portion in the world to come, provided that he accepts them and performs them because the Holy One, blessed be He, commanded them in the law and made known through Moses our teacher that the observance thereof had been enjoined upon the descendants of Noah even before the law was given. But if his observance thereof is based upon a reasoned conclusion, he is not deemed a resident alien, or one of the pious of the Gentiles, but one of their wise men.[239]

The same point of view underlies the following evaluation of the repentant sinner:

> Let not the penitent suppose that he is kept far away from the degree attained by the righteous because of the iniquities and sins that he has

---

239. *Mĕlakim*, viii, 10–11. The problem was noted by R. Isaac Arama, *'Ăkedat Yiṣḥak̠*, *ša'ar* 100. R. Moses Almosnino, *Tĕfillah lĕ-Mošeh* (Salonica, 1563), p. 13a, also questions Maimonides' solution. R. Moses Alashkar, *Tĕšubot*, 117, uses Maimonides' emphasis on heteronomy generally and this formulation concerning Noachides in particular to rebut the charges of excessive intellectualism leveled at Maimonides by R. Shem Ṭob in the *Sefer 'Ĕmunot* (see below, n. 380). See generally M. Guttmann, *REJ*, LXXXIX (1935), 34, who calls attention to the *Mišnat R.'Eli'ezer*, ed. H. Enelow (New York, 1934); J. Katz, "Šĕlošah Mišpaṭim," *Zion*, XXIII (1958), 174ff., and idem, *Exclusiveness and Tolerance*, pp. 175ff. S. Schwarzschild, "Do Noachites Have to Believe in Revelation?", *JQR* LII (1962), 297ff.; LIII (1963), 30ff. Also D. Revel, "Lĕ-Ḇerur Da'at ha-RaMBaM," *Ḥoreḇ*, II (1935), 112ff. The exclusiveness of Mosaic authority, which may be seen as a corollary of the uniqueness of Mosaic prophecy (see, e.g., *Yĕsode hat-Torah*, vii, and MN, II, 32), is strongly emphasized—there is no other source of legislative authority; other prophets could only exhort. See *Yĕsode hat-Torah*, ix; *'Akum*, i; *'Aḇel*, i, 1; *Mĕlakim*, ix, 1; MN, II, 39; PhM, Ḥul 7:6 (p. 212); *Tĕšubot*, 148 (p. 282); *Koḇeṣ*, II, 15b; MTH, 31 (and cf. *Kuzari*, III, 43). This inviolable Maimonidean principle is further fortified by our passage which extends the exclusiveness of Mosaic authority to non-Jews as well. Practically all texts support our reading "one of their wise men." The variant "not even one of their wise men" was in the text which Moses Mendelssohn had and he was greatly agitated by it; see A. Altmann, *Moses Mendelssohn* (University, Alabama, 1973), p. 294. Spinoza also had that reading; see *Theologico-Political Treatise*, ed. R. Elwes (New York, 1951), chap. V (pp. 79–80). On the special role of Moses, note also *Ḥameṣ u-Maṣṣah*, vii, 2.

committed. This is not so. He is beloved by the Creator, desired by Him, as if he had never sinned. Moreover, his reward is great; since, though having tasted sin, he renounced it and overcame his evil passions. The Sages say, "Where penitents stand, the completely righteous cannot stand." This means that the degree attained by penitents is higher than that of those who had never sinned, the reason being that the former have had to put forth a greater effort to subdue their passions than the latter.[240]

The full force of this statement is felt if we realize further that there was no compelling reason or precedent for Maimonides to codify the opinion that the penitent attains a higher degree than the innately and uniformly righteous; predecessors, such as R. Bahya ibn Pakuda, opted for the other view.[241] Furthermore, the reason he gives seems to be his own, in support of the imperatival awareness and submission.[242] No distinction is made between *ḥukkim* and *mišpaṭim;* in the context of his Code, heteronomy seems to be nobler with regard to both.

This now gives a clue also to the proper perspective on whether or not Maimonides operates with a concept of natural law. Maimonides' insistence upon the imperatival aspect, even with regard to those ethical virtues and actions which are perfectly rational and practically universal, unequivocally rules out complete autonomy for law. G. F. Moore, in an entirely different context, submitted that "the Jewish teachers recognized the distinction between acts which the common conscience of mankind condemns as morally wrong and such as are wrong only because they are made so by statute: but the former are not the more properly sin because of their moral quality nor the latter less so because in themselves they are morally indifferent."[243] Needless to say,

240. *Tešubah,* vii, 4.
241. *Ḥoboṯ hal-Lĕbaboṯ,* VIII, 8 (II, 160). The position of R. Abraham bar Ḥiyya, *Hegyon han-Nefeš, 'amud* III (Eng. tr. G. Wigoder [London, 1969], p. 92) is similar to that of Maimonides; ham-Me'iri, *Ḥibbur hat-Tešubah,* p. 56. See also Wolfson, *Philo,* II, 258. And cf. E. Simon, "Pflicht und Neigung bei Maimonides und in der neuen deutschen Ethik," *Horizons of a Philosopher: Essays in Honor of David Baumgardt* (Leiden, 1963), pp. 391–421.
242. A possible source or antecedent is R. Nissim Gaon, *Ḥibbur Yafeh,* ed. H. Hirschberg (Jerusalem, 1954), p. 84; see *Tarbiz,* XXXVII (1968), 326.
243. G. F. Moore, *Judaism* (Cambridge, 1958), I, 465.

"natural reason is not a sufficient and authoritative source of the rules of morality."[244] That was never the issue. We are not dealing with an Enlightenment concept which insists that religion is not revealed but discovered only by human reason, and that inasmuch as truths are rational and knowable by reason, they are not part of revelation; this is for Moses Mendelssohn but not for Rabbi Moses ben Maimon. All that the Rabbis and philosophers contend is that natural reason is in agreement with divine authority. There is an all-important parallelism here between reason and revelation. *All* legislation is divine from the point of view of authority, but if it can be shown to be congruent with reason, it may be described as rational and natural. Ground for obligation and authoritativeness is unquestionably the divine command—no Jewish thinker would dispute this or introduce distinctions concerning source and validity, authenticity and normativeness—but philosophers of the Maimonidean kind will try to show that the laws per se are rational. This makes them "in accordance with nature." They should not be described as "natural" for they are "divine," but only divine law can be completely "in accordance with nature," for both are universal and immutable.[245] Law is natural if it is modeled after laws implanted by God in nature. Whereas Maimonides would agree with R. Judah hal-Levi that *all* ritual is from God and not man's rationalization, they disagree radically concerning the resultant role of reason: for hal-Levi reasons discovered by philosophical investigation and teleological explanation are not very useful or significant, since all depends on revelation, whereas for Maimonides these reasons add an important depth-dimension to the religious experience.[246] For Maimonides, laws are true by divine sanction, but reason discovers their wisdom and intelligibility. Reason does not replace

---

244. Cf. M. Fox, "Maimonides and Aquinas on Natural Law," *Dine Israel*, III (1972), viii; idem, "Law and Ethics in Modern Jewish Philosophy," *PAAJR*, XLIII (1976), 1–2. On whether there was a pre-Mosaic natural religion, see '*Akum*, i; MN, III, 29, and I, 63.

245. MN, II, 40; see Wolfson, *Philo*, II, 310ff. and 179–80; I. Heinemann, "Die Lehre vom ungeschriebenen Gesetz," *HUCA*, IV (1927), 149ff.

246. *Kuzari*, I, 56 (end); also I, 98, 99; II, 60; III, 53. This resembles the view repudiated by Maimonides in MN, III, 31. It is possible that hal-Levi would welcome the MT type of rationalizations and ethicizations which are, after all, close to hal-Levi's joy-love-fear syndrome; see *Kuzari*, II, 50; III, 19.

divine authority but convinces man of the utility and rationality of the laws which he would obey even if they were peremptory prescriptions. This is analogous to the way Maimonides approached the relationship between Scripture and philosophy: Scripture contains philosophic truths which human reason can arrive at independently, but this does not diminish the revealed quality or force of these truths. It is man's duty—and if he is wise, his aspiration—to rationalize revealed truths. The intellect is a tool for uncovering the congruence between reason and revelation and the ultimate meaning of divine laws, and there is no doubt about the existence of this meaning. Just as the scientist operates on the assumption that the universe—i.e., natural law created by God—is rational and intelligible, the religious philosopher operates on the assumption that the Torah—i.e., moral-ritual law created by God—is rational and intelligible. The same mode of thinking and feeling about the cosmic order carried over to the moral order; the same axiological-ontological postulates governed both realms.

We must explain Maimonides' statement that moral principles are "conventional" and not "rational" in the same way.[247] Human morality is based on convention and is therefore beyond reason. This is a commonplace of classical Greek thought. Divinely ordained morality is, like philosophically or humanly ordained morality, *generically* describable as conventional, but like all other divine actions, it is immanently reasonable and its rationality is discoverable. Maimonides objected strenuously to those predecessors who said that *some* commandments were rational laws, *miṣwoṯ śikliyyoṯ* (the phrase introduced into Jewish philosophic literature by R. Saadiah Gaon). What should be understood is that his strenuous objection is nourished by his own passionate conviction that not *some* but *all* laws are rational. He does not, as is ordinarily assumed, object to the use of the term and its clear implication that laws are rational; he objects to its

---

247. MN, I, 2. For the meaning of *muśkaloṯ* (primary rational notions) see *Milloṯ ha-Higgayon*, chap. 8; MN, I, 51; II, 33; Wolfson, *Studies*, I, 566, 590. The statement in MN, II, 33 (p. 364), that only the first two of the Ten Commandments are rational, needs special study. See I. Arama, Ḥazuṯ Ḳaśah (Pressburg, 1841), p. 10a; *Kuzari*, III, 11 (concerning the first commandment). Cf. L. Strauss, *Persecution and the Art of Writing*, pp. 96ff.; J. Faur, *Tarbiz*, XXXVIII (1968), 49.

*limited* application and the resultant implication that other laws are nonrational.[248] *All* laws are rational, and with intellectual exertion and insight we are able to discover this necessary rationality of revelation.

In any event, the apodictic affirmation that there is rationality in the law is not yet the final goal or the ultimate vindication. As we have noted, religious commandments are self-validating, and their observance is unconditional. However, fathoming their intent and purpose, thoroughly rationalizing them, is a means to perfection and a basic component of the knowledge of God— hence a central feature of Maimonides' religious intellectualism.

## Attitude toward asceticism

A final example, of great importance per se, is the Maimonidean posture on asceticism. At first blush it would appear that Maimonides' theory of the golden mean as the foundation of ethics would categorically eliminate all tendencies or traces of extremism. Virtues are defined as the psychological dispositions between the extremes of excess and deficiency: "Good deeds are such as are equibalanced, maintaining the mean between two equally bad extremes." Generosity, for example, is the virtuous mean between stinginess and extravagance, just as courage is the mean between recklessness and cowardice. However, Maimonides does recognize certain exceptions. For therapeutic reasons one may adopt extremism. If one is ill by being addicted to extreme stinginess, he should move to the extreme of extravagance, and only subsequently will he be ready to return to the median position. If one is fearful of being corrupted by an irremediably immoral society, one may withdraw completely, even though antisocial behavior is generally eschewed. The examples and emphases are noteworthy:

When, at times, some of the pious ones deviated to one extreme by fasting, keeping nightly vigils, refraining from eating meat or drinking

---

248. ŠP, chap. VI; see his surprising use of the cognate term *miṣwah šim'iṭ* in PhM, Ber 5:3 (p. 75); and cf. MN, III, 48. Note the striking formulation in *Ma'ăḵaloṯ 'Ăsuroṯ*, xvii, 29, 30: "The Sages have forbidden the consumption of food and drink of the kind that is revolting to most people. . . . They have also forbidden eating and drinking out of filthy utensils which offend against one's natural fastidiousness." This is natural law, but its source of authority is divine.

wine, renouncing sexual intercourse, clothing themselves in woolen and hairy garments, dwelling in the mountains, and wandering about in the wilderness, they did so partly as a means of restoring the health of their souls, as we have explained above, and partly because of the immorality of the townspeople. When the pious saw that they themselves might become contaminated by association with evil men or by constantly seeing their actions, fearing that their own morals might become corrupt on account of contact with them, they fled to the wildernesses far from their society, as the prophet Jeremiah said, *Oh that I were in the wilderness, in a lodging place of wayfaring men, that I might leave my people, and go from them! For they are all adulterers, an assembly of treacherous men* (Jer. 9:1).[249]

This historical description from the Šěmonah Pěrakim should be correlated with a contemporary formulation in Hilkot De'ot, where the advice or aspiration of Jer. 9:1 is also underscored:

> It is natural to be influenced, in sentiments and conduct, by one's neighbors and associates, and observe the customs of one's fellow citizens. Hence a person ought constantly to associate with the righteous and frequent the company of the wise, so as to learn from their practices, and shun the wicked who are benighted, so as not to be corrupted by their example . . . . So, too, if one lives in a country where the customs are pernicious and the inhabitants do not go in the right way, he should leave for a place where the people are righteous and follow the ways of the good. If all the countries of which he has personal knowledge, or concerning which he hears reports, follow a course that is not right, as is the case in our times, or if military campaigns or sickness debar him from leaving for a country with good customs, he should live by himself in seclusion, as it is said, *Let him sit alone and keep silence* (Lam. 3:28). And if the inhabitants are wicked reprobates who will not let him stay in the country unless he mixes with them and adopts their evil practices, let him withdraw to caves, thickets, or deserts, and not habituate himself to the ways of sinners, as it is said, *Oh that I were in the wilderness, in a lodging place of wayfaring men* (Jer. 9:1).[250]

While moral and cultural pessimism is not uncommon— many tend to see their own times as "the acme of

---

249. ŠP, chap. IV; De'ot, ii, 2.
250. De'ot, vi, 1.

unrighteousness"[251]—Maimonides' remark "as is the case in our times" is significant and may have influenced his son and other ascetically inclined contemporaries.[252] One's historical perception may thus accentuate the desire to interiorize ethical norms and justify asceticism in repudiation of the world and its "unrighteousness."

Elsewhere, the examples of maladies which may have to be cured by extremism relate to more frequent problems or conditions of ethical theory and practice:

> What is the method of effecting their cure? If one is irascible, he is directed so to govern himself that even if he is assaulted or reviled, he should not feel affronted. And in this course he is to persevere for a long time till the choleric temperament has been eradicated. If one is arrogant, he should accustom himself to endure much contumely, sit below everyone, and wear old and ragged garments that bring the wearer into contempt, and so forth, till arrogance is eradicated from his heart and he has regained the middle path, which is the right way. And when he has returned to this path, he should walk in it the rest of his days. On similar lines, he should treat all his dispositions. If, in any of them, he is at one extreme, he should move to the opposite extreme, and keep to it for a long time till he has regained the right path which is the normal mean in every class of dispositions.[253]

In any event, all this is fully elaborated in the *Šĕmonah Pĕraķim* as well as in the *Hilķot De'ot*, and in this regard the two are really mutually supplementary and supportive.

There is, however, a glaring discrepancy between these two major sources. Regular deviation from the middle course is recognized in the *Mishneh Torah* as a legitimate ethical alternative. Besides the wise man (*ḥakam*), who "observes in his dispositions

---

251. E.g., R. C. Petry, "Medieval Eschatology and Social Responsibility in Bernard of Morval's De Contemptu Mundi," *Speculum*, XXIV (1949), 207–17; K. Giocarinis, "Bernard of Cluny and the Antique," *Classica et Medievalia*, XXVII (1966), 34; he sees "his times as the acme of unrighteousness."

252. G. Cohen, "Soteriology of R. Abraham Maimuni," *PAAJR*, XXXVI (1968), 54.

253. *De'ot*, ii, 2; *Nĕḏarim*, xiii, 33. In ŠP, chap. IV, Maimonides states: "This subtle point, which is a canon and secret of the science of medicine, tells us that it is easier for a man of profuse habits to moderate them to generosity, than it is for a miser to become generous. Likewise, it is easier for one who is apathetic (and eschews sin) to be excited to moderate enjoyment, than it is for one burning with passion to curb his desires."

the mean," there is the *ḥasid*, who is "particularly scrupulous and deviates somewhat from the exact mean in disposition":

> For example, if one avoids haughtiness to the utmost extent and is exceedingly humble, he is termed a saint, and this is the standard of saintliness. If one only departs from haughtiness as far as the mean, and is humble, he is called wise, and this is the standard of wisdom. And so with all other dispositions. The ancient saints trained their dispositions away from the exact mean toward the extremes: in regard to one disposition in one direction, in regard to another in the opposite direction. This was supererogation. We are bidden to walk in the middle paths which are the right and proper ways, as it is said, *And thou shalt walk in His ways* (Deut. 28:9).[254]

This ethical option—a perfectly legitimate, if not superior, alternative—is not put forth in the *Šěmonah Pěraḳim*, where deviation from the mean is purely therapeutic or else prudential, i.e., in order to preserve the mean one moves a bit to either side. Preservation of the mean is a tightrope balancing act, hence the need for a measure of latitude and expansiveness. The goal remains adherence to the mean:

> On this account, the saintly ones were not accustomed to cause their dispositions to maintain an exact balance between the two extremes, but deviated somewhat, by way of (caution and) restraint, now to the side of exaggeration, now to that of deficiency. Thus, for instance, abstinence would incline to some degree toward excessive denial of all pleasures; valor would approach somewhat toward temerity; generosity to lavishness; modesty to extreme humility, and so forth. This is what the Rabbis hinted at, in their saying, "Do more than the strict letter of the law demands" (B.BM 35a).

There was no desire for, nor is this cited in defense of, permanent forms of asceticism or extremism. As a matter of fact, Maimonides unequivocally discountenances such a distorting application of these Rabbinic episodes and anecdotes:

---

254. *De'ot*, i, 5 (and see MN, III, 53). See, generally, H. Cohen, "Charakteristik der Ethik Maimunis," *Juedische Schriften* (Berlin, 1924), III, 269ff.; D. Rosin, *Die Ethik des Maimonides* (Breslau, 1876); S. Rawidowicz, *'Iyyunim bě-Maḥšebet Yiśra'el* (Jerusalem, 1969), I, 424ff.

When the ignorant observed saintly men acting thus, not knowing their motives, they considered their deeds virtuous in and of themselves; and so, blindly imitating their acts, thinking thereby to become like them, they chastised their bodies with all kinds of afflictions, imagining that they had acquired perfection and moral worth, and that by this means man would approach nearer to God, as if He hated the human body and desired its destruction. It never occurred to them, however, that these actions were bad and resulted in moral imperfection of the soul. Such men can only be compared to one ignorant of the art of healing, who sees skillful physicians curing patients at the point of death by administering [purgatives known in Arabic as] colocynth, scammony, aloe, and the like, and depriving them of food, and foolishly concludes that since these things cure sickness, they must be all the more efficacious in preserving health or prolonging life. If a person should take these things constantly and treat himself as a sick person, he would really become ill. Likewise, those who are spiritually well but have recourse to remedies will undoubtedly become morally ill.[255]

In short, the ethical type of *ḥasid*, the consistent and healthy radical and extremist, is conspicuously missing from the *Šĕmonah Pĕraḳim*.

The reason for this discrepancy—and it should not be glossed over or attenuated—is rather straightforward. In the *Šĕmonah Pĕraḳim*, Maimonides tries to rebut the contention of certain Jews that they are compelled by a desire for deeper spirituality to adopt non-Jewish ascetic practices. Here is an assimilation that seeks more rather than less, that wants a more stringent regimen rather than an unstructured life-style! In describing the Torah as the perfect embodiment of the golden mean, Maimonides is polemicizing against those Jewish contemporaries who were attracted by Sufi-inspired asceticism and renunciation of this-worldliness, and he argues energetically that the Torah is a delicately constructed instrument, designed to produce perfect spirituality through moderation; necessary restraint or self-denial and spur to spirituality has already been incorporated in this ideal constitution: "The perfect law which leads us to perfection—as one who knew it well testifies by the words, *The law of the Lord is*

---

255. ŠP, chap. IV. The interpretation of the Talmudic passage (B.BM 35a) does not, on the face of it, support Maimonides. See PhM, 'Ab 5:6 (p. 458), and 2:10 (p. 425).

*perfect, restoring the soul; the testimony of the Lord is sure, making wise the simple* (Ps. 19:9)—recommends none of these things (such as self-torture, flight from society, etc.)." One should not presume to improve upon perfection. Asceticism has been obviated by the built-in spirituality of the law. At one point, Maimonides is most explicit and blunt:

> But to resume. Should those of our coreligionists—*and it is of them alone that I speak*—who imitate the followers of other religions maintain that when they torment their bodies and renounce every joy, they do so merely to discipline the faculties of their souls by inclining somewhat to the one extreme, as is proper and in accordance with our own recommendations in this chapter, our answer is that they are in error, as I shall now demonstrate. The law did not lay down its prohibitions or enjoin its commandments except for just this purpose, namely, that by its disciplinary effects we may persistently maintain the proper distance from either extreme.

The concluding paragraph is also emphatic and unequivocal: "Now let me return to my subject. If a man will always carefully discriminate as regards his actions, directing them to the medium course, he will reach the highest degree of perfection possible to a human being, thereby approaching God and sharing in His happiness. This is the most acceptable way of serving God."[256] Obviously, recognition of the *ḥasid* type, with the possible implication that it is even superior to the *ḥakam* type, would dull the edge of the polemical thrust. Ascetic behavior or monastic lifestyle are only tolerable for limited purposes and restricted periods of time, but should never be adopted permanently or imitated indiscriminately.

We might add that one corollary of this distinction is to recognize the extent to which Maimonides' essentially favorable attitude to asceticism *is* reflected in the *Mishneh Torah*. The assertion that "qua philosopher, though not qua teacher of the

---

256. ŠP, chap. IV. The conclusion here is unequivocal: the *ḥasid* type of the MT is not superior. In the MT itself this is not clear. On Jews imitating Sufis, see S. D. Goitein, "A Jewish Addict to Sufism,"*JQR*, XLIV (1953), 37–49; and idem, "Abraham Maimonides and His Pietist Circle,"*Jewish Medieval and Renaissance Studies*, pp. 145–64. On the meaning of "perfect" as "equibalanced," see MN, II, 39, 40; note *Kuzari*, II, 50, on the equivalence of fear, joy, and love in the service of God. The emphasis that Maimonides is addressing his coreligionists is crucial in this context.

halakah, he favored asceticism" need not be qualified or hedged in this way. Halakah, which is antiascetic, imposes certain inescapable constraints, but what we are dealing with is divergent emphasis rather than contradiction.[257]

The motto of Book Twelve (Acquisitions) indirectly reveals the extent to which this attitude is mirrored also in the Code: *The beginning of wisdom is: Get wisdom; yea, with all thy getting, get understanding* (Prov. 4:7). The verse is prima facie irrelevant to a book concerned with the modes of acquisition of property and other goods, as well as the rights and responsibilities of ownership.[258] Recognition of its moralistic intent, however, makes it relevant. The only true acquisition is intellectual, as Maimonides, echoing the philosophers (Aristotle) and the prophets, contends in the concluding chapter of the *Moreh*. Of the four kinds of perfection, the "most defective" is the "perfection of possessions, that is, of what belongs to the individual in the manner of money, garments, tools, slaves, land, and other things of this kind." Maimonides continues to teach that "between this perfection and the individual himself there is no union whatever. . . . For if he considers his own individual self, he will find that all this is outside his self, and that each of these possessions subsists as it is by itself. . . . The philosophers have explained that the endeavor and the efforts directed by man toward this kind of perfection are nothing but an effort with a view to something purely imaginary, to a thing that has no permanence."[259] This must be the thrust and message of the verse: in all one's acquisitions, which are transitory and imaginary, only the acquisition of knowledge is real and abiding. Remember that acquisiton is one of the most practical and popular parts of halakah, a fact which is reflected in the special attention paid to post-Talmudic developments in the application of halakic principles, in the discussion of significant Gaonic precedents and contemporary practices. Waving the flag of learning and knowledge is thus especially meaningful and apposite—effective, subtle preaching.

257. Cf. S. Pines, translator's introduction, MN, p. lxvii.
258. On the introductory verses, see above, chap IV, and cf. D. Feuchtwang, Maimonides Supplement to *Haaretz*, 14 Nisan, 5695/1935. See G. Cohen, "Soteriology," *PAAJR*, XXXV (1967), 92, n.50.
259. MN, III, 54 (p. 634); A. Altmann, "Maimonides' Four Perfections," pp. 17–18.

Further, in opposition to most halakists, for example, Maimonides considered the case of Ben Azzai, who refused to marry lest marriage hinder or limit his study, as a normative precedent.[260] Generally, his attitude to sex is very stringent. Only "fools" indulge in "sexual excess."[261] The following generalization from the *Moreh* is completely applicable to the Code: "Similarly one of the intentions of the law is purity and sanctification; I mean by this renouncing and avoiding sexual intercourse and causing it to be as infrequent as possible."[262] Maimonidean critics find fault not only with his warm endorsement in the *Moreh* of the Aristotelian dictum that "the sense of touch is a shame for us," but also with certain halakic formulations of the *Mishneh Torah* as well.[263]

To be sure, Maimonides, in common with R. Bahya ibn Pakuda and Ibn Ezra, recognized the destructive potential of general asceticism and withdrawal—the motto was *Be not righteous overmuch; neither make thyself overwise; why shouldst thou destroy thyself?* (Eccles. 7:16)[264] He also knew, as did R. Saadiah Gaon[265] and other predecessors, that a monk who is not involved with his fellow man in trials and tribulations cannot show morality. Yet "withdrawing from the world," the specter of desolation notwithstanding, remained a lofty ideal. The potential prophet—and every individual is a potential prophet—is always "sanctifying himself, withdrawing from the ways of the ordinary run of men who walk in the obscurities of the time, zealously training himself not to have a single thought of the vanities of the age and its intrigues."[266] The clearest need seems to be the differ-

---

260. *'Iśut*, xiv, 15; xv, 2, 3; *Talmud Torah*, i, 5.
261. *De'ot*, iv, 19; *Mĕlakim*, iii, 6; see *Tĕšubah*, iv, 4; *Tĕfillah*, iv, 4; *'Issure Bi'ah*, xxi, 11. In PhM, Ḥag 2:1 (p. 378), Maimonides characterizes concupiscence as a rejection of reason.
262. MN, III, 33 (p. 533), and see III, 49 (p. 606); ŠP, chap. IV.
263. MN, III, 8 (p. 432). Cf. *De'ot*, iii, 2; and RABD, ad loc. See pseudo-Naḥmanides; *'Iggeret hak-Kodeš* in *Kitbe RaMBaN;* II, 323.
264. *Yĕsode hat-Torah*, v, 11; *Ḥobot hal-Lĕbabot*, viii, 3 (II, 260); R. Abraham ibn Ezra, to Eccles. 7:16; see B. Hor 13b. Note the use of this verse in MN, I, 32.
265. *'Ĕmunot wĕ-De'ot*, x, 1, 4.
266. *Yĕsode hat-Torah*, vii, 1, also ii, 12; *Talmud Torah*, iii, 12; and MN, III, 51. H. Blumberg, "Alfarabi, Ibn Bajjah, wĕha-RaMBaM 'al Hanhagot ham-Mitboded," *Sinai*, LXXVIII (1976), 135–45.

entiation between asceticism as a goal, reflecting contempt of the world, and asceticism as a means to achieve ethical inwardness and intellectual perfection or to intensify religious sensibility.

We have here a multifaceted dialectical attitude, but it is freely unfolded in the *Mishneh Torah,* and it is gratuitous to impose this dialectic upon an alleged ambivalence between the teacher of halakah and the disciple of Aristotle. Nor is it defensible to see it as an esoteric elitist view reserved for the *Moreh.* The treatment of vows and oaths in the *Mishneh Torah* is expressive of this. When formulating the ethical theory of the golden mean, Maimonides not only frowns upon but practically forbids the use of vows which increase abstinence and self-mortification:

> Of the Nazirite, it is said, *He (the priest) shall make atonement for him, for that he sinned by reason of the dead* (Num. 6:11). On this text, the Sages comment, "If the Nazirite who only abstained from wine stands in need of an atonement, how much more so one who deprives himself of all legitimate enjoyments." The Sages accordingly enjoined us that we should only refrain from that which the Torah has expressly withdrawn from our use. And no one should, by vows and oaths, inhibit to himself the use of things permitted. "Do not the prohibitions of the Torah," say our Sages, "suffice you, that you add others for yourself?"[267]

The opposition is sociological and theological, as reflected in Rabbinic hermeneutics. However, in the treatise on vows, there is a different climate and a changed and supple sensibility: "Whosoever makes vows in order to discipline his moral disposition and to improve his conduct displays commendable zeal and is worthy of praise. . . . All such vows are ways of serving God, and of them and their like the Sages have said, 'Vows are a fence around (for) self-restraint.' "[268] Concerning the Nazirite, previously unqualifiedly dismissed as a sinner, we are now reminded that there is need to ascertain his motive before passing judgment upon him:

> Whosoever says, "I intend to become a Nazirite if I do," or "do not do a certain thing," or something similar, is a wicked person, and this

---

267. *De'ot,* iii, 1; also ŠP, chap. IV.
268. *Nĕdarim,* xiii, 23.

type of Naziriteship is accounted the Naziriteship of the wicked. On the other hand, whosoever vows to God in the way of holiness does well and is praiseworthy. Of such a one Scripture says, *His consecration unto God is upon his head . . . he is holy unto the Lord* (Num. 6:7–8). Indeed Scripture considers him the equal of a prophet, for it says, *And I raised up of your sons for prophets, and of your young men for Nazirites* (Amos 2:11).[269]

In short, the immanently dialectical attitude toward carefully regulated and properly motivated vows and the balanced exposition of Naziriteship, undeniably elitist, are basically congruent with the philosophic stance of the *Moreh*. Use of vows is "training with a view to achieving temperance and to restraining the appetite for eating and drinking." The same Rabbinic source is cited: "Vows are a fence around (for) self-restraint [or abstinence]." As always, literary or exegetical overlap is noteworthy.[270]

*Overt acknowledgment of elitism*

It is perhaps most important to stress at this point that the recognition of elitism—the difference between the beliefs and motives of the masses and the insights and stimuli of philosophers—is a completely exoteric doctrine. The nature of some of its teachings may on occasion be ambiguous, but the phenomenon per se is unmistakable. The *Mishneh Torah* makes it perfectly clear that such differences exist and that hopefully there will be some ethical-intellectual mobility from the lower to the higher levels. There is, at the very outset, a definite elitist ethos for the wise man, the "man great in the knowledge of the Torah and reputed for his piety" or the "worthy one" who preoccupies himself only with the "words of Torah and wisdom."[271] It even finds expression in such specific matters as returning lost property: "If one follows the good and upright path and does more than the strict letter of the law requires, he will return lost property in all cases, even if it is not in keeping with his dignity."[272] There are also clearly formulated laws which should not be taught

---

269. *Nĕzirut*, x, 14; cf. J. Levinger, " 'Al Ṭa'am han-Nĕzirut," pp. 299ff. See *Kuzari*, II, 50, and III, 1.
270. MN, III, 48 (p. 600); also III, 35 (p. 537), and Maimonides' reference to ŠP.
271. *Yĕsode hat-Torah*, v, 11; *Ṭumĕ'at Ṣara'at*, xvi, 10; *De'ot*, v.
272. *Gĕzelah wa-'Abedah*, xi, 7, 17; *Roṣeaḥ*, xiii, 4. See also *Ta'ăniyyot*, v, 9.

# LAW AND PHILOSOPHY

publicly.[273] More remarkable is the fact that differences between the scientifically trained and the unlearned or innocent have even normative-halakic repercussions:

> It is well known to wise men endowed with understanding and knowledge that the sun is 170 times larger than the earth. If an ordinary person swears that the sun is larger than the earth, he is not liable to a flogging because of a false oath. For although the fact is as stated, this is not commonly known to any but the most eminent scholars, and no person is liable unless he swears about a thing well known to at least three ordinary persons, e.g., that a man is a man, or a stone a stone. Similarly, if he swears that the sun is smaller than the earth, even though this is not so, he is not liable to a flogging. For this subject is not familiar to all men, and it is therefore not like swearing that a man is a woman, as he is merely swearing about the way the sun appears to him, and he does indeed see it small. This holds good in all similar cases connected with calculations dealing with astronomical cycles, constellations, and geometrical measurements, and other scientific matters which are known only to some men.[274]

With regard to all matters of theory and practice, Maimonides tells us that the "greatest Sages" would have special exhortations and teaching for "their disciples who were understanding and intelligent." "The young, women, or the illiterate" should be guided and instructed differently in the hope that they will gradually advance from literalism and improper motivation to spiritualism and nobility of purpose.[275] The goals are identical but the media diverge, for the message, although precise, was not easily communicable; the actions are similar but the motives are dissimilar. Maimonides frequently contrasts the vulgar view, which he condemns, with the view of wise and knowledgeable people, which he advocates: "Let not the notion, expressed by foolish Gentiles and most of the *senseless folk* among Israelites, pass through your mind . . ." Concerning the spirituality of the future life, he urges the reader not to be influenced by the "foolish and silly Arabs" who imagine a corporeal hedonistic existence, but rather to adopt the view of the *ḥakamim* and the intelligent

---

273. *YomṬob*, iv, 9.
274. *Šĕbu'ot*, v, 22.
275. *Tĕšubah*, x, 1, 4.

who appreciate the beauty and purity of spiritual bliss.[276] The same contrast is underscored concerning belief in the "false and deceptive" magical practices.[277] Even the *Mishnah Commentary* reveals the duality between the philosophic view and the vulgar opinion.[278] Not only in the *Moreh* but also in his letters Maimonides emphasizes that he will not be deterred from the truth by mass criticism or disagreement. *Gĕnut he-hamon*, the contempt which the masses feel toward the elite, must be ignored.[279] Yet the initiated teacher must be patient with the unenlightened "till their knowledge increases and they have attained a large measure of wisdom. Then we reveal to them this secret truth, little by little.[280] What a lucid and unequivocal statement concerning esoteric doctrine and elitist status! There is a secret truth which is gradually revealed. Torah contains subjects of study for everybody, "those gifted with great intellectual capacity as well as those whose intelligence is limited."[281] Maimonides' sympathies are clearly with the former—they constitute the ideal religious type—and his hopes are that everyone, "according to his capacity," will try to approximate this ideal. There are "exceedingly profound topics, and not every intellect is able to grasp them."[282] In the light of these candid declarations, it seems that "suppression" of facts in certain contexts is an avowed pedagogic device and a necessity, rather than a calculated distortion.

276. *Tĕšubah*, v, 2 (italics mine); viii, 6. In MTH, 7, 37, Maimonides emphasized strongly that the average person is unable to think abstractly.
277. *'Akum*, xi, 16; see R. Abraham ibn Ezra, to Lev. 19:3.
278. PhM, Sanh, chap. 10 (p. 203).
279. MN, introduction (p. 16): "I am the man who, when the concern pressed him and his way was straitened, and he could find no device by which to teach a demonstrated truth other than by giving satisfaction to a single virtuous man, while displeasing ten thousand ignoramuses—I am he who prefers to address that single man by himself, and I do not heed the blame of those many creatures." *Koḇeṣ*, II, 16; MTH, 20. See R. Saadiah, *Sefer Hag-Galuy* (*Haś-Śarid wĕhap-Paliṭ*, ed. A. Harkavy), p. 152. The MN statement is reminiscent of Plato (*Gorgias*, 482): "Since I am one, it is better for me to disagree with the whole world than to be in disagreement with myself."
280. *Tĕšubah*, x, 5; the theme is not uncommon, but see Song Rabbah, i, 17: בשעה שתלמידיך קטנים תהי' מכבש לפניהם דברי תורה. הגדילו ונעשו ת'׳ח תהי' מגלה להם סתרי תורה.
281. *Yĕsode hat-Torah*, iv, 13.
282. Ibid., ii, 12.

# LAW AND PHILOSOPHY

Any esotericism by definition involves *suppressio veri*[283] and gradual unfolding of the truth. Since it is difficult to move abruptly from a strictly literal interpretation to a delicately allegorical understanding, the gap is, at best, slowly bridged. The cumulative effect of one allusion after another, a string of insights and flashes, will be noticeable: "I shall explain some large rules . . . that they may provide an opening for the understanding person."[284] Maimonides paints a picture of an exoteric reality, often pale and platitudinous, brightened, hopefully in increasing measure, by the rays of a luminous, exciting, but necessarily circumscribed esotericism.

### OTHER FEATURES: EXPLANATION OF DECREES

There are various other nonhalakic features which supplement the theme of philosophy and law and show its full scope and suppleness. One which grows directly out of our discussion of *ṭaʿame ham-miṣwot* is Maimonides' attempt, really restrained and rhetorically hedged, to confront those laws which, even more than *ḥukkim*, seem to defy explanation—decrees (*gĕzerat hak-Katub*).[285] Two examples which attracted the attention of the *riśonim* may suffice to illustrate this matter.

Concerning the sounding of the shofar, Maimonides writes:

Although the sounding of the shofar on New Year's Day is a decree of the Written Law, still it has a deep meaning, as if saying, "Awake, awake, O sleeper, from your sleep; O slumberers, arouse yourselves from your slumbers; examine your deeds, return in repentance, and remember your Creator. Those of you who forget the truth in the follies of the times, and go astray the whole year in vanity and emptiness which neither profit nor save, look to your souls; improve your ways and works. Abandon, every one of you, his evil course and the thought that is not good."

---

283. Cf. S. Pines, translator's introduction, MN, p. lviii; MN, introduction: causes of contradiction (p. 17).
284. *Yĕsode hat-Torah*, ii, 1; for "the understanding person," see *Deʿot*, vii, 7; *Kidduš ha-Ḥodeš*, xix, 16; MN, III, 49 (p. 613); *Tešubot*, II, 436 (p. 715): מבין ולבו נכון לטול דרך האמת.
285. *ʿIšuṭ*, xxv, 2: *gĕzerat hak-Katub* as opposite of *dibre ṭaʿam*. Also, LA, 229. See R. Abraham Maimonides, *Tešubot*, 97 (p. 144). See also the famous crux *Tĕfillah*, ix, 7.

## 472 INTRODUCTION TO THE CODE OF MAIMONIDES

There is a cross-reference in the *Moreh* to this explanation of the shofar as a symbolic call to awakening from lethargy and sharpening of sensitivity.[286] In explaining this decree, Maimonides does not emphasize flagrant transgression as much as he excoriates diversion from high purpose, immersion in drab unfruitful routine, and consequent deflection from creative-redeeming enterprise. The shofar helps one to return by deepening the aspiration to purposive action.

The decree which affirms that self-incrimination leading to capital punishment is halakically void is another case in point. Maimonides grapples with this principle and rather haltingly rationalizes it by recognizing a latent suicidal impulse in man:

> It is a Scriptural decree that the court shall not put a man to death or flog him on his own admission (of guilt). This is done only on the evidence of two witnesses. It is true that Joshua condemned Achan to death on the latter's admission, and that David ordered the execution of the Amalekite stranger on the latter's admission. But those were emergency cases, or the death sentence pronounced in those instances was prescribed by the state law. The Sanhedrin, however, is not empowered to inflict the penalty of death or of flagellation on the admission of the accused. For it is possible that he was confused in mind when he made the confession. Perhaps he was one of those who are in misery, bitter in soul, who long for death, thrust the sword in their bellies, or cast themselves down from the roofs. Perhaps this was the reason that prompted him to confess to a crime he had not committed, in order that he might be put to death. To sum up the matter, the principle that no man is to be declared guilty on his own admission is a divine decree.[287]

It is noteworthy that while Maimonides specifically mentions in the *Moreh* that it is possible to rationalize a *gĕzerat ḥak-Katub*, these specific attempts are made in the *Mishneh Torah*.[288]

---

286. *Tĕšubah*, iii, 4; MN, III, 43 (p. 571). See R. Joshua ibn Shu'ayb, *Dĕrašot*, 89b (for New Year's Day); R. Isaac Laṭif, " 'Iggereṭ hat-Tĕšubah," *Ḳobeṣ 'al Yad*, I (1885), 55, with emphasis on the great potential of creative interpretation.

287. *Sanhedrin*, xviii, 6; and RaDBaZ, ad loc., who actually utilizes *Roṣeaḥ*, i, 4. See N. Lamm, "The Fifth Amendment and its Equivalent in the Halakah," *Judaism*, V (1956), 53ff. A. Enker ("Self-Incrimination in Jewish Law," *Dine Israel*, IV [1974], cviii ff.) has properly distinguished between the confessing defendant and the confessing witness; they are legally different. See above, chap. II, n. 197.

288. LA, 229; see also 'Eduṭ, xiii, 15; xviii, 3; *Mamrim*, vi, 7; *Miḵwa'oṭ*, xi, 12.

After all, Maimonides did state in a famous responsum that his objective in composing the *Mishneh Torah* was to "bring matters close to reason" (*lĕ-ḳareb 'el haś-śekel*).[289] This objective—natural for a jurisprudent, a wise interpreter of law—was basic and all-encompassing: explaining laws, formulating them clearly and intelligibly, and generally riveting attention not only on the compatibility of religious law and reason but also on their interrelatedness. This is, in my opinion, how the programmatic declaration, apparently simple but really quite sticky, at the beginning of the *Mishneh Torah* should be understood: *dĕbarim bĕrurim, ḳĕrobim, nĕḳonim. Ḳĕrobim* means rational and intelligible, and like *bĕrurim* (clear), characterizes the entire *Mishneh Torah*. In one of his last references to the *Mishneh Torah*, Maimonides also emphasizes that he has explained and rationalized (again, *ḳarob*) difficult and profound matters. This rationalization is thus a leitmotif, as well as a major motive, of Maimonides' juridical activity.[290]

*Interpolation of ḥokmah*

Moving completely away from the realm of *ṭa'ăme ham-miṣwoṭ*, we may note a few instances where Maimonides demonstratively underscores the importance of extrahalakic learning by interpolating *ḥokmah* or some equivalent emphasis into his halakic formulations. Again, three interesting examples, selected from many, may suffice to concretize this persistent Maimonidean tendency.

---

289. *Tĕšubot*, 252 (p. 461); and III, p. 168 (S. Abramson's notes). Recent discussions include B. Benedikt, "Lĕ-Darko šel ha-RaMBaM," *Torah Šebbĕ-'al Peh* (Jerusalem, 1964), pp. 96 ff.; J. Levinger, *Darke ham-Maḥšabah ha-Hilḳaṭiṭ* (Jerusalem, 1965), pp. 21ff.; S. Rosenthal, " 'Al Dereḳ ha-Rob," *Pĕraḳim*, I (1968), 183ff. For *dereḳ ha-rob*, see, e.g., *Tĕšubot*, 224 (p. 399); PhM, 'Ed 2:9 (p. 299); *Yom Ṭob*, i. 20; *Tĕfillah*, vi, 7; MN, II, 39; III, 34; III, 49. Whatever this phrase means, *'el haś-śekel* is quite clear. See Simeon Duran, *Magen 'Abot*, introduction (p. 1a): אשר לא נמצא כמוהו מקרב הדברים אל המושכל. Note also R. Moses Isserles, *Toraṭ ha-'Olah*, I, chap. 2 (p. 21a): ובכל מה שאפשר לפרש דברי; חכמים ז"ל שלא יחלקו על המפורסם ולקרבן אל השכל, מה טוב ומה נעים, idem, *Tĕšubot*, 6 (statement of R. Solomon Luria). Of course, if one takes *dereḳ ha-rob* and *'elhaś-śekel* as expressing one idea—as do Benedikt and Levinger, each for a different reason—the sentence would refer to "that which is close to reason" because it is "a matter of frequent occurrence." Rosenthal's interpretation assumes that Maimonides would be free to do with the law that which the Lawgiver did initially—make it beneficial for the majority!

290. MT, introduction. See Twersky, "Sefer MT," p. 19, and above, p. 78.

## 474 INTRODUCTION TO THE CODE OF MAIMONIDES

First, the incorrigible professional dice thrower is decried and his "profession" discountenanced in the Talmud. Two explanations are offered for the strong disapproval: (a) gambling approximates robbery, inasmuch as the high odds are unjust and indefensible; (b) the gamblers themselves are not engaged in constructive work beneficial to humanity or in professions which further the welfare of society. In Maimonides' formulation of this law, which happens to be studded with difficulties, we need only note again the casual insertion and implicit exaltation of *ḥokmah:* "Playing dice . . . entails the prohibition of wasting time on useless pursuits, for it is not fitting for a person to spend any part of his life other than on studying wisdom and furthering civilization."[291]

Second, Maimonides' description of the procedure of conversion to Judaism vividly reflects his uniform insistence upon the indispensability of knowledge of the theoretical bases and theological premises of religion. A potential convert must be carefully informed about Judaism and instructed in its ritualistic patterns and, most emphatically, its metaphysics, its dogmatic principles—Maimonides emphasizes that the latter must be presented at great length.[292] Now the need to expatiate concerning the theological foundations, in contradistinction to the ritual commandments, is not mentioned in the Talmud. Some scholars were inclined to assume that Maimonides found these details in his text of the tractate *Gerim,* inasmuch as a few other variants can be traced to this source, but this seems to be a gratuitous assumption.[293] Given the Maimonidean stance, this emphasis is a logical

---

291. *Gĕzelah wa-'Ăbedah,* vi, 11; and see the emphatic formulation in PhM, Sanh 3:3 (p. 158).
292. *'Issure Bi'ah,* xiv, 2; see B. Yeḇ 47a, and the tractate *Gerim.* For another problem concerning conversion (*'Issure Bi'ah,* xiii, 10), see A. Munk, "Tĕšubah Ḥădašah la-RaMBaM," *Pĕraḳim,* II (1969–74), 329ff. See above, n.174.
293. See S. Rappaport, *'Oṣar Neḥmad,* I (1856), 30; F. Baer, *Tolĕdot hay-Yĕhudim bis-Sĕfarad han-Noṣriṭ* (Tel Aviv, 1945), p. 482. In *Zion,* XV (1950), 5, Baer has noted a striking parallel with Philo. The *Migdal 'Oz, 'Issure Bi'ah,* xiv, 2, offers no corroborative evidence for Rappaport, whose methodological assumption that every phrase and nuance of the MT is explicit in some source, is misleading. It fails to acknowledge the interpretative-derivative aspects of the MT. See MM, *'Issure Bi'ah,* xiv, 2: אינו מבואר בגמ' רק שפשוט הוא מעצמו; RaDBaZ, *Mattĕnot 'Ăniyyim,* x, 17. This is not in the category of a Maimonidean novelty, usually heralded by the formula "it seems to me," but an

corollary or even a self-evident component of the underlying text, which stipulates that the convert be informed about "some commandments." Selective instruction concerning Judaism and its commandments would be ludicrously inadequate or warped if it omitted the first and most important commandment of all—a true conception of the oneness of God. That this is a sustained emphasis is corroborated further in the same chapter, where Maimonides defines a truly righteous person, the person for whom the world to come was prepared, as the wise man (ba'al hă-ḥokmah) who practices and understands these commandments. This is also Maimonides' expository interpolation.[294] As a matter of fact, the entire presentation bristles with suggestive Maimonidean novelties which should not be glossed over and obscured.[295]

Third, the Talmud states that the unintentional killer who flees to a city of refuge should be provided with all the necessities and amenities of life. This statement is based on the verse *that he shall flee thither and live (wa-ḥay)* (Deut. 19:4), which is interpreted to mean "see to it that he lives properly."[296] The halakah subsumes under this provision that when a student flees to a city of refuge, his master is exiled with him. At this point Maimonides sounds his bell. Whereas the Talmud derives from this the admonition to teachers to screen their students,[297]

---

interpretative elaboration which in Maimonides' opinion is implicit in the text; see Twersky, "Beginnings," p. 164. See also RaDBaZ, *Šĕmiṭṭah wĕ-Yoḇel*, xiii, 13; MM, *Mĕkirah*, xiv, 14; *LM*, *Sanhedrin*, ii, 7. The MT clearly does not efface Maimonides' personality. It should be noted that when Maimonides says in his responsum (*Tĕšuḇot*, 345 [p. 618]) לא נגיח תלמוד ערוך ונפסוק הלכה ממשא ומתן של גמרא, this does not eliminate or minimize the role of his interpretative elaborations. See also *Tĕšuḇot*, 89. *Talmud 'aruk* presumes certain interpretations. See above, n. 182 and chap II, n. 188.

294. B. Yeḇ 47a, reads: אומרים לו הוי יודע שהעולם הבא אינו עשוי אלא לצדיקים. ומודיעין אותו שבעשית מצות אלו יזכה לחיי העולם הבא, xiv, 3, reads: *Issure Bi'ah*. See also *Tĕšuḇah*, ix, 1: ושאין שום צדיק גמור אלא בעל החכמה שעושה מצות אלו ויודען. העושה כל הכתוב בה ויודעו דעה גמורה (and above chap. III).

295. E.g., the application and interpretation of Hos. 11:4 in *Issure Bi'ah*, xiv, 2 (see the Talmudic use of this verse in B. Shab 89). It is noteworthy that many of these interpretative additions and philosophic amplifications were omitted by medieval writers, even those who lean heavily on Maimonides and often quote him verbatim. See ham-Me'iri, *Bet hab-Bĕḥirah*, *Yĕḇamot* (Jerusalem, 1962), p. 189; *Sefer Miṣwot Gadol*, negative 115; *Ṭur* and *Šulḥan 'Aruk*, *Yoreh De'ah*, 268.

296. Mak 10a; Deut. 4:42.

297. B. Ḥul 133a.

Maimonides underscores that the seekers of wisdom cannot live without study, inasmuch as such an unintellectual existence is tantamount to death.[298]

Maimonides' political conception of the Messianic period as an instrument of intellectual achievement should be mentioned here. Like every utopia it includes man's most profound aspirations, and by implication, his deepest fears. It is a dream not for a *renovatio imperii Judaeorum* but for a *renovatio studii;* the dread of obstacles, such as "sickness, war, famine, and other calamities" that hinder one in the study and fulfillment of the law, will be removed. It is restorative in a formal sense, in the same way that Abraham's promulgation of monotheism restored the primordial theological purity that prevailed at the time of Adam, or in the way that the medieval resuscitation of philosophy restored the classical state of affairs at the time of the early Talmudic Sages. In actuality, it is reformative, and hence quite innovative.[299]

Just as political adversity and abnormal historical conditions contributed to the eclipse of intellectual achievement in antiquity, so political normalcy will be supportive of intense intellectualism and spiritual elevation. As noted, the correlation of normalcy with intellectual grandeur and of adversity with atrophy is a constant of Maimonidean historiography and philosophy. In the light of this emphasis—applied, for example, to the disappearance of philosophy,[300] the decline of Talmudic learning,[301] and the contemporary intellectual deterioration of his own period[302]—his characterization of the Messianic period is natural and consistent. It will redress a serious imbalance: "Hence all Israelites and their prophets and Sages longed for the advent of Messianic times, that they might have relief from the wicked tyranny that does not permit them to occupy themselves properly

---

298. *Roṣeaḥ*, vii, 1: וחיי בעלי חכמה . . . בלא תלמוד תורה כמיתה חשובין. By leaving the remaining Talmudic inferences for *Roṣeaḥ*, viii, 8, this one is made even more emphatic (cf. *Sefer Miṣwot Gadol*, positive 76). Note also the very significant emphases in *Mĕkirah*, xiv, 14; *Sanhedrin*, ii, 1; iii, 7; *Gĕnebah*, viii, 1. Also *'Edut*, xvii, 1.

299. *Tĕšubah*, ix, 1. Arthur Ekirch has underscored the relationship between *Ideologies and Utopias* (Chicago, 1969); also R. Elliott, *The Shape of Utopia* (Chicago, 1970).

300. MN, I, 71; II, 32, 36; III, 6; IT, ii, xx. See above, chap. I.

301. MT, introduction; *Mamrim*, ii, 4; Twersky, "Sefer MT," p. 8, n.31.

302. *Ḳobeṣ*, II, 44. See A. Toynbee, *A Study of History* (London, 1954), VII, 279.

with the study of the Torah and the observance of the commandments; that they might have ease, devote themselves to getting wisdom, and thus attain to life in the world to come. For in those days knowledge, wisdom, and truth will increase." The *Mishneh Torah* concludes on the same note: "The Sages and prophets did not long for the days of the Messiah that Israel might exercise dominion over the world, or rule over the heathens, or be exalted by the nations, or that it might eat and drink and rejoice. Their aspiration was that Israel be free to devote itself to the law and its wisdom, with no one to oppress or disturb it, and thus be worthy of life in the world to come."[303] Unlike Philo,[304] for example, who sees prosperity per se as a self-contained component of the Messianic success, for Maimonides prosperity is merely instrumental, productive of congenial material conditions which make possible man's self-fulfillment. We may note, finally, that his conception is another pointed illustration of the balanced relationship between the overt collective orientation of religious goals and their ultimate individual orientation and purposiveness—an axial theme and challenge of all religious philosophy.[305]

Indeed, to mention a related example, just as intellectual achievement is the means to ultimate bliss—"Hence Israelites will be very wise, they will know the things that are now concealed, and will attain an understanding of their Creator to the utmost capacity of the human mind"—so intellectual lapse is the prime cause of monotheistic corruption and theological deviation.[306]

People, because of a false inference and generally faulty reasoning, assumed that cosmic forces, as divine agents, should be revered. This led ultimately to the memory of God's existence being lost. As idols, originally intermediaries, became objects of worship, the masses, easily satisfied with externals, allowed the

---

303. *Těšubah*, ix, 2; *Mělakim*, xii, 4.
304. Wolfson, *Philo*, II, 408.
305. There is really no need to differentiate between individual or collective emphasis in these areas, for the two are interrelated. This is the theme of J. Morrall, *The Medieval Imprint* (London, 1970), pp. 97ff.
306. '*Akum*, i (and ham-Me'iri, *Bet hab-Běḥirah*, '*Abot*, 22–23, for paraphrase and commentary); see above, chap. III. For another example (concerning Job), see MN, III, 22.

memory of God to be obscured and obliterated. Maimonides' historical conceptions are thus fully congruent with his contemporary perceptions and emphases—the value of intellectual probity on the one hand and the hazard of ritual externalization or routinization on the other. We see again how the reciprocity of action and knowledge, of moral virtue and intellectual virtue, appears in Maimonidean writing with the emphatic regularity of a poetic refrain.[307]

Maimonides' philosophic interpretation of Biblical books, elaborately developed in the *Guide,* and briefly stated or alluded to in the *Mishneh Torah,* adds another significant dimension. The Song of Songs, for example, depicts the soul's passionate yearning for communion with God. It describes the "love of God that is befitting," i.e., "to love the Eternal with a great and exceeding love, so strong that one's soul shall be knit up with the love of God, and one should be continually enraptured by it, like a lovesick individual whose mind is at no time free from his passion for a particular woman.... Even more intense should be the love of God in the hearts of those who love Him.... The entire Song of Songs is indeed an allegory descriptive of this love."[308] Similarly, the Book of Proverbs is to be understood as an allegory of the

---

307. PhM, AZ 4:7 (p. 357); 'Akum, i, 1; MN, I, 6, 36. Maimonides is very much concerned about Jews who still believe in charms—see 'Akum, xi, 16—hence the thrust of this section in PhM as well as the MT emphasis. His philosophical digressions are usually indispensable, in his opinion, for establishing or refining true opinions; see PhM, Ber 9:7 (p. 92). His struggle against anthropomorphic belief is of the same order (Tešubah, iii, 7; MN, I, 31, 36).

This intellectualism—the emphasis upon the importance of cognitive perceptions, of the purity of theory and theoretical guidelines—is not constricted to history or eschatology but has halakic repercussions as well. Note these two examples: (1) In 'Akum, iv, 6, Maimonides concludes, to the amazement of most commentators, that even women and children of an 'ir han-niddaḥat (a city all of whose inhabitants have been led into idolatry) are put to death. In MN, I, 54 (p. 127), Maimonides himself provides the explanation for his ruling: the ideological source of contamination must be eliminated in toto because its practical consequences are so damnable. (2) In 'Eḍuṭ, xi, 1–3, Maimonides emphasizes that an 'am ha-'areṣ (an ignorant person) is untrustworthy because his ignorance leads him to sin; cf. B. Ḳid 40b, and commentaries. Rashi explains it in terms of lack of self-respect (*bizzuy*); see 'Eḍuṭ, xi, 5. Note finally that Karaism also began as an intellectual error, as a simple misunderstanding, and then two unscrupulous individuals converted it into a tough sectarianism for purposes of personal benefit and profit; PhM, 'Aḅ 1:3 (p. 409).

308. Tešubah, x, 3 (cf. Yĕsoḍe hat-Torah, ii, 2, where it is not mentioned); MN, III, 51 (pp. 623, 628), and see above, chap. II, n. 159.

conflict between matter and form. While its "external meaning contains wisdom that is useful in many respects, among which is the welfare of human societies," its deeper meaning warns against "the pursuit of bodily pleasures and desires. . . . Accordingly he (Solomon) likens matter, which is the cause of all these bodily pleasures, to a harlot. . . . In fact his entire book is based on this allegory." Maimonides' intellectualistic exegesis of Job—Job was morally virtuous and righteous but not wise, for "knowledge is not attributed to him"—is also discernible.[309] As we have seen, the *Mishneh Torah* is relatively well stocked with philosophic interpretations of individual verses as well as aggadic passages, and their cumulative impact is significant.

*Attitude to "popular religion"*

Maimonides' elimination of objectionable beliefs and unworthy practices (perhaps vestigial pagan custom) is a pivot of his rationalistic-spiritualistic program. Anything which reflects gross theological error or smacks of magic or superstition—anthropomorphism, astrology, myth—must be exorcised or at the very least neutralized in order to maintain the purity of Jewish religious belief and ritual. Interpretation or omission are equally useful in pursuing this goal; one may criticize or condemn by stricture as well as by silence, by vehemently indicting or sardonically ignoring something. Scholars have already called attention to Talmudic dicta which are quoted by other codifiers but are omitted by Maimonides.[310] There are also dicta which are included in the *Mishneh Torah* but are given different reasons or contexts.[311] Most interesting are the instances of Maimonidean reinterpretation of well-known statements, often streaked with vehement criticism of perverse or deviant behavior resulting from improper understanding of the intent and integrity of a commandment.

---

309. MN, introduction (pp. 12–13); III, 8; and see below, n. 358. Naḥmanides (*Kitḇe RaMBaN*, I, 185) called attention to this Maimonidean interpretation. For Job, see MN, III, 22–24, and above, n. 179. Note also MN, III, 11; and *Mĕlaḵim*, xii, 1 (the use of Isa. 11:6). See I. Heinemann; "Die wissenschaftliche Allegoristik," *HUCA*, XXIII (1950–51), 626, n. 46. See below, n. 358.
310. See above, chap. III.
311. *Roṣeaḥ*, xii, 4, and RABD, *ad loc.*

A comprehensive example concerning theological naiveté and anthropological roguery is the treatment of the mĕzuzah. One chapter arraigns those who abuse this commandment:

> It is a universal custom to write the word *Šadday* ("Almighty") on the other side of the mĕzuzah, opposite the blank space between the two sections. As this word is written on the outside, the practice is unobjectionable. They, however, who write names of angels, holy names, a Biblical text, or inscriptions usually found on seals within the mĕzuzah, are among those who have no portion in the world to come. For these fools not only fail to fulfill the commandment but also treat an important precept that expresses the oneness of God, the love of Him, and His worship, as if it were an amulet to promote their own personal interests; for according to their foolish minds, the mĕzuzah is something that will secure for them advantage in the vanities of the world.

It is noteworthy that this theme is repeated in the *Moreh* as well as in the *Mishnah Commentary,* and the latter is even more vehement than the former.[312] Maimonides' opposition to this kind of popular religion was uniform and uncompromising. While he may look indulgently at divergent customs concerning the *Hallel,* he cannot but look censoriously at what he considers superstitious customs concerning the mĕzuzah.

The concluding paragraph of the next chapter in the *Mishneh Torah* suggests the proper perspective:

> A person should pay heed to the precept of the mĕzuzah, for it is an obligation perpetually binding upon all. Whenever one enters or leaves a home with the mĕzuzah on the doorpost, he will be confronted with the declaration of God's oneness, blessed be His holy name, will remember the love due to God, and will be aroused from his slumbers and his foolish absorption in temporal vanities. He will realize that nothing endures to all eternity save knowledge of the Ruler of the universe. This thought will immediately restore him to his right senses and he will

---

312. *Mĕzuzah,* v, 4; PhM, Soṭ 7:4 (p. 267); MN, I, 61 (p. 149). Generally, we are in a position to learn something about popular religion from the criticism, censure, calculated omission, and special pleading found in such a comprehensive work. See, e.g., *De'ot,* iii, 1; vi, 1; *Talmud Torah,* iii, 10; *'Akum,* xi, 16; *Tĕšubah,* v, 1; *Yom Ṭob,* vi, 18; *'Abel,* iv, 2; *Zĕkiyah u-Mattanah,* xii, 17 and MM. Such statements supplement the more obvious documents; cf. S. D. Goitein, "Religion in Everyday Life as Reflected in the Documents of the Cairo Genizah," *Religion in a Religious Age* (Cambridge, 1974), pp. 3ff.

walk in the paths of righteousness. Our ancient teachers said: He who has phylacteries on his head and arm, fringes on his garment, and a mĕzuzah on his door may be presumed not to sin, for he has many monitors, angels that save him from sinning, as it is said, *The angel of the Lord encampeth round about them that fear Him and delivereth them* (Ps. 34:8).

In the process the underlying Talmudic text is reinterpreted, transmuting the "angels" of the verse into the spiritual effects of the commandments.[313] Spiritualization and intellectualization are firmly allied.

Related to this is the unqualified prohibition of other quasi-magical uses—incantations, spells—of religious objects: "One who whispers a spell over a wound, at the same time reciting a verse from the Torah, one who recites a verse over a child to save it from terrors, and one who places a Scroll or phylacteries on an infant to induce it to sleep, are not only in the category of sorcerers and soothsayers, but are included among those who repudiate the Torah; for they use its words to cure the body, whereas these are only medicine for the soul, as it is said, *So shall they be life unto thy soul* (Prov. 3:22)." It is almost as if the recognition of intrinsic sacral qualities, and resultant efficacy in the natural realm, compromises the transcendence of God.[314]

Furthermore, Maimonides not only insisted upon the total repudiation of astrology and other superstitious practices but also demanded that this repudiation be motivated by rational conviction rather than reluctant compliance with a decree. One who believes these "false and deceptive" practices to have been arbitrarily forbidden by the Torah is "a fool, deficient in understanding":

These practices are all false and deceptive and were means employed by the ancient idolaters to deceive the peoples of various countries and induce them to become their followers. It is not proper for Israelites who

---

313. *Mĕzuzah*, vi, 13; see *Sefer Miṣwot Gadol*, positive 3.
314. *'Akum*, xi, 12, and MN, I, 42; see J. Avida, "Rĕfu'ah Šĕlemah," *Sinai*, VI (1959), 50ff. Note the following concessions: *'Akum*, xi, 11; *Šabbat*, xix, 14; *'Issure Bi'ah*, xxi, 31. None of these, however, relate to sacral objects—e.g., *Mĕzuzah*, vi, 4, and *Tĕšubot*, 268 (pp. 511ff.). *'Akum*, xi, 2, is preventive but not curative (and cf. MN, III, 51 [p. 626], for a totally different view of Ps. 91).

are highly intelligent to suffer themselves to be deluded by such inanities or imagine that there is anything in them, as it is said, *For there is no enchantment with Jacob, neither is there any divination with Israel* (Num. 23:23); and further, *For these nations, that thou art to dispossess, hearken unto soothsayers and unto diviners; but as for thee, the Lord thy God hath not suffered thee so to do* (Deut. 18:14). Whoever believes in these and similar things and in his heart holds them to be true and scientific and only forbidden by the Torah, is nothing but a fool, deficient in understanding, who belongs to the same class with women and children whose intellects are immature. Sensible people, however, who possess sound mental faculties, know by clear proofs that all these practices which the Torah has prohibited have no scientific basis but are chimerical and inane; and that only those deficient in knowledge are attracted by these follies and for their sake leave the ways of truth. The Torah, therefore, in forbidding all these follies, exhorts us, *Thou shalt be wholehearted (tamim) with the Lord thy God* (Deut. 18:13).[315]

This is a significant component of Maimonides' entire approach to the role of reason in religion, and hence his distaste for various manifestations of popular religion. There is a passionate insistence upon the purity of method, not only the correctness of result. The procedure, the modality, the motive—all are intrinsically significant,[316] and this unites the nature of his rejection of astrological practices, his attempt to maximize intention and inwardness, his indictment of poetry and hymnology,[317] his condemnation of *kalām* philosophy,[318] and his quest for reasons for the commandments. The echoes and reverberations of the cognitive motif are uniformly loud and clear.

We may, with a convenient sense of symmetry, proceed to link up this unconditionally negative attitude to assorted magical practices with an uncompromisingly positive attitude toward

---

315. *'Akum,* xi, 16; R. Abraham ibn Ezra, to Lev. 19:31. Cf. Naḥmanides, *Peruš,* Deut. 18:10, and R. Elijah Gaon, *Yoreh De'ah,* 179:13. For various interpretations of Deut. 18:13, cf. commentaries ad loc.; *Ḥobot hal-Lĕbabot,* introduction, p. 36. See, generally, J. Bazak, *Lĕ-ma'ălah min ha-Ḥušim* (Tel Aviv, 1968). Also L. Edelstein, "Greek Medicine in Its Relation to Religion and Magic," *Bulletin of the Institute of the History of Medicine,* V (1937), 201ff., especially p. 231.
316. *Tĕšubah,* x, 1.
317. MN, I, 59. *Tĕšubot,* 224 (pp. 398ff.). See above, chap. IV, n. 29.
318. MN, dedicatory epistle (p. 4); I, 71, 74.

medical practice. It is, first of all, forbidden to try to derive natural hygienic benefits from sacred objects. The Torah, while interested in the well-being of the body (*tiķķun hag-guf*), is medicine for the soul.[319] Furthermore, there is no need to attempt, or be tempted, to rely upon supernatural effects flowing from sacred objects inasmuch as the Torah commands and commends natural science. Cures for the body are readily available and should be utilized. Of course, in his insistence upon the preservation of life by maximum use of the best medicine, Maimonides is in the mainstream of traditional Jewish thought.[320] Nevertheless, his formulations and interpolations add nuances and emphases. Also, he frequently, sometimes in unexpected contexts, mentions doctors and medicine.[321]

The following classic formulation concerns the Sabbath and should be read in its entirety:

> The commandment of the Sabbath, like all other commandments, may be set aside if human life is in danger. Accordingly, if a person is dangerously ill, whatever a skilled local physician considers necessary may be done for him on the Sabbath.
>
> If it is uncertain whether the Sabbath needs to be violated or not, or if one physician says that violation is necessary and another says that it is not, the Sabbath should be violated, for the mere possibility of danger to human life overrides the Sabbath.

319. '*Akum*, xi, 12. Three points should be made: (1) While Maimonides emphasizes the well-being of the body as the goal of the law, he rules out magical procedures but finds natural-scientific procedures perfectly congruent with the overall pursuit of individual welfare and social good. (2) He particularly wants to rule out the therapeutic-practical use of sacred objects, so that they be not converted into amulets. *Ķĕdušah* generally (see above, chap. IV) means transcendence (cf., however, *Bet hab-Bĕḥirah*, vi, 16); it is not consequently an intrinsic quality which can be transferred. Note, in this context, *Šĕķenim*, vi, 6, where Maimonides uses the phrase "ha-Torah šomartam" (and see B. BB 7b). (3) The criticism of such people as R. Jacob ben Sheshet ('*Oṣar Neḥmad*, III [1860], 153ff.), that philosophers reduced laws to hygienic measures, does not apply to Maimonides (cf. MN, III, 48 [p. 599]). See also *Minḥat Ķĕna'ot*, 41, 46, 133, 153; I. Polgar, '*Ezer had-Dat* (reprinted, Jerusalem, 1970), chap. 2 (p. 7).

320. PhM, Ned 4:4 (p. 129); Pes 4:10 (p. 177), where Maimonides forcefully polemicizes with the view that condemns the use of medicine on religious grounds; Kel 1:5, and above, n.28. See *Kĕle ham-Miķdaš*, vii, 14 (and cf. Sheķ 5:1). See *Yoreh De'ah*, 336:1. The passage in PhM, Pes, has remained a locus classicus to this day; see, e.g., the criticism of R. Abraham Karelitz, *Ḥazon 'Iš: 'Inyĕne 'Ĕmunah u-Biṭṭaḥon*, chap. V.

321. E.g., *Malweh wĕ-Loweh*, xv, 1; *Roṣeaḥ*, ii, 8. Medicine could not impinge upon halakic tradition; see *Šĕḥiṭah*, x, 12.

If it is estimated on the Sabbath that a certain treatment is necessary and will have to be continued for eight days, one should not say, "Let us wait until evening, so as not to violate two Sabbaths"; rather, one should begin the treatment from that very Sabbath day, and as long as treatment is necessary and danger, or possibility of danger, persists, even a hundred Sabbaths may be violated. One may light a lamp, extinguish a lamp that is disturbing the patient, slaughter an animal, bake, cook, or heat water for the patient to drink or to wash with. In general, insofar as the needs of a person who is dangerously ill are concerned, the Sabbath is the same as a weekday.

When such things have to be done, they should not be left to heathens, minors, slaves, or women, lest these should come to regard Sabbath observance as a trivial matter. They should rather be done by adult and scholarly Israelites. Furthermore, it is forbidden to delay such violation of the Sabbath for the sake of a person who is dangerously ill, for Scripture says, *Which if a man do, he shall live by them* (Lev. 18:5), that is to say, he shall not die by them. Hence you learn that the ordinances of the law were meant to bring upon the world not vengeance but mercy, loving-kindness, and peace. It is of heretics, who assert that this is nevertheless a violation of the Sabbath and therefore prohibited, that Scripture says, *Wherefore I gave them also statutes that were not good, and ordinances whereby they should not live* (Ezek. 20:25).

The passage combines significant exegesis with sharp polemics.[322]

---

322. *Šabbaṭ*, ii, 1–3. The halakic components of this formulation and their relation to the Talmudic sources (especially B. Yoma 84b, Men 64a, and Alfasi, ad loc.) require careful analysis. Note also *Yĕsoḏe hat-Torah*, v, 1–6; *Šĕḥiṭaṭ 'Asor*, ii, 8 (and R. Aḥai Gaon, *Šĕ'iltoṭ*, i, 67); *Ma'ăḵaloṯ 'Asuroṯ*, xiv, 13–15; also *Roṣeaḥ*, i, 11; xii, 7. See the Gaonic text in L. Ginzberg, *Ginze Schechter*, I, 19.

The statement that the law is not vengeance must be intended to repudiate the old Christian contention that the law was punishment for Jewish recalcitrance and could therefore be abrogated in due time; see Justin Martyr, *Dialogue with Trypho*, n. 19; E. Goodenough, *The Theology of Justin Martyr* (Amsterdam, 1968), pp. 89, 92; and L. Barnard, in *Vetus Testamentum*, XIV (1964), 395ff. The verse from Ezekiel is commonly used in polemical literature. See the lengthy, three-fold discussion of this verse by R. Saadiah Gaon in the fragment edited by M. Zucker, *PAAJR*, XL (1972), 6–7. "Kofĕrim" (heretics) usually refers to Ḥiwi al-Balki. Note the use of this verse by Abraham ibn Daud, *Sefer hak-Kabbalah*, ed. G. Cohen, p. 49. As for the contrast between vengeance and mercy, note *Tĕfillah*, ix, 7. In *Mamrim*, iii, 1, " 'Epikoros" is equated with Karaite, but see above, n.183. See also S. Pines, "Some Traits of Christian Theological Writing in Relation to Moslem Kalām and to Jewish Thought," *Proceedings of Israel Academy of Sciences*, V (1973), 107ff.

## PERSONAL-PHILOSOPHIC INCLINATIONS AND HALAKIC FORMULATIONS

Caution is, however, called for in the correlation of cherished personal or philosophic views with decisions formulated in a halakic or exegetical context. As we have seen, it is possible to identify the nexus of ideas, sentiments, and motives which give Maimonides' juridical work its unique coherence. This nexus combined an awesome erudition, a conscious legal method, and an ingrained philosophic sensibility. A codifier may adopt deliberate anonymity up to a point, but then his individuality becomes visible. It does not have to be ceremoniously announced or emphatically underscored; it just breaks through and shines forth even without autobiographical reminiscence or ideological confession.

One must not automatically assume a purely philosophic impetus in everything, particularly when there might be compelling, or at least supporting, interpretative reasons. Halakah, after all, has objective constraints—special norms, canons, and categories. For example, Maimonides codifies the view that the proselyte may bring the first fruits (*bikkurim*) to Jerusalem and recite the appropriate Scriptural passage (Deut. 26), for it was said to Abraham, *The father of a multitude of nations have I made thee* (Gen. 17:5). Abraham is thus the father of all those in the entire world who convert to Judaism (come under the wings of the Divine Presence). A proselyte is thus considered a descendant of Abraham, is part of the covenantal community, and may legitimately and meaningfully repeat such expressions as *the land which the Lord swore unto our fathers to give us* (Deut. 26:3). These first person plural statements include the proselyte, who becomes a full-fledged member of this historic group, sharing its experiences and rememberances of things past as well as its expectations and hopes.[323] To be sure, this coincides with Maimonides' view, expressed with forceful eloquence in his letter to Obadiah the proselyte—a conscious or unconscious rebuttal of R. Judah hal-Levi—that converts to Judaism enjoy complete equality and are

---

323. *Bikkurim*, iv, 3. See J. Wijnhoven, "The Zohar and the Proselyte," *Texts and Responses*, ed. M. Fishbane (Leiden, 1975), pp. 120ff.

in fact objects of special love. This is a major thrust of Maimonides' spiritual conception of Judaism, in which biological factors are rather insignificant:

> You ask me if you, too, are allowed to say in the blessings and prayers you offer alone or in the congregation, *"Our God"* and *"God of our fathers,"* "Thou who hast sanctified *us* through Thy commandments," "Thou who hast separated *us*," "Thou who hast chosen *us*," "Thou hast inherited *us*," "Thou who hast brought *us* out of the land of Egypt," "Thou who hast worked miracles for *our* fathers," and more of this kind.
>
> Yes, you may say all this in the prescribed order and not change it in the least. In the same way as every Jew by birth says his blessing and prayer, you, too, may bless and pray alike, whether you are alone or pray in the congregation. The reason for this is that Abraham our father taught the people, opened their minds, and revealed to them the true faith and the oneness of God; he rejected the idols and abolished their adoration; he brought many children under the wings of the Divine Presence; he gave them counsel and advice, and ordered his sons and the members of his household after him to keep the ways of the Lord forever, as it is written, *For I have known him, to the end that he may command his children and his household after him, that they may keep the way of the Lord, to do righteousness and justice* (Gen. 18:19). Ever since then, whoever adopts Judaism and confesses the oneness of the Divine Name, as it is prescribed in the Torah, is counted among the disciples of Abraham our father, peace be upon him. These men are Abraham's household, and he it is who converted them to righteousness.[324]

However, this opinion concerning the status of proselytes could have been arrived at independently, using purely halakic categories and considerations. It is discussed in the Palestinian Talmud, and the normative conclusion is a subject of controversy between two prominent Tosafists, among whom there is no discernible difference in philosophic posture. While Maimonides' halakic formulation fits beautifully and naturally into the interstices of his philosophic outlook, the latter need not have determined the normative conclusion.[325]

In explanation of a certain case where it is recommended to persuade and compel a person, by use of sanctions and punish-

---

324. *Tĕšubot*, 448 (p. 727); also 293 (p. 549); see *Kuzari*, I, 27. Also *'Akum*, i, 3.
325. *Tosafot*, BB 81a. In *Ma'ăśer Šeni*, xi, 17, a *ger* is excluded. For the problem of correlation, see my *Rabad*, p. 49. Also J. Levinger, *Darke*, pp. 182 ff.

ments, to abide by the law, Maimonides defends the essential propriety, validity, and long-range prudence of this severe procedure:

> If a person who may be legally compelled to divorce his wife refuses to do so, an Israelite court may scourge him until he says "I consent". . . . And why is this writ of divorce not null and void, seeing that it is the product of duress . . . ? Because duress applies only to him who is compelled and pressed to do something which the Torah does not obligate him to do, for example, one who is lashed until he consents to sell something or give it away as a gift. On the other hand, he whose evil inclination induces him to violate a commandment or commit a transgression, and who is lashed until he does what he is obligated to do, cannot be regarded as a victim of duress; rather, he has brought duress upon himself by submitting to his evil intention. Therefore, this man who refuses to divorce his wife, inasmuch as he desires to be of the Israelites, to abide by all the commandments, and to keep away from transgressions—it is only his inclination that has overwhelmed him—once he is lashed until his inclination is weakened and he says "I consent," it is the same as if he had given the divorce voluntarily.[326]

Man's irrational nature overpowers him and leads him to transgression; he should be controlled, even by extreme coercion, for we assume that he really does not want to sin. One may detect here rumblings of a philosopher's insistence upon rigid discipline and impatience with moral or intellectual flabbiness; Maimonides unequivocally demands thought control just as he insists upon emotional discipline.[327] One may also read this passage as an emphatic restatement of the legal power of the court to force and enforce compliance with the law. Compulsion (*kĕfiyyah*) is a basic juridical concept.[328]

---

326. *Gerušin*, ii, 20 (and note Tos Sheḵ 1:6). See also *Yĕsoḏe hat-Torah*, v, 4; cf. Wolfson, *Philo*, I, 76.

327. ŠP, chap. I; ShM, negative 58 (and criticism of RABD in the MT listing); *Mĕlaḵim*, vii, 15. Naḥmanides, *Peruš*, Deut. 20:4, reports RABD's comment; also ShM, negative 47; MN, II, 46 (p. 589). See also *Gĕzelah wa-'Aḇedah*, i, 9, 10, and RABD. R. Abraham ibn Ezra and R. Abraham Maimonides disagree with the Maimonidean view. Maimonides' treatment of anthropomorphism is analogous; *Tĕšuḇah*, iii, 7; RABD, ad loc., and see my *Rabad*, pp. 282ff. Note ham-Me'iri, *Beṯ hab-Bĕḥirah*, *Kiddušin*, 202 (יש דברים שהמחשבה מעשה גמור).

328. E.g., *Sanhedrin*, xxiv, 4; *Mĕlaḵim*, iii, 10; xi, 4 (concerning the Messiah).

## 488 INTRODUCTION TO THE CODE OF MAIMONIDES

Similarly, any a priori attempt to straitjacket Maimonides or impose a modern "critical" stereotype on his work is indefensible. For example, one might expect a measure of historical criticism, the discernment of historical strata, etc., in the explanation of law. The fact is that there is relatively little of this in Maimonides even in cases where other Talmudists use it.[329] Nor is the assumption or conjecture that Maimonides the philosopher would always adopt a lenient interpretation tenable or profitable. Here too there are numerous examples to the contrary.[330] There are halakic definitions in the *Mishneh Torah*—e.g., the teleological definition of a *šoṭeh* (mentally incompetent person)—which differ radically from the definitions proposed by other interpreters or codifiers, but again the philosophic impetus remains moot.[331] Finally, any implication that Maimonides used *ṭa'āme ham-miṣwoṯ* to tamper with the halakah must be firmly resisted. *Ṭa'āme ham-miṣwoṯ* were not seen as an instrument of reform or change or as a license for laxity and flippancy, even though they could be misused and misconstrued. Their purpose was to invigorate the law, add a philosophic sensibility, but not to violate it.[332]

PHILOSOPHY AS AN INTEGRAL PART OF TALMUD

The legitimacy, cohesiveness, and inner consistency of these assorted references, explanations, and emphases, apparently be-

---

329. *Gĕzelah*, i. 4; and *Tosafoṯ*, BK 94a. For another issue (polygamy), see RIṬBA, *Ḥiddušim*, Yeb 44a, where he refers to the influence of Muslim custom, and M. Friedman, *Tarbiz*, XL (1971), 320–59. See above, n.123. Note also RaDBaZ, *Mĕlakim*, vii, 4.

330. *Šabbaṯ*, xix, 8; and *Tosafoṯ*, Shab 64b. For the contrary assumption, and allegation, that Maimonides shrewdly presented the image of a stringent codifier, see I. Twersky, "R. Joseph Ashkenazi," *Salo Baron Jubilee Volume* (Jerusalem, 1975), p. 194. Maimonidean antagonists—see above, n.224, concerning R. Shem Ṭob—assumed that Maimonides was smart enough to pretend and to concede in certain areas. See Maimonides' own statement about leniency in *Tĕšuboṯ*, 310 (p. 578).

331. *'Edut*, ix, 9; and see Bazak (cited in n.40, above). The elimination of prophecy from halakah is another interesting case; see *Yĕsode hat-Torah*, ix, 1, 4; PhM, introduction (p. 4). Cf. R. Judah hal-Levi, *Kuzari*, III, 41, and see E. Urbach, "Halakah u-Nĕbu'ah" *Tarbiz*, XVIII (1947), 1ff. As for the selection of one or another Talmudic view, see B. Ker 5a (R. Jose) and *Kĕle ham-Mikdaš*, i, 2, which eliminates a miraculous feature (note ibid., vii, 14). Note also *Roṣeah*, i, 9 (especially the phrase *tib'o šel 'olam*), and *Tĕšuboṯ Ḥawwoṯ Ya'ir*, n.31. Also, *Ṭumĕ'at Ṣara'at*, xvi, 10; *Tĕšuboṯ*, 436 (p. 715).

332. This is the question of *daršinan ṭa'āma' di-kĕra'*; e.g., *Malweh wĕ-Loweh*, iii, 1.

# LAW AND PHILOSOPHY

yond the scope of the Oral Law, can perhaps be clarified in the light of one axial statement in the *Mishneh Torah,* a statement which was capable of working a silent revolution in Jewish intellectual history:

> The time allotted to study should be divided into three parts. A third should be devoted to the Written Law; a third to the Oral Law; and the last third should be spent in reflection, deducing conclusions from premises, developing implications of statements, comparing dicta, studying the hermeneutical principles by which the Torah is interpreted, till one knows the essence of these principles, and how to deduce what is permitted and what is forbidden from what one has learned traditionally. This is termed Talmud.
>
> For example, if one is an artisan who works at his trade three hours daily and devotes nine hours to the study of the Torah, he should spend three of these nine hours in the study of the Written Law, three in the study of the Oral Law, and the remaining three in reflecting on how to deduce one rule from another. The words of the prophets are comprised in the Written Law, while their exposition falls within the category of the Oral Law. The subjects styled *Pardes* (esoteric studies) are included in Talmud. This plan applies to the period when one begins learning. But after one has become proficient and no longer needs to learn the Written Law, or be continually occupied with the Oral Law, he should, at fixed times, read the Written Law and the traditional dicta, so as not to forget any of the rules of the Torah, and should devote all his days exclusively to the study of Talmud, according to his breadth of mind and maturity of intellect.

This unusually expansive, almost prolix, formulation is based on the following concise, almost epigrammatic, saying in the Talmud: "One should always divide his years into three: [devoting] a third to Scripture, a third to Mishnah, and a third to Talmud."[333] Maimonides has here dramatically inverted the usual procedure which leads him to condense lengthy Talmudic statements.

The Maimonidean paraphrase is highly problematic and the following items require explication: (a) the nonchalant substitution of what appears to be the genus for a species, in other words "Oral Law" for "Mishnah"; (b) the designation of "Gemara" or

---

333. *Talmud Torah,* i, 11, 12; B. Ḳid 30a. See above, chap. I, n. 170.

"Talmud"[334] as an independent unit of study, distinct from the "Oral Law," and the inclusion of metaphysics and the natural sciences in this third unit of study. A precise definition of the terms "Mishnah" and "Gemara" according to Maimonides, determination of their scope, and definition of their relations will help resolve these difficulties. It would be helpful perhaps to indicate the conclusions and then provide the documentation:

First, Mishnah and Gemara are exactly coterminous in scope—complete, unabridged summaries of Oral Law.

Secondly, they differ in method and form, Mishnah being apodictic and popular while Gemara is analytic and technical, but they are alike in purpose and actual achievement. Gemara is to Mishnah what rational demonstration (*mofet*) is to traditional belief (*kabbalah*). Its essence is independent reflection, conceptualization, and interpretative elaboration or innovation.

Finally, philosophy is an integral, even paramount component of this Oral Law, and like halakah proper, can be presented either in apodictic and catechetic summary or in analytic and demonstrative elaboration.

That Maimonides equates Mishnah with the Oral Law in his paraphrase of B. Kid 30, interpreting it to mean the authoritative corpus of the entire Oral Law, is not really perplexing upon closer scrutiny. The basic text of the Oral Law in toto is the work redacted by R. Judah han-Naśi', the Mishnah. *Every other work*—Tannaitic or Amoraic—stands in interpretative-commentatorial, but not actually innovating, relation to the Mishnah. Maimonides repeats this assertion, carefully and consistently, in his introductions to the *Commentary on the Mishnah* and the *Mishneh Torah*. The purpose of the Sifra and Sifre is "to explain the principles of the Mishnah," while the function of the Tosefta is "to explain the subject matter of the Mishnah." The same is true for the Baraita, whose purpose is "to elucidate the words of the Mishnah." This interpretative relation characterizes also the Talmud, the Palestinian as well as the Babylonian; both continue the task of explanation. One of the four goals that R. Ashi set for

---

334. The terms are interchangeable; see variants on this passage of *Talmud Torah* in the new edition of *Sefer ham-Madda'* (Jerusalem, 1964; editor-in-chief, S. Lieberman).

himself in the compilation of the Talmud was to reveal the principles, methods, and proofs utilized in the Mishnah.[335] Explanation (be'ur) is the major feature of all these works. In the light of this we may perhaps explain the fact that Maimonides frequently uses the term "Talmud" when he is actually quoting the Tosefta,[336] for they are generically identical. Mishnah, in brief, represents the entire Oral Law.

Mishnah differs from Gemara only in that its contents are cast in an apodictic mold—and this is the second characteristic or connotation of the term. Mishnah includes the normative conclusion, the obligatory *miṣwah*, without excessive explanation or review of the process of exegesis and inference. It is for this reason that in many different contexts the terms *mishnah*, *miṣwah*, and *halakah* (or *hilkĕta'*) are interchangeable and used freely as equivalents.[337] The following instance is especially significant. The introduction to the *Mishneh Torah* begins: "All the precepts which Moses received on Sinai were given together with their interpretation, as it is said, *And I will give thee the tables of stone, and the law (Torah), and the commandment (miṣwah)* (Exod. 24:12). 'The law' refers to the Written Law, 'and the commandment' to its interpretation. God bade us fulfil 'the law' in accordance with 'the commandment.' This commandment refers to that which is called the Oral Law." Here the equation of *mishnah*, *miṣwah*, and *Torah šebbĕ-'al peh* is sharply delineated. That this is a conscious equation, carefully reasoned and consistently maintained, is clear from the cross reference to it in a subsequent book of the *Mishneh Torah*.[338] The Talmudic source (B. Ber 5a) for this was noted for

---

335. PhM, introduction (pp. 34–35). In *Ḳobeṣ*, I, 25b, Maimonides refers to "the Talmud which is *peruš ham-Mišnah*"—a phrase found in R. Abraham ibn Ezra, *Yĕsod Mora'*, I, 12. On Mishnah as synonymous with Oral Law in later kabbalistic literature, see R. J. Z. Werblowsky, *Joseph Karo* (London, 1962), pp. 268ff., especially the quotation from R. Moses Cordovero on p. 273. See also S. Abramson, "Mišnah u-Talmud," *Sefer Dov Sĕdan* (Jerusalem, 1977), pp. 23ff.

336. See, e.g., S. Lieberman, *Tosefta ki-Fĕšuṭah, Zĕra'im*, p. 637, n.1; p. 642, n.25; p. 645, n.38; and others.

337. B. Ḳid 49b, and *'Išuṭ*, viii, 4. Also *Tĕfillah*, vii, 10–11. See R. Hai Gaon in *Tĕšubot hag-Gĕ'onim*, ed. A. Harkavy, 262 (p. 135); ibid., ed. S. Assaf (Jerusalem, 1927), 58 (p. 68).

338. "*Miṣwah zu . . . nikreṭ Torah šebbĕ-'al peh*"; *Šĕḥiṭah*, i, 4.

the first time apparently by R. Elijah Gaon of Vilna.[339] Happily, we now have the explicit testimony of R. Abraham Maimonides to the effect that this "explanation of the *tradentes*" indeed underlies the opening statement of the *Mishneh Torah*. What is more, our general thesis which has Maimonides equating Mishnah with the Oral Law as a whole (or *mishnah* and *miṣwah*) is fully corroborated by R. Abraham, who asserts very forcefully, almost dramatically, that *mishnah* refers not to a given text but to the "principles [sources] of tradition."[340] Mishnah refers to the traditional corpus of the Oral Law, and Talmud is its ever-expanding commentary.

As a final illustration we turn to the passage in the oft-quoted letter of Maimonides to R. Phinehas, the judge of Alexandria.[341] In defending the purpose and nature of the *Mishneh Torah*, Maimonides defined the structural and stylistic differences between *peruš* and *ḥibbur*, discursive commentary and monolithic code, justifying his own opus by characterizing it as *ḥibbur*. What has not been stressed in this passage is the telling equation of *ḥibbur* with the "way of the Mishnah" and *peruš* with the "way of the Talmud"; in other words, two approaches to, or two presentations of, the same material. Maimonides then proceeds to equate his own work not only with the Mishnah but with the "way of the Mishnah," which can now be paraphrased as follows: the *Mishneh Torah*, a complete summary of Oral Law, is equal to the Mishnah in its comprehensive scope and apodictic method. This is further substantiated by all Maimonidean descriptions of his Code.[342] If one were to conflate them, the following characterization would emerge: an authoritative summary and guide for the entire Oral Law, practical and nonpractical, modeled upon the genre as well as the style of the Mishnah and obviating the need for exacting analysis of Talmudic demonstration and ar-

---

339. *'Ăbodat ham-Melek*, ad loc. Cf. W. Bacher, "Die Agada in Maimunis Werken," *MbM*, II, 145, n.1, who treats this as Maimonides' own formulation.
340. R. Abraham Maimonides, *Peruš*, pp. 382–84.
341. *Ḳobeṣ*, I, 25b.
342. See chap. I, above. On the term "Mishneh Torah" as "a presentation (or formulation) of the Torah," see R. Solomon Duran, *Milḥemet Miṣwah* (1869), end. He cites the phrase *mišneh tĕfillah* used in *Tĕfillah*, i, 2.

gumentation, and on the basis of which one will be able to know in capsule form the contents of *Torah šebbĕ-'al peh*. Especially significant is the elimination of Talmudic "depth study."

A component of Gemara, which deserved special mention alongside of that "which is forbidden or permitted, clean or unclean," is philosophy, or *Pardes*. Let us note immediately a formal resemblance between these two parts of Gemara: both are uniformly described as demanding "a broad mind, a wise soul, and prolonged study." The same qualities of mind and prerequisites of knowledge are prescribed for both branches of Gemara study.[343]

The inclusion of philosophy in the Oral Law had already been established by Maimonides in an earlier chapter of the *Sefer ham-Madda'* where, following what he elaborated in his *Commentary on the Mishnah*, he reiterated the identification of *ma'ăśeh bĕre'šit* with physics and *ma'ăśeh merkabah* with metaphysics:

> The topics connected with these five precepts, treated in the above four chapters, are what our wise men called *Pardes*, as in the passage, "Four went into the *Pardes*" (B. Ḥag 14b). And although those four were great men of Israel and great Sages, they did not all possess the capacity to know and grasp these subjects clearly. Therefore, I say that it is not proper to dally in the *Pardes* till one has first filled oneself with bread and meat; by which I mean knowledge of what is permitted and what is forbidden, and similar distinctions in other classes of precepts. Although these last subjects were called by the Sages "a small thing" (when they say, "a great thing, *ma'ăśeh merkabah*; a small thing, the discussion of Abbaye and Raba"), still they should have the precedence. For the knowledge of these things gives primarily composure to the mind. They are the precious boon bestowed by God, to promote social well-being on earth, and enable men to obtain bliss in the life hereafter. Moreover, the knowledge of them is within the reach of all, young and old, men and women, those gifted with great intellectual capacity as well as those whose intelligence is limited.[344]

I would call attention, however, to a proof-text which Maimonides introduces here for the first time and whose relevance

---

343. ShM, introduction; MT, introduction; *Yĕsode hat-Torah*, iv, 13; *Talmud Torah*, i, 13.
344. *Yĕsode hat-Torah*, iv, 13.

is established by his interpreting it with a crushing literalism. The Talmud reports in praise of R. Johanan ben Zakkai that he studied everything: "He did not leave (unstudied) Scripture, Mishnah, Gemara, Halakah, Aggadah, details of the Torah, details of the Scribes, inferences a *minore ad majus*, analogies, calendrical computations, *gĕmaṭriyyoṭ*, the speech of the ministering angels, the speech of spirits, and the speech of palm trees, fullers' parables and fox fables, great matters or small matters. 'Great matters' mean the *ma'ăśeh merkabah*, 'small matters' the discussions of Abbaye and Raba."[345] The consensual explanation of this concluding passage, which describes the Talmudic deliberations (Abbaye and Raba symbolizing all the Amoraim) as a "small matter," is that all the future queries of the Amoraim were crystal clear to R. Johanan ben Zakkai and his Tannaitic colleagues. They did not have to struggle with these questions because they had all the answers and the subject matter was smooth and unproblematic. Later generations, further removed from the original teachings, were marked by a decline in knowledge and insight and therefore had many sharp questions. This explanation is found in the *'Iggereṭ R. Sherira Gaon*, the commentaries of R. Hananeel, R. Gershom, and Rashi, and in the *Peruš Sefer Yĕṣirah* of R. Judah of Barcelona,[346] and continues to prevail in post-Maimonidean writing. It should be noted that R. Judah hal-Levi also quotes this passage but, fortuitously or prudentially, cites a shorter version,[347] omitting the crucial conclusion, and thereby evades the interpretative issue. Maimonides, realizing that this passage provided him with a powerful prop for his position, takes the phrases "great matter" and "small matter" at face value, thereby buttressing his argument concerning the nobility and superiority of metaphysics. As in the famous palace metaphor of the *Guide*, *ma'ăśeh merkabah* emerges as the summit of *Torah šebbĕ-'al peh*. The need for arduous preparation for the ascent, a pervasive theme of Maimonides, is also stressed in passing.[348] That

---

345. B. Suk 28a, BB 134b, and commentaries.
346. *'Iggereṭ R. Šerira Gaon*, ed. B. M. Lewin (Haifa, 1921), pp. 8–9; *'Oṣar hag-Gĕ'onim* on *Sukkah*, *Perušim*, 28a (p. 95); *Peruš Sefer Yĕṣirah*, ed. S. J. Halberstam (Berlin, 1885), p. 101.
347. *Kuzari*, III, 65; see ARN, xiv; Sof xvi.
348. MN, III, 51; I, 31–34; PhM, introduction (p. 38).

Maimonides maintained this unprecedented explanation of the Talmudic passage is seen from his repetition of it in one of his letters to Ibn Aknin.[349] His ardent protagonist R. Jacob Anatoli also repeats this literal explanation as if it were routine.[350] The mainstream of Talmudic exegesis, however, continues to carry the standard Gaonic explanation.[351] One writer, in obvious deprecation of the Maimonidean view, even adds that the Gaonic explanation is "true and correct for every believer, and not as others have explained".[352] R. Joseph Karo bemoans the fact that Maimonides wrote what he did.[353]

This conviction that *Pardes* is an integral and indispensable part of Oral Law led Maimonides to frequent tours de force in interpreting Talmudic maxims. In his commentary on *Pirḳe 'Aḇot*, a rich hunting ground not yet explored systematically, Torah is regularly interchanged with *ḥokmah*. Maimonides introduces *ḥokmah* into the opening statement of Simeon the Just and notes curtly, "This is what he meant by Torah."[354] When only "Torah" appears in the underlying passage, Maimonides interprets it to include *ḥokmah* as well. When "Torah" and "*ḥokmah*" both appear, their separate identity or autonomy is maintained. The Rabbinic description of Moses as "a father in Torah, a father in wisdom (*ḥokmah*), and a father in prophecy" is a favorite theme for Maimonides, because, he says, it vigorously differentiates between Torah and *ḥokmah* while establishing their precise relation.[355] All this interpretative energy, skill, and pressure are compressed in Maimonides' adaptation of the following Talmudic maxim: "The Holy One, blessed be He, has nothing in His world but the four cubits of halaḵah alone." Halaḵah is, of course, metamorphosed by Maimonides so that it emerges several pages later as including not only positive law but also all other sciences

---

349. *'Iggĕrot*, 57.
350. Jacob Anatoli, *Malmaḏ hat-Talmiḏim* (Lyck, 1866), p. 11; Profiat Duran, *Ma'ăśeh 'Efoḏ*, p. 7, alludes to it.
351. E.g., ham-Me'iri, *Bet hab-Běḥirah*, *'Aḇot*, p. 59.
352. *Ḥidduše ha-RIṬBA, Sukkah*, 28a. See *Ḥiddušim* of R. Aaron hal-Levi (who was RIṬBA's teacher) in *Ginze Rišonim*, ed. M. Hershler (Jerusalem, 1967), p. 95.
353. *KM, Yěsoḏe hat-Torah*, iv, 13.
354. 'Aḇ 1:2. See above, n.97.
355. B. Meg 13a; MN, III, 54; PhM, 'Aḇ 4:4 (p. 439). See R. Simeon Duran, *Magen 'Aḇot* on 'Aḇ 3:13.

as well.[356] No comprehensive description of the components of Torah will be allowed to omit ḥokmah.[357]

A striking illustration of the ease with which Maimonides identified and interchanged Torah and ḥokmah is found in two adjacent chapters of the *Mishneh Torah*. One proven way to avoid or escape from distracting thoughts, particularly sexual fantasy, is to turn one's mind to the "words of the Torah, which is *a lovely hind and a graceful doe* (Prov. 5:19)." The section then concludes with an amalgamation of Torah and ḥokmah: "But above all this, as the Sages have declared, a man should direct his mind and thoughts to the words of Torah and enlarge his understanding with wisdom, for unchaste thoughts prevail only in a heart devoid of wisdom, and of wisdom it is said, *A lovely hind and a graceful doe.*"[358] Concupiscence is thwarted by study of Torah and/or ḥokmah.

There are many other instances where Maimonides demonstratively interpolates ḥokmah or an equivalent emphasis into his formulations: "One should always cultivate the habit of silence and only converse on words of wisdom. . . . So too in discussing Torah and wisdom";[359] "But the conversation of the worthy ones of Israel is none other than words of Torah and wisdom."[360] Whereas Ibn Daud, for example, consistently speaks of Torah and ḥokmah as two separate entities, Maimonides regularly fuses them.[361]

Furthermore, Maimonides' halakic formulation, which grafts philosophy onto the substance of the Oral Law, dovetails perfectly with his view on the history of philosophy. In common with many medieval writers, Jewish, Christian, and Muslim,

---

356. B. Ber 8a; PhM, introduction (p. 39). See RaSHBA, *Ḥiddušé 'Aggadot* (Jerusalem, 1966), introduction.

357. For ḥokmah in Talmudic sources, see L. Ginzberg, *Perušim wĕ-Ḥiddušim* (New York, 1961), IV, 19–31; S. Lieberman, in *Biblical and Other Studies*, p. 132. It is obvious that Maimonides could have easily read his meaning of ḥokmah into a good number of the original sources.

358. *'Issure Bi'ah*, xxi, 19; xxii, 21. See *Kobeṣ*, I, 12a (49). This use of the Book of Proverbs reflects the Maimonidean perception (MN, introduction, [p. 12]) of the book as an allegory of the conflict between matter and form. See also MN, I, 30.

359. *De'ot*, ii, 4, 5.

360. *Ṭumĕ'at Ṣara'at*, xvi, 10.

361. Abraham ibn Daud, *Sefer haḳ-Ḳabbalah*, ed. G. Cohen (Philadelphia, 1967), p. 87.

## LAW AND PHILOSOPHY

Maimonides is of the opinion that Jews in antiquity cultivated the science of physics and metaphysics, which they later neglected for a variety of reasons, historical and theological. He does not, however, repeat the widespread view, as does hal-Levi, that all sciences originated in Judaism and were borrowed or plagiarized by the ancient philosophers. Hal-Levi, echoing a Philonic view, states: "The roots and principles of all sciences were handed down from us first to the Chaldeans, then to the Persians and Medes, then to Greece, and finally to the Romans."[362] That Maimonides does not subscribe to this view of the Jewish origin of all wisdom has been inferred—a kind of argument *ex silentio*—from his formulation in the *Guide,* where he merely establishes the antiquity of philosophy per se. It seems to me that this is clearly noted by Maimonides in the introduction to his *Commentary on the Mishnah,* where, in buttressing an argument, he says that this matter is known to us not only from the prophets but also from the wise men of the ancient nations "even though they did not see the prophets or hear their words."[363] Maimonides does not care to trace all philosophic wisdom back to an ancient Jewish matrix. His sole concern is to establish *ḥokmah* as an original part of the Oral Law, from which it follows that the study of the latter in its encyclopedic totality—that is, Gemara—includes philosophy. This is the position—a harmonistic position unifying the practical, theoretical, and theological parts of the law—which Maimonides codified in the *Mishneh Torah.*

However, whether or not all science originated in Hebrew lore, whether or not the Torah is the *principium sapientiae* of the whole world, philosophy is by nature universal. Hence Maimonides naturally assumes the *identity* of that classical philosophic tradition of Judaism which was lost with that study of philosophy

---

362. MN, I, 71; *Kuzari*, II, 66. See Wolfson, *Philo*, I, 163.
363. PhM, introduction (p. 42). The same independent parallelism is reflected in the following parenthetic remark concluding a long and passionately polemical chapter concerning human freedom (*Teŝubah*, v, 5): "It is not because of religious tradition alone that this is known, but also by clear proofs furnished by the works of wisdom (*ḥokmah*)." See MN, I, 8 (p. 34). Also LA, 233 ("It is one of the roots of the religion of Moses, and one that all the philosophers also acknowledge").

which was in his own day being restored under foreign influence. He need not be uncomfortable or apologetic when in his reconstruction of the history of philosophy he acknowledges the non-Jewish, primarily Muslim, stimulus for the medieval revival of Jewish philosophy:

> As for the Andalusians (Spaniards) among the people of our nation, all of them cling to the affirmation of the philosophers and incline to their opinions, in so far as these do not ruin the foundations of the law. You will not find them in any way taking the paths of the *Mutakallimūn*. In many things concerning the scanty matter of which the later ones among them had knowledge, they have therefore approximately the same doctrine that we set forth in this treatise.[364]

The following conclusion to a technical discussion of astronomy is even more revealing:

> We have already explained that all these views do not contradict anything said by our prophets and the sustainers of our law. For our community is a community that is full of knowledge and is perfect, as He, may He be exalted, has made clear through the intermediary of the master who made us perfect, saying, *Surely this great nation is a wise and understanding people* (Deut. 4:6). However, when the wicked from among the ignorant communities ruined our good qualities, destroyed our words of wisdom and our compilations, and caused our men of knowledge to perish, so that we became ignorant, as we had been threatened because of our sins, for Scripture says, *And the wisdom of their wise men shall perish, and the prudence of their prudent men shall be hid* (Isa. 29:14).... When in consequence of all this we grew up accustomed to the opinions of the ignorant, these philosophic views appeared to be, as it were, foreign to our law, just as they are foreign to the opinions of the ignorant. However, matters are not like this.[365]

Awareness of the universality of true philosophic views and the conceptual-methodological parallelism between Jewish and non-Jewish sources puts Maimonides' seemingly bold statement about the use of "foreign" materials into perspective.[366] These are not

---

364. MN, I, 71 (p. 177). The phrase *principium sapientiae* is from F. M. Cornford, *Principium Sapientiae: a Study of the Origins of Greek Philosophical Thought* (Cambridge, 1952).
365. MN, II, 11 (p. 276). This explicit statement is very significant.
366. *Kidduš ha-Ḥodeš*, xvii, 25; also xi, 3, which reflects the same parallelism.

really "foreign" sources, just as certain philosophic views are not really "foreign" to the Torah. These views are displaced; the sources are complementary.

The final dividend from this awareness, from taking Maimonides' conception seriously, is that his actual use in the Code of "foreign" sources, which he does not mention, need not be seen as so terribly problematic. It is a consequence of this entire historiography, whose salient feature is the inseparability of halakah and philosophy, twin parts of the Oral Law.[367]

In sum, Maimonides saw himself as the *reconditor philosophiae*. The crucial point is that this wisdom is universal; it is this universality of philosophy which makes its medieval recrudescence as legitimate as its original version.

On a number of subsequent occasions, Maimonides seems to be reflecting upon or justifying this inclusive concept of Gemara. In the *Guide* he refers to the fact that the "foundations of religion" were reviewed in his Talmudic works.[368] Elsewhere he explains why he was compelled to begin the *Mishneh Torah* with the *Sefer ham-Madda',*[369] and in the same vein some of his immediate successors called attention to the twofold but unified objective of the Maimonidean Code: halakic and philosophic.[370] As a matter of fact, both goals are depicted in the letter to Ibn Aknin, where Maimonides uses the term *diwān* to describe the *Mishneh Torah*, asserting that the Jewish people lacked such an authoritative compilation, and then adds that the people also lacked "true and

367. E.g., Rabbi I. Herzog in *Moses Maimonides*, ed. I Epstein (London, 1935), p. 149, n.1; G. Scholem, *The Messianic Idea in Judaism*, p. 28. Perhaps Maimonides' famous statement in his letter to R. Jonathan (see above, chap. I) about sciences as handmaidens should be interpreted to refer to the ancillary sciences in the original sense of the term *ancilla*, i.e., logic and related arts. *Ḥokmah* per se, the core of metaphysics, is not alien. The concluding line of the letter, praying for divine aid in the "study of His Torah and knowledge of His oneness" (*talmud Torato wi-yĕdi'at yiḥudo*) is noteworthy in this respect.
368. MN, I, introduction (p. 10); I, 71, and elsewhere.
369. MTH, 2.
370. R. Isaac ibn Latif, *Ša'ar haš-Šamayim*, introduction; *he-Ḥaluṣ*, VII (1865), 91; R. Levi ben Abraham, *Pardes ha-Ḥokmah*, in *'Oṣar haṣ-Sifrut*, III (1890), 19. Inasmuch as he later singles out the MN for individual consideration, this reference ("the law of the Torah and its secrets [*razeha*]") must apply exclusively to Maimonides' Talmudic works. Also *'Iggeret* of R. Sheshet han-Nasi', *JQR*, XXV (1935), 417. Note IT, 1: "May the Lord divulge unto you its secrets (*maṣpuneha*). . . ."

## 500 INTRODUCTION TO THE CODE OF MAIMONIDES

accurate opinions."[371] The implication is that these beliefs can be presented in the same summary fashion as the details of law. Indeed, the Talmudists (people of the *fiqh*, the third group in the palace metaphor) are not without true beliefs; rather they possess true beliefs by means of tradition. In other words, the *fiqh*, the Oral Law, contains philosophic truths presented descriptively or apodictically as articles of tradition instead of being elaborated demonstratively as syllogistic premises and conclusions.[372] These articles of tradition may ultimately be rationalized, just as the judicial part of *Torah šebbě-'al peh* is subject to amplification. Both expansive processes take place in the domain of Gemara, which had been explicitly defined as consisting of (a) the study and application of hermeneutic principles, and (b) the subject matter of *Pardes*. In this respect the *Moreh Něbukim* may be described as part of the Gemara of the *Mishneh Torah*, just as the actual Talmud and its commentaries are the other part.

### NOBILITY OF PHILOSOPHICAL KNOWLEDGE

Maimonides has thus unequivocally committed himself to the nobility of philosophical knowledge.[373] The provocative statement in the *Mishneh Torah* concerning the hierarchical relationship of Talmud study to *ma'ǎśeh merkabah* (small matters and great matters) is identical not only with the emphasis of the *Mishnah Commentary* concerning *gufe Torah* and *yěsodot gufe Torah* but also with the axiology outlined in the famous palace metaphor:

> Those who have come up to the habitation and walk around it are the jurists who hold true opinions on the basis of traditional authority and

---

371. *'Iggěrot*, 50 and 51, especially the reference to *yěsode ha-'ěmunah hak-kělulim bo*. Such a reference is missing from Maimonides' definition of Mishnah in *Talmud Torah*, i, 12, or perhaps it is self-evident.

372. MN, III, 51; MTH, 4.

373. This should not be translated as "the rule of reason," a flashy motto which is misleading, because medieval religious philosophers were concerned with "faith and reason," never with "religion within the limits of reason alone." For a good definition, see H. A. Wolfson, "The Double Faith Theory," *JQR*, XXXIII (1942), 231ff., reprinted in *Studies in the History of Philosophy and Religion*, I, 583ff. Maimonides' view would be classified as the "single faith theory of the rationalist type," and this covers the MT as well as the MN.

## LAW AND PHILOSOPHY

study the law concerning the practices of divine service, but do not engage in speculation concerning the fundamental principles of religion and make no inquiry whatever regarding the rectification of belief.

Those who have plunged into speculation concerning the fundamental principles of religion have entered the antechambers. People there indubitably have different ranks. He, however, who has achieved demonstration, to the extent that that is possible, of everything that may be demonstrated; who has ascertained in divine matters, to the extent that that is possible, everything that may be ascertained; and who has come close to certainty in those matters in which one can only come close to it—has come to be with the ruler in the inner part of the habitation.[374]

Of course, the scale of values established by the halakah, with its ideal of study, would not require radical transfiguration to accommodate the philosophic ideal of the *vita contemplativa*.[375] At least formally, no drastic transvaluation was involved. If, in addition, we recall that philosophy was considered to be a major integral component of Torah, the Maimonidean ideal could be presented as firmly entrenched in the Jewish tradition. In any event, the message of the *Mishneh Torah* concerning philosophy and law, their interaction and interrelatedness, seems to be loud and clear; it mirrors the strength and serene consistency of his life's work, or with an altered metaphor, it echoes the *Mishnah Commentary* and adumbrates the *Moreh*.[376]

There is little doubt that contemporary intellectual forces and pressures led Maimonides to intensify rationalism, to galvanize that which was dormant, to be discursive and communicative where the sources were elliptical or allusive. Maimonides clearly felt—and the general milieu nurtured this—that Judaism had strayed, had depreciated its intellectual content, and had

---

374. MN, III, 51; *Yĕsode hat-Torah*, iv, 13; PhM, Ḥag 2:1.

375. *Talmud Torah*, i, 3, 8, 10; iii, 3; *Tĕšubah*, ix, 1; *Mĕlakim*, xi, 4; cf. F. Rosenthal, *Knowledge Triumphant* (Leiden, 1970), p. 95; L. Berman, "Maimonides, the Disciple of Alfarabi," p. 159; G. Scholem, *The Messianic Idea in Judaism* (New York, 1972), p. 25.

376. In studying the Maimonidean corpus, there is no need, as we have noted, to attenuate real contradictions or ambiguities, but neither is there any need to seek skeletons in the closet. Whatever "intentional perplexities" there may be in the exposition of certain philosophic doctrines in the *Moreh*—e.g., providence, prophecy—there do not seem to be any in the thematic relationship analyzed in this chapter. We have rather a tense and delicate structure. See below, n.383.

shortchanged itself philosophically. The legitimacy of philosophy in religion was not the issue; rather the legitimacy of religion without philosophy was the issue. Maimonides thus saw himself as restoring, perhaps consummating, a philosophic tradition not only of metaphysics but of jurisprudence. The outer-directed motive, which was sharp and influential, was naturally sustained by inner forces. As we have noted, religious rationalism was not merely a response to external pressures, not only an enterprise of apologetics and polemics; it was also a fulfillment of the inner need for understanding and rationalizing.[377] As a movement of spiritual insurgence, this intellectualism was not qualitatively different from medieval kabbalah.

At this point, the *Ma'āmar Tĕḥiyyat ham-Metim*,[378] certainly a strange and problematic document in so many respects, should be mentioned again. The specificity of the issue (belief in, or denial of, corporeal resurrection) notwithstanding, Maimonides couches it in a very broad context, and writes a long and pathos-charged prologue defending and glorifying the philosophical approach to religion. Had he followed his own canons about the rigid economy of language, with the intention of producing a pointed polemical tract, he could have simply introduced the epistle as follows: "I have had occasion, in previous writings, to discuss resurrection and its relation to immortality. My statements have been misinterpreted, mindlessly or maliciously, and here is how I

---

377. See above, chap. I, p. 87; M. Weber, *Sociology of Religion* (Boston, 1963), p. 117: "Intellectualism, as such, more particularly the metaphysical needs of the human mind as it is driven to reflect on ethical and religious questions, driven not by material need but by an inner compulsion to understand the world as a meaningful cosmos and to take up a position toward it. . . ."

378. See the bibliography of editions, translations, and studies by J. Dienstag, *KS*, XLVIII (1973), 730ff. There are three possible approaches to this work. It may be seen as (1) a "forgery," (2) a genuine, representative summary, or (3) an intentionally distorted composition striving to mollify critics and gain adherents. See S. A. Shapiro, "The Dark Continent of Literature: Autobiography," *Comparative Literature Studies*, V (1968), 421ff., especially p. 425: "autobiography is an imaginative organization of experience for aesthetic and for various intellectual and moral purposes." Close study of the text absolutely dispels Teicher's contention (*JJS*, I [1948], 42) that the MTH makes Maimonides "conform to that standard of 'orthodox' religion which a preponderant section of Jewry in Christian countries accepted as their own under the influence of 13th century Christian theology." This is by no means a conventional 'orthodox' document.

would set the record straight." Instead, he converts the letter into a poignant spiritual-intellectual autobiography, a genuine *apologia pro vita sua* belonging, mutatis mutandis, to the genre of Plato's *Seventh Letter,* Avicenna's *Autobiography,* or Peter Abelard's *Historia.* It emerges as a vigorous restatement of his standard and life-long approach to issues of law, religion, and metaphysics, alerting us to the fact that the opposition in this case is not an eccentric or isolated matter but symptomatic of divergent and irreconcilable religious conceptions. The issue is not resurrection but religious phenomenology and axiology. That is why he again, with a few broad strokes, characterizes his major Code and its achievement in classification and rationalization, and emphasizes the inclusion of theological-philosophical principles in all his works. He has never dealt with any aspect of Judaism without paying attention to philosophical issues or implications; and his treatment of resurrection, he affirms, should be seen from that vantage point. It was particularly impossible for him to compose a comprehensive work on the details of practical precepts while ignoring the fundamentals of essential beliefs. His pejorative characterization of those people who think that they are scholars but who are actually engaged in trivial scholastic endeavors, also reflects his conception of proper Talmudism and his repeated criticism of scholarly stereotypes.[379] The achievement of his *Mishneh Torah,* in which he lays bare the inner formative forces and motive powers of the halakah and brings it "close to reason," is axial. It is quite significant for our analysis that much of this Treatise on Resurrection revolves around the *Mishneh Torah,* which is almost a microcosm of his life's work.

When younger contemporaries, immediate successors, and later students of Maimonides condemned the *Moreh* and the *Sefer ham-Madda'* in one breath, this was not the result of blind animosity or overzealousness. Nor was uniform and unified praise predicated upon blind partisanship. The correspondence of ideological emphases and aspirations was, to their minds, clear.

---

379. PhM, Bek 4:6 (p. 247); Ned 4:3 (p. 128); 'Ab 4:7 (p. 441); *Talmud Torah,* iii, 10; see above, chap. I, n.6. In his criticism of R. Samuel ben Ali Gaon he focuses on methodology; MTH, 12–13.

## 504 INTRODUCTION TO THE CODE OF MAIMONIDES

They realized that for better or for worse the *Mishneh Torah* contained a condensed but uncamouflaged précis of his views on religious philosophy, particularly religion and law, and this produced a sense of malaise and anxiety for some while it provided comfort and encouragement for others.[380] We may further note simply that the main intention of the *Moreh* was to elucidate the real meaning of *ma'aśeh běre'šit* and *ma'aśeh merkabah*, i.e., the true science of the law. These disciplines were, as we have seen, referred to by Maimonides as *yěsodot gufe Torah*. The integrity and reciprocal influence of these areas of study are clear. *Yěsode hat-Torah*, other parts of Book One, and related theoretical sections of the *Mishneh Torah* are *yěsodot*. This is what Maimonides had in mind when he said that the "foundations of religion" were reviewed in his Talmudic works.[381] While the *Moreh* is his philosophic opus par excellence, unique, difficult, and challenging, the *Mishneh Torah* may be described as the consummate expression of the relationship between *gufe Torah* and their formative-informative *yěsodot*.

To say this is not to suggest or demand complete one-to-one correspondence of contents or of method between these works. We must avoid the fallacy of misplaced concreteness. The *Mishneh Torah* is first and foremost a code, and everything else is subordinate. To be sure, it sets the law in a framework of ethical, philosophical, and spiritual dimensions—compared to the *Šulḥan 'Aruk*, the non-halakic aspects of the *Mishneh Torah* are quite substantive and unusually expansive—but to treat it as a philosophical manual or ethical treatise would be like treating poets as philosophers, lawyers as historians, or even psychologists as theologians and scientists as metaphysicians.[382] Overlap is not

---

380. See the discussion in Twersky, "Beginnings," pp. 178ff., with references to such figures as R. Meir hal-Levi Abulafia, R. David Ḳimḥi, R. Judah al-Fakhar, Naḥmanides, RaSHBA, and others. Note also the skillful use of MT by R. Moses Alashkar, *Těšubot*, 117, in refutation of philosophic criticisms (particularly those of R. Shem Ṭob in *Sefer ha-'Ĕmunot*). He uses MT passages to rebut the charge of intellectualism, i.e., the superiority and autonomy of intellectual achievement. In quoting Maimonides, R. Shem Ṭob has fused *Sefer ham-Madda'* with MN. On the other hand, R. Solomon Luria, *Yam šel Šělomoh, Baba Ḳamma*, introduction, attacks Maimonides for inserting philosophic views into the MT.

381. MN, I, introduction, 34, 71; II, 29 (p. 346); III, introduction (p. 415).

382. See Twersky, "The Shulḥan 'Aruk," p. 153.

identity; there are obviously many philosophic problems not treated in the *Mishneh Torah*.[383] The *Moreh*, on the other hand, is a philosophical or metaphysical work, devoted to an elucidation of the secrets of the prophetic books, or in different words, of the esoteric meaning of Scripture and Talmud, by means of careful allegorical interpretation predicated on select philosophic premises.[384] It is *not* a "religious" book in terms of halakah or ethics.

383. E.g., the problem of evil (MN, III, 8–12); and see H. Blumberg, "Theories of Evil in Medieval Jewish Philosophy," *HUCA*, XLIII (1972), 149ff. See above, n.236 (on prayer). For the theory of providence and its contradictions (MN, III, 13ff.), see, e.g., Z. Diesendruck, "Samuel and Moses ibn Tibbon on Maimonides' Theory of Providence," *HUCA*, XI (1936), 341–66. There is no parallel in the MT.

384. There is not, to my mind, much value in the semantic squabble as to whether the MN is a "philosophic" book in the modern sense (see, e.g., L. Strauss, "How to Begin to Study the Guide," MN, p. xiv, and passim). It is philosophic by the author's standards and prepossessions; it grapples with problems of faith and reason (see above, n.373) and attaches primacy to purity of method and analysis: "My purpose in this was that the truth should be established in your mind according to the proper methods, and that certainty should not come to you by accident" (MN, dedicatory epistle [p. 4]). Maimonides is careful not to "run counter to the nature of existence" or to "violate that which is perceived by the senses" as do the exponents of *kalām* (MN, I, 71 [p. 182]). Assent to tradition is part of the epistemology of medieval religious philosophy; LA, 228. Philosophy and theology are related. The book is philosophic in its own context, with its categories and objectives.

The following, rather unusual statement, inserted in the middle of MN, II, 2 (pp. 253–54) as a "preface," should be carefully pondered: "Now before all that, it is obligatory to set forth a preface, which is like a lamp illuminating the hidden features of the whole of this treatise, both of those of its chapters that come before and of those that come after. This preface is as follows:

Know that my purpose in this treatise of mine was not to compose something on natural science, or to make an epitome of notions pertaining to the divine science according to some doctrines, or to demonstrate what has been demonstrated in them. Nor was my purpose in this treatise to give a summary and epitomized description of the disposition of the spheres, or to make known their number. For the books composed concerning these matters are adequate. If, however, they should turn out not to be adequate with regard to some subject, that which I shall say concerning that subject will not be superior to everything else that has been said about it. My purpose in this treatise, as I have informed you in its introduction, is only to elucidate the difficult points of the law and to make manifest the true realities of its hidden meanings, which the multitude cannot be made to understand because of these matters being too high for it. Hence if you perceive that I speak about the establishment of the existence of the separate intellects and about their number, or about the number of the spheres and the causes of their motions, or about investigating the true reality of the notion of matter and form, or about the notion of divine overflow and about other such notions, you ought not to think, and it ought not to occur to you, that I intended only to investigate that true reality of that particular philosophic notion. For these notions have been expounded in many books, and the correctness of most of them has been demonstrated. I only intend to mention matters, the understanding of which may elucidate some difficulty of the law; in fact, many knots will be unraveled

It does not ordinarily treat these themes. At one point Maimonides even apologizes for a digression with the following words: "In the greater part of the chapter we *have turned aside from the purpose of the treatise to deal with moral and also religious matters.* However, though these matters do not wholly belong to the purpose of the treatise, the order of the discourse had led to that."[385]

Furthermore, the Code, although intended for "small and great"—the latter should not be overlooked in the rush to emphasize the Code's popularity, or even its imprecision—was certainly more accessible and readable than the *Moreh*. Maimonides clearly communicates the fact that he could not, and need not, be excessively exacting or minutely exact and fastidious in his treatment of certain technical matters in the *Mishneh Torah:*

> Some (readers of this book) who have studied Greek science, be they Gentile scholars or Jewish scholars, will perhaps notice that some of the methods used by me for the calculation of the visibility of the new moon operate by more or less close approximation, and they would suspect that this is due to inadvertence or ignorance on our part. Let them not give room to such a suspicion; for if we have not striven for complete exactitude (in our computations), it was only because we knew by positive mathematical proofs that such a procedure need not alarm us, since it will by no means affect the correct determination of the time of the visibility of the new moon, and this is why we have not aimed at minute exactness. . . . In this way we were able to avoid long and complicated calculations which are of no practical value for the determination of the

---

through the knowledge of a notion of which I give an epitome. Now you know already from the introduction of this my treatise that it hinges on the explanation of what can be understood in the *Account of the Beginning* and the *Account of the Chariot* and the clearing-up of the difficulties attaching to prophecy and to the knowledge of the Deity. Accordingly, in whatever chapter you find me discoursing with a view to explaining a matter already demonstrated in natural science, or a matter demonstrated in divine science, or an opinion that has been shown to be the one fittest to be believed in, or a matter attaching to what has been explained in mathematics—know that that particular matter necessarily must be a key to the understanding of something to be found in the books of prophecy, I mean to say of some of their parables and secrets. The reason why I mentioned, explained, and elucidated that matter would be found in the knowledge it procures us of the *Account of the Chariot* or of the *Account of the Beginning*, or would be found in an explanation that it furnishes of some root regarding the notion of prophecy, or would be found in the explanation of some root regarding the belief in a true opinion belonging to the beliefs of law."

385. MN, III, 8 (p. 436) (italics mine).

visibility of the new moon, and may only lead to the confusion and bewilderment of the layman, who is not trained in such matters.[386]

Hence the conclusion that "the *Mishneh Torah* is primarily addressed to the general run of man, while the *Guide* is addressed to the small number of people who are able to understand by themselves" is indisputable. What needs to be explored is, given the exoteric character of the Code and the frank avowal that there is indeed a gap between popular and elitist views, how is one to assess the "brief and allusive discussion of the basic truths of the law" found in the Code? How did Maimonides present his original views and press his convictions while being fully cognizant of the needs, tastes, and preconceptions of the masses?[387] Would a wise man, studying the *Mishneh Torah* after he mastered the *Moreh*, accuse Maimonides of inconsistency or acclaim his skill? Would he be able to conclude that Maimonides had skillfully and effectively incorporated some of his major philosophic motifs and favorite rationalistic theories into the *Mishneh Torah*, thereby charting a course for everyone to advance toward religious-intellectual perfection? The selection of motifs, the decisions concerning inclusion or exclusion, detailed presentation or allusiveness, would have to be considered independently, in the light of the theme, text, and context.

CONCLUSION

In sum, to put the matter in a purely literary frame of reference, anyone who reads Maimonides' works, particularly the *Mishneh Torah*, carefully, and takes such passages as *Yĕsode hat-Torah*, iv, 13, or *Talmud Torah*, i, 12, seriously; who notes the regular systolic-diastolic rhythm of *Tĕšubah*, ix, 1, with its interlocking of performance and knowledge, or the resounding peroration to *Sefer ham-Madda'*, which presents knowledge of God (attained through the "understanding and comprehension" of physics and metaphysics) as an indispensable prerequisite of love of God, or the pronounced theoretical emphasis of *'Issure Bi'ah*,

---

386. *Kiddus ha-Hodeš*, xi, 5, 6. It is a mistake to generalize from this specific context to the entire MT; cf. J. Levinger, *Darke ham-Maḥšabah*, p. 22.
387. Cf. L. Strauss, *Persecution and the Art of Writing*, pp. 82, 93, 94.

xiv, 2, where a premium is placed upon knowledge of the theological foundations of Judaism; who thoughtfully follows the masterful elaboration of the general blueprint as well as many details of the system of *ṭa'ăme miṣwoṯ*, particularly those geared to moral improvement and intellectual perfection; who understands the spiritualistic interpretation of the law suggested in such passages as *Ṭumē'aṯ Ṣara'aṯ*, xvi, 10, *Ṭumē'aṯ 'Oḵlin*, xvi, 12, and *Miḵwa'oṯ*, xi, 12; who studies the strategic use of such key concepts as *'ahăḇah* and *yir'ah* and *'ăḇodah*, *de'ah* and *ḥoḵmah*, *ḥăsiḏuṯ*, *ḵěḏušah*, and *ḵidduš haš-Šem;* who ponders the philosophic interpretation of Biblical books (Song of Songs as an allegory of the soul's love of God; Proverbs as an allegory of the conflict between matter and form); who is attentive to the thorough elimination of objectionable beliefs and practices (anthropomorphism, astrology, demonology, myth, magic), the consistent coupling of spiritualization and intellectualization as an antidote to vulgarization or distortion; who takes to heart the passionate message that one's act has impact on one's moral-intellectual achievement and vice versa; who reacts sensitively to the ideal types, prophetic model, and Messianic hope as portrayed in the *Mishneh Torah*—such a person cannot doubt the depth of Maimonides' intellectualism and philosophically motivated spirituality. One who studies the *Mishneh Torah* in its entirety, from the affirmation of the existence, oneness, and incorporeality of God at the very beginning of the work ("the basic principle of all basic principles and the pillar of all sciences is to realize that there is a First Being who brought every existing thing into being") to the eschatological vision of universal knowledge of God at the very end ("Israelites will be very wise, they will . . . attain an understanding of their Creator to the utmost capacity of the human mind, as it is written, *For the earth shall be full of the knowledge of the Lord, as the waters cover the sea* [Isa. 11:9]"), will resist any denial or attenuation of this intellectualism as tendentious.

However, by the same token, anyone who has lived with the massive halaḵah of the *Mishneh Torah* and has been stimulated by its grandeur; has experienced its profundity, confronted its originality, appreciated its scope, discovered, time and again, the delicacy, dynamism, and detail of innumerable explanations embedded in its normative summaries; has savored its felicity of style and power of compression; has basked in the warmth and light of its allusions and subtleties; has been enthralled by a provocative formulation or temporarily agitated by a seemingly unintelligible equation which suddenly, after prolonged attempts at analysis and repeated frustrations, reveals its meaning and intention—such a person will not be able to characterize the *Mishneh Torah* as a task necessarily or tactically performed by a "philosopher-statesman." If it were merely a question of "political" tokenism, of a statesmanlike gesture on the part of a philosopher toward law, Maimonides could have chosen a different option. The Spanish-Gaonic tradition of pragmatically oriented condensation and codification allowed him a path of less resistance, of minimal collection of Talmudic data. He chose rather to maximize the role of law by pushing back the frontiers of Talmudic learning. He reintroduced the study of *Ḳodašim* and grappled with the complexities of *Ṭōharot*, hardly a prudent act for a philosopher with an allegedly congenital distaste for law. He reestablished the totality of the fragmented concept of *talmud Torah* and by his conceptual classification as well as painstaking interpretation opened up new vistas in halakic study. The scope of his halakic achievement is both awesome and exhilarating. The closely textured *Mishneh Torah* remains a magisterial demonstration of sweeping synthesis emerging from minute analysis. It is fair to say that the vocabulary, indeed the morphology, of halakic study were reshaped by the *Mishneh Torah*. New concepts and definitions, emphases and interpretations—e.g., the classification of vows (*nidre 'issur* and *nidre hekdeš*), prayer and *'ăbodah šebbĕ-leb*, *těšubah* and *talmud Torah*, laws concerning the calendar, the sanctity of Jerusalem, interrogation of witnesses (status of *děrišot* alongside of *ḥăḳirot* and *bědiḳot*), the structuring and numbering of the 613 commandments—were injected into the bloodstream of halakic study, hermeneutics, and exegesis. Our analysis, therefore, suggests that the best way to approach Maimonides is to view him as a scholar vigorously pursuing and creatively uniting two inseparable disciplines. The issue, in short, seems to be not merely the calculated involvement of an Alfarabian-Platonic philosopher in nonphilosophic activities but also a firmly held conviction about the abiding reciprocity and complementarity of law and philosophy.

Historically, the emerging problem was whether this complementarity is necessary or desirable. Is it possible to spiritualize and rationalize without jeopardizing normativeness? Is it possible to be a Talmudist and a philosopher simultaneously? Many thought that Maimonides' synthesis was subversive, really favoring what Kierkegaard was to describe pejoratively as the "intellectual categorical imperative"[388]—the synthesis would break down or would be misunderstood; rationalization would produce laxity and flippancy; philosophy would undercut the study of Rabbinic literature. Others, per contra, considered it a spiritually invigorating formula—routinization would calcify the system which originally was, and should be, marked by spiritual excitement, emotional sensitivity, and intellectual elan; metaphysics would complement Rabbinics. Consensus or conflict revolved around the definition of *yĕsodot* and the importance of intellectualism. In Maimonidean terms, the question may perhaps be phrased with reference to the ideal, the philosopher-king or metaphysician-jurisprudent, depicted at the very end of the *Moreh:*

It is clear that the perfection of man that may truly be gloried in is the one acquired by him who has achieved, in a measure corresponding to his capacity, apprehension of Him, may He be exalted, and who knows His providence extending over His creatures as manifested in the act of bringing them into being and in their governance as it is. The way of life of such an individual, after he has achieved this apprehension, will always have in view loving-kindness, righteousness, and judgment, through assimilation to His actions, may He be exalted, just as we have explained several times in this treatise.[389]

Was this a real and realizable religious-philosophic formula? Can the circuit be completed or will it be short-circuited?

---

388. S. Kierkegaard, *Sickness unto Death,* p. 220, beautifully analyzed by G. Clive, *The Romantic Enlightenment* (New York, 1960), p. 123.

389. MN, III, 54 (p. 638). Note also MN, I, 69 (p. 170): "Consequently He, may He be exalted, is the ultimate end of everything; and the end of the universe is similarly a seeking to be like unto His perfection as far as is in its capacity"; see H. Blumberg, "Muśśag ha-Raṣon ha-'Eloḳi bĕ-Mišnato šel ha-RaMBaM," *Peraḳim,* IV (1966), 43ff. (especially p. 52); and A. Nuriel, "Ha-Raṣon ha-'Eloḳi," *Tarbiz,* XXXIX (1970), 39–61. For the influence of MN, III, 51, see also G. Vajda, "The Mystical Doctrine of R. Obadyah, Grandson of Maimonides," *JJS,* VI (1955), 213ff.

## LAW AND PHILOSOPHY

Maimonides believed that knowledge stimulates and sustains proper prescribed conduct which in turn is a conduit for knowledge, and this intellectual achievement in return *raises* the level and motive of conduct.[390] Even in the *Moreh*, after "affecting the Aristotelian manner and . . . dwelling upon the finality of the contemplative life . . . he is soon forced to admit that the knowledge of God is to be taken to mean the knowledge of God's ways and attributes, which ought to serve us as a guide for our actions. Logically, Maimonides could have repeated with R. Abraham ibn Daud that 'the end of all philosophy is right conduct.' "[391] He could also have echoed R. Joseph ibn Ṣaddiḳ's statement: "The purpose of philosophy is to lead one to know the Creator, but the fruit and the effect of its teaching is to cause one to imitate according to one's ability the Creator's moral qualities."[392] Philo's formulation that "philosophy is the practice of wisdom" could also have been adopted by him.[393] In other

[390]. The resultant conduct is not ordinary and routine—perfunctory behavior in which one acts out of conformity and inertia—but rather reflects a higher order in which tradition is substantiated by independent thought and understanding. The first is, in the terms of R. Baḥya ibn Paḳuda, a follow-the-leader system: "The believer having faith in those from whom he has received the tradition, not however knowing the truth by the exercise of his own intellect and understanding, such a person is like a blind man led by one that can see" (*Ḥobot hal-Lĕbabot*, I, 2 [I, p. 25]). By frequent repetition of inherently desirable and edifying acts, every person, even a blind one, may achieve a degree of ethical perfection (ŠP, chap. IV). There is a higher moral excellence attainable by select persons after arduous intellectual efforts. Cf. S. Pines, translator's introduction, MN, p. cxxii, who questions the view (noted, e.g., by J. Guttmann) that there is here (in MN, III, 54) a Kantian redirection and reformulation, which insists upon adding a moral dimension to knowledge; he rejects the conclusion that "ordinary moral virtues and moral actions are of greater importance and value than the intellectual virtues and theoretical way of life." The point is, as we have emphasized, that these are by no means "ordinary moral virtues" but extraordinary, intellectually rooted virtues reflecting the excellences of the theoretical way of life. In "Spinoza's Tractatus, Maimonides, and Kant," *Scripta Hierosolymitana*, XX (1968), p. 27, Professor Pines suggests a different position: the *imitatio Dei*, clearly outlined at the end of the *Guide*, is intended for "a small minority . . . credited with the intellectual superiority" necessary for this attainment. Here again, it should be noted that inasmuch as this minority is not a closed caste, the goal remains open and universal and this special kind of *imitatio Dei* is a true mirror of Maimonideanism. See also *Yĕsode hat-Torah*, vii, 7 (prophecy may be for individual perfection, without the obligation to communicate its message).

[391]. H. A. Wolfson, "Classification of Sciences," p. 313; R. Abraham ibn Daud, *ha-'Ĕmunah ha-Ramah*, introduction (p. 4).

[392]. R. Joseph ibn Ṣaddiḳ, *'Olam Ḳaṭan*, p. 64.

[393]. Wolfson, *Philo*, I, 147; II, 195. Philo speaks of "knowledge of the Maker of the world" from which one gains piety. See also R. Abraham Maimonides, *Tĕšubot*, n.63.

words, *imitatio Dei* means assimilating God's ways and attributes so that as a result one lives in accord with the law, which constantly propels the individual towards a contemplative goal.

All this happens to coincide with the Platonic-Alfarabian ideal, well known and influential as well as controversial in the philosophic milieu of the twelfth century. Whether or not this ideal—which is, in any event, open to divergent emphases: one may unequivocally prefer the contemplative aspect while another may stress the active aspect—is the Maimonidean model is not the major issue in our context. More significant is the fact that the same fusion of action and contemplation characterizes the Messianic figure depicted by Maimonides at the end of the Code: "If there arise a king from the House of David who meditates on the Torah, occupies himself with the commandments, as did his ancestor David, observes the precepts prescribed in the Written and the Oral Law, prevails upon Israel to walk in the way of the Torah and to repair its breaches, and fights the battles of the Lord, it may be assumed that he is the Messiah." Earlier in the same work, the Messiah is described as follows: "Because the king who will arise from the seed of David will possess more wisdom than Solomon and will be a great prophet, approaching Moses our teacher, he will teach the whole of the Jewish people and instruct them in the way of God."[394] The Patriarchs and Moses are also shown to be exemplars of philosophic excellence and practical distinction; they exhibit social activism together with nearness to God achieved by sustained contemplation. Neither their knowledge nor their love of God turned them into recluses. In the *Moreh* Maimonides states that "the end of the efforts (of Abraham, Isaac, and Jacob) was to bring into being a religious community that would know and worship God"—the same dual program and objective emphasized in *Hilkot Tĕšubah*. In the *Mishneh Torah* Maimonides graphically describes how Abraham, having "attained the way of truth," "began to proclaim to the whole world with great power and to instruct the people that the entire universe had but one Creator, and that Him it was right to worship. . . . He would instruct each one accord-

394. *Mĕlakim*, xi, 4; *Tĕšubah*, ix, 2.

ing to his capacity until he brought him to the way of truth [i.e., until they reached the common goal]. . . . And so it went on with ever increasing vigor among Jacob's children and their adherents until they became a people that knew God."[395] Maimonides must have had this ideal type in mind when in an earlier chapter he wrote: "How well put is the phrase *ascending and descending* (Gen. 28:12), in which ascent comes before descent. . . . For after the ascent and the attaining of certain rungs of the ladder that may be known, comes the descent with whatever decree the prophet has been informed of, with a view to governing and teaching the people of the earth."[396] Cognitive attainment is not the ultimate, for it too is self-transcending; it is, however, indispensable for religious perfection.

The ideal is clear; the intellectual-spiritual gap between this and "the mind of the multitude" and its behavior is both a reality and a challenge, creating great tension.

Maimonides made no secret of his spiritual elitism, but he did not seal it off from all aspirants either. Again, there seems to be a common feature of philosophical and mystical programs; any abstract, nonliteral system is esoteric. In common with kabbalists who passionately espouse esoteric teachings while hoping that these would be spread gradually among increasing numbers of people, Maimonides did not camouflage or compromise his elitist standards; the heirarchical structure of disciplines, attainments, and objectives is firm. The vision of a meaningful observance of *miṣwot* together with genuine appreciation of philosophy is consistently clear. Routine piety and unreflective behavior—the unexamined life—are denigrated. The nobility of philosophic religion (*Torah—ḥokmah*), in which rationalism and piety are natural companions and through which man's two perfections (of body and soul) are advanced, is emphasized. Nevertheless, he hoped that these elitist standards and goals would be progressively democratized. He was fully aware of the difficulties and inevitable limitations in the process of combining the philosophic *vita contemplativa* with the religious *vita activa,* but this awareness did

---

395. MN, III, 51 (p. 624); *'Akum,* i, 2.
396. MN, I, 15.

not blur the theoretical blueprint and did not dampen the hope that there would be ethical-intellectual mobility from the lower to the higher levels. Ordinary ethical behavior would become sensitized and inspired; traditional beliefs would be individualized and rationalized through philosophic demonstration; knowledge would have fear give way to love, so that one would "occupy himself with the Torah for its own sake" or reach that special service of God described in the *Guide:* "After apprehension, total devotion to Him and the employment of intellectual thought in constantly loving Him should be aimed at."[397] Whenever (in the *Moreh,* the *Mishneh Torah,* or the *Epistle to Yemen* and other small writings) he had occasion to refer to rational analysis of religious belief or action, to emphasize the importance of understanding the purposiveness of the Commandments, or to discuss the pure motives for service of God, Maimonides noted that everyone should progress "according to his capacity." The assumption is that the "knowledge [of all] increases and they have attained a large measure of wisdom." Inasmuch as individual capabilities vary greatly, the reality would remain checkered, full of glaring gaps and inequalities. The theory and ideal were egalitarian; the reality sharpened the difference between the *hamon* and the elite. Consequently, esotericism (i.e., the use of rhetorical devices, expository skills, and instructional tricks, gradual unfolding of abstract conceptions, shaded-nuanced revelation of profound meanings and spiritual-intellectual objectives) was a pedagogic necessity but not an ideological finality.

The motto of the *Moreh, Open ye the gates, that the righteous nation that keepeth faithfulness may enter in* (Isa. 26:2),[398] and the motto of the *Mishneh Torah, Then should I not be ashamed, when I have regard unto all Thy commandments* (Ps. 119:6), form a natural montage.

397. MN, III, 51.
398. The second of the introductory verses to the MN (p. 5) is Prov. 8:4: *Unto you, O men ('išim), I call, and my voice is to the sons of men (bĕne 'aḏam).* The goal is to progress from the select few, *'išim,* to larger numbers of people; see MN, I, 14. On these verses, see R. Isaac ben Sheshet, *Tešuḇot,* 45.

# VII

# Epilogue*

A TRUE CLASSIC: UNPRECEDENTED AND UNRIVALED

The *Mishneh Torah* represents a quantum jump in the development of Rabbinic literature as a whole and the history of codification in particular. While general historians of medieval thought and doctrine frequently periodize the era in terms of prescholasticism, high scholasticism, and late scholasticism, the natural and more meaningful counterparts in Jewish history would be pre-Maimonidean and post-Maimonidean. The juridical-philosophical oeuvre of Maimonides in toto is literally epochal, acknowledged by both protagonists and antagonists. The statement of R. Jonathan hak-Kohen of Lunel, "Thou hast gained fame through the treasure of thy learning everywhere," rings true and is representative. Yet unlike the *Moreh*, which had an oscillating, seesaw-like history, its course resembling a wadi whose waters sometimes rage and overflow and sometimes subside and even evaporate completely, the *Mishneh Torah*—all the criticism and demurrals notwithstanding—exercised a decisive, extensive, nearly constant influence on the study and practice of halakah, that is to say, on Judaism and Jewish history. Moreover, in thinking further about the historical impact of these two seminal creations, we may note that although the dispute concerning philosophy was exacerbated, there was no corresponding attack on

---

*This epilogue is a composite and highly compressed essay alluding to facts and characterizations presented fully in the previous chapters or condensing material treated comprehensively in other works of mine (particularly "The Beginnings of Mishneh Torah Criticism," "The Shulḥan 'Aruk," *Rabad*) and my Hebrew article on R. Joseph Ashkenazi (see below, n. 1). Documentation and basic bibliographic references contained therein are not reproduced here. The few notes in this chapter serve to avoid extended digressions or to provide a few references not mentioned elsewhere. Much of this material will be elaborated, together with the analysis of new material, in a separate monograph on the study of MT through the ages. Studies of the commentaries on MT are major desiderata; see, e.g., Y. Spiegel's article on MM, *KS*, XLVI (1971), 554–80.

the *Mishneh Torah*; indeed, the initial tide of criticism receded.[1] There were avid admirers of the *Mishneh Torah* who frequently connected the philosophical-theological achievement with the juridical-halakic achievement—the laudatory statements of R. Jonathan hak-Kohen of Lunel and R. Moses of Coucy illustrate this—but even those (e.g., R. Judah al-Fakhar of Toledo and R. Solomon of Montpellier) who were heatedly hostile, or, if such an attitude is conceivable, outwardly indifferent to the *Moreh* and the accelerated propagation of philosophy, praised the Code genuinely or even unstintingly. Everyone who studied it was affected by it; no one viewed it impassively or nonchalantly.

Hebrew literature, of all ages and genres, provides abundant material for a long and impressive list of honorific references to Maimonides, encomiastic pronouncements about his work, unqualified praise for his genius, erudition, and intellectual daring —extraordinary epithets, brimful of esteem and reverence, concerning his unique position in Jewish history. We may note one single instance of the progression or intensification of this praise: R. Jedaiah hap-Penini states that there was no comparable scholar among all the sages of Israel since the completion of the Talmud, while R. Joseph del Medigo (*Miktab 'Aḥuz*) states that there has been no leader like him since "the time of the prophets." Yet a sober and dispassionate historical judgment concerning the importance, innovation, and influence of the *Mishneh Torah*—a judgment which, all its intrinsic rigor and discipline, facticity and easy demonstrability notwithstanding, would be quite extraordinary and intense—need not be nurtured by such plaudits and acclamations, sincere or stereotyped, studied or spontaneous. Study of the fate of the *Mishneh Torah* and analysis of its role, even of the periodic resentment which it aroused, demonstrate force-

---

[1]. There is need to differentiate between the textual-substantive criticism—e.g., that of RABD—which zeroes in on hundreds of issues and cruxes, and the a priori ideologically-tinted indictment—e.g., of such a modern anti-Maimonidean as S. D. Luzzatto—which finds the Code per se uncongenial. See also the suspicious and condemnatory attitude of the sixteenth-century scholar R. Joseph Ashkenazi described by me in the *Salo Baron Jubilee Volume* (Jerusalem, 1975), III, 183ff. Chapter II, above, reviews some of the reservations concerning *total* reliance upon the MT without supportive knowledge of the sources.

fully that the influence of this rich and resonant work was, in fact, unusually widespread and multifaceted, both specific and general; its impact—direct or indirect—on later codes was massive, even if not decisive in the strict Maimonidean sense, while it also crucially and creatively impinged upon other genres of halakic writing (commentary, responsa, novellae) as well as many cognate disciplines (e.g., Biblical exegesis, aggadah commentary, homilies, and ethical works). The very idiom of halakic writing—style, syntax, allusions—showed Maimonides' imprint. His work, in effect, changed the entire landscape of Rabbinic literature. Ongoing preoccupation with the *Mishneh Torah*—and it was used in an amazing variety of ways—reinforced the recognition that it constituted an unparalleled achievement, hence it was increasingly treated as an inexhaustible treasure, yielding practical religious guidance, intellectual stimulus, and edifying insight. This tightly structured and multidimensional work, unmistakably marked by vastness of erudition, subtlety of discernment, delicacy of interpretation, fastidiousness of classification, and sensitivity of formulation became rather rapidly a prism through which passed practically all reflection and analysis of Talmudic study. There is hardly a major literary development in the broad field of Rabbinic literature which does not relate in some way to the *Mishneh Torah*. Its influence is mirrored and echoed through many works in various genres by a steady succession of authors. One could, for example, make an index of all major collections of responsa in terms of *Mishneh Torah* references, or note the extent to which Talmudic commentary (from R. Meir hal-Levi Abulafia, through the great triumvirate of Naḥmanides, RaSHBA, and RIṬBA, and on to the twentieth century) relates to the *Mishneh Torah*. Regardless of whether one accepted Maimonides' premises and goals, aspirations and projections, whether one rejected or endorsed his ideological positions and commentatorial presuppositions, the Code became a universal frame of reference for all kinds of study (Mishnah, Tosefta, Talmud, Geonica), for criticism, innovation, or summation. Practically every subsequent treatment of a problem, whether theoretical or practical, casuistic or normative, was approached through the concepts and formulations of the *Mishneh Torah*, which displayed all the qualities and strengths of a classic: timely yet timeless, clear yet suggestive, firm yet endlessly stimulating for ongoing interpretation. As can be shown, even commentaries on the text were sometimes a pretext for other literary purposes. Moreover, no one has ever attempted to duplicate Maimonides' achievement. R. Hasdai Crescas and R. Joseph del Medigo talked about composing a new comprehensive code à la the *Mishneh Torah*, combining halakah and philosophy, and intimated that their works would supersede the Maimonidean Code, but neither implemented his plan. The *Mishneh Torah* remained sui generis, unprecedented and unrivaled. In terms of John Ruskin's useful, if slightly hackneyed, division of all books into "books of the hour and books of all time," we may say that the *Mishneh Torah* fits into both classes—the true test of a classic.

RAPID DISSEMINATION OF THE *Mishneh Torah:* CRITICS AND COMMENTATORS

Clearly, the first step toward understanding the unique and predominant position of the *Mishneh Torah* is to establish the facts concerning its rapid dissemination.

Completed in 1178, or possibly 1180, it became known with amazing rapidity, first in Oriental countries (Palestine, Syria, Babylon [Iraq], Yemen), then in the Mediterranean area (including Spain and Provence), and finally in the Franco-German orbit as well. By 1191 Maimonides spoke of its renown in all corners of the earth, even though in 1193 it had apparently not yet reached southern France. By the turn of the century it was firmly rooted in the Provençal-Castile region and was the subject of intense study. Actually, as we shall see, the systematic and critical study of the *Mishneh Torah* was interwoven with that of the *Hălakot* of Alfasi. One may say that both of these works were "launched" on their careers in Provence; the most sustained and fruitful activity in the realm of Rabbinic literature resulted from the preoccupation with these works. Consequently, in order to get an accurate gauge we must pay attention not merely to the animadversions of RABD and his younger contemporary R. Moses hak-Kohen, but also to such works as the *Sefer ha-Hašlamah* of R. Meshullam ben Moses of Béziers, the *Sefer ham-Mě'orot* of R. Meir ben Simeon of Narbonne, the *Sefer ham-Miktam* of R. David ben Levi, and the

# EPILOGUE

commentaries of R. Abraham of Montpellier, all of which use the *Mishneh Torah* seriously and substantively. Even the *Sefer ham-Manhig* of R. Abraham ben Nathan, a younger contemporary of Maimonides, refers regularly to the *Mishneh Torah*. The *Sefer ham-Měnuḥah* of R. Manoah early initiated the literary tradition of full commentary and defense (particularly against the strictures of RABD). We may almost say that from the moment that the *Mishneh Torah* arrived in southern France, the only area on which a somewhat gloomy Maimonides pinned his hopes for the survival of Rabbinic scholarship, the main contours of its future influence and study were fixed. Its value as a commentary as well as a code was promptly appreciated. The scene was one in which the above-mentioned scholars, and others, worked side by side in the exhaustive study, searching analysis, and honest appraisal of the *Mishneh Torah,* which thus became a highly charged "instrument of legal process."

In northern France also it quickly established itself and circulated widely. One can discern the transition, in a matter of decades, from casual and irregular use and selective study of the *Mishneh Torah* to habitual, almost routine, reference to it on all occasions. The earliest quotations, those by R. Judah ben Isaac of Paris, R. Isaac ben Abraham (RIṢBA), and R. Samson of Sens, appear as sporadic references to "the book of R. Moses." By 1236, R. Moses of Coucy refers to that praiseworthy composition of Maimonides which has "enlightened the eyes of Israel" and strengthened Talmudic study as it spread "in the lands of Christendom and Islam"; his *Sefer Miṣwot Gadol,* a major and influential work moving primarily in the orbit of Maimonidean concepts, definitions, and interpretations, may be seen as a high watermark in the spread of the *Mishneh Torah* in northern Europe while simultaneously signaling the increasing impact of the Tosafists. Indeed, his avowed aim of grafting the insights and novellae of the latter onto the Maimonidean material is emblematic of much subsequent Talmud study. Still later, by the time of R. Meir of Rothenburg, it had achieved special prominence as an indispensable reference work, comparable metaphorically to the *'Urim wĕ-Tummim.* The *Haggahot Maymuniyyot,* a glossarial-interpretative work from the school of R. Meir of Rothenburg, which purported to give Franco-German customs and precedents

## INTRODUCTION TO THE CODE OF MAIMONIDES

a fair view alongside of the predominantly Spanish-African views formulated by Maimonides, clearly attests to the entrenched centrality and acknowledged authoritativeness of the Maimonidean Code. This is analogous to the motives and assumptions which led R. Moses Isserles to append his glosses—strictures, supplements, and variants—to the *Šulḥan 'Aruk*: together they would be universally accepted and validated. Such annotation unqualifiedly recognizes the intrinsic prestige and increasing predominance of the core creation while it allows for expansion and innovation. One notes how in the course of the century extensive quotations from the *Mishneh Torah*, sometimes anonymous, turn up in the *'Ărugat hab-Bośem* of R. Abraham ben 'Azriel, certain versions of the *Sefer Ḥăsidim*, the *Sefer ha-Rokeaḥ* of R. Eleazar of Worms, and the responsa collections of R. Meir of Rothenburg. In short, less than a century after its composition, the *Mishneh Torah* was well on its way to becoming "the most celebrated codification of Jewish law."

Next, there is great need to clarify and realign the range of attitudes to the *Mishneh Torah* (all the nuances, intimations, and allusions) which were implicit in this vast literary output; particularly to determine not ad hominem gibes or panegyrics but the specific roles and expressions of criticism and commentary, curt repudiation and elaborate explication, and the various combinations thereof. As is known, Maimonides himself was not serene or sanguine in expecting immediate and widespread acceptance of his Code; he anticipated criticism and opposition, envy and recrimination—in a word, a rather tempestuous reaction. He not only feared that inbred conservatism which instinctually leads people to oppose innovation and change but also foresaw specific reasons for *Mishneh Torah* criticism. We recall how, in his letter to his favorite disciple Joseph ben Judah, he enumerated the following types of critics:

> I knew, and it was perfectly clear to me at the time that I composed it, that it would undoubtedly fall into the hands of a wicked and jealous person who would defame its praiseworthy features and pretend that he does not need it or is in a position to ignore it; and (that it would fall) into the hands of a foolish ignoramus who will not recognize the value of this project and will consider it worthless; and (that it would fall) into

the hands of a deluded and confused tyro to whom many places in the book would be incomprehensible, inasmuch as he does not know their source or is unable to comprehend in full the inferences which I inferred with great precision; and (that it would fall) into the hands of a reactionary and obtuse man of piety who will assail the explanations of the fundamentals of faith included in it.

This sensitive and perceptive prediction—singling out scholarly rivalry and jealousy, methodological reservations concerning undocumented codification, and ideological malaise concerning his exposition of the "fundamentals of faith"—is noteworthy, but there should be no mistake about the fact that the categories of criticism, although relevant, are by no means exhaustive. The same is true of other motivational analyses, sometimes variations of the above, suggested by medieval scholars and/or modern historians. The Maimonidean allegation of jealousy—begrudging Maimonides the honor which was almost universally bestowed upon him—is often repeated; it was echoed immediately by R. Aaron hak-Kohen of Lunel and R. Sheshet of Saragossa. Instinctive polemicism, critique for critique's sake, is sometimes suggested. Responsibility is also placed upon ideological convictions: suspicion of heresy and antipathy to unbridled popular philosophic inquiries. Arbitrary opposition to codification, to any definitive and systematic formulation of halakah, is also submitted in explanation of the anti-Maimonidean critique. All these motivational analyses, to my mind, merely skirt the periphery, without really coming to grips with the crux of the problem: how much of the opposition was personal and petty, psychological and ideological, and how much was scholarly and methodological? What was objectionable even to scholars who themselves excelled in codification and were not averse to philosophizing? What made a student move from obviously great admiration to reservation and even rejection?

Deeper study would indicate that the nature and motives of this criticism can be determined only in the broad perspective of the total reception of the *Mishneh Torah,* where stricture and supplement, criticism and commentary, dissent and elaboration are inseparable. Scholars everywhere turned to its exhaustive study rather than its exclusive criticism, as had previously been the case with Alfasi's *Hălakot*. Bias and personal temperament, to be sure, may play a part; scholars are "involved" persons with likes and dislikes, individual traditions and local customs, deep-seated sentiments and decided propensities, and do not always write with emotional detachment. Often unknowingly these subjective factors impinge upon the objective process of interpretation. However, reaction to the *Mishneh Torah* was motivated primarily by a sense of intellectual freedom and independence which expressed itself in pointed criticism and/or reasoned corroboration—animadversions or scholia. As indicated above (at the end of Chapter II), the concept of *mĕleket šamayim* with its double-edged thrust of caution and creativity, respectful recognition of authoritative achievement together with relentless reexamination, was relevant. Add to this the triumphant advance of the Tosafistic school and the stage is fully set for ongoing creativity. The common purpose of all Maimonidean literature was to scrutinize Maimonidean statements, criticize them, interpret them, modify them, relate them to the sources or to new insights. Most of the twelfth- and thirteenth-century writers—R. Daniel hab-Babli, R. Abraham ben David of Posquières, R. Moses hak-Kohen, R. Jonathan of Lunel, R. Meshullam ben Moses of Béziers, R. Samson of Sens, R. Meir hak-Kohen—are as much commentators as they are critics, while to a measurable extent the writings of the Maimonidean "armbearers" of the fourteenth century and later, starting with R. Manoah (*Sefer ham-Mĕnuḥah*), R. Vidal of Tolosa (*Maggid Mishneh*), R. Shem Ṭob ibn Gaon (*Migdal 'Oz*), and on to R. David ibn Abi Zimra (*Lĕšonot ha-RaMBaM; Yĕkar Tif'eret*), R. Joseph Karo (*Kesef Mishneh*), and R. Abraham de Boton (*Leḥem Mishneh*), or such less influential sixteenth-century commentators as R. Judah Albutini, R. Levi ben Ḥabib, R. David Arama, or R. Joseph Corcos, contain much substantive critique. The same is true with regard to the Maimonidean statements quoted and discussed in the general halakic literature of the period, such as the *Sefer ha-'Iṭṭur* of R. Isaac ben Abba Mari, the responsa of R. Meir hal-Levi Abulafia, the collective studies of the sages of Lunel, the early *Tosafot* of R. Judah ben Isaac of Paris, R. Isaac ben Abraham, and R. Solomon ben Judah of Dreux, the *'Or Zaru'a* of R. Isaac ben Moses of Vienna, the commentaries of R. Jonah

# EPILOGUE

Gerondi and his disciples, the novellae and codificatory writings of Naḥmanides and RaSHBA, and the compendium of R. Asher ben Jehiel. The common characteristic of this heterogeneous literature vis-à-vis Maimonides is neither unquestioning subservience nor uninformed rejection but rather searching analysis of the subject under consideration. The results—blanket endorsement, qualified approval, partial dissent, or relentless criticism—vary. *Variae erunt hominum voces.*

We have earlier depicted RABD as a good example of the early critic-commentator. The axiological orientation and literary achievements of R. Jonathan hak-Kohen of Lunel, younger contemporary and erstwhile student of RABD, illustrate the same dialectical position from a slightly different vantage point. On the one hand, he is the spokesman for the Lunel scholars and communicates the famous twenty-four questions, respectful but trenchant, to Maimonides. These questions, many of which are repeated in the *Haśśagot* of RABD and RaMaK, reflect the cooperative-critical endeavor of the Lunel school (and indicate parenthetically the immediacy with which they turned to the study of the *Mishneh Torah*). On the other hand, R. Jonathan hak-Kohen is described by contemporaries and successors as a zealous and erudite champion of the *Mishneh Torah* who "explained and corroborated the words of Maimonides." R. David Messer Leon puts his writings in the same category as the *Maggid Mishneh* and *Migdal 'Oz*, which usually "refute the criticisms." R. Moses Botarel characterizes him as a defender who arose to "save" the Code from its detractors. Actually, his attitude to the *Mishneh Torah* should be correlated with his treatment of Alfasi's *Hălakot*. His commentaries on Alfasi's compendium of law initiated that process whereby the *Hălakot* were transformed into a "miniature Talmud," embellished with commentaries just like the Talmud itself. Nonetheless, although operating within a theoretical framework which was overtly favorable to Alfasi, he periodically modified or dissented from certain views.

The ramified activity of R. Jonathan suggests an extension of the dialectical principle we have just formulated with regard to the *Mishneh Torah:* all writing on major works (Rashi's Commentary and Alfasi's *Hălakot* take their places alongside of

Maimonides' *Mishneh Torah*) was of this character—partly approbatory, partly negative. First of all, the terminology itself is significant. The literature stimulated by the aforementioned epochal works consists of *tosafot, sifre tašlum, hašlamah, haggahot,* and *haśśagot.* Even the latter term, which in the course of time and contrary to its original connotation acquired the sense of negative critique—demolition tactics exclusively—originally denoted supplements of all kinds, fairly objective and frequently favorable. It is noteworthy that many scholars—R. Samuel has-Sardi, R. David ben Levi of Narbonne, Naḥmanides, R. Aaron hak-Kohen of Lunel, R. Manoah, RaSHBA, ham-Me'iri, the author of *Kol Bo,* R. David ibn Abi Zimra, R. Jacob Landau (*'Agur*)—use the words *haśśagot* and *haggahot* interchangeably. RABD himself uses both terms to designate his scholia. Secondly, a number of authors publicly declare their intention of devoting their works to exhaustive review rather than exclusive criticism of a given text. The avowed goal of the *Sefer ha-Hašlamah* (פעם לחזק דבריו ופעם לתמוה עליהם) is not, in theory, very different from the alleged purpose of the *Sefer ham-Ma'or:* דורש ושואל וחוקר ומאיר ומעורר, פעם סומך ועוזר ופעם כמשיב ושובר.

RABD also introduces his criticism of Alfasi in similar terms: לא נמנעתי לחפש אחריו כאשר תשיג ידי, פעם לסתור ופעם לחזק. What is more, even if such an a priori declaration of intent is not forthcoming, the actual literary practice is the same. For example, in his defense of Alfasi against the *Sefer ham-Ma'or,* RABD frequently supports RaZaH, expands his statements or elaborates his theories. He points out correlations and coincidences between their views, refers to his own criticisms of Alfasi, and even has an occasional word of praise for RaZaH. A striking indication of the complexity or dialectical involvement of this defense-criticism is the statement of Naḥmanides, most vigilant guardian and comprehensive expounder of Alfasi, that RABD's attempted defense of Alfasi is futile, for Alfasi's position is really indefensible. The critical attitude of Rashi's descendants and disciples toward his epochal commentaries is, of course, another case in point.

This characterization and conclusion notwithstanding, further precision requires that we not camouflage the marked critical tendency which was operative in the early decades of *Mishneh Torah* study. By the middle of the thirteenth century there must already have been a considerable volume of criticism, for by approximately that time Naḥmanides, in the introduction to his criticisms on the *Sefer ham-Miṣwot,* observed in passing that Maimonides' "great treatise" (*ḥibburo hag-gaḏol*) had been subject to sustained questioning. Such a statement as the one coming from R. Meshullam ben Moses of Béziers (who died about 1230), that he will not "put himself into pawn" for the sake of the *Mishneh Torah,* is also emblematic. Earlier R. Judah Alḥarizi, in the famous chapter XLVI of his *Taḥkĕmoni,* had commented rather amorphously on the widespread criticism of Maimonides' work, suggesting with transparent partisanship that it was *all* biased and inconsequential. The early debate was apparently quite heated; R. Meir hal-Levi Abulafia already notes the quip whether the title should be *Mishneh Torah* or *Mĕšanneh Torah* (one who changes the Torah). In any event, whatever the motives or perceptions, the fact of criticism must be clearly noted. RABD and R. Moses hak-Kohen are, as we have tried to demonstrate, critics-commentators, but the critical dimension, the impetus to trim and contain, to expose flawed interpretations or vulnerable foundations is paramount, while the motive of R. Manoah (*Sefer ham-Mĕnuḥah*) or R. Vidal (*Maggiḏ Mishneh*) is predominantly commentatorial and explicative, supportive and defensive. Actually, as noted briefly in Chapter II, the motive is dual: to embellish the *Mishneh Torah* with the necessary sources and explanations, to supply the interpretative-critical apparatus which would clarify ambiguous, or vindicate controversial, statements and thereby rehabilitate it as an authoritative code. This literary effort would counter the thrust of those who spotlighted the general lack of sources and explanations in the *Mishneh Torah* and also dissented from specific rulings, and thereby disqualified it as an ultimate guide in codification. Special mention should, of course, be made of those commentators, particularly in modern times, who have no axe to grind and whose concern is purely theoretical: to understand and explicate the Maimonidean view as well as that of his critics, to show how a Talmudic passage lends itself to multiple interpretations. Suffice it to refer to the three great works, already classics in their own right, of the twentieth century: *Ḥidduše R. Ḥayyim hal-Levi, 'Or Sameaḥ,* and *Ṣofnat Pa'ăneaḥ.*

DESIGN AND REALITY: THE ACTUAL IMPACT

Now if we return to Maimonides' own scenario of the spread and impact of his Code, we must qualify it further. He soberly anticipated a tempestuous reaction but steadfastly believed that the tempest would subside, the raging waters recede, and his great Code would then sail smoothly.[2] Its value would finally be acknowledged and its axial role would become both conspicuous and consistent. Actually, the story is more checkered. There was immediately a period of intensive study reflected in selective (serene or severe) criticism, probing commentary, extensive quotation, and varied imitation (seen to some extent in the proliferation of partial codes). There followed a succession of full-fledged commentaries initiated in the thirteenth century and continuing to our own days. The *Mishneh Torah* is reputedly second only to the Bible in the number of commentaries and studies it has elicited. It was adopted as a legal guide in certain communities. Communal ordinances (*takkanot*) and responsa officially recognized its authoritative-regulatory role, stipulating that all religious-judicial issues be decided in accord with Maimonidean views. Its impact on certain exegetical compilations is most substantive and noteworthy: the *Midraš hag-Gadol,* for example, contains extensive (often anonymous) quotations from the *Mishneh Torah,* while practically all the halakic matters introduced into the *Midraš Berešit Zuṭa* of R. Samuel ben Nissim are also lifted from the Maimonidean Code. In some places it is reported that

---

2. The analysis in Chapter II of exceptions to the codificatory form—the double-barreled reality that the *Mishneh Torah* has extensive commentatorial material, and that Maimonides acknowledged that total finality was a wistful goal—does not change the basic central fact. All our talk about judicial indeterminacy should not be taken out of context. Maimonides' repeated references convey the impression that he was eager to see this opus established as a standard manual and uniform reference book for practically all issues. He recognized, in addition, that a code must have some immanent uncertainties which the jurist decides, matters "which require due deliberation" and give the jurist a creative-interpretative role. However, the basic use and value of the Code remains. For the MaHaRaL, *Dĕrašot* (Jerusalem, 1959), p. 104, see also S. Assaf, in *ḲS,* XX (1943/44), 41.

people were accustomed to study only "the books of Maimonides and not the books of the Talmud." The MaHaRaL denounces "those who say that it is possible to resolve all the problems in the world by the *Mishneh Torah* of Maimonides" and that there is no need to study the Talmud. We also know that in the early stages of the circulation of the *Šulḥan ʿAruk* there was a measure of rivalry and some tension as communities reviewed their options and weighed whether or not to substitute the new code for the *Mishneh Torah*. It did thus have a measure of success in becoming an authoritative code.

It may well be, however, that the main point about the massive and enduring influence of the *Mishneh Torah* is the fact that it was pivotal even in ways which Maimonides did not anticipate. An author's work often bears unintended as well as intended fruits; its total influences and repercussions need not be designed, directed, or even desired by the author. Great literary compositions, like works of music and art, take on a life of their own. They are filtered through the personality and mentality of the reader or interpreter, who frequently transforms the work in consonance with his own predilections and insights. To claim the vast literature surrounding the *Mishneh Torah* as an integral part of Maimonides' influence would be inaccurate if not bizarre, in the light of Maimonides' intentions and aspirations;[3] nevertheless, the historical record must be established and evaluated. As opposition to the Code faded, it was not replaced by bland acceptance. Lingering reservations, if not resentments, are reflected in the relentless refusal of Talmudists to use the name *Mishneh Torah*. They conspicuously and persistently substituted the title *Yad ha-ḥăzakah* or else used personal references (R. Moses) and literary circumlocutions ("his composition") in order to avoid mentioning the name *Mishneh Torah*. Even those who relied on it, explicated and defended it, reconstructed its assumptions and unearthed its sources, dissociated themselves from the title given by

---

3. Cf. L. Strauss, *Persecution*, p. 47: "And just as the *Mishneh Torah*, far from terminating the halakic discussions, actually served as a new starting point for them, in the same way the *Guide*, far from offering a final interpretation of the secret teaching of the Bible, may actually have been an attempt to revive the oral discussion thereof by raising difficulties which intentionally were left unsolved."

Maimonides and its implications. There is not too much explicit debate concerning Maimonides' intention—i.e., whether the *Mishneh Torah* should supersede the Talmud—an issue which can be traced from the letter to R. Phinehas, through the statement of R. Solomon Duran (*Milḥemet Miṣwah*), and on to the accusations and allegations of R. Joseph Ashkenazi, not to mention the vehement charges of such a modern anti-Maimonidean as Samuel D. Luzzatto. The fact is—even discounting this sporadic and principled opposition to the very enterprise—that it did *not* become, as he hoped, *the* monolithic and authoritative code of Judaism, even though its codificatory influence, often channeled through later codes or responsa collections, was great, but became instead a dynamo generating an endless variety of works. The increasing awe with which his opus was viewed—the recognition that the *Mishneh Torah* was unique in so many ways, that nobody before or after had attempted a work of such scope and exactitude—and the nearly consensual assumption that its formulations and conclusions were exceedingly meticulous and harmonious meant that any study and analysis (commentary or criticism) must be equally meticulous and geared to uncovering the implicit interpretations or resolving the apparent contradictions. All assumed the existence of an interpretative-hermeneutical infrastructure as well as a conceptual-classificatory superstructure. Hence the study of the *Mishneh Torah* through the ages combined scholarly sleuthing—quest for unknown or unnoticed sources together with variant readings of conventional texts—with interpretative hypothesis, conceptual inference, and reconstruction of Maimonidean interpretations and deductions. Maimonides, the magisterial codifier, was usually honored and heeded, his views weighing heavily; in addition, Maimonides, the versatile but laconic and allusive interpreter, was regularly, often laboriously, studied, his views being microscopically analyzed. There was need to align his sententious, sometimes seemingly ambiguous halakot with the Talmudic sources as well as to determine the inner consistency and harmoniousness of his formulations (e.g., the relation of a Maimonidean formulation in *Hilkot Ḥăgigah* with one in *Hilkot Parah,* or one in *Hilkot ʿĂbadim* with *Ḳorban Pesaḥ* and *Ḥăgigah*).

We may perhaps note—examples are legion—that this heterogeneous influence of, and divergent approaches to, the *Mishneh Torah* are telescoped in the sixteenth-century preoccupation with it in the renascent and burgeoning center of Safed.[4] The *Mishneh Torah* was used both as a basis for and a source of codificatory conclusions in accord with the author's original intention, but also served as a pivot for expansive Talmud study, for interpretative amplification—for commentary which, on occasion, assumed a wide-ranging, "free association" form of writing, for the exercise of identifying "difficult passages" and proposing solutions, for the whole gamut of *pilpul, ḥidduš*, etc. There was also methodological investigation, the literature of *kĕlalim* (rules and norms of codification and exposition). It was also a text for popular public study, with daily readings; the Rabbi would be asked to "explain a chapter of Maimonides in the synagogue, as was their custom." R. Solomon Duran reports that he studied two laws of the Code daily. In a word, it hovered over popular study, codificatory activity, jurisprudential reflection, and exegetical enterprise, and the same is true for other places and for other periods. The works of R. Jonathan Eybeschütz, R. Jacob Emden, R. Solomon of Chelm (*Mirkebet ham-Mishneh*), and R. Judah Rosanes (*Mishneh lĕ-Melek*) could also be shown to illustrate the range of attitudes, goals, and achievements. Suffice it to mention, for example, that the real goal of the *Mishneh lĕ-Melek* was to preserve and popularize the teachings of R. Judah Rosanes' master. As he was looking for an effective way to do this systematically and with dignity, he chose to use the prestigious *Mishneh*

---

4. See, e.g., M. Benayahu, *'Areševt*, II (1960), pp. 109–29; Z. Dimitrovsky, *Sĕfunot*, VII (1963), especially pp. 80ff. The interest in the MT goes back to the time of R. Shem Ṭob ibn Gaon (*Migdal 'Oz*); see D. Löwinger, *Sĕfunot*, VII (1963), especially pp. 24ff. As for the sixteenth century itself, one might add a variety of additional examples: e.g., R. Abraham Portaleone (*Šilṭe Gibborim*), in describing his education, singles out the halakic works of Maimonides; R. Azariah Figo (*Giddule Tĕrumah*)—an author-commentator in search of a text—informs us that he abandoned his initial inclination to write on either the *Mishneh Torah* or the *Ṭurim* because he felt that R. Joseph Karo's commentaries left little room for significant contribution, and yet most discussions in his work (a commentary on the *Sefer hat-Tĕrumot*) revolve around the *Mishneh Torah* and its commentaries. R. Moses Isserles (in his *Torat ha-'Olah*) declares that in all halakic matters relating to the Temple and its ritual he will invariably follow the *Mishneh Torah*, ignoring Talmudic controversy; see also J. Avida, *'Areševt*, III (1961), pp. 31–47 (concerning use of MT as a text book).

*Torah*, which was not really his primary interest. The Maimonidean text is thus a good pretext, and a sturdy springboard, for ramified literary achievement.

Needless to say, this reverential conception and the resultant attempts to harmonize passages, illuminate obscurities, and eliminate difficulties harbored the danger of overinterpretation. The very fact that so much is unarticulated, invisible, and implicit attracted creative scholars who relished the opportunity for untrammeled speculation and investigation; the *Mishneh Torah* was an ideal point of departure. In the face of this, the critic-commentator can only fall back upon internal evidence and the general trends and traits of the work, as well as upon conceptual discipline and interpretative restraint. The search for sources or the elaboration of hypothetical interpretations of problematic and/or provocative passages must be guided and disciplined by Maimonides' explicit statements concerning method or meaning, substance or structure. Farfetched theories, however subtle or ingenious, are not the prime goal. A full history of the various approaches to the *Mishneh Torah* and the differing methods of exposition would almost yield a history of Rabbinic literature.[5]

One notable result of the surge of literary achievement and creativity which mirrored the multifaceted approach to the *Mishneh Torah* is that the feeling of historical loneliness, the fear of depletion, of not being able to create or contribute anything new, which overcomes many writers when they confront and contemplate great and overpowering classical achievements,[6] did not

---

5. The non-Jewish use and study of the *Mishneh Torah* is, in its own right, an interesting and often piquant chapter of the history of Maimonidean influence. One could note its use in the Barcelona disputation of 1263 as well as the Tortosa disputation of 1413. It played a dominant role in Christian Hebraism and along with other works was translated into Latin and vernaculars. See the bibliography by J. Dienstag, "Christian Translators of Maimonides' *Mishneh Torah* into Latin," *Salo Baron Jubilee Volume*, I, 287ff. For the attempt of the Czarist government to impose study of the MT as a substitute for the Talmud and the adamant opposition of Jewish religious leaders, see the memoirs of R. Joseph Schneersohn, *The Tzemach Tzedek and the Haskalah* (New York, 1962).

6. See, e.g., W. Jackson Bate, *The Burden of the Past* (New York, 1972). Of course, one must distinguish between theoretical innovation (offering new conceptualizations, interpretations, and insights) and practical innovation (changing halakic observance as a result of a novel understanding of the sources). The latter was rare and subject to numerous restraints. Hence, creative Rabbinic writing is often hedged by an author's caveat: what I

# EPILOGUE

become a serious obstacle or deterrent for Rabbinic writers. In this case, the challenges presented by the *Mishneh Torah*—search for sources and reconstruction of interpretations—were a spur to creativity. Actually, creativity, the possibility of new insight and fresh perception, is a hallmark of Rabbinic literature in general and *ḥidduš* (novel interpretation) is its motto. When scholars, even master and disciple, met, they would greet each other by inquiring about the *ḥidduš* which was propounded in the house of study (see, e.g., B. Ḥag 3a). Rabbinic literature is cumulative but also open-ended; the past is not a burden but a pulsating heritage, and hence the composition of novellae (*ḥiddušim*) is a dominant literary trait. Given these dynamic features of halakic writing, a seminal achievement such as the *Mishneh Torah* would not stultify but stimulate further achievement.

The support which the critical-commentatorial literature on the *Mishneh Torah* gave to the sense of intellectual freedom is also noteworthy. The fact that the revered Maimonides could be criticized, and that students could dissent from his rulings, encouraged independence. R. Ḥayyim Jair Bacharach, for example, posits that his periodic criticism of predecessors should not alarm his readers, for fallibility is a universal human trait—witness the great Maimonides and the criticism directed against him.

## THE *Mishneh Torah* AND SUBSEQUENT CODIFICATION

The specific influence of Maimonides' great Code on subsequent codification—apart from its nearly ubiquitous influence on responsa and novellae and its use as a commentary or spur to commentary (attested already by ham-Me'iri)—is conveniently narrated as a classical tale of convergence and divergence, or even fulfillment and frustration. All the encomia concerning his Code notwithstanding, Maimonides had no followers in the precise sense. There was no school of Maimonidean codification. It should be clear that this assertion refers not only to imitators and continuators but also to users; even when somebody like R. Moses

---

write is pure theory, not for practical application. A good statement concerning the pros and cons of innovative enterprises in Rabbinic literature is found in R. Israel of Shklov, *Pĕ'at haĭ-Šulḥan* (Safed, 1836), p. 6. See also above, chap. I, n. 126.

## 532 INTRODUCTION TO THE CODE OF MAIMONIDES

Ḥayyim Luzzatto in the eighteenth century or R. Moses Sofer in the nineteenth century recommended regular use of the *Mishneh Torah*, it was as a masterful summary of the Oral Law, to be reviewed quickly and conveniently. The same is true for the use of select sections, e.g., *Hilkot Těšubah*, to be read between New Year's Day and the Day of Atonement. This is certainly the case with abridgments and condensations; the son of R. Samuel Aboab (*Děbar Šěmu'el*) mentions in the introduction to his father's work that the latter prepared an abridged footnoted edition of the *Mishneh Torah*. Such use is not identical with the codificatory model which Maimonides had in mind, and therefore concurs with the statement that the *Mishneh Torah* did not initiate a codificatory school. Whereas in philosophy Maimonideanism is a fundamental and formative reality, an aggressive ideology and methodology which attracted or repelled, there is no equivalent or counterpart in halakic codification. Pragmatism prevailed and Maimonides' soaring ideal of compressed but all-embracing study of Torah, including laws and ideas temporarily impractical, was eclipsed; his program of comprehensive, albeit simplified and systematized, Talmud study was not implemented and his vision never became a reality. There is no antagonism, merely benign neglect and different study habits. RaDBaZ apologizes and R. Joseph Karo complains, but the shrunken curriculum, which Maimonides tried with such force and passion to expand, remained in vogue.[7] R. Ḥayyim of Volozhin, in his introduction to the commentary of R. Elijah Gaon of Vilna on *Šěkalim*, comments on the continued neglect of extensive portions of the Talmud. Functionality prevailed and Maimonides' unique attempt at topical-conceptual classification yielded to more utilitarian and totally relevant arrangement of codes.[8] As noted in Chapter IV,

---

7. In modern times, the expansive and theoretically oriented study of *Zěra'im, Kodašim,* or *Ṭohărot*—represented in the works of such creative figures as R. Israel of Shklov (*Pě'at haš-Šulḥan*), R. Gershon Enoch of Radzin (*Sidre Ṭohărot*), or R. Baruch Epstein ('*Ăruk haš-Šulḥan he-'Atid*), or in the schools of Radin and Brisk—is, of course, heavily indebted to the MT but hardly a continuation of its method. This is another instance of fulfillment and frustration.

8. The unqualified statement concerning the uniqueness of Maimonides' classification, underscored also in Chapter IV, especially n. 93, is easily substantiated by a rapid review of

## EPILOGUE

the conceptual refinement and theoretical orientation of the *Mishneh Torah* were amply admired and loudly acclaimed, but more pragmatic-utilitarian conceptions and conventions determined the form and structure of post-Maimonidean codes. The paradox, however, is that while the *Ṭurim* of R. Jacob ben Asher—and the same is true, of course, for the *Šulḥan 'Aruk* and the *Lĕbuš*, which are modelled on the *Ṭurim*—differed from the *Mishneh Torah* in arrangement and scope as well as in the conception of philosophy and law, the Maimonidean influence is pervasive. The retreat from the *Mishneh Torah* was a two-pronged affair. When R. Joseph Karo decided to compose his *Bet Yosef*, motivated by the need to review "all the *practical* laws of Judaism, explaining their roots and origins in the Talmud" (italics mine) and all the conflicting interpretations concerning them, he identified himself with the critics of the worth and desirability of an oracular type of code containing curt staccato directives and summations. Such manuals were neither adequate nor reliable. Moreover, when he chose to build his expansive work around an existing code that

---

the structure and arrangement of other codes, pre- as well as post-Maimonidean. In order for the comparison to be instructive and meaningful, we should consider only the works which (a) abandoned the Talmudic sequence and (b) made some attempt at comprehensiveness. The first stipulation excludes from our overview such works as the *Hălakot* of Alfasi or of R. Asher ben Jehiel, for although comprehensive (with regard to the practicable portions of the law) they remained, with minor exceptions, within the Mishnaic-Talmudic framework. The second eliminates monographs on specific topics, such as the halakic compendia of R. Saadiah Gaon, R. Hai Gaon, and R. Samuel ben Hofni Gaon, or such later works as the *Sefer hat-Tĕrumot* of R. Samuel has-Sardi and the *Torat hab-Bayit* of RaSHBA, for while original in definition and perception their restricted scope gave them no chance, or challenge, to classify and integrate thematically disparate material. Such works as the *'Iṭṭur* of R. Isaac ben Abba Mari may be included, because they at least develop some rationale for combining several areas of halakah, however artificial the combination.

The result of such a review—moving from the *Sefer ha-'Iṭṭim* of R. Judah al-Bargeloni and the *Sefer ha-'Eškol* of R. Abraham ben Isaac of Narbonne to the *Sefer ha-Roḳeaḥ* of R. Eleazar of Worms and the *Sefer Yĕre'im* of R. Eleazar ben Samuel of Metz, the *'Orḥot Ḥayyim* of R. Aaron ha-Kohen of Lunel and the *Tolĕdot 'Adam wĕ-Ḥawwah* of R. Jeroham, the *Ṣedah lad-Derek* of R. Menahem ben Zerah and the *'Agur* of R. Jacob Landau, through the *Ṭurim* of R. Jacob ben Asher and the *Šulḥan 'Aruk*—provides overwhelming and unimpeachable proof for the uniqueness of the MT classification.

Of course, even comparison with monographs of restricted scope would illustrate the advance in Maimonides' conceptualization and presentation of smaller units of halakah. His treatment of *šĕbu'ot*, *'erubin*, or *bĕrakot* are good examples.

was popular and authoritative, and proceeded to select the *Ṭurim* of R. Jacob ben Asher rather than the more famous and widespread *Mishneh Torah,* his decision tilted the scales toward practicability. He urged expansive and full-orbed study, taking into account alternate views and divergent explanations rather than the review of undocumented, usually unilateral, decisions, but the scope remained limited, determined by the practical orientation of the *Ṭurim*. Maimonides' all-inclusive goals and programs, obliterating distinctions between practice and theory, were thus aborted and thwarted, and the practical or relevant orientation, addressing oneself only to those concrete problems and issues whose applicability was not confined either temporally or geographically, received semicanonical status. Even when R. Joseph Karo then reversed himself—having persuasively argued against the utility and wisdom of the apodictic compendium, he later convincingly conceded its need and efficacy—he still did not return to Maimonides' comprehensive scope. When he himself abridged the voluminous *Bet Yosef* and produced the *Šulḥan 'Aruk,* in which the "reader will find all kinds of delicacies" fastidiously arranged, systematized, and clarified, the structure was fixed by the practical contours of the *Ṭurim* and the frame of reference remained utilitarian. The crucial step thus was the initial predilection for the *Ṭurim:* by adopting the scope and classification of the *Ṭurim,* R. Joseph Karo capitulated unconditionally to the practical orientation. While both Maimonides and R. Jacob ben Asher were of one mind in abandoning the sequence of the Talmudic treatises and seeking an independent classification of halakah, they differed radically in their goals: Maimonides sought to create a topical-conceptual arrangement that would provide a new interpretative mold for study, and would also be educationally sound and practically useful. R. Jacob ben Asher was guided only by functionality, and as a result was less rigorous conceptually. He did not hesitate to group disparate items together, inasmuch as a code, according to this conception, should facilitate the understanding of the operative laws and guide people in translating concepts into rules of conduct.

Nevertheless, Maimonides' imprints are scattered throughout the *Šulḥan 'Aruk*. The content, the norm, the style are notably Maimonidean; R. Yom Ṭob Lipman Heller (*Ma'ădane Yom Ṭob*) has already underscored this. R. Joel Sirkes (*Tešubot BaH ha-Ḥădašot*) notes critically the nearly total reliance of R. Joseph Karo on Maimonides, especially in laws of monetary matters. Entire paragraphs (halakot) or snippets from the *Mishneh Torah* are quoted verbatim on every page. Traces of the Maimonidean formulations are easily and regularly visible. It is almost a special kind of *pars pro toto*—the whole is rejected, while the parts are kept in a clear and decisive preponderance. The *Mishneh Torah* view, whether lenient or stringent, is a major factor in any codificatory decision; even in cases where it is a minority view, it is rarely rejected peremptorily. The history of halakah is replete with instances of "Maimonidean stringencies" (*ḥumrot*) or, generally, Maimonidean interpretations and emphases which were absorbed into the bloodstream of halakic observance. Even R. Moses Isserles, whose glosses are designed to guarantee that the Ashkenazic tradition be fully represented in the *Šulḥan 'Aruk*, respected and relied extensively on Maimonides. The failure of the *Mishneh Torah* to become the standard authoritative reference work, or at least to become the paradigm for subsequent codification, is part of the story. The depth and extent of Maimonidean influence, which have been repeatedly studied and generally acknowledged, are the other part of the story.

## Adherence and Divergence: the Example of *Talmud Torah*

It may be appropriate, in conclusion, to focus on one specific instance which illustrates adherence as well as divergence in all major aspects, thereby summarizing the tale of fulfillment and frustration. Maimonides included *Hilkot Talmud Torah* in Book One, the *Sefer ham-Madda'*, aiming to summarize the essential beliefs and guiding concepts which provide the theoretical and experiential substructure of Judaism. The section on study overflows with pathos, underscoring the universality of the obligation of study and its precedence over other preoccupations. However, not only is the classification novel, but the very definition of study, of the scope of *talmud Torah*, is overwhelming. The implications of this, in which philosophy is presented as an integral, even paramount, component of Oral Law, have been fully discussed in Chapter VI.

A quick glance at the treatment of *talmud Torah* in the *Šulḥan 'Aruk* reveals first of all the divergence or incongruence in the realm of classification. *Hilkot Talmud Torah* are tucked away, almost inconspicuously, in the last section (*Yoreh Déah*, 246). There is not the faintest resemblance to the *Mishneh Torah*'s conceptual classification. Yet most of the passages which are included have been lifted verbatim from the *Mishneh Torah*. It is a pastiche of Maimonidean formulations. When, however, we come to Maimonides' daring and ideologically charged formulation concerning the scope of *talmud Torah* and the central role of philosophical pursuits, we are struck by the difference. To be sure, post-Maimonidean writers generally either ignore this formulation, camouflage it, or blunt its edges.[9] In keeping with this trend, R. Joseph Karo quotes both long paragraphs of *Hilkot Talmud Torah* (i, 11, 12) verbatim with the single flagrant deletion of the sentence, which obviously caused him more than a twinge of discomfiture, about *Pardes*. R. Moses Isserles, author of the *Torat ha-'Olah* and moderate protagonist of philosophic study, reinserts this reference less conspicuously and more restrainedly toward the end of his gloss. In sum, having in mind contemporary discussions concerning "the structure of scientific revolutions" (T. Kuhn), it may be proposed that Maimonides' revolution remained primarily "literary"; there was maximum dissemination of the *Mishneh Torah* itself but more limited acceptance of its premises and goals: it did not basically transform modes of thought or redirect the course of codification, but it impinged, directly and indirectly, on methods of study and norms of observance and provided a nearly universal referent for discussion of halakah.

AN ORIGINAL, DYNAMIC FORCE IN JEWISH LIFE

This brief tale of complex and multifaceted influence, often differing drastically from the directions which the author anticipated, should not divert our attention from what is probably

---

9. One may consult, e.g., *Sefer Miṣwot Gadol*, 12; '*Orḥot Ḥayyim*, I, 28b; ham-Me'iri in *Bet hab-Beḥirah* on *Kiddušin*, 30a; *Toledot 'Adam wĕ-Ḥawwah*, *netib* 2; *Ṭur Yoreh De'ah*, 246:4; *Ṣedah lad-Derek*, I, 4:7.

the central historical fact: acknowledgment of the underlying force and the intrinsic originality of his work, its creative underived elements and innovative emphases, its rejection of mediocrity, timidity, and conventionality, the newness of its scope, structure, style, and intellectual sovereignty. For us to recognize individual genius is not to subscribe to the "great man" theory of history but to avoid the snares of geneticism, precursorism, and reductionism, to move beyond generalizations, abstractions, and typologies to the realities and dynamisms of history. The *Mishneh Torah* is one of these original dynamic realities of Jewish history.

# Abbreviations

## General

B.  Babylonian Talmud
HTR  *Harvard Theological Review*
HUCA  *Hebrew Union College Annual*
JAOS  *Journal of the American Oriental Society*
JJS  *Journal of Jewish Studies*
JQR  *Jewish Quarterly Review*
KM  Kesef Mishneh (Commentary on MT)
KS  *Ḳiryat Sefer*
LM  Leḥem Mishneh (Commentary on MT)
MbM  *Moses ben Maimon, Sein Leben, Seine Werke und Sein Einfluss*, ed. W. Bacher, M. Brann, and D. Simonsen (Leipzig, 1908–14; reprinted, Hildesheim, 1971), 2 vols.
MGWJ  *Monatsschrift für Geschichte und Wissenschaft des Judenthums*
MM  Maggid Mishneh (Commentary on MT)
P.  Palestinian (Yerushalmi) Talmud
PAAJR  *Proceedings of the American Academy for Jewish Research*
R.  Rabbi
REJ  *Revue des Études Juives*
Twersky, "Beginnings"  I. Twersky, "The Beginnings of Mishneh Torah Criticism," *Biblical and Other Studies*, ed. A. Altmann (Cambridge, Mass., 1963), pp. 161–83.
Twersky, "Non-Halakic Aspects"  I. Twersky, "Some Non-Halakic Aspects of the Mishneh Torah," *Jewish Medieval and Renaissance Studies*, ed. A. Altmann (Cambridge, Mass., 1967), pp. 95–119.
Twersky, *Rabad*  I. Twersky, *Rabad of Posquières* (Cambridge, Mass., 1962).
Twersky, "Sefer MT"  I. Twersky, "Sefer Mishneh Torah la-RaMBaM; Měḡammato wě-Tafḳido," Israel Academy of Sciences, *Dibre (Proceedings)*, V (1972), 1–22.
Twersky, "The Shulḥan 'Aruḵ"  I. Twersky, "The Shulḥan 'Aruḵ: Enduring Code of Jewish Law," *Judaism*, XVI (1967), 141–59.
YJS  Yale Judaica Series

## Personal Names

MaHaRaL  R. Judah Loew ben Bezaleel of Prague
RABD  R. Abraham ben David of Posquières

## 540 INTRODUCTION TO THE CODE OF MAIMONIDES

| | |
|---|---|
| RaDBaZ | R. David ibn Abi Zimra |
| RaMaK | R. Moses hak-Kohen |
| RaMBaM | R. Moses ben Maimon (Maimonides) |
| RaMBaN | R. Moses ben Naḥman (Naḥmanides) |
| RaSHBA | R. Solomon ben Abraham ibn Adret |
| RaSHBaM | R. Samuel ben Meir |
| RaZaH | R. Zerahiah hal-Levi (*Ba'al ham-Ma'or*) |
| RIF | R. Isaac Alfasi |
| RIṢBA | R. Isaac ben Abraham |
| RIṬBA | R. Yom Ṭob ben Abraham Ishbili |

TRACTATES OF *Mishnah, Tosefta,* AND *Talmud*

| | | | | | |
|---|---|---|---|---|---|
| 'Ab | '*Abot* | Ker | *Kĕritot* | Sanh | *Sanhedrin* |
| 'Ar | '*Ărakin* | Ket | *Kĕtubbot* | Shab | *Šabbat* |
| ARN | '*Abot dĕ-Rabbi Nathan* | Ḳid | *Ḳiddušin* | Shebi | *Šĕbi'it* |
| AZ | '*Ăbodah Zarah* | Mak | *Makkot* | Shebu | *Šĕbu'ot* |
| BB | *Baba Batra* | Meḡ | *Mĕgillah* | Sheḵ | *Šĕkalim* |
| Beḵ | *Bĕkorot* | Men | *Mĕnahot* | Sof | *Sofĕrim* |
| Ber | *Bĕrakot* | Miḵ | *Mikwa'ot* | Soṭ | *Soṭah* |
| BḲ | *Baba Ḳamma* | MḲ | *Mo'ed Ḳaṭan* | Suk | *Sukkah* |
| BM | *Baba Mĕṣi'a* | Ned | *Nĕdarim* | Ta | *Ta'ănit* |
| 'Ed | '*Eduyyot* | Neḡ | *Nĕga'im* | Tam | *Tamid* |
| 'Er | '*Erubin* | Nid | *Niddah* | Ter | *Tĕrumot* |
| Giṭ | *Giṭṭin* | 'Oh | '*Ŏhalot* | Ṭoh | *Ṭohărot* |
| Ḥaḡ | *Ḥăḡiḡah* | Par | *Parah* | 'Uḵ | '*Uḳṣin* |
| Ḥal | *Ḥallah* | Pe | *Pe'ah* | Yeb | *Yĕbamot* |
| Hor | *Horayot* | Pes | *Pĕsahim* | Zeb | *Zĕbahim* |
| Ḥul | *Ḥullin* | RH | *Roš haš-Šanah* | | |
| Kel | *Kelim* | | | | |

B. prefixed to the name of a tractate indicates a reference to the Babylonian Talmud; P. indicates a reference to the Palestinian (Jerusalemite) Talmud; and Tos a reference to the Tosefta (ed. Zuckermandel, Pasewalk, 1880; 2d ed., Jerusalem, 1937). Otherwise the reference is to tractates of the Mishnah.

### WORKS BY MAIMONIDES

'*Iggĕrot*   '*Iggĕrot ha RaMBaM* (*Letters of Maimonides*), ed. D. H. Baneth. Jerusalem, 1946. References are to the pages of this edition.

IT   '*Iggeret Teman* (*Epistle to Yemen*). The Arabic Original and Three Hebrew Versions, ed. A. S. Halkin, English tr. B. Cohen. New

# ABBREVIATIONS

York, 1952. Page references (in Roman numerals) are to the English translation unless otherwise specified.

Ḳobeṣ     *Ḳobeṣ Tĕšuḇot ha-RaMBaM we-'Iggĕrotaw* (*Collection of Maimonides' Responsa and Letters*), ed. A. Lichtenberg. Leipzig, 1859. References are to parts (I–III) and page.

LA     *Letter on Astrology*. Page references are to the English translation in *Medieval Political Philosophy*, ed. R. Lerner and M. Mahdi. Glencoe, 1963, pp. 227–37. The English translation was made from the Hebrew text published by A. Marx, *HUCA*, III (1926), 349–58.

MN     *Moreh Nĕḇuḵim* (*Guide of the Perplexed*). References are to parts (I–III) and chapters of the work. Page references in parentheses, when a passage from a long chapter is cited, are to *The Guide of the Perplexed*, tr. S. Pines. Chicago, 1963.

MT     *Mishneh Torah*. References give name of treatise, chapter, and section (*halaḵah*), e.g., *Šabbaṯ*, i, 5. The List of Treatise Titles in MT, below, will enable the reader to correlate these references with the Yale Judaica Series (YJS), which refers numerically to the volumes of the MT by book, treatise, chapter, and section, e.g., III, 1, i, 5 = Book III, *Šabbaṯ*, i, 5.

MTH     *Ma'ămar Tĕḥiyyaṯ ham-Meṯim* (*Treatise on Resurrection*), ed. J. Finkel. *PAAJR*, IX (1939). References are to the pages of this edition.

PhM     *Peruš ham-Mišnayoṯ* (*Mishnah Commentary*). Citations are to treatise, chapter, and section (mishnah). Page references are to the seven-volume edition (which includes the Arabic original and a Hebrew translation) of J. Ḳāfiḥ. Jerusalem, 1963. Abbreviations conform to the YJS system of Mishnah references.

ShM     *Sefer ham-Miṣwoṯ* (*Book of Commandments*). Citations indicate either a positive or a negative commandment and its number. The fourteen principles (*šorašim*) are cited by number. Page references are to *The Commandments* (*Sefer ham-Miṣwoṯ of Maimonides*). 2 vols., tr. C. Chavel, London, 1967.

ŠP     *Šĕmonah Pĕraḵim* (*Eight Chapters*), ed. J. Gorfinkle. New York, 1912. References are to chapters of the work.

*Tĕšuḇot*     *Tĕšuḇot ha-RaMBaM* (*Responsa of Maimonides*), 3 vols., ed. J. Blau. Jerusalem, 1958. References are to the responsum number, with the page in parentheses. Vol. III, which contains a variety of supplementary material, is cited by page only.

## List of Treatise Titles in MT

(Roman numerals refer to Book and Treatise as cited in the Yale Judaica Series)

'Ăḇaḏim   XII, v
'Aḇel   XIV, iv
'Ăḇoḏaṯ Yom haḵ-Kippurim   VIII, viii
'Aḇoṯ haṭ-Ṭumē'oṯ   X, v
'Akum ('Ăḇoḏaṯ Kokaḇim)   I, iv
'Ărakin   VI, iv
Běḵoroṯ   IX, iii
Běrakoṯ   II, v
Beṯ hab-Běḥirah   VIII, i
Bi'aṯ Mikdaš   VIII, iii
Bikkurim   VII, vi
De'oṯ   I, ii
'Eḏuṯ   XIV, ii
'Eruḇin   III, ii
Gěneḇah   XI, ii
Gerušin   IV, ii
Gězelah wa-'Ăḇeḏah   XI, iii
Ḥăḡiḡah   IX, ii
Ḥameṣ u-Maṣṣah   III, v
Ḥănukkah   III, x
Ḥoḇel u-Mazziḵ   XI, iv
'Issure Bi'ah   V, i
'Issure Mizbeaḥ   VIII, iv
'Išuṯ   IV, i
Kěle ham-Mikdaš   VIII, ii
Kelim   X, vii
Ķěri'aṯ Šěma'   II, i
Ķidduš ha-Ḥoḏeš   III, viii
Kil'ayim   VII, i
Ķorban Pesaḥ   IX, i
Lulaḇ   III, vi
Ma'ăḵaloṯ 'Ăsuroṯ   V, ii
Ma'ăśeh haḵ-Korbanoṯ   VIII, v
Ma'ăśer   VII, iv
Ma'ăśer Šeni   VII, v

Malweh wě-Loweh   XIII, iii
Mamrim   XIV, iii
Mattěnoṯ 'Ăniyyim   VII, ii
Měḡillah   III, x
Měḥusre Kapparah   IX, v
Mě'ilah   VIII, ix
Měkirah   XII, i
Mělaḵim   XIV, v
Měṭamme' Miškaḇ u-Mošaḇ   X, iv
Mězuzah   II, iii
Mikwa'oṯ   X, viii
Milah   II, vi
Na'ărah Běṯulah   IV, iv
Naḥăloṯ   XIII, v
Něḏarim   VI, ii
Něziruṯ   VI, iii
Nizke Mamon   XI, i
Parah 'Ăḏumah   X, ii
Pěsule ham-Mukdašin   VIII, vii
Roṣeaḥ   XI, v
Šabbaṯ   III, i
Sanhedrin   XIV, i
Šě'ar 'Aḇoṯ haṭ-Ṭumē'oṯ   X, v
(usually referred to merely as 'Aḇoṯ haṭ-Ṭumē'oṯ)
Šěḇiṯaṯ 'Aśor   III, iii
Šěḇu'oṯ   VI, i
Šě'elah u-Fikkaḏon   XIII, ii
Sefer Torah   II, iii
Šěḡaḡoṯ   IX, iv
Šěḥiṭah   V, iii
Šěkalim   III, vii
Šěkenim   XII, iii
Śěkiruṯ   XIII, i
Šěluḥin wě-Šutafin   XII, iv
Šěmiṭṭah wě-Yoḇel   VII, vii

# LIST of TREATISE TITLES IN MT

Ṣiṣit  II, IV
Šofar  III, VI
Soṭah  IV, V
Sukkah  III, VI
Ta'ăniyyot  III, IX
Talmud Torah  I, III
Tĕfillah  II, II
Tĕfillin  II, III
Tĕmidin u-Musafin  VIII, VI
Tĕmurah  IX, VI

Tĕrumot  VII, III
Tĕšubah  I, V
Ṭo'en wĕ-Niṭ'an  XIII, IV
Ṭumĕ'at Met  X, I
Ṭumĕ'at 'Oklin  X, VI
Ṭumĕ'at Ṣara'at  X, III
Yĕsode hat-Torah  I, I
Yibbum  IV, III
Yom Ṭob  III, IV
Zĕkiyyah u-Mattanah  XII, II

# Glossary*

*'Ăbodah*
 worship (of God); literally "service"
*'Ăbodah šebbĕ-leb*
 prayer; literally "service of the heart" (cf. Deut. 11:13)
*'Aggadah*
 nonlegal part of the Talmud
*'Ăguddot*
 factions
*'Ahăbah*
 love
*'Al derek ha-rob*
 preponderantly
*'Am ha-'areṣ*
 ignorant (unlearned) person
*Amoraim* (sing. *Amora*)
 authorities cited in the Gemara who flourished about 200–500 C. E.
*'Aral śĕfatayim*
 *of uncircumcised lips* (Exod. 6:12); i.e., a person whose speech is stilted
*'Ărukim bak-kol u-šĕmurim, sĕdurim u-bĕrurim*
 set up in everything and guarded, ordered and clear
*'Arum bĕ-yir'ah*
 "cunning in the fear (of the Lord)"; i.e., seeking ways of supererogatory service
*'Asmakta*
 surety, unsecured pledge of no legal force
*'Asmaktot*
 Scriptural proof-verses cited in support of Rabbinic enactments
*'Awen*
 iniquity (Ps. 119:133)
*'Azharot*
 poetic enumerations of the 613 precepts; literally "warnings"

*Ba'al hă-ḥokmah*
 wise man

---

*I thank Dr. Nemoy for suggesting and actually compiling this glossary. The terms are Hebrew or Aramaic, except when otherwise designated.

# GLOSSARY

*Ba'ăle de'ah*
persons endowed with knowledge
*Baraita* (pl. *Baraitot*)
an extraneous Mishnah; i.e., Tannaitic teaching not cited in the Mishnah
*Bĕdikot, dĕrišot, ḥăkirot*
examinations, inquiries, investigations (of witnesses)
*Bĕ-lo' kušyah wĕ-lo' peruk*
eliminating questions and solutions
*Bĕrakot*
benedictions, blessings
*Bet din*
judicial court
*Be'ur*
explanation
*Bikkurim*
first fruits
*Birkat bĕtulim*
benediction over virginity
*Biṭṭul ham-mĕ'orĕrim*
abolition of the awakeners (the Levites who sang *Awake, why sleepest Thou, O Lord* [Ps. 44:24])
*Bizzuy*
lack of self-respect
*Da'at*
knowledge, consciousness
*Da'at ḥiṣoni*
external (i.e., heretical) opinion
*Da'at maknah*
mental resolve which transfers possession or ownership
*Darke 'Ĕmori*
"the ways of the Amorites"; i.e., superstitious practices
*Daršinan ṭa'ăma' di-kĕra'*
we interpret the Scriptural passage in accordance with its (logical) reason
*Dat ha-'emet*
true religion
*Dayyan*
judge
*De'ah*
knowledge (of God)

*Dĕbar halakah*
    discussion of halakah
*Dĕbarim bĕrurim, kĕrobim, nĕkonim*
    clear, rational, and correct matters
*De'ot*
    moral-intellectual qualities
*Derek ha-rob*
    see *'Al derek ha-rob*
*Dĕrišot*
    see *Bĕdikot*
*Dibre 'aggadah*
    matters relating to Aggadah
*Dibre ḥăsidut*
    matters (or practices) of piety (sometimes in the sense of supererogatory practices)
*Dibre ḥokmah*
    words of wisdom
*Dibre Torah*
    Torah study
*Debre Torah*
    Torah study
*Dīwān* (Arabic)
    compendium, all-inclusive collection

*'Eglah 'ărufah*
    heifer whose neck is to be broken
*'El de'ot*
    God who knows the opinions (of man [see above, p. 444, n.213])
*'Ĕlohe ruḥot*
    God of spirits
*'Enam nĕkamah*
    are not vengeance
*'Epikoros*
    Epicurean, skeptic, heretic
*'Erub*
    the "blending" of several domains or limits together in order to permit movement from one to the other on the Sabbath
*'Erub ḥăṣerot*
    *'erub* of courtyards
*'Erub tabšilin*
    *'erub* of foods; i.e., food prepared on the eve of the festival and on the festival itself (see *'Erubin*, vi)

# GLOSSARY

*'Eruḇ tĕḥumim*
  'eruḇ of limits

*Fiqh* (Arabic)
  jurisprudence

*Gas ruaḥ*
  "crude of spirit"; i.e., boor, fool, or haughty
*Gassuṯ ha-ruaḥ*
  haughtiness
*Gĕmaṭriyyoṯ*
  homiletic interpretations based on the numerical values of letters
*Gĕnuṯ he-hamon*
  contempt felt by the masses (toward the elite)
*Gĕ'one ham-ma'ăraḇ*
  Geonim of the West
*Gĕ'onim 'aḥăronim*
  later Geonim
*Ger*
  proselyte
*Geṭ*
  bill of divorcement
*Gĕzeraṯ hak-Kaṯuḇ*
  Scriptural edict, decree which apparently has no explanation
*Gilgul*
  associationism
*Gufe Torah*
  essentials of Torah; see also *Yĕsoḏoṯ gufe Torah*

*Haḇdalah*
  separation (the ceremony marking the end of the Sabbath and the beginning of the following weekday)
*Haḇle haz-zĕman*
  follies of the times
*Haḇle 'olam*
  worldly inanities
*Hafla'ah*
  utterance (of one's lips), asseveration (form of oath)
*Haggahoṯ*
  corrections, comments, glosses
*Ḥăḵamim* (sing. *ḥaḵam*)
  wise men, sages, Talmudic Sages

*Ḥăḳiroṯ*
 see *Bĕḏiḳoṯ*
*Halaḵah*
 that part of Talmudic (and of later Rabbinic) literature which deals with legal matters
*Halaḵoṯ gĕḏoloṯ, halaḵoṯ ḳĕṣuḇoṯ, halaḵoṯ ḳĕṭu'oṯ, halaḵoṯ pĕsuḵoṯ*
 titles of Gaonic compendia and codes of law; literally "fixed defined rules"
*Ḥăliṣah*
 ceremony signifying the levir's refusal to marry his widowed sister-in-law
*Hallel*
 Psalms 113–18, as used for liturgical recitation
*Hamon*
 multitude (as distinguished from the elite), unlearned
*Ḥăsiḏim* (sing. *ḥasiḏ*)
 pious men
*Ḥăsiḏuṯ*
 piety
*Hašlamah*
 complement
*Haskamah*
 consensus; see also *Ijmā'*
*Haśśaḡah* (pl. *haśśaḡoṯ*)
 stricture, animadversion, supplement
*Ḥayil*
 substance
*Heḇel*
 vanity, folly, futility
*Heḇel wa-hăḇay*
 vanity and folly
*Hefḳer*
 ownerless or abandoned property; the act of renunciation of ownership
*Heḵal*
 temple
*Heḳḳeš ḥămiši*
 the fifth, poetic, syllogism
*Ḥibbur*
 composition, compendium
*Ḥidduš* (pl. *ḥiddušim*)
 novella, new interpretation

*Higgayon*
  logic
*Ḥikmah* (Arabic)
  wisdom; see also *Sophia*
*Hiḵtiran bĕ-miṣwoṯ*
  He crowned them with precepts
*Hilḵĕta'*
  rule of law
*Ḥilluḵ*
  classification; literally "division (of materials)"
*Ḥoḵmah*
  science, wisdom
*Hores*
  wrecker
*Ḥuḵḵim*
  laws which appear to be beyond reason, statutes (in contrast with *mišpaṭim*)
*Ḥumroṯ*
  stringencies

*'Ibbur*
  intercalation
*Ijmā'* (Arabic)
  consensus; see also *Haskamah*
*'Iḵḵar*
  root, principle
*'Illĕḡim* (sing. *'illeḡ*)
  stammerers
*'Ilm* (Arabic)
  science, wisdom, knowledge
*'Innuy*
  dirge
*'Ir han-niddaḥaṯ*
  city led into idolatry
*'Iṭran bĕ-miṣwoṯ*
  He crowned them with precepts
*'Iyyun*
  careful study

*Ḵabbalah*
  tradition; mystic theosophy (= cabala)
*Ḵaddiš*
  sanctification prayer

550 INTRODUCTION TO THE CODE OF MAIMONIDES

*Ḳal wa-ḥomer*
  from the minor to the major (a principle of logic and hermeneutics)
*Kalām* (Arabic)
  Muslim scholastic philosophy
*Kapparah*
  atonement
*Ḳaton wĕ-gadol*
  small and great, unlearned and learned
*Kawwanah*
  intention, attention, inwardness
*Ḳĕdušah*
  holiness, self-restraint, transcendence
*Kĕfiyyah*
  compulsion
*Kĕlal u-fĕraṭ*
  a general proposition and a particular one
*Kĕlalim*
  rules and principles of adjudication and codification; see also *Sifre kĕlalim*
*Kĕlalim 'ămitiyyim*
  true generalities
*Ḳĕrobim* (sing. *ḳarob*)
  reasonable; literally "close (to reason)"
*Ḳerub*
  facilitation or rationalization
*Keṣad*
  how (is this)?
*Kĕsil* (pl. *kĕsilim*)
  fool
*Kĕṭoreṭ*
  incense
*Kĕ-zayiṭ*
  bulk of an olive
*Kibbud' ab*
  honoring one's father
*Ḳibbuṣ*
  collecting
*Ḳidduš*
  Sanctification benediction
*Ḳidduš haš-Šem*
  sanctification of the Name (of God) (usually through martyrdom, but also by morally impeccable behavior)

*Kil'ayim*
  mixed kinds (of seeds, etc.)
*Ḳinah*
  lament
*Ḳodše mizbeaḥ*
  sacred offerings pertaining to the altar
*Kohen* (pl. *kohănim*)
  priest, person descended from Aaron
*Kolel*
  comprehensive
*Ḳuppah*
  charity fund
*Lašon ṣaḥah*
  precise, elegant language
*Lĕ-har'oṯ han-nes*
  to show (publicize) the miracle
*Lĕ-ḳareḇ 'el haś-śeḵel*
  to bring (matters) close to reason
*Lešeḇ bas-sukkah*
  (benediction) concerning the precept to dwell in the festal booth (on the Festival of Tabernacles)
*Lĕšon haḳ-ḳodeš*
  holy tongue; i.e., Hebrew
*Lifnim miš-šuraṯ had-din*
  beyond the letter (literally "line") of law, supererogatory action
*Lišna' dĕ-rabbanan*
  language of the Rabbis; i.e., the mixed Hebrew-Aramaic style

*Ma'ăśeh*
  action, deed
*Ma'ăśeh 'aḵum*
  idolatrous practice
*Ma'ăśeh bĕre'šiṯ*
  work of creation (Gen. 1); i.e., physics or natural science
*Ma'ăśeh merkaḇah*
  work of the (heavenly) chariot (Ezek. 1); i.e., metaphysics
*Ma'ăśeh raḇ*
  guiding precedent; literally "the deed of a master"
*Maḥloḵeṯ yĕšanah*
  old controversy
*Mal'iḡ 'al ham-miṣwoṯ*
  pours mockery upon the precepts

*Maśkil*
  intellectually cognizing subject
*Masorah*
  Biblical textual tradition; oral tradition
*Maśśa' u-mattan*
  debate, argumentation
*Maṭṭarah*
  purpose
*Mĕḥazzeh rabbotaw*
  treats his masters contemptuously
*Mĕḡammah*
  aim
*Mĕḥilah*
  forgiveness (used in the sense of overlooking a mistake made by an author)
*Mĕḳomot*
  places, *topoi*
*Mĕleḵet haš-Šem*
  labor for the sake of the (Holy) Name
*Mĕleḵet šamayim*
  labor for the sake of heaven (used to denote religious study)
*Miḡbaʿat*
  head-gear
*Miḵreh*
  chance
*Min* (pl. *minim*)
  heretic
*Minhaḡ*
  custom
*Minhaḡ pašuṭ bĕ-roḇ ham-mĕdinot*
  custom prevalent in most countries
*Minhaḡ ṭaʿuṭ*
  custom rooted in error
*Minhaḡ Yiśra'el bĕ-metim*
  Israelite custom regarding the dead
*Minyan ham-miṣwot*
  enumeration of precepts
*Mishnah* (pl. *mishnayot*)
  individual passage in the Mishnah
*Mishnah lo' zazah mim-mĕḳomah*
  mishnah not moved from its place; i.e., a ruling cited verbatim even if its meaning changes

# GLOSSARY

*Mišneh těfillah*
  order (text) of prayer
*Mišpaṭ*
  law, judgment
*Mišpaṭim*
  judgments which are eminently reasonable, ordinances
*Miṣwah* (pl. *miṣwoṯ*)
  religious duty, commandment
*Mišwah šim'iṯ*
  ordinance not subject to rational explanation; literally "traditional commandment"; see also *Ḥukkim*
*Miṣwoṯ śikliyyoṯ*
  rational commandments; see also *Mišpaṭim*
*Miṯaṯ něšikah*
  death by a kiss; i.e., death as the ultimate spiritual consummation
*Miṯyašḥin bě-daḥar zeh*
  this matter requires due, or ample, deliberation
*Mofeṯ*
  rational demonstration
*Molaḏ*
  birth of the new moon
*Morašah*
  inheritance
*Musaf prayer*
  additional prayer (in the festival liturgy)
*Muśkal* (pl. *muśkaloṯ*)
  primary rational notion, intellectually cognized object
*Mutakallimūn* (Arabic)
  Muslim scholastic philosophers (Ash'arites or Mu'tazilites)

*Nahăloṯ*
  inheritances
*Něḇelah*
  an animal slaughtered not according to ritual rules
*Něḇone laḥaš*
  skillful enchanters (cf. Isa. 3:3), persons who are able to express their views in clear and well-chosen words
*Něğinoṯ*
  musical accentuation
*Ně'ilah*
  prayer recited at the "closing" of the gates of heaven at the end of the Day of Atonement

*Nešek̲*
  usury; literally "biting"
*Nĕṭirah*
  grudge
*Ni̲dre hek̲deš*
  vows of consecration
*Ni̲dre 'issur*
  vows of prohibition
*Nomos* (pl. *nomoi*) (Greek)
  law (man-made law)

*'Olam hab-ba'*
  world to come
*'Omer*
  sheaf offering (Lev. 23:11ff.)
*'Omru ḥak̲amim*
  the Sages said
*'Ona'aṭ dĕb̲arim*
  oral deception
*'Ona'aṭ mamon*
  fiscal deception

*Pardes*
  esoteric studies, philosophy
*Paršane Sĕfara̲d*
  the interpreters (Biblical exegetes) from Spain
*Pĕraṭim* (sing. *pĕraṭ*)
  details
*Peruš*
  explication, commentary
*Peruš ham-Mišnah*
  explanation of the Mishnah
*Pĕsak̲, pĕsak̲ halak̲ah*
  normative guidance, practical conclusion
*Pĕšarah*
  compromise
*Pĕšaṭ*
  literal meaning (of Scripture)
*Pĕšaṭe hat-Torah*
  literal (external) meanings of the Torah
*Pidyon šĕb̲uyim*
  ransoming of captives

*Piggul*
  abomination, an offering invalid by reason of an improper intention on the part of the officiating priest
*Pikkudim*
  precepts
*Pilpul*
  subtle or oversubtle exegesis
*Piyyuṭ*
  liturgical poetry

*Rabbanan Sěḫora'e*
  our masters the Seboraim; see *Sěḫoraim*
*Razeha*
  its (the Torah's) secrets
*Rěḇi'iṯ*
  ¼ of a loḡ (measure of liquid)
*Remez*
  hint, indication
*Rěṣon hab-Bore'*
  the will of the Creator
*Rišonim*
  early authorities

*Šadday*
  Almighty (God)
*Ṣaddiḳim* (sing. *ṣaddiḳ*)
  righteous men
*Ṣaḥuṯ*
  clear and precise expression
*Sakal*
  fool, literalist
*Sěḇarah*
  theory
*Sěḇoraim*
  scholars of the Babylonian academies in the period (sixth century) following that of the Amoraim
*Šěḇu'aṯ had-dayyanim*
  judicial oath
*Sědarim* (sing. *seḏer*)
  orders (of the Mishnah)
*Sefer kolel*
  all-inclusive book, summa; see also *Diwan*

*Sefer Torah*
  Scroll of the Torah
*Sĕḡullah*
  special quality or nature
*Šĕḥiṭah*
  ritual slaughtering
*Śeḵel*
  intellect
*Šem he-'amur bĕ-šuttafuṯ*
  homonym
*Sĕmiḵah*
  Rabbinic ordination
*Šĕmirah*
  observance (of law) (used also to mean esteem of its worth and wisdom)
*Sĕtam*
  acronym of Scroll (*Sefer*) of Torah, tĕfillin, and mĕzuzah
*Siddur*
  prayer book
*Sifre kĕlalim*
  works dealing with rules and principles of adjudication and codification
*Sifre tašlum*
  complementary books
*Siḵluṯ*
  ignorance, literalism
*Ṣiṣiṯ*
  ritual fringe attached to garments (Num. 15:38ff.)
*Siṯre Torah*
  mysteries of the Torah
*Ši'ur ḵomah*
  measurement of (God's) stature
*Soleṯ nĕḵiyyah*
  clean (fine) flour (used to designate a code)
*Šomrim*
  trustees
*Sophia* (Greek)
  wisdom, knowledge, science
*Šoreš* (pl. *šorašim*)
  root, principle
*Soṭah*
  wayward wife

# GLOSSARY

*Šoṭeh*
    fool, incompetent

*Ṭa'am had-daḇar*
    reason for the matter
*Ṭa'ăme hălakah (hălakot)*
    reasons for (details of) the rule(s)
*Ṭa'ăme miṣwah (miṣwot)*
    reasons for the commandment(s)
*Ṭa'ăme Torah*
    reasons of the Torah
*Ta'ănit (pl. ta'ăniyyot)*
    fast
*Ta'ănit Esther*
    Fast of Esther
*Takkanat (pl. takkanot) hak-kahal*
    communal ordinance
*Talmiḏe ḥăḵamim*
    disciples of the wise, scholars
*Talmud 'aruk*
    explicit Talmudic statement
*Talmud Torah*
    study of Torah
*Talmud Torato wi-yĕdi'at yiḥudo*
    study of His (God's) Torah and knowledge of His oneness
*Tamḥuy*
    charity plate
*Tamiḏ*
    always; daily sacrifice offered at the Temple in Jerusalem
*Tannaim (sing. Tanna)*
    authorities cited in the Mishnah and the Baraita who flourished up to about the year 200 C.E.
*Taqlīd (Arabic)*
    following recognized authorities
*Ṭeḇel*
    produce from which the priestly and Levitical dues have not yet been set aside
*Tĕhillat ḥibbur zeh*
    the beginning (part) of this composition
*Ṭĕ'inah u-pĕriḳah*
    loading and unloading

Ṭĕrefah (pl. ṭĕrefot)
: animal lawfully unfit for consumption because of fatal disease or defect

Tĕrumah
: heave offering

Tĕšubah
: repentance

Ṭib'o šel 'olam
: the natural way of the world

Tikkun
: well-being, welfare, improvement

Tikkun hag-guf
: well-being (care) of the body

Tikkun han-nefeš
: well-being of the soul

Ṭippeš (pl. tippĕšim)
: simpleton, fool, literalist

Tiš'ah bĕ-'Ab
: (Fast of) the Ninth of Ab

Todah
: thanksgiving sacrifice

Torah
: (1) the Pentateuch, (2) the totality of Jewish law

Torah li-šĕmah
: Torah for its own sake

Torah šebbĕ-'al peh
: Oral Law

Ṭoref
: seizor of debtor's property in satisfaction of debt

Tosafot
: additions; Talmudic glosses by medieval Franco-German scholars

'Ulam
: Temple vestibule

Uṣul (Arabic)
: principles; see also Yĕsodot

Wĕ-ken kol hay-yoṣe' baz-zeh
: so also anything similar to this

Widduy
: confession, declaration made upon the completion of tithing

*Yĕfat to'ar*
  beautiful (captive) woman
*Yĕšibot* (sing. *yĕšibah*)
  academies
*Yĕsode ha-'ĕmunah hak-kĕlulim bo*
  the principles of faith contained therein
*Yĕsode hat-Torah*
  principles of the Torah
*Yĕsodot*
  foundations, principles; see also *Uṣūl*
*Yĕsodot gufe Torah*
  foundations of the essentials of the Torah
*Yibbum*
  levirate marriage (Deut. 25:5ff.)
*Yir'ah*
  fear (of God)
*Yode'a*
  knowing

*Zaken mamreh*
  rebellious elder
*Ẓawāhir al-sharī'ah* (Arabic)
  externals of the law
*Zed* (pl. *zedim*)
  wicked person
*Zeh hak-kĕlal*
  this is the rule
*Zugot*
  pairs

# BIBLIOGRAPHY*

This bibliography is not a mere alphabetical listing of works cited in the footnotes. Some works referred to only once, in a special context, are not included. On the other hand, articles and books generally relevant or especially useful, which provide basic information or suggest divergent interpretations, are listed, although they have not been mentioned in the footnotes. As noted in the preface, the footnotes originally consisted for the most part of primary source references; secondary works were cited to identify important contributions, to indicate consensus, or occasionally to call attention to noteworthy differences. Although I did not consider it necessary to underscore every instance where my interpretation or use of a Maimonidean passage differed from the way in which others have approached it, I have included here items whose relevance the interested readers will surely detect.

Selectivity is the hallmark of this bibliography, not only because of the obvious limitations of my own reading but also because the subject is so central and so repercussive that all the major areas of Jewish learning relate to it. Literary genres such as Rabbinics, philosophy, exegesis, and ethics are vital; geographic centers, such as Spain, Provence, Egypt, Land of Israel, Yemen, must be covered; all Geonica are obviously relevant background; as Maimonides' works spread, and one attempts to chronicle their abiding and multifaceted influence, it is almost impossible to delimit the areas of inquiry, significance, and relevance. "Post-Maimonidean" literature or thought is a precise and expressive designation, historically very meaningful but bibliographically very formidable, almost intractable. This means that practically all Rabbinic literature, down to the most recent volume of *ḥiddušim*, is a potential contributor to a fuller understanding of Maimonides' historical impact or often of his original intent. It also means that practically every book or article on Jewish law (*mišpaṭ ‘ibri* or halakah) devotes considerable attention to Maimonides. The interested reader need only glance at the burgeoning literature—scores of books and specialized periodicals, such as *Dine Yiśra'el, Mišpaṭim,* and *Šěnaton ham-Mišpaṭ ha-‘Ibri*, as well as articles on Jewish law in general scholarly periodicals—to convince himself that these new publications should be consulted regularly. While

---

*I thank Rabbi Mordecai Feuerstein for his invaluable help in polishing and systematizing the bibliography.

forcefully and dramatically sustaining my statement in Chapter I and my summation in Chapter VII about the centrality of the *Mishneh Torah*, this complicates the problems and multiplies the difficulties and frustrations of compiling a reasonable bibliography. Inasmuch as it is not feasible or sensible to try to encompass everything, my efforts have been sustained by a dual hope: (a) that the listing is sufficiently broad and representative; (b) that the bibliographical studies included in it— i.e., Dienstag, Kasher, Rackover, etc., or those books which include substantial bibliographies—will provide further guidance. In keeping with this, no attempt was made to list all *Mishneh Torah* editions, commentaries, etc. (see., e.g., Dienstag's bibliography, S. Frankel's edition of *Zĕmanim*, or the bibliographic supplement to the Schulsinger edition). Nor was it deemed necessary to reproduce a list of *Opera Omnia* of Maimonides, to which reference is made in many of the books on his life and works; for those editions used in this volume, see the list of abbreviations. Some volumes of the YJS have good concise bibliographies. The annual bibliographical volumes *Rĕšimat Ma'ămarim bĕ-Madda'e hay-Yahădut*, published by the KS editorial board, are very helpful. I have, finally, included a fair number of important general works which should suggest additional readings.

Articles in collectanea or special (usually jubilee) volumes, e.g., *Moses ben Maimon* or *Kobes RaMBaM*, have not, with very few exceptions, been listed separately; the reader must thus examine the contents of these works carefully.

The typescript was submitted in 1976. During the long period of editing I selected certain books and articles published since 1976 for inclusion in the bibliography, but I did not make a comprehensive effort to update or revise bibliographical references, which were in any event selective.

PRIMARY SOURCES

Aaron hak-Kohen, of Lunel. *'Orḥot Ḥayyim*, vol. I, Florence, 1750; vol. II, ed. M. Schlesinger, Berlin, 1912.
Aaron hal-Levi, of Barcelona. *Sefer ha-Ḥinnuk*, ed. C. Chavel, Jerusalem, 1952.
Abba Mari ben Moses, of Lunel. *Minḥat Kĕna'ot*, Pressburg, 1838.
Abraham bar Ḥiyya. *Hegyon han-Nefeš*, Leipzig, 1860; English tr. G. Wigoder, London, 1969.
———. *Mĕğillat ham-Mĕğalleh*, ed. A. Poznanski, Berlin, 1924.
Abraham ben 'Azriel. *'Arugat hab-Bośem*, ed. E. Urbach, 4 vols., Jerusalem, 1939–63.

## BIBLIOGRAPHY

Abraham ben David (RABD). *Ba'ăle han-Nefeš*, ed. J. Ḳāfiḥ, Jerusalem, 1964.
———. *Haśśagot*, printed in standard editions of the *Mishneh Torah*.
———. *Tĕšubot u-Fĕsakim*, ed. J. Ḳāfiḥ, Jerusalem, 1964.
Abraham ben Isaac, of Narbonne. *Sefer ha-'Eškol*, ed. C. Albeck, Jerusalem, 1935.
———. *Tĕšubot*, ed. J. Ḳāfiḥ, Jerusalem, 1961–62.
Abraham ben Nathan hay-Yarḥi. *Sefer ham-Manhig*, ed. I. Refael, 2 vols., Jerusalem, 1978.
Abraham Bibago. *Derek 'Ĕmunah*, Constantinople, 1522.
Abraham ibn Daud. *Ha-'Ĕmunah ha-Ramah*, ed. S. Weil, Frankfurt, 1852; reprinted, Jerusalem, 1966.
———. *Sefer hak-Ḳabbalah*, ed. G. Cohen, Philadelphia, 1967.
Abraham ibn Ezra. *Moznayim*, Vilna, 1809.
———. *Peruš hat-Torah*, ed. A. Weiser, Jerusalem, 1976; printed also in standard editions of the Bible with commentaries.
———. *Yĕsod Mora'*, Prague, 1833.
Abraham ibn Megas. *Kĕbod 'Ĕlohim*, Constantinople, 1583; reprinted, Jerusalem, 1976 (with introduction by H. H. Ben-Sasson).
Abraham Maimonides. *Birkat 'Abraham*, ed. B. Goldberg, Lyck, 1859.
———. *Highways to Perfection*, vol. I, New York, 1927; vol. II, Baltimore, 1938.
———. *Milḥamot haš-Šem*, ed. R. Margaliyot, Jerusalem, 1953.
———. *Peruš*, ed. A. Wiesenberg and S. Sasson, London, 1959.
———. *Tĕšubot*, ed. A. Freimann and S. Goitein, Jerusalem, 1937.
Aḥai Gaon. *Šĕ'iltot*, 3 vols., Jerusalem, 1947–52; ed. S. K. Mirsky, Jerusalem, 1959–.
Almosnino, Moses. *Tĕfillah lĕ-Mošeh*, Salonica, 1563.
Aristeas. *Letter*, ed. M. Hadas, New York, 1951.
Asher ben Jeḥiel. *Hilkot ha-ROŠ*, printed in standard editions of the Talmud.
———. *Šĕ'elot u-Tĕšubot ha-ROŠ*, ed. E. Urbach, *Šĕnaton ham-Mišpaṭ ha-'Ibri*, II (1975), 1–153.
———. *Tĕšubot*, Venice, 1595.
Ashkenazi, Eliezer. *Ma'ăśe haš-Šem*, Jerusalem, 1972.
Assaf, S., ed. *Mĕḳorot lĕ-Tolĕdot ha-Ḥinnuk bĕ-Yiśra'el*, 4 vols., Tel Aviv, 1926–45.
Averroes. *Averroes on the Harmony of Religion and Philosophy*, tr. G. Hourani, London, 1961.
Babad, Joseph. *Minḥat Ḥinnuk*, Lemberg, 1889; New York, 1952 (with various additions).

# 564 INTRODUCTION TO THE CODE OF MAIMONIDES

Baḥya ben Asher. *Kitḇe R. Baḥya*, ed. C. Chavel, Jerusalem, 1969.
———. *Peruš hat-Torah*, ed. C. Chavel, Jerusalem, 1968.
Baḥya ibn Paḳuda. *Ḥoḇot hal-Lĕḇaḇot*, ed. A. Zifroni, Jerusalem, 1928; ed. and tr. M. Hyamson, New York, 1925.
——— (pseudo-Baḥya). *Sefer Toraṯ han-Nefeš*, ed. I. Broide, Paris, 1896.
Cases, Ḥananiah. *Ḳin'aṯ Sofĕrim*, Livorno, 1738.
Cordovero, Moses. *Tomer Dĕḇorah*, Petah-Tikvah, 1953.
David ben Joseph. *Sefer 'Abudarham*, Warsaw, 1878.
David ben Samuel Koḳabi. *Sefer hab-Batim*, ed. M. Blau, New York, 1978.
David ibn Abi Zimra (RaDBaZ). *Commentary on Mishneh Torah*, printed in standard editions of the *Mishneh Torah*.
———. *Tĕšuḇoṯ*, New York, 1947.
———. *Yĕḳar Tif'ereṯ*, ed. S. B. Werner, Jerusalem, 1945.
David Ḳimḥi. *'Eṯ Sofer*, Lyck, 1864.
———. *Peruš*, printed in standard editions of the Bible (see also below, under F. Talmage).
———. *Sefer ham-Miḳlol*, Jerusalem, 1965.
Dawidowicz, S. and D. Baneth, eds., *Pĕraḳim bĕ-Haṣlaḥah*, Jerusalem, 1939.
De Modena, Leo. *'Ări Nohem*, Jerusalem, 1929.
Del Medigo, Elijah ben Moses. *Bĕḥinaṯ had-Daṯ*, Vienna, 1833; reprinted, Jerusalem, 1969.
Del Medigo, Joseph Solomon. *Sefer Noḇĕloṯ Ḥoḵmah*, Basel, 1631; reprinted, Jerusalem, 1970.
Eleazar ben Judah, of Worms. *Sefer ha-Roḳeaḥ*, ed. B. Schneerson, Jerusalem, 1966.
Eleazar ben Samuel, of Metz. *Sefer Yĕre'im*, reprinted, Jerusalem, 1973.
Emden, Jacob. *Miṭpaḥaṯ Sĕfarim*, Jerusalem, 1969/70.
Ephraim ben Israel Alnakawa. *Ša'ar Kĕḇoḏ haš-Šem*, Tunis, 1902.
Epstein, Baruch. *'Aruḵ haš-Šulḥan he-'Aṯiḏ*, Jerusalem, 1969–75.
Fano, Menahem Azariah. *Šĕ'eloṯ u-Tĕšuḇoṯ*, Jerusalem, 1963.
Ganz, David. *Neḥmad wĕ-Na'im*, Jessnitz, 1743.
*Genesis Rabbah*, ed. J. Theodor and H. Albeck, 3 vols., Jerusalem, 1965.
Goitein, S., ed. "Miḵtaḇ 'el ha-RaMBaM," *Tarbiz*, XXXIV (1965), 232–56.
Hai, Gaon. *Mišpĕṭe Šĕḇu'oṯ*, Venice, n.d.
———. *Musar Haśkel*, ed. H. Gollancz, London, 1922.
*Halaḵoṯ Gĕḏoloṯ*, ed. A. S. Traub, Warsaw, 1874; ed. E. Hildesheimer, Berlin, 1888–92.

*Halakot Pĕsukot*, ed. S. Sasson, Jerusalem, 1973.
Hananeel ben Hushiel. *Peruše R. Hananĕ'el 'al hat-Torah*, ed. C. Chavel, Jerusalem, 1972.
Hasdai Crescas. *Sefer 'Or haš-Šem*, Vienna, 1860.
Hayyim Eliezer ben Isaac. *'Or Zaru'a, Piske Halakah*, Jerusalem, 1972.
*Hebrew Ethical Wills*, ed. I. Abrahams, 2 vols., Philadelphia, 1926, 1948.
Hefeṣ ben Yaṣliaḥ. "Mis-Sefer ham-Miṣwot," *PAAJR*, XXIX (1960–61), 1–68.
———. *Sefer ham-Miṣwot*, ed. B. Halper, Philadelphia, 1915.
Heller, Yom-Tob Lipmann. *Ma'ădane Yom-Tob* (commentary on Asher ben Jehiel), printed in standard editions of the Talmud.
———. *Tosafot Yom-Tob* (commentary on the Mishnah), printed in standard editions of the Mishnah.
*Hilkot Rĕ'u*, ed. L. Schlossberg, Versailles, 1886; reprinted, Jerusalem, 1966.
Hillel, of Verona. *Tagmule han-Nefeš*, Lyck, 1874.
Immanuel Benevento. *Liwyat Ḥen*, Mantua, 1557.
Immanuel ben Solomon, of Rome. *Maḥbĕrot 'Immanu'el*, ed. D. Yarden, Jerusalem, 1957.
Isaac Abarbanel. *Naḥlat 'Abot*, New York, 1953.
———. *Roš 'Ămanah*, Tel Aviv, 1958.
———. *Yĕšu'ot Mĕšiḥo*, Koenigsberg, 1861.
Isaac Aboab. *Mĕnorat ham-Ma'or*, ed. J. Fries-Horeb, Jerusalem, 1961.
Isaac Albalag. *Sefer Tikkun had-De'ot*, ed. G. Vajda, Jerusalem, 1973.
Isaac Alfasi (RIF). *Sefer ha-Halakot*, ed. N. Zaks, 2 vols., Jerusalem, 1969; printed also in standard editions of the Talmud.
———. *Tĕšubot*, ed. D. Rotstein, New York, 1975.
Isaac Arama. *'Akedat Yiṣḥak*, ed. H. J. Pollack, Pressburg, 1849; reprinted, Jerusalem, 1960.
———. *Ḥazut Kašah*, Pressburg, 1849.
Isaac ben Abba Mari. *Sefer ha-'Iṭṭur*, New York, 1955.
Isaac ben Joseph Israeli. *Yĕsod 'Olam*, ed. B. Goldberg, Berlin, 1851.
Isaac ben Melchizedek. *Peruš Zĕra'im*, ed. N. Zaks, Jerusalem, 1975.
Isaac Canpanton. *Darke Gĕmara'*, Vienna, 1891; reprinted, Jerusalem, 1969.
Isaac ibn Ghiyāth. *Ša'åre Śimḥah*, ed. I. Bamberger, Fürth, 1861.
Isaac ibn Laṭif. "'Iggeret hat-Tĕšubah," *Kobeṣ 'al Yad*, I (1885), 45–70.
———. *Ša'ar haš-Samayim*, *He-Ḥaluṣ*, XII (1887), 114–24.
Isaac Polgar. *'Ezer had-Dat*, Jerusalem, 1970.
Isaiah di Trani. *Kiryat Sefer*, Warsaw, 1902.
———. *Peruš Nĕbi'im u-Kĕtubim*, 3 vols., Jerusalem, 1959–.

## 566 INTRODUCTION TO THE CODE OF MAIMONIDES

———. *Sefer ham-Makri'a*, ed. Y. Z. Reichman, Jerusalem, 1970.
Israel Al-Nakawa, *Měnorat hām-Ma'or*, ed. H. Enelow, 4 vols., New York, 1929–32.
Israel, of Shklov. *Pě'at haš-Šulḥan*, Safed, 1836.
Jacob Anatoli. *Malmaḏ hat-Talmiḏim*, Lyck, 1866.
Jacob ben Asher. *Ṭurim*, standard editions.
Jacob ben Judah Hazan, of London. *'Eṣ Ḥayyim*, ed. I. Brodie, 3 vols., Jerusalem, 1962–67.
Jacob ben Sheshet. *Mešiḇ Děḇarim Někoḥim*, Jerusalem, 1967.
Jacob Landau. *Sefer ha-'Aḡur*, Venice, 1546.
Jedaiah hap-Penini. *Běḥinaṯ 'Olam*, Berlin, 1927.
Jellinek, A., ed. *Bet ha-Midrash*, Jerusalem, 1967.
Jeroham ben Meshullam. *Sefer Mešarim*, Kopys, 1908.
———. *Tolěḏoṯ 'Aḏam wě-Ḥawwah*, Venice, 1553.
Jonah ibn Janāḥ. *Opuscules et Traités*, ed. J. and H. Derenbourg, Paris, 1880.
———. *Peruš lě-Kiṯḇe hak-Ḳoḏeš*, ed. A. S. Rabinovitz, Tel Aviv, 1936.
———. *Sefer ha-Riḳmah*, ed. M. Wilensky, Berlin, 1929.
Jonathan hak-Kohen, of Lunel. "Commentary on Sanhedrin", *Sanheḏri Gěḏolah*, ed. Y. Kuperberg, Jerusalem, 1969, II, 1–168.
———. "Commentary on 'Aḇoṯ," *Sanheḏri Gěḏolah*, ed. I. Ralbag, Jerusalem, 1973, vol. I.
———. "Commentary on Roš haš-Šanah, Yoma, and Ta'ăniṯ", *Ginze Rišonim*, ed. M. Herschler, Jerusalem, 1963, vol. II.
———. "Commentary on Sukkah, *Ginze Rišonim*, ed. M. Herschler, Jerusalem, 1962, vol. I.
———. "Commentary on Baḇa Ḳamma", ed. S. Y. Friedman, Jerusalem, 1969.
———. "Commentary on Běraḵoṯ", ed. M. Y. Blau, New York, 1957.
Joseph Albo. *Sefer ha-'Iḳḳarim*, ed. J. Husik, Philadelphia, 1930.
Joseph ben Judah ibn Aknin. *Hiṯgaluṯ has-Soḏoṯ, Peruš Šir haš-Širim*, ed. A. S. Halkin, Jerusalem, 1964.
———. *Sefer Musar, Peruš 'Aḇoṯ*, ed. W. Bacher, Berlin, 1910; reprinted, Jerusalem, 1966.
Joseph ben Shem Ṭob. *Sefer Kěḇoḏ 'Ělohim*, Ferrara, 1552.
Joseph Gikatilia. *Ginaṯ 'Eḡoz*, Hanau, 1615.
Joseph ibn Kaspi. *'Ăśārah Kěle Kesef*, ed. I. Last, Pressburg, 1903.
———. *Mišneh Kesef*, ed. I. Last, reprinted, Jerusalem, 1970.
———. *Tam hak-Kesef*, Jerusalem, 1970.
Joseph ibn Megas. *Těšuḇoṯ*, Warsaw, 1870.
Joseph ibn Ṣaddiḳ. *Sefer ha-'Olam haḳ-Ḳaṭan*, ed. S. Horovitz, Breslau, 1903.

Joseph Jabez. *'Or ha-Ḥayyim*, Lublin, 1913.
———. *Peruš 'Aḇot*, Jerusalem, 1957.
Joseph Ḳimḥi. *Sefer hag-Galuy*, ed. H. Mathews, Berlin, 1887.
Joseph Ṭob 'Elem. *Ṣofnaṯ Pa'neaḥ*, ed. D. Herzog, Heidelberg, 1911.
Joshua ben Abraham Maimonides. *Tešuḇot*, ed. A. Freimann and J. Rivlin, Jerusalem, 1971.
Joshua ibn Shu'ayb. *Dĕrašoṯ*, Jerusalem, 1969 (with introduction by Sh. Abramson).
Judah ben Asher (ROŠ). *Zikron Yĕhuḏah (Tešuḇot)*, Berlin, 1846.
Judah ben Barzilai. *Peruš Sefer Yĕṣirah*, ed. S. J. Halberstamm, Berlin, 1885.
———. *Sefer ha-'Ittim*, ed. J. Shore, Berlin, 1903.
Judah ben Solomon al-Ḥarīzī. *Taḥkĕmoni*, Tel Aviv, 1952.
Judah Hadassi. *'Eškol hak-Kofer*, Eupatoria, 1836.
Judah hal-Levi. *Dīwān*, ed. H. Brody, Berlin, 1901.
———. *Kuzari*, Hebrew tr. Judah ibn Tibbon, ed. A. Zifroni, Tel Aviv, 1948; English tr. H. Hirschfeld, New York, 1946; Hebrew tr. J. Ibn Shemuel, Tel Aviv, 1972.
Judah Ḥayyūj. *Šĕlošah Sifre Diḳduḳ*, Hebrew tr. Moses ibn Gikatilia, ed. J. W. Nutt, London, 1870.
Judah ibn Ḳureish. *'Iggereṯ*, ed. M. Katz, Tel Aviv, 1952.
Judah Loew ben Bezaleel (MaHaRaL). *Dĕrašoṯ MaHaRaL*, Jerusalem, 1959.
———. *Sifre MaHaRaL*, 12 vols., Jerusalem, 1972.
Aviv, 1936.
Kanofsky, R. S. *Kiryaṯ Meleḵ*, Jerusalem, 1964.
Karo, Joseph. *Šulḥan 'Aruḵ*, standard editons.
———. *Šĕ'elot u-Tešuḇot 'Aḇkat Roḵel*, Jerusalem, 1960 (with introduction by B. Landau).
Khadduri, M., tr. *Islamic Jurisprudence: Shāfi'ī's Risāla*, Baltimore, 1961.
Ḳolon, Joseph. *Ḥidduše u-Feruše ha-MₐHₐRiK*, ed. E. Pines, Jerusalem, 1971.
———. *Šĕ'elot u-Fiske MaHaRiK ha-Ḥăḏašim*, ed. E. Pines, Jerusalem, 1970.
———. *Tešuḇot*, Lemberg, 1798.
Krakowski, Menahem. *'Aḇoḏaṯ ham-Meleḵ*, Jerusalem, 1971.
Landau, Ezekiel. *Noda' bi-Yĕhuḏah*, 2 vols., Jerusalem, 1960.
Leiner, Gershon Enoch, of Radzin. *Šĕlošeṯ Sifre hat-Tĕḵeleṯ*, Jerusalem, 1963.
———. *Sidre Ṭohăroṯ*, Piotrkow, 1903; New York, 1960.
Leo de Modena, *see* De Modena, Leo.

## 568 INTRODUCTION TO THE CODE OF MAIMONIDES

Levi ben Abraham. "Pardes ha-Ḥokmah," in *'Oṣar haṣ-Sifruṯ*, III (1890), 19–23.
Levi ben Gershon (RaLBaG). *Milḥamoṯ haš-Šem*, Leipzig, 1866.
———. *Peruš*, printed in standard editions of the Bible.
Levi ibn Ḥabib. *Tešuḇoṯ*, Lemberg, 1865.
Lewin, B. M., ed. *'Oṣar hag-Gĕ'onim*, 13 vols., Haifa, 1928–43.
Lifshitz, Israel, *Tif'ereṯ Yiśra'el*, printed in standard editions of the Mishnah.
Luria, Solomon. *Tešuḇoṯ*, Jerusalem, 1969.
———. *Yam šel Šĕlomoh, Baḇa Ḳamma*, New York, 1953.
Luzzatto, M. H. *Mĕsillaṯ Yĕšarim*, ed. M. Kaplan, Philadelphia, 1948.
Luzzatto, S. *Ma'ămar 'al Yĕhuḏe Winiṣi'ah*, ed. A. Aescoly, Jerusalem, 1951.
*Maḥzor Vitry*, ed. S. Hurwitz, Berlin, 1893.
Maimon ben Joseph. *'Iggereṯ han-Nĕḥamah*, Hebrew tr. B. Klar, ed. J. Maimon (Fishman), Jerusalem, 1945.
———. "Letter of Consolation," tr. L. M. Simmons, *JQR*, I (1910), 62–101.
Manoah ben Simeon, of Narbonne. *Sefer ham-Mĕnuḥah*, Pressburg, 1879.
———. *Sefer ham-Mĕnuḥah*, in *Ḳobeṣ Rišonim 'al Mishneh Torah*, Jerusalem, 1967.
———. *Sefer ham-Mĕnuḥah*, ed. E. Hurvitz, Jerusalem, 1970.
*Masseḵeṯ Soferim*, ed. M. Higger, New York, 1937.
Mat, Moses. *Maṭṭeh Mošeh*, Warsaw, 1876.
Medigo, see Del Medigo.
Meir Aldabi. *Šĕḇile 'Ĕmunah*, Tel Aviv, 1965.
Meir ben Todros Abulafia. *Kitāb al-Rasā'il* (with letters by Aaron hak-Kohen of Lunel, Samson of Sens, and others), ed. J. Brill, Paris, 1871.
———. *Masoreṯ Sĕyaḡ lat-Torah*, Berlin, 1760.
———. *Yaḏ Ramah, Sanheḏrin*, Warsaw, n.d.
Meir hak-Kohen, of Narbonne. *Sefer ham-Mĕ'oroṯ*, ed. M. Y. Blau, 4 vols., New York, 1964–66.
Meir ibn Gabbai. *'Aḇoḏaṯ haḳ-Ḳodeš*, Jerusalem, 1973.
———. *Tola'aṯ Ya'ăḳoḇ*, Warsaw, 1876.
Menahem ben Saruḳ. *Maḥbereṯ*, ed. Z. Filipovsky, Edinburgh, 1854.
Menahem ben Zerah. *Ṣeḏah laḏ-Dereḵ*, Warsaw, 1880.
Menahem ham-Me'iri. *Beṯ hab-Bĕḥirah* (on *'Aḇoṯ*), ed. S. Waxman, New York, 1944.
———. *Beṯ hab-Bĕḥirah* (on *Bĕrakoṯ*, with author's general introduction), Jerusalem, 1964.

———. *Bet hab-Běhirah* (on various other tractates of the Talmud).
———. *Hibbur hat-Těšubah*, ed. A. Sofer, New York, 1950.
———. *Kiryat Sefer*, ed. M. Herschler, Jerusalem, 1956.
———. *Magen 'Abot*, ed. I. Last, London, 1909.
Mendelssohn, Moses. *'Or li-Nětibah*, Berlin, 1782.
Meshullam ben Moses, of Béziers. *Sefer ha-Hašlamah*, ed. M. Y. Blau, 4 vols., New York, 1964–66.
———. *Sefer ha-Hašlamah* (on Běrakot), *Ginze Rišonim*, ed. M. Herschler, Jerusalem, 1967, IV, 197–250.
———. *Sefer ha-Hašlamah* (on Roš haš-Šanah, Yoma, and Ta'anit), *Ginze Rišonim*, ed. M. Herschler, Jerusalem, 1963, II, 135–72.
———. *Sefer ha-Hašlamah* (on Sukkah), *Ginze Rišonim*, ed. M. Herschler, Jerusalem, 1962, I, 121–72.
*Mišnat R. 'Eli'ezer*, ed. H. Enelow, New York, 1934.
Mizrahi, Elijah. *Těšubot*, Salonica, 1805.
Moses Alaškar. *Těšubot*, Sabbioneta, 1554.
Moses ben Jacob, of Coucy. *Sefer Miswot Gadol*, Venice, 1522.
Moses ben Nahman (Nahmanides). *Hidduše RaMBaN*, standard editions.
———. *Kitbe RaMBaN*, ed. C. Chavel, Jerusalem, 1963 (includes his *Torat ha-'Adam*).
———. *Milhāmot haš-Šem*, printed in standard editions of the Talmud.
———. *Peruš hat-Torah*, ed. C. Chavel, Jerusalem, 1966–67.
———. *Těšubot ha-RaMBaN*, ed. C. Chavel, Jerusalem, 1975.
Moses hak-Kohen (RaMaK). *Haśśagot ha-RaMaK 'al ha-RaMBaM: Madda', 'Ahăbah, Zěmanim*, ed. S. Atlas, Jerusalem, 1969.
Moses ibn Ezra. *Širat Yiśra'el*, Hebrew tr. B. Halper, Leipzig, 1924.
———. *Sefer ha-'Iyyunim wěha-Diyyunim (Širat Yiśra'el)*, ed. A. Halkin, Jerusalem, 1975.
Moses Isserles. *Darke Mošeh*, printed in standard editions of Jacob ben Asher's *Turim*.
———. *Těšubot*, ed. A. Ziv, Jerusalem, 1971.
———. *Torat ha-'Olah*, Prague, 1871.
Moses of Narbonne. *Be'ur lě-Sefer Moreh Nebukim*, ed. J. Goldenthal, Vienna, 1850.
———. *Ma'ămar bi-Šělemut han-Nefeš*, ed. A. Ivry, Jerusalem, 1977.
Moses Taku. "Kětab Tamim," *'Osar Nehmad*, III (1860), 54–99 (with introduction by R. Kircheim).
Nathan ben Jehiel, of Rome. *'Aruk haš-Šalem*, ed. A. Kohut, Vienna, 1926.
Neubauer, A., ed. *Medieval Jewish Chronicles*, Oxford, 1887.
Nieto, David. *Matteh Dan, Kuzari Šeni*, Jerusalem, 1975.

Nissim ben Jacob ibn Shāhīn. *An Elegant Composition Concerning Relief after Adversity (Ḥibbur Yafeh)*, English tr. W. Brinner, New Haven, 1977 (YJS, 20).

———. *Ḥamiššah Sĕfarim*, ed. Sh. Abramson, Jerusalem, 1965.

———. *Ḥibbur Yafeh*, Hebrew tr. J. Hirschberg, Jerusalem, 1953/54.

———. *Sefer ham-Mafteaḥ lĕ-Man'ule hat-Talmud*, ed. J. Goldenthal, Vienna, 1847; Jerusalem, 1971.

Nissim Gerondi. *Dĕrašot ha-RaN*, Jerusalem, 1959; ed. L. Feldman, Jerusalem, 1973.

———. *Ḥiddušim*, standard editions.

———. *Peruš hat-Torah*, ed. L. Feldman, Jerusalem, 1968.

———. *Peruš Hilkot 'Alfasi*, standard editions.

———. *Šĕ'elot u-Tĕšubot*, Cremona, 1557.

*'Oṣar hag-Gĕ'onim* (on Sanhedrin), ed. Z. Taubes, Jerusalem, 1966.

Pardo, David. *Ḥasde Dawid*, Jerusalem, 1890.

*Peruš hag-Gĕ'onim 'al Seder Ṭohărot*, ed. J. N. Epstein, Berlin, 1921.

Pinsker, S. *Likkute Kadmoniyyot*, Vienna, 1860.

*Pirke dĕ-Rabbi 'Eli'ezer*, Vilna, 1838; ed. H. M. Horowitz, Jerusalem, 1972.

Profiat Duran. *Ma'ăseh 'Efod*, Vienna, 1865; reprinted, Jerusalem, 1969.

Rosen, Meir Simḥah. *'Or Sameaḥ* (commentary on *Mishneh Torah*), Jerusalem, 1966.

Rossi, Azariah dei. *Me'or 'Enayim*, 3 vols., reprinted, Jerusalem, 1970.

Saadiah ben Joseph Gaon. *'Ĕmunot wĕ-De'ot*, Józefów, 1885; ed. and tr. J. Ḳāfiḥ, Jerusalem, n.d.

———. *Mišle, Targum u-Peruš*, ed. J. Ḳāfiḥ, Jerusalem, 1975/76.

———. *Peruš Masseket Bĕrakot*, ed. S. Wertheimer, Jerusalem, 1927.

———. *Peruš Tĕhillim*, ed. J. Ḳāfiḥ, Jerusalem, 1965.

———. *Sefer ha-'Igron*, ed. N. Aloni, Jerusalem, 1969.

———. *Sefer hag-Galuy*, ed. A. Harkavy, Petersburg, 1892.

———. *Sefer ham-Miṣwot lĕ-RaSaG*, ed. J. Perla, reprinted, New York, 1962.

———. *Siddur*, ed. I. Davidson, S. Assaf, and B. I. Joel, Jerusalem, 1941.

———. *Tĕšubot RaSaG 'al Šĕ'elot Ḥiwi al-Balki*, ed. I. Davidson, New York, 1915.

Sacks, J. L. ed. *Ḥidduše ha-RaMBaM lat-Talmud*, Jerusalem, 1963.

Samau'al al-Maghribī. *Ifḥām al-Yahūd ("Silencing the Jews")*, ed. and tr. M. Perlmann, New York, 1964 (*PAAJR*, XXXII).

Samuel ben Ḥofni Gaon. *Peruš hat-Torah*, ed. A. Greenbaum, Jerusalem, 1979.

# BIBLIOGRAPHY

Samuel ben Meir (RaSHBaM). *Peruš hat-Torah*, printed in standard editions of the Bible; ed. A. Bromberg, Jerusalem, 1969.
Samuel han-Nagid. *Diwan*, ed. D. Yarden, Jerusalem, 1966.
———. *Sefer Hilkot han-Nagid*, Jerusalem, 1962.
Samuel has-Sardi, *Sefer hat-Tĕrumot (u-Peruš Giddule Tĕrumah)*, Jerusalem, 1961.
Samuel ibn Tibbon. *Peruš ham-Millot ha-Zarot*, ed. J. Ibn Shemuel, Jerusalem, 1947.
———. *Yikkawu ham-Mayim*, Pressburg, 1837.
Saphir, Jacob. *'Eben Sappir*, 2 vols., Lyck, 1866–74; reprinted, 1969.
Schwartz, I., ed. *Peruš Rišonim*, Berlin, 1868.
*Šeba' Massektot Kĕtanot*, ed. M. Higger, New York, 1930.
*Sefer Ḥăsidim*, ed. R. Margulies, Jerusalem, 1957; ed. J. Wistinetzki, Frankfurt, 1924.
*Sefer Tĕšubot Talmide Mĕnahem*, ed. S. Z. Stern, Vienna, 1890.
*Sefer wĕ-Hizhir*, ed. I. M. Freimann, 2 vols., Leipzig, 1873–80.
Shem Tob ben Joseph Falaquera. *Moreh ham-Moreh*, Pressburg, 1837.
———. *Rešit Ḥokmah*, Berlin, 1902; reprinted, Jerusalem, 1969/70.
———. *Sefer ham-Ma'ălot*, Berlin, 1894; reprinted, Jerusalem, 1969/70 (*Kitbe Shem Tob Falaquera*).
Shem Tob ben Shem Tob. *Sefer ha-'Ĕmunot*, Ferrara, 1556; reprinted, Jerusalem, 1969.
Shem Tob ibn Shaprut. *Sefer Pardes Rimmonim*, Sabbioneta, 1514.
Sherira Gaon. *'Iggeret R. Sherira*, ed. B. M. Lewin, Haifa, 1921.
Sheshet han-Naśi'. *'Iggeret*, ed. A. Marx, *JQR*, XXV (1935), 414–28.
Simeon ben Joseph. "Ḥošen Mišpat," ed. J. Kaufmann, *Zunz Jubelschrift*, Berlin, 1884, pp. 142–74.
Simeon ben Ṣemaḥ Duran. *Tĕšubot (TaŠBeṢ)*, Amsterdam, 1741.
———. *Zohar ha-Raki'a*, Vilna, 1879.
Solomon al-'Ami. *'Iggeret Musar*, ed. A. M. Habermann, Jerusalem, 1946.
Solomon ben Abraham ibn Adret (RaSHBA). *Ḥidduše RaSHBA*, standard editions.
———. *Torat hab-Bayit haš-Šalem*, ed. M. Herschler, Jerusalem, 1963.
Solomon ben Simeon Duran. *Milḥemet Miṣwah* (bound with *Kešet u-Magen*), Jerusalem, 1969.
———. *Tĕšubot (Sefer ha-RaŠBaŠ)*, Jerusalem, 1967.
Solomon ibn Gabirol. *Improvement of the Moral Qualities*, ed. S. S. Wise, New York, 1903.
———. *Širim*, ed. H. N. Bialik and J. C. Ravnitzky, Tel Aviv, 1927–28.
Solomon ibn Parhon. *Maḥberet he-'Aruk*, Pressburg, 1844; reprinted,

Jerusalem, 1970.
Soloveitchik, Ḥayyim, Ḥidduše R. Ḥayyim hal-Lewi, n.p., n.d..
Soloveitchik, Joseph B. Beṯ hal-Lewi, Tešuḇoṯ, New York, 1943.
Tanḥum hay-Yerushalmi. Ham-Madriḵ ham-Maspiḵ, ed. B. Toledano, Jerusalem, 1921; ed. H. Shy, 3 vols., unpublished dissertation, Jerusalem, 1975.
Tešuḇoṯ Gĕ'one Mizraḥ u-Ma'ăraḇ, ed. J. Mueller, Berlin, 1888.
Tešuḇoṯ Gĕ'onim Ḳadmonim, ed. D. Cassel, Berlin, 1848.
Tešuḇoṯ hag-Gĕ'onim, ed. J. Musafia, Lyck, 1864.
———, ed. N. Coronel, Vienna, 1871.
———, ed. A. Harkavy, Berlin, 1887; reprinted, New York, 1959.
———, ed. S. Assaf, Jerusalem, 1927, 1928, 1942.
———, ed. A. Marmorstein, Deva, 1928.
Tešuḇoṯ Ḥaḵme Provence, ed. A. Schreiber, Jerusalem, 1967.
Tešuḇoṯ R. Śar Šalom Ga'on, ed. R. Weinberg, Jerusalem, 1975.
Toraṯam šel Rišonim, ed. C. M. Horowitz, Frankfurt, 1881.
"Tosafoṯ Yĕšanim 'al Masseḵeṯ Yĕḇamoṯ, Pereḳ Šeliši," ed. B. S. Wacholder, Texts and Responses, Studies Presented to Nahum Glatzer, ed. M. Fishbane, Leiden, 1975, pp. 285–306.
Wessely, Naphtali H. Diḇre Šalom wĕ-'Emeṯ, Berlin, 1782–88.
Yom Ṭob ben Abraham Ishbili (RIṬBA). Ḥiddušim, standard editions.
———. Sefer Zikkaron, ed. K. Kahana, Jerusalem, 1955.
Zacuto, Abraham. Yuḥasin haš-Šalem, Jerusalem, 1953.
Zerahiah ben Shealtiel, of Barcelona. Peruš, in Perušim 'al Sefer Iyyoḇ, ed. I. Schwartz, Jerusalem, 1970.
Zerahiah hal-Levi. Sefer ham-Ma'or, ed. with commentary by S. Z. Ehrenreich, Jerusalem, 1967; printed also in standard editions of the Talmud.
———. Sefer haṣ-Ṣaḇa', in Tĕmim De'im, Jerusalem, 1960.

SECONDARY LITERATURE

Abramson, Sh. "'Ăgaḇ Ḳĕri'ah," Lĕšonenu, XXXVII (1973), 317–18; XXXVIII (1974), 158–89.
———. "'Al haš-Šimmuš bi-lĕšon Mišnah wĕ-Talmud," Sinai, LXXVII (1975), 193–212.
———. "Arba'ah Pĕraḳim bĕ-'Inyan ha-RaMBaM," Sinai, LXX (1972), 24–33.
———. Bam-Merkazim u-baṯ-Tĕfuṣoṯ, Jerusalem, 1965.
———. Ḥamiššah Sĕfarim lĕ-R. Nissim Ga'on, Jerusalem, 1965.
———. "'Iggĕroṯ Gĕ'onim," Tarbiz, XXXI (1961–62), 43–58, 191–214.

———. "'Inyanoṯ bĕ-Sefer Miṣwoṯ Gaḏol," *Sinai*, LXXX (1976–77), 203–13.
———. *'Inyanoṯ bĕ-Sifruṯ hag-Gĕ'onim*, Jerusalem, 1974.
———. "Lĕ-Feruš R. Yiṣḥaḳ 'ibn Giyyaṯ lĕ-Ḳoheleṯ," *ḲS*, LII (1977), 156–72.
———. "Lĕ-maḇo' hat-Talmuḏ lĕ-Raḇ Šĕmu'el ben Ḥofni," *Tarbiz*, XXVI (1957), 421–24.
———. "Mafṯĕḥoṯ li-Tĕšuḇoṯ hag-Gĕ'onim," *Harry Wolfson Jubilee Volume, Jerusalem*, 1965, Hebrew section, pp. 7–23.
———. "Min ham-Maḳor ha-'Āraḇi šel Sefer ham-Meḳaḥ wĕham-Mimkar," *Tarbiz*, XX (1950), 296–315.
———. "Mišnah u-Talmuḏ bĕ-Fi Ḳaḏmonim," *Sefer Doḇ Sĕḏan*, Jerusalem, 1977, pp. 23–43.
———. "Mis-Sifre Raḇ Šĕmu'el ben Ḥofni," *Tarbiz*, XVII (1946), 138–64.
———. "R. Joseph Roš has-Seḏer," *ḲS*, XXVI (1950), 72–96.
Adar, Z. *Mišnaṯ ha-RaMBaM*, Tel Aviv, 1957.
Albeck, H. "Ḳĕṣaṯ Mĕḵoroṯ wĕ-He'aroṯ lĕ-Sefer Yaḏ ha-Ḥăzaḳah," *Sefer hay-Yoḇel lĕ-Professor S. Krauss*, Jerusalem, 1936, pp. 145–55.
———. *Maḇo' lam-Mišnah*, Jerusalem, 1959.
———. *Maḇo' lat-Talmuḏim*, Tel Aviv, 1969.
Albeck, S. "Mĕḥoḳĕḳe Yĕhuḏah," *Festschrift zu Israel Lewys 70sten Geburtstag*, ed. M. Brann and J. Elbogen, Breslau, 1911, pp. 104–31.
———. "Yaḥăso šel R. Tam," *Zion*, XIX (1954), 109–41.
———. "Yesoḏoṯ Mišṭar haḳ-Ḳĕhilloṯ bi-Sĕfaraḏ," *Zion*, XXV (1960), 85–121.
Allard, M. "Le rationalisme d'Averroes d'après une étude sur la création," *Bulletin d'Études Orientales*, XIV (1952–54), 7–59.
Aloni, N. "Šaloš Hora'oṯ 'Oṭografiyyoṯ la-RaMBaM," *Sinai*, LXXIX (1976), 1–7.
Altmann, A. "Eternality of Punishment, a Theological Controversy within the Amsterdam Rabbinate in ... the Seventeenth Century," *PAAJR*, XL (1972), 1–88.
———. "Ma'ămar bĕ-yiḥuḏ hab-Bore'," *Tarbiz*, XXVII (1958), 301–09.
———. "Maimonides and Aquinas: Natural or Divine Prophecy," *Association for Jewish Studies Review*, III (1978), 1–19.
———. "Maimonides' 'Four Perfections,' " *Israel Oriental Studies*, II (1972), 15–24.
———. *Moses Mendelssohn*, University, Alabama, 1973.

———. "Moses Narboni's 'Epistle on Shi'ur Qomah,' " *Medieval and Renaissance Studies,* ed. A. Altmann, Cambridge, Mass., 1967, pp. 225-89.

———. "The Religion of the Thinkers: Free Will and Predestination in Maimonides," *Religion in a Religious Age,* ed. S. D. Goitein, Cambridge, Mass., 1974, pp. 25-53.

———. "Saadya's Conception of the Law," *Bulletin of the John Rylands Library,* XXVIII (1944), 320-39.

———. *Studies in Religious Philosophy and Mysticism,* New York, 1969.

———. "Das Verhältnis Maimunis zur jüdischen Mystik," *MGWJ,* LXXX (1936), 305-30.

Ankori, Z. *Karaites in Byzantium,* New York, 1959.

Apel, K. O. *Die Idee der Sprache in der Tradition des Humanismus von Dante bis Vico,* Bonn, 1963.

Appel, G. *A Philosophy of Mizvot,* New York, 1975.

Aptowitzer, A. *Maḇo' lĕ-Sefer Ra'ḇiyah,* Jerusalem, 1932.

Arieli, T. "Hat-Tĕfiśah has-Statiṯ wĕhat-Tĕfiśah had-Dinamiṯ bam-Mišpaṭ ha-'Iḇri," *Diḇre ha-Congress lĕ-Madda'e hay-Yahăḏuṯ,* I (1967), 175-79.

Arnaldez, R. *Grammaire et théologie chez Ibn Ḥazm,* Paris, 1956.

Ashkenazi, S. *Ha-RaMBaM ki-Mĕṯargem,* Jerusalem, 1965 (*Lĕšonenu la-'Am,* XVI, no. 6).

Ashtour (Strauss), E. "Kawim li-Dĕmuṯah šel haḳ-Ḳĕhillah hay-Yĕhudiṯ bĕ-Miṣrayim," *Zion,* XXX (1965), 61-157.

———. *Ḳoroṯ hay-Yĕhudim bi-Sĕfaraḏ ham-Muslemiṯ,* 2 vols., Jerusalem, 1966.

———. "The Number of Jews in Medieval Egypt," *JJS,* XVIII (1967), 9-42; XIX (1968), 1-22.

———. "Saladin and the Jews," *HUCA,* XXVII (1956), 305-26.

Assaf, Ś. *Baṯe had-Din wĕ-Siḏrehem,* Jerusalem, 1924.

———. *Bĕ-'Ohŏle Ya'ăḳoḇ,* Jerusalem, 1943.

———. "Ḳeṭa' mi-Ḥibburo šel Ibn al-Jasūm," *ḲS,* XXVIII (1952-53), 101-09.

———. "Ḳobeṣ šel 'Iggeroṯ R. Šĕmu'el ben 'Ali," *Tarbiz,* I (1929), pt. 1, 102-30; pt. 2, 43-84; pt. 3, 15-80.

———. "Mip-Perušo šel ha-RaMBaM lĕ-Masseḵeṯ Šabbaṯ," *Sinai,* II (1940), 103-34.

———. "Mip-Perušo šel Sĕ'adyah ben Dawiḏ Al'aḏani 'al ha-RaMBaM," *ḲS,* XXII (1942), 240-44.

———. "Miš-Šĕyare Sifruṯam šel hag-Gĕ'onim," *Tarbiz,* XV (1943), 27-35.

———. Review of "Peruš R. Ḥănaně'el lĕ-Masseket Zĕbaḥim," KS, XIX (1942–43), 229–31.
———. "Sefer ha-Ḥob lĕ-Rab Hay Ga'on," Tarbiz, XVII (1945), 28–31.
———. "Šĕlošah Sĕfarim Niftaḥim lĕ-Rab Šĕmu'el ben Ḥofni," Sinai, XVII (1939), 113–55.
———. Sifran šel Rišonim, Jerusalem, 1935.
———. "Sifre R. Hay u-Tĕšubotaw kĕ-Makor lĕha-RaMBaM," Sinai, II (1938), 522–26.
———. Tĕkufat hag-Gĕ'onim wĕ-Sifrutah, Jerusalem, 1955.
———. "Zutot: Tĕšubah neḡed Ḥibbur Sifre Dinim," KS, XX (1943–44), 41–42.
Atlas, S. "The Contemporary Relevance of the Philosophy of Maimonides," CCAR Yearbook, LXIV (1954), 186–213.
———. ed., Keṭa'im mis-Sefer Yad ha-Ḥăzakah lĕha-RaMBaM, London, 1940.
———. "Maimon and Maimonides," HUCA, XXII (1950–51), 517–48.
———. "Moses in the Philosophy of Maimonides, Spinoza, and Solomon Maimon," HUCA, XXV (1954), 369–400.
———. Nĕtibim bam-Mišpaṭ ha-'Ibri, New York, 1978.
Auerbach, E. Literary Language and Its Public in Late Latin Antiquity and in the Middle Ages, New York, 1965.
Avida, J. "Mispar hap-Pĕrakim bĕ-Sefer Mishneh Torah," Sura, II (1955), 267–76.
———. "Rĕfu'ah Šĕlemah," Sinai, XXII (1959), 50–55.
———. "Sefer Mishneh Torah lĕha-RaMBaM kĕ-Sefer Limmud," 'Ărešeṭ, III (1961), 31–47.
Avineri, I. Gĕnazim Mĕgullim, Tel Aviv, 1968.
Bacher, W. (B.Z.). Die Bibelexegese der jüdischen Religonsphilosophen des Mittelalters vor Maimuni, Strasbourg, 1892.
———. 'Erke Midraš, Tel Aviv, 1923, Supplement: "Lĕšon ha-RaMBaM."
———. "Hebräische Verse von Maimuni," MGWJ, LIII (1909), 581–88.
———. R. 'Abraham 'ibn 'Ezra' ham-Mĕdakdek, tr. A. Z. Rabinovitz, Tel Aviv, 1931.
———. Ha-RaMBaM Paršan ham-Mikra', tr. A. Z. Rabinovitz, TelAviv, 1932.
———, Brann, M., and Simonsen, D., eds. Moses ben Maimon, 2 vols., Leipzig, 1914; reprinted, Hildesheim, 1971.

Baer, Y. "'Ăbodaṯ haḵ-Ḵorbanoṯ," *Zion*, XL (1975), 95–153.
———. *Galuṯ*, New York, 1947.
———. "Ha-Hatḥaloṯ wĕhay-Yĕsodoṯ šel 'Irgun haḵ-Ḵĕhilloṯ," *Zion*, XV (1950), 1–41.
———. *A History of the Jews in Christian Spain*, 2 vols., Philadelphia, 1961.
———. "Lĕ-Beruro šel Toraṯ 'Aḥăriṯ hay-Yamim biy-Yĕme hab-Bayyiṯ haš-Šeni," *Zion*, XXIII (1958), 3–34.
Baldwin, John W. *Masters, Princes, and Merchants: The Social Views of Peter the Chanter and His Circle*, 2 vols., Princeton, 1970.
———. *The Scholastic Culture of the Middle Ages*, Lexington, 1971.
Baneth, D. "Hatḥalaṯ Sefer ham-Miṣwoṯ lĕ-RaSaG," *Ḳoḇeṣ R. Sĕ'adyah Gaon*, ed. J. L. Fishman, Jerusalem, 1943, pp. 365–82.
———. "Jehuda Hallewi und Gazali," *Korrespondenzblatt der Akademie für die Wissenchaft des Judentums*, Berlin, 1923, pp. 27–45.
———. "Laṯ-Terminoloğiyah hap-Pilosofiṯ šel ha-RaMBaM," *Tarbiz*, VI (1935), 10–40.
———. "Me-Ḥălifaṯ ham-Miḵtaḇim šel ha-RaMBaM," *Sefer Zikkaron lĕ-Gulak u-Klein*, Jerusalem, 1942, pp. 50–56.
———. "Ha-RaMBaM kĕ-Mĕtargem Diḇre 'Aṣmo," *Tarbiz*, XXIII (1951–52), 170–91.
Bardowicz, A. "Die rationale Schriftauslegung des Maimonides," *Magazin für die Wissenschaft des Judenthums*, XIX (1892), 139–70; XX (1893), 50–76.
Barnard, L. W. "The Old Testament and Judaism in the Writings of Justin Martyr," *Vetus Testamentum*, XIV (1964), 395–406.
Barnett, R. D., ed. *The Sephardi Heritage*, New York, 1971.
Baron, S. W. *Ancient and Medieval Jewish History, Essays*, ed. L. A. Feldman, New Brunswick, 1972.
———, ed. *Essays on Maimonides*, New York, 1941.
———. "The Historical Outlook of Maimonides," *PAAJR*, VI (1935), 5–113; reprinted in his *History and Jewish Historians*, Philadelphia, 1964, pp. 109–67.
———. *A Social and Religious History of the Jews*, New York, 1958– (especially vols. VI–VII).
Barzilay, I. *Between Reason and Faith*, The Hague, 1967.
———. "The Ideology of the Berlin Haskalah," *PAAJR*, XXV (1956), 1–37.
———. "The Treatment of the Jewish Religion in the Literature of the Berlin Haskalah," *PAAJR*, XXIV (1955), 39–68.
———. *Yoseph Shlomo Delmedigo* (Yashar of Candia), Leiden, 1974.

# BIBLIOGRAPHY

Bazak, J. *'Aḥărayuṭo hap-Pĕliliṭ šel hal-Laḵuy bĕ-Nafšo*, Jerusalem, 1964.
———. *Lĕ-Ma'ălah min ha-Ḥušim*, Tel Aviv, 1968.
Bechler, Z. "Hatḵafaṭo šel ha-RaMBaM," *'Iyyun*, XVII (1966), 34–41.
Becker, J. *Mišnaṭo hap-Pilosofiṭ šel RaMBaM*, Tel Aviv, 1955.
Beit-Arié, M. "A Maimonides Autograph in the Rylands Gaster Genizah Collection," *Bulletin of the John Rylands University Library*, LVII (1974), 1–6.
Belkin, S. "Ham-Midraš hag-Gaḏol u-Midrĕše Philo," *Joshua Finkel Festschrift*, ed. S. Hoenig and L. Stitskin, New York, 1974, Hebrew section, pp. 7–59.
———. "Ham-Midraš has-Simli 'ešel Philo," *Harry A. Wolfson Jubilee Volume*, ed. S. Lieberman, Jerusalem, 1965, Hebrew section, pp. 33–68.
———. *Philo and the Oral Law*, Cambridge, Mass., 1940.
Ben-David, A. *Lĕšon Miḵra' u-Lĕšon Ḥăḵamim*, Tel Aviv, 1967.
Ben-Ezra, A. "Ḥidduše Millim šel RaSaG," *Ḥoreḇ*, VIII (1944), 135–47.
Ben-Jacob, Abraham. *Yĕhuḏe Baḇel*, Jerusalem, 1965.
Benjacob, I. *Oṣar has-Sĕfarim*, Vilna, 1880.
Ben-Menahem, N. *'Inyĕne 'ibn 'Ezra'*, Jerusalem, 1978.
———. "Yĕsod Mora' šel R. 'Aḇraham ben 'Ezra'," *Essays Presented to Israel Brodie*, ed. H. C. Zimmels, London, 1967, pp. 67–78.
Ben-Sasson, H. H. *Haḡuṭ wĕ-Hanhaḡah*, Jerusalem, 1959.
———. "Ha-RaMBaM: Hanhaḡaṭ 'Iš ha-Ruaḥ," *Ha-'Išiyyuṭ wĕ-Dorah*, Jerusalem, 1964, pp. 93–106.
———. "The Reformation in Contemporary Jewish Eyes," *Proceedings of the Israel Academy of Sciences*, IV (1970), 239–326.
———. "Yiḥud 'Am Yiśra'el," *Pĕraḵim*, II (1971), 145–218.
Ben-Sasson, Y. "Le-Ḥeḵer Mišnaṭ Ṭa'ăme Miṣwoṭ," *Tarbiz*, XXIX (1960), 268–82.
———. "Mišnaṭo ha-Hisṭoriṭ šel R. Yĕhudah hal-Lewi," *Mišnaṭo he-Haḡuṭiṭ šel R. Yĕhudah hal-Lewi*, Jerusalem, 1978, pp. 151–72.
———. "Haš-Šabbaṭ bĕ-Maḥšeḇeṭ hay-Yahăḏuṭ," *Ma'ăyanoṭ*, Jerusalem, 1974, pp. 78–116.
———. "Toraṭ han-Nĕḇu'ah šel ha-RaMBaM," *Haḡuṭ ham-Miḵra'*, Jerusalem, 1977, pp. 27–71.
———. "Yĕsoḏe Toraṭ ham-Musar šel Ḥeḇrah u-Mišpaḥah bĕ-Mišnoṭehem šel RaMBaM wĕhal-Lewi," *Mišpĕḥoṭ Beṭ Yiśra'el*, Jerusalem, 1976, pp. 77–132.
Ben-Shammai, H. "Hăluḵaṭ ham-Miṣwoṭ u-Muśśaḡ ha-Ḥoḵmah bĕ-Mišnaṭ RaSaG," *Tarbiz*, XXXXI (1972), 170–82.

## 578 INTRODUCTION TO THE CODE OF MAIMONIDES

Benayahu, M. "Ḥiddušah šel has-Sĕmiḵah," *Y. Baer Jubilee Volume*, ed. S. Ettinger and others, Jerusalem, 1961, pp. 248–69.

———. *Marbiṣ Torah*, Jerusalem, 1953.

———. "R. Ḥiyya' Rofe' wĕ-Sifro Ma'ăśeh Ḥiyya'," 'Ărešĕṭ, II (1960), 109–29.

———. *Sefer Tolĕdoṯ ha-'ARI*, Jerusalem, 1967.

Benedict, B. Z. " 'Al Darko šel ha-RaMBaM," *Sefer hay-Yobel lĕ-R. Ḥănoḵ Albeck*, Jerusalem, 1963, pp. 52–71.

———. " 'Al Dereḵ ha-Hagdarah bĕ-Mišnaṯ ha-RaMBaM," *Šanah bĕ-Šanah*, (1965), 223–36.

———. [Annual essays in] *Torah šebbĕ-'al Peh*, IV (1962)–XIX (1977) (an important series on aspects of the *Mishneh Torah*).

———. "Lĕ-Tolĕdoṯaw šel Merkaz hat-Torah bĕ-Provence," *Tarbiz*, XXII (1951), 85–109.

———."Sefer hat-Tašlum šel R. 'Efrayim," *ḲS*, XXVI (1949–50), 322–36.

Berlin, C. *Index to Festschriften in Jewish Studies*, New York, 1971.

Berman, L. "Maimonides, the disciple of Alfarabi," *Israel Oriental Studies*, IV (1974), 154–78.

———. "Maimonides' Statement on Political Science," *Journal of the American Oriental Society*, LXXXIX (1969), 106–12.

———. "Medieval Jewish Religious Philosophy," *Study of Judaism: Bibliographical Essays in Medieval Jewish Studies*, New York, 1976, pp. 231–65.

———. "The Political Interpretation of the Maxim: The Purpose of Philosophy is the Imitation of God," *Studia Islamica*, XV (1961), 53–61.

Berman, S. J. "Lifnim miš-Šuraṯ had-Din," *JJS*, XXVI (1975), 86–105; XXVIII (1977), 181–94.

Bernstein, B. *Die Schrifterklärung des Bachja b. Ascher ibn Chalawa und ihre Quellen*, Berlin, 1891.

Bialoblocki, S. *'Em lĕ-Masoreṯ*, Ramat Gan, 1971.

———. *Materialien zum islamischen und jüdischen Eherecht*, Giessen, 1928.

Birnbaum, P. *Karaite Studies*, New York, 1971.

Blau, J. *The Emergence and Linguistic Background of Judeo-Arabic* (Scripta Judaica, V), Oxford, 1963.

———. "Ma'ămaḏan šel ha-'Ibriṯ wĕha-'Ărabiṯ," *Lĕšonenu*, XXVI (1962), 281–84.

Bleich, J. "Ethico-Halakhic Considerations in the Practice of Medicine," *Dine Yiśra'el*, VII (1976), 87–137.

Blidstein, G. *Honor Thy Father and Mother,* New York, 1975.
Bloch, M. *Sefer Ša'are Toraṯ haṯ-Taḳḳanoṯ,* 3 vols., Vienna, 1879–86.
———. "Les 613 Préceptes," *REJ,* 1 (1886) 196–214.
Blumberg, H. "Alfarabi, Ibn Bajjah, wěha-RaMBaM 'al Hanhaḡaṯ ham-Miṯboḏeḏ," *Sinai,* LXXVIII (1976), 135–45.
———. "Muśśaḡ ha-Raṣon ha-'Ěloḳi bě-Mišnaṯo šel ha-RaMBaM," *Pěraḳim,* IV (1966), 43–56.
———. "The Problem of Immortality in Avicenna, Maimonides, and St. Thomas Aquinas," *Harry A. Wolfson Jubilee Volume,* ed. S. Lieberman, Jerusalem, 1965, I, 165–85.
———. "Theories of Evil in Medieval Jewish Philosophy," *HUCA,* XLIII (1972), 149–68.
———. "Toraṯ ham-Musar be-Mišnaṯam šel 'Aḇráham bar Ḥiyya, Yosef 'ibn Ṣaddiḳ, wě-'Ibn Dauḏ," *Tarbiz,* XLVI (1977), 231–45.
Blumenfeld, S. M. "Toward a Study of Maimonides the Educator," *HUCA,* XXIII (1950–51), 555–91.
Blumenthal, D. R. *The Commentary of R. Ḥōṭer ben Shelōmo to the Thirteen Principles of Maimonides,* Leiden, 1974.
Boksboim, J. "Těšuḇoṯ Ḥaḳme Sěfaraḏ bě-Din Ḳaṭlaniṯ," *Moriah,* VII (1977), 11–13.
Bokser, B. Z. *The Legacy of Maimonides,* New York, 1962.
———. "Morality and Religion in the Theology of Maimonides," *Essays on Jewish Life in Honor of Salo W. Baron,* New York, 1959, pp. 139–57.
Bolgar, R. *The Classical Heritage and its Beneficiaries,* New York, 1964.
Born, L. "The Perfect Prince, a Study in Thirteenth and Fourteenth Century Ideals," *Speculum,* III (1928), 470–504.
Bourke, V. *History of Ethics,* vol. I, New York, 1970.
Braude, W. "Maimonides' Attitudes to Midrash," *Studies . . . in Honor of I. Edward Kiev,* ed. C. Berlin, New York, 1971, pp. 75–83.
Breuer, M. *Keṯer 'Aram Ṣoḇah,* Jerusalem, 1976.
———. "Miněʿu Beneḵem min ha-Higgayon," *Miḵtam lě-Dawiḏ,* Ramat Gan, 1978, pp. 242–61.
Brody, H. "Miḵtamim 'al ha-RaMBaM u-Sěfaraw," *Moznayim,* III (1935), 402–13.
Bromberg, A. J. "Hašpa'aṯ R. Hananěʾel 'al ha-RaMBaM," *Sinai,* XXXIII (1953), 43–55.
———. *Měḳoroṯ lě-Fisḳe ha-RaMBaM,* Jerusalem, 1947.
———. R. Hananěʾel wěha-RaMBaM," *Sinai,* XXII (1948), 4–13.
Brüll, N. "Iggeret Teman," *Jahrbücher für jüdische Geschichte und Literatur,* I (1876), 194–98.

———. "Die Polemik für und gegen Maimuni," *Jahrbücher*, IV (1879), 1–53.
Brumer, J. "Minyan hag-Giḍim ha-'Ăsurim lĕ-RaSaG," *PAAJR*, XXX (1962), 1–8.
Buchholz, J. "Historischer Überblick über die mannigfachen Codificationen," *MGWJ*, XIII (1864), 201ff., 241ff.
Büchler, A. "The Reading of the Law . . . in a Triennial Cycle," *JQR*, V (1893), 420–68; VI (1894), 1–73.
Bürgel, C. *Averroes contra Galenum*, Göttingen, 1968.
Burke, P. "Tradition and Experience: the Idea of Decline from Bruni to Gibbon," *Daedalus*, Summer 1976), 137–153.
Cairns, H. *Legal Philosophy from Plato to Hegel*, Baltimore, 1949.
Callus, D. *The Condemnation of St. Thomas at Oxford*, Oxford, 1946.
Cassuto, M. D. *Hay-Yĕhuḍim bĕ-Firenze bi-Tĕḳufaṯ ha-Renaissance*, Jerusalem, 1967.
Castro, A. *The Structure of Spanish History*, Princeton, 1954.
Chajes, Z. H. *Kol Sifre . . . Chajes*, 2 vols., Jerusalem, 1958.
Chenu, M. D. *Nature, Man, and Society in the Twelfth Century*, Chicago, 1968.
Chomsky, W. "Hebrew during the Middle Ages," *JQR Seventy-Fifth Anniversary Volume* (1967), 121–36.
Cohen, A. *The Teachings of Maimonides*, reprinted, New York, 1968 (with prolegomenon by Marvin Fox).
Cohen, B. "Classification of Law in the *Mishneh Torah*," *JQR*, XXV (1935), 519–40.
———. *Law and Tradition in Judaism*, New York, 1959.
Cohen, G. D. "Esau as Symbol in Early Medieval Thought," *Jewish Medieval and Renaissance Studies*, ed. A. Altmann, Cambridge, Mass., 1967, pp. 19–48.
———. *Messianic Postures of Ashkenazim and Sephardim* (Leo Baeck Memorial Lecture), New York, 1967.
———. "The Soteriology of R. Abraham Maimuni," *PAAJR*, XXXV (1967), 75–98; XXXVI (1968), 33–56.
———. "The Story of the Four Captives," *PAAJR*, XXIX (1960–61), 55–131.
Cohen, H. "Charakteristik der Ethik Maimunis," *Jüdische Schriften*, III (1924), 221–89.
———. *Daṯ hat-Tĕḇunah mim-Mĕḳorot hay-Yahăḍut* (Hebrew translation of his *Religion der Vernunft aus den Quellen des Judentums*), ed. S. Bergman and N. Rotenstreich, Jerusalem, 1971.

Corcos, D. "Lĕ-'Ofi Yaḥăsam šel Šĕliṭe ha-Almuwaḥḥidun lay-Yĕhuḏim," *Zion*, XXXII (1967), 137-60.
Coulson, N. J. *A History of Islamic Law*, Edinburgh, 1964.
Cronbach, A. "The Maimonidean Code of Benevolence," *HUCA*, XX (1947), 471-540.
Curtius, E. *European Literature and the Latin Middle Ages*, New York, 1953.
*Da'aṯ* (Journal of Jewish Philosophy and Kabbalah), ed. N. Arieli, I (1978).
Dan, J. *Sifruṯ ham-Musar wĕha-Dĕruš*, Jerusalem, 1975.
———. *Toraṯ has-Soḏ šel Ḥasiḏe 'Aškĕnaz*, Jerusalem, 1968.
Daube, D. "The Self-Understood in Legal History," *Juridical Review*, LXXXV (1973), 126-34.
David, A. "R. Šĕmu'el 'Aṭiyyah," *Tarbiz*, XXXIX (1970), 415-19.
Davidson, H. A. "The Active Intellect in the *Cuzari*," *REJ*, CXXXI (1972), 351-96.
———. "Alfarabi and Avicenna on the Active Intellect," *Viator*, III (1972), 109-78.
———. "Maimonides' *Shemonah Peraḳim* and Alfārābi's *Fuṣūl al-Madanī*," *PAAJR*, XXXI (1963), 33-51.
———. *The Philosophy of Abraham Shalom*, Los Angeles, 1964.
———. "The Study of Philosophy as a Religious Obligation," *Religion in a Religious Age*, ed. S. D. Goitein, Cambridge, Mass., 1974, pp. 53-69.
Denari, Y. "'Aḇiḏ 'Enaš Dina' lĕ-Nafšeh," *Dine Yiśra'el*, IV (1973), 91-107.
———. "Ham-Minhāḡ wĕha-Halaḳah," *Sefer Zikkaron B. de Vries*, Jerusalem, 1969, pp. 168-98.
Dienstag, J. I. "Be'ur Milloṯ ha-Higgayon," *'Ărešeṯ*, II (1960), 7-34.
———. "Biblical Exegesis of Maimonides in Jewish Scholarship," *Samuel K. Mirsky Memorial Volume*, New York, 1970, pp. 151-90.
———. "Christian Translators of Mainmonides' *Mishneh Torah* into Latin," *Salo W. Baron Jubilee Volume*, ed. S. Lieberman, Jerusalem, 1974, I, 287-309.
———. *'En ham-Miṣwoṯ*, New York, 1969.
———. "Ha-'im Hiṯnaḡeḏ hag-GĕRa' lĕ-Mišnaṯo hap-Pilosofiṯ šel ha-RaMBaM," *Talpiyoṯ*, IV (1949), 253-68.
———. "'Iggereṯ Teman," *'Ărešeṯ*, III (1961), 48-70.
———. "Lĕ-Yaḥas Maran 'el Mišnaṯ ha-RaMBaM," *Sinai*, LIX (1966), 54-75.

582 INTRODUCTION TO THE CODE OF MAIMONIDES

———. "Ma'ămar Tĕḥiyyăṯ ham-Meṯim lĕha-RaMBaM," *ḲS*, XLVIII (1973), 730–40.

———. "Mishneh Torah lĕha-RaMBaM" (bibliography of editions), *Studies in Jewish Bibliography, History, and Literature in Honor of I. E. Kiev*, ed. C. Berlin, New York, 1971, pp. 21–108.

———. "Moreh Nĕḇukim wĕ-Sefer ham-Madda' bas-Sifruṯ ha-Ḥăsiḏiṯ," *Abraham Weiss Jubilee Volume*, New York, 1964, pp. 307–30.

———. "Moses Maimonides, a Topical Bibliography," *Studies in Bibliography and Booklore*, I (1961), 12–29.

———. "The Prayer Book of Maimonides," *Leo Jung Jubilee Volume*, ed. M. Kasher, N. Lamm, and L. Rosenfeld, New York, 1962, pp. 53–63.

———. "Sefer ham-Miṣwoṯ," *'Ăreṣeṯ*, V (1972), 34–80.

———. ed. *Studies in Maimonides and St. Thomas Aquinas*, New York, 1975.

———. "Tĕrumaṯam šel Ḥakme Liṭa' lĕ-Sifruṯ hay-Yaḏ ha-Ḥăzaḵah," *Ḥesed lĕ-Aḇraham, Yoḇel lĕ-Aḇraham Golomb*, Los Angeles, 1970, pp. 445–96.

———. "Yaḥăsam šel Ba'ăle hat-Tosafoṯ lĕha-RaMBaM," *Samuel K. Mirsky Jubilee Volume*, New York, 1958, pp. 350–79.

Diesendruck, Z. "On the Date of the Composition of the *Moreh Nebukim*," *HUCA*, XII–XIII (1937–38), 461–97.

———. "The Philosophy of Maimonides," *CCAR Yearbook*, XLV (1935), 355–68.

———. "Samuel and Moses ibn Tibbon on Maimonides' Theory of Providence," *HUCA*, XI (1936), 341–66.

Dimitrovsky, Z. " 'Al Dereḵ hap-Pilpul," *Salo W. Baron Jubilee Volume*, ed. S. Lieberman, Jerusalem, 1975, Hebrew section, pp. 111–82.

———. "Beṯ Midrašo šel R. Ya'aḵoḇ Beraḇ," *Sĕfunoṯ*, VII (1963), 41–102.

Dinur, B. *Yiśra'el bag-Golah*, Jerusalem, 1969–.

Dozy, R. *Spanish Islam*, tr. G. Stokes, London, 1913.

Dykan, P. *Dine Niśśu'in u-Gerušin*, Tel Aviv, 1956.

Edelstein, L. "Greek Medicine in Its Relation to Religion and Magic," *Bulletin of the Institute of the History of Medicine*, V (1937), 210–46.

Efros, I. " 'Iyyunim bĕ-Sefer 'Ĕmunoṯ wĕ-De'oṯ," *Sefer Yoḇel lĕ-Šim'on Federbush*, ed. J. L. Maimon, Jerusalem, 1961, pp. 69–89.

———. *Philosophical Terms in the Moreh Nĕḇukim*, New York, 1924.

———. "Saadia's General Ethical Theory and its Relation to Sufism," *JQR Seventy-Fifth Anniversary Volume* (1967), 166–77.

———. *Studies in Medieval Jewish Philosophy*, New York, 1974.
———. "Ṭebaʿ wa-Ruaḥ bĕ-Mišnaṭ ha-RaMBaM," *Sefer Yobel lĕ-Yiśra'el Elfenbein*, ed. J. Maimon, Jerusalem, 1963, pp. 14–20.
Eidelberg, S. *Jewish Life in Austria in the XVth Century*, Philadelphia, 1962.
Elbaum, J. "Rabbi Judah Loew of Prague and his Attitude to the Aggadah," *Scripta Hierosolymitana*, XXII (1971), 28–47.
Elbogen, I. *Hat-Tĕfillah bĕ-Yiśra'el* (Hebrew translation of his *Der jüdische Gottesdienst*), Tel Aviv, 1972.
———. "Moses ben Maimons Persönlichket," *MGWJ*, LXXIX (1935), 76–79.
Elon, M. *Ḥeruṭ hap-Pĕraṭ bĕ-Darke Gĕbiyaṭ Ḥob bam-Mišpaṭ ha-ʿIbri*, Jerusalem, 1964.
———. *Ham-Mišpaṭ ha-ʿIbri*, 3 vols., Jerusalem, 1973.
———, ed. *The Principles of Jewish Law*, Jerusalem, 1975.
———. "Taḳḳanoṭ haḳ-Ḳahal," *Meḥḳĕre Mišpaṭ lĕ-'Abraham Rosenthal*, ed. G. Tedeschi, Jerusalem, 1964, pp. 1–55.
Elstein, Y. "Toraṭ ham-Miṣwoṭ bĕ-Mišnaṭ Rab Sĕʿadyah," *Tarbiz*, XXXVIII (1968–69), 120–35.
Enelow, H. *Selected Works*, 4 vols., Kingsport, 1935.
Engelard, I. "Tannuro šel ʿAknaʿi," *Šĕnaṭon ham-Mišpaṭ ha-ʿIbri*, I (1974), 45–56.
Enker, A. "Reṣaḥ mit-Toḳ Heḳraḥ wĕ-Ṣoreḳ," *Šĕnaṭon ham-Mišpaṭ ha-ʿIbri*, V (1975), 154–74.
———. "Self-Incrimination in Jewish Law," *Dine Yiśra'el*, IV (1974), cvi–cxxiv.
Eppenstein, S. *ʿIyyun wĕ-Ḥeḳer*, Jerusalem, 1976.
Epstein, A. "Sefer 'Eldad had-Dani," *Kitbe 'A. Epstein*, ed. A. M. Habermann, Jerusalem, 1950, pp. 1–186.
Epstein, I. "The Distinctiveness of Maimonides' Halakah," *Leo Jung Jubilee Volume*, ed. M. Kasher, N. Lamm, and L. Rosenfeld, New York, 1962, pp. 65–75.
———, ed. *Moses Maimonides*, London, 1935.
Epstein, J. N. *Diḳduḳ 'Aramiṭ Bablit*, Jerusalem, 1960.
———. *Mabo' lĕ-Nusaḥ ham-Mishnah*, 2 vols., Jerusalem, 1948.
———. "Mĕkilta wĕ-Sifre bĕ-Sifre ha-RaMBaM," *Tarbiz*, VI (1935), 99–138.
Epstein, L. M. *The Jewish Marriage Contract*, New York, 1927.
———. *Sex Laws and Customs in Judaism*, New York, 1949.
Etziony, M. "Apropos of Maimonides' Aphorisms," *Bulletin of the History of Medicine*, XXXV (1961), 163–68.

Fakhry, M. "The Antinomy of the Eternity of the World in Averroes, Maimonides, and Aquinas," *Muséon*, LXVI (1953), 139–55.
———. *A History of Islamic Philosophy*, New York, 1970.
Faur, J. "La Doctrina de la Ley Natural," *Sefarad*, XXVII (1967), 239–68.
———. *'Iyyunim bĕ-Mišneh Torah lĕha-RaMBaM: Sefer ham-Madda'*, Jerusalem, 1978.
———. "Mĕḳor Ḥiyyuban šel ham-Miṣwot lĕ-Da'at ha-RaMBaM," *Tarbiz*, XXXVIII (1969), 43–53.
———. "The Origin of the Classification of Rational and Divine Commandments in Medieval Jewish Philosophy," *Augustinianum*, IX (1969), 299–304.
Federbush, S., ed. *Ha-RaMBaM: Torato wĕ-'Išiyyuto*, New York, 1956 (includes his "Yaḥaso šel ha-RaMBaM lal-Lašon ha-'Ibrit").
Feldman, Leon. " 'Oṣar hak-Kabod haš-Šalem," *Salo W. Baron Jubilee Volume*, ed. S. Lieberman, Jerusalem, 1975, Hebrew section, pp. 297–317.
Feldman, Louis. "Abraham the Greek Philosopher in Josephus," *Transactions of the American Philological Association*, IC (1968), 143–56.
Finkel, E. R. *Obadja Sforno als Exeget*, Breslau, 1896.
Finkel, J. "A Link between Hasidism and Hellenistic and Patristic Literature," *PAAJR*, XXVI (1957), 1–24; XXVII (1958), 19–41.
———. "Maimonides' Treatise on Resurrection: a Comparative Study," *Essays on Maimonides*, ed. S. Baron, New York, 1941, pp. 93–123.
Finkelstein, L. "Maimonides and the Tannaitic Midrashim," *JQR*, XXV (1935), 469–517.
Fishman, J., ed. "Rab Sĕ'adyah Ga'on," *Ḳobeṣ Torani-Madda'i*, Jerusalem, 1943.
———. "Rabbi Yĕhudah hal-Lewi," *Ḳobeṣ Torani-Madda'i*, Jerusalem, 1943.
Fleischer, E. "'Iyyunim bĕ-Širato šel R. Hay Ga'on," *Šay lĕ-Heman (Habermann)*, ed. Z. Mal'aki, Jerusalem, 1977, pp. 239–75.
———. "Lĕ-'Inyan Šir hap-Pĕtiḥah šel R. 'Abraham 'ibn 'Ezra'," *Lĕšonenu*, XXXVI (1977), 314–15.
———. *Širat haḳ-Ḳodeš*, Jerusalem, 1975.
———. "Unpublished Poems by Rav Hai Gaon," *JQR*, LXV (1974), 1–17.
Fox, M. "Law and Ethics in Modern Jewish Philosophy," *PAAJR*, XLIII (1976), 1–13.
———. "Maimonides and Aquinas on Natural Law," *Dine Yiśra'el*, III (1972), V–XXXVI.

———. "On the Rational Commandments in Saadia's Philosophy, a Re-Examination," *Modern Jewish Ethics: Theory and Practice*, ed. M. Fox, Columbus, 1975, pp. 174–87.

———. "Hat-Těfillah bě-Maḥšabto šel ha-RaMBaM," *Hat-Těfillah ha-Yěhudit*, Ramat Gan, 1978, pp. 142–67.

Frankel, J. *Darko šel RaSHI bě-Fěrušo lě-Talmud Babli*, Jerusalem, 1975.

Frankel, Z. *Darke ham-Mišnah*, Warsaw, 1923.

Freimann, A. *Seder Ḳidduš́in wě-Niśśu'in*, Jerusalem, 1945.

———. "Těšubot R. Maimon had-Dayyan 'Abi ha-RaMBaM," *Tarbiz*, VI (1935), 164–76.

Friedenwald, H. *The Jews and Medicine*, 2 vols., Baltimore, 1944.

Friedlander, I. *Past and Present: Selected Essays*, New York, 1961.

Friedman, M. "Ribbuy Našim bě-Mismake hag-Gěnizah," *Tarbiz*, XL (1971), 320–59.

———. "Šělošah Ḳěṭa'im Ḥadašim mit-Těšubot ha-RaMBaM," *Tarbiz*, XLIV (1977), 145–50.

Friedman, S. "Mit-Tosěfot ha-RaSHBaM la-RIF," *Ḳobeṣ 'al Yad*, VIII (1976), 187–226.

Fuchs, L. S. *Studien ueber . . . Ibn Bal'am*, Berlin, 1893.

Fuerstenthal, R. D. *Das jüdische Traditionswesen*, Breslau, 1842.

Funkenstein, A. "Gesetz und Geschichte, zur historisierenden Hermeneutik bei Moses Maimonides und Thomas von Aquin," *Viator*, I (1970), 147–78.

———. "Maimonides: Political Theory and Realistic Messianism," *Miscellanea Mediaevalia*, XI (1977), 81–103.

———. "Hat-Těmurot bě-Wikkuaḥ had-Dat šeb-ben Yěhudim lě-Noṣrim," *Zion*, XXXIII (1968), 125–44.

Gabriel, A. *Garlandia* (Studies in the History of the Medieval University), Notre Dame, 1969.

Gandz, D. "Date of the Composition of Maimonides' Code," *PAAJR*, XVII (1948), 1–7; reprinted in his *Studies in Hebrew Astronomy and Mathematics*, ed. S. Steinberg, New York, 1970, pp. 113–20.

Gardet, L. *Études de philosophie et de mystique comparées*, Paris, 1972.

———. *La pensée religieuse d'Avicenne*, Paris, 1951.

Gaster, M., ed. "Be'ur Šěmot Ḳodeš wě-Ḥol," *Dvir*, I (1923), 191–222.

Gevaryahu, H. "Ha-'Ělilut lě-fi Těfiśat ha-RaMBaM," *Sefer Karl*, ed. A. Weiser, Jerusalem, 1960, pp. 353–60.

Gibb, H. "The Structure of Religious Thought in Islam," *Muslim World*, XXXVIII (1948), 113–19.

Gilson, E. *History of Christian Philosophy in the Middle Ages*, London, 1955.

———. "Humanisme médiéval et Renaissance," *Les idées et les lettres*, Paris, 1955.
———. *The Spirit of Medieval Philosophy*, New York, 1948.
Ginzberg, A. "The Supremacy of Reason," *Maimonides Octocentennial Series*, New York, 1935.
Ginzberg, L. *Geonica*, 2 vols., New York, 1909.
———. *Ginze Schechter*, 2 vols., New York, 1928.
———. *On Jewish Law and Lore*, Philadelphia, 1955.
———. *Perušim wĕ-Ḥiddušim bi-Yĕrušalmi*, 3 vols., New York, 1941; vol. 4, ed. D. Weiss-Halivni, New York, 1961.
Giocarinis, K. "Bernard of Cluny and the Antique," *Classica et Medievalia*, XXXVII (1966), 310–48.
Gössmann, E. *Antiqui und Moderni im Mittelalter*, Munich, 1974.
Goitein, S. D. "Abraham Maimonides and his Circle," *Jewish Medieval and Renaissance Studies*, ed. A. Altmann, Cambridge, Mass., 1967, pp. 145–65.
———. "Ḥayye ha-RaMBaM lĕ-'Or Giluyim Ḥădašim," *Pĕraḳim*, IV (1966), 29–42.
———. "A Jewish Addict to Sufism," *JQR*, XLIV (1953), 37–49.
———. "Maimonides as Chief Justice," *JQR*, XLIX (1959), 191–203.
———. "The Medical Profession in the Light of the Cairo Genizah Documents," *HUCA*, XXXIV (1963), 177–94.
———. *A Mediterranean Society, the Jewish Communities of the Arab Word as Portrayed in the Documents of the Cairo Geniza*, vols. I–III, Berkeley and Los Angeles, 1967–78.
———. A "Miḵtab 'el ha-RaM BaM bĕ-'Inyane ha-Heḳdešot," *Tarbiz*, XXXIV (1965), 232–56.
———. "Religion in Everyday Life as Reflected in the Documents of the Cairo Geniza," *Religion in a Religious Age*, ed. S. D. Goitein, Cambridge, Mass., 1974, pp. 3–19.
———. *Sidre Ḥinnuḵ mit-Tĕḵufat hag-Gĕ'onim u-Bet ha-RaMBaM*, Jerusalem, 1962.
———. "Temanim bi-Yĕrušalayim," *Har'el*, ed. I. Razhaby, Tel Aviv, 1962, pp. 133–49.
———. "Tĕmiḳatam šel Yĕhude Teman . . . bi-Yĕšibat ha-RaMBaM," *Tarbiz*, XXXI (1962), 347–71.
———. "Tiḳḳun Nosaf ba-'Otograf šel ha-RaMBaM," *Tarbiz*, XXXIV (1965), 195.
———. "Tiḳḳunim . . . la-RaMBaM," *Tarbiz*, XXVIII (1959), 190–97; XXXII (1963), 188–97.

Golb, N. *Tolĕḏoṯ hay-Yĕhuḏim bĕ-'Ir Rouen*, Tel Aviv, 1976.

Goldberger, P. *Die Allegorie in ihrer exegetischen Anwendung bei M. Maimonides*, Breslau, 1901.

Goldman, E. "Ha-'Ăḇoḏah ham-Mĕyuḥe'ḏeṯ bĕ-Massiḡe ha-'Ămiṯoṯ," *Bar Ilan Annual*, VI (1968), 287–313.

———. "Nĕḇu'ah u-Bĕḥirah," *Samuel K. Mirsky Memorial Volume*, ed. G. Appel, Jerusalem, 1970, pp. 203–10.

Goldman, S. "The Halachic Foundations of Maimonides' Thirteen Principles," *Essays Presented to Israel Brodie*, ed. H. J. Zimmels, London, 1967, pp. 111–18.

Goldziher, I. *Gesammelte Schriften*, ed. J. de Somogyi, Hildesheim, 1967.

———. "Proben muhammedanischer Polemik gegen den Talmud," *Jeschurun*, VIII (1872), 76–104.

———. ed. *Pseudo-Baḥya: Kitāb ma'ānī al-nafs*, Berlin, 1907.

———. "Ueber eine Formel in der juedischen Responsenliteratur und in den muhammedanischen Fatwâs," *Zeitschrift der Deutschen Morgenländischen Gesellschaft*, LIII (1899), 645–52.

———. *Vorlesungen über den Islam*, Heidelberg, 1910 (Hebrew translation: *Harṣa'oṯ*, Jerusalem, 1951).

Golinski, G. *Das Wesen des Religionsgesetzes in der Philosophie des Bachja*, Würzburg, 1935.

Goode, A. "The Exilarchate in the Eastern Caliphate, 637–1258," *JQR*, XXXI (1940–41), 149–69.

Goodenough, E. *The Theology of Justin Martyr*, Amsterdam, 1968.

Goshen-Gottstein, M. "The Authenticity of the Aleppo Codex," *Textus*, I (1966), 17–58.

———. "Ha-'Iḳḳarim lĕha-RaMBaM bĕ-Targum 'Alḥarizi," *Tarbiz*, XXVI (1957), 185–96, 335–36.

———. "Mid-darke hat-Targum wĕham-Mĕtargĕmim," *Tarbiz*, XXIII (1953), 210–16.

———. *Taḥbirah u-Milonah šel hal-Lašon ha-'Iḇriṯ*, Jerusalem, 1951.

Gottlieb, E. *Meḥḳarim bĕ-Sifruṯ haḳ-Ḳabbalah*, ed. J. Hacker, Tel Aviv, 1976.

———. "Peruše Ma'ăśeh Bĕrešiṯ bĕ-Rešiṯ haḳ-Ḳabbalah," *Tarbiz*, XXXVII (1968), 294–317.

Grabmann, M. "Aristoteles im 12. Jahrhundert," *Mittelalterliches Geistesleben*, III (1956), 64–124.

Graetz, H. *Darke ha-Hisṯoriyah hay-Yĕhuḏiṯ*, Jerusalem, 1969.

———. *Diḇre Yĕme Yiśra'el*, tr. S. Ph. Rabinowitz (addenda by A. Harkavy), 8 vols., Warsaw, 1890–99.

Gray, H. "Renaissance Humanism: the Pursuit of Eloquence," *Renaissance Essays*, ed. P. Kristeller and P. Weiner, New York, 1968, pp. 199–217.
Gray, J. C. *The Nature and Sources of the Law*, Boston, 1963.
Greenbaum, A. "Halaḵoṯ bě-'Abeluṯ le-R. Šěmu'el ben Ḥofni," *Samuel K. Mirsky Memorial Volume*, ed. G. Appel, Jerusalem, 1970, pp. 53–69 (with lists of recently published fragments).
———. "Šělošim Miṣwoṯ šel Běne Noaḥ lě-fi Raḇ Šěmu'el ben Ḥofni," *Sinai*, LXXII (1973), 205–21.
Greive, H. *Studien zum jüdischen Neuplatonismus: Die Religionsphilosophie des Abraham ibn Ezra*, Berlin, 1973.
Grintz, J. M. "Lo' Toḵlu 'al had-Dam," *Zion*, XXXI (1966), 1–17.
Groner, Z. "Těšuḇoṯ lě-R. Hay Ga'on," *Sinai*, LXXIX (1976), 229–42.
Gross, B. *Neṣaḥ Yiśra'el, Haškafaṯo ham-Měšiḥiṯ šel ha-MaHaRaL*, Tel Aviv, 1974.
Gross, H. *Gallia Judaica*, reprinted, Amsterdam, 1969 (with bibliographical supplement by S. Schwarzfuchs).
Grunebaum, G. E. von. *Medieval Islam*, Chicago, 1953.
Gulak, A. "Gěḏarim Mišpaṭiyyim," *Tarbiz*, VI (1935), 139–51.
———. *Yěsoḏe ham-Mišpaṭ ha-'Iḇri*, Tel Aviv, 1967.
Guttmann, Jakob. *Die religionsphilosophischen Lehren des Isaak Abravanel*, Breslau, 1916.
———. *Ueber Dogmenbildung in Judenthum*, Breslau, 1894.
———. *Das Verhältnis des Thomas von Aquino zum Judenthum und zur jüdischen Litteratur*, Göttingen, 1891.
Guttmann, Julius. *Daṯ u-Madda'*, Jerusalem, 1955.
———. *Philosophies of Judaism*, New York, 1964.
———. "Das Problem der Kontingenz in der Philosophie des Maimonides," *MGWJ*, LXXXIII (1939), 406–30.
Guttmann, M. "Die Bedeutung der Tradition . . . bei Maimonides," *MGWJ*, LXXX (1936), 206–15.
———. *Běḥinaṯ Ḳiyyum ham-Miṣwoṯ*, Breslau, 1931.
———. *Das Judentum und seine Umwelt*, Breslau, 1927.
———. "Maïmonide sur l'universalité de la morale religieuse," *REJ*, LXXXIX (1935), 34–43.
———. "Maimonides über das biblische 'jus talionis'," *Eduard Mahler Jubilee Volume*, ed. A. Wertheimer, Budapest, 1937, pp. 415–26.
———. "Yěsoḏe hay-Yahăḏuṯ bě-Fisḵe ha-RaMBaM," *Has-Soḵer*, III (1936–40), 3–62.
———. "Zur Quellenkritik der Mishnah Tora," *MGWJ*, LXXIX (1935), 148–59.

Hajdu, H. *Das mnemotechnische Schrifttum des Mittelalters,* Amsterdam, 1961.
Ha-Kohen, M. "'Or Ḥadaš 'al Yĕšiḇaṯ ha-RaMBaM bĕ-Miṣrayim," *Šanah bĕ-Šanah* (1963), 325–44.
Halkin, A. S. "Ha-Ḥerem 'al Limmuḏ hap-Pilosofiyah," *Pĕraḳim,* I (1967), 35–55.
———. "Lĕ-Tolĕḏoṯ haš-Šĕmaḏ," *Joshua Starr Memorial Volume,* ed. S. Baron, New York, 1953, pp. 101–10.
———. "Li-Dĕmuṯo šel R. Yosef ben Yĕhuḏah 'ibn 'Aḳnin," *Harry A. Wolfson Jubilee Volume,* ed. S. Lieberman, Jerusalem, 1965, Hebrew section, pp. 93–112.
———. "The Medieval Jewish Attitude toward Hebrew," *Biblical and Other Studies,* ed. A. Altmann, Cambridge, Mass., 1963, pp. 232–48.
———. "Mip-Pĕṯiḥaṯ RaSaG lĕ-feruš hat-Torah," *Louis Ginzberg Jubilee Volume,* New York, 1946, Hebrew section, pp. 129–57.
———. "Saneḡoriyah 'al Sefer Mishneh Torah," *Tarbiz,* XXV (1956), 413–28.
———. "Why Was Levi ben Ḥayyim Hounded?" *PAAJR,* XXXIV (1966), 65–77.
———. "Yedaiah Bedershi's Apology," *Jewish Medieval and Renaissance Studies,* ed. A. Altmann, Cambridge, Mass., 1967, pp. 165–84.
Harasta, K. "Die Bedeutung Maimuns für Thomas von Aquin," *Judaica,* XI (1965), 65–83.
Harkavy, A. *Ḥăḏašim gam Yĕšanim,* reprinted, Jerusalem, 1970.
———. "Ḥeleḳ mis-Sefer ham-Miṣwoṯ le-Raḇ Šĕmu'el ben Ḥofni Ga'on," *Haḳ-Ḳeḏem,* III (1909–10), 107–10.
———. *Mĕ'assef Niddaḥim,* reprinted, Jerusalem, 1970 (with a bibliography of works of R. Samuel ben Ḥofni Gaon).
Hartman, D. *Maimonides: Torah and Philosophic Quest,* Philadelphia, 1976.
Harvey, W. "Holiness: a Command to Imitatio Dei," *Tradition,* XVI (1977), 7–28.
Haskins, C. H. *The Renaissance of the Twelfth Century,* New York, 1962.
Havazelet, M. "Hištalšĕluṯ Minhaḡ . . . Ba 'ale Ḳeri," *Talpiyyoṯ* VIII (1963), 531–38.
———. *Ha-RaMBaM wĕhag-Gĕ'onim,* Jerusalem, 1967.
———. "Ziḳaṯ ha-RaMBaM lĕ-'Ereṣ Yiśra'el," *Pĕraḳim,* II (1960), 65–86.
Havlin, S. "Lĕ-Tolĕḏoṯ had-Dĕfusim ha-Rišonim," introduction to the reprint of the Constantinople, 1509 edition of the *Mishneh Torah,* Jerusalem, 1973.

———. "Mishneh Torah Sof Gĕ'onut̠," *Ham-Ma'ăyan,* V (1965), 41–59.

———. Taḳḳanot̠ R. Geršom," *Šĕnat̠on ham-Mišpat̠ ha-'Ib̠ri,* II (1975), 200–58.

Heinemann, I. "Die Lehre vom Ungeschriebenen Gesetz im Jüdischen Schrifttum," *HUCA,* IV (1927), 149–71.

———. *Die Lehre von der Zweckbestimmung des Menschen im griechisch-römischen Altertum und im jüdischen Mittelalter,* Breslau, 1926.

———. "Maimuni und die arabischen Einheitslehrer," *MGWJ,* LXXIX (1935), 102–48.

———. *Ṭa'ăme Miṣwot̠ bĕ-Sifrut̠ Yiśra'el,* Jerusalem, 1949.

———. "Tĕmunat̠ ha-Hisṭoriyah šel R. Yĕhuḏah hal-Lewi," *Zion,* IX (1944), 147–77.

———. "Die Wissenschaftliche Allegoristik des jüdischen Mittelalters," *HUCA,* XXIII (1950–51), 611–43.

Heinemann, J. "Yaḥăso šel R. Sĕ'aḏyah le-Šinnuy Maṭbe'a hat-Tĕfillah," *Bar Ilan,* I (1963), 220–33.

Heller, J. "Maimonides' Theory of Miracles," *Between East and West,* ed. A. Altmann, London, 1958, pp. 112–27.

Herschler, M. "Ḳeṭa' mip-Perušo šel ha-RaMBaM lĕ-Ḥăḡiḡah," *Sinai,* LVI (1964), 185–90.

Hershman, A. *Rabbi Isaac ben Sheshet Perfet,* New York, 1943.

———. "Textual Problems of Book Fourteen of the Mishneh Torah," *JQR,* XL (1950), 401–13.

Herskovis, M. "Yaḥas ḤaZaL lĕ-Targum 'Onḳĕlos," *Joshua Finkel Festschrift,* ed. S. Hoenig, New York, 1974, Hebrew section, pp. 169–76.

Herzog, D. "The Polemic Treatise against Saadya Ascribed to Dunash ben Labrat," *Saadya Studies,* ed. E. I. J. Rosenthal, Manchester, 1943, pp. 26–46.

Herzog, I. "John Selden and Jewish Law," *Journal of Comparative Legislation,* XIII (1931), 236–45.

———. *Judaism, Law, and Ethics,* London, 1975.

———. *Main Institutions of Jewish Law,* 2 vols., London, 1965.

———. "Ha-RaMBaM ba-Halak̠ah," *Sinai,* XXXVI (1956), 439–46.

———. "Seḏer has-Sĕfarim," *Ḳob̠eṣ ha-RaMBaM,* ed. J. L. Maimon, Jerusalem, 1935, pp. 257–64.

Heschel, A. J. "Ha-He'ĕmin ha-RaMBaM šez-Zak̠ah li-Nĕb̠u'ah," *Louis Ginzberg Jubilee Volume,* New York, 1946, Hebrew section, pp. 159–88.

———. *The Insecurity of Freedom,* New York, 1966.

———. *Maimonides,* Berlin, 1935.

———. *Torah min haš-Šamayim*, 2 vols., London, 1962.
Hilvitz, A. *Li-Lĕšonot ha-RaMBaM*, Jerusalem, 1950.
———. "Seder ham-Miṣwot bĕ-Minyan šel ha-RaMBaM," *Sinai*, XIX (1946), 258–67.
Hirschberg, H. Z. "ʿAl Gĕzerot ham-Mĕyaḥădim wĕ-Saḥar Hodi," *Sefer Yobel lĕ-Baer*, Jerusalem, 1960, pp. 134–53.
———. " ʿAl Mĕḵomam šel hat-Targumim ha-'Ărămiyyim," *Bar Ilan*, I (1963), 16–23.
———. " ʿAl R. Zĕḵaryah 'Aḡmati," *Tarbiz*, XLII (1973), 379–89.
———. *History of the Jews in North Africa*, Leiden, 1974.
———. "Review of M. Zucker's *'Al Targum Rab Sĕʿadyah . . . lat-Torah*," *Tarbiz*, XXXI (1962), 414–22.
Hoffmann, E. *Die Liebe zu Gott bei Moses ben Maimon*, Breslau, 1937.
Horodezky, S. A. "Hašpaʿat ha-RaMBaM ʿal ha-RaMaʾ," *'Emet lĕ-Yaʿăḵob, Sefer Yobel . . . Jacob Freimann*, Berlin, 1937, pp. 42–57.
Horovitz, S. *Die Psychologie bei den jüdischen Religionsphilosophen des Mittelalters*, Breslau, 1898.
Hurvitz, E. "Dĕrašot HaZaL lĕ-Rabbenu 'Abraham ben ha-RaMBaM," *Joshua Finkel Festschrift*, ed. S. Hoenig, New York, 1974, Hebrew section, pp. 139–69.
———. "Šĕridim Nosafim mis-Sefer Mishneh Torah," *had-Darom*, XXXVIII (1974), 4–44.
Husik, I. *A History of Medieval Jewish Philosophy*, New York, 1958.
———. *Philosophical Essays*, Oxford, 1952.
Hyman, A. "Maimonides' Thirteen Principles," *Jewish Medieval and Renaissance Studies*, ed. A. Altmann, Cambridge, Mass., 1967, pp. 119–45.
———. "Spinoza's Dogmas of Universal Faith in Light of Their Medieval Jewish Background," *Biblical and Other Studies*, ed. A. Altmann, Cambridge, Mass., 1963, pp. 183–95.
Ibn Shemuel, Judah. "Taʿănato ha-ʿIḵḵarit šel ha-RaMBaM neḡed 'Aristo," *Sinai, Sefer Yobel*, ed. J. L. Maimon, Jerusalem, 1958, pp. 126–41.
Idel, M. "Rabbi Abraham Abulafia" (unpublished dissertation, Jerusalem, 1976).
Jaeger, W. *Aristotle, Fundamentals of the History of His Development*, London, 1948.
———. "Aristotle's Use of Medicine as a Model of Method in his Ethics," *Journal of Hellenic Studies*, LXXVII (1957), 54–61.
———. *Paideia*, New York, 1944.
Jay, E. G. *The Existence of God, Commentary on St. Thomas Aquinas' Five Ways of Demonstrating the Existence of God*, London, 1946.

Jellinek, A. *Ḳunṭres hak-Kĕlalim,* Jerusalem, 1971.
———. *Maftĕḥoṯ lĕ-Sifruṯ Yiśra'el,* reprinted, Jerusalem, 1972.
*Jewish Law Annual,* ed. B. Jackson, I (1978).
Joel, M. *Lewi ben Gerson als Religionsphilosoph,* Breslau, 1862.
Jones, J. R. "From Abraham to Andrenio (Observations on the Evolution of the Abraham Legend, Its Diffusion in Spain, and Its Relation to the Theme of the Self-Taught Philosopher)," *Comparative Literature Studies,* VI (1969), 69–101.
Jones, J. W. *The Law and Legal Theory of the Greeks,* Oxford, 1956.
Ḳafîḥ, J. *Ham-Miḳra' ba-RaMBaM,* Jerusalem, 1972.
Kahana, I. "Hap-Polĕmos mis-Sabib li-Ḳĕbi'aṯ ha-Hălaḵah kĕha-RaMBaM," *Sinai,* XXVI (1955), 391–411, 530–37; reprinted in his *Meḥḳarim bĕ-Sifruṯ haṯ-Tĕšuḇoṯ,* Jerusalem, 1973.
———. "Hay-Yaḥas ben ha-Hălaḵah wĕham-Minhāḡ," *Mazkereṯ,* ed. S. Zevin, Jerusalem, 1962, pp. 554–64.
Kahana, K. "'Al Ḥazaroṭaw šel ha-RaMBaM," *Ham-Ma'ăyan,* XVII (1977), 5–27.
———. *Ḥeḳer wĕ-'Iyyun,* Tel Aviv, 1960.
———. "Lĕ-Maḥăšeḇeṯ haḳ-Ḳorbanoṯ," *Sinai,* LIII (1963), 314–23.
Kaplan, A. A. *Bĕ-'Iḵḇoṯ hay-Yir'ah,* Jerusalem, 1960.
Kaplan, Z. "'Iyyunim bĕ-'Ahăḇah," *Sefer Adam Noah Braun,* Jerusalem, 1969, pp. 159–64.
Karl, Z. "Ha-RaMBaM kĕ-Faršan hat-Torah," *Tarbiz,* VI (1935), 99–138.
Kasher, M. *Haggaḏah Šĕlemah,* Jerusalem, 1961.
———. *Ha-RaMBaM wĕham-Mĕḵilta dĕ-RaSHBI,* New York, 1943.
———. *Śare ha-'Elef,* New York, 1952.
Katz, J. "'Af 'al Pi še-Ḥaṭa' Yiśra'el Hu'," *Tarbiz,* XXVII (1958), 203–17.
———. *Exclusiveness and Tolerance,* Oxford, 1961.
———. "Ma'ariḇ bi-Zĕmano," *Zion,* XXXV (1970), 35–60.
———. "Maḥăloḳeṯ has-Sĕmiḳah," *Zion,* XVI (1951), 28–45.
———. *Massoreṯ u-Mašber,* Jerusalem, 1958.
———. "Šĕlošah Mišpaṭim 'Apologetiyim," *Zion,* XXIII (1958), 174–93.
———. "Sublanuṯ Daṯiṯ bĕ-Šiṭaṯo šel R. Mĕnaḥem ham-Me'iri," *Zion,* XVIII (1953), 15–30.
Kaufmann, D. "The Etz Chayim of Jacob b. Jehudah of London," *JQR,* V (1893), 353–75.
———. *Geschichte der Attributenlehre in der jüdischen Religionsphilosophie von Saadja bis Maimuni,* Gotha, 1877.

———. "Jewish Informers in the Middle Ages," *JQR*, VIII (1898), 217–38.
———. *Meḥḳarim bas-Sifrut ha-'Ibrit*, tr. I. Eldad, Jerusalem, 1965.
———. *Die Sinne*, Budapest, 1884.
Kellner, M. "Maimonides and Gersonides on Mosaic Prophecy," *Speculum*, LII (1977), 62–79.
———. "Rabbi Isaac bar Sheshet's Responsum Concerning the Study of Greek Philosophy," *Tradition*, XIV (1975), 110–18.
Kirschenbaum, A. "Hab-Bĕriṯ 'im Bĕne Noaḥ," *Dine Yiśra'el*, VI (1975), 31–49.
———. *Self-Incrimination in Jewish Law*, New York, 1970.
Klar, B. *Meḥḳarim wĕ-'Iyyunim*, Tel Aviv, 1954.
Klein, A. "Replik," *Nachlath Z'wi*, II (1932), 162–67.
Klein, H. "Die Begründung der Gebote durch RaMBaM und S. R. Hirsch," *Nachlath Z'wi*, II (1932), 155–62.
Klein-Braslavsky, S. "Mĕṣi'uṯ haz-Zĕman,"*Tarbiz*, XLV(1976), 106–27.
———. *Peruš ha-RaMBaM lĕ-Sippur Bĕri'aṯ ha-'Olam*, Jerusalem, 1978.
Knoller, L. *Das Problem der Willensfreiheit in der aelteren juedischen Religionsphilosophie*, Leipzig, 1884.
Knowles, D. *The Evolution of Medieval Thought*, New York, 1962.
Kokowzoff, P. "The Date of Life of Baḥya," *Livre d'Hommage à la Mémoire du Dr. Samuel Poznanski*, Warsaw, 1927, pp. 13–21.
Kook, S. H. *'Iyyunim u-Meḥḳarim*, 2 vols., Jerusalem, 1963.
Kopf, L. "Religious Influences on Medieval Arabic Philology," *Studia Islamica*, V (1956), 33–59.
Koplowitz, E. S. *Die Abhängigkeit Thomas von Aquins von R. Mose ben Maimon*, Mir, 1935.
Kraemer, J. "A Lost Passage from Philoponus' Contra Aristotelem," *JAOS*, LXXXV (1965), 318–27.
Kramer, J. *Das Problem des Wunders im Zusammenhang mit dem der Providenz . . . von Saadia bis Maimuni*, Strasbourg, 1903.
Kupfer, E. "Hašlamah lĕ-feruš RaMBaM lĕ-Roš haš-Šanah," *Sinai*, LV (1964), 230–35.
———. "Tĕšuḇoṯ bilti Yĕdu'oṯ šel ha-RaMBaM," *Tarbiz*, XXXIX (1970), 170–83.
Kuttner, S. "Methodological Problems Concerning the History of Canon Law," *Speculum*, XXX (1955), 539–49.
———. "Sur les origines du terme 'droit positif,'" *Revue Historique de Droit Français et Étranger*, XV (1936), 728–40.
———, and Rathbone, E. "Anglo-Norman Canonists of the Twelfth Century," *Traditio*, VII (1949–51), 279–358.

Lahover, R. "Ha-RaMBaM wĕha-Haśkalah," *Moznayim*, III (1935), 539–46.
Lamm, N. "The Fifth Amendment and its Equivalent in the Halakah," *Judaism*, V (1956), 53–59.
———. *Torah li-Šĕmah*, Jerusalem, 1972.
Lasker, D. *Jewish Philosophical Polemics Against Christianity in the Middle Ages*, New York, 1977.
Lazarus-Yafeh, H. "The Place of the Religious Commandments in the Philosophy of al-Ghazālī," *Muslim World*, LI (1961), 173–84.
Leeuw, G. van der. *Religion in Essence and Manifestation*, tr. J. E. Turner, New York, 1963.
Le Goff, J. *Les intellectuels au Moyen Age*, Paris, 1957.
Lehman, J. "Maimonides, Mendelssohn, and the Me'asfim," *Leo Baeck Year Book*, XX (1975), 87–108.
Lemay, R. *Abu Ma'shar and Latin Aristotelianism in the Twelfth Century*, Beirut, 1962.
Lerner, R. "Maimonides' Letter on Astrology," *History of Religions*, VIII (1968), 143–58.
———, and Mahdi, M. *Medieval Political Philosophy, a Sourcebook*, Glencoe, 1963.
Lesne, E. *Les écoles de la fin du VIII$^e$ siècle à la fin du XII$^e$*, Lille, 1940.
Le Tourneau, R. *The Almohad Movement in North Africa in the Twelfth and Thirteenth Centuries*, Princeton, 1969.
Levey, I. "Maimonides as Codifier," *CCAR Yearbook*, XLV (1935), 368–96.
Levi, J. "'Issur Hăna'ah mit-Talmud Torah," *Ham-Ma'ăyan*, XVII (1977), 13–23.
Levine, H. I. "The Experience of Repentance: The Views of Maimonides and William James," *Tradition*, I (1958), 40–63.
Levinger, A. "Ha-RaMBaM bĕ-Tor Rofe' u-Fosek̲," *Ha-Rĕfu'ah*, VIII (1935), 150–62.
Levinger, J. "'Al Ṭa'am han-Nĕzirut bĕ-Moreh Nĕbukim," *Bar Ilan Annual*, IV–V (1967), 299–305.
———. "'Al Torah šebĕ-'al Peh bĕ-Haguto šel ha-RaMBaM," *Tarbiz*, XXXVII (1968), 282–93.
———. *Darke ham-Maḥăšabah ha-Hilk̲atit šel ha-RaMBaM*, Tel Aviv, 1965.
———. "Nĕbu'at Mošeh Rabbenu bĕ-Mišnat ha-RaMBaM," *Proceedings of Fourth World Congress of Jewish Studies*, II (1969), 335–39.
Levy, S. "English Students of Maimonides," *Miscellanies of the Jewish Historical Society of England*, IV (1942), 61–84.

Lewis, B. "Maimonides, Lionheart, and Saladin," *Eretz-Israel*, VII (1964), 70–75.
Lewis, H. "The Golden Mean in Judaism," *Jewish Studies in Memory of Israel Abrahams*, New York, 1927, pp. 283–95.
Lichtenstein, A. "Does Jewish Tradition Recognize an Ethic Independent of Halakha," *Modern Jewish Ethics*, ed. M. Fox, Columbus, 1975, pp. 62–89.
Lieberman, S. *Hellenism in Jewish Palestine*, New York, 1962.
———. "How Much Greek in Jewish Palestine?" *Biblical and Other Studies*, ed. A. Altmann, Cambridge, Mass., 1963, pp. 123–41.
———. *Midrěše Tēman*, Jerusalem, 1940.
———. *Šěḳi'in*, Jerusalem, 1970.
———. *Tosefet Rišonim*, Jerusalem, 1937.
———. *Tosefta ki-Fěšuṭah*, 13 vols., New York, 1955–73.
Liebeschutz, H. "The Significance of Judaism in Peter Abelard's Dialogues," *JJS*, XII (1961), 1–18.
Lipschütz, E. M. *Kětabim*, 3 vols., Jerusalem, 1947.
Loewe, R. "Potentialities and Limitations of Universalism in the Halakah," *Studies in Rationalism, Judaism, and Universalism*, ed. R. Loewe, London, 1966, pp. 115–51.
Loewinger, D. S. "Rabbi Šem-Toḇ ben 'Aḇraham ben Ga'on," *Sěfunot*, VII (1963), 7–39.
Loucel, H. "L'origine du langage d'après les grammairiens arabes," *Arabica*, X (1963), 188–208, 253–81; XI (1964), 47–72, 151–87.
Lovejoy, A. *The Great Chain of Being*, Cambridge, Mass., 1936; reprinted, New York, 1960.
Luzki, M. *Pěrāḳim mis-Sefer Mishneh Torah*, New York, 1947 (appendix to the Schulsinger edition).
———. "Wě-Kataḇ Mošeh," *Hat-Těḳufah*, XXX–XXXI (1946), 679–704.
Luzzatto, S. D. "Ḥăḳiroṯ Šonoṯ," *Kerem Ḥemed*, III (1838), 61–76.
———. *Yěsode hat-Torah*, Lemberg, 1880; reprinted, Jerusalem, 1947.
Macht, D. "Moses Maimonides, physician and scientist," *Jewish Academy of Arts and Sciences Jubilee Volume*, ed. M. Soltes, New York, 1954, pp. 107–19.
Mahdi, M. *Ibn Khaldūn's Philosophy of History*, Chicago, 1964.
———. "Language and Logic in Classical Islam," *Logic in Classical Islamic Culture*, ed. G. E. von Grunebaum, Wiesbaden, 1970, pp. 51–83.
Mahler, R. *Haḳ-Ḳara'im*, Merhavya, 1949.
Maimon, A. *Ḥidduš has-Sanhedrin*, Jerusalem, 1957.

Maimon, J., ed. *Ḳobeṣ ha-RaMBaM*, Jerusalem, 1935.
———. *RaMBaM*, Jerusalem, 1960.
Malter, H. *Saadya Gaon*, Philadelphia, 1942.
Mandelbaum, J. "Ḳuntres Hašlamah lĕ-Sefer Śare ha-'Elef," *Sefer Adam Noah Braun*, Jerusalem, 1969, pp. 213–96.
Mann, J. *The Bible as Read and Preached in the Old Synagogue*, Cincinnati, 1943.
———. "'Inyanim Šonim lĕ-Ḥeḳer Tĕḳufaṯ hag-Gĕ'onim," *Tarbiz*, VI (1935), 66–88, 238–42, 543.
———. *The Jews in Egypt*, 2 vols., reprinted, New York, 1970.
———. "Roš hag-Golah bĕ-Baḇel bĕ-Sof Tĕḳufaṯ hag-Ge'onim," *Sefer Zikkaron lĕ-S. Poznanski*, Warsaw, 1927, pp. 18–32.
———. *Texts and Studies in Jewish History and Literature*, 2 vols., reprinted, New York, 1972.
Marcus, I. G. "The Recensions and Structure of Sefer Ḥăsiḏim," *PAAJR*, XLV (1978), 131–54.
Margalit, D. "Minyan ham-Miṣwoṯ," *Sinai*, XL (1956), 96–102.
Margaliyot, M. *Ha-Ḥillukim šeb-ben 'Anše Mizraḥ u-Ḇĕne 'Ereṣ Yiśra'el*, Jerusalem, 1938.
———, ed. *Sefer ha-Razim*, Jerusalem, 1967.
———, ed. *Sefer Hilḵoṯ han-Nağiḏ*, Jerusalem, 1962.
Margaliyot, R. *Ha-RaMBaM wĕhaz-Zohar*, Jerusalem, 1954.
———. *Yĕsoḏ ham-Mišnah wa-'Ăriḵaṯah*, Jerusalem, 1955.
Marmorstein, A. "The Place of Maimonides' *Mishneh Torah* in the History and Development of the Halachah," *Moses Maimonides*, ed. I. Epstein, London, 1935, pp. 159–79.
———. "Sefer Dine Tĕfillah u-Mo'ăḏim šel R. Maymon 'Aḇi ha-RaMBaM," *Tarbiz*, VI (1934–35), 182–84.
Marx, A. "The Correspondence between the Rabbis of Southern France and Maimonides about Astrology," *HUCA*, III (1926), 311–58.
———. *Essays in Jewish Biography*, Philadelphia, 1947.
———. "Texts by and about Maimonides," *JQR*, XXV (1935), 371–428.
Medan, M. "Millonam ham-Miḳra'i šel Ḥaḵme Yiśra'el bi-Sĕfaraḏ," *Lĕšonenu*, XVII (1950), 110–14
Merhavyah, H. *Hat-Talmuḏ bi-Rĕ'i han-Naṣruṯ*, Jerusalem, 1970.
Meron, Y. "Nĕḳuḏoṯ Magga' ben ham-Mišpaṭ ha-'Iḇri lĕ-ben ham-Mišpaṭ ham-Muslĕmi," *Šĕnaṯon ham-Mišpaṭ ha-'Iḇri*, II (1975), 343–60.
Meyerhoff, M. "The Medical Works of Maimonides," *Essays on Maimonides*, ed. S. Baron, New York, 1941, pp. 265–301.

---. "L'Oeuvre médicale de Maimonide," *Archeion*, XI (1929), 136-55.
Mittwoch, E. "Ein Genīza-Fragment," *Zeitschrift der Deutschen Morgenländischen Gesellschaft*, LVII (1903), 61-67.
Moore, G. F. *Judaism*, 3 vols., Cambridge, Mass., 1958.
Morag, S. "Rešit ham-Millona'uṯ ha-'Iḇriṯ wĕha-'Ărabiṭ", *Molaḏ*, XXVI (1970), 575-80.
Münz, J. *Maimonides: the Story of His Life and Genius*, tr. H. Schnittkind, Boston, 1935.
Munk, A. "Tĕšubah Hăḏašah la-RaMBaM," *Pĕraḵim*, II (1969-74), 329-34.
Munk, S. *Mélanges*, Paris, 1859.
Muntner, Z. *Sefer 'Assaf ha-Rofĕ'*, Jerusalem, 1958.
Murdoch, J. E., and Sylla, E. D. *The Cultural Context of Medieval Learning*, Dordrecht, 1975.
Nemoy, L. "Al-Qirqisānī's Account of the Jewish Sects," *HUCA*, VII (1930), 317-98.
---. *Karaite Anthology*, New Haven, 1952.
Netanyahu, B. *Don Isaac Abravanel*, Philadelphia, 1953.
---. *The Marranos of Spain*, New York, 1966.
Neubauer, A. "Miscellanea Liturgica, II: Azharoth on the 613 Precepts," *JQR*, VI (1894), 698-709.
Neubauer, J. *Ha-RaMBaM 'al Diḇre Sofĕrim*, Jerusalem, 1957.
Neuburger, C. *Das Wesen des Gesetzes in der Philosophie des Maimonides*, Danzig, 1933.
Neugebauer, O. "The Astronomy of Maimonides and Its Sources," *HUCA*, XXII (1949), 322-64.
Neuhausen, S. *Torah 'Or la-RaMBaM*, Baltimore, 1941.
Neuman, A. *The Jews in Spain*, 2 vols., Philadelphia, 1948.
Neumark, D. *Essays in Jewish Philosophy*, Cincinnati, 1929.
Neustadt, D. "'Inyĕne Nĕḡiḏuṯ bĕ-Miṣrayim," *Zion*, IV (1939), 126-49.
---. Nĕḡiḏuṯo šel ha-RaMBaM," *Zion*, XI (1946), 147-48.
Newman, L. I. *Jewish Influences on Christian Reform Movements*, New York, 1955.
Nuriel A. "Ḥidduš ha-'Olam 'o Ḳaḏmuṯo 'al Pi ha-RaMBaM," *Tarbiz*, XXXIII (1964), 372-87.
---. "Ha-Raṣon ha-'Eloḳi bĕ-Moreh Nĕḇuḵim," *Tarbiz*, XXXIX (1970), 39-61.
Ochs, D. "Haḡdaraṯ ham-Muśaḡ Ḥinnuḵ," *Sefer Zikkaron lĕ-R. Y. Weinberg*, ed. K. Kahana, Jerusalem, 1970, pp. 237-40.

Packard, S. *Twelfth-Century Europe, an Interpretive Essay,* Amherst, 1973.
Pagis, D. *Ḥidduš u-Massoret bě-Širat ha-Ḥol,* Jerusalem, 1976.
———. *Širat ha-Ḥol wě-Torat haš-Šir,* Jerusalem, 1970.
Panofsky, Erwin. *Gothic Architecture and Scholasticism,* New York, 1957.
Pearl, C. *The Medieval Jewish Mind,* London, 1971.
Peters, F. E. *Aristotle and the Arabs,* New York, 1968.
Petry, R. "Medieval Eschatology and Social Responsibility in Bernard of Morval's *De Contemptu Mundi,*" *Speculum,* XXIV (1949), 207–17.
Petuchowski, J. *The Theology of Haham David Nieto,* New York, 1970.
Pines, S. "Aristotle's 'Politics' in Arabic Philosophy," *Israel Oriental Studies,* V (1975), 150–60.
———. *Ben Maḥšebet Yiśra'el lě-Maḥšebet ha-'Amin,* Jerusalem, 1977.
———. "Ibn Khaldūn and Maimonides," *Studia Islamica,* XXXII (1970), 265–74.
———. "Nathanel ben al-Fayyumi et la théologie Ismaélienne," *Bulletin des Études Historiques Juives,* I (1946), 5–22.
———. *Nouvelles études sur . . . Abu-l-Barakāt al-Baghdādi,* Paris, 1955.
———. "Has-Skolastikah . . . u-Mišnatam šel Ḥasday Crescas wě-šel Ḳodĕmaw," *Proceedings of the Israel Academy of Sciences,* I (1966), v–xi, 1–73.
———. "Some Traits of Christian Theological Writing in Relation to Moslem Kalām and to Jewish Thought," *Proceedings of the Israel Academy of Sciences,* V (1973), 143–52.
———. "Spinoza's *Tractatus,* Maimonides, and Kant," *Scripta Hierosolymitana,* XX (1968), 3–54.
———. "Studies in Abul-Barakāt al-Baghdādi's Poetics and Metaphysics," *Scripta Hierosolymitana,* VI (1960), 120–99.
Pinsker, S. *Likkuṭe Ḳadmoniyyot,* Vienna, 1860.
Post, G. "Masters' Salaries and Student Fees in Mediaeval Universities," *Speculum,* VII (1932), 181–98.
Potolsky, M. "'En Lěmēdim mik-Ḳodem Mattan Torah," *Dine Yiśra'el,* VI (1975), 195–231.
Poznanski, S. *Babylonische Geonim im nachgaonäischen Zeitalter,* Berlin, 1914.
———. *Eine hebräische Grammatik,* Berlin, 1894.
———. *The Karaite Literary Opponents of Saadia Gaon,* London, 1908.
———. *Maḇo' 'al Ḥakme Ṣarfat,* Warsaw, 1913.
Rabinovitch, N. "Ham-Mussag 'Efšar bě-Mišnato šel ha-RaMBaM," *Tarbiz,* XLIV (1975), 159–71.
———. *Probability and Statistical Inference in Ancient and Medieval Jewish Literature,* Toronto, 1973.

Rabinovitz, H. "Paršanut ham-Miḵra' bĕ-Mishneh Torah lĕha-RaMBaM," *Šanah bĕ-Šanah* (1967), 223–33.
Rabinowitz, A. H. *Taryag*, Jerusalem, 1967.
Rabinowitz, J. *Jewish Law, its Influence on the Development of Legal Institutions*, New York, 1956.
Rackover N. *Haḵ-Ḵĕhillah* (Bibliography), Jerusalem, 1978.
———. *'Oṣar ham-Mišpaṭ (Mafteaḥ Bibliyografi)*, Jerusalem, 1975.
———. *Haŕ-Šĕlihuṭ wĕha-Harša'ah bam-Mišpaṭ ha-'Iḇri*, Jerusalem, 1972.
Rahman, F. *Islam*, New York, 1965.
———. *Prophecy in Islam*, London, 1958.
Rappaport, S. "Miḵtaḇ," *'Oṣar Neḥmaḏ*, I (1856), 22–32.
———. *Tolĕdot Gĕḏole Yiśra'el*, 2 vols., reprinted, Jerusalem, 1969.
Ratzhaby, J. "Haḡahoṭ li-Tĕšuḇoṭ bilti Yĕḏu'oṭ šel ha-RaMBaM," *Tarbiz*, XXXIX (1970), 318–20.
———. "Sifruṭ Yĕhuḏe Teman," *ḴS*, XXVIII (1953), 255–78, 394–406; XXXIII (1957), 111–17.
Ravitsky, E. "Ḥidduš 'o Ḳadmuṭ ha-'Olam bĕ-Toraṭ ha-RaMBaM," *Tarbiz*, XXXV (1966), 333–48.
———. "Kĕṭaḇ Niškaḥ lĕ-R. Ḥasdai Crescas," *ḴS*, LI (1976), 705–11.
Rawidowicz, S. *'Iyyunim bĕ-Maḥšeḇeṭ Yiśra'el*, 2 vols., Jerusalem, 1969.
———. *Studies in Jewish Thought*, Philadelphia, 1974.
Ray, R. "Medieval Historiography through the Twelfth Century, Problems and Progress of Research," *Viator*, V (1974), 33–59.
Refael, I. *Rišonim wĕ-'Aḥăronim*, Tel Aviv, 1957.
Reifman, Jacob. *'Arba'ah Ḥorašim*, Prague, 1860.
———. *Tolĕdoṭ Rabbenu Zĕraḥyah hal-Lewi*, Prague, 1853.
Reines, A. J. *Maimonides and Abrabanel on Prophecy*, Cincinnati, 1970.
———. "Maimonides' Concept of Mosaic Prophecy," *HUCA*, XL–XLI (1969–70), 325–61.
———. "Maimonides' Concepts of Providence and Theodicy," *HUCA*, XLIII (1977), 169–206.
Reines, H. Z. "Ha-Muḇan šel wĕ-'Ahaḇta lĕ-Re'ăḵa Kamoḵa," *Sefer Yoḇel lĕ-Šim'on Federbush*, ed. J. Maimon, Jerusalem, 1961, pp. 304–15.
Revel, B. "Lĕ-Berur Da'aṭ ha-RaMBaM," *Ḥoreḇ*, II (1935), 112–16.
———. "'Oneš Šĕḇu'aṭ Šeḵer lĕ-Da'aṭ Philo wĕha-RaMBaM," *Ḥoreḇ*, II (1935), 1–5.
Roensch, F. J. *Early Thomistic School*, Dubuque, 1964.
Rosenberg, S. "Logic and Ontology in Fourteenth Century Jewish Philosophy," (unpublished dissertation, Jerusalem, 1974).
———. "Tĕfillah wĕ-Haḡuṭ Yĕhuḏiṭ," *Hat-Tĕfillah ha-Yĕhuḏiṭ*, Ramat Gan, 1978, pp. 85–130.

Rosenbloom, N. "Hirsch's *Torot* and Maimonides' *Sefer Hamada*," *Samuel K. Mirsky Memorial Volume*, ed. G. Appel, Jerusalem, 1970, pp. 53–74.

———. *Tradition in an Age of Reform, the Religious Philosophy of Samson Raphael Hirsch*, Philadelphia, 1976.

Rosenthal, E. I. J. *Studia Semitica*, 2 vols., London, 1971.

———. "Torah and Nomos in Medieval Jewish Philosophy," *Studies in Rationalism, Judaism, and Universalism*, ed. R. Loewe, London, 1966, pp. 215–31.

Rosenthal, E. S. "'Al Derek ha-Rob," *Pĕrakim*, I (1968), 183–224.

———. "Li-Šĕmu'at hap-Pĕtihah šel Babli Ta 'anit," *Sefer Zikkaron lĕ-Ya'ăkob Friedman*, ed. S. Pines, Jerusalem, 1974, pp. 237–48.

Rosenthal, F. *The Classical Heritage in Islam*, London, 1975.

———. "The Defense of Medicine in the Medieval Muslim World," *Bulletin of the History of Medicine*, XLIII (1969), 519–32.

———. *Knowledge Triumphant, the Concept of Knowledge in Medieval Islam*, Leiden, 1970.

———. *The Muslim Concept of Freedom*, Leiden, 1960.

———. Review of Galen, *On Medical Experience* (tr. R. Walzer, 1944), *Isis*, XXXVI (1945–46), 251–55.

———. *The Technique and Approach of Muslim Scholarship*, Rome, 1947.

Rosenthal, J. "Kara'im wĕ-Kara'ut bĕ-'Eyropah ham-Ma'ărabit," *C. Albeck Jubilee Volume*, Jerusalem, 1963, pp. 425–42.

———. *Mehkarim u-Mĕkorot*, 2 vols., Jerusalem, 1966.

Rosenzweig, Franz. *Naharayim*, Jerusalem, 1960.

Rosin, D. *Ein Compendium der jüdischen Gesetzeskunde aus dem vierzehnten Jahrhundert*, Breslau, 1871.

———. *Die Ethik des Maimonides*, Breslau, 1876.

———. *Rabbi Samuel ben Meir als Schrifterklärer*, Breslau, 1880.

Rosner, F. "Maimonides the Physician, a Bibliography," *Bulletin of the History of Medicine*, XLIII (1969), 221–35.

———. *Sex Ethics in the Writings of Moses Maimonides*, New York, 1974.

Rotenstreich, N. *Jewish Philosophy in Modern Times*, New York, 1968.

———. *Ham-Mahšabah hay-Yĕhudit ba-'Et ha-Hădašah*, Tel Aviv, 1945.

Roth, A. N. "Keta'im mim-Mishneh Torah," *Ginze Kaufmann*, Budapest, 1948; reprinted, Jerusalem, 1971, pp. 62–70.

Roth, E., and Abramson, S. "Mis-Sifre R. Nissim Ga'on," *Tarbiz*, XXVI (1956), 49–71.

Roth, L. *Judaism, a Portrait*, New York, 1962.

———. *Spinoza, Descartes, and Maimonides*, New York, 1963.

Samuels, N. "On Knowing God: Maimonides, Gersonides, and the Philosophy of Religion," *Judaism*, XVIII (1969), 64–77.
Sandmel, S. *Philo's Place in Judaism, a Study in Conceptions of Abraham in Jewish Literature,* Cincinnati, 1956.
Sarachek, J. *The Doctrine of the Messiah in Medieval Jewish Literature,* New York, 1932.
———. *Faith and Reason: Conflict over the Rationalism of Maimonides,* Williamsport, 1935.
Sarfatti, G. *Munaḥe ham-Matematiḳah bas-Sifruṯ ham-Madda'iṯ ha-'Iḇriṯ šel Yĕme hab-Benayim,* Jerusalem, 1969.
Sarton, G. *Introduction to the History of Science,* 2 vols., Washington, D.C., 1931.
Schacht, J. *An Introduction to Islamic Law,* Oxford, 1964.
———. *The Origins of Muslim Jurisprudence,* Oxford, 1951.
———. and Meyerhof, M. "Maimonides against Galen, on Philosophy and Cosmogony," *Bulletin of the Faculty of Arts of the University of Egypt,* V (1937).
Schechter, S. *Saadyana,* Cambridge, Mass., 1903.
———. *Studies in Judaism,* Philadelphia, 1960.
Scheiber, A. "Bibliographisches aus der Genisa," *Studies . . . in Honor of J. Edward Kiev,* ed. C. Berlin, New York, 1971, pp. 415–25.
———. "'Iggereṯ bilti-Yĕdu'ah lĕha-RaMBaM," *Sĕfunoṯ,* VIII (1964), 137–42.
———. "Pĕraḳim mis-Sefer ham-Miṣwoṯ lĕ-RaSaG," *Sefer Yoḇel lĕ-Šim'on Federbush,* ed. J. Maimon, Jerusalem, 1961, pp. 330–36.
———. "The Rabbanite Prayer Book Quoted by Qirqisānī," *HUCA,* XXII (1949), 307–20.
Scheindlin, R. "Rabbi Moshe ibn Ezra on the Legitimacy of Poetry," *Medievalia et Humanistica,* VII (1976), 101–17.
Schepansky, I. *Rabbenu 'Efrayim, Talmiḏ Ḥaḇer šel ha-RIF,* Jerusalem, 1976.
Schereschevsky, B. Z. *Dine Mišpaḥah,* Jerusalem, 1958.
Schirman, H. "Ḳinoṯ 'al hag-Gĕzeroṯ," *Ḳoḇeṣ 'al Yaḏ,* III, [Part I] (1939), 23–74.
———. "Ha-RaMBaM wĕhaš-Širah ha-'Iḇriṯ," *Moznayim,* III (1935), 433–36.
———. *Haš-Širah ha-'Iḇriṯ bi-Sĕfaraḏ u-Provence,* 2 vols., Jerusalem, 1954–56.
Schlanger, J. *La philosophie de Salomon ibn Gabirol,* Leiden, 1968.
Schmiedl, A. *Studien über jüdische . . . Religionsphilosophie,* Vienna, 1869.

Schneersohn, J. *The Tzemach Tzedek and the Haskalah Movement*, tr. Z. I. Posner, New York, 1962.

Scholem, G. *Jewish Gnosticism, Merkabah Mysticism, and Talmudic Tradition*, New York, 1960.

———. "Joseph ibn Waqar," *KS*, XX (1943), 153–62.

———. *Major Trends in Jewish Mysticism*, New York, 1941.

———. *The Messianic Idea in Judaism*, New York, 1971.

———. "Mi-ḥoḳer li-Mĕḳubbal," *Tarbiz*, VI (1935), 90–98.

———. *On Jews and Judaism*, New York, 1976.

———. *On the Kabbalah and Its Symbolism*, New York, 1969.

———. "Yĕdi'ot Ḥădašot 'al R. Yosef 'Aškĕnazi," *Tarbiz*, XXVIII (1958), 59–90, 201–35.

Schreiner, M. *Der Kalam in der jüdischen Literatur*, Berlin, 1895.

Schulz, M. *Die Lehre von der historischen Methode bei den Geschichtschreibern des Mittelalters*, Berlin, 1909.

Schwarz, A. *Der Mischneh Thorah*, Vienna, 1905.

———. "Das Verhältnis Maimuni's zu den Gaonen," *Moses ben Maimon*, ed. W. Bacher, Hebrew tr. M. Havatzelet, *Sura*, IV (1964), 156–91.

Schwarzfuchs, S. "Les Lois Royales de Maimonide," *REJ*, CXI (1951–52), 63–86.

Schwarzschild, S. "Do Noachites Have to Believe in Revelation?" *JQR*, LII (1962), 297–308; LIII (1962), 30–65.

Schweid, E. *'Iyyunim bi-Šĕmonah Pĕraḳim*, Jerusalem, 1969.

———. *Ṭa'am wĕ-Haḳḳašah*, Tel Aviv, 1970.

Seigel, J. E. *Rhetoric and Philosophy in Renaissance Humanism*, Princeton, 1968.

*Šĕnaton ham-Mišpaṭ ha-'Iḇri*, ed. M. Elon, vols. III–IV (1976–77).

Septimus, B. "Meir Abulafia and the Maimonidean Controversy" (unpublished dissertation, Harvard University, 1975).

Shamir, Y. "Allusions to Muhammed in Maimonides' Theory of Prophecy in his *Guide*," *JQR*, LXIV (1974), 212–24.

———. *Rabbi Moses hak-Kohen and his Book 'Ezer ha-'Ĕmunah*, Leiden, 1975.

Shapiro, D. S. "A Note on the Guide for the Perplexed," *Sefer hay-Yoḇel Me'ir Waksman*, ed. J. Rosenthal, Chicago, 1966, pp. 113–21.

Sharf, A. *The Universe of Shabbetai Donnolo*. New York, 1976.

Shatzmiller, J. "'Iggarto šel R. 'Ašer ben R. Geršon," *Meḥḳarim le-Zeḵer Ṣĕḇi 'Aḇner*, Haifa, 1970, 129–40.

———. "Li-Tĕmunat ham-Maḥloḳet ha-Rišonah 'al Kitḇe ha-RaMBaM," *Zion*, XXXIV (1969), 126–44.

Shefer, S. *Ha-RIF u-Mišnaṯo*, Jerusalem, 1967.
Sherwin, B. "In the Shadow of Greatness, Rabbi Hayyim ben Betsalel of Friedberg," *JSS*, XXXVII (1975), 35–60.
Shifman, P. "Has-Safek ba-Hălakah ubam-Mišpaṭ," *Šĕnaṯon ham-Mišpaṭ ha-'Iḇri*, I (1974), 328–52.
Shiloh, S. *Dina' dĕ-Malkuṯa'*, Jerusalem, 1975.
———. "Yaḥăso šel R. Yosef 'ibn Meḡas lag-Gĕ'onim," *Sinai*, LXVI (1970), 263–68.
Shochetman, E. "Ḥozeh šen-Na'ăśeh bĕ-Šabbaṯ," *Šĕnaṯon ham-Mišpaṭ ha-'Iḇri*, I (1974), 300–13.
Shoḥet, A. "Bĕrurim bĕ-Farašaṯ hap-Pulĕmos ha-Rišon," *Zion*, XXXVI (1971), 26–60.
———. *'Im Ḥillufe Tĕkufoṯ*, Jerusalem, 1961.
Shunami, S. *Mafteaḥ ham-Maftĕḥoṯ*, Jerusalem, 1969.
Shy, H. "R. Tanḥum hay-Yĕrušalmi," 3 vols. (unpublished dissertation, Jerusalem, 1975).
Silver, A. H. *A History of Messianic Speculation in Israel*, Boston, 1959.
Silver, D. J. *Maimonidean Criticism and the Maimonidean Controversy*, Leiden, 1965.
Silverstein, Arthur J. "Censorship of Medical Works: Hezekiah and 'The Book of Remedies'," *Dine Yiśra'el*, VII (1976), 151–57.
Simon, E. "Pflicht und Neigung bei Maimonides und in der neuen deutschen Ethik," *Horizons of a Philosopher, Essays in Honor of David Baumgardt*, ed. Joseph Frank, Leiden, 1963, pp. 391–421.
Simonsohn, S. *Tolĕdoṯ hay-Yĕhuḏim bĕ-Dukkasuṯ Mantua*, Jerusalem, 1965.
Sirat, C. *Les théories des visions sur-naturelles dans la pensée juive du moyen-age*, Leiden, 1969.
Smalley, B. *English Friars and Antiquity in the Early Fourteenth Century*, Oxford, 1960.
———. *Historians in the Middle Ages*, London, 1974.
———. *The Study of the Bible in the Middle Ages*, New York, 1950.
———. "William of Auvergne, John of La Rochelle, and St. Thomas Aquinas on the Old Law," *Aquinas Commemorative Studies*, Toronto, 1974, II, 11–73.
Solomon, N. "Definition and Classification in the Works of the Lithuanian Halakhists," *Dine Yiśra'el*, VI (1975), lxxiii–cv.
Soloveitchik, H. "Can Halakic Texts Talk History," *Association for Jewish Studies Review*, III, (1978), 152–97.
———. "Maimonides' Iggeret ha-Shemed: Law and Rhetoric," *Joseph H. Lookstein Jubilee Volume*, New York, 1979, pp. 1–39 (Offprint circulated before publication of volume).

———. "Three Themes in the Sefer Ḥăsidim," *Association for Jewish Studies Review*, I (1976), 311–57.
Soloveitchik, J. B. "'Iš ha-Halakah," *Talpiyot*, I (1944), 651–736.
———. "U-Biḳḳaštem miš-Šam," *Had-Darom*, XLIII (1978), 1–70.
Sonne I. "Ein Beitrag zu der verschollenen Kuzari Übersetzung des Jehuda ben Cardinal," *MGWJ*, LXXII (1928), 66–70.
———. "'Iggeret ha-RaMBaM li-Šĕmu'el 'ibn Tibbon," *Tarbiz*, X (1939), 135–54, 309–32.
———. "A Scrutiny of the Charges of Forgery against Maimonides' Letter on Resurrection," *PAAJR*, XXI (1952), 101–17.
———. "Ṭiyyulim bĕ-Hisṭoriyah u-Bibliyografiyah," *Alexander Marx Jubilee Volume*, New York, 1950, pp. 209–35.
Southern, R. W. "Aspects of the European Tradition of Historical Writing: Hugh of St. Victor and the Idea of Historical Development," *Transactions of the Royal Historical Society*, 5th series, XXI (1971), 159–79.
Spiegel, S. "Lĕ-Parašat hap-Pulĕmos šel Pirḳoi ben Baboi," *Harry A. Wolfson Jubilee Volume*, ed. S. Lieberman, Jerusalem, 1965, Hebrew section, pp. 243–64.
Spiegel, Y. "Gilgule ha-Hăḡahot šebbi-Dĕfuse Mishneh Torah," *Taḡim*, V–VI (1975), 25–39.
———. "Ma-šehu 'al Mishneh Torah la-RaMBaM," *ḲS*, XLVII (1972), 493–501.
———. "Sefer Maggid Mishneh," *ḲS*, XLVI (1971), 554–80.
Spitzer, L. *Essays in Historical Semantics*, New York, 1948.
Steenberghen, F. van. *Aristotle in the West, the Origins of Latin Aristotelianism*, tr. L. Johnston, Louvain, 1955.
Stein, L. *Die Willensfreiheit und ihr Verhältniss zur göttlichen Präscienz und Providenz bei den jüdischen Philosophen des Mittelalters*, Berlin, 1882.
Stein, S. "The Development of the Jewish Law of Interest from the Biblical Period to the Expulsion of the Jews from England," *Historia Judaica*, XVII (1955), 3–40.
Steinschneider M. *Die arabische Literatur der Juden*, Frankfurt, 1902.
———. *Gesammelte Schriften*, Berlin, 1925.
———. "Die hebräischen Commentare zum Führer des Maimonides," *Festschrift zum siebzigsten Geburtstage A. Berliner's*, Frankfurt, 1903, pp. 345–63.
———. *Die hebräischen Übersetzungen des Mittelalters*, Berlin, 1893.
———. *Jewish Literature from the Eighth to the Eighteenth Century*, London, 1857.
———. *Polemische und Apologetische Literatur*, Leipzig, 1877.

Stern, S. M. "Ḥălifat ham-Miḵtabim ben ha-RaMBaM wĕ-Ḥakme Provence," *Zion*, XVI (1951), 19–28.
———. "Ḳeṭa' Ḥadaš . . . lĕ-RaSaG," *Mĕlilah*, V (1955), 133–47.
———. "Peruš ham-Mishnah bi-Kĕtab Yado šel ha-RaMBaM," *Tarbiz*, XXIII (1953), 72–88.
Strashun, M. *Mibḥar Kĕtabim*, Jerusalem, 1969.
Strashun, S. *Mĕḵore ha-RaMBaM*, ed. Z. Harkavy, Jerusalem, 1957.
Strauss, L. "Notes on Maimonides' Book of Knowledge," *Studies in Mysticism and Religion Presented to G. Scholem*, ed. E. Urbach, Jerusalem, 1967, pp. 269–83.
———. *Persecution and the Art of Writing*, Glencoe, 1952.
———. *Philosophie und Gesetz*, Berlin, 1935.
———. *Spinoza's Critique of Religion*, New York, 1965.
Swartz, M. "The Position of Jews in the Arab Lands Following the Rise of Islam," *Muslim World*, LX (1970), 6–24.
———. *Tĕšubat ha-RaMBaM bi-Šĕ'elat hak-Ḳeṣ*, Tel Aviv, 1979 (Hebrew tr. of G. Weil, *Maimonides über die Lebensdauer*).
Ta-Shema, I. "Heḵan Nithaber Sefer 'Ălilot Dĕbarim," *'Ale Sefer*, III (1977), 44–53.
———. "Šippuṭ 'Ibri," *Šĕnaton ham-Mišpaṭ ha-'Ibri*, I (1974), 353–72.
———. "Yĕṣirato has-Sifruṭit šel Rabbenu Yosef 'ibn Megaš," *ḲS*, XLVI (1970–71), 136–46, 541–53; XLVII (1972), 318–22.
———, and Ben-Shammai, H. "Šĕmoneh Tĕšubot Ḥadašot lĕ-Rabbenu Yosef 'ibn Megas," *Ḳobeṣ 'al Yad*, VIII (1976), 167–85.
Talmage, F. *David Ḳimḥi*, Cambridge, Mass., 1975.
———. "David Ḳimḥi and the Rationalist Tradition," *HUCA*, XXXIX (1968), 177–218.
———. "David Ḳimḥi and the Rationalist Tradition, II: Literary Sources," *Studies in Honor of I. Kiev*, New York, 1972, pp. 435–78.
Taubes, H. Z. *Liḳḳuṭe R. Yiṣḥaḳ 'ibn Ghiyath: Bĕraḵot*, Zürich, 1952.
Tchernowitz, C. "Lu lo Ḳam kĕ-Mošeh," *Moznayim*, III (1935), 381–401.
———. "Maimonides as Codifier," *Maimonides Octocentennial Series*, New York, 1935.
———. "Mišnato šel ha-RaMBaM bĕ-Halaḵah," *Miḵlaṭ*, V (1921), 348–85.
———. *Tolĕdot hap-Posĕḳim*, 3 vols., New York, 1946.
Tchernowitz, G. *Hay-Yaḥas ben Yiśra'el la-Goyim lĕ-Fi ha-RaMBaM*, New York, 1950.
Teicher J. L. "The Arabic Original of Maimonides' Rejoinder to Samuel ben 'Ali," *JJS*, IV (1953), 141–42.

———. "Christian Theology and Jewish Opposition to Maimonides," *Journal of Theological Studies*, XLIII (1942), 68–76.

———. "The Latin-Hebrew School of Translators in Spain in the Twelfth Century," *Homenaje a Millás-Vallicrosa*, Barcelona, 1956, II, 401–44.

———. "Maimonides' Letter to Joseph b. Jehudah—a Literary Forgery," *JJS*, I (1948), 35–54.

———. "Ziyyuf Sifruti: Ma'ămar Těḥiyyat ham-Metim," *Mělilah*, I (1944), 81–92.

Temkin, O. *Galenism, Rise and Decline of a Medical Philosophy*, Ithaca, 1973.

Tishby, I., and Dan, J. *Mibḥar Sifrut ham-Musar*, Jerusalem, 1971.

Toledano, J. *'Oṣar Gěnuzim*, Jerusalem, 1960.

———. *Yěhude 'Aleksandriyah wěham-Maymuni*, Alexandria, 1936.

Touati, C. *La pensée théologique et philosophique de Gersonide*, Paris, 1973.

———. "Le problème de l'inerrance prophétique dans la théologie juive du Moyen Age," *Revue de l'Histoire des Religions*, CLXXIII (1968), 169–87.

Tuby, I. "Širah bě-Šebaḥ ha-Ḥibbur lěha-RaMBaM," *'Ăfiḳim*, XLVI (1972), 19–20.

Twersky, I. "'Al Haśśagot ha-RaBaD lě-Mishneh Torah," *Harry A. Wolfson Jubilee Volume*, ed. S. Lieberman, Jerusalem, 1965, Hebrew section, pp. 169–86.

———. "The Beginnings of Mishneh Torah Criticism," *Biblical and Other Studies*, ed. A. Altmann, Cambridge, Mass., 1963, pp. 161–83.

———. "Ḥamiššah Sěfarim lě-Rab Nissim Ga'on," *Tarbiz*, XXXVII (1968), 318–27.

———. "Joseph ibn Kaspi," *Juifs et judaïsme de Languedoc*, ed. B. Blumenkranz, Toulouse, 1977, pp. 185–204.

———. *Rabad of Posquières*, Cambridge, Mass., 1962.

———. "R. Yosef 'Aškěnazi wě-Sefer Mishneh Torah la-RaMBaM," *Salo W. Baron Jubilee Volume*, ed. S. Lieberman, Jerusalem, 1975, Hebrew section, pp. 183–94.

———. "Religion and Law," *Religion in a Religious Age*, ed. S. D. Goitein, Cambridge, Mass., 69–82.

———. "Sefer Mishneh Torah la-RaMBaM, Měğammato wě-Tafḳido," Israel Academy of Sciences, *Dibre (Proceedings)*, V (1972), 1–22.

———. "The Shulḥan 'Aruk, Enduring Code of Jewish Law," *Judaism*, XVI (1967), 141–59.

———. "Sidduro šel Sefer Mišneh Torah la-RaMBaM," *Proceedings of the Sixth World Congress of Jewish Studies*, Jerusalem, 1977, III, 179–91.

———. "Some Aspects of the Jewish Attitude toward the Welfare State," *Tradition*, V (1963), 137–58.

———. "Some Non-Halakic Aspects of the Mishneh Torah," *Jewish Medieval and Renaissance Studies*, ed. A. Altmann, Cambridge, Mass., 1967, pp. 95–119.

———. "Yĕdaʻyah hap-Pĕnini u-Ferušo la-ʼAggadah," *Alexander Altmann Jubilee Volume*, ed. R. Loewe and S. Stein, University, Alabama, 1979, pp. 73–93.

Tykocinski, H. *Takkanot hag-Gĕʼonim*, Jerusalem, 1959.

Ullmann, I. M. *Die Medizin im Islam*, Leiden, 1970.

Unna, M. *RaMBaN*, Jerusalem, 1954.

Urbach, E. *Baʻăle hat-Toʼsafot*, Jerusalem, 1955.

———. "Halakah u-Nĕbuʼah," *Tarbiz*, XVIII (1947), 1–27.

———. "Haśśagot ha-RABD," *KS*, XXXIII (1958), 360–75; XXXIV (1959), 101–08.

———. *ḤaZaL*, Jerusalem, 1969.

———. "Ḥelkam šel ḥakme ʼAškĕnaz . . . ba-Pulĕmos ʻal ha-RaMBaM," *Zion*, XII (1947), 149–59.

———. "The Laws Regarding Slavery," *Annual of the Institute of Jewish Studies*, I (1964), 1–94.

———. "Matay Paskah han-Nĕbuʼah," *Tarbiz*, XVIII (1946), 1–11.

Urbach, S. B. "Ha-ʼAdam ha-ʻElyon had-Dati lĕ-Fi R. Baḥya wĕha-RaMBaM," *Ḥinnuk ha-ʼAdam wĕ-Yĕʻudo*, Jerusalem, 1967, pp. 341–57.

Uryan, M. *Ham-Moreh lĕ-Dorot*, Jerusalem, 1956.

Vajda, G. *L'amour de Dieu dans la théologie juive du Moyen Age*, Paris, 1957.

———. *Deux commentaires karaïtes sur l'Ecclésiaste*, Leiden, 1971.

———. "Les études de philosophie juive du Moyen Age depuis la synthèse de Julius Guttmann," *HUCA*, XLIII (1972), 125–47; XLV (1974), 205–42.

———. *Introduction à la pensée juive du Moyen Age*, Paris, 1947.

———. *Isaac Albalag*, Paris, 1960.

———. "Le ʻKalam' dans la pensée religieuse juive du Moyen Age," *Revue de l'Histoire des Religions*, CLXXXIII (1973), 143–60.

———. "Lĕ-Tolĕdot hap-Pulĕmos ben hap-Pilosofiyah wĕhad-Dat," *Tarbiz*, XXIV (1965), 307–22.

———. "The Mystical Doctrine of R. Obadyah, Grandson of Maimonides," *JJS*, VI (1955), 213–25.

———. "Le pensée religieuse de Moïse Maimonide: unité ou dualité?" *Cahiers de Civilisation Médiévale*, IX (1966), 29–49.

———. "La philosophie juive en Espagne," *The Sephardi Heritage*, ed. R. D. Barnett, London, 1971, I, 81–111.

———. *Recherches sur la philosophie et la Kabbale dans la pensée juive du Moyen Age*, Paris, 1962.

———. *La théologie ascétique de Bahya ibn Pakuda*, Paris, 1947.

Viner, J. *The Role of Providence in the Social Order* (Memoirs of the American Philosophical Society, vol. 90), Philadelphia, 1972.

Wacholder, B. "Attitudes Towards Proselytizing in the Classical Halakah," *Historia Judaica*, XX (1958), 77–96.

Walzer, R. *Greek into Arabic*, Cambridge, Mass. 1962.

Warhaftig, Z. *Ha-Ḥazaḳah bam-Mišpaṭ ha-'Iḇri*, Jerusalem, 1964.

Watt, M. *Muslim Intellectual, a Study of al-Ghazālī*, Edinburgh, 1963.

Waxman, M. "Maimonides as Dogmatist," *CCAR Yearbook*, XLV (1935), 397–418.

Weiler, M. C. "'Iyyunim bat-Terminoloğiyah," *HUCA*, XXXVII (1966), 13–45.

Weinberg, Y. *Śěriḏe 'Eš*, 4 vols., Jerusalem, 1969.

Weis, P. R. "Abraham ibn Ezra wěhak-Ḳara'im," *Mělilah*, I (1944), 35–53; II (1946), 121–34; III–IV (1950), 188–203.

Weisblatt, S. "Pěsuḵe TaNaḴ u-Ma'ămare HaZaL kě-'Asmaḵta'oṯ lě-De'oṯ Pilosofiyoṯ," *Beṯ Miḵra'*, XXXVII (1969), 59–79.

———. "R. 'Aḇraham bar Ḥiyya' ki-Měfareš ham-Miḵra'," *Beṯ Miḵra'*, XXII (1977), 365–70.

Weiss, I. H. *Dor Dor wě-Dorěšaw*, vol. IV, Vilna, 1904.

———. "Raḇ Hay wěha-Ḥoḵmoṯ ha-Ḥiṣoniyyoṯ," *He-'Asif*, III (1886), 148–52.

———. "Tolěḏoṯ ha-RaMBaM," *Beṯ Talmuḏ*, I (1881), 161–69, 193–200, 225–33, 257–65, 289–96.

Weiss, J. G. "'Ḥăḵamim Rišonim' bě-Mishneh Torah la-RaMBaM," *Dine Yiśra'el*, IV (1973), 125–41.

Weiss, R. L. "Language and Ethics: Reflections on Maimonides' Ethics," *Journal of the History of Philosophy*, IX (1971), 425–33.

———. *Wisdom and Piety: The Ethics of Maimonides*, Chicago, 1966.

Werblowsky, R. J. Z. *Joseph Karo*, London, 1962.

———. "Rešiṯ ham-Monote'ism," *'Iyyun*, IX (1958), 152–62.

Wessely, N. H. *Diḇre Šalom wa-'Emeṯ*, Berlin, 1782–88.

Wieder, N. *Hašpa'oṯ 'Islamiyyoṯ 'al hap-Pulḥan hay-Yěhuḏi*, Oxford, 1947.

Wilensky, S. *Hap-Pilosofiyah šel Yiṣḥaḳ 'Aramah*, Jerusalem, 1956.

Wischnitzer, R. "Les manuscrits à miniatures de Maimonide," *Gazette des Beaux-Arts*, VI (1935), 47–52.
Wolfson, H. A. "The Classification of Sciences in Medieval Jewish Philosophy," *Hebrew Union College Jubilee Volume*, Cincinnati, 1925, pp. 263–315.
———. "Hallevi and Maimonides on Design, Chance, and Necessity," *PAAJR*, XI (1941), 105–63.
———. "Hallevi and Maimonides on Prophecy," *JQR*, XXXIII (1942), 49–82.
———. "The Jewish Kalām," *JQR Seventy-Fifth Anniversary Volume* (1967), 544–73.
———. *Philo: Foundations of Religious Philosophy in Judaism, Christianity, and Islam*, 2 vols., Cambridge, Mass., 1962.
———. *The Philosophy of Spinoza*, Cambridge, Mass., 1934.
———. *The Philosophy of the Kalam*, Cambridge, Mass., 1976.
———. *Repercussions of the Kalam in Jewish Philosophy*, Cambridge, Mass., 1979.
———. *Studies in the History of Philosophy and Religion*, ed. I. Twersky and G. Williams, 2 vols., Cambridge, Mass., 1973–76.
Worman, E. J. "Notes on the Jews in Fustat," *JQR*, XVIII (1905), 1–39.
Wynhoven, J. "The Zohar and the Proselyte," *Texts and Responses*, ed. M. Fishbane, Leiden, 1975, pp. 120–40.
Ya'ari, A. *'Iggĕrot̲ 'Ereṣ Yiśra'el*, Tel Aviv, 1953.
———. "Peruš ham-Mišnah lĕha-RaMBaM bi-Mĕḵoro," *ḲS*, IX (1932), 101–09, 228–35.
Yawitz, Z. *Tolĕdot̲ Yiśra'el*, Tel Aviv, 1935.
Yellin, D., and Abrahams, I. *Maimonides, His Life and Works*, Philadelphia, 1903; reissued with bibliographical supplement by J. Dienstag, New York, 1972.
Yerushalmi, Y. "The Inquisition and the Jews of France in the Time of Bernard Gui," *HTR*, LXIII (1970), 317–76.
Zak, B. "Yaḥăso šel R. Šĕlomoh 'Alḵabeṣ la-Ḥăḵirah hap-Pilosofiṯ," *'Ešel*, I (1976), 288–304.
Zaslanski, A. *Wĕ-Zot̲ li-Yĕhudah*, Jerusalem, 1946.
Zeidman, J. "Signon Mishneh Torah," *Sinai*, III (1938), 112–21.
Zevin, I. *'Išim wĕ-Šiṯot̲*, Tel Aviv, 1952.
Zilberg, M. *Ham-Ma'amad̲ ha-'Iši bĕ-Yiśra'el*, Jerusalem, 1965.
———. *Kak̲ Darko šel Talmud̲*, Jerusalem, 1961.
Zimmels, H. J. *Ashkenazim and Sephardim, Their Relations, Differences, and Problems as Reflected in the Rabbinical Responsa*, London, 1958.

———. *R. David ibn Abi Simra*, Breslau, 1932.

Zinberg, I. *Tolĕḏoṯ Sifruṯ Yiśra'el*, vol. I, Tel Aviv, 1955.

Zlotnik (Avida), J. L. "Lĕ-Tolĕḏoṯ ha-Hoṣa'oṯ ha-Rišonoṯ šel Mishneh Torah," *Sinai*, XV (1951), 138–43, 247–48.

Zucker, M. *'Al Targum RaSaG lat-Torah*, New York, 1959.

———. "Ḥelḳo šel RaSaG bĕ-Pulĕmos mim-Moḥăraṯ haš-Šabbaṯ," *PAAJR*. XX (1951), Hebrew section, 1–26.

———. "Ḳeṭa' . . . lĕ-R. Sĕ'aḏyah," *PAAJR*, XLIII (1976), Hebrew section, 29–36.

———. "Lĕ-Bĕ'ayaṯ ham-Maḥloḳeṯ," *Salo W. Baron Jubilee Volume*, ed. S. Lieberman, Jerusalem, 1975, Hebrew section, pp. 319–29.

———. "Lĕ-Mašma'uṯo šel Šem has-Sefer 'Ĕmunoṯ wĕ-De'oṯ," *Bitzaron*, VII (1943), 255–70.

# GENERAL INDEX*

Aaron ben Meshullam, 3n4, 191n9
Aaron hak-Kohen of Lunel (*Orḥot Ḥayyim*), 18n24, 53n76, 284n97, 521, 524, 533n8, 536n9
Aaron hal-Levi, 193n15, 495n352
Abelard, Peter: *Historia*, 503
'Ăḇodah, 364n18
Abraham, 208, 225, 449, 451, 476, 486; biographies of, 226n80
Abraham Abulafia, 324n1
Abraham bar Ḥiyya, 54, 86, 275, 456n241
Abraham ben 'Azriel (*'Ărugat hab-Bośem*), 451n231, 520
Abraham ben David (RABD), 52n76, 102–07, 121n75, 144, 145n156, 159–61, 169n205, 189n2, 190n6, 242n8, 280, 300, 304, 318, 319, 320, 353n81, 431n186, 466n263, 487n327, 516n1, 518, 522–25; on Maimonides' reliance on Alfasi, 8n8; on Maimonides' use of Palestinian Talmud, 10n12; on resurrection, 43n55; on custom, 133n116; on MT as commentary, 158nn189–90; on *mĕleḵet šamayim*, 171
Abraham ben Isaac (*Sefer ha-'Eškol*), 533n8
Abraham ben Nathan (*Sefer ham-Manhig*), 519
Abraham de Boton (*Leḥem Mishneh*), 106, 429n182, 475n293, 522
Abraham Farisol, 452n235
Abraham ibn Daud, 8n9, 63n103, 85, 86, 89, 100n5, 194n16, 199, 202, 356, 484n322, 496n361, 511; '*Ĕmunah Ramah*, 200n28, 216n63, 276n81, 356n2, 384n73, 388n80, 411n139, 511n391; on Deut. 4:6, 383–84; on Torah and ḥokmah, 496
Abraham ibn Ezra, 58, 86, 88n165, 152n176, 190n7, 195–97, 199, 204, 223n78, 228n83, 247n20, 267n59, 275n75, 294n122, 324n1, 325n4, 327n10, 328n14, 330n17, 390n85, 429n181, 447n220, 466n264, 470n277, 482n315; *Yĕsod Mora'*, 54n86, 90, 196n21, 209n50, 249n25, 252n33, 287n109, 364n18, 385n74, 491n335; and Karaites, 85; attitude to *'Azharot*, 247n20, 252, 324n1; on Hebrew language, 326, 327n10; on Deut. 4:6, 385; and asceticism, 466
Abraham ibn Megas, 8n9, 384n73, 452n235
Abraham Kook, 358n6
Abraham Karelitz (*Ḥazon 'Iš*), 483n320
Abraham Maimonides, 104n15, 107n22, 115n62, 122n81, 133n16, 140n142, 368n33, 386n78, 396n99, 403n122, 419n153, 436n197, 437n198, 438, 443n209, 471n285, 492, 511n393
Abraham of Montpellier, 519
Abraham Portaleone (*Šilṭe Gibborim*), 529n4
Abraham Zacuto, 19n28
Aggadah, 11–12, 46, 48, 203, 411n139; use in MT, 150–53, 154n179, 219–20; Deut. 4:6 as stimulus for interpretation of, 386–87
Aha of Šabha, 245n15
'Akiba, R., 110
Alfarabi, 95, 512
Allegory, 366–67n31, 393, 478, 508; and Song of Songs, 145, 478–79; Christian, 393; and Job, 427n179; in Proverbs, 496n358, 508
Altar, 153, 436
Anatoli, 63n103
Animal blood, covering of, 436
Anonymity, 61, 98n3, 100
Anonymous *Apologia* (for MT), 45–47, 99n5; on self-sufficiency of MT, 46
Anthropomorphism, 84
Antinomianism: philosophic, 392–93; agnostic or sceptical, 393; and *ṭa'ăme miṣwot*, 394–97
Arabic language, 327, 329, 330, 333–36

---

*Prepared by Mordecai Feuerstein. I am grateful for his hard work, accompanied by great energy, skill, sensitivity, and meticulousness.

Names of authors cited in the footnotes or listed in the bibliography are not listed. Primary sources in the footnotes are indexed because the context is usually significant.

## GENERAL INDEX

Aramaic language, 26, 325, 329, 332
Aristotle, 50, 223, 465
Asceticism, 405; in SP and *Hilkot De'ot*, 459–68
Asher ben Jehiel, 104, 523, 533n8
Ashi, Rab, 490
Astrology, 420, 481, 482
Astronomy, 59, 122, 216–17, 368n33, 498, 506–07; astronomical calculation, 189–90
Avicenna: *Autobiography*, 503
Azariah dei Rossi, 432n190
Azariah Figo (*Giddule Terumah*), 529n4
'Azharot, 25, 248, 250–52

Bahya ben Asher, 395n397
Bahya ibn Pakuda, 24n37, 54, 74–75, 86, 121n74, 135, 197n24, 204, 210, 221n74, 249n25, 275n79, 276n81, 335n26, 356, 406n130, 417n148, 422n169; outer-directed motif, 88n165; typology of students, 90–91; critique of Talmudism, 199, 201–02; on love and fear of God, 216n63, 262n49, 284n98; and R. Hefeṣ, 247n20; on *ṭa'ăme miṣwot*, 373n47; on Deut 4:6, 383–84; on King David, 414n141; on supererogatory practice, 429n181; on penitents, 456; on asceticism, 466; on rationalism, 511n390
Baneth, D., 365
*Ba'ot*, 407, 408, 409
Baruch Epstein (*Aruk haš-Šulḥan he-'Atid*), 57n90, 532n7
Baruch ibn al-Balia, 356
Ben Asher, 110–11, 119
Ben Azzai, 466
Benedictions. *See* Blessings
Biblical narratives, interpretation of, 147–48, 397–400. *See also* Allegory
*Birkat 'Abraham*, 9n9, 312n185
Blessings (*berakot*), 421–22
*Book of Correspondence*, 11
*Book of Prophecy*, 11

Charity, 265, 272, 290–91, 305, 369n39, 426, 447; taught to convert, 425; act of giving, 425–26
Christianity, 393, 403–04, 484; polemicists for, 84, 341; not monotheistic, 452; historical function of, 452–53
Circumcision, 152–53, 261, 283, 422
Classification, 238ff., 532n8. *See also* Moses ben Maimon, *Mishneh Torah*
Compassion: emphasis on, in MT, 424–29
Contingency, theory of, 398
Conversion, 295, 425, 474–75
Court of law: qualifications for appointment to, 146–47; judicial discretion of, 139, 143, 156–67
Creation of world, 410, 448n224
Curriculum: Talmud and cognate subjects, 89–92, 195–204, 359–61
Cursing, 440–41
Custom (*minhag*), 124–34, 228

Daniel hab-Babli, 522
*Darke 'Emori*, 431n186
*Daršinan ṭa'ăma' di-ḳera'*, 488n332
*Dat ha-'emet*, 403n183
David Arama, 522
David ben Joseph, 415n145
David ben Levi (*sefer ham-Miktam*), 518, 524
David Gans, 385n76
David ibn Abi Zimra (RaDBaZ), 10n12, 57n90, 66n113, 76n141, 106, 143n148, 154n179, 159n191, 191n10, 250n29, 285n105, 289n115, 306n169, 308n172, 309, 315, 316, 342n1, 474n293, 488n329, 522, 524, 532
David Kimḥi, 267n59, 271n65, 288n111, 326n7, 377n58, 395n97, 405n128, 408n133; on Deut. 4:6, 385
David Messer Leon, 523
David Nieto, 100n5
David Pardo, 52n76
David Tevele, 192n13
Death and mourning, 154–55, 306; divergent attitudes towards, in MN and MT, 438–39
*De'ot*, 416, 417n148
*Derek ha-rob*, 473n289
Deuteronomy 4:6, interpretations of, 381–87, 498
"Discussions (*hawwayot*) of Abbaye and Raba," 493–94
Disputations: use of MT in, at Barcelona and Tortosa, 530n5
*Diwān*, 77, 97, 191, 499

# GENERAL INDEX

Dunash ben Labrat, 353n81
'Eğlah 'ărufah, 445–46
Egyptian codex of Bible, 119
Eldad had-Dani, 110n25
Eleazar ben Samuel of Metz (Sefer Yĕre'im), 247n19, 533n8
Eleazar haḳ-Ḳalir, 328n14
Eleazar of Worms (Sefer ha-Roḳeaḥ), 520, 533n8
Elijah Gaon (of Vilna), 10n12, 55n87, 191n10, 314, 357n5, 482n315, 492
Elijah Mizraḥi, 382n68, 450n228
Elitism, 135, 468–71, 507, 512–13
Enoch, Rabbenu, 54
Ephraim, Rabbenu, 12n16
'Epiḳoros, 430n183, 484n322
Eschatology. See Messiah and Messianism
Esotericism, 400, 471
Ethics, 226, 511n390; free will, 366, 410; beyond the letter of the law, 428–29; autonomy vs. heteronomy, 453–56; golden mean, theory of, 459, 467. See also Ṭa'ăme miṣwot
Exempla, 121, 137–39
Ezekiel Landau, 192n13, 337n31
Ezra and the Great Assembly, 110

Fasting, 302–04; and prayer, 422
Festivals: manner of rejoicing on, 423–24
Free will and predestination, 366, 410

Gamaliel, Rabban, 110, 113
Gambling, 474
Genetic fallacy, 95, 537
Gĕnut he-hamon, 470. See also Elitism
Geometry, 59, 217
Geonim, 7, 62, 78, 81–83, 91, 107, 121, 169, 171, 221, 253, 330; Maimonides' criticism of, 9, 29, 50, 115–16, 124, 129, 133, 156, 453n236; and MT, 26, 36, 49, 53–55, 110, 160, 188, 254, 256, 465; nature of their works, 33, 88, 101, 245n15, 255, 333; Maimonides' definition of, 66, 78; opposition to piyyuṭ, 251n29
Gershom, Rabbenu, 494
Gershon Enoch of Radzin (Sidre Ṭŏharot), 191n10, 532n7
Gĕzerat hak-Katub, 471–73
al-Ghazālī, 202

Gilgul, 295
God: love of, 47, 215, 216n63, 262, 284, 301, 363, 478; knowledge of, 47, 261, 511; fear of, 272, 284n98, 363n18; names of, 328; profanation of name of, 428
Gradualism (or accommodation), 390
Gufe Torah, 361, 500; yĕsodot gufe Torah, 361, 371, 500, 504

Haggahot. See Haśśagot
Haggahot Maymuniyyot, 127n94, 316, 519–20
Hai Gaon, 55n87, 81, 82, 160n193, 250n29, 254, 277n82, 278, 353n81, 491n335, 533n8; apocalyptic Messianism, 451n231
Ḥakam, 461, 464
Halakot Gĕdolot, 24, 55n87, 56n89, 101, 211, 241n6, 248, 295nn127–29; classification of laws in, 244–45; listing of miṣwot in, 246–49; criticism of, 248–49
Halakot Ḳĕṭu'ot, 101, 245n15
Halakot Pĕsukot, 101, 107, 166, 245n15, 255
Hallel, 126–27, 480
Hananeel, Rabbenu, 13n17, 53, 160n193, 417n148, 494; Maimonides' reliance on, 88
Hananiah Cases (Ḳin'at Sofĕrim), 168n204
Ḥāros, hārisah, 407, 408, 409
Ḥasdai Crescas, 73, 105, 518
Ḥasid, 111, 134, 152, 460, 462–64
Ḥăsidut, 135, 427, 429
Haskamah, 129n100
Haśśagot, 159; used interchangeably with haggahot, 524
Hayyim ibn 'Aṭṭar, 74
Hayyim Jair Bacharach (Tĕšubot Ḥawwot Ya'ir), 100n5, 162n196, 531
Hayyim of Volozhin, 191n10, 199, 532
Ḥayyim 'Or Zaru'a, 424n172
Hebel, 419–20
Hebrew language: Biblical, 26, 325–27, 329; Mishnaic, 26, 325, 330–33; purity of, 331. See also Language
Ḥefeṣ ben Yaṣliaḥ, 16, 245n16, 247, 248, 253
Heteronomy. See Ethics
Ḥibbur, 16, 18, 20, 33, 191, 239, 492

*Ḥidah*, 366n31
*Ḥidduš*, 529, 531
*Higgayon*, 241n6
*Hilkot 'Akum* (Laws of Idolatry), 27, 28, 261, 283
*Hilkot De'ot:* asceticism, 460–64
*Hilkot 'Issure Mizbeaḥ*, 27
*Hilkot Rē'u*, 329n15
*Hilkot Talmud Torah*, 114, 535–36
*Hilkot Tešubah*, 532
Hillel of Verona, 403n122
Hillel the Elder, 110, 113
*Ḥilluk*, 252
Hippocrates: theory of climates, 69
Historical motifs, 153–54, 220–228. See also Moses ben Maimon, *Mishneh Torah*
*Ḥokmah ('ilm)*, 219, 341, 366n31, 367–68, 427, 428, 429, 473–76, 495–97, 499n367, 513; science, 7, 10, 87, 203
*Ḥokmah yěwanit*, 366n25
*Ḥukkim*, 377, 378, 382, 385, 386, 387, 391, 402, 413, 414, 415, 427, 429, 456

Ibn al-Jasūm, 53
Ibn Bajjah, 50, 466n266
Ibn Jābir, 16n21, 45n59, 59, 352, 368n38
Idolatry, history of. See Religion, history of
*'Ikkar*, 260, 261n47
*'Ilm*. See *Ḥokmah*
Immortality, 366, 368n38
Immanuel Benevento, 379n62
Immanuel of Rome, 18n25
Intentional fallacy, 21, 22n34
Isaac Abarbanel, 12n15, 70, 163n197, 190n7, 228n83, 341n49, 352n77, 362n12, 395n97; on Deut 4:6, 385n76, 403
Isaac Aboab, 203
Isaac Alfasi (*Halakot*), 8, 13n7, 88, 89, 111, 116, 157n188, 168, 236n96, 239–40, 343, 419n153, 518, 522, 523, 524, 533n8; and Maimonides, 9, 12, 14, 32, 54, 160–61, 169–70, 245; criticism of Geonim, 171; *mēleket šamayim*, 173–74; restricted scope of Talmud study, 193–94
Isaac Arama, 198n25, 455n239, 458n247
Isaac ben Abba Mari (*Sefer ha-'Iṭṭur*), 120n72, 522, 533n8
Isaac ben Abraham (RIṢBA), 519, 522

Isaac ben Baruch al-Balia, 54
Isaac ben Joseph Israeli, 193n13
Isaac ben Moses (of Vienna) (*'Or Zaru'a*), 522
Isaac ben Reuben al-Bargeloni, 248
Isaac ben Sheshet Perfet, 105, 514n398
Isaac Canpanton, 8n9, 21n32
Isaac Gikatilia, 248
Isaac ibn Ghiyāth, 54, 254, 356n1
Isaac ibn Latif, 347n65, 476n286, 499n370
Isaac of Corbeille, 253
Isaac Polgar (*'Ezer had-Dat*), 105n16, 483n19
Isaiah di Trani, 108n24
Islam, 403–04; historical function of, 452–53; Sufi influence, 463
Israel Lifshitz (*Tif'eret Yiśra'el*), 191n10
Israel of Shklov (*Pē'at haš-Šulḥan*), 191n10, 531n6, 532n7
*'Iyyun*, 170

Jacob Anatoli, 75, 104n15, 495
Jacob ben Asher (*Ṭurim*), 171n208, 234, 281, 284, 475n295, 533, 534, 536n9
Jacob ben Sheshet, 331n18, 394n93, 483n19
Jacob Emden, 432n190, 529
Jacob Ḥazzan, 104n11
Jacob ibn Gabbai, 385n73
Jacob Landau (*Sefer ha-'Agur*), 171n208, 524, 533n8
Japeth: Maimonides' letter to, 4n5, 5n6, 10n10
Jedaiah hap-Penini, 386n78, 516
Jeroham ben Meshullam (*Sefer Mešarim; Tolēdot 'Adam wĕ-Ḥawwah*), 104n14, 280n88, 281n92, 284n97, 295n126, 533n8, 536n9
Job, Book of, 427n179, 479
Joel Sirkes, 535
Johanan ben Zakkai, 110, 494
Johanan the High Priest, 110
Jonah Gerondi, 522–23
Jonah ibn Janāḥ, 58, 203, 204n36, 323n11, 331n17, 337n31, 348n67, 349n69, 408n132; and Mishnaic Hebrew, 330
Jonathan ben Uzziel (*Targum*), 58n92
Jonathan Eybeschütz, 73n129, 529

# GENERAL INDEX

Jonathan hak-Kohen of Lunel, 4, 37–41, 62n101, 65, 76, 78n149, 93, 250n29, 257, 336n30, 417n148, 419n153, 499n367, 515, 516, 522
Joseph Abulafia, 104n11, 370n54
Joseph Albo, 190n6, 226n8, 228n83, 234n92, 341n49, 405n128
Joseph Ashkenazi, 488n330, 515, 516n1, 528
Joseph ben Judah, 41–43, 45n59, 62n101, 73, 74, 76, 169, 210n53, 365, 368, 520
Joseph ben Todros Abulafia, 103
Joseph Corcos, 522
Joseph del Medigo, 516, 518
Joseph Gikatilia, 384n73
Joseph hal-Levi, 63n103
Joseph ham-Ma'arabi, 41n50
Joseph ibn Abitur, 248
Joseph ibn Aknin, 5n6, 368, 495, 499
Joseph ibn Kaspi, 104, 190n6, 197n24, 228n83, 324n1, 337n31, 341n49, 368n33, 440n204
Joseph ibn Megas, 7, 8, 9, 11n12, 13n17, 54, 55, 63n103, 88–89, 102n23, 107, 111, 115n62, 160, 247, 343n51; influence on Maimonides, 8, 9, 247
Joseph ibn Plat, 415n145
Joseph ibn Ṣaddik, 86, 356, 511
Joseph Jabez, 198n25, 200, 201n30, 385n76
Joseph Karo, 60n99, 71, 79n149, 105, 106, 127n94, 148n164, 159, 191n110, 254, 281, 316, 495, 522, 529n4, 532, 533, 534, 536; *Beṭ Yosef*, 71n127, 105n18, 430n132; KM, 106n21, 110n27, 129n100, 148n164, 159n191, 162n197, 236n96, 308n172, 316n192, 317n194, 422n168, 429–430n182, 431n186, 446n18, 495n353
Joseph Ḳimḥi, 168n204, 326n7, 328n14, 331n17, 348n67, 356n1
Joseph Kolon, 10n12, 147n164
Joseph Roš has-Seder, 70, 211, 240n4
Joseph Rozin (Rosen) (*Ṣofnaṭ Pa'ăneaḥ*), 526
Joseph Ṭob 'Elem, 328n14
Joshua ben Levi: on Deut. 4:6, 382–83
Joshua han-Naǵid, 250n29, 312n185, 315
Joshua ibn Shu'ayb, 120n72, 408n133, 472n286
Judah Albutini, 106n21, 257n41, 522

Judah al-Fakhar, 504n380, 516
Judah Alḥarizi, 367n32, 525
Judah ben Barzillai al-Bargeloni, 54, 171n208, 203, 211, 254, 494, 533n8
Judah ben Isaac (of Paris), 519
Judah del Bene, 453n235
Judah hak-Kohen, 324n1
Judah hal-Levi, 71, 73, 86, 150n171, 198n25, 228n83, 239n2, 365n21, 366n29; theory of climates, 70; on Hebrew language, 324n1, 328n14, 331n18, 332; on Deut 4:6, 385n73; on miracles, 390n84; and philosophic antinomianism, 393; on *miṣwoṭ*, 405n128, 406n130; on asceticism, 405n129; and theory of chance, 422n169; attitude to Christianity and Islam, 453; role of reason, 457; on proselytes, 485; and history of philosophy, 497
Judah han-Naśi', 30, 33, 34, 35, 64–65, 110, 167, 168n203, 191, 256, 347, 354, 490; extolled by Maimonides, 238–39
Judah Ḥayyūj, 327n13, 331n17
Judah ibn Aknin, 67n115
Judah ibn Bal'am, 58, 146n161, 249n25
Judah ibn Tibbon, 74, 327, 328n14, 351
Judah Loew ben Bezaleel (MaHaRaL), 12n15, 105n20, 526n2, 527
Judah Rosanes (*Mishneh lĕ-Melek*), 529–30

Kabbalah: oral traditions, 59, 111, 490
*Kalām (Mutakallimūn)*, 482, 498, 505n384
Kalonymos ben Kalonymos, 197n24
Kant, E., 79
Karaites, 77, 81, 84–86, 145, 204, 215, 234, 344, 362n13, 403n123, 484n322; anti-Karaite polemic in MT, 31, 35, 57, 109, 344; and Sadduceanism, 85, 133; MT not an anti-Karaite work, 86
*Kĕduśah*, 264, 286–88, 324n1, 442n209, 483n319
*Kĕfiyyah*, 487
*Kĕlalim*, literature of, 158n189, 529
*Kĕnesseṭ hag-Gĕdolah*, 158n189
*Keruḇ (karoḇ, kĕroḇim)*, 78, 79n149, 473
*Kĕsilim* (fools, literalists), applied to Karaites, 85
*Kibbuṣ*, 78–79, 257, 278
Kierkegaard, S., 510

# 616 GENERAL INDEX

Ḳiryaṭ Sefer, 361n10
Kol Bo, 524
Ḳušyah u-peruḳ, 166

Language: natural or conventional, 324n1;
  Maimonides' attitude to, 324, 354
Lĕ-ḥappoṭ dĕḥarim, 407, 408, 409
Leo de Modena, 72n129
Leprosy, 446, 447n220
Levi, tribe of, 441–42
Levi ben Abraham, 499n370
Levi ben Gershom (RaLBaG, Gersonides),
  57n91, 253n35, 403n122, 417n148
Levi ben Ḥabib, 159n191, 522
Lex talionis, 437n198
Lifnim miš-šuraṭ had-din, 428, 511n390
Liturgy, 127; Nĕ'ilah, 144; Shema', 150–51. See also Prayer
Luzzatto, Moses Hayyim, 190n7, 531–32
Luzzatto, Samuel David, 243n11,
  441n306, 516n1, 528

Ma'ăśeh 'akum, 306
Ma'ăśeh bĕre'šit, ma'ăśeh merkabah, 361, 493,
  500, 504, 505n384; identified with
  physics and metaphysics, 365–66
Ma'ăśeh Roḳeaḥ, 292n118
Magic, 366, 479–82
Maimon had-Dayyan, R., 7, 8, 9n9, 116,
  117
Maimonides. See Moses ben Maimon
Mannheim, Karl, 76
Manoah, Rabbenu (Sefer ham-Mĕnuḥah),
  106, 280
Mašal, 366n31, 367n31
Masorites, 54
Maśśa' u-mattan, 39, 47, 99
Mattithiah hay-Yiṣhari, 76n141
Medicine, 2n2, 51, 94, 216, 219, 366;
  medical literature, 59; on Sabbath,
  483–84
Meir Aldabi, 228n83, 408n133
Meir ben Simeon (Sefer ham-Mĕ'oroṭ), 518
Meir hak-Kohen, 522
Meir hal-Levi Abulafia, 3n4, 107n23,
  119n68, 191n9, 367n30, 504n380,
  517, 522, 525; and mĕleket šamayim, 171
Meir ibn Gabbai, 100n5, 422n165
Meir of Rothenburg, 519, 520
Meir Simḥah hak-Kohen ('Or Śameaḥ),
  292n188, 526

Mĕleket šamayim (mĕleket haš-šem), 170–75;
  as spur to criticism, 522, 531
Menahem ben Saruḳ, 326, 328n14, 330
Menahem ben Zerah, (Ṣedah lad-Derek),
  3n4, 28n41, 193n15, 357n5, 432n190,
  533n8
Menahem ham-Me'iri, 54n82, 100n6,
  119n68, 133n116, 194n17, 385n73,
  405n128, 475n285, 487n327, 524,
  531; on MT, 3n4, 48n65, 65n111, 104,
  158, 191n9, 235n98, 257n41, 274n74,
  279n85, 293, 295; history of Rabbinic
  literature, 28n41; oral culture, 73n31;
  on custom, 133n116; on Talmud commentary,
  157n188, 319n202; on history
  of religion, 226n80, 447n306; on
  kĕdušah, 288n172; on Hebrew language,
  347n65; on Ps. 19, 377n58; on antinomism,
  394n13; on penitents,
  456n241; on talmud Torah in MT,
  495n351, 536n9
Menahem Krakowski ('Aḇoḏat ham-melek),
  52n73, 54n86
Meshullam ben Moses (Sefer ha-Hašlamah),
  169n205, 518, 522, 524, 525
Messiah and Messianism, 43, 54n86, 58,
  59, 67–68, 272; natural law and, 145–46,
  451, 476–77, 502, 512; treated as
  halakic reality in MT, 207, 227; immortality,
  368n38; in IT, 450–51;
  apocalyptic view of R. Hai Gaon,
  451n231
Mĕzuzah, 125, 275, 421, 480–81
Midrash: halakic Midrashim, 52;
  Maimonides' attitude to, 437. See also
  Aggadah; Book of Correspondence
Midraš hag-Gaḏol, 526
Minhaḡ. See Custom
Minhaḡ ṭa'uṭ, 59, 132–33
Minḥat Ḥinnuḳ, 231n87, 317n198
Minḥat Ḳĕna'oṭ, 483n319
Minim, 35, 85, 113, 133
Miracles, 366, 389, 390n84; in Messianic
  era, 451nn231, 233
Mishnah, study of, 88–89, 205–07
Mishneh lĕ-Melek, 191n10, 257n41
Mishneh Torah. See Moses ben Maimon,
  Mishneh Torah
Mišpaṭim, 377, 382, 391, 415n145, 427,
  429; autonomy vs. heteronomy, 454,
  456

## GENERAL INDEX

*Miṣwot.* See Oral Law
*Miṣwot śikliyyot,* 458
Mittwoch, E., 75
*Mofet,* 490
Moore, G. F., 456
Mordecai Jaffe (*Lĕbuš*), 234, 281, 533
Moses Alashkar, 56n89, 455n239, 504n380
Moses Almosnino, 455n239
Moses ben Enoch, 54, 88, 194n16
Moses ben Jacob of Coucy (*Sefer Miṣwot Gadol*), 28n41, 103–04, 192n13, 209–10, 246, 253, 394n95, 414n143, 475n295, 476n298, 516, 519, 536n9
Moses ben Maimon, works of: *Animadversions Against R. Isaac Alfasi,* 12, 14; *Commentary on Difficult Halakot in Talmud,* 12–13; *Commentary on Talmud,* 7–8, 12; *Hilkot Yĕrušalmi,* 10, 12, 165; *'Iggeret haš-Šĕmad* (Epistle on Conversion), 14–15, 277; *'Iggeret Teman* (Epistle to Yemen), 14–15, 19, 63, 75, 227n81, 249n26, 334, 417–18, 450–51, 453; *Letter on Astrology,* 15n19, 249, 391n87, 420; Letters (see *Kobeṣ, 'Iggĕrot,* in Index of Passages); *Millot ha-Higgayon* (Treatise on Logic), 15, 365n22, 375n52, 376n54; *Siddur,* 54n82, 131; *Tĕšubot* (see Index of Passages); *Treatise on the Intercalation of the Calendar,* 15
—*Ma'amar Tĕḥiyyat ham-Metim* (Treatise on Resurrection), 43–45; attitude to the masses, 43; defense of Maimonides' life's work, 44, 502–03; philosophic motive of MT, 77–78; classification, 257; language, 345
—Medical writings: *Pirḳe Mošeh,* 75; *On Asthma,* 240n6
—*Mishneh Torah:* attitude to predecessors, 9, 83 (see also *Geonim*; Isaac Alfasi); Palestinian Talmud in, 10, 52, 266; centrality of, in Maimonides' oeuvre, 14–15, 515–16; in Yemen, 19; and Talmud, 30n42, 31 ff., 46, 65, 99–102, 108, 211, 368, 528; *Sefer hab-Be'ur* as supplement to, 36, 107; brevity as goal in, 45, 99; philosophic themes in, 47, 356 ff.; Scriptural exegesis in, 57–58, 145–50; oral traditions in, 58–59, 112; non-Jewish sources, 59–60; motives and goals of, 61–81; *Sefer Madda',* 78, 212–13, 260–61, 372, 493, 499, 503; and Karaism, 86 (see also Karaites); as Talmud commentary, 87–88, 157–59, 528; analysis of Maimonides' introduction to, 97, 166, 188; criticism of, 102 ff., 522, 525; various attitudes toward, 102–08, 518–26; *Yad ha-ḥăzaḳah* as title of, 105, 527; commentaries on, 106–07, 518–26; judicial discretion, 140; aggadah in, 150–53; *ta'ăme halakot* in, 162–64; *mĕleket haš-šem,* 173; classification, description of, 260–80; problems of, 281–300; contradictions in, 311–20; *ta'ăme miṣwot* in, 374n48 (see also *Ta'ăme miṣwot*); differences between MY and MN, 430 ff.; outer-directed awareness, 432, 502; explanation of term MT, 492n342; influence of, 515–18
—*Moreh Nĕbukim* (Guide of the Perplexed), 3, 37, 41, 44, 50, 68; and projected commentary on aggadah, 11, 220; as "Gemara" of MT, 19, 500; references to MT in MN, 47; date of composition, 47n64; *ta'ăme miṣwot* in, 374–406; historicism, 389–91, 431–39; *sitre Torah,* 397–400; erroneous views of the masses in Torah, 440; theory of gradualism (or accomodation), 448; four kinds of perfection, 465; and *gĕnut he-hamon,* 470; as philosophic book, 505n384; history of, compared to MT, 515–16
—*Peruš ham-Mishnah* (Commentary on the Mishnah), 7, 10, 11, 14, 25, 55, 63–64, 137, 145, 165, 220; corrected in light of MT, 16, 17; restricted to Arabic readers, 19; and scope of Talmud study, 88–89, 205–07; rationalism in, 44–45, 87, 219, 360, 364–68, 493, 497, 501; *mĕleket šamayim* in, 169, 172–74; systematization and classification of law in, 258
—*Sefer ham-Miṣwot* (Book of Commandments): introduction to, 7, 13–14, 24–28, 74, 97–98, 167, 188–89, 236, 253n35; motives for composition of, 27–28; temporary laws, 229–34
—*Šĕmonah Pĕraḳim,* 367, 453; on asceticism, 460–64
Moses ben Naḥman. See Naḥmanides
Moses Botarel, 315n187, 523
Moses Cordovero, 53, 100n5, 491n355

## GENERAL INDEX

Moses di Trani, 253, 361n10
Moses hak-Kohen (RaMaK), 37, 103, 125n80
Moses ibn Ezra, 54, 73n130, 202n32, 324n1, 326, 327n10, 330, 331n18, 348n67, 353
Moses ibn Gikatilia, 58, 146n161, 327n13, 335
Moses ibn Tibbon, 16n21, 249n24, 251
Moses Isserles, 127n94, 210n52, 221n74, 250n27, 473n289, 520, 529n4, 535, 536
Moses Mendelssohn, 457
Moses Met, 385n73
Moses Provençalo, 361n10
Moses Sofer, 532
Moses Taku, 380n64
Murder, 148, 443–44, 445; unintentional, 475–76
Muśkalot, 458n247

Naḥmanides, Moses, 10n12, 16n21, 25n39, 55n87, 173n211, 190n6, 228n83, 242n8, 249nn24–25, 251–52, 257n41, 263n50, 264n52, 271n65, 273n70, 287n109, 294n122, 304, 319n202, 324n1, 328n14, 337n33, 341n49, 373n45, 414n144, 422n168, 429n181, 432n190, 466n263, 479n309, 482n315, 487n327, 504n380, 517, 523, 524, 525; concept of relativism, 168, 172
Natural law, 456–59; and moral law, 376n57. See also Oral Law
Nazirite, 467–68
Nehorai had-Dayyan: Maimonides' responsum to, 7
Ninth of Ab, 119
Nissim Gaon (Sefer ham-Mafteah), 53
Nissim Gerondi, 385n76, 440n204
Niṣṣuaḥ, 161n195
Noahide commandments, 147–48
Non-Jewish sources, 59–60, 122, 216–218, 367, 498–99, 506. See also Moses ben Maimon, Mishneh Torah

Obadiah Sforno, 445n215
Obadiah the Proselyte, 485
Odofredus, 345n62

'Olam hab-ba', 430n183
Onkelos (Targum), 57, 58n92
"Opinion of the Multitude": and Torah, 440
Oral Law (and halakah), 26, 99, 233, 271; intellectual dynamism, 17, 25; 613 commandments, 24, 30, 135, 197, 229, 249, 275; superiority of oral study, 27, 66, 72–73, 112, 240n6; histories of, 28n41, 29; two components: positive law and metalegal, 77–79, 150n171, 203, 360–62, 394, 491–93; Karaite charges against, 84; controversy in, 99; relativism in study of, 170–75; as "burden," 404–05; teleology of, 418–20; interpretation of ritual laws, 420–29; Mosaic authority for, 455; rationality of, 458–59; embodied in Mishnah, 489–92. See also Mishnah; Ṭa'ăme halakot; Ṭa'ăme miṣwot; Talmud 'aruk; Talmud study
Originality, 3, 49–61, 97n2
Outer-directed awareness, 88n165, 385–87, 502; in MT and MN, 432, 502

Palestinian Talmud, 10, 11n12, 36, 52, 53, 57, 62, 149, 165n201, 266
Paltoi Gaon, 255n37
Pardes, 489, 493, 495, 536
Penitents, 455–56
Pĕraḳim bĕ-Haṣlaḥah, 358n6
Peruš, 18n25, 33, 161, 492
Pĕsaḳ, 80, 102, 203
Pĕṣat, 197
Philo, 288, 477, 511
Philosophy: history of, 29, 370, 496; handmaiden of theology, 38; and aggadah, 46; disappearance in ancient Israel, 69; study of, 77, 89–90, 94, 195–204; integral part of Talmud, 489–500. See also Curriculum; Oral Law; Rationalism
Phinehas ben Meshullam (had-Dayyan), 18n25, 30–37, 42, 45n59, 49, 62n101, 65, 74, 98n3, 99, 100, 108, 109, 118, 157n188, 206, 241–42, 257, 492, 528. See also Ḳobeṣ, I, 25b in Index of Passages
Pilpul, 35, 210, 529
Plato, 73, 347, 503
Poetry, 482; Maimonides' attitude toward,

# GENERAL INDEX

250; liturgical (*piyyuṭ*), 409n135
Polemics: and *ṭa'ăme miṣwoṭ*, 403–06. *See also* Christianity; Islam; Karaites
Prayer: origin of statutory, 9n9, 223–25, 233–34, 303; Maimonides' *Siddur*, 54n82; and fasting, 422; history and paradox of, 453n236. *See also* Liturgy
Profiat Duran (*Ma'ăśeh 'Efoḏ*), 100n5, 191n9, 324n1, 377n58, 413n140, 495n350
Prophecy, 11, 47, 365; cessation of, 67–68; uniqueness of Mosaic, 455
Proselytes, 474–75, 485–86
Prostitution, 446
Providence, 303, 422, 505n383; Epicurean theory of chance, 422; related to intellectual achievement, 423n169

Rabbinate, professionalization of, 82–83, 89, 94, 453n236; Maimonides' ideal type of, 5, 134n123
Rashi. *See* Solomon ben Isaac (RaSHI)
Rationalism, 86–88, 356 ff.
Religion, history of, 150n171, 225–26, 366, 477–78. *See also* Sabians
Resurrection, 43, 502
Revenge, prohibition of seeking, 441
Reward: and *summum bonum*, 228
"Righteous heathen," 455
Ritual cleanness and uncleanness (purity and impurity), 268; divergent emphases in MN and MT, 434–35

Saadiah ben David, 357n5
Saadiah Gaon, 3n3, 20, 55n87, 56, 58, 70, 81, 82, 85, 86, 172n210, 258n45, 356, 470n279, 533n8; on history of tradition, 28n41; on *translatio studii*, 38; *Siddur*, 53–54, 225n79, 251n30; on reward, 228n83; *Sefer ham-Miṣwoṯ*, 247n19, 248, 251, 253–54; *miṣwoṯ*, 276n18, 458; Hebrew language, 326, 328, 330n17, 335, 348n67, 349nn69–70, 350n72, 353n81; pioneer of religious philosophy, 356n2; *ṭa'ăme miṣwoṯ*, 373n47, 446n219, 447n222; on Epicureanism, 422n169; Maimonides' characterization of, 449n227; asceticism, 466
Sabbath: honoring of, 113–14; and *ṭa'ăme*

*halakoṯ*, 163–64; reasons for observance of, 363, 447; violation of, to save life, 483–84
Sabians, 389, 391, 399, 402, 403n121, 431
Sacrifices, 56n89, 390–91, 413–15; historical explanation of, in MN, 432; ethical explanation of, in MT, 433
Sadducees: name applied to Karaites, 85
"Sages of Spain," 111
*Ṣaḥuṯ*, 347–49
Samson of Sens, 103, 175n213, 519, 522
Samson Raphael Hirsch, 432n190
Samuel Aboab (*Dḇar Šĕmu'el*), 532
Samuel ben Ali Gaon, 43, 207n46, 503n379
Samuel ben Ḥofni Gaon, 28n41, 53, 81, 147n164, 246, 247n19, 248, 254, 276n80, 533n8
Samuel ben Meir (RaSHBaM), 123n83, 196, 385n75
Samuel ben Nissim (*Midraš Berešiṯ Zuṭa*), 526
Samuel han-Nagid, 13n17, 28n41, 85, 109n25, 197n24, 204, 239n2, 348n67, 350n72; *Sefer Hilkoṯ han-Naḡiḏ*, 254n36
Samuel has-Sardi, 524, 533n8
Samuel ibn Tibbon, 37, 69n118, 327, 333n20, 351, 367n32, 385n74; letter from Maimonides to, 4, 50, 353, 356n2
Sanhedrin, 83, 129, 472. *See also* Court of law
"Scholars of the West," 111
Schneersohn, Joseph, 530n5
"Science of the law," 360
*Seder 'Olam Zuṭa*, 102n9
*Sefer dinim* (Mishnah), 168n203
*Sefer ha-Ḥinnuḵ*, 231n87, 246, 317n198, 403n122, 420n160, 440n204
*Sefer ha-Razim*, 54n84
*Sefer Ḥăsiḏim*, 429n181, 520
*Sefer kolel*, 97, 191
*Sefer wĕ-Hizhir*, 329n15
*Šĕḥiṭah*, 126
Self-incrimination: and capital punishment, 472
*Sĕmiḵah*, 117
*Šĕmirah*, 413, 414
Shabbethai Donnolo, 351
Shem Ṭoḇ ben Shem Ṭoḇ, 403n122,

Shem Ṭob ben Shem Ṭob (cont'd)
449n224, 488n330, 504n380, 529n4
Shem Ṭob ibn Falaquera, 75, 105n16,
210n53, 332n19, 336n30
Shem Ṭob ibn Gaon (Migdal 'Oz), 106,
522, 529n4
Shem Ṭob ibn Shaprut, 12n15
Sherira Gaon, 28n41, 242, 494; letter of,
71
Sheshet han-Naśi' (of Saragossa), 103,
336n30, 499n370, 521
Shneur Zalman of Ladi, 199
Shofar, 471–72
Simeon Duran, 122n81, 347n65, 357n5,
395n97, 473n289, 495n355; Zohar
ha-Raḳi'a, 249nn24–25, 251, 252n32,
403
Šimmuša Rabbah, 53
Simon the Just, 110, 495
Ṣiṣit, 113, 126, 134
Sitre Torah, 397–98. See also Aggadah;
Huḳḳim; Ma'aśeh bere'šit
Ši'ur Ḳomah, 54, 369n39
Slaves: treatment of, 427; fugitive, 439
Solomon al-'Ami, 200
Solomon ben Isaac (RaSHI), 12, 13n17,
56n89, 162n197, 312n185, 413n140,
424n174, 478n307, 484, 523, 524
Solomon ben Judah (of Dreux), 522
Solomon del Medigo (Nobĕlot Ḥokmah),
100n5, 105n16
Solomon Duran (Milḥemet Miṣwah),
105n19, 209n50, 528, 529; explanation
of term MT, 492n342
Solomon ibn Adret (RaSHBA), 157n188,
235n93, 236n96, 280, 357n5,
408n133, 440n204, 496n356,
504n380, 517, 523, 524, 533n8
Solomon ibn Gabirol, 86, 328; 'Azharot,
248, 251
Solomon Luria, 100nn5–6, 105n20,
119n69, 257n41, 504n380
Solomon of Chelm (Mirkebet ham-Mishneh),
529
Solomon of Montpellier, 516
Solomon Parḥon, 331n17, 335
Soloveitchik, Hayyim (of Brisk), 94n171,
159n191, 450n230, 526
Soloveitchik, Joseph B. (Bet hal-Lewi),
53n76
Šoṭeh, 370n40, 488

Sufism, 463
Sulḥan 'Aruḳ, 112n48, 234, 281, 309,
475n295, 527, 533, 534, 535, 536
Supererogatory conduct, 135n123, 427–
29, 435, 462. See also Ḥasid; Lifnim miš-
šurat had-din

Ṭa'ăme halakot, 162–64
Ṭa'ăme miṣwot: key Maimonidean passages,
374nn48–49; proofs for, 375–80; teleological
motif, 376, 418; vs. futility of
pagan practices, 380, 404–05, 418–20;
use of Deut. 4:6 as outer-directed Scriptural
imperative, 381–87, 414;
philosophic and historical methods of interpretation,
387–91; dangers of antinomianism,
391–94; and sitre Torah,
397–99; interpretation of generalities,
not details, 398 (see also ṭa'ăme halakot);
monolithic vs. multiple explanation,
401–03; and polemics, 403–06;
paradigm for analysis of, 407; ethical perfection
as goal, 416–18, 440–43 (see also
Cursing; Revenge); miṣwot as antidote to
ḥebel, 419–20; methodological differences
between MT and MN, 431 ff., 440
(see also Death and mourning; Ritual
cleanness and uncleanness; Sacrifices;
Slaves); socially-oriented explanations,
443–47 (see also Charity; 'Eglah 'ărufah;
Leprosy; Murder; Prostitution; Sabbath).
See also Antinomianism; Outer-directed
awareness; Sacrifices; Tiḳḳun hag-guf;
Tiḳḳun han-nefeš
Taḳḳanot: taḳḳanat hak-ḳahal, 129; to adopt
MT as a legal guide, 526
Talmud 'aruḳ, 157–58
Talmud study: difficulties of, 17n22, 32,
42, 65, 241, 295, 329; and philosophy,
77–79, 89, 198, 360; and codes, 101,
104, 107, 169–70, 211; text criticism,
115n62; and Scripture, 149, 196–97,
206n44, 209; MT as spur to, 157–59,
528; restricted scope of, 192–94; Torah
li-šĕmah, 196; dangers of Talmudism,
200–03; ostentation and pragmatism in,
205; Maimonides' objection to pilpul,
210
Tanḥum Yerushalmi, 330n17, 333n22,
337n33, 347n65
Tĕfillin, 113, 421

## GENERAL INDEX

Ten Commandments: reading of, 133; daily recitation of, 165–66
*Tikkun hag-guf*, 417, 483
*Tikkun han-nefeš*, 300, 417
*Tippeš, tippēšim*, 369n40
Todros, R., 362n68
*Torah li-šĕmah*, 196
Torah reading: triennial cycle of, 125–26; *kohen* vs. scholar in, 132. *See also* Ten Commandments
Torah scroll (*Sefer Torah*), 421
Tosafot, 13n17, 486n375, 488nn329–30, 519, 522
Toynbee, Arnold, 72
*Translatio studii*, 38
Vidal of Tolosa (*Maggid Mishneh*), 53n76, 106, 155n182, 164n199, 175n213, 189n2, 236n96, 279–80, 294n125, 309n176, 310n179, 343n51, 429n182, 475n293, 480n312, 522, 525

Wellek, René, 95
Wessely, N. H., 147n164
"Will" of Maimonides, 358n6

*Yad ha-Ḥăzakah* as title for MT, 105, 527
*Yad Mal'aki*, 158n189
*Yĕfat to'ar* (beautiful [captive] woman), 446n219
Yefet of Acco, 75
*Yĕsodot* (*uṣūl*), 44, 261n47, 360n10, 510; defined, 361, 362n12; *Yĕsode hat-Torah*, 361; *Yĕsodot gufe Torah*, 361, 500, 504, 510
Yom Ṭob ben Abraham Ishbili (RIṬBA), 168n204, 252n33, 319n202, 363n17, 403n122, 431n187, 432n190, 488n329, 495n352, 517
Yom Ṭob Lipman Heller (*Ma'ădane Yom Ṭob, Tosafot Yom Ṭob*), 347n65, 534–35
*Zaken mamreh*, 228
Zechariah, R., 207
*Zedim*: term applied to Karaites, 85
Zerahiah ben Shealtiel, 352n77, 362n13
Zerahiah hal-Levi (*Sefer ham-Ma'or*), 13n17, 168, 175n213, 195, 236n96, 316n193, 319n202, 524

# INDEX OF MAIMONIDEAN PASSAGES

**MISHNEH TORAH**
Introduction  13n17, 29, 42n53, 49n67, 50n70, 62n102, 64n108, 66n113, 78n148, 82n153, 85n159, 89n166, 97n2, 129n100, 159n191, 188n1, 229n85, 232n90, 233, 241n7, 252n34, 256n39, 275n75, 337n33, 473n290, 476n301, 493n343

**I. Sefer Madda'**
**1. Yĕsode hat-Torah**
i–iv  341n48, 351
i,1  199
i,5  448n224
i,6  261n47
i,9  366n31
ii,1  210n52, 364n18, 471n284
ii,1–2  216n63
ii,2  478n308
ii,7  351n74
ii,10  361n10
ii,12  470
iii,5  216n64, 368n33, 382n68
iii,12  466n266
iv,12  216n63, 362n14, 364n18
iv,13  62n102, 65n111, 78n147, 110n34, 345n62, 359n7, 374n49, 406n130, 417n148, 418, 430n183, 443n211, 470n281, 493, 501n374, 507
v,1–6  484n322
v,4  487n326
v,10  430n183
v,11  5n6, 54n86, 135n123, 428–29, 466n264, 468
vi,8  58n93, 408n132, 429n182
vii–x  351
vii  455n239

vii,1  65n111, 239n2, 435n195, 466
vii,4  68n117
vii,7  51n390
ix  455n239
ix,1  234n92, 488n331
ix,4  54n86
x,4  111n43

**II. De'ot**
i  341n48
i,5  287n110, 462
i,6  405n128
i,7  370n40, 417n148, 426n177
i,8  370n40
ii,2  460, 461
ii,4  324n1, 339n42, 409n135, 496
ii,5  337n32, 496
iii,1  53n76, 54n86, 429n181, 431n186, 467, 480n312
iii,2  280n89, 466n263
iii,3  420
iii,4  145n160
iii,15  145n160
iii,19  145n160
iv,1  216n65
iv,2  110n33
iv,15  57n90
iv,19  466n261
iv,20  2n2, 216n65, 366n28
iv,21  2n2, 59n97, 94n172
iv,23  294n123
v  468n271
v,1  150n172, 424n172
v,4  435n195
v,5  417n148, 435n195
v,8  150n172
v,11  417n148
v,12  369n39
v,13  5n6, 135n123, 428n180
vi,1  480n312
vi,2  287n110
vi,4  430n183
vi,8  280n91

622

# INDEX OF PASSAGES 623

| | | | |
|---|---|---|---|
| vii,1 | 7, 443n210 | | 447n306 |
| vii,4 | 145n160 | i,1 | 430n183, 478n307 |
| vii,7 | 146n163, 206, 374n49, 396n100, 417n148, 419, 443, 471n284 | i,2 | 146n163, 449, 513n395 |
| | | i,3 | 451, 486n324 |
| | | ii,1 | 306n167 |
| vii,8 | 419, 443n210 | ii,3 | 430n183 |
| **III. Talmud Torah** | | ii,4 | 261n47, 431n185 |
| i,3 | 320n205, 501n375 | ii,5 | 361n12, 430n183 |
| i,5 | 466n260 | ii,6 | 282n94, 283 |
| i,9 | 110n28 | iv | 57n90 |
| i,8 | 501n375 | iv,6 | 308n172, 478n307 |
| i,9 | 114n58 | vi,1 | 55n84 |
| i,10 | 501n375 | vi,6 | 431n186 |
| i,11 | 5n6, 78n147, 93n170, 395n97, 489, 500n371, 536 | ix,1 | 306n167 |
| | | ix,4 | 404n123 |
| | | x,1 | 85n159 |
| i,12 | 5n6, 78n147, 150n171, 205n40, 395n97, 489, 500n371, 536 | x,7 | 70n124 |
| | | xi,1 | 417n148, 431n186 |
| | | xi,2 | 481n314 |
| i,13 | 65n111, 114n58, 374n49, 429n182, 493n343 | xi,11 | 481n314 |
| | | xi,12 | 125n88, 419, 481, 483n319 |
| ii,3 | 172n211 | | |
| ii,7 | 165n200 | xi,15 | 431n185 |
| iii,1–2 | 114n61, 177 | xi,16 | 412, 420n158, 470n277, 478n307, 480n312, 482 |
| iii,3 | 114n61 | | |
| iii,5 | 177 | xii,1 | 306n167, 431n186 |
| iii,6 | 114n61, 177, 454n238 | xii,6 | 112n49 |
| iii,8 | 114n58, 114n61, 178 | xii,13 | 294n122 |
| iii,10 | 5n6, 60, 61, 114n59, 125n88, 178, 340n47, 453n236, 480n312, 503n379 | **V. Teshubah** | |
| | | i,1 | 332n19 |
| | | i,2 | 212n58 |
| | | ii,2 | 332n19 |
| iii,11 | 430n183 | ii,4 | 94n173 |
| iii,12 | 114n61, 145n160, 178 | ii,10 | 425n173 |
| iii,13 | 114n61, 179, 409n135, 419 | iii,1–2 | 444n213 |
| | | iii,4 | 292n118, 419, 472n286 |
| v,1 | 314 | iii,5 | 430n183 |
| v,4 | 173n212 | iii,6 | 153n77 |
| v,7 | 55n87 | iii,7 | 55n84, 478n307, 487n327 |
| v,13 | 111n40, 114n60, 210n53 | iii,8 | 85n159, 430n183 |
| vi,3 | 5n6, 135n123 | iii,11 | 130n103 |
| vi,11 | 409n135 | iv,2 | 408n133, 409n135 |
| vi,12 | 295n127 | iv,4 | 466n261 |
| vii,1 | 111n41 | iv,5 | 213n59, 417n148 |
| vii,13 | 111n41 | v–viii | 351 |
| **IV. 'Akum** | | v | 390n84 |
| i | 150n171, 226n80, 389n81, 431n185, 455n239, 457n244, | v,1 | 344n57, 369n40, 414n142, 480n312 |
| | | v,2 | 125n88, 136n125, 239n2, |

# INDEX OF PASSAGES

**Tĕšuḇah** (*continued*)
    417n148, 470n276
v,4   136n125
v,5   136n125, 410, 452n235, 497n363
vi,1   136n125
vi,5   213n59
vii,2   136n125
vii,4   136n132, 456
vii,7   417n148
vii,8   293
viii,1   430n183
viii,2   43n55, 366n31
viii,3   417n148
viii,4   366n31
viii,6   414n142, 419
viii,8   470n276
ix,1   176, 228n83, 341, 380n64, 417n148, 419, 430n183, 475n294, 476n299, 501n375
ix,2   67n116, 430n183, 477, 512
x   216n63, 359n7
x,1   112n47, 469n275, 482n316
x,2   145n159, 226n80, 262n49, 364n18
x,3   478
x,4   111n41, 469n275
x,5   470n280
x,6   54n86, 87n163, 261n47, 262n49, 362n14, 394n95

**II. Sefer 'Ahăḇah**
**I. Ḳĕri'aṭ Šĕma'**
i,2   261n47, 394n95
i,4   146n163, 151n174, 177
i,7   144n153, 313
ii,8   134n118
ii,9   144n153
ii,10   324n1, 328n14
iii,4   287n109, 293n119, 324n1, 334n23
iii,5   293n119, 324n1, 334n23
iii,6   10n12
iv,8   132n110

**II. Tĕfillah**
i   453n236

i,1   105n19, 350n71
i,2   492n342
i,1–4   177
i,4   9n8, 224, 328n14, 348n68
i,19   144n155
ii,1   110n29, 113n54
ii,16   127n95
iii,7   280n89
iv   310n181
iv,4   110n26, 466n261
iv,5   111n41, 370n40
iv,6   132nn110–11
iv,15–19   453n236
iv,18   66n114, 101n8
v   310n181
v,5   428n180, 429n182
v,6   235n93
v,14   213n59
v,15   127n96
vi,1   421n162
vi,7   349n70, 473n289
vii,9   127n96, 133n114
vii,10–11   491n337
vii,11–13   127n96
vii,15   430n183
vii,18   134n119
viii,2   362n14
ix,7   301n153
xi   310n179
xi,4   130n102
xi,5   131n105
xii,1   111n44
xii,8   132n112
xii,10   110n26
xiii,1   110n26, 126n90, 127n95
xiii,5   429n182
xiii,6   438n200
xiii,11   162n197
xiv–xv   295n129
xiv,6   110n30
xiv,10   110n27
xiv,13   293n119
xv,1   310n181, 349n69
xv,6   429n182
xv,7   344n57

**IIIa. Tĕfillin**
i,3   310n181
i,13   429n182, 430n183
i,19   231n87

# INDEX OF PASSAGES

| | | | |
|---|---|---|---|
| ii,11 | 113n55 | viii,14 | 121n75, 127n95 |
| ii,13 | 110n28 | xi,11 | 138n136 |
| iii,5 | 125n89 | xi,12 | 138n136 |
| iii,6 | 53n77 | xi,16 | 146n163 |
| iii,8 | 53n78 | VI. *Milah* | |
| iii,10 | 53n78 | i,18 | 162n197 |
| iii,19 | 134n120 | ii,1 | 85n159 |
| iv,14 | 287n109 | iii,1 | 123n83, 127n95 |
| iv,25 | 110nn32–33, 113n56, | iii,9 | 153n177 |
| | 387n109, 409n135, 421 | III. *Sefer Zĕmannim* | |
| v,5 | 419n153 | I. *Šabbat* | |
| IIIb. *Mĕzuzah* | | i,7 | 53n80, 169n205 |
| v,4 | 125n88, 324n1, 369n40, | ii,1 | 344n58, 484 |
| | 396n101, 480 | ii,2 | 344n58, 484 |
| v,7 | 292 | ii,3 | 85n159, 143n148, |
| vi,4 | 481n314 | | 344n58, 430n183, |
| vi,13 | 292n118, 421, 481 | | 432n190, 484 |
| IIIc. *Sefer Torah* | | ii,4 | 431n186 |
| vii,10 | 111n43, 112n46 | ii,22 | 287n109 |
| vii,16 | 313 | ii,24 | 227n81 |
| viii,4 | 54n83, 111n36, 119n68, | iii,8 | 125n89 |
| | 282n95, 343n55 | viii,8 | 349n70 |
| ix,10 | 119n68 | x,10 | 349n70 |
| x,1 | 310n181 | xii,8 | 362n12 |
| x,2 | 287n109 | xix,8 | 488n330 |
| x,10 | 287n109, 324n1 | xix,14 | 481n314 |
| x,11 | 114n58, 141n145, | xix,20 | 343n51 |
| | 287n109, 324n1, 421 | xxiii,24 | 58n93 |
| IV. *Ṣiṣit* | | xxiv,1 | 164n198 |
| i,6 | 53n79 | xxiv,12 | 164n198, 177 |
| i,9 | 126n91 | xxiv,13 | 164n198, 177 |
| i,17 | 111n42 | xxv,13 | 8n8 |
| iii,9 | 287n109 | xxviii,17 | 217n66 |
| iii,11 | 152n176 | xxix,14 | 120n73, 121n77 |
| iii,12 | 134n121, 152n176 | xxix,29 | 162n197 |
| V. *Bĕrakot* | | xxx,2 | 111n41 |
| i,3 | 284n98, 422 | xxx,6 | 114n57 |
| i,4 | 284n98, 313 | xxx,10 | 111n41 |
| i,5 | 313 | xxx,15 | 164n199, 431n185 |
| i,6 | 334n23 | II. *'Erubin* | |
| i,13 | 430n183 | i,4 | 111n45, 155n182, |
| i,17 | 111n42 | | 429n182 |
| ii,4 | 121n75 | i,6 | 162n197 |
| ii,10 | 315n190 | i,13 | 136n129 |
| ii,11 | 315n190 | i,16 | 145n156 |
| vi,1 | 280n89 | ii,16 | 85n159 |
| vi,2 | 86n160 | III. *Šĕbitat 'Aśor* | |
| vii,4 | 134n119 | i,3 | 131n109 |
| viii,5 | 121n76 | i,4 | 158n190 |

# INDEX OF PASSAGES

Šĕḇiṭaṯ 'Aśor (continued)
| | |
|---|---|
| ii,8 | 55n87, 484n322 |
| iii,3 | 132n110 |
| iii,10 | 127n95 |

IV. Yom Ṭoḇ
| | |
|---|---|
| i,14 | 169n205 |
| i,20 | 473n289 |
| i,24 | 138n136 |
| ii,12 | 124n85, 145n160 |
| iii,8 | 169n205 |
| iv,9 | 469n273 |
| vi,2 | 162n197, 300n151 |
| vi,16 | 263n50, 287n109 |
| vi,17 | 212n56, 263n50 |
| vi,18 | 150n172, 177, 423, 480n312 |
| vi,22 | 280n89 |
| vi,24 | 144n150 |
| vii,1 | 287n109 |
| vii,12 | 162n197 |

V. Ḥameṣ u-Maṣṣah
| | |
|---|---|
| v,3 | 131n109 |
| v,7 | 131n169 |
| v,17 | 130n102 |
| vi,12 | 54n86 |
| vii | 299n149 |
| vii,1 | 53n76, 319n204 |
| vii,2 | 420n158, 455n239 |
| viii,8 | 127n95, 169n205 |

VIa. Šofar
| | |
|---|---|
| iii,4 | 169n205 |
| iii,10 | 131n106 |

VIb. Sukkah
| | |
|---|---|
| vi,11 | 319n202 |
| vi,12 | 120n72 |

VIc. Lulaḇ
| | |
|---|---|
| vii,15 | 110n30 |
| vii,23 | 131n106 |
| viii,14 | 180 |
| viii,15 | 54n86, 181, 190n7, 210n52, 262n49, 370n40, 414n141, 422 |

VII. Šĕḳalim
| | |
|---|---|
| i,3 | 111n44 |
| i,4 | 136n128, 279n87 |
| i,8 | 298n141 |
| ii,10 | 134n123, 144n154 |
| iii,9 | 121n75 |

VIII. Ḳidduš ha-Ḥodeš

| | |
|---|---|
| iii,6 | 110n30 |
| iv,9 | 213n60 |
| v,3 | 110n34, 111n42 |
| vi,1 | 144n151 |
| vi,14 | 136n125 |
| viii,9 | 136n125 |
| ix,1 | 122n79 |
| xi,1 | 218n67 |
| xi,2 | 218n67 |
| xi,3 | 59n95, 218n67, 498n366 |
| xi,4 | 136n125, 218n67, 298n142 |
| xi,5 | 414n142, 507n386 |
| xi,6 | 507n386 |
| xi,8 | 136n125 |
| xi,16 | 28n41 |
| xvii,24 | 368n33 |
| xvii,25 | 59n97, 218n67, 382n68, 498n366 |
| xviii,6 | 111n43 |
| xviii,14 | 165n200 |
| xviii,16 | 298n142 |
| xix,13 | 190n5 |
| xix,16 | 471n284 |

IX. Ta'āniyyoṯ
| | |
|---|---|
| i,1–3 | 145n158, 422n168 |
| i,3 | 303n160 |
| i,14 | 309n176 |
| ii,3 | 155n180 |
| iv | 299n150 |
| iv,1–3 | 180 |
| v,1 | 422n168 |
| v,2 | 429n182 |
| v,3 | 280n91, 343n53, 430n183 |
| v,6 | 127n95 |
| v,9 | 119n69, 468n272, 343n55 |
| v,14 | 162n197, 250n29 |

Xa. Mĕġillah
| | |
|---|---|
| i,5 | 162n197, 165n201 |
| ii,12 | 429n182 |
| ii,17 | 287n110, 426 |
| iii | 240n5 |

Xb. Ḥănukkah
| | |
|---|---|
| ii,1 | 223n77 |
| iii,3 | 297n137 |
| iii,6 | 294n124, 339n43 |
| iii,14 | 126n93 |
| iv,3 | 131n108 |
| iv,14 | 158n190 |

| | | | |
|---|---|---|---|
| v,14 | 120n71 | xiii,29 | 136n131, 344n57 |

IV. *Sefer Našim*

I. *'Išuṭ*

III. *Yibbum*

| | | | |
|---|---|---|---|
| | | intro. | 145n156 |
| i,2 | 145n156 | iv,5 | 313 |
| ii,12 | 53n79 | vi,8 | 279n86 |
| ii,21 | 213n60 | vi,27 | 169n205 |
| ii,27 | 136n126, 279n87 | viii,12–13 | 140n140 |
| iii,23 | 123n84 | xi,22 | 137n134 |
| iv,7 | 347n64 | | |

IV. *Naʻărah Bĕṯulah*

| | | | |
|---|---|---|---|
| v,15 | 122n80 | i,13 | 353n80 |
| vi,13 | 130n132, 137n134, 343n54 | V. *Soṭah* | |
| | | iii,7 | 334n23 |
| vi,14 | 83n153, 123n83 | iii,19 | 263n51, 299n146 |
| viii,4 | 110n34, 491n337 | | |

V. *Sefer Kĕḏušah*

I. *'Issure Bi'ah*

| | | | |
|---|---|---|---|
| viii,5 | 110n31, 110n34 | i,10 | 145n156 |
| x,3 | 315n190 | ii,6 | 158n190 |
| x,4 | 127n95 | iii,13 | 189n2 |
| xi,13 | 111n43, 116n63, 241n7 | vii,12 | 136n130 |
| xii,5 | 289n114 | vii,14 | 136n130 |
| xiv,14 | 111n43, 130nn101–02 | xi,3 | 111n42 |
| xiv,15 | 466n260 | xi,5 | 127n95, 130n102, 131n107 |
| xv,2–3 | 466n260 | | |
| xv,13 | 110n34 | xi,6 | 111n42, 127n95 |
| xv,20 | 435n195 | xi,7 | 112n53, 127n95, 131n107 |
| xvi,9 | 140n143 | xi,15 | 85n159, 124n86, 133n116, 344n58, 430n183 |
| xvii,8 | 8n8 | | |
| xviii,19 | 169n205 | | |
| xviii,28 | 169n205 | | |
| xx,6–7 | 214n62 | xi,16 | 299n148, 280n89 |
| xxiii,11 | 127n97 | xii–xiv | 295n129 |
| xxv,2 | 112n52, 156n185, 414n142, 432n187, 471n285 | xii,1 | 110n26 |
| | | xii,7 | 443n210 |
| | | xii,13 | 58n92, 443n210 |
| | | xii,23 | 110n26, 111n45, 116n26 |

II. *Gerušin*

| | | | |
|---|---|---|---|
| i,1 | 155n181, 310n180 | xii,24 | 425 |
| i,16 | 123n83 | xiii,8 | 158n190 |
| i,24 | 162n197 | xiii,9 | 132n111 |
| i,27 | 130n102 | xiii,14 | 145n160, 227n81, 405n128 |
| ii,7 | 136n127 | | |
| ii,20 | 143n148, 162n197, 417n148, 487 | xiv,2 | 425, 474n292, 475n295 |
| | | xiv,3 | 78n147, 430n183, 475n294 |
| iii,8 | 121n78, 123n83, 171n207 | | |
| iii,19 | 294n125 | xiv,5 | 212n57 |
| iv,11 | 130n102 | xiv,7 | 213n59 |
| viii,4 | 344n60 | xv,29 | 156n183 |
| ix,25 | 160n193 | xix,17 | 425 |
| ix,31 | 116n63 | xx,14 | 110n32 |
| x,1–3 | 137n134 | xx,17 | 139n139 |
| x,21 | 369n39 | xxi | 435n195 |

## INDEX OF PASSAGES

'Issure Bi'ah (continued)
xxi,8 446n219
xxi,11 134n122, 466n261
xxi,19 419n157, 496n358
xxi,24 111n41
xxi,31 481n314
xxii 435n195
xxii,3 110n28
xxii,11 279n86
xxii,20 111n41, 417n148, 432n189
xxii,21 417n148, 496n358
xxi,24 419n157

II. Ma'ăkalot 'Ăsurot
i,24 235n93
iii,1 121n75
iii,13 111n42, 343n51
iv,8 136n131
iv,12 134n119
vi,7 130n102
vi,19 145n156
vii,9 121n75
viii,15–16 158n190
ix,1–2 158n190
ix,4 314
x,1 278n84
x,8 278n84
x,9 317n197
x,10 278n84
x,15 156n184
x,18 150n184, 343n54
x,22 317n197
x,23 278n84
x,24 317n197
xi,3 317n196
xi,7 404n123
xi,10 110n35
xiv,13–15 484n322
xiv,18 158n190
xv,12 136n131
xv,29 279n86
xvi,9 432n187
xvii,12 131n107
xvii,28 435n195
xvii,29 459n248
xvii,30 435n195, 459n248

III. Šĕḥiṭah
i,4 85n159, 213n59
iii,7 136n130

iv,14 213n59, 430n183
iv,16 85n159
iv,17,18 232n88
vi,13 333n20
viii,16 56n88
x,9 310n181
x,12 94n172, 483n321
xi,6 122n81
xi,7 111n42
xi,10 117n66
xi,11 9n8, 126n92
xi,15 125n88
xiii,1 282n95, 290
xiv,6 436
xiv,15 418
xiv,16 78n146, 262n49, 374n49

VI. Sefer Hafla'ah
I. Šĕḇu'ot
i,4 316n191
i,5 313
i,6 344n56
iv,3 317n198
iv,4 318n198
v,22 313, 469n274
vii,7 334n23
viii,9 214n62, 297n138
x,10 214n62, 297n138
xi,1 304n164
xi,2 304n163
xi,3 265
xi,6 214n62
xi,8 343n53
xi,14 324n1, 334n23
xii,2 212n58, 213n59, 443n210
xii,12 57n91, 85n159, 344n58

II. Nĕḏarim
i,1–2 278
i,3–4 285n104
i,16 349n69
i,26 265n54
ii,4 121n75
ii,6 121n75
ii,14 282n95, 285
iii,1 310n181
iii,8 57n91, 136n132
iii,9 294n125
vi,8 366n28
ix,13 136n132
xii,23 265n54, 417n148,

## INDEX OF PASSAGES

|  |  |  |  |
|---|---|---|---|
|  | 432n188, 467 | xi,5 | 334n23 |
| xiii,24–25 | 306n166 | xi,15 | 426 |
| xiii,33 | 461n253 | xi,17 | 486n325 |
| III. *Nězirut* |  | VI. *Bikkurim* |  |
| i,1 | 282n95, 285 | i,7 | 136n130 |
| ii,11 | 279n86 | i,12 | 279n85 |
| v,2–3 | 317n195 | ii,1 | 299n147 |
| x,14 | 265n54, 285n103, | iv,3 | 485n323 |
|  | 287n109, 306n166, 468 | vii,9 | 319n202 |
| IV. *'Ărakin* |  | x,17 | 116n64 |
| i,1 | 282n95, 285n105 | xi,6 | 299n147 |
| vi,33 | 57n90, 146n163 | VII. *Šĕmiṭṭah wĕ-Yobel* |  |
| viii,12 | 432n188 | ix,8 | 10n12 |
| viii,13 | 369n39, 417n148 | ix,17 | 110n34 |
| VII. *Sefer Zěra'im* |  | ix,22 | 16n21 |
| I. *Kil'ayim* |  | x,4 | 28n41 |
| ii,9 | 160n193 | x,5 | 111n43 |
| v,20 | 138n137 | x,6 | 130n104 |
| x,27 | 214n62 | xii,16 | 207n48, 451n233 |
| x,29 | 353n79 | xiii,12 | 379n63, 442 |
| II. *Mattěnot 'Ăniyyim* |  | xiii,13 | 442 |
| i,14 | 111n43 | VIII. *Sefer 'Ăbodah* |  |
| viii,1 | 282n95 | I. *Bet hab-Běḥirah* |  |
| viii,10 | 340n45 | i,3 | 267 |
| ix,2 | 145n156 | i,13 | 436 |
| ix,3 | 120n70 | i,17 | 306n168 |
| ix,10 | 134n123 | ii,2 | 153n178 |
| x,1 | 181, 426, 430n183 | ii,3 | 207n48 |
| x,2 | 181, 426 | vi,12 | 267n59 |
| x,3 | 54n82 | vi,13 | 287n109 |
| x,4 | 182, 426 | vi,16 | 214n62, 267, 483n319 |
| x,5 | 182 | vii | 434n193 |
| x,7 | 311n182 | vii,1 | 262n49 |
| x,8 | 110nn31,34 | viii | 434n193 |
| x,18 | 5n6 | II. *Kĕle ham-Miķdaš* |  |
| III. *Tĕrumot* |  | i,1 | 111n42, 149n168, 231n87 |
| ix,10 | 214n62 | i,2 | 488n331 |
| x,25 | 214n62 | ii,4 | 144n152, 333n21 |
| xii,2 | 214n62 | iii,1–3 | 155n181 |
| xii,11 | 214n62 | iii,8 | 232n88 |
| xii,18–19 | 428n180 | iii,9–10 | 111n45 |
| xiv,21 | 214n62 | iii,19 | 154n179 |
| xv,19 | 156n187 | iv,1–3 | 154n179 |
| xv,22 | 112n51 | iv,2 | 287n109 |
| IV. *Ma'ăśer* |  | vi,11 | 280n91 |
| ix,1 | 110n27 | viii,2 | 144n152 |
| V. *Ma'ăśer Šeni* |  | x,2 | 58n92 |
| ii,5 | 317n195 | x,13 | 149n168 |
| ix,12 | 124n86 | III. *Bi'at Miķdaš* |  |

# INDEX OF PASSAGES

| i,3 | 85n159, 293n121 |
|---|---|
| i,4 | 100n8, 293n121 |
| i,12 | 280n91 |
| iii,8 | 301n153 |
| iv,2 | 280n91 |
| v,14 | 317n194 |
| vii–viii | 310n181 |
| viii,7 | 55n84 |
| ix,13 | 235n93 |
| ix,14 | 235n93 |

IV. *'Issure Mizbeaḥ*

| i,11 | 287n109 |
|---|---|
| v,1 | 121n77 |
| vii,11 | 417n148, 426n175, 429n182, 432n188, 433 |

V. *Ma'áśeh haḳ-Ḳorbanot*

| i,5–6 | 267n57 |
|---|---|
| ii,14 | 207n48, 232n88 |
| ii,15 | 232n88 |
| iii,7 | 279n86 |
| v,2 | 214n62 |
| viii,11 | 235n93 |
| ix,5 | 267 |
| ix,25 | 214n62 |
| x,15 | 57n91, 155n182 |
| xii,1 | 282n95 |
| xviii,4 | 158n190 |

VI. *Těmidin u-Musafin*

| i,10 | 306n168, 431n186 |
|---|---|
| iv,3 | 13n17 |
| vii | 344n58 |
| vii,11 | 55n87, 85n159, 112n53, 145n157, 227n81, 369n40 |
| vii,22 | 299n143 |

VII. *Pěsule ham-Muḳdašin*

| iii,8 | 287n109 |
|---|---|

VIII. *'Ăḇodat Yom haḳ-Ḳippurim*

| i,7 | 85n159 |
|---|---|

IX. *Mě'ilah*

| viii,8 | 78n148, 176, 190n7, 374n49, 378n59, 394n95, 400, 407–08, 413, 430n183, 432n190 |
|---|---|

IX. *Sefer Ḳorbanot*

I. *Ḳorban Pesaḥ*

| v,5 | 349n70 |
|---|---|
| vi,7 | 212n57 |

II. *Ḥăḡiḡah*

| ii,10 | 214n62 |
|---|---|
| ii,14 | 423 |
| iii,1 | 210n52 |
| iii,5 | 334n23 |
| iii,6 | 210n52, 421n164 |
| iii,14 | 212n56 |

III. *Běḵorot*

| intro. | 267n58, 282n95, 285–86 |
|---|---|

IV. *Šěḡaḡot*

| i,4 | 279n85 |
|---|---|
| ii,5 | 349n70 |
| iii,10 | 408n132 |
| vi,4 | 158n190 |

VI. *Těmurah*

| iv,13 | 78n146, 176, 374n49, 400n112, 416, 417n148 |
|---|---|

X. *Ṭohărah*

II. *Parah 'Ădumah*

| i,14 | 85n159 |
|---|---|
| i,15 | 85n159 |
| iii,4 | 207n48, 451n233 |
| x,5 | 85n159 |
| xiii,2 | 110n34 |

III. *Ṭume'at Ṣara'at*

| vi,10 | 261n47 |
|---|---|
| x,6 | 58n92 |
| x,7 | 447n220 |
| xvi,10 | 176, 282n95, 349n70, 351n75, 374n49, 409, 419n157, 430n183, 447n220, 468n271, 488n331, 496n360 |

IV. *Meṭamme' Miškaḇ u-Mošaḇ*

| vi,1 | 337n36 |
|---|---|
| vi,15 | 136n125 |
| vii,8 | 279n86 |

V. *'Aḇot haṭ-Ṭume'ot*

| ii,10 | 156n183 |
|---|---|
| iv,8 | 280n89 |
| ix,6 | 145n159 |
| xii,1 | 311n182 |
| xii,7 | 288n111 |

VI. *Ṭume'at 'Oḵlin*

| xvi,12 | 287n110, 374n49, 435 |
|---|---|

VII. *Kelim*

| x,15 | 144n154 |
|---|---|
| xiii,1 | 189n2 |

VIII. *Miḵwa'ot*

# INDEX OF PASSAGES

| | | | |
|---|---|---|---|
| i,8 | 269n61, 435n194 | V. Roṣeaḥ | |
| ii,16 | 110n26 | i,4 | 296n133, 429n182, 472n287 |
| iv,9 | 110n38, 122n81 | | |
| xi,1 | 213n61 | i,9 | 430n183, 488n331 |
| xi,12 | 176, 269, 288n11, 374n49, 434–35, 472n288 | i,11 | 484n322 |
| | | i,16 | 443n210 |
| | | ii,8 | 94n172 |

**XI. Sefer Nĕziḳin**

**I. Nizḳe Mamon**

| | | | |
|---|---|---|---|
| | | ii,14 | 308n172, 430n182 |
| | | iii,4 | 308n172 |
| i,1 | 53n76 | iv,8 | 444 |
| v,3 | 111n44 | iv,9 | 148n166, 177, 296n133, 340n46, 444 |
| v,4 | 111n45 | | |
| viii,5 | 162n197, 414n142, 429n182 | v,4 | 213n61 |
| | | vii,1 | 78n147, 476n298 |
| xii,8 | 169n205 | viii,8 | 476n298 |
| xiii,22 | 111n41 | ix,12 | 299n145 |

**II. Gĕnebah**

| | | | |
|---|---|---|---|
| | | x,2 | 445n217 |
| i,4 | 162n197 | xi,4–5 | 296n134 |
| i,10 | 162n197, 429n182 | xii,4 | 479n311 |
| vii,7 | 111n44 | xii,5,6 | 235n93 |
| vii,9 | 147n164 | xii,7 | 484n322 |
| vii,12 | 429n182, 444–45 | xii,8 | 149n167 |
| viii,1 | 59n97, 217n66, 476n298 | xii,12 | 432n190 |
| viii,2 | 217n66 | xiii,4 | 468n272 |
| ix | 310n179 | xiii,14 | 261n47, 289n115 |

**III. Gĕzelah wa-'Ăbedah**

**XII. Sefer Ḳinyan**

**I. Mĕkirah**

| | | | |
|---|---|---|---|
| i,4 | 488n329 | v,7 | 212n57 |
| i,9,10 | 487n327 | vii,8 | 134n122 |
| i,11,13 | 270 | vii,12 | 212n57, 216n63 |
| iv,11 | 297n138 | x,5 | 297n138 |
| iv,13 | 8n8 | xi,12 | 114n58 |
| v,10 | 135n123 | xi,13 | 333n20 |
| vi,11 | 78n147, 474 | xi,18 | 55n87, 111n37, 121n73 |
| xi,2 | 296n132, 430n183 | xiii,1 | 10n12 |
| xi,7 | 468 | xiv,12 | 293n120 |
| xi,17 | 135n124, 468 | xiv,14 | 368n35, 476n298 |
| xii,2 | 314, 317n194 | xxii,15 | 116n65, 434n192 |
| xvi,7 | 182 | xxii,17 | 116n65 |
| xvi,8 | 183 | xxvii,11 | 136n124 |

**IV. Ḥobel u-Mazziḳ**

**II. Zĕkiyyah u-Mattanah**

| | | | |
|---|---|---|---|
| i,6 | 57n91, 112n53, 301n153, 437n198, 448n224 | iii,5 | 8n8 |
| | | iii,8 | 83n153, 122n80 |
| iii,6 | 111n37 | vii,1 | 130n102 |
| iii,7 | 280n91, 443n210 | vii,4 | 349n70 |
| iv,8 | 162n197 | viii,2 | 333n20 |
| v,10 | 425n173 | viii,18 | 137n134 |
| v,13 | 162n197, 345n62 | x,2 | 169n205 |
| vii,19 | 297n138 | xii,17 | 5n6, 111n41, 480n312 |
| viii,9 | 280n91 | | |

# INDEX OF PASSAGES

Zĕkiyyah u-Mattanah (*continued*)
xiv,7   297n138
III. *Sĕkenim*
iv,13   110n35
vi,6   483n319
IV. *Šĕluḥin wĕ-Šutafin*
iii,7   123n83, 343n54
vi,5   122n80
V. *'Ăbadim*
vi,5   214n62
vi,6   85n159, 162n197
vii,6   189n2, 280n89
viii,10   439
viii,11   293n120
ix,8   146n163, 427

XIII. *Sefer Mišpaṭim*
I. *Šĕkirut*
ii,3   122n80, 343n52
v,8   139n139
x,11   8n8
xiii,7   57n90, 146nn162–63
II. *Šĕ'elah u-Fikkadon*
v,6   81n9, 111n39
vi,4   140n141
III. *Malweh wĕ-Loweh*
i,3   114n58
ii,1–2   221–23
ii,4   140n143, 141n144
iii,1   488n332
iv,1   144n149
v,8   134n122
vi,7   111n43, 156n183
xi,10   111n38
xi,11   110n35
xiv,13   111n39
xv,1   94n172, 366n28, 483n321
xv,2   111n43, 115n62
xvi,4   214n62
xviii,1   144n149
xxi,1   122n80
xxi,3   8n8
xxiii,2   141n144
xxv,13   110n35, 122n80
xxv,14   117n66, 122n80
xxvi,11   110n35, 123n83
xxvii,1   111n39, 122n80
IV. *Ṭo'en wĕ-Niṭ'an*
iii,2   111n39
viii,9   136n131

viii,10   110n34, 123n83, 343n54
ix,1   343n54
ix,7   138n137, 448n224
ix,8   138n137
xii,12   55n87
xiv,2   297n138
xiv,7   175n213
V. *Naḥălot*
vi,1   289n114
vi,11   134n122
vi,12   112n48, 114n59
vi,13   146n163
vii,3   112n50, 121n74
x,7   129n100
xi,12   134n123

XIV. *Sefer Šofeṭim*
I. *Sanhedrin*
i,3   83n154, 162n197, 163n197
ii   341n58
ii,1–7   141n146, 147n164, 177
ii,1   122n79, 219n70, 272n67, 368n33, 476n298
ii,6   347n64
ii,7   428n180, 445n215
iii,5   289n114
iii,7   272n67, 476n298
iii,8   147n164, 429n182
iii,9   429n182
iii,10   111n41
iv,1   111n44, 117n67
iv,2   117n67
iv,5   110n28
iv,11   117n67
iv,15   429n182
v,1   280n91, 316n191
vi,9   112n48
xi,5   420n158
xii,3   111n4, 183
xiv,10   140n143
xiv,12   154n179, 296n135
xv   155n180
xv,8   293n119
xviii,6   163n197, 280n91, 472
xix   310n181
xx,1   398n107
xx,4   272, 296n135
xx,7   370n40
xxi,1   272n69

# INDEX OF PASSAGES 633

| | | | |
|---|---|---|---|
| xxi,5 | 111n43, 112n50 | vi,15 | 59n95 |
| xxi,11 | 140n143, 272n69 | IV. *'Aḇel* | |
| xxii,10 | 293n119 | intro. | 282n95, 286 |
| xxiii,1 | 139n138 | i,1 | 234n92, 455n239 |
| xxiii,3 | 139n138 | iii,12 | 435n195 |
| xxiii,5 | 5n6 | iv,1 | 130n102 |
| xxiv,2 | 129n100 | iv,2 | 134n121, 306n169, 370n40, 431n186, 480n312 |
| xxiv,4 | 487n328 | | |
| xxiv,5 | 110n26, 428n180 | | |
| xxiv,6 | 429n182 | iv,7 | 134n121 |
| xxiv,10 | 5n6, 135n123, 141n145, 272n67 | iv,9 | 155n180 |
| | | v | 310n179 |
| xxv,1 | 5n6 | v,1 | 155n180, 185 |
| xxv,4 | 125n88 | v,3–7 | 185 |
| xxvi,1,2 | 440n205 | v,15 | 186 |
| xxvi,7 | 283n96 | v,18 | 155n180 |
| II. *'Edut* | | v,19–20 | 186 |
| v,1 | 297n138 | vi | 310n179 |
| vi,4 | 59n95, 112n50 | xiii,3 | 162n197 |
| ix,3 | 279n86 | xiii,10 | 110n32, 239n2 |
| ix,9 | 370n40, 488n331 | xiii,11 | 430n183 |
| ix,10 | 140n142 | xiii,12 | 439 |
| x,2 | 345n62 | xiv,2 | 426 |
| xi,1–2 | 443n212, 478n307 | xiv,5 | 94n172, 162n197, 308n172, 429n182 |
| xi,3 | 421n163, 443n212, 478n307 | V. *Mĕlaḵim* | |
| xi,4–5 | 443n212, 478n307 | i,3 | 280n91, 316n191 |
| xii,9 | 345n62 | ii,5 | 187, 272n68 |
| xiii,15 | 472n288 | ii,6 | 5n6, 239n2, 272n68, 445n216 |
| xvi,4 | 140n143 | | |
| xvi,5 | 213n60 | iii,5 | 272n68 |
| xvii,1 | 476n298 | iii,6 | 370n40, 466n261 |
| xviii,3 | 472n288 | iii,7 | 272n67 |
| III. *Mamrim* | | iii,10 | 444n213, 445n216, 487n328 |
| i,1 | 234n92 | | |
| i,4 | 98n3 | iv,4 | 345n62 |
| ii,2 | 129n100, 234n92 | iv,8 | 451n233 |
| ii,4 | 114n58, 143n148, 177, 476n301 | iv,10 | 5n6, 62n101, 135n123, 272n68, 445n216 |
| ii,9 | 314 | v,4 | 230n86 |
| iii,1 | 430n183 | v,7 | 31n44 |
| iii,3 | 85n159 | v,11 | 54n86, 146n163, 439n203 |
| iii,4–5 | 299n144 | v,12 | 439n203 |
| iii,7 | 143n148 | vi,1 | 435n195 |
| v | 295n127 | vi,14–15 | 301n153 |
| v,15 | 57n90, 112n52, 148n164, 429n182 | vii,1 | 367n31 |
| | | vii,15 | 152n175, 177, 429n182, 430n183, 487n327 |
| vi,1 | 299n144 | | |
| vi,7 | 472n288 | viii,5 | 446n216 |

## INDEX OF PASSAGES

Mĕlakim (*continued*)
| | | | |
|---|---|---|---|
| viii,8 | 148n165, 227n81 | | 250n29, 324n1, 354n82, 409n135 |
| viii,10 | 229n84, 234n92, 455 | 1:17 | 135n124, 388n80 |
| viii,11 | 430n182, 455 | 2:5 | 337n32, 344n60 |
| ix,1 | 226n80, 227n81, 455n239 | 2:7 | 447n221 |
| ix,14 | 148n165, 227n81 | 2:10 | 463n255 |
| x,12 | 427n179 | 2:12 | 114n58 |
| xi | 341n48 | 2:15 | 400n111 |
| xi,1 | 207n47, 298n140 | 3:11 | 435n195 |
| xi,2 | 280n91 | 3:13 | 395n97 |
| xi,3 | 110n31, 298n140, 343n53, 376n55, 429n182, 430n183 | 3:20 | 360n10 |
| | | 4:4 | 395n97, 409n135, 414n141, 495n355 |
| xi,4 | 298n140, 414nn141–42, 452, 487n328, 501n375, 512 | 4:5 | 362n13 |
| | | 4:6 | 114n58 |
| | | 4:7 | 5n6, 8n9, 83n154, 110n28, 205n41, 503n379 |
| xii,1 | 146n161, 451n231, 479n309 | | |
| xii,2 | 59n96, 437n199 | 4:22 | 430n183 |
| xii,4 | 67n116, 213n59, 477n303 | 5:5 | 366n29, 390n84 |
| xii,5 | 227n82, 261n48, 451 | 5:6 | 360n10, 463n255 |
| xiii,8 | 207n48 | AZ | |
| *PERUŠ HAM-MIŠNAYOṮ* * | | 1:1 | 404n123 |
| Introduction | | 2:5 | 389n83 |
| | 3n3, 7, 8, 9n8, 41n50, 49n67, 50n70, 65n112, 82n153, 89n166, 98n3, 99n5, 110n27, 114n58, 114n61, 161n211, 168n203, 169n205, 219n69, 238n1, 239n2, 240n4, 241nn6–7, 243n12, 245n15, 285n103, 294n125, 296n135, 309n176, 337nn35–36, 338n38, 348n66, 365nn23–24, 368nn34–35, 400n11, 411, 438n200, 488n331, 491n335, 494n348, 496n356, 497n363 | 4:7 | 226n80, 366n27, 389n81, 478n307 |
| | | *Bek* | |
| | | 4:4 | 82n152 |
| | | 4:6 | 503n379 |
| | | 8:8 | 9n8, 112n49 |
| | | 9:3 | 281n91 |
| | | *Ber* | |
| | | 1:1 | 366n31 |
| | | 5:3 | 459n248 |
| | | 7:1 | 236n94 |
| | | 8:8 | 136n128, 362n13 |
| | | 9:3 | 366n31, 374n48, 398n107 |
| | | 9:7 | 33n30, 258n44, 338n39, 360n10, 366n26, 478n307 |
| | | *BK* | |
| | | 4:3 | 366n31 |
| *Ab* | | *BM* | |
| 1:2 | 395n97 | 2:8 | 396n97 |
| 1:3 | 85n159, 366n26, 478n307 | 4:2 | 440n205 |
| 1:5 | 301n154 | 4:8 | 213n61 |
| 1:16 | 73n130, 134n121, | 4:10 | 368n35 |

*Arranged alphabetically, not by order of tractates.

## INDEX OF PASSAGES

| | | | | |
|---|---|---|---|---|
| *'Ed* | | 1:2 | 349n69 | |
| 1:3 | 9n8, 117n66, 349n69 | 3:10 | 153n177 | |
| 1:5–6 | 125n87, 168n203 | 4:3 | 5n6, 503n379 | |
| 2:9 | 473n289 | 4:4 | 366n28, 483n320 | |
| 2:10 | 258n44 | 8:6 | 432n187 | |
| 4:7 | 117n66 | *Neg* | | |
| 8:7 | 336, 451n231 | 12:5 | 366n31, 409n135, | |
| *'Er* | | | 447n220 | |
| 6:2 | 85n159 | *Par* | | |
| *Git* | | 3:9 | 59n95 | |
| 5:7 | 140n141 | *Pe* | | |
| 5:8 | 132n112 | 1:1 | 275n75, 369n39, 442n209 | |
| 9:10 | 369n39 | *Pes* | | |
| *Hag* | | 2:2 | 112n48, 131n107, | |
| 2:1 | 205n40, 361nn11–12, | | 134n117 | |
| | 366n25, 400n11, | 4:10 | 2n2, 366n28, 483n320 | |
| | 403n121, 466n261, | 10:3 | 119n69 | |
| | 501n374 | 10:4 | 226n80, 366n27 | |
| 2:3 | 85n159, 162n197 | *RH* | | |
| 3:2 | 277n82 | 2:7 | 10n10, 190n5, 277n82, | |
| *Hal* | | | 366n31 | |
| 4:9 | 279n85 | 3:6 | 365n32 | |
| *Hul* | | 4:7 | 339n43 | |
| 1:2 | 85n159 | *Sanh* | | |
| 7:6 | 455n239 | 1:3 | 451n231 | |
| *Kel* | | 1:6 | 172n211 | |
| 1:5 | 10n10, 366n31 | 3:3 | 366n31, 374n48, 474n291 | |
| 1:6 | 310n179 | 7:4 | 16n2, 258n44 | |
| 2:1 | 337n32 | 10 | 11n13, 216n63, 277n82, | |
| *Ker* | | | 365n24, 366nn30, 31, | |
| 1:1 | 279n85 | | 374n48, 380n64, | |
| 3:4 | 158n190, 258n44 | | 386n78, 388n80, | |
| 3:5 | 111n43 | | 414n142 | |
| 10:5 | 145n156 | 10:3 | 61n100 | |
| *Mak* | | *Shab* | | |
| 3:6 | 366n31 | 1:1 | 258n44 | |
| 3:17 | 165n200, 216n63, | 4:1 | 241n7 | |
| | 430n183 | 6:2 | 366n28 | |
| *Meg* | | *Shebi* | | |
| 1:1 | 105n201 | 10:5 | 16n21 | |
| 2:1 | 231n87 | *Shebu* | | |
| *Men* | | 1:4 | 61n100, 366n31 | |
| 4:1 | 16n21, 168n203, 236n94 | 6:7 | 9n8, 117n66 | |
| 4:4 | 145n156 | *Sot* | | |
| 13:10 | 110n27 | 1:6 | 11n12, 165n201 | |
| 13:11 | 206n43, 210n52 | 2:4 | 59n95 | |
| *Mik* | | 3:2 | 227n81 | |
| 4:4 | 195n20 | 3:3 | 61n100, 146n163, | |
| *Ned* | | | 204n39, 216n63, | |

## INDEX OF PASSAGES

Soṭ (continued)
        366n31, 419n157
5:1    100n6, 338n39, 339n43
5:5    58n93
7:4    125n88, 480n312
9:15    366n25

Suk
1:1    10n10, 366n31
1:4    366n31
4:1    190n5

Tam
3:4    11n12
5:1    10n11, 165n201

Ter
1:1    328n14, 330n17
1:2    10n10, 366n31

Ṭoh
intro.    3n3, 73n133, 115n61, 136n128, 137n135, 206n44, 208–09, 258n44, 277n82, 337n32, 339n43

'Uḳ
    64n106, 75n139, 172nn210–11, 288n111

Yadayim
intro.    136n128

Yoma
2:1    3n3, 13n17, 277n82
8:4    366n28

Zeb
intro.    209n50

### SEFER HAM-MIṢWOT
Introduction
    3n3, 14n18, 25, 49n66, 97n1, 98n3, 167n202, 189nn2–3, 240n6, 247n20, 249n24, 253n35, 326n5, 328n14, 354n82, 493n343

Šoreš
3    229n84, 288n111
4    264n52, 288n112, 442n209
9    47n63, 275n76, 441n206
14    236n95, 325n4, 337n32, 337n36

positive
2    363n18
3    216n63, 262n49, 394n95
4    136n133
5    422n168
56–57    136n133
75    136n133
77    136n133
82    136n133
108    189n2
111    136n133
153    85n159
157    253n35, 319n204
159    136n133
161    136n133
167    136n133
187    231n87, 253n35
209    136n133

negative
40    59n97
43    253n35
47    487n327
133    61n100
187    136n133, 158n190
199    115n61
254    439
290    398n107
306    290
317    374n48, 440n205
353    16n21
365    253n35, 374n48, 377n58, 392

### MOREH NEBUKIM
Dedicatory
  epistle    41n51, 362n14, 482n318, 505n384
Introductory
  verses    514n398
Intro.    3n3, 11n14, 16n20, 18n27, 47nn61–63, 78n148, 90n168, 206n44, 277n82, 315n187, 336n30, 353n78, 360n9, 362nn13, 14, 365n22, 399n109, 470n279, 471n283, 479, 496n358, 499n368
I,2    57n91, 58n92, 149n170,

# INDEX OF PASSAGES

|  |  |  |  |
|---|---|---|---|
|  | 354n83, 362n13, 394n94, 458n247 | I,74 | 85n159, 354n82, 482n318 |
|  |  | II, intro. | 398n108 |
| I,5 | 250n29, 409n134 | II,1 | 362n14 |
| I,6 | 478n307 | II,2 | 505n384 |
| I,8 | 497n363 | II,8 | 368n33 |
| I,9 | 250n29 | II,9 | 59n97 |
| I,14 | 514n398 | II,10 | 47n62 |
| I,15 | 513 | II,11 | 385n76, 498 |
| I,16 | 226n80 | II,16 | 410 |
| I,17 | 362n14 | II,20 | 422n169 |
| I,21 | 47n64, 121n75 | II,25 | 156n187, 369n40 |
| I,30 | 496n358 | II,28 | 430n183 |
| I,31–34 | 362n14, 400n11, 494n348 | II,29 | 352n77, 366n29, 390n84, 447n220, 504n381 |
| I,31 | 45n59, 226n80, 250, 375n52, 478n307 | II,30 | 324n1, 366n31 |
| I,32 | 411, 466n264 | II,31 | 363n16, 376n54, 447 |
| I,33 | 452n235 | II,32 | 68n117, 239n2, 455n239, 476n300 |
| I,34 | 42n53, 347n64, 435n195, 504n381 | II,33 | 58n92, 458n247 |
| I,36 | 58n92, 226n80, 362n13, 478n307 | II,35 | 47n64 |
|  |  | II,36 | 68n117, 435n195, 476n300 |
| I,39 | 364n18 |  |  |
| I,40 | 414n141 | II,37 | 373n45 |
| I,42 | 481n314 | II,38 | 378n60 |
| I,48 | 58n92, 112n53 | II,39 | 266, 305n165, 376n54, 405–06, 439n203, 442, 455n239, 464n256, 473n289 |
| I,50 | 325n4, 338n41 |  |  |
| I,51 | 360n10, 419n153, 458n247 |  |  |
| I,53 | 362n13 | II,40 | 364n19, 374n49, 396n102, 457n245, 464n256 |
| I,54 | 287n110, 325n4, 338n41, 362n14, 427n178, 478n307 |  |  |
|  |  | II,41 | 162n197 |
| I,59 | 250n29, 409n135, 482n317 | II,45 | 47n64, 414n141 |
|  |  | II,46 | 487n327 |
| I,61 | 125n88, 328n14, 366n27, 480n312 | II,47 | 362n13, 374n49, 376n56 |
|  |  | II,48 | 430n183 |
| I,62 | 125n88, 250n27 | III,intro. | 366n31, 397n105, 424n171, 504n381 |
| I,63 | 226n80, 389n81, 457n244 |  |  |
| I,67 | 324n1, 328n14 | III,6 | 69n118 |
| I,68 | 360n10 | III,8–12 | 505n383 |
| I,69 | 510n389 | III,8 | 324n1, 328n14, 325n3, 406n131, 466n263, 479n309, 506 |
| I,71 | 3n3, 29, 30n42, 47n61, 59n97, 69n119, 72n129, 98n3, 99n5, 326n8, 337n36, 360n9, 448n224, 476n300, 482n318, 497n362, 498, 504n381, 505n384 |  |  |
|  |  | III,11 | 227n82, 369n40, 479n309 |
|  |  | III,12 | 250n29 |
|  |  | III,17 | 413n140 |
|  |  | III,22–24 | 479n309 |
|  |  | III,22 | 477n306 |
| I,72 | 250n29 | III,24 | 226n80, 363n18 |

## INDEX OF PASSAGES

| | | | |
|---|---|---|---|
| III,25 | 379n62 | III,43 | 47n64, 164n199, 284n98, 322n207, 437n199 |
| III,26–50 | 374n49 | III,44 | 152n176, 250n29, 422 |
| III,26 | 164n199, 276n81, 375n51, 375n53, 376n55, 378n59, 378n61, 387n79, 392n88, 398n106, 398n108, 399n110, 400n113, 402n117 | III,45 | 153n178, 250n29, 354n82, 389n81, 390n85, 431n186, 436, 437n199 |
| | | III,46 | 389n81, 390n85, 433n191, 436, 437n198 |
| | | III,47 | 269n61, 404n126, 419n157, 434n193, 437n199, 447 |
| III,27 | 276n81, 300n152, 363n18, 388, 394, 397n104, 419n152, 430n183, 435n195, 445n216 | III,48 | 285n103, 290n166, 301n153, 306n166, 322n207, 402n121, 448n224, 459n248, 468n270, 483n319 |
| III,28 | 47n64, 276n81, 362n13, 375n51, 380n64, 388n80, 394n94, 400n113, 402n118 | III,49 | 153n177, 302n155, 362n14, 369n39, 375n51, 376n54, 376n57, 380n65, 389n82, 391n87, 399n110, 401n114, 402n121, 404n127, 437n198, 446, 466n262, 471n284, 473n289 |
| III,29 | 47n62, 118n120, 226n80, 362n13, 363n18, 380n66, 389nn81–82, 391n86, 457n244 | | |
| III,30 | 389n82, 404n125 | | |
| III,31 | 88n165, 276n81, 375n51, 380n64, 385n77, 388n80, 414n142 | | |
| III,32 | 226n80, 363n16, 389n81, 389n83, 390n84, 430n183 | III,50 | 221n74, 337n37, 398n106, 399n110 |
| | | III,51–54 | 359n7 |
| III,33 | 435n195, 466 | III,51 | 90n168, 145n159, 205n40, 216n63, 226n80, 307, 362n14, 364n18, 395n98, 421, 423n169, 438, 466n266, 478n308, 481n314, 494n348, 500n372, 501n374, 510n386, 513n395, 514n397 |
| III,34 | 143n148, 234n92, 362n14, 376n57, 473n289 | | |
| III,35 | 265, 276n81, 301n154, 303n158, 388n80, 419, 439n201, 442n209, 447 | | |
| III,36 | 303nn158–59, 303n161, 304n162, 422n168 | | |
| III,37 | 235n93, 389n81, 401n115, 402n119, 402n121 | III,52 | 114n58, 363n18 |
| | | III,53 | 462n254 |
| III,38 | 321n206 | III,54 | 287n110, 308n172, 360n9, 394n96, 395n97, 396n99, 427, 465, 495n355, 510, 511n390 |
| III,40 | 446 | | |
| III,41 | 272, 283n96, 301n153, 310n179, 416n146, 437n198, 439n201, 440, 443n210, 446n219, 448n224 | | |
| | | TĚŠUBOT | |

## INDEX OF PASSAGES 639

| | | | |
|---|---|---|---|
| 1 | 141n145 | 265 | 85n159, 362n13 |
| 66 | 53n79 | 267 | 58n93, 134n117 |
| 70 | 110n35, 112n52, 160n192 | 268 | 20n29, 59n95, 85n159, |
| 82 | 161n194 | | 134n121, 273n70, |
| 89 | 475n293 | | 481n314 |
| 91 | 236n94 | 269 | 8n9, 54n85, 111n37 |
| 98 | 100n5 | 286 | 53n79 |
| 110 | 59n95 | 289 | 53n77, 125n89, 160n192 |
| 117 | 54n84, 369n39 | 293 | 486n324 |
| 119 | 337n32, 344n59 | 294 | 8n9, 54n85 |
| 121 | 18n25, 50n68, 191n8 | 299 | 10n12 |
| 122 | 161n195 | 301 | 53n80 |
| 126 | 9n8, 13n17, 111n39 | 304 | 125n89, 134n117 |
| 128 | 54n85, 356n1 | 310 | 14n18, 17n22, 24n36, |
| 129 | 191n8 | | 38n46, 54n85, |
| 130 | 18n26 | | 165n200, 172n211, |
| 135 | 132n112, 135n123, | | 188n330, 277n82, |
| | 141n146 | | 311n184 |
| 136 | 119n69, 421n164 | 313 | 53n81 |
| 138 | 125n87, 134n117 | 315 | 56n88, 156n187, 312n185 |
| 141 | 236n95 | 320 | 59n95, 85n159 |
| 148 | 455n239 | 326 | 156nn186, 187 |
| 149 | 414n142, 452n234 | 332 | 214n62, 312n185, |
| 150 | 216n63, 374n48, 382n68 | | 315n188 |
| 152 | 129n100 | 334 | 292n118 |
| 153 | 145n156 | 344 | 156n187, 312n185, |
| 154 | 54n83, 111n38 | | 319n204 |
| 156 | 54n85, 111n38, 112n52 | 345 | 17n22, 157n188, |
| 180 | 250n29 | | 315n189, 475n293 |
| 198 | 20n29 | 346 | 31n44 |
| 201 | 20n29 | 351 | 85n159 |
| 207 | 133n114, 250n29 | 355 | 18n24, 31n44, 249n26 |
| 208 | 250n29 | 373 | 18n26 |
| 212 | 16n21 | 389 | 130n104 |
| 213 | 18n25 | 390 | 190n5 |
| 215 | 134n122 | 395 | 135n123, 236n96 |
| 217 | 247n20, 314n187 | 423 | 344n60 |
| 218 | 134n122 | 433 | 18n24 |
| 224 | 162n197, 264n52, 374n48, | 436 | 18n25, 318n199, 374n48, |
| | 473n289, 482n317 | | 378n60, 471n284, |
| 233 | 31n44 | | 488n331 |
| 242 | 85n159 | 442 | 115n61 |
| 251 | 12n16, 169n205 | 447 | 249n26, 253n35, 334n24 |
| 252 | 78n149, 374n48, 473n289 | 448 | 414n142, 452n234, 486 |
| 254 | 250n29, 409n135 | 449 | 85n159 |
| 259 | 125n87 | 458 | 437n199 |
| 263 | 133n115 | 469 | 172n211 |
| 264 | 156n187, 170n206, | III,15 | 18nn24–25 |
| | 312n185 | III,42–43 | 94n171 |

# INDEX OF PASSAGES

| Těšuḇoṯ (continued) | | | | |
|---|---|---|---|---|
| III,52 | 78n149 | | I,26a | 18n25, 30n42, 45n59, 52n75, 86n160, 105n20, 107n22, 132n111, 157n188, 242n8, 295n126, 404n123 |
| III,56 | 250n29, 366n28 | | | |
| III,57 | 4n5, 257n41, 414n142 | | | |

*'IGGĚROṮ*

| 2 | 47n64 | I,26b | 43n57 |
|---|---|---|---|
| 4 | 365n21 | I,30a | 82n152, 134n117 |
| 5–6 | 365n20 | I,50b | 82n152 |
| 14 | 348n66 | II,9b | 58n93 |
| 15 | 363n18 | II,12a | 324n1, 325n3, 339n43 |
| 16 | 38n47, 57n91, 150n171, 336n30 | II,12b | 277n82 |
| | | II,15b | 18n25, 324n1, 333n22, 335n28, 352n76, 455n239 |
| 49 | 43n57 | | |
| 50 | 42–43, 77n144, 78n148, 97n1, 172n210, 336n30, 500n371 | II,16a | 43n56, 59n95, 368n38, 470n279 |
| 51 | 64n109, 107n22, 500n371 | II,16b | 16n21, 41n50, 43n57, 363n18 |
| 52 | 18n25 | | |
| 56 | 210n53 | II,23a | 165n200, 419n153 |
| 57 | 205n41, 495n349 | II,23b | 374n48, 376n54, 382n68 |
| 58 | 17n22, 160n192, 247n20, 369n39 | II,24a | 355n98 |
| | | II,26a | 4n5 |
| 59 | 207n46 | II,27a | 58n93 |
| 61 | 43n57 | II,27b | 333n20, 349n69, 353n81 |
| 63 | 205n41 | II,28b | 8n8, 366n28 |
| 65 | 205n41 | II,31b | 5n6 |
| 66 | 43n56 | II,37b | 4n5, 149n169 |
| 68 | 5n6, 73n132, 210n53, 360n9 | II,44a | 38nn48–49, 63n103, 335n27, 476n302 |
| 69 | 51, 170n206, 210n53, 240n4, 241n7 | II,54b | 430n183 |
| | | III,27a | 348n66 |
| 90 | 43n57 | | |

*MA'ĂMAR TĚḤIYYAṮ HAM-MEṮIM*

| | | 1 | 43n57, 190n6 |
|---|---|---|---|
| *ḲOḆEṢ* | | 2 | 43n57, 44, 78n149, 190n6, 205n41, 257n41, 401n116, 499n369 |
| I,3b | 5n6, 123n84 | | |
| I,4b | 18n25 | | |
| I,8a | 333n21 | | |
| I,12a | 496n358 | | |
| I,23b | 18n25, 134n117 | 3 | 43n57, 44, 362n13 |
| I,25a–27a | 32 | 4 | 18n25, 44, 47n63, 78n145, 205n41, 257n41, 261n47, 365n23, 401n116, 500n372 |
| I,25a | 50n68 | | |
| I,25b | 3n4, 16n20, 24n36, 60n98, 97n1, 100n6, 168n23, 206n45, 239n3, 240n4, 256n39, 257n47, 333n21, 337n32, 491n335, 492n341 | | |
| | | 5 | 18n25 |
| | | 6 | 137n134, 344n60, 379n63 |
| | | 7 | 346n63, 470n276 |
| | | 8 | 205n41, 346n63 |

## INDEX OF PASSAGES

| | | | |
|---|---|---|---|
| 9 | 362n13, 366n31, 386n78 | | 454n237, 459n248 |
| 10 | 18n25, 362n13, 366n31 | chap. VIII | 366n26 |
| 12–13 | 503n379 | | |
| 12 | 346n63 | *'IGGERET TEMAN* | |
| 14 | 386n78, 409n134 | i | 499n370 |
| 15 | 337n32, 346n63 | ii | 476n300 |
| 18 | 379n63 | iii | 63n104, 334n25 |
| 19 | 54n86, 58nn93–94 | iv | 374n48, 396n103, 418 |
| 21 | 54n86, 58nn93–94, 146n161 | v | 406n130 |
| | | xii | 356n2, 451n231, 449n227 |
| 23 | 58n93, 419n157 | xiv | 249n26 |
| 24 | 45, 98–99n3 | xv | 112n49, 451n231 |
| 25 | 98–99n3 | xvii–xix | 419n153 |
| 26 | 98–99n3, 386n78 | xviii | 227n81, 414n141 |
| 31 | 69n118, 389n81, 455n239 | xx | 9n8, 117n66, 476n300 |
| 32 | 390n85 | | |
| 36 | 303n160 | *MILLOT HA-HIGGAYON* | |
| 37 | 325n3, 337n32, 344n61, 470n276 | | 251n29, 365n22, 375n52, 376n54, 458n247 |
| 39 | 409n134 | *LETTER ON ASTROLOGY* | |
| *ŠĔMONAH PĔRAḲIM* | | 22 | 376n54 |
| intro. | 98n3, 219n68, 367n33 | 228 | 18n25, 505n384 |
| chap. IV | 3n3, 53n76, 301n154, 374n48, 376n54, 388n80, 405n129, 416n147, 419n153, 432n188, 460, 461n253, 463, 464, 466n262, 467n267, 511n390 | 339 | 51, 233, 249n26, 374n48, 376n56, 391n87, 401n116, 420n159, 471n285, 472n288 |
| | | 230 | 382n68 |
| | | 233 | 303n160, 422n169, 497n363 |
| chap. V | 216n63, 250n29, 377nn32, 34 | *TREATISE ON ASTHMA* | |
| chap. VI | 380n64, 415n145, | 3 | 109n25, 240n6 |